Let the Nations
Be Glad!

Other Books by John Piper

Let the Nations Be Glad!

The Supremacy
of God
in Missions

Second Edition
Revised and Expanded

John Piper

Baker Academic
A Division of Baker Book House Co
Grand Rapids, Michigan 49516

Published by Baker Academic
a division of Baker Book House Company
P.O. Box 6287, Grand Rapids, MI 49516-6287
www.bakeracademic.com

Printed in the United States of America

Library of Congress Cataloging-in-Publication Data
Piper, John, 1946–
    Let the nations be glad! : the supremacy of God in missions / John Piper.—2nd ed.
        p.   cm.
    Includes bibliographical references and indexes.
    ISBN 0-8010-2613-X
    1. Missions. 2. Providence and government of God. 3. Glory of God. I. Title.
    BV2063.P55 2003
    266'.001—dc21   2002032650

To
Tom Steller

in the precious partnership
of worship, prayer, and suffering
for the supremacy of God in all things,
for the joy of all peoples
through Jesus Christ

Contents

Preface

My passion is to see people, churches, mission agencies, and social ministries become God-centered, Christ-exalting, Spirit-powered, Bible-saturated, missions-mobilizing, soul-winning, and justice-pursuing. The supremacy of God in all things for the joy of all peoples through Jesus Christ is the central, driving, all-unifying commitment of my life. This vision is clearer and more firm in my heart today than when this book was first published in 1993. I am thankful that God has been merciful to use *Let the Nations Be Glad!* to make himself more central in missions. And I thank Baker Book House for letting me revise and expand this new edition.

John Stott has sounded the note I love to hear and echo:

> The highest of missionary motives is neither obedience to the Great Commission (important as that is), nor love for sinners who are alienated and perishing (strong as that incentive is, especially when we contemplate the wrath of God . . .), but rather zeal—burning and passionate zeal—for the glory of Jesus Christ. . . . Only one imperialism is Christian . . . and that is concern for His Imperial Majesty Jesus Christ, and for the glory of his empire.[1]

He said this in relation to Romans 1:5. There the apostle Paul sums up his calling as a missionary: "[I am called] to bring about the obedience of faith *for the sake of his name* among all the nations." Notice: "For the sake of his name!" Stott exults again in this great Pauline passion: "We should be 'jealous' . . . for the honour of his name—troubled when it remains unknown, hurt when it is ignored, indignant when it is blasphemed. And all the time anxious and determined that it shall be given the honor and glory which are due to it."[2] O for the

---

1. John Stott, *Romans: God's Good News for the World* (Downers Grover, Ill.: Inter-Varsity, 1994), 53.
2. Ibid.

day when more pastors and scholars and missionaries would not just say that but feel it as the driving force of their lives!

The apostle John applies this Christ-exalting passion to all missionaries when he says, "They have gone out *for the sake of the name*" (3 John 1:7). My friend and comrade in the Greatest Cause for over twenty-five years, Tom Steller, wrote an afterword for this text. I have dedicated this book to Tom with deep affection. Together we want to give our lives to creating, sending, and sustaining world Christians who live and die "for the sake of the name." Increasingly what burns inside us is the question: Where do such God-centered, Christ-exalting, missions-driven people come from? We believe they come from God-besotted, Christ-addicted, Bible-breathing homes and churches and schools and ministries. That is what this book aims to nurture.

There is a God-enthralled, Christ-treasuring, all-enduring love that pursues the fullness of God in the soul and in the service of Jesus. It is not absorbed in anthropology or methodology or even theology—it is absorbed in God. It cries out with the psalmist, "Let the peoples praise you, O God; let all the peoples praise you! Let the nations be glad and sing for joy. . . . Sing praises to our King, sing praises! For God is the King of all the earth" (Pss. 67:3–4; 47:6–7). There is a distinct God-magnifying mind-set. It is relentless in bringing God forward again and again. It is spring-loaded to make much of God in anthropology and methodology and theology. It cannot make peace with God-ignoring, God-neglecting planning or preaching or puttering around.

Such God-entranced people are what we need. For example, *Let the Nations Be Glad!* is like a little skiff riding on the wake of the massive undertaking of Patrick Johnstone and Jason Mandryk in publishing *Operation World*. Would that every Christian used this book to know the nations and pray. I look at this great, church-wakening, mission-advancing book, and I ask, "What kind of mind-set unleashes such a book?" Listen.

> All the earth-shaking awesome forces unleashed on the world are released by the Lord Jesus Christ. He reigns today. He is in the control room of the universe. He is the only Ultimate Cause; all the sins of man and machinations of Satan ultimately have to enhance the glory and kingdom of our Saviour. This is true of our world today—in wars, famines, earthquakes, or the evil that apparently has the ascendancy. All God's actions are just and loving. We have become too enemy-conscious, and can over-do the spiritual warfare aspect of intercession. We need to be more God-conscious, so that we can laugh the laugh of faith knowing that we have power over all the power of the enemy (Luke 10:19). He has already lost control because of Calvary where the Lamb

was slain. What confidence and rest of heart this gives us as we face a world in turmoil and such spiritual need.[3]

There it is. Where are the teachers and preachers and mission executives and seminary presidents who talk like that? Their number is increasing. I want to be one. I want to breathe any little spark of Godward zeal I can into the reader's soul. Feel free to ransack this book for wherever you feel that breath. It doesn't have to be read straight through.

Let it be clear: This book is not just for missionaries. It is for pastors who (like me) want to connect their fragile, momentary, local labors to God's invincible, eternal, global purposes. It's for laypeople who want a bigger motivation for being world Christians than they get from statistics. It's for college and seminary classes on the theology of missions that really want to be *theo*logical as well as anthropological, methodological, and technological. And it's for leaders who need the flickering wick of their vocation fanned into flame again with a focus on the supremacy of God in all things.

Tom Steller and I love Jesus Christ, we love the church, and we love missionaries. Our united prayer and commitment, from the base of a missions-mobilizing local church, is that God will be merciful to us and make our labors fruitful for Christ's "Imperial Majesty." May he raise up generations of world Christians who are willing to lay down their lives to make the nations glad in the glory of God through Jesus Christ.

3. Patrick Johnstone, *Operation World* (Kent, England: STL, 1987), 21. See the new 2001 edition first published by Paternoster Lifestyle, P.O. Box 300, Carlisle, Cumbria, CA3 OQS, UK. Johnstone and Mandryk say, "We reckon now that, in all five editions and in over 12 languages, nearly 2 million copies had been printed by 2000" (xi in the 2001 edition).

Acknowledgments

I am surrounded by people who energize me because they share the vision to spread a passion for the supremacy of God in all things for the joy of all peoples through Jesus Christ.

Thank you to Bethlehem Baptist Church, who, under the leadership of visionary, globally minded, God-centered elders, gave the assignment to leave off preaching for a month and finish this new edition.

Thank you, Carol Steinbach, friend and fellow-fighter for joy, for making the book more accessible and useful with the text and person indexes. And thanks, Matt Perman, for giving your eagle eye to the creation of the subject index.

Thank you, Justin Taylor, for pulling everything together from the old edition, making dozens of valuable suggestions, and giving every assistance needed.

Thank you, Noël, that even in weakness you strengthen my hand and set me free to write.

Thank you most of all, dear Jesus, that you have buttressed the command, "Teach them to observe all that I have commanded you," with the double promise, "All authority in heaven and on earth has been given to me," and, "I am with you always, to the end of the age" (Matt. 28:18–20).

PART 1

Making God Supreme in Missions

*The Purpose,
the Power,
and the Price*

1

The Supremacy of God in Missions through Worship

Missions is not the ultimate goal of the church. Worship is. Missions exists because worship doesn't. Worship is ultimate, not missions, because God is ultimate, not man. When this age is over, and the countless millions of the redeemed fall on their faces before the throne of God, missions will be no more. It is a temporary necessity. But worship abides forever.[1]

Worship, therefore, is the fuel and goal of missions. It's the goal of missions because in missions we simply aim to bring the nations into the white-hot enjoyment of God's glory. The goal of missions is the gladness of the peoples in the greatness of God. "The LORD reigns, let the earth *rejoice;* let the many coastlands *be glad!*" (Ps. 97:1). "Let the peoples praise you, O God; let all the peoples praise you! Let the nations *be glad and sing for joy!*" (Ps. 67:3–4).

But worship is also the fuel of missions. Passion for God in worship precedes the offer of God in preaching. You can't commend what you don't cherish. Missionaries will never call out, "Let the nations *be glad!*" who cannot say from the heart, "*I rejoice* in the LORD. . . . *I will be glad and exult in you,* I will sing praise to your name, O Most High" (Ps. 104:34; 9:2). Missions begins and ends in worship.

---

1. In the 2003 edition of this book, I have added a chapter to clarify in great detail and application what I mean by "worship" and how it relates to "worship services" and the worship of practical obedience (Rom. 12:1–2). It is titled "The Inner Simplicity and Outer Freedom of Worldwide Worship." The thesis is that the New Testament is stunningly silent about the outward forms of worship and radically focused on the inner experience of treasuring God, because it is a book of vision for missions in all cultures, not a worship manual for how to "do worship" in our culture.

If the pursuit of God's glory is not ordered above the pursuit of man's good in the affections of the heart and the priorities of the church, man will not be well served, and God will not be duly honored. I am not pleading for a diminishing of missions but for a magnifying of God. When the flame of worship burns with the heat of God's true worth, the light of missions will shine to the darkest peoples on earth. And I long for that day to come!

Where passion for God is weak, zeal for missions will be weak. Churches that are not centered on the exaltation of the majesty and beauty of God will scarcely kindle a fervent desire to "declare *his glory* among the nations" (Ps. 96:3). Even outsiders feel the disparity between the boldness of our claim upon the nations and the blandness of our engagement with God.

Albert Einstein's Indictment

For example, Charles Misner, a scientific specialist in general relativity theory, expressed Albert Einstein's skepticism over the church with words that should waken us to the shallowness of our experience with God in worship:

> The design of the universe . . . is very magnificent and shouldn't be taken for granted. In fact, I believe that is why Einstein had so little use for organized religion, although he strikes me as a basically very religious man. *He must have looked at what the preachers said about God and felt that they were blaspheming. He had seen much more majesty than they had ever imagined, and they were just not talking about the real thing.* My guess is that he simply felt that religions he'd run across did not have proper respect . . . for the author of the universe.[2]

The charge of blasphemy is loaded. The point is to pack a wallop behind the charge that in our worship services God simply doesn't come through for who he is. He is unwittingly belittled. For those who are stunned by the indescribable magnitude of what God has made, not to mention the infinite greatness of the One who made it, the steady diet on Sunday morning of practical how-to's and psychological soothing and relational therapy and tactical planning seem dramatically out of touch with Reality—the God of overwhelming greatness.

It is possible to be distracted from God in trying to serve God. Martha-like, we neglect the one thing needful and soon begin to present God as busy and fretful as we are. A. W. Tozer warned us about this:

2. Quoted in *First Things* 18 (December 1991): 63 (emphasis added).

We commonly represent God as a busy, eager, somewhat frustrated Father hurrying about seeking help to carry out His benevolent plan to bring peace and salvation to the world. . . . Too many missionary appeals are based upon this fancied frustration of Almighty God.[3]

Scientists know that light travels at the speed of 5.87 trillion miles a year. They also know that the galaxy of which our solar system is a part is about 100,000 light-years in diameter—about 587,000 trillion miles. It is one of about a million such galaxies in the optical range of our most powerful telescopes. It has been estimated that in our galaxy there are more than 200 billion stars. The sun is one of them, a modest star burning at about 6,000 degrees centigrade on the surface and traveling in an orbit at 135 miles per second, which means it will take about 250 million years to complete a revolution around the galaxy.

Scientists know these things and are awed by them. And they say, "If there is a personal God, as the Christians say, who spoke this universe into being, then there is a certain respect and reverence and wonder and dread that would have to come through when we talk about him and when we worship him."

We who believe the Bible know this even better than the scientists because we have heard something even more amazing:

"To whom then will you compare me, that I should be like him?" says the Holy One. Lift up your eyes on high and see: who created these [stars]? He who brings out their host by number, calling them all by name, by the greatness of his might, and because he is strong in power not one is missing.

Isaiah 40:25–26

Every one of the billions of stars in the universe is there by God's specific appointment. He knows their number. And most astonishing of all, he knows them by name. They do his bidding as his personal agents. When we feel the weight of this grandeur in the heavens, we have only touched the hem of his garment. "Behold, these are but the outskirts of his ways, and how small a whisper do we hear of him!" (Job 26:14). That is why we cry, "Be exalted, O God, above the heavens!" (Ps. 57:5). God is the absolute reality that everyone in the universe must come to terms with. Everything depends utterly on his will. All other realities compare to him like a raindrop compares to the ocean or like an anthill compares to Mount Everest. To ignore him

3. Quoted in Tom Wells, *A Vision for Missions* (Carlisle, Pa.: Banner of Truth Trust, 1985), 35.

or belittle him is unintelligible and suicidal folly. How shall one ever be the emissary of this great God who has not trembled before him with joyful wonder?

The Second Greatest Activity in the World

The most crucial issue in missions is the centrality of God in the life of the church. How can people who are not stunned by the greatness of God be sent with the ringing message, "*Great* is the Lord, and *greatly* to be praised; he is to be feared above all gods" (Ps. 96:4)? Missions is not first and ultimate; God is. And these are not just words. This truth is the lifeblood of missionary inspiration and endurance. William Carey, the father of modern missions, who set sail for India from England in 1793, expressed the connection:

> When I left England, my hope of India's conversion was very strong; but amongst so many obstacles, it would die, unless upheld by God. Well, I have God, and His Word is true. Though the superstitions of the heathen were a thousand times stronger than they are, and the example of the Europeans a thousand times worse; though I were deserted by all and persecuted by all, yet my faith, fixed on the sure Word, would rise above all obstructions and overcome every trial. God's cause will triumph.[4]

Carey and thousands like him have been moved and carried by the vision of a great and triumphant God. That vision must come first. Savoring it in worship precedes spreading it in missions. All of history is moving toward one great goal, the white-hot worship of God and his Son among all the peoples of the earth. Missions is not that goal. It is the means. And for that reason it is the second greatest human activity in the world.

God's Passion for God Is the Foundation for Ours

One of the things God uses to make this truth take hold of a person and a church is the stunning realization that it is also true for God himself. Missions is not *God's* ultimate goal, worship is. And when this sinks into a person's heart everything changes. The world is often turned on its head, and everything looks different—including the missionary enterprise.

4. Quoted in Iain Murray, *The Puritan Hope* (Edinburgh: Banner of Truth Trust, 1971), 140. For an introduction to Carey's life, see Timothy George, *Faithful Witness: The Life and Mission of William Carey* (Birmingham, Ala.: New Hope, 1991).

The ultimate foundation for our passion to see God glorified is his own passion to be glorified. God is central and supreme in his own affections. There are no rivals for the supremacy of God's glory in his own heart. God is not an idolater. He does not disobey the first and great commandment. With all his heart and soul and strength and mind he delights in the glory of his manifold perfections.[5] The most passionate heart for God in all the universe is God's heart.

This truth, more than any other I know, seals the conviction that worship is the fuel and goal of missions. The deepest reason why our passion for God should *fuel* missions is that God's passion for God fuels missions. Missions is the overflow of our delight in God because missions is the overflow of God's delight in being God. And the deepest reason why worship is the *goal* in missions is that worship is God's goal. We are confirmed in this goal by the biblical record of God's relentless pursuit of praise among the nations. "Praise the LORD, all nations! Extol him, all peoples!" (Ps. 117:1). If it is God's goal, it must be our goal.

The Chief End of God Is to Glorify God and Enjoy Himself Forever

All my years of preaching and teaching on the supremacy of God in the heart of God have proved that this truth hits most people like a truck laden with unknown fruit. If they survive the impact, they discover that this is the most luscious fruit on the planet. I have unpacked this truth with lengthy arguments in other places.[6] So here I will give just a brief overview of the biblical basis. What I am claiming is that the answer to the first question of the Westminster Catechism is the same when asked concerning God as it is when asked concerning man. Question: "What is the chief end of man?" Answer: "The chief end of man is to glorify God and enjoy him forever." Question: "What is the chief end of God?" Answer: "The chief end of God is to glorify God and enjoy himself forever."

Another way to say it is simply that God is righteous. The opposite of righteousness is to value and enjoy what is not truly valuable or rewarding. This is why people are called unrighteous in Romans 1:18. They suppress the truth of God's value and exchange God for created things. So they belittle God and discredit his worth. Righteousness is

---

5. I have tried to unfold this wonderful truth of the Father's delight in himself in *The Pleasures of God: Meditations on God's Delight in Being God*, rev. and exp. ed. (Sisters, Ore.: Multnomah, 2000), chap. 1, "The Pleasure of God in His Son" (25–45).

6. See especially "Appendix 1: The Goal of God in Redemptive History," in *Desiring God: Meditations of a Christian Hedonist* (Sisters, Ore.: Multnomah, 1996), 255–66; and the entirety of *The Pleasures of God*.

the opposite. It means recognizing true value for what it is and esteeming it and enjoying it in proportion to its true worth. The unrighteous in 2 Thessalonians 2:10 perish because they refuse to *love* the truth. The righteous, then, are those who welcome a *love* for the truth. Righteousness is recognizing and welcoming and loving and upholding what is truly valuable.

God is righteous. This means that he recognizes, welcomes, loves, and upholds with infinite jealousy and energy what is infinitely valuable, namely, the worth of God. God's righteous passion and delight is to display and uphold his infinitely valuable glory. This is not a vague theological conjecture. It flows inevitably from dozens of biblical texts that show God in the relentless pursuit of praise and honor from creation to consummation.

Probably no text in the Bible reveals the passion of God for his own glory more clearly and bluntly than Isaiah 48:9–11, where God says:

> *For my name's sake* I defer my anger, *for the sake of my praise* I restrain it for you, that I may not cut you off. Behold, I have refined you, but not as silver; I have tried you in the furnace of affliction. *For my own sake, for my own sake,* I do it, for *how should my name be profaned? My glory I will not give to another.*

I have found that for many people these words come like six hammer blows to a man-centered way of looking at the world:

For *my* name's sake!
For the sake of *my* praise!
For *my* own sake!
For *my* own sake!
How should *my* name be profaned!
My glory I will not give to another!

What this text hammers home to us is the centrality of God in his own affections. The most passionate heart for the glorification of God is God's heart. God's ultimate goal is to uphold and display the glory of his name.

Biblical Texts to Show God's Zeal for His Own Glory

God chose his people for his glory:

> He chose us in Him before the foundation of the world, that we should be holy and blameless before Him. In love He predestined us to adop-

tion as sons through Jesus Christ to Himself, according to the kind intention of His will, to the praise of the glory of His grace.

Ephesians 1:4–6 NASB; cf. vv. 12, 14

God created us for his glory:

Bring my sons from afar and my daughters from the end of the earth, everyone who is called by my name, *whom I created for my glory.*

Isaiah 43:6–7

God called Israel for his glory:

You are my servant, Israel, in whom I will be glorified.

Isaiah 49:3

I made the whole house of Israel and the whole house of Judah cling to me, declares the LORD, *that they might be for me a people, a name, a praise, and a glory.*

Jeremiah 13:11

God rescued Israel from Egypt for his glory:

Our fathers, when they were in Egypt, did not consider your wondrous works . . . but rebelled by the Sea, at the Red Sea. Yet he saved them *for his name's sake, that he might make known his mighty power.*

Psalm 106:7–8

God raised Pharaoh up to show his power and glorify his name:

For the Scripture says to Pharaoh, "For this very purpose I have raised you up, that I might show my power in you, and that my name might be proclaimed in all the earth."

Romans 9:17

God defeated Pharaoh at the Red Sea to show his glory:

And I will harden Pharaoh's heart, and he will pursue them, and *I will get glory over Pharaoh* and all his host, and the Egyptians *shall know that I am the LORD. . . . And the Egyptians shall know that I am the LORD, when I have gotten glory* over Pharaoh, his chariots, and his horsemen.

Exodus 14:4, 18; cf. v. 17

God spared Israel in the wilderness for the glory of his name:

I acted for the sake of my name, that it should not be profaned in the sight
of the nations, in whose sight I had brought them out.

Ezekiel 20:14

God gave Israel victory in Canaan for the glory of his name:

Who is like your people Israel, the one nation on earth whom God went
to redeem to be his people, *making himself a name* and doing for them
great and awesome things by driving out before your people, whom you
redeemed for yourself from Egypt, a nation and its gods?

2 Samuel 7:23

God did not cast away his people for the glory of his name:

Do not be afraid; you have done all this evil. Yet do not turn aside from
following the LORD. . . . For the LORD will not forsake his people, *for his
great name's sake.*

1 Samuel 12:20, 22

God saved Jerusalem from attack for the glory of his name:

For I will defend this city to save it, *for my own sake* and for the sake of
my servant David.

2 Kings 19:34; cf. 20:6

God restored Israel from exile for the glory of his name:

Thus says the Lord GOD: It is not for your sake, O house of Israel, that I
am about to act, but *for the sake of my holy name.* . . . *And I will vindicate the holiness of my great name.* . . . And the nations will know that I
am the LORD.

Ezekiel 36:22–23; cf. v. 32

Jesus sought the glory of his Father in all he did:

The one who speaks on his own authority seeks his own glory, but *the
one who seeks the glory of him who sent him* is true, and in him there is
no falsehood.

John 7:18

Jesus told us to do good works so that God gets glory:

In the same way, let your light shine before others, so that they may see
your good works and *give glory to your Father who is in heaven.*

Matthew 5:16; cf. 1 Peter 2:12

Jesus warned that not seeking God's glory makes faith impossible:

How can you believe, when you receive glory from one another and do not *seek the glory that comes from the only God?*

John 5:44

Jesus said that he answers prayer that God would be glorified:

Whatever you ask in my name, this I will do, *that the Father may be glorified in the Son.*

John 14:13

Jesus endured his final hours of suffering for God's glory:

"Now is my soul troubled. And what shall I say? 'Father, save me from this hour?' *But for this purpose I have come to this hour. Father, glorify your name.'"* Then a voice came from heaven: *"I have glorified it, and I will glorify it again."*

John 12:27–28

Father, the hour has come; *glorify your Son that the Son may glorify you.*

John 17:1; cf. 13:31–32

God gave his Son to vindicate the glory of his righteousness:

God put [Christ] forward as a propitiation by his blood . . . *to show God's righteousness.* . . . It was to show his righteousness at the present time.

Romans 3:25–26

God forgives our sins for his own sake:

I, I am he who blots out your transgressions *for my own sake,* and I will not remember your sins.

Isaiah 43:25

For *your name's sake,* O LORD, pardon my guilt, for it is great.

Psalm 25:11

Jesus receives us into his fellowship for the glory of God:

Welcome one another as Christ has welcomed you, *for the glory of God.*

Romans 15:7

The ministry of the Holy Spirit is to glorify the Son of God:

He will glorify me, for he will take what is mine and declare it to you.

John 16:14

God instructs us to do everything for his glory:

So, whether you eat or drink, or whatever you do, *do all to the glory of God.*

1 Corinthians 10:31; cf. 6:20

God tells us to serve in a way that will glorify him:

Whoever serves, [let him do it] as one who serves by the strength that God supplies—*in order that in everything God may be glorified* through Jesus Christ. To him belong glory and dominion forever and ever. Amen.

1 Peter 4:11

Jesus will fill us with fruits of righteousness for God's glory:

It is my prayer that . . . [you be] filled with the fruit of righteousness that comes through Jesus Christ, *to the glory and praise of God.*

Philippians 1:9, 11

All are under judgment for dishonoring God's glory:

They became fools, and *exchanged the glory of the immortal God for images.*

Romans 1:22–23

For all have sinned and *fall short of the glory of God.*

Romans 3:23

Herod is struck dead because he did not give glory to God:

Immediately an angel of the Lord struck him down, because *he did not give God the glory.*

Acts 12:23

Jesus is coming again for the glory of God:

They will suffer the punishment of eternal destruction, away from the presence of the Lord and from the glory of his might, when he comes on that day *to be glorified in his saints, and to be marveled at among all who have believed.*

2 Thessalonians 1:9–10

Jesus' ultimate aim for us is that we see and enjoy his glory:

Father, I desire that they also, whom you have given me, may be with me where I am, *to see my glory* that you have given me because you loved me before the foundation of the world.

John 17:24

Even in wrath God's aim is to make known the wealth of his glory:

Desiring to show his wrath and to make known his power, [God] has endured with much patience vessels of wrath prepared for destruction, *in order to make known the riches of his glory* for vessels of mercy, which he has prepared beforehand for glory.

Romans 9:22–23

God's plan is to fill the earth with the knowledge of his glory:

For the earth will be filled with *the knowledge of the glory of the* LORD as the waters cover the sea.

Habakkuk 2:14

Everything that happens will redound to God's glory:

From him and through him and to him are all things. *To him be glory forever.* Amen.

Romans 11:36

In the New Jerusalem, the glory of God replaces the sun:

And the city has no need of sun or moon to shine on it, for *the glory of God gives it light,* and its lamp is the Lamb.

Revelation 21:23

God's passion for God is unmistakable. God struck me with this most powerfully when I first read Jonathan Edwards's book titled *The Dissertation Concerning the End for Which God Created the World.*[7] There he piles reason upon reason and Scripture upon Scripture to show this truth:

7. For an introduction to the life of Edwards, the implications of his theology for evangelicalism, and the complete text of *The End for Which God Created the World,* see John Piper, *God's Passion for His Glory: Living the Vision of Jonathan Edwards* (Wheaton: Crossway, 1998).

The great end of God's works, which is so variously expressed in Scripture, is indeed but ONE; and this one end is most properly and comprehensively called, THE GLORY OF GOD.[8]

In other words, the chief end of God is to glorify God and enjoy himself forever.

The Belittling of God's Glory and the Horrors of Hell

The condition of the human heart throws God's God-centeredness into stark relief. Man by nature does not have a heart to glorify God. "All have sinned and *fall short of the glory of God*" (Rom. 3:23). In our wickedness, we suppress the truth that God is our Sovereign and worthy of all our allegiance and affection. By nature we exchange the glory of the immortal God for dim images of it in creation (Rom. 1:18, 23). We forsake the fountain of living waters and hew out for ourselves broken cisterns that can hold no water (Jer. 2:13).

The nations "are darkened in their understanding, alienated from the life of God because of the ignorance that is in them, due to their hardness of heart" (Eph. 4:18). By nature we were all once dead in trespasses and sins, following the slave master Satan, and therefore children of wrath (Eph. 2:1–3). Our end was "eternal punishment" (Matt. 25:46), exclusion "from the presence of the Lord" (2 Thess. 1:9), and endless torments in "the lake that burns with fire and sulfur, which is the second death" (Rev. 21:8; cf. 14:11; 20:10).[9]

The infinite horrors of hell are intended by God to be a vivid demonstration of the infinite value of the glory of God. The biblical assumption of the justice of hell is a clear testimony to the infiniteness of the sin of failing to glorify God. All of us have failed. All the nations have failed. Therefore, the weight of infinite guilt rests on every human head because of our failure to cherish the glory of God. The biblical vision of God, then, is that he is supremely committed, with infinite passion, to uphold and display the glory of his name. And the biblical vision of man without grace is that he suppresses this truth and by nature finds more joy in his own glory than he does in God's. God exists to be worshiped, and man worships the work of his own hands. This twofold reality creates the critical need for missions. And the very God-centeredness of God, which creates the crisis, also creates the solution.

8. Ibid., 246.
9. In defense of the reality of eternal conscious torment in hell for those who reject the truth of God, see chapter 4.

How Can Self-Exaltation Be Love?

For over thirty years I have tried to present to Christians in various places this central biblical truth of God's passion for the glory of God. The major objection has been that it seems to make God unloving. The merciful, kind, loving heart of God seems to disappear in the passions of an overweening ego. Doesn't the Bible say, "Love . . . does not seek its own" (1 Cor. 13:5 NASB)? How then can God be loving and seek his own glory? It's a good question. And in answering it we will see how the supremacy of God in the heart of God is the spring of mercy and kindness and love—which means the spring of missions.

There are two ways to see harmony between God's passion for his own glory and Paul's statement "Love . . . does not seek its own." One is to say that Paul doesn't mean that every way of seeking your own is wrong. Some ways are, and some ways aren't. The other is to say that God is unique and that Paul's statement does not apply to him the way it does to us. I think both of these are true.

Love Seeks Its Own Joy in the Joy of Others

First, "Love . . . does not seek its own" was not meant by Paul to condemn every possible way of "seeking your own." He did not mean that seeking your own happiness in loving others is loveless. We know this because in Acts 20:35 Paul told the elders of the church of Ephesus to "remember" the word of the Lord Jesus: "It is more blessed to give than to receive." If it were unloving to be motivated by the blessedness of loving, then Paul would not have told the elders to "remember" this word, that is, to keep it in their minds where it could function as a conscious motive. If seeking your own blessing in giving to others ruined the act, Paul would not have told us to keep this blessing in mind.

Those who have thought most deeply about motivation realize this and have interpreted Paul's words in 1 Corinthians 13:5 with great wisdom. For example, Jonathan Edwards pointed out that what Paul is opposing in the words "Love . . . does not seek its own" is not

> the degree in which [a person] loves his own happiness, but in his placing his happiness where he ought not, and in limiting and confining his love. Some, although they love their own happiness, do not place that happiness in their own confined good, or in that good which is limited to themselves, but more in the common good—in that which is the good of others, or in the good to be enjoyed in and by others. . . . And when it is said that *Charity seeketh not her own*, we are to understand it of her own private good—good limited to herself.[10]

10. Jonathan Edwards, *Charity and Its Fruits* (1852; reprint, Edinburgh: Banner of Truth Trust, 1969), 164.

In other words, Paul did not mean to condemn every possible way of seeking your own. He had in mind the selfish attitude that finds its happiness not in helping others but in using others or ignoring others for personal gain. He did not have in mind the attitude that *seeks its own* joy precisely in doing good to others. In fact, he appeals to that motive two verses earlier when he says, "If I give away all I have, and if I deliver up my body to be burned, but have not love, I *gain nothing*" (1 Cor. 13:3). He is saying, "Surely you do not want to 'gain nothing,' do you? Well, then be sure that you love. Then you will gain much." So he actually appeals to the very motive that some say he is denouncing. But he is not appealing to low, selfish, materialistic motives. He is calling for the radical transformation of heart that finds its joy in the act of love and all the goodness that comes from it.

So the way is opened perhaps for God to "seek his own" and still be loving. But I said there are two ways to see harmony between God's passion for his own glory and Paul's statement "Love seeks not its own." We've seen one, namely, that Paul is not opposing "seeking one's own" if "one's own" is really the good of others.

The Sin of Imitating God

The other way to see this harmony is to say that God is unique and that Paul's statement does not apply to him the way it does to us. This is true. Things are forbidden to us that are not forbidden to God precisely because we are not God and he is. The reason we are not to exalt our own glory but God's is because he is God and we are not. For God to be faithful to this same principle means that he too would exalt not our glory but his. The unifying principle is not, Don't exalt your own glory. The unifying principle is, Exalt the glory of what is infinitely glorious. For us that means exalt God. And for God that means exalt God. For us it means don't seek your own glory. For God it means *do* seek your own glory.

This can be very slippery. Satan saw this and used it in the Garden of Eden. He came with the temptation to Adam and Eve: If you eat from the forbidden tree, "you will be like God, knowing good and evil" (Gen. 3:5). Now, what Adam and Eve should have said was, "We are already like God. We have been created *in his image*" (Gen. 1:27). But instead of putting this truth against Satan's temptation, they allowed the truth to make error look plausible: "If we are in the image of God, then it can't be wrong to want to be like God. So the suggestion of the serpent that we will be like God can't be bad." So they ate.

But the problem is that it is *not* right for humans to try to be like God in every way. God's God-ness makes some things right for him to do that are not right for us to do. In Adam and Eve's case, it is God's right to decide for them what is good and what is evil, what is helpful and what is harmful. They are finite and do not have the wisdom to know all the factors to take into account in living a happy life. Only God knows all that needs to be known. Therefore, humans have no right to be independent of God. Independent judgment about what is helpful and harmful is folly and rebellion. That was the temptation. And that was the essence of their disobedience.

The point is simply that even though we are created in the image of God, and even though in some ways we are to "be imitators of God" (Eph. 5:1), we are mistaken to think that God does not have some rights that we do not have. A father wants his child to imitate his manners and courtesies and integrity, but he does not want the child to imitate his authority, neither toward his parents nor toward his brothers and sisters.

Thus, it is right for God to do some things that we are forbidden to do. And one of those things is to exalt his own glory. He would be unrighteous if he did not do so, because he would not be prizing what is infinitely valuable. He would in fact be an idolater if he esteemed as his infinite treasure something less precious than his own glory.

God Is Most Glorified in Us
When We Are Most Satisfied in Him

But is it loving for God to exalt his own glory? Yes, it is. And there are several ways to see this truth clearly. One is to ponder this sentence: *God is most glorified in us when we are most satisfied in him.* This is perhaps the most important sentence in my theology.[11] If it is true, then it becomes plain why God is loving when he seeks to exalt his glory in my life, for that would mean that he would seek to maximize my satisfaction in him, since he is most glorified in me when I am most satisfied in him. Therefore, God's pursuit of his own glory is not at odds with my joy, and that means it is not unkind or unmerciful or unloving of him to seek his glory. In fact, it means that the more passionate God is for his own glory, the more passionate he is for my

11. For an extended elaboration of this thesis, see Piper, *Desiring God,* and its abbreviated version, *The Dangerous Duty of Delight: The Glorified God and the Satisfied Soul* (Sisters, Ore.: Multnomah, 2001). See also Sam Storms, *Pleasures Evermore: The Life-Changing Power of Enjoying God* (Colorado Springs: NavPress, 2000).

satisfaction in that glory. And therefore, God's God-centeredness and God's love soar together.

To illustrate the truth that God is most glorified in us when we are most satisfied in him, consider what I might say on a pastoral visit when entering the hospital room of one of my people. They look up from their bed with a smile and say, "Oh, Pastor John, how good of you to come. What an encouragement." And suppose I lift my hand, as it were to deflect the words, and say matter-of-factly, "Don't mention it. It's my duty as a pastor." Now, what is wrong here? Why do we cringe at such a thoughtless pastoral statement? It is my duty. And duty is a good thing. So why does that statement do so much damage?

It damages because it does not honor the sick person. Why? Because delight confers more honor than duty does. Doing hospital visitation out of mere duty honors duty. Doing it out of delight honors the patients. And they feel that. The right pastoral response to the patient's greeting would have been, "It's a pleasure to be here. I'm glad I could come." Do you see the paradox here? Those two sentences would show that I am "seeking my own." "It's *my* pleasure to be here. *I'm* glad I could come." And yet the reason these statements are not selfish is that they confer honor on the patient, not on the pastor. When someone delights in you, you feel honored. When someone finds happiness in being around you, you feel treasured, appreciated, glorified. Visiting the sick because you are glad to be there is a loving thing to do.

This then is the answer to why God is not unloving to magnify his glory. God is glorified precisely when we are satisfied in him—when we delight in his presence, when we like to be around him, when we treasure his fellowship. This is an utterly life-changing discovery. It frees us to pursue our joy in God and God to pursue his glory in us because they are not two different pursuits. God is most glorified in us when we are most satisfied in him.

God's Self-Exaltation: Signpost to Human Satisfaction

Therefore, when we read hundreds of texts in the Bible that show God passionately exalting his own glory, we no longer hear them as the passions of an overweening, uncaring ego. We hear them as the rightful exaltation of One who is infinitely exalted, and we hear them as God's pursuit of our deepest satisfaction in him. God is utterly unique. He is the only being in the universe worthy of worship. Therefore, when he exalts himself he directs people to true and lasting joy.

"In your presence there is fullness of joy; at your right hand are pleasures forevermore" (Ps. 16:11). But when we exalt ourselves, we are distracting people from what will bring true and lasting joy. So for us to be loving we must exalt God, and for God to be loving he must exalt God. Love is helping people toward the greatest beauty and the highest value and the deepest satisfaction and the most lasting joy and the biggest reward and the most wonderful friendship and the most overwhelming worship—love is helping people toward God. We do this by pointing to the greatness of God. And God does it by pointing to the greatness of God.

God Exalts Himself in Mercy

There is another way to see how God's passion for his own glory is loving, and here the connection between the supremacy of God and the cause of missions becomes explicit. The connection between missions and the supremacy of God is found in this sentence: *The glory God seeks to magnify is supremely the glory of his mercy.* The key text is Romans 15:8–9:

> I tell you that Christ became a servant to the circumcised [Jewish people] to show God's truthfulness, *in order to confirm the promises given to the patriarchs, and in order that the Gentiles might glorify God for his mercy.*

Notice three interlocking truths in these great missionary verses.

1. *Zeal for the glory of God motivates world missions.* Paul gives three reasons why Christ humbled himself as a servant and came into the world on that first great missionary journey from heaven to earth. First, "Christ became a servant . . . *to show God's truthfulness.*" Second, he came "in order *to confirm [God's] promises.*" Third, he came "in order that the [nations] *might glorify God* for his mercy."

In other words, Christ was on a mission to magnify God. He came to show that *God* is truthful. He came to show that *God* is a promisekeeper. And he came to show that *God* is glorious. Jesus came into the world for *God's sake*—to certify *God's* integrity, to vindicate *God's* Word, to magnify *God's* glory. Since God sent his Son to do all this, it is plain that the primary motive of the first great mission to unreached peoples—the mission of Jesus from heaven—was God's zeal for the glory of God. That's the first truth from Romans 15:8–9: Zeal for the glory of God motivates world missions.

2. *A servant spirit and a heart of mercy motivate world missions.*

"Christ became a *servant* . . . in order that the Gentiles might glorify God for his *mercy.*" Christ became a servant . . . and Christ brought mercy. He was a servant not only in that he humbled himself to do what the Father wanted him to do at great cost to himself. He was also a servant in that he lived his life for the sake of extending mercy to the nations. During his lifetime, he showed the connection between compassion and missions. We see this, for example, in Matthew 9:36–38:

> When he saw the crowds, he had compassion for them, because they were harassed and helpless, like sheep without a shepherd. Then he said to his disciples, "The harvest is plentiful, but the laborers are few; therefore pray earnestly to the Lord of the harvest to send out laborers into his harvest."

Jesus' compassion came to expression in the call to pray for more missionaries. From first to last, mercy was moving missions in the life of Jesus. And not only in his life but also in his death. "You were slain, and by your *blood* you ransomed people for God from every tribe and language and people and nation" (Rev. 5:9). Mercy was the very heart of Jesus' mission. No one deserved his mission. It was all mercy and all servanthood. That's the second truth from Romans 15:8–9: A servant spirit and a heart of mercy motivate world missions.

3. *The third truth is that the first and second truths are one truth.* Zeal for the glory of God and a servant heart of mercy for the nations are one. This is plain from the wording of verse 9: Christ came "in order that the Gentiles might glorify God." Yes! That was the passion of Christ, and it should be our passion—that the nations might love the glory of God and praise the glory of God. But the verse goes on: Christ came "that the Gentiles might glorify God *for his mercy.*" The motive of mercy and the motive of God's glory are not two different motives, because the glory we want to see exalted among the nations is supremely the glory of God's mercy.

Mercy is the apex of God's glory the way the overflow of a fountain is the apex of the fountain's fullness. God is free to be merciful because he is full and utterly self-sufficient in himself. He has no deficiencies or needs or defects. He relies totally on himself for all that he is. He never had a beginning or underwent any process of improvement through some influence outside himself. The glory of his all-sufficiency overflows in the freedom of his mercy to the nations. Therefore, extending God's mercy and exalting God's glory are one.[12]

12. For a more extended treatment of how God's God-centeredness is the ground of his mercy, see *Pleasures of God,* 104–9.

A heart for the glory of God and a heart of mercy for the nations make a Christlike missionary.[13] These must be kept together. If we have no zeal for the glory of God, our mercy becomes superficial, man-centered human improvement with no eternal significance. And if our zeal for the glory of God is not a reveling in his mercy, then our so-called zeal, in spite of all its protests, is out of touch with God and hypocritical (cf. Matt. 9:13).

He Does Everything for the Praise of the Glory of His Grace

This wonderful agreement between God's passion to be glorified and his passion to be gracious is also strikingly evident in the first chapter of Ephesians. Three times Paul says that God is doing all his saving work "to the praise of His glory" (NASB). And verse 6 makes clear that this glory is "the glory of His grace." Election, predestination, adoption, redemption, sealing by the Spirit, working all things according to the counsel of his will—God does all this to elicit praise for the glory of his grace. Verses 5–6: "He predestined us to adoption as sons through Jesus Christ . . . *to the praise of the glory of His grace.*" Verses 11–12: "[God] works all things after the counsel of His will, to the end that we who were the first to hope in Christ should be *to the praise of His glory.*" Verse 14: "[The Holy Spirit] is given as a pledge of our inheritance, with a view to the redemption of God's own possession, *to the praise of His glory.*"

This is just what we saw in Romans 15:9. There the nations glorify God for his mercy. Here they praise God for his grace. In both cases, God gets the glory and humans get the joy. So the more passionate God is for his glory, the more passionate he is for meeting our need as sinners. Grace is our only hope and the only hope of the nations. Therefore, the more zealous God is for his grace to be glorified, the more hope there is that missions will succeed.

The Power of Missions Is Worship

What we have been showing is that God's supremacy in his own heart is not unloving. It is, in fact, the fountain of love. God's full delight in his own perfections overflows in his merciful will to share that delight with the nations. We may reaffirm then the earlier truth that worship is the fuel and the goal that drive us in missions because it is

13. For further reflection on the interconnectedness of mercy and magnifying God in missions, see chapter 6 of this book, "A Passion for God's Supremacy and Compassion for Man's Soul."

the fuel and the goal that drive God in missions. Missions flows from the fullness of God's passion for God, and it aims at the participation of the nations in the very passion that he has for himself (cf. Matt. 25:21, 23; John 15:11; 17:13, 26). The power of the missionary enterprise is to be caught up into God's fuel and God's goal. And that means being caught up in worship.

Only One God Works for People Who Wait for Him

This remarkable vision of God as one who "exalts himself to show mercy" (Isa. 30:18) impels world missions in more ways than one. One way we have not pondered is the sheer uniqueness of this God among all the gods of the nations. Isaiah realizes this and says, "From of old no one has heard or perceived by the ear, no eye has seen a God besides you, who acts for those who wait for him" (Isa. 64:4). In other words, Isaiah is stunned that the greatness of God has the paradoxical effect that he does not need people to work for him but rather magnifies himself by working for them, if they will renounce self-reliance and "wait for him."

Isaiah anticipated the words of Paul in Acts 17:25: "[God is not] served by human hands, as though he needed anything, since he himself gives to all mankind life and breath and everything." The uniqueness at the heart of Christianity is the glory of God manifest in the freedom of grace. God is glorious because he does not need the nations to work for him. He is free to work for them. "The Son of Man came not to be served but to serve, and to give his life as a ransom for many" (Mark 10:45). Missions is not a recruitment project for God's labor force. It is a liberation project from the heavy burdens and hard yokes of other gods (Matt. 11:28–30).

Isaiah says that such a God has not been seen or heard anywhere in the world. "From of old no one has heard or perceived by the ear, no eye has seen a God besides you, who acts for those who wait for him" (Isa. 64:4). What Isaiah sees everywhere he looks are gods who have *to be served* rather than serve. For example, the Babylonian gods Bel and Nebo: "Bel bows down; Nebo stoops; their idols are on beasts and livestock; these things you carry are borne as burdens on weary beasts. They stoop; they bow down together; they cannot save the burden, but themselves go into captivity. Listen to me, O house of Jacob, all the remnant of the house of Israel, who have been borne by me from before your birth, carried from the womb; even to your old age I am he, and to gray hairs I will carry you. I have made, and I will bear; I will carry and will save" (Isa. 46:1–4; cf. Jer. 10:5).

The difference between the true God and the gods of the nations is that the true God carries and the other gods must be carried. God serves; they must be served. God glorifies his might by showing mercy. They glorify theirs by gathering slaves. So the vision of God as one whose passion for his glory moves him to mercy impels missions because he is utterly unique among all the gods.

The Most Shareable Message in the World

There is yet another way that such a God motivates the missionary enterprise. The gospel demand that flows from such a God to the nations is an eminently shareable, doable demand, namely, to rejoice and be glad in God. "The LORD reigns; let the earth *rejoice;* let the many coastlands *be glad!*" (Ps. 97:1). "Let the peoples praise you, O God; let all the peoples praise you! Let the nations *be glad and sing for joy!*" (Ps. 67:3–4). "Let the oppressed see it and *be glad;* you who seek God, *let your hearts revive*" (Ps. 69:32 RSV). "May all who seek you *rejoice and be glad in you!* May those who love your salvation say evermore, 'God is great!'" (Ps. 70:4). What message would missionaries rather take than the message, "Be glad in God! Rejoice in God! Sing for joy in God! For God is most glorified in you when you are most satisfied in him! God loves to exalt himself by showing mercy to sinners."

The liberating fact is that the message we take to the frontiers is that people everywhere should seek their own best interest. We are summoning people to God. And those who come say, "In your presence there is fullness of joy; at your right hand are pleasures forevermore" (Ps. 16:11). God glorifies himself among the nations with the command, "Delight yourself in the LORD!" (Ps. 37:4). His first and great requirement of all men everywhere is that they repent from seeking their joy in other things and begin to seek it only in him. A God who cannot be served[14] is a God who can only be enjoyed. The great sin of the world is not that the human race has failed to work for God so as to *increase* his glory but that we have failed to delight in God so as to *reflect* his glory, for God's glory is most reflected in us when we are most delighted in him.

The most exhilarating thought in the world is that God's inexorable purpose to display his glory in the mission of the church is virtually

---

14. I am aware that the Bible is replete with pictures of God's people serving him. I have dealt in some detail with the way service can be conceived biblically so as not to put God in the category of an employer who depends on wage earners. See *Desiring God*, 144–49.

the same as his purpose to give his people infinite delight. The glory of a Mountain Spring is seen in how many people (and how many different peoples!) find satisfaction and life in its overflowing streams. Therefore, God is committed to the holy joy of the redeemed, gathered from every tribe and tongue and people and nation, with the same zeal that moves him to seek his own glory in all that he does. The supremacy of God in the heart of God is the driving force of his mercy and the missionary movement of his church.

Biblical Expressions of the Supremacy of God in Missions

Against the background we have developed so far, we may now be able to feel the full force of those biblical texts that emphasize the supremacy of God in the missionary impulse of the church. The motives we see will confirm the centrality of God in the missionary vision of the Bible.

We have seen some of the Old Testament texts that make the glory of God the centerpiece of missionary proclamation: "Declare his glory among the nations, his marvelous works among all the peoples!" (Ps. 96:3). "Proclaim that his name is exalted" (Isa. 12:4). There are many others.[15] But we have not yet seen the straightforward statements of Jesus, Paul, and John that say the same thing.

Leaving Family and Possessions for the Sake of the Name

When Jesus turned the rich young ruler away because he was not willing to leave his wealth to follow Jesus, the Lord said, "Only with difficulty will a rich person enter the kingdom of heaven" (Matt. 19:23). The apostles were amazed and said, "Who then can be saved?" (v. 25). Jesus answered, "With man this is impossible, but with God all things are possible." (v. 26). Then Peter, speaking as a kind of missionary who had left his home and business to follow Jesus, said, "See, we have left everything and followed you. What then will we have?" (v. 27). Jesus answered with a mild rebuke of Peter's sense of sacrifice: "Everyone who has left houses or brothers or sisters or father or mother or children or lands, *for my name's sake,* will receive a hundredfold and will inherit eternal life" (v. 29).

The one point of focus for us here is the phrase "for my name's sake." The motive that Jesus virtually takes for granted when a missionary leaves home and family and possessions is that it is *for the sake of the name of Jesus.* That means for the sake of Jesus' reputation. God's goal is that his Son's name be exalted and honored among all

---

15. See an extensive list of these texts in chapter 5.

the peoples of the world, for when the Son is honored, the Father is honored (Mark 9:37). When every knee bows at the name of Jesus, it will be "to the glory of God the Father" (Phil. 2:10–11). Therefore, God-centered missions exists for the sake of the name of Jesus.

A Missionary Prayer for God's Name to Be Hallowed

The first two petitions of the Lord's Prayer are perhaps the clearest statements in the teachings of Jesus that missions is driven by the passion of God to be glorified among the nations. "Hallowed be your name. Your kingdom come" (Matt. 6:9–10). Here Jesus teaches us to ask God to hallow his name and to make his kingdom come. This is a missionary prayer. Its aim is to engage the passion of God for his name among those who forget or revile the name of God (Pss. 9:17; 74:18). To hallow God's name means to put it in a class by itself and to cherish and honor it above every claim to our allegiance or affection. Jesus' primary concern—the very first petition of the prayer he teaches—is that more and more people, and more and more peoples, come to hallow God's name. This is the reason the universe exists. Missions exists because this hallowing does not.

How Much He Must Suffer for the Name

When Paul was converted on the Damascus road, Jesus Christ became the supreme treasure and joy of his life. "I count everything as loss because of the surpassing worth of knowing Christ Jesus my Lord" (Phil. 3:8). It was a costly allegiance. What Paul learned in Damascus was not only the joy of sins forgiven and fellowship with the King of the universe but also how much he would have to suffer. Jesus sent Ananias to him with this message: "I will show him how much he must suffer *for the sake of my name*" (Acts 9:16). Paul's missionary sufferings were "for the sake of the name." When he came near the end of his life and was warned not to go to Jerusalem, he answered, "What are you doing, weeping and breaking my heart? For I am ready not only to be imprisoned but even to die in Jerusalem *for the name of the Lord Jesus*" (Acts 21:13). For Paul, the glory of the name of Jesus and his reputation in the world were more important than life.

"For the Sake of His Name among All the Nations"

Paul makes crystal clear in Romans 1:5 that his mission and calling are for the name of Christ among all the nations: "We have received grace and apostleship to bring about the obedience of faith *for the sake of his name among all the nations.*"

The apostle John described the motive of early Christian missionaries in the same way. He wrote to tell one of his churches that they should send out Christian brothers in a manner "worthy of God." And the reason he gives is that "they have gone out *for the sake of the name,* accepting nothing from the Gentiles" (3 John 6–7).

John Stott comments on these two texts (Rom. 1:5; 3 John 7): "They knew that God had superexalted Jesus, enthroning him at his right hand and bestowing upon him the highest rank, in order that every tongue should confess his lordship. They longed that Jesus should receive the honor due to his name."[16] This longing is not a dream but a certainty. At the bottom of all our hope, when everything else has given way, we stand on this great reality: The everlasting, all-sufficient God is infinitely, unwaveringly, and eternally committed to the glory of his great and holy name. For the sake of his fame among the nations he will act. His name will not be profaned forever. The mission of the church will be victorious. He will vindicate his people and his cause in all the earth.

May the Blessed Redeemer See the Travail of His Soul!

David Brainerd, the missionary to the Indians in New Jersey in the 1740s, was sustained by this confidence to his death at age twenty-nine. Seven days before he died in 1747, he spoke of his longing for the glory of God in the world. These are the last words he had the strength to write with his own hand:

> Friday, October 2. My soul was this day, at turns, sweetly set on God: I longed to be "with him" that I might "behold his glory." . . . Oh, that his kingdom might come in the world; that they might all love and glorify him for what he is in himself; and that the blessed Redeemer might "see of the travail of his soul, and be satisfied." Oh, "come, Lord Jesus, come quickly! Amen."[17]

The absence of Brainerd's passion for God is the great cause of missionary weakness in the churches. This was Andrew Murray's judgment a hundred years ago:

16. John R. W. Stott, "The Bible in World Evangelization," in *Perspectives on the World Christian Movement: A Reader,* 3d ed., ed. Ralph D. Winter and Steven C. Hawthorne (Pasadena, Calif.: William Carey Library, 1999), 22.

17. Jonathan Edwards, *The Life of David Brainerd,* ed. Norman Pettit, vol. 7 of *The Works of Jonathan Edwards* (New Haven: Yale University Press, 1985), 474. For a more accessible version of Brainerd's diary, see Philip E. Howard Jr., *The Life and Diary of David Brainerd, ed. by Jonathan Edwards with a Biographical Sketch of the Life and Work of Jonathan Edwards* (Grand Rapids: Baker, 1989).

As we seek to find out why, with such millions of Christians, the real army of God that is fighting the hosts of darkness is so small, the only answer is—lack of heart. The enthusiasm of the kingdom is missing. And that is because there is so little enthusiasm for the *King*.[18]

This is still true today. Peter Beyerhaus also sees it clearly and calls us to put the glory of God at the center of our life and mission.

> We are called and sent to glorify the reign of God and to manifest His saving work before the whole world. . . . Today it is extremely important to emphasize the priority of this doxological aim before all other aims of mission. Our one-sided concern with man and his society threatens to pervert mission and make it a secular or even a quasi-atheistic undertaking. We are living in an age of apostasy where man arrogantly makes himself the measuring rod of all things. Therefore, it is a part of our missionary task courageously to confess before all enemies of the cross that the earth belongs to God and to His anointed. . . . Our task in mission is to uphold the banner of the risen Lord before the whole world, because it is his own.[19]

The zeal of the church for the glory of her King will not rise until pastors and mission leaders and seminary teachers make much more of the King. When the glory of God himself saturates our preaching and teaching and conversation and writings, and when he predominates above our talk of methods and strategies and psychological buzzwords and cultural trends, then the people might begin to feel that he is the central reality of their lives and that the spread of his glory is more important than all their possessions and all their plans.

The Power of Missions When Love for the Lost Is Weak

Compassion for the lost is a high and beautiful motive for missionary labor. Without it we lose the sweet humility of sharing a treasure we have freely received. But we have seen that compassion for people must not be detached from passion for the glory of God. John Dawson, a leader in Youth With a Mission, gives an additional reason why this is so. He points out that a strong feeling of love for "the lost" or "the world" is a very difficult experience to sustain and is not always recognizable when it comes.

18. Andrew Murray, *Key to the Missionary Problem* (Fort Washington, Pa.: Christian Literature Crusade, 1979), 133.
19. Peter Beyerhaus, *Shaken Foundations: Theological Foundations for Missions* (Grand Rapids: Zondervan, 1972), 41–42.

Have you ever wondered what it feels like to have a love for the lost? This is a term we use as part of our Christian jargon. Many believers search their hearts in condemnation, looking for the arrival of some feeling of benevolence that will propel them into bold evangelism. It will never happen. It is impossible to love "the lost." You can't feel deeply for an abstraction or a concept. You would find it impossible to love deeply an unfamiliar individual portrayed in a photograph, let alone a nation or a race or something as vague as "all lost people."

Don't wait for a feeling of love in order to share Christ with a stranger. You already love your heavenly Father, and you know that this stranger is created by Him, but separated from Him, so take those first steps in evangelism because you love God. It is not primarily out of a compassion for humanity that we share our faith or pray for the lost; it is first of all, love for God. The Bible says in Ephesians 6:7–8: "With good will doing service, as to the Lord, and not to men, knowing that whatever good anyone does, he will receive the same from the Lord, whether he is a slave or free."

Humanity does not deserve the love of God any more than you or I do. We should never be Christian humanists, taking Jesus to poor sinful people, reducing Jesus to some kind of product that will better their lot. People deserve to be damned, but Jesus, the suffering Lamb of God, deserves the reward of His suffering.[20]

The Miracle of Love

Dawson's words are a wise and encouraging warning not to limit our mission engagement to the level of compassion we feel for people we do not know. However, I don't want to minimize what the Lord is able to do in giving people a supernatural burden of love for distant peoples. For example, Wesley Duewel of OMS International tells the story of his mother's remarkable burden for China and India:

My mother for years carried a hunger for the people of China and India. For many years practically every day as she prayed during family prayer for these two nations she would break down and weep before she finished praying. Her love was deep and constant, and she will be rewarded eternally for her years of love-burden for those lands. This is the love of Jesus reaching out and mediated through Christians by the Holy Spirit.[21]

I emphasize again that the motive of compassion and the motive of zeal for the glory of God are not separate. The weeping of compassion

20. John Dawson, *Taking Our Cities for God* (Lake Mary, Fla.: Creation House, 1989), 208–9.

21. Wesley Duewel, *Ablaze for God* (Grand Rapids: Francis Asbury Press of Zondervan, 1989), 115–16.

is the weeping of joy in God impeded in the extension of itself to another.[22]

The Call of God

God is calling us above all else to be the kind of people whose theme and passion is the supremacy of God in all of life. No one will be able to rise to the magnificence of the missionary cause who does not feel the magnificence of Christ. There will be no big world vision without a big God. There will be no passion to draw others into our worship where there is no passion for worship.

God is pursuing with omnipotent passion a worldwide purpose of gathering joyful worshipers for himself from every tribe and tongue and people and nation. He has an inexhaustible enthusiasm for the supremacy of his name among the nations. Therefore, let us bring our affections into line with his, and, for the sake of his name, let us renounce the quest for worldly comforts and join his global purpose. If we do this, God's omnipotent commitment to his name will be over us like a banner, and we will not lose, in spite of many tribulations (Acts 9:16; Rom. 8:35–39). Missions is not the ultimate goal of the church. Worship is. Missions exists because worship doesn't. The Great Commission is first to "delight yourself in the LORD" (Ps. 37:4) and then to declare, "Let the nations *be glad and sing for joy*" (Ps. 67:4). In this way, God will be glorified from beginning to end, and worship will empower the missionary enterprise until the coming of the Lord.

> Great and amazing are your deeds,
>   O Lord God the Almighty!
> Just and true are your ways,
>   O King of the nations!
> Who will not fear, O Lord,
>   and glorify your name?
> For you alone are holy.
>   All nations will come
>   and worship you,
> for your righteous acts have been revealed.
>
> Revelation 15:3–4

---

22. On this theme, see chapter 6 of this book, "A Passion for God's Supremacy and Compassion for Man's Soul."

2

The Supremacy of God
in Missions through Prayer

We cannot know what prayer is for until we know that life is war.

Life is war. That's not all it is. But it is always that. Our weakness in prayer is owing largely to our neglect of this truth. Prayer is primarily a wartime walkie-talkie for the mission of the church as it advances against the powers of darkness and unbelief. It is not surprising that prayer malfunctions when we try to make it a domestic intercom to call upstairs for more comforts in the den. God has given us prayer as a wartime walkie-talkie so that we can call headquarters for everything we need as the kingdom of Christ advances in the world. Prayer gives *us* the significance of frontline forces and gives *God* the glory of a limitless Provider. The one who gives the power gets the glory. Thus, prayer safeguards the supremacy of God in missions while linking us with endless grace for every need.

Life Is War

When Paul came to the end of his life, he said in 2 Timothy 4:7, "I have fought *the good fight*, I have finished the race, I have kept the faith." In 1 Timothy 6:12, he tells Timothy, *"Fight the good fight* of the faith. Take hold of the eternal life to which you were called." For Paul, all of life was war. Yes, he used other images as well—farming, athletics, family, building, shepherding, and so on. And yes, he was a man who loved peace. But the pervasiveness of war is seen precisely in the fact that one of the weapons of war is the gospel of peace! (Eph. 6:15).

45

Yes, he was a man of tremendous joy. But this joy was usually a "rejoicing in the sufferings" of his embattled mission (Rom. 5:3; 12:12; 2 Cor. 6:10; Phil. 2:17; Col. 1:24; cf. 1 Peter 1:6; 4:13).

Life is war because the maintenance of our faith and the laying hold on eternal life is a constant fight. Paul makes clear in 1 Thessalonians 3:5 that Satan targets our faith for destruction. "I sent to learn about your *faith*, for fear that somehow the tempter had tempted you and *our labor would be in vain*." Satan's attack in Thessalonica was against the Christians' faith. His aim was to make Paul's work there "vain"—empty, destroyed.

It's true that Paul believed in the eternal security of the elect ("Those whom [God] justified he also glorified" [Rom. 8:30]). But the only people who are eternally secure are those who "make their calling and election sure" by fighting the good fight of faith and laying hold on eternal life (1 Tim. 6:12; 2 Peter 1:10). Jesus said, "The one who endures to the end will be saved" (Mark 13:13). And Satan is fighting always to bring us to ruin by destroying our faith.

The word for "fight" in 1 Timothy, *agōnizesthai*, is used repeatedly in describing the Christian life. Jesus said, "*Strive* to enter through the narrow door. For many, I tell you, will seek to enter and will not be able" (Luke 13:24). Hebrews 4:11 says, "Let us therefore *strive* to enter that rest, so that no one may fall by the same sort of disobedience." Paul compares the Christian life to a race and says, "Every athlete *strives* and uses self-control in all things. They do it to obtain a perishable crown, but we do it to obtain an imperishable one" (1 Cor. 9:25, author's translation). He describes his ministry of proclamation and teaching in these terms: "For this I toil, *struggling* with all his energy that he powerfully works within me" (Col. 1:29). And he says that prayer is part of this fight: "Epaphras, who is one of you, a servant of Christ Jesus, greets you, always *struggling* on your behalf in his prayers" (Col. 4:12). "*Strive* together with me in your prayers to God on my behalf" (Rom. 15:30). It's the same word each time: the word for "fight."

Paul is even more graphic at times with other warfare language. Concerning his own life of warfare he said, "I do not run aimlessly; I do not *box* as one beating the air. But I discipline my body and keep it under control, lest after preaching to others I myself should be disqualified" (1 Cor. 9:26–27). He runs a race, he fights a boxing match, and he strives against the forces of his own body. Concerning his ministry he said, "Though we walk in the flesh, we are not waging *war* according to the flesh. For the *weapons of our warfare* are not of the flesh but have divine power to destroy strongholds. We destroy arguments and every lofty opinion raised against the knowledge of God, and take every thought captive to obey Christ" (2 Cor. 10:3–5).

Paul encouraged Timothy to see his whole ministry as war: "This charge I entrust to you, Timothy, my child, in accordance with the prophecies previously made about you, that by them you may *wage the good warfare*" (1 Tim. 1:18). "No *soldier* gets entangled in civilian pursuits" (2 Tim. 2:4). In other words, missions and ministry are war.

Probably the most familiar passage on our daily warfare is Ephesians 6:12–18, where Paul lists the pieces of the "whole armor of God." We must not miss the forest for the trees here. The simple assumption of this familiar passage is this: Life is war. Paul simply assumes this and then tells us what kind of war it is: not "against flesh and blood, but against the rulers, against the authorities, against the cosmic powers over this present darkness, against the spiritual forces of evil in the heavenly places. Therefore take up the whole armor of God" (vv. 12–13).

Then all the precious blessings of life that could be thought of in contexts other than war are drafted for the battle. If we know *truth*, it is for a belt in the armor. If we have *righteousness*, we must wear it as a breastplate. If we cherish *the gospel of peace*, it must become a soldier's footwear. If we love *resting* in the promises of God, that faith must be fastened on our left arm as a shield against flaming arrows. If we delight in our *salvation*, we must fit it securely on our head as a helmet. If we love *the Word of God* as sweeter than honey, we must make the honey a sword. Virtually every "civilian" blessing in the Christian life is conscripted for the war. There is not a warfare part of life and a non-warfare part. Life is war.[1]

The Absence of Austerity

But most people do not believe this in their heart. Most people show by their priorities and their casual approach to spiritual things that they believe we are in peacetime, not wartime.

In wartime, the newspapers carry headlines about how the troops are doing. In wartime, families talk about the sons and daughters on the front lines and write to them and pray for them with heart-wrenching concern for their safety. In wartime, we are on the alert. We are armed. We are vigilant. In wartime, we spend money differently—there is austerity, not for its own sake but because there are more strategic ways to spend money than on new tires at home. The

---

1. There are other texts we could look at besides those cited, for example, Rev. 6:2; 12:17; 17:14.

war effort touches everybody. We all cut back. The luxury liner becomes a troop carrier.

Very few people think that we are in a war that is greater than World War II or any imaginable nuclear war. Few reckon that Satan is a much worse enemy than any earthly foe or realize that the conflict is not restricted to any one global theater but is in every town and city in the world. Who considers that the casualties of this war do not merely lose an arm or an eye or an earthly life but lose everything—even their own soul—and enter a hell of everlasting torment?

In the *Screwtape Letters* by C. S. Lewis, Screwtape (the devil) tells Wormwood (a subordinate evil spirit) "not to hope for too much from a war." He was referring to the agonies of the Second World War. He explains that war will not destroy the faith of real believers and will, thanks to God's high-handed ways, produce a good deal of unwanted seriousness about life, death, and the issues of eternity. "How disastrous for us," the devil complains, "is the continual remembrance of death which war enforces. One of our best weapons, contented worldliness, is rendered useless. In wartime not even a human can believe that he is going to live forever."[2] So it may even take a lesser war—such as a World War III or a war of sheer terrorism—to waken us to the more serious war that rages daily for the soul.

Prayer Is for Wielding the Word

Until we feel the force of this, we will not pray as we ought. We will not even know what prayer is. In Ephesians 6:17–18, Paul makes the connection between the life of war and the work of prayer: "Take . . . the sword of the Spirit, which is the word of God, praying at all times in the Spirit, with all prayer and supplication. To that end keep alert with all perseverance, making supplication for all the saints." Notice that, true to the original Greek, verse 18 does not begin a new sentence. It connects with verse 17 like this: "Take the sword of the Spirit, which is the word of God, praying at all times in the Spirit, with all prayer and supplication." Take the sword . . . praying! This is how we are to wield the word—by prayer.

Prayer is the communication with headquarters by which the weapons of warfare are deployed according to the will of God. That's the connection between the weapons and prayer in Ephesians 6. Prayer is for war.

2. C. S. Lewis, *Screwtape Letters* (London: Geoffrey Bles: The Centenary Press, 1942), 32.

Missions Is Given as a Field for Prayer

The connection between prayer and missions can be seen in a passage that doesn't use warfare words but deals with the same reality, namely, John 15:16. Jesus said, "You did not choose me, but I chose you and appointed you that you should go and bear fruit and that your fruit should abide, *so that* whatever you ask the Father in my name, he may give it to you."

The logic of this sentence is crucial. Why is the Father going to give the disciples what they ask in Jesus' name? Answer: Because they have been sent to bear fruit. The reason the Father gives the disciples the instrument of prayer is because Jesus has given them a mission. In fact, the grammar of John 15:16 implies that the reason Jesus gives them their mission is so that they will be able to use the power of prayer. "I appointed you that you should go and bear fruit . . . *so that* whatever you ask the Father in my name, he may give it to you." This is just another way of saying that prayer is a wartime walkie-talkie. God designed it and gave it to us for use on a mission. You can say the mission is to "bear fruit," or you can say the mission is to "set the captives free." The point stays the same: Prayer is designed to extend the kingdom into fruitless enemy territory.

Why Prayer Malfunctions

Probably the number one reason prayer malfunctions in the hands of believers is that we try to turn a wartime walkie-talkie into a domestic intercom. Until you know that life is war, you cannot know what prayer is for. Prayer is for the accomplishment of a wartime mission. It is as though the field commander (Jesus) called in the troops, gave them a crucial mission (go and bear fruit), handed each of them a personal transmitter coded to the frequency of the General's headquarters, and said, "Comrades, the General has a mission for you. He aims to see it accomplished. And to that end he has authorized me to give each of you personal access to him through these transmitters. If you stay true to his mission and seek his victory first, he will always be as close as your transmitter, to give tactical advice and to send air cover when you need it."

But what have millions of Christians done? We have stopped believing that we are in a war. No urgency, no watching, no vigilance. No strategic planning. Just easy peace and prosperity. And what did we do with the walkie-talkie? We tried to rig it up as an intercom in our houses and cabins and boats and cars—not to call in firepower for conflict with a mortal enemy but to ask for more comforts in the den.

Times of Great Distress

In Luke 21:34–35, Jesus warned his disciples that times of great distress and opposition were coming. Then he said, "But stay awake at all times, *praying* that you may have strength to escape all these things that are going to take place, and to stand before the Son of Man" (v. 36). In other words, following Jesus will lead us into severe conflict with evil. It will mean war. Evil will surround us and attack us and threaten to destroy our faith. But God has given us a transmitter. If we go to sleep, it will do us no good. But if we are alert, as Jesus says, and call for help in the conflict, the help will come and the Commander will not let his faithful soldiers be denied their crown of victory before the Son of Man. Thus, repeatedly we see the same truth: We cannot know what prayer is for until we know that life is war.

Praying for Peace Is Part of the War

But 1 Timothy 2:1–4 looks as though it might conflict with this battlefield image of prayer. Paul says that he wants us to pray for kings and for all who are in high positions "that we may lead a peaceful and quiet life, godly and dignified in every way" (v. 2). Now, that sounds very domestic and civilian and peaceful.

But read on. The reason for praying this way is highly strategic. Verses 3–4 say, "This [praying for peace] is good, and it is pleasing in the sight of God our Savior, who desires all people to be saved and to come to the knowledge of the truth." God aims to save people from every tribe and tongue and people and nation. But one of the great obstacles to victory is when people are swept up into social, political, and militaristic conflicts that draw away their attention, time, energy, and creativity from the real battle of the universe.

Satan's aim is that no one be saved and come to a knowledge of the truth. And one of his key strategies is to start battles in the world that draw our attention away from the real battle for the salvation of the lost and the perseverance of the saints. He knows that the real battle, as Paul says, is not against flesh and blood. So the more wars and conflicts and revolutions of "flesh and blood" he can start, the better, as far as he is concerned.

So when Paul tells us to pray for peace precisely because God desires all men to be saved and to come to a knowledge of the truth, he is not picturing prayer as a kind of harmless domestic intercom for increasing our civilian conveniences. He is picturing it as a strategic appeal to headquarters to ask that the enemy not be allowed to draw any firepower away to decoy conflicts of flesh and blood.

The Crying Need of the Hour

So the truth is reaffirmed: God has given us prayer because Jesus has given us a mission. We are on this earth to press back the forces of darkness, and we are given access to headquarters by prayer to advance this cause. When we try to turn it into a civilian intercom to increase our conveniences, it stops working, and our faith begins to falter. We have so domesticated prayer that for many of us it is no longer what it was designed to be—a wartime walkie-talkie for the accomplishment of Christ's mission.

We simply must seek for ourselves and for our people a wartime mentality. Otherwise the biblical teaching about the urgency of prayer and the vigilance of prayer and the watching in prayer and the perseverance of prayer and the danger of abandoning prayer will make no sense and find no resonance in our hearts. Until we feel the desperation of a bombing raid or the thrill of a new strategic offensive for the gospel, we will not pray in the spirit of Jesus.

The crying need of the hour is to put the churches on a wartime footing. Mission leaders are crying out, "Where is the church's concept of militancy, of a mighty army willing to suffer, moving ahead with exultant determination to take the world by storm? Where is the risk-taking, the launching out on God alone?"[3] The answer is that it has been swallowed up in a peacetime mentality.

We are a "third soil century." In the parable of the soils, Jesus says that the seed is the Word. He sows his urgent Word of kingdom power. But instead of taking it up as our sword (or bearing fruit), we "are those who hear the word, but the cares of the world and the deceitfulness of riches and the desires for other things enter in and choke the word, and it proves unfruitful" (Mark 4:18–19).

This is why Paul says that *all* of life is war—every moment. Before we can even engage in the mission of the church, we have to fight against the "the deceitfulness of riches" and "desires for other things." We must fight to cherish the kingdom above all "other things"—that is our first and most constant battle. That is the fight of faith. Then, when we have some experience in that basic battle, we join the fight to commend the kingdom to all the nations.

God Will Win the War

Now, into this warfare God asserts himself for the triumph of his cause. He does this in an unmistakable way so that the victory will re-

---

3. James Reapsome, "What's Holding Up World Evangelization?" *Evangelical Missions Quarterly* 24, no. 2 (April 1988): 118.

dound to his glory. His purpose in all of history is to uphold and display his glory for the enjoyment of his redeemed people from all the nations. Therefore, God engages in the battle so that the triumphs are manifestly his. As we saw in chapter 1, the chief end of God is to glorify God and enjoy his excellence forever. This is what guarantees the victory of his cause. In order to magnify his glory, he will exert his sovereign power and complete the mission he has commanded.

Power of the Puritan Hope

This confidence in the sovereignty of God and the triumph of his cause is essential in the prayers of God's people and the mission of the church. It has proven to be a powerful force in the history of missions. The first missionary endeavor of the Protestants in England burst forth from the soil of Puritan hope. The Puritans were those pastors and teachers in England (and then New England), roughly between the years 1560 and 1660, who wanted to purify the Church of England and bring it into theological and practical alignment with the teachings of the Reformation.[4]

They had a view of God's sovereignty that produced an undaunted hope in the victory of God over all the world. They were deeply stirred by a passion for the coming of God's kingdom over all the nations. Their hearts really believed the truth of the promises that Christ's cause would triumph. "I will build my church, and the gates of hell shall not prevail against it" (Matt. 16:18). "This gospel of the kingdom will be proclaimed throughout the whole world as a testimony to all the nations, and then the end will come" (Matt. 24:14). "All the nations you have made shall come and worship before you, O Lord, and shall glorify your name" (Ps. 86:9). "In you all the families of the earth shall be blessed" (Gen. 12:3). "I will make the nations your heritage" (Ps. 2:8). "All the ends of the world shall remember and turn to the LORD, and all the families of the nations shall worship before you" (Ps. 22:27). "All the earth will worship You, And will sing praises to You; They will sing praises to Your name" (Ps. 66:4 NASB). "To him shall be the obedience of the peoples" (Gen. 49:10).[5]

---

4. For introductions to Puritanism, see Leland Ryken, *Worldly Saints: The Puritans as They Really Were* (Grand Rapids: Zondervan, 1991); J. I. Packer, *A Quest for Godliness: The Puritan Vision of the Godly Life* (Wheaton: Crossway, 1994); Peter Lewis, *The Genius of Puritanism* (Morgan, Pa.: Soli Deo Gloria, 1998); and Erroll Hulse, *Who Are the Puritans, and What Do They Teach?* (Darlington, England: Evangelical Press, 2000).

5. For additional texts concerning the promise of Christ's victory over the nations and their eventual turning to him, see chapter 5.

This tremendous confidence that Christ would one day conquer hearts in every nation and be glorified by every people on earth gave birth to the first Protestant missionary endeavor in the English-speaking world, and it happened 150 years before the modern missionary movement began with William Carey in 1793.

Between 1627 and 1640, 15,000 people emigrated from England to America, most of them Puritans, carrying this great confidence in the worldwide reign of Christ. In fact, the seal of the colonists of Massachusetts Bay had on it a North American Indian with these words coming out of his mouth: "Come over into Macedonia and help us," which was taken from Acts 16:9. What this shows is that in general the Puritans saw their emigration to America as part of God's missionary strategy to extend his kingdom among the nations.

The Prayers and Pain of John Eliot

One of those hope-filled Puritans who crossed the Atlantic in 1631 was John Eliot. He was twenty-seven years old and a year later became the pastor of a new church in Roxbury, Massachusetts, about a mile from Boston. But something happened that made him much more than a pastor.

According to Cotton Mather, there were twenty tribes of Indians in that vicinity. John Eliot could not avoid the practical implications of his theology: If the infallible Scriptures promise that all nations will one day bow down to Christ, and if Christ is sovereign and able by his Spirit through prayer to subdue all opposition to his promised reign, then there is good hope that a person who goes as an ambassador of Christ to one of these nations will be the chosen instrument of God to open the eyes of the blind and to set up an outpost of the kingdom of Christ.

And so when he was slightly over forty (not twenty but forty!) years old, Eliot set himself to study Algonquin. He deciphered the vocabulary, grammar, and syntax and eventually translated the entire Bible as well as books that he valued such as Richard Baxter's *Call to the Unconverted.* By the time Eliot was eighty-four years old, there were numerous Indian churches, some with their own Indian pastors. It is an amazing story of a man who once said, "Prayers and pains through faith in Christ Jesus will do any thing!"[6]

The reason I tell this story is to highlight the tremendous importance of solid biblical *hope* on the basis of which we pray in the cause

6. Cotton Mather, *The Great Works of Christ in America*, vol. 1 (1702; reprint, Edinburgh: Banner of Truth Trust, 1979), 562.

of world missions. God has promised and God is sovereign: *"All the nations . . . shall come and worship before you, O Lord, and shall glorify your name"* (Ps. 86:9).

This is what gripped the Puritan mind and eventually gave birth to the modern missionary movement in 1793. William Carey was nourished on this tradition, as were David Brainerd[7] and Adoniram Judson, Alexander Duff and David Livingstone, John Paton[8] and a host of others who gave their lives to reach the unreached peoples of the world. The modern missionary movement did not arise in a theological vacuum. It grew out of a great Reformation tradition that put the sovereignty of God square in the center of human life. In the warfare of world missions, God bares his arm and triumphs for his own glory.[9]

Missions Is Supremely the Work of God

It is even more important to see how God triumphs for his own glory in Scripture than in the faith of great missionaries. The New Testament makes clear that God has not left his Great Commission to the uncertainties of the human will. The Lord said from the beginning, "I will build my church" (Matt. 16:18). World missions is supremely the work of the risen Lord Jesus.

7. For a brief overview of Brainerd's life and ministry, refer to John Piper, "'Oh, That I May Never Loiter on My Heavenly Journey!' Misery and Mission in the Life of David Brainerd," in John Piper, *The Hidden Smile of God: The Fruit of Affliction in the Lives of John Bunyan, William Cowper, and David Brainerd* (Wheaton: Crossway, 2001), 123–59. An earlier version of this biographical sketch may be found at www.DesiringGod.org. Also see Jonathan Edwards, *The Life of David Brainerd*, ed. Norman Pettit, vol. 7 of *The Works of Jonathan Edwards* (1749; reprint, New Haven: Yale University Press, 1985).

8. For a brief overview of Paton's life and ministry, refer to John Piper, "'You Will Be Eaten By Cannibals!' Courage in the Cause of World Missions: Lessons from the Life of John G. Paton" at www.DesiringGod.org. Also see *John G. Paton: Missionary to the New Hebredes, An Autobiography Edited by His Brother* (1889, 1891; reprint, Edinburgh: Banner of Truth Trust, 1965).

9. Whether one is a postmillennialist, as were most of the Puritans (though not all, e.g., William Twisse, Thomas Goodwin, William Bridge, and Jeremiah Burroughs, who were all premillennial Westminster divines in the seventeenth century), or whether one is a pre- or amillennialist, my point remains the same. Hope for the unstoppable success of Christ's mission (whether you see it as a golden age of gospel sway on earth or as an ingathering of the elect from every people group on earth) is a crucial element in motivation and power for missions. Iain Murray's book, *The Puritan Hope* (Edinburgh: Banner of Truth Trust, 1971), is an inspiring and compelling account of this truth. Its thesis is: "We believe it can be conclusively shown that the inspiration which gave rise to the first missionary societies of the modern era was nothing other than the doctrine and outlook which, revitalized by the eighteenth-century revival, had come down from the Puritans" (135).

"I Have Other Sheep . . . I Must Bring Them Also"

In the Gospel of John, Jesus put it like this: "I have other sheep that are not of this fold. I must bring them also, and they will listen to my voice" (John 10:16). This is the great missionary text in the Gospel of John. It is full of hope and power. It means that Christ has people besides those already converted. "I have *other sheep* that are not of this fold." This is a reference to the doctrine of election.[10] God chooses who will belong to his sheep, and they are already his before Jesus calls them. "All that the Father gives me will come to me, and whoever comes to me I *will* never cast out" (John 6:37; cf. 6:44–45; 8:47; 10:26–27; 17:6; 18:37). These sovereign "wills" of the Lord Jesus guarantee his invincible engagement in world missions.

There will always be people who argue that the doctrine of election makes missions unnecessary. But they are wrong. It does not make missions unnecessary; it makes missions hopeful. John Alexander, a former president of InterVarsity Christian Fellowship, said in a message at Urbana '67 (a decisive event in my own life), "At the beginning of my missionary career I said that if predestination were true I could not be a missionary. Now after twenty some years of struggling with the hardness of the human heart, I say I could never be a missionary *unless I believed in the doctrine of predestination.*"[11] It gives hope that Christ most certainly has "other sheep" among the nations.[12]

When Jesus says, "I must bring them also," he does not mean that he will do it without missionaries. That's plain from the fact that salvation comes through faith (John 1:12; 3:16; 6:35), and faith comes through the word of his disciples (John 17:20). Jesus brings his sheep into the fold through the preaching of those whom he sends, just as the Father sent him (John 20:21). So it is just as true today as in that day, "My sheep hear my voice, and I know them, and they follow me" (John 10:27). It is *Christ* who calls in the gospel. *Christ* gathers his sheep in world missions. That is why there is complete assurance that they will come.

10. I have given an extensive biblical defense of this truth in "The Pleasure of God in Election," in *The Pleasures of God* (Sisters, Ore.: Multnomah, 2000), 121–55.

11. This is a paraphrase of a sentence that is emblazoned on my memory because of the effect it had on my life at the time.

12. It was precisely this truth that encouraged the apostle Paul when he was downcast in Corinth. "And the Lord said to Paul one night in a vision, 'Do not be afraid, but go on speaking and do not be silent, for I am with you, and no one will attack you to harm you, for I have many in this city who are my people" (Acts 18:9–10). In other words, there are sheep here, and Jesus will call them through you, and they *will* come. Take heart.

Clothed with Power for Missions

When Jesus ascended to heaven, he told the disciples, "All authority in heaven and on earth has been given to me. . . . I am with you always, to the end of the age" (Matt. 28:18, 20). That's the authority with which he calls his sheep.

Then to make it plain that it would be his authority and his presence that would give success to the mission, he told his disciples to wait in Jerusalem until they were clothed with his power from on high (Luke 24:49). He said that the coming of that power through the Holy Spirit would enable them to be his witnesses "in Jerusalem and in all Judea and Samaria, and to the end of the earth" (Acts 1:8). When the Spirit comes, it is the Lord himself fulfilling the promise to build his church. Accordingly, Luke says, "The *Lord* added to their number day by day those who were being saved" (Acts 2:47). The Lord did it. And he continued to do it by converting the greatest missionary of all time (Acts 26:16–18) and directing the missionaries in their travels (Acts 8:26, 29; 16:7, 10) and giving them the words that they needed (Mark 13:11; Acts 6:10).

"Not I, but the Grace of God That Is with Me"

Paul was deeply aware that the success of his mission was the Lord's work and not his own. He said, "I will not venture to speak of anything except *what Christ has accomplished through me* to bring the Gentiles to obedience—by word and deed, by the power of signs and wonders, *by the power of the Spirit of God*" (Rom. 15:18–19). Paul's passion, as always, was to focus all glory on the supremacy of Christ in the mission of the church. The Lord was building his church.

How did Paul then speak of his own labors? He said, "By the grace of God I am what I am, and his grace toward me was not in vain. On the contrary, I worked harder than any of them, *though it was not I, but the grace of God that is with me*" (1 Cor. 15:10). Paul worked. Paul fought the fight and ran the race. But he did so, as he said in Philippians 2:13, because beneath and within his willing, God was at work to will and to do his good pleasure. Using a farming image, Paul put it like this: "I planted, Apollos watered, but God gave the growth. So neither he who plants nor he who waters is anything, but only God who gives the growth" (1 Cor. 3:6–7). Paul was jealous to uphold the supremacy of God in the mission of the church.

This jealousy for the glory of God in the mission of the church drove the apostles to minister in a way that would always magnify God and not themselves. For example, Peter taught the young churches, "Whoever serves [should do so] as one who serves by the strength that God supplies—in order that in everything God may be glorified through Jesus Christ" (1 Peter 4:11; cf. Heb. 13:20–21). The one who gives the strength gets the glory. So Peter drove home the absolute necessity of serving in the strength that God supplies and not our own. If God did not build his church, he would not get the glory, and all would be in vain, no matter how "successful" the work may look to the world.

New Covenant Confidence in the Sovereignty of God

The apostles knew that what was happening in their mission was the fulfillment of the promises of the new covenant. "[God] has made us competent to be ministers of a new covenant" (2 Cor. 3:6). And the new covenant promises were that God would overcome hardness of heart and make people new on the inside. "And I will give you a new heart, and a new spirit I will put within you. And I will remove the heart of stone from your flesh and give you a heart of flesh. And I will put my Spirit within you, and cause you to walk in my statutes and be careful to obey my rules" (Ezek. 36:26–27).

So as Luke tells how the Christian movement spread, he repeatedly records God's sovereign initiative in the growth of the church. When Cornelius and his household are converted, it is described as God's doing. "Then to the Gentiles also *God has granted repentance* that leads to life" (Acts 11:18). "God first visited the Gentiles, to take from them a people for his name" (Acts 15:14). When the gospel broke loose on European soil in Philippi beginning with Lydia, it was God who did it: "*The Lord opened her heart* to pay attention to what was said by Paul" (Acts 16:14).

In all these ways the supremacy of God in the mission of the church is clear. God does not put his gospel and his people in the world and leave them to wage war on their own. He is the main combatant, and the battle is to be fought in a way that gives him the glory.

Prayer Proves the Supremacy of God in Missions

This is why God has ordained prayer to have such a crucial place in the mission of the church. The purpose of prayer is to make clear to all the participants in this war that the victory belongs to the Lord. Prayer is God's appointed means of bringing grace to us and glory to himself. This is crystal clear in Psalm 50:15. God says, "Call upon me in the day of trouble; I will deliver you, and you shall glorify me." Charles Spurgeon makes the point unavoidable:

God and the praying man take shares. . . . First, here is your share: "Call upon me in the day of trouble." Secondly, here is God's share: "I will deliver thee." Again, you take a share—for you shall be delivered. And then again it is the Lord's turn—"Thou shalt glorify me." Here is a compact, a covenant that God enters into with you who pray to Him, and whom He helps. He says, "You shall have the deliverance, but I must have the glory. . . ." Here is a delightful partnership: we obtain that which we so greatly need, and all that God getteth is the glory which is due unto His name.[13]

Prayer puts God in the place of the all-sufficient Benefactor and puts us in the place of the needy beneficiaries. So when the mission of the church moves forward by prayer, the supremacy of God is manifest and the needs of the Christian troops are met.

Prayer Is for the Glory of the Father

Jesus had taught this to his disciples before he left. He had told them, "Whatever you ask in my name, this I will do, *that the Father may be glorified in the Son*" (John 14:13). In other words, the ultimate purpose of prayer is that the Father be glorified. The other side of the purpose comes out in John 16:24. Jesus says, "Until now you have asked nothing in my name. Ask, and you will receive, *that your joy may be full.*" The purpose of prayer is that our joy may be full. The unity of these two goals—the glory of God and the joy of his people— is preserved in the act of prayer.

The zeal that the apostles had for the exaltation of God's supreme influence in all their missionary work was built into them by Jesus. In John 15:5, Jesus says, "I am the vine; you are the branches. Whoever abides in me and I in him, he it is that bears much fruit, *for apart from me you can do nothing.*" So we really are totally ineffective as missionaries in ourselves. We may have many human strategies and plans and efforts, but the spiritual effect for the glory of Christ will be nothing. But according to John 15:5, God does not intend for us to be fruitless but to "bear much fruit." So he promises to do for us and through us what we can't do in and of ourselves.

How then do we glorify him? Jesus gives the answer in John 15:7: "If you abide in me, and my words abide in you, *ask* whatever you wish, and it will be done for you." We *pray*. We *ask* God to do for us through Christ what we can't do for ourselves—bear fruit. Then verse 8 gives the result: "*By this my Father is glorified*, that you bear much fruit." So how is God glorified by prayer? Prayer is the open admis-

13. Charles Spurgeon, *Twelve Sermons on Prayer* (Grand Rapids: Baker, 1971), 105.

sion that without Christ we can do nothing. And prayer is the turning away from ourselves to God in the confidence that he will provide the help we need. Prayer humbles *us* as needy and exalts *God* as all-sufficient.

This is why the missionary enterprise advances by prayer. The chief end of God is to glorify God. He will do this in the sovereign triumph of his missionary purpose that the nations worship him. He will secure this triumph by entering into the warfare and becoming the main combatant. And he will make that engagement plain to all the participants *through prayer,* because prayer shows that the power is from the Lord. The range of his powerful engagement in the warfare of missions becomes evident from the range of things that the church prays for in her missionary enterprise. Consider the amazing scope of prayer in the vibrant missionary life of the early church. How greatly was God glorified in the breadth of his provision!

God Was Sought in Everything

They called on God to exalt his name in the world: "Pray then like this: 'Our Father in heaven, hallowed be your name'" (Matt. 6:9).

They called on God to extend his kingdom in the world: "Your kingdom come, your will be done, on earth as it is in heaven" (Matt. 6:10).

They called on God that the gospel would speed ahead and be honored: "Finally, brothers, pray for us, that the word of the Lord may speed ahead and be honored, as happened among you" (2 Thess. 3:1).

They called on God for the fullness of the Holy Spirit: "If you then, who are evil, know how to give good gifts to your children, how much more will the heavenly Father give the Holy Spirit to those who ask him!" (Luke 11:13; cf. Eph. 3:19).

They called on God to vindicate his people in their cause: "And will not God vindicate his elect, who cry to him day and night?" (Luke 18:7 RSV).

They called on God to save unbelievers: "Brothers, my heart's desire and prayer to God for them is that they may be saved" (Rom. 10:1).

They called on God to direct the use of the sword: "Take . . . the sword of the Spirit, which is the word of God, praying at all times in the Spirit, with all prayer and supplication" (Eph. 6:17–18).

They called on God for boldness in proclamation: "Praying at all times in the Spirit . . . and also for me, that words may be given to me in opening my mouth boldly to proclaim the mystery of the gospel" (Eph. 6:18–19). "And now, Lord, look upon their threats and grant to your servants to continue to speak your word with all boldness" (Acts 4:29).

They called on God for signs and wonders: "And now, Lord, . . . grant to your servants to continue to speak your word with all boldness, while you stretch out your hand to heal, and signs and wonders are performed through the name of your holy servant Jesus" (Acts 4:29–30). "Elijah was a man with a nature like ours, and he prayed fervently that it might not rain, and for three years and six months it did not rain on the earth. Then he prayed again, and heaven gave rain, and the earth bore its fruit" (James 5:17–18).

They called on God for the healing of wounded comrades: "Let them pray over him, anointing him with oil in the name of the Lord. And the prayer of faith will save the one who is sick, and the Lord will raise him up" (James 5:14–15).

They called on God for the healing of unbelievers: "It happened that the father of Publius lay sick with fever and dysentery. And Paul visited him and prayed, and putting his hands on him healed him" (Acts 28:8).

They called on God for the casting out of demons: "And he said to them, 'This kind cannot be driven out by anything but prayer'" (Mark 9:29).

They called on God for miraculous deliverances: "So Peter was kept in prison, but earnest prayer for him was made to God by the church. . . . When he realized [he had been freed], he went to the house of Mary, the mother of John whose other name was Mark, where many were gathered together and were praying" (Acts 12:5, 12). "About midnight Paul and Silas were praying and singing hymns to God, and the prisoners were listening to them, and suddenly there was a great earthquake" (Acts 16:25–26).

They called on God for the raising of the dead: "But Peter put them all outside, and knelt down and prayed; and turning to the body he said, 'Tabitha, arise.' And she opened her eyes, and when she saw Peter she sat up" (Acts 9:40).

They called on God to supply his troops with necessities: "Give us this day our daily bread" (Matt. 6:11).

They called on God for strategic wisdom: "If any of you lacks wisdom, let him ask God, who gives generously to all without reproach, and it will be given him" (James 1:5).

They called on God to establish leadership in the outposts: "And when they had appointed elders for them in every church, with prayer and fasting they committed them to the Lord in whom they had believed" (Acts 14:23).

They called on God to send out reinforcements: "Therefore pray earnestly to the Lord of the harvest to send out laborers into his harvest" (Matt. 9:38). "While they were worshiping the Lord and fasting, the Holy Spirit said, 'Set apart for me Barnabas and Saul for the work to which I have called them.' Then after fasting and praying they laid their hands on them and sent them off" (Acts 13:2–3).

They called on God for the success of other missionaries: "I appeal to you, brothers, by our Lord Jesus Christ and by the love of the Spirit, to strive together with me in your prayers to God on my behalf, that I may be delivered from the unbelievers in Judea, and that my service for Jerusalem may be acceptable to the saints" (Rom. 15:30–31).

They called on God for unity and harmony in the ranks: "I do not ask for these only, but also for those who will believe in me through their word, that they may all be one, just as you, Father, are in me, and I in you, that they also may be in us, so that the world may believe that you have sent me" (John 17:20–21).

They called on God for the encouragement of togetherness: "We pray most earnestly night and day that we may see you face to face and supply what is lacking in your faith" (1 Thess. 3:10).

They called on God for a mind of discernment: "And it is my prayer that your love may abound more and more, with knowledge and all discernment, so that you may approve what is excellent, and so be pure and blameless for the day of Christ" (Phil. 1:9–10).

They called on God for a knowledge of his will: "And so, from the day we heard, we have not ceased to pray for you, asking that you may be filled with the knowledge of his will in all spiritual wisdom and understanding" (Col. 1:9).

They called on God to know him better: "[We have not ceased to pray for you to be] increasing in the knowledge of God" (Col. 1:10; cf. Eph. 1:17).

They called on God for power to comprehend the love of Christ: "I bow my knees before the Father . . . [that you] may have strength to comprehend with all the saints what is the breadth and length and height and depth, and to know the love of Christ that surpasses knowledge" (Eph. 3:14, 18–19).

They called on God for a deeper sense of assured hope: "I do not cease to give thanks for you, remembering you in my prayers . . . that you may know what is the hope to which he has called you, what are the riches of his glorious inheritance in the saints" (Eph. 1:16, 18).

They called on God for strength and endurance: "[We have not ceased to pray for you to be] strengthened with all power, according to his glorious might, for all endurance and patience with joy" (Col. 1:11; cf. Eph. 3:16).

They called on God for a deeper sense of his power within them: "I do not cease to give thanks for you, remembering you in my prayers . . . that you may know . . . what is the immeasurable greatness of his power toward us who believe" (Eph. 1:16, 18–19).

They called on God that their faith not be destroyed: "I have prayed for you that your faith may not fail. And when you have turned again, strengthen your brothers" (Luke 22:32). "But stay awake at all times, praying that you may have strength to escape all these things that are going to take place, and to stand before the Son of Man" (Luke 21:36).

They called on God for greater faith: "Immediately the father of the child cried out and said, 'I believe; help my unbelief!'" (Mark 9:24; cf. Eph. 3:17).

They called on God that they might not fall into temptation: "Lead us not into temptation" (Matt. 6:13). "Watch and pray that you may not enter into temptation. The spirit indeed is willing, but the flesh is weak" (Matt. 26:41).

They called on God that he would complete their resolves: "To this end we always pray for you, that our God may make you worthy of his calling and may fulfill every resolve for good and every work of faith by his power" (2 Thess. 1:11).

They called on God that they would do good works: "[We have not ceased to pray for you that you] walk in a manner worthy of the Lord, fully pleasing to him, bearing fruit in every good work" (Col. 1:10).

They called on God for forgiveness of their sins: "Forgive us our debts, as we also have forgiven our debtors" (Matt. 6:12).

They called on God for protection from the evil one: "Deliver us from evil" (Matt. 6:13).

Since the Giver gets the glory, what all this prayer shows is that the early church meant to make God supreme in the mission of the church. She would not live on her own strength or her own wisdom or even her own faith. She would live on God. God would be the one who would give the power and the wisdom and the faith. And therefore God would get the glory.

God's Ultimate Goal Will Come Only through Prayer

This crucial place of prayer reaffirms the great goal of God to uphold and display his glory for the enjoyment of the redeemed from all the nations. God has made it the ground of his oath: "All the earth shall be filled with the glory of the LORD" just as surely as that the Lord lives (Num. 14:21). The missionary purpose of God is as invincible as the fact that he is God. He will achieve this purpose by creating white-hot worshipers from every people, tongue, tribe, and nation (Rev. 5:9; 7:9). And he will be engaged to do it through prayer.

But *the* Work of Missions Is Not Prayer

Therefore, it is almost impossible to overemphasize the awesome place of prayer in the purposes of God for the world. But a caution is needed here. I sense the danger of overstating the role of prayer in relation to the Word of God and the preaching of the gospel. I am not comfortable, for example, with calling prayer *"the* work of missions." We will not jeopardize its awesome indispensability if we deny this claim. I do not deny it because of any desire to minimize the place of prayer but out of a zeal for the place of the Word of God in world missions. So let me say loud and clear that I believe the proclamation of the gospel in Word and deed is *the* work of missions. Prayer is the power that wields the weapon of the Word, and the Word is the weapon by which the nations will be brought to faith and obedience.

The frontline work of missions is the preaching of the Word of God, the gospel. If this public act is displaced by prayer, the supremacy of Christ in the mission of the church will be compromised. Jesus said, "When the Spirit of truth comes . . . he will glorify me" (John 16:13–14). This is why the Spirit becomes active to save people precisely where the gospel of Jesus is preached. His mission is to glorify Jesus. Where Jesus and his saving work are not proclaimed, there is no truth for the Holy Spirit to empower and no knowledge of Christ for him to exalt. Therefore, it is vain to pray that the hearts of people will be opened where there is no gospel portrait of Christ to see.

> "Everyone who calls on the name of the Lord will be saved." But how are they to call on him in whom they have not believed? And how are they to believe in him of whom they have never heard? And how are they to *hear* without *someone preaching*. . . . Faith comes from *hearing*, and hearing through the word of Christ.
>
> Romans 10:13–14, 17

God has ordained that saving faith comes by hearing the Word of Christ because faith is a response to Christ. If Christ is to be glorified in the mission of the church, he must be heard and known.[14] This happens only through the Word. No prayer can replace it. Prayer can only empower it. The New Testament pattern is: "Take . . . the sword of the Spirit, which is the word of God, *praying* . . ." (Eph. 6:17–18). "When they had *prayed* . . . they were all filled with the Holy Spirit and continued to *speak the word of God with boldness*" (Acts 4:31).

Prayer Releases the Power of the Gospel

But even the power that comes from the Holy Spirit through prayer is in some sense the unique power of the Word of God itself: *"The gospel . . . is the power of God* for salvation" (Rom. 1:16). Perhaps we should speak of prayer as God's instrument to *release* the power of the gospel, for it is clear that the Word of God is the immediate regenerating instrument of the Spirit: "You have been born again, not of perishable seed but of imperishable, through the living and abiding *word of God*" (1 Peter 1:23). "[God] brought us forth by the *word of truth,* that we should be a kind of firstfruits of his creation" (James 1:18).

The central promise of world missions in the teaching of Jesus concerns the spreading of the *Word:* "This *gospel of the kingdom* will be *proclaimed* throughout the whole world as a *testimony* to all nations, and then the end will come" (Matt. 24:14). In his parable about sowing, Jesus said, "The seed is *the word of God*" (Luke 8:11). When he prayed for the future mission of his disciples, he said, "I do not ask for these only, but also for those who will believe in me *through their word*" (John 17:20). And after his resurrection in his risen lordship over the mission of his church, he continued to exalt the Word: "The Lord . . . bore witness to the word of his grace, granting signs and wonders to be done by [the apostles'] hands" (Acts 14:3).

As the Christian movement spread, Luke repeatedly described its growth as the growth of the Word of God. "And *the word of God* continued to increase, and the number of disciples multiplied greatly in Jerusalem" (Acts 6:7). *"The word of God* increased and multiplied" (Acts 12:24). *"The word of the Lord* was spreading throughout the whole region" (Acts 13:49). *"The word of the Lord continued to increase* and prevail mightily" (Acts 19:20).

This is why I am jealous to say that the proclamation of the gospel is *"the* work of missions." It is the weapon that God designed to use in penetrating the kingdom of darkness and gathering the children of

---

14. This is what I argue for in chapter 4.

light from all the nations (Acts 26:16–18). His whole redemptive plan for the universe hangs on the success of his Word. If the proclamation of the Word aborts, the purposes of God fail.

The Word of God Cannot Fail

But that cannot happen:

> For as the rain and the snow come down from heaven and do not return there but water the earth, making it bring forth and sprout, giving seed to the sower and bread to the eater, *so shall my word be that goes out from my mouth*; it shall not return to me empty, but it shall accomplish that which I purpose, and shall succeed in the thing for which I sent it.
>
> Isaiah 55:10–11

God is sovereign. Yes, he has made all his plans hang on the success of his Word proclaimed by frail and sinful men and women; nevertheless, his purposes cannot fail. This is the essence of the new covenant oath: "I will put my Spirit within you, and cause you to walk in my statutes" (Ezek. 36:27). "The LORD your God will circumcise your heart and the heart of your offspring, so that you will love the LORD your God with all your heart and with all your soul" (Deut. 30:6). The Lord will work in his church "to will and to work for his good pleasure" (Phil. 2:13). A generation may be passed over in their disobedience, but none can undermine the plan of God. Job learned this long ago: "I know that you can do all things, and that no purpose of yours can be thwarted" (Job 42:2). Whenever God wills, his Word stands, and none can stay his hand.[15]

Victory Even from Inside the Tomb

It will often look as though Christ is defeated. That's the way it looked on Good Friday. He *let* himself be libeled and harassed and scorned and shoved around and killed. But in it all he was in control. "No one takes [my life] from me" (John 10:18). So it will always be. If China was closed for forty years to the Western missionaries, it was not as though Jesus accidentally slipped and fell into the tomb. He *stepped* in. And when it was sealed over, he saved fifty million Chinese from inside—without Western missionaries. And when it was time, he pushed the stone away so we could see what he had done.[16]

---

15. I have tried to argue extensively for the sovereignty of God in this irresistible sense in "The Pleasure of God in All He Does," in *The Pleasures of God,* 47–75.

16. "The growth of the Church in China since 1977 has no parallels in history. . . . Mao Zedong unwittingly became the greatest evangelist in history. . . . [He] sought to

When it looks as though he is buried for good, Jesus is doing something awesome in the dark. "The kingdom of God is as if a man should scatter seed on the ground. He sleeps and rises night and day, and the seed sprouts and grows; he knows not how" (Mark 4:26–27). The world thinks Jesus is done for—out of the way. They think his Word is buried and his plans have failed.

But Jesus is at work in the dark places: "Unless a grain of wheat falls into the earth and dies, it remains alone; but if it dies, it bears much fruit" (John 12:24). He lets himself be buried, and he comes out in power when and where he pleases. And his hands are full of fruit made in the dark. "God raised him up, loosing the pangs of death, because *it was not possible for him to be held by it*" (Acts 2:24). Jesus goes about his invincible missionary plan "by the power of an *indestructible life*" (Heb. 7:16).

For twenty centuries, the world has given it their best shot to hold him in. They can't bury him. They can't hold him in. They can't silence him or limit him. Jesus is alive and utterly free to go and come wherever he pleases. All authority in heaven is his. All things were made through him and for him, and he is absolutely supreme over all other powers (Col. 1:16–17). "He upholds the universe by the word of his power" (Heb. 1:3). And the preaching of his Word is *the* work of missions that cannot fail.

The Truly Awesome Place of Prayer in the Purpose of God

Now we can say again, safely and stunningly, what the awesome place of prayer is in the purpose of God to fill the earth with his glory. Not only has God made the accomplishment of his purposes hang on the preaching of the Word, but he has also made the success of that preaching hang on prayer. God's goal to be glorified will not succeed without the powerful proclamation of the gospel. And that gospel will not be proclaimed in power to all the nations without the prevailing, earnest, faith-filled prayers of God's people. This is the awesome place of prayer in the purpose of God for the world. That purpose won't happen without prayer.

---

destroy all religious 'superstition' but in the process cleared spiritual roadblocks for the advancement of Christianity. Deng [Xiaoping] reversed the horrors inflicted by Mao and in freeing up the economy, gave more freedom to the Christians. . . . [Today] the Church of the Lord Jesus is larger than the Communist Party of China." Patrick Johnstone and Jason Mandryk, *Operation World: When We Pray God Works* (Carlisle, Cumbria, England: Paternoster, 2001), 161. The second sentence is from the 1993 edition of *Operation World*, 164.

This accounts for Paul's repeated call for prayer in support of the Word. "Finally, brothers, *pray* for us, that the word of the Lord may speed ahead and be honored" (2 Thess. 3:1). *Pray* "also for me, that *words* may be given to me in opening my mouth boldly to proclaim the mystery of the *gospel*" (Eph. 6:19). "*Pray* also for us, that God may open to us a door for the *word*" (Col. 4:3). "[God] will deliver us [to go on preaching the Word, if you] help us by *prayer*" (2 Cor. 1:10–11; cf. Phil. 1:19).

Prayer is the walkie-talkie of the church on the battlefield of the world in the service of the Word. It is not a domestic intercom to increase the temporal comforts of the saints. It malfunctions in the hands of soldiers who have gone AWOL. It is for those on active duty. And in their hands it proves the supremacy of God in the pursuit of the nations. When missions moves forward by prayer, it magnifies the power of God. When it moves by human management, it magnifies man.

The Return to Prayer in Our Day

The return to prayer at the beginning of the twenty-first century is a remarkable work of God. It is full of hope for the awakening of the church and the finishing of the Great Commission. Looking back on the way God aroused and honored seasons of prayer in the past should enlarge our expectation that wonderful works of power are on the horizon. A hundred years ago, A. T. Pierson made this point exactly the way I would like to make it, namely, by highlighting the connection between prayer and the supremacy of God. He said:

> Every new Pentecost has had its preparatory period of supplication. . . . God has compelled his saints to seek Him at the throne of grace, so that every new advance might be so plainly due to His power that even the unbeliever might be constrained to confess: "Surely this is the finger of God!"[17]

More recently, there were movements in the twentieth century that kindled expectation of significant breakthroughs in missions. Thousands of us have been stirred deeply by the missionary credo of Jim Elliot: "He is no fool who gives what he cannot keep to gain what he cannot lose." But not as many of us know the atmosphere of prayer from which the missionary passions in the late 1940s and 1950s came. David Howard, the General Director of the World Evangelical Fellowship, was in that atmosphere and tells part of the story of what God was doing to magnify himself in the prayers of students in those days.

17. A. T. Pierson, *The New Acts of the Apostles* (New York: Baker and Taylor, 1894), 352ff.

I still have a small, faded World Evangelism Decision Card dated 1946, with my signature. Unfortunately, I did not record the day, but it is quite possible that I signed this card at the close of the first student missionary convention at the University of Toronto.

The card used to be green. I can tell by the small green circle where a thumb tack used to hold this card above my desk throughout the rest of my college days. It served as a daily prayer reminder that I had committed myself to serve God overseas unless he were clearly to direct otherwise. The fact that I had 15 years of exciting service in Latin America is attributable in large measure to prayer—much of it stimulated by that little card.

Upon returning to college after the Toronto convention students began to meet regularly to pray for missions. My closest friend in college was Jim Elliot. Jim was only to live for a few years beyond college, but in that short life he would leave a mark for eternity on my life and the lives of hundreds of others. Exactly 10 years to the week when the Toronto convention ended, Jim and his four companions were speared to death by the Huaorani Indians on the Curaray River in Ecuador. In his death he would speak to multiplied thousands, although we did not know that in our college days. Jim encouraged a small group of us to meet every day at 6:30 a.m. to pray for ourselves and our fellow students on behalf of missions. This became a regular part of my college life.

Jim Elliot also organized a round-the-clock cycle, asking students to sign up for a 15 minute slot each day when he or she would promise to pray for missions and for mission recruitment on our campus. The entire 24 hours were filled in this way. Thus, every 15 minutes throughout the day and night at least one student was on his knees interceding for missions at Wheaton College.

Art Wiens was a war veteran who had served in Italy and planned to return as a missionary. He decided to pray systematically through the college directory, praying for 10 students by name every day. Art followed this faithfully through his college years.

I did not see Art again until we met in 1974 at the Lausanne Congress on World Evangelization in Switzerland. As we renewed fellowship and reminisced about old times, he said, "Dave, do you remember those prayer meetings we used to have at Wheaton?"

"I certainly do," I replied.

Then Art said, "You know, Dave, I am still praying for 500 of our college contemporaries who are now on the mission field." "How do you know that many are overseas?" I asked. "I kept in touch with the alumni office and found out who was going as a missionary, and I still pray for them."

Astounded, I asked Art if I could see his prayer list. The next day he brought it to me, a battered old notebook he had started in college days with the names of hundreds of our classmates and fellow students.[18]

18. David Howard, "The Road to Urbana and Beyond," *Evangelical Missions Quarterly* 21, no. 1 (January 1985): 115–16.

When I first read that account of prevailing prayer and the remarkable fruit that has come of it to the glory of Christ through the lives of radical, Spirit-empowered missionaries, I felt a surge of longing to set my hand to the plow and never take it off. I long to be like George Mueller in the tenacity of prayer and missions. Mueller wrote in his *Autobiography:*

> I am now, in 1864, waiting upon God for certain blessings, for which I have daily besought Him for 19 years and 6 months, without one day's intermission. Still the full answer is not yet given concerning the conversion of certain individuals. In the meantime, I have received many thousands of answers to prayer. I have also prayed daily, without intermission, for the conversion of other individuals about ten years, for others six or seven years, for others four, three, and two years, for others about eighteen months; and still the answer is not yet granted, concerning these persons [whom I have prayed for nineteen years and six months]. . . . Yet I am daily continuing in prayer and expecting the answer. . . . Be encouraged, dear Christian reader, with fresh earnestness to give yourself to prayer, if you can only be sure that you ask for things which are for the glory of God.[19]

The call of Jesus is for prevailing prayer: "Always . . . pray and [do] not lose heart" (Luke 18:1). By this his Father will be glorified (John 14:13). The supremacy of God in the mission of the church is proved and prized in prevailing prayer. I believe Christ's word to his church at the beginning of the twenty-first century is a question: "Will not God give justice to his elect, who cry to him day and night? Will he delay long over them? I tell you, he will give justice to them speedily" (Luke 18:7–8).

Do you ever cry out to the Lord, "How long, O Lord? How long till you vindicate your cause in the earth? How long till you rend the heavens and come down with power on your church? How long till you bring forth victory among all the peoples of the world?"

Is not his answer plain: "When my people cry to me *day and night*, I will vindicate them, and my cause will prosper among the nations." The war will be won by God. He will win it through the gospel of Jesus Christ. This gospel will run and triumph through prevailing prayer—so that in everything God might be glorified through Jesus Christ.

---

19. George Mueller, *Autobiography*, comp. G. Fred Bergin (London: J. Nisbet, 1906), 296.

3

The Supremacy of God in Missions through Suffering

We measure the worth of a hidden treasure by what we will gladly sell to buy it. If we will sell all, then we measure the worth as supreme. If we will not, what we have is treasured more. "The kingdom of heaven is like treasure hidden in a field, which a man found and covered up. Then *in his joy* he goes and sells *all that he has* and buys that field" (Matt. 13:44). The extent of his *sacrifice* and the depth of his *joy* display the worth he puts on the treasure of God. Loss and suffering, joyfully accepted for the kingdom of God, show the supremacy of God's worth more clearly in the world than all worship and prayer.

This is why the stories of missionaries who gladly gave their all have made God more real and precious to many of us. The life of Henry Martyn has had this remarkable effect for almost two hundred years.

Henry Martyn Submits to God

Martyn was born in England on February 18, 1781. His father was well-to-do and sent his son to a fine grammar school, as they called them in those days, and then to Cambridge in 1797, when he was sixteen. Four years later Martyn took highest honors in mathematics, and the year after that first prize in Latin prose composition.

He had turned his back on God as a youth, and during these days of academic achievement, he became disillusioned with his dream. "I obtained my highest wishes, but was surprised to find that I had grasped a shadow." The treasure of the world rusted in his hands. The death of his father, the prayers of his sister, the counsel of a godly minister, and the diary of David Brainerd brought him to his knees in submission to God. In 1802, he resolved to forsake a life of academic prestige and ease and become a missionary. That was the first measure of the kingdom's worth in his life.

Martyn served as the assistant to Charles Simeon, the great evangelical preacher at Trinity Church in Cambridge, until he departed for India on July 17, 1805. His ministry was to be a chaplain with the East India Company. He arrived in Calcutta on May 16, 1806, and the first day ashore found William Carey.

Martyn was an evangelical Anglican; Carey was a Baptist. And there was some tension over the use of liturgy. But Carey wrote that year, "A young clergyman, Mr. Martyn, is lately arrived, who is possessed of a truly missionary spirit. . . . We take sweet counsel together, and go to the house of God as friends."

Alongside his chaplain's duties, Martyn's main work was translation. Within two years, by March 1808, he had translated part of the Book of Common Prayer, a commentary on the parables, and the entire New Testament into "Hindostanee." He was then assigned to supervise the Persian version of the New Testament. It was not as well received as the other, and his health gave way in the process. So he decided to return to England for recovery and to go by land through Persia in the hope of revising his translation on the way.

He became so sick, however, that he could barely press on. He died among strangers in the city of Tocat in Asiatic Turkey on October 16, 1812. He was thirty-one years old.

Martyn's Hidden Pain

What you can't see in this overview of Martyn's life are the inner flights and plunges of spirit that make his achievement so real and so helpful to real people. I am persuaded that the reason David Brainerd's *Life and Diary* and Henry Martyn's *Journal and Letters* have such abiding and deep power for the cause of missions is that they portray the life of the missionary as a life of constant warfare in the soul, not a life of uninterrupted calm. The suffering and struggle make us feel the supremacy of God in their lives all the more.

Listen to how he felt on the boat on the way to India:

I found it hard to realize divine things. I was more tried with desires after the world, than for two years past. . . . The sea-sickness, and the smell of the ship, made me feel very miserable, and the prospect of leaving all the comforts and communion of saints in England, to go forth to an unknown land, to endure such illness and misery with ungodly men for so many months, weighed heavy on my spirits. My heart was almost ready to break.

On top of this there is a love story to tell. Martyn was in love with Lydia Grenfell. He didn't feel right taking her along without going before her and proving his own reliance on God alone. But two months after he arrived in India on July 30, 1806, he wrote and proposed and asked her to come.

He waited fifteen months (!) for the reply. His journal entry on October 24, 1807, reads:

> An unhappy day; received at last a letter from Lydia, in which she refuses to come, because her mother will not consent to it. Grief and disappointment threw my soul into confusion at first; but gradually, as my disorder subsided, my eyes were opened, and reason resumed its office. I could not but agree with her, that it would not be for the glory of God, nor could we expect his blessing, if she acted in disobedience to her mother.

He took up his pen and wrote her that same day:

> Though my heart is bursting with grief and disappointment, I write not to blame you. The rectitude of all your conduct secures you from censure. . . . Alas my rebellious heart—what a tempest agitates me! I knew not that I had made so little progress in a spirit of resignation to the Divine will.

For five years he held out hope that things might change. A steady stream of letters covered the thousands of miles between India and England. His last known letter, written two months before his death (August 28, 1812), was addressed as usual to "My dearest Lydia." It closed:

> Soon we shall have occasion for pen and ink no more; but I trust I shall shortly see thee face to face. Love to all the saints.
>
> Believe me to be yours ever,
most faithfully and affectionately,
H. Martyn

Martyn never saw her again on this earth. But dying was not what he feared most, nor seeing Lydia what he desired most. His passion was to make known the supremacy of Christ in all of life. Near the very end he wrote, "Whether life or death be mine, may Christ be magnified in me! If he has work for me to do, I cannot die." Christ's work for Martyn was done. And he had done it well. His losses and pain made the supremacy of God in his life powerful for all time.[1]

"He Bids Him Come and Die"

Some suffering is the calling of every believer but especially of those God calls to bear the gospel to the unreached. Dietrich Bonhoeffer's famous lines are biblical: "The cross is not the terrible end to an otherwise God-fearing and happy life, but it meets us at the beginning of our communion with Christ. When Christ calls a man, he bids him come and die."[2] This is simply a paraphrase of Mark 8:34: "If anyone would come after me, let him deny himself and *take up his cross* and follow me." To take up a cross and follow Jesus means to join Jesus on the Calvary road with a resolve to suffer and die with him. The cross is not a burden to bear; it is an instrument of pain and execution. It would be like saying, "Pick up your electric chair and follow me to the execution room." Or "Pick up this sword and carry it to the place of beheading." Or "Take up this rope and carry it to the gallows."

The domestication of cross-bearing into coughs and cranky spouses takes the radical thrust out of Christ's call. He is calling every believer to "renounce all that he has," to "hate his own life" (Luke 14:33, 26), and to take the road of obedience joyfully, no matter the loss on this earth. Following Jesus means that wherever obedience requires it, we will accept betrayal and rejection and beating and mockery and crucifixion and death. Jesus gives us the assurance that if we will follow him to Golgotha during all the Good Fridays of this life, we will also rise with him on the last Easter day of the resurrection. "Whoever loses his life for my sake and the gospel's will save it" (Mark 8:35). "Whoever hates his life in this world will keep it for eternal life" (John 12:25).

Do We Need Martyr Models?

The question about martyrdom is dangerous given the new rise of terrorism in the twenty-first century. There is a fundamental difference between Christian martyrs and those who have gained notoriety through terrorism. First, the life of a Christian martyr is taken by those whom he wants to save. He does not fall on his own sword, and he does not use it against his adversary. Second, Christian mar-

---

1. All the quotes in this account are from Henry Martyn, *Journal and Letters of Henry Martyn* (New York: Protestant Episcopal Society for the Promotion of Evangelical Knowledge, 1851).
2. Dietrich Bonhoeffer, *The Cost of Discipleship* (New York: Macmillan, 1963), 99.

tyrs do not pursue death; they pursue love. Christians do not advance the cause of the gospel of Christ by the use of the sword: "For all who take the sword will perish by the sword" (Matt. 26:52). Jesus said, "My kingdom is not of this world. If my kingdom were of this world, my servants would have been fighting. . . . But my kingdom is not from the world" (John 18:36). Christianity advances not by shedding the blood of others, even if it is mingled with ours. It advances by suffering to bring life, not suffering to cause death (Mark 10:45; Col. 1:24).

One of the most stunning and sobering words spoken at the second Lausanne Congress on World Evangelization in Manila in 1989 was spoken by George Otis concerning the call to martyrdom. He asked, "Is our failure to thrive in Muslim countries the absence of martyrs? Can a covert church grow in strength? Does a young church need martyr models?" Many places in the world today feel the words of Jesus with all their radical impact: To choose Christ is to choose death, or the very high risk of death. David Barrett has estimated that in 2002 approximately 164,000 Christians will die as martyrs and that the average number of Christian martyrs each year will grow to 210,000 by the year 2025.[3] In the 2001 edition of *World Christian Encyclopedia*, he says there were 45,400,000 martyrs in the twentieth century.[4]

"I Am Crucified with Christ"

It's true that taking up our cross involves a spiritual transaction by which our "old nature" or "the flesh" dies with Christ and a "new creature" comes into being. This is one way the apostle applies the call of Jesus to take up our cross. "Those who belong to Christ Jesus have *crucified the flesh* with its passions and desires" (Gal. 5:24). "*I have been crucified with Christ*. It is no longer I who live, but Christ who lives in me. And the life I now live in the flesh I live by faith in the Son of God, who loved me and gave himself for me" (Gal. 2:19–20). "Our old self *was crucified with him* in order that the body of sin might be

3. David Barrett, "Annual Statistical Table on Global Mission: 2002," *International Bulletin of Missionary Research* 26, no. 1 (January 2002): 23.

4. David Barrett, George T. Kurian, and Todd M. Johnson, *World Christian Encyclopedia: A Comparative Survey of Churches and Religions—AD 30 to 2200*, vol. 1 (Oxford: Oxford University Press, 2001), 11. Lest we think Christians are the only ones who endure martyrdom in huge numbers, Barrett compares Islam to Christianity: 80 million Muslim martyrs, 70 million Christian martyrs over the history of their two religions. He observes that there are 210 countries that have lengthy histories of martyrdom and are now fully evangelized (11).

brought to nothing, so that we would no longer be enslaved to sin" (Rom. 6:6). "Set your minds on things that are above, not on things that are on earth. For *you have died,* and your life is hidden with Christ in God" (Col. 3:2–3).

But the point of this spiritual death is not that it takes the place of a real, practical application of Jesus' teaching to physical suffering and death but that it makes that application possible. Precisely because our old, selfish, worldly, unloving, fearful, proud self has died with Christ and a new, trusting, loving, heaven-bent, hope-filled self has come into being—precisely because of this inner death and new life, we are able to take risks, and suffer the pain, and even die without despair but full of hope.

"If They Persecuted Me, They Will Persecute You"

So we must not water down the call to suffer. We must not domesticate the New Testament teaching on affliction and persecution just because our lives are so smooth. It may be that we have not chosen to live in all the radical ways of love that God wants us to. It may be that our time of suffering is just around the corner. But it will not do to take our own comfortable lives and make them the measure of what we allow the Bible to mean.

Jesus came into the world to give his life as a ransom for many (Mark 10:45). There was a divine necessity upon him to suffer: "The Son of Man *must* suffer many things" (Mark 8:31; cf. Luke 17:25). Because this was his vocation, suffering also becomes the vocation of those who follow him. It is implied in the words, "As the Father has sent me, even so I am sending you" (John 20:21). And Jesus made it explicit when he said, "Remember the word that I said to you: 'A servant is not greater than his master.' If they persecuted me, they will also persecute you" (John 15:20). "If they have called the master of the house Beelzebul, how much more will they malign those of his household?" (Matt. 10:25).

Does His Suffering for Us Mean We Escape Suffering?

It would be easy to make a superficial mistake about the death of Christ as a substitutionary atonement. The mistake would be to say that since Christ died for me, I don't need to die for others. Since he suffered for me, I don't need to suffer for others. In other words, if his death is really substitutionary, shouldn't I escape what he bore for me? How can his death be a call for my death if his death took the place of my death?

The answer is that Christ died for us so that we would not have to die for sin, *not* so that we would not have to die for others. Christ bore the punishment of our sin so that our death and suffering are never punishment from God. The call to suffer with Christ is not a call to bear our sins the way he bore them but to love the way he loved. The death of Christ for the sin of my selfishness is not meant to help me escape the suffering of love but to enable it. Because he took my guilt and my punishment and reconciled me to God as my Father, I do not need to cling any longer to the comforts of earth in order to be content. I am free to let things go for the sake of making the supremacy of God's worth known.

Christ's Death: Substitution and Pattern

Peter shows us the connection between the death of Christ as a substitution to be received and a pattern to be followed. He speaks to Christian slaves who may be mistreated by their unbelieving masters:

> For what credit is it if, when you sin and are beaten for it, you endure? But if when you do good and suffer for it you endure, this is a gracious thing in the sight of God. *For to this you have been called, because Christ also suffered for you, leaving you an example, so that you might follow in his steps.*
>
> 1 Peter 2:20–21

Notice the all-important little phrase "for you." Christ suffered "for you." This is the substitutionary atonement. He took our place and did for us what we could not do for ourselves. "He himself bore our sins in his body on the tree" (1 Peter 2:24). This is a work nobody else but the Son of God could do for us (Rom. 8:3). It cannot be imitated or duplicated. It happened once for all. "He has appeared *once for all* at the end of the ages to put away sin by the sacrifice of himself" (Heb. 9:26). This is the foundation of all our hope and joy and freedom and love. Our sins are forgiven, and we have eternal life (John 3:16; Eph. 1:7). God is for us, and nothing can separate us from him (Rom. 8:31, 35–39).

Therefore, when Peter says that Jesus "left you an example that you should follow in his steps," he did not mean that you are called to make atonement for sin. He meant that you are called to love as Jesus did and be willing to suffer for doing right as he did. The pattern we follow is not the atonement but the love and the pain. The relationship between the two is crucial. The substitution is the foundation of the imitation, not vice versa. We do not earn our forgiveness by suffering as Jesus did. We are freed to love as Jesus did because our sins are forgiven. Because he suffered *for* us, we can suffer *like* him.

In fact, Peter says, "To this [way of suffering] you have been *called.*" It is our vocation. Don't make the mistake of saying, "Oh, that was addressed to slaves with cruel masters and does not apply to us." That is a mistake because 1 Peter 3:8–9 is addressed to all believers but makes the same point: "Finally, *all of you* . . . do not repay evil for evil or reviling for reviling, but on the contrary, bless, *for to this you were called,* that you may obtain a blessing." This is not the calling of slaves only. It is the calling of all Christians. The way Christ lived and suffered and died places a calling on us to show with our lives the supremacy of his love by living in the same way.

So Peter goes on to describe how Jesus handled unjust suffering. We are called to do it the way he did it: "He committed no sin, neither was deceit found in his mouth. When he was reviled, he did not revile in return; when he suffered, he did not threaten, but continued entrusting himself to him who judges justly" (1 Peter 2:22–23).

Arm Yourselves with This "Thought"

Then to make the call even more clear, Peter says later on, "Since therefore Christ suffered in the flesh, arm yourselves with the same thought" (1 Peter 4:1 RSV). The suffering of Christ is a call for a certain mind-set toward suffering, namely, that it is normal and that the path of love and missions will often require it. Thus, Peter says, "Beloved, do not be surprised at the fiery trial when it comes upon you to test you, as though something strange were happening to you" (1 Peter 4:12). Suffering with Christ is not strange; it is your calling, your vocation. The "same kinds of suffering are being experienced by your brotherhood throughout the world" (1 Peter 5:9). This is the "thought" that we need to put on like armor, lest we be vulnerable to suffering as something strange.

Preparing for Suffering—Now!

Richard Wurmbrand endured fourteen years of imprisonment and torture in his homeland of Romania between 1948 and 1964. He had been leading a secret underground ministry when the Communists seized Romania and tried to control the church for their purposes.

Wurmbrand, like the apostle Peter, stressed the tremendous need to get spiritually ready to suffer.

> What shall we do about these tortures? Will we be able to bear them? If I do not bear them I put in prison another fifty or sixty men whom I know, because that is what the Communists wish from me, to betray those around me. And here comes the great need for the role of preparation for suffering which must start now. *It is too difficult* to prepare yourself for it when the Communists have put you in prison.
>
> I remember my last Confirmation class before I left Romania. I took a group of ten to fifteen boys and girls on a Sunday morning, not to a church, but to the zoo. Before the cage of lions I told them, "Your forefathers in faith were thrown before such wild beasts for their faith. Know that you also will have to suffer. You will not be thrown before lions, but you will have to do with men who would be much worse than lions. Decide here and now if you wish to pledge allegiance to Christ." They had tears in their eyes when they said yes.
>
> We have to make the preparation now, before we are imprisoned. In prison you lose everything. You are undressed and given a prisoner's suit. No more nice furniture, nice carpets, or nice curtains. You do not have a wife any more and you do not have your children. You do not have your library and you never see a flower. Nothing of what makes life pleasant remains. Nobody resists who has not renounced the pleasures of life beforehand.[5]

Paul tried to prepare his converts for suffering. Like Peter he armed them with this "thought"—that suffering is our calling. He said to the newer believers in Thessalonica, "We sent Timothy . . . to . . . exhort you in your faith that no one be moved by these afflictions. For you yourselves know that *we are destined for this*" (1 Thess. 3:2–3). That is, it is our calling.

Similarly, as Paul returned from his first missionary journey, he stopped at the young churches and encouraged them with this "thought." He was "strengthening the souls of the disciples, encouraging them to continue in the faith, and saying that *through many tribulations we must enter the kingdom of God*" (Acts 14:22). It was important for the new believers to be "armed with this thought": that the road to the kingdom is the Calvary road; there are many tribulations. There is a divine necessity: "We *must* enter" this way. It is our calling. "All who desire to live a godly life in Christ Jesus *will* be persecuted" (2 Tim. 3:12).

5. Richard Wurmbrand, "Preparing the Underground Church," *Epiphany Journal* 5, no. 4 (summer 1985): 46–48.

"Let Us Go to Him outside the Camp"

The writer to the Hebrews connects the atoning work of Christ and the pattern of his suffering the same way Peter does, only with vividly different words.

> So Jesus also suffered outside the gate in order to sanctify the people through his own blood. Therefore let us go to him outside the camp and bear the reproach he endured. For here we have no lasting city, but we seek the city that is to come.
>
> Hebrews 13:12–14

Jesus suffered first in a way that we cannot: "to sanctify the people through his own blood." The death of the Son of God is absolutely unique in its effect. But then notice the word "therefore." Because Jesus died for us in this way, *therefore* let us go forth with him outside the camp and bear the abuse he endured. It does not say, since he suffered for us, *therefore* we can have an easy life free from suffering and abuse and danger. Just the opposite. Jesus' suffering is the *basis* of our going with him and bearing the same abuse he bore.

This is above all a missionary text. Outside the camp means outside the borders of safety and comfort. Outside the camp are the "other sheep" that are not of this fold. Outside the camp are the unreached nations. Outside the camp are the places and the people who will be costly to reach and will require no small sacrifice. But to this we are called: "Let us go and bear the reproach he endured." It is our vocation.

Bearing the Abuse He Endured in Sudan

The abuse may range from the slightest ostracism to agony of torture and death. Both are probably happening every day in our world. We hear only a tiny fraction of the "reproach he endured." For example, *Mission Frontiers* carried this report in 1988.

> In 1983, the Sudan was declared an Islamic republic. At that time, Islamic Sharia law was imposed on all the country's citizens. Since then, dozens of Christian pastors have been killed and countless Christian churches burned. . . .
>
> This past March 27 and 28 [1987], according to a 33 page report filed by Khartoum University professors Drs. Ushari Ahmad Mahmud and Suleyman Ali Baldo (both Muslims), more than 1,000 Dinka men, women, and children were slaughtered and burned to death in the western Sudan town of Diein.

The massacre erupted when 25 Christian Dinka worshipers were driven from their evening prayer service by a mob of Rizeigat Muslims wielding sticks, spears, axes, and Soviet-made Klasmnikov guns. That evening, five to seven Dinkas were murdered, and dozens of homes were burned.

Early the next morning, as many Dinkas were being loaded into rail boxcars for safe evacuation from the troubled town, hundreds of armed Rizeigats converged on the train station and began attacking the defenseless Dinkas. Burning mattresses were heaped on the top of huddled Dinkas. Others were shot, mutilated, and clubbed to death. By nightfall, more than one thousand Dinkas were dead.[6]

As horrible as this is, Peter said that when the fiery ordeal comes, we should not be surprised as though something strange were happening to us. We live in such relative ease that such thinking seems incomprehensible to us. But I believe God is calling us to arm ourselves with this very thought: Christ suffered outside the gate brutally and without justice, leaving us an example that we should follow in his steps.

May We Spend the Night on Death Row?

Charles Wesley gives us an example of how one might obey Hebrews 13:13 and go "outside the camp" and bear the abuse he endured. On July 18, 1738, two months after his conversion, Charles Wesley did an amazing thing. He had spent the week witnessing to inmates at the Newgate prison with a friend named "Bray," whom he described as "a poor ignorant mechanic." One of the men they spoke to was "a black [slave] that had robbed his master." He was sick with a fever and was condemned to die.

On Tuesday, Wesley and Bray asked if they could be locked in overnight with the prisoners who were to be executed the next day [this is outside the camp!]. That night they spoke the gospel. They told the men that "One came down from heaven to save lost sinners." They described the sufferings of the Son of God, his sorrows, agony, and death.

The next day the men were loaded onto a cart and taken to Tyburn. Wesley went with them. Ropes were fastened around their necks so that the cart could be driven off, leaving them swinging in the air to choke to death.

The fruit of Wesley and Bray's nightlong labor was astonishing. Here is what Wesley wrote:

6. *Mission Frontiers* 10, no. 1 (January 1988): 29.

They were all cheerful; full of comfort, peace and triumph; assuredly persuaded Christ had died for them, and waited to receive them into paradise. . . . The black [slave] . . . saluted me with his looks. As often as his eyes met mine, he smiled with the most composed, delightful countenance I ever saw.

We left them going to meet their Lord, ready for the Bridegroom. When the cart drew off, not one stirred, or struggled for life, but meekly gave up their spirits. Exactly at twelve they were turned off. I spoke a few suitable words to the crowd; and returned, full of peace and confidence in our friends' happiness. That hour under the gallows was the most blessed hour of my life.[7]

Two things in this story amaze and inspire me. One is the astonishing power of Wesley's message about the truth and love of Christ. All the condemned prisoners were converted, and they were so deeply converted that they could look death in the face (without a long period of "follow up" or "discipling") and give up their lives with confidence that Christ would receive them. Their suffering was not for righteousness' sake, but the same dynamics were at work to sustain them. They looked on their suffering as something they must pass through on the way to heaven, and the hope of glory was so real that they died in peace. Oh, for such power in witness!

The other thing that amazes me is the sheer fact that Wesley went to the prison and asked to be locked up all night with condemned criminals who had nothing more to lose if they killed another person. Wesley had no supervisor telling him that this was his job. He was not a professional prison minister. It would have been comfortable and pleasant to spend the evening at home conversing with friends. Then why did he go?

God put it in his heart to go. And Wesley yielded. There are hundreds of strange and radical things God is calling his people to do in the cause of world missions. Not everyone will hear the same call. Yours will be unique. It may be something you never dreamed of doing. It may be something you have only dreamed of doing. But I urge you to listen to the leading of the Spirit to see where "outside the camp" he may be taking you "to bear the reproach he endured."

"I Will Show Him How Much He Must Suffer"

Afflictions are our vocation, whether we are missionaries or not. But this is especially the calling of those appointed to reach the unreached peoples of the world. Paul is the prototype of such missionar-

7. Charles Wesley, *Journal*, vol. 1 (Grand Rapids: Baker, 1980), 120–23.

ies. When the Lord sent Ananias to Paul in Damascus, he sent him with the armor of this "thought" mentioned in 1 Peter 4:1. Only it was intensified for Paul. The Lord said, "Go, for he is a chosen instrument of mine to carry my name before the Gentiles and kings and the children of Israel. For *I will show him how much he must suffer for the sake of my name*" (Acts 9:15–16). Then God kept on pressing this "thought" on Paul: "The Holy Spirit testifies to me in every city that *imprisonment and afflictions await me*" (Acts 20:23).

Suffering was part of Paul's calling. It became so much a part of his identity and ministry that he took it as a badge of his apostolic authenticity. It was like part of his visa papers to prove his right to do what God had called him to do.

> As servants of God we commend ourselves in every way: by great endurance, in afflictions, hardships, calamities, beatings, imprisonments, riots, labors, sleepless nights, hunger; by purity, knowledge, patience, kindness, the Holy Spirit, genuine love, by truthful speech, and the power of God; with the weapons of righteousness for the right hand and for the left; through honor and dishonor, through slander and praise. We are treated as impostors, and yet are true; as unknown, and yet well known; as dying, and behold, we live; as punished, and yet not killed; as sorrowful, yet always rejoicing; as poor, yet making many rich; as having nothing, yet possessing everything.
>
> 2 Corinthians 6:4–10

The extraordinary suffering of the apostle Paul staggers the mind. The litany of 2 Corinthians 11:23–28 is overwhelming, especially if we think of the pain of each part and the multiplied pain upon pain as the parts mount up. It is a rare glimpse into the cumulative pain and sorrow of Paul's missionary life:

> . . . with far greater labors, far more imprisonments, with countless beatings, and often near death. Five times I received at the hands of the Jews the forty lashes less one. Three times I was beaten with rods. Once I was stoned. Three times I was shipwrecked; a night and a day I was adrift at sea; on frequent journeys, in danger from rivers, danger from robbers, danger from my own people, danger from Gentiles, danger in the city, danger in the wilderness, danger at sea, danger from false brothers; in toil and hardship, through many a sleepless night, in hunger and thirst, often without food, in cold and exposure. And, apart from other things, there is the daily pressure on me of my anxiety for all the churches.

Lest we pass over this too quickly, without having the breath knocked out of us, consider what it meant to receive "forty lashes less one." It meant that he was stripped and tied to some kind of stake so that he could not run or fall. Then a person trained in flogging would take a whip, maybe with or without shards in the leather, and lash Paul's back thirty-nine times. Halfway through, or earlier perhaps, the skin would begin to break and tear. By the end, parts of Paul's back would be like jelly. The lacerations would not be clean, as with a razor blade. The skin would be torn and shredded, so that healing would be slow and perhaps complicated by infection. They knew nothing of sterilization in those days and had no antiseptics. It would take perhaps months before his garments could hang on his back without pain.

Now, with that in view, consider that this happened a second time on the same back, opening all the scars. It healed more slowly the second time. Then consider that some months later it happened a third time. Imagine what his back must have looked like. Then it happened again. And finally it happened a fifth time. And this was just one of Paul's sufferings.

Does God Allow or Appoint the Suffering of His Messengers?

Why does God allow this? No, that is not quite the right question. We have to ask, Why does God *appoint* this? These things are part of God's plan for his people just as the suffering and death of Jesus were part of God's plan for salvation (Isa. 53:10; Acts 4:27–28). It is true that Satan can be the more immediate agent of suffering, but even he may do nothing without God's permission.[8]

Paul describes suffering as a gift of God: "It has been granted to you that for the sake of Christ you should not only believe in him but also *suffer for his sake*" (Phil. 1:29). Twice Peter spoke of suffering as being God's will: "It is better to suffer for doing good, *if that should be God's will*, than for doing evil. . . . Let those who suffer *according to God's will* entrust their souls to a faithful Creator while doing good" (1 Peter 3:17; 4:19).[9]

8. Demons cannot even speak without the permission of Jesus: "He would not permit the demons to speak" (Mark 1:34). How much less may they do anything more harmful without permission, as Job 1:12, 21; 2:6–7, 10 makes plain. Nevertheless, Satan does persecute the church. "Behold, the devil is about to throw some of you into prison, that you may be tested" (Rev. 2:10). For a more extensive treatment of this problem of how God's sovereignty relates to the evil things men do, see John Piper, *The Pleasures of God* (Portland, Ore.: Multnomah, 2000), 66–75.

9. For a discussion of two different ways of talking about God's will (his will of decree and his will of command), see John Piper, "Are There Two Wills in God? Divine

James placed all of life, including the seemingly accidental hindrances to our plans, under the sovereign will of God: "Come now, you who say, 'Today or tomorrow we will go into such and such a town and spend a year there and trade and make a profit. . . .' Instead you ought to say, '*If the Lord wills*, we will live and do this or that'" (James 4:13, 15). Flat tires, car accidents, road construction—whatever can keep you from doing your plan—are the will of God. *If God wills*, you will live and do this or that.

The writer to the Hebrews puts all our suffering under the banner of God's loving discipline. It is not an accident that he permits; it is a plan for our holiness.

> In your struggle against sin you have not yet resisted to the point of shedding your blood. And have you forgotten the exhortation that addresses you as sons? "My son, do not regard lightly the discipline of the Lord, nor be weary when reproved by him. For the Lord disciplines the one he loves, and chastises every son whom he receives."
>
> Hebrews 12:4–6

The suffering that missionaries meet is not something unforeseen by the Lord. He saw it clearly, embraced it for himself, and sent his disciples into the same danger. "Behold, I am sending you out as sheep in the midst of wolves" (Matt. 10:16). "I will send them prophets and apostles, some of whom they will kill and persecute" (Luke 11:49). As Paul says in 1 Thessalonians 3:3, we are "destined" or "appointed" for these things.

Election and God's Desire for All to Be Saved," in *The Pleasures of God: Meditations on God's Delight in Being God* (Sisters, Ore.: Multnomah, 2000), 313–40. (This essay is also found in Thomas R. Schreiner and Bruce A. Ware, eds., *Still Sovereign: Contemporary Perspectives on Election, Foreknowledge, and Grace* [Grand Rapids: Baker, 2000], 107–31.) The point is that when we think about the will of God, we must distinguish between actions that he commands to be done, such as "You shall not murder" (Exod. 20:13), and actions that he ordains in his sovereignty to come to pass, such as the death of his Son at the hands of murderers (Acts 2:23; 4:27–28). In other words, God sometimes ordains that things happen according to his *will of decree* that are against his *will of command*. That is surely the case in the crucifixion of his Son, which was planned from of old and yet necessarily involved the sins of men in the act of crucifixion. But most Christians have always believed that it is not sin in God to will that sin be. This is a difficult issue, and I only mention it here because it may trouble some readers that suffering is described as God's will. It *is* in one sense, and it may *not be* in another. And yet man always remains responsible for it. I hope the troubled reader will seek help in the essay referred to above and in other parts of that same book, for example, chapter 2, "The Pleasure of God in All That He Does," 47–75.

Six Reasons God Appoints Suffering for His Servants

So our question is Why? Why did God appoint for Paul to suffer so much as the prototype of the frontier missionary? God is sovereign. As every child knows, he could toss Satan into the pit today if he wanted to, and all his terrorizing of the church would be over. But God wills that the mission of the church advance through storm and suffering. What are the reasons? I will mention six.

1. Suffering Deepens Faith and Holiness

As we have just seen in Hebrews 12, God disciplines his children through suffering. His aim is deeper faith and deeper holiness. "He disciplines us for our good, that we may share his holiness" (v. 10). Jesus experienced the same thing. "Although he was a son, he learned obedience through what he suffered" (Heb. 5:8). This does not mean that Jesus grew from disobedience to obedience. The same writer says Jesus never sinned (Heb. 4:15). Rather, the process through which he grew in deeper and deeper obedience was the process of suffering. For us there is the need not only to have our obedience tested and proven but also to be purified of all remnants of self-reliance and entanglement with the world.

Paul described this experience in his own life like this:

For we do not want you to be ignorant, brothers, of the affliction we experienced in Asia. For we were so utterly burdened beyond our strength that we despaired of life itself. Indeed, we felt that we had received the sentence of death. But *that was to make us rely not on ourselves but on God who raises the dead.*

2 Corinthians 1:8–9

Paul does not concede his suffering to the hand of Satan but says that God ordained it for the increase of his faith. God knocked the props of life out from under Paul's heart so that he would have no choice but to fall on God and receive his hope from the promise of the resurrection. This is the first purpose of missionary suffering: to wean us from the world and set our hope fully in God alone (cf. Rom. 5:3–4). Since the freedom to love flows from this kind of radical hope (Col. 1:4–5), suffering is a primary means of building compassion into the lives of God's servants.

Thousands of missionaries throughout the centuries have found that the sufferings of life have been the school of Christ where lessons of faith were taught that could not be learned anywhere else. For example, John G. Paton, who was born in 1824 in Scotland, was a missionary to the New Hebrides (today's Vanuatu) in the South Seas from

1858 almost until his death in 1907. He lost his wife four months after he landed on the island of Tanna at the age of thirty-four. Two weeks later his newborn son died. He buried them alone with his own hands. "But for Jesus, and the fellowship he vouchsafed to me there, I must have gone mad and died beside the lonely grave!"[10] He stayed on the island for a harrowing four years of dangers. Finally, an uprising was mounted against him, and he believed it was right to try to escape. He sought help from the one person he could trust on the island, his friend Nowar. His escape was an unforgettable discovery of grace that left a lifelong spiritual mark. Nowar told Paton to flee the village and hide in a tree that Nowar's son would show him and to stay there till the moon rose.

> Being entirely at the mercy of such doubtful and vacillating friends, I, though perplexed, felt it best to obey. I climbed into the tree and was left there alone in the bush. The hours I spent there live all before me as if it were but of yesterday. I heard the frequent discharging of muskets, and the yells of the Savages. Yet I sat there among the branches, as safe in the arms of Jesus. Never, in all my sorrows, did my Lord draw nearer to me, and speak more soothingly in my soul, than when the moonlight flickered among these chestnut leaves, and the night air played on my throbbing brow, as I told all my heart to Jesus. Alone, yet not alone! If it be to glorify my God, I will not grudge to spend many nights alone in such a tree, to feel again my Savior's spiritual presence, to enjoy His consoling fellowship. If thus thrown back upon your own soul, alone, all alone, in the midnight, in the bush, in the very embrace of death itself, have you a Friend that will not fail you then?[11]

2. Suffering Makes Your Cup Increase

By enduring suffering with patience, the reward of our experience of God's glory in heaven increases. This is part of Paul's meaning in 2 Corinthians 4:17–18:

> For this slight momentary affliction is preparing for us an eternal weight of glory beyond all comparison, as we look not to the things that are seen but to the things that are unseen. For the things that are seen are transient, but the things that are unseen are eternal.

Paul's affliction is "preparing" or "effecting" or "bringing about" a weight of glory beyond all comparison. We must take seriously Paul's

10. James Paton, ed., *John G. Paton: Missionary to the New Hebrides, an Autobiography* (1889, 1898; reprint, Edinburgh: Banner of Truth Trust, 1965), 80.

11. Ibid., 200. For a brief overview of Paton's life and ministry, refer to John Piper, "'You Will Be Eaten by Cannibals!' Courage in the Cause of World Missions: Lessons from the Life of John G. Paton" at www.DesiringGod.org.

words here. He is not merely saying that he has a great hope in heaven that enables him to endure suffering. That is true. But he also says that the suffering has an effect on the weight of glory. There seems to be a connection between the suffering endured and the degree of glory enjoyed. Of course the glory outstrips the suffering infinitely, as Paul says in Romans 8:18: "I consider that the sufferings of this present time are *not worth comparing with the glory* that is to be revealed to us." Nevertheless, the weight of that glory, or the experience of that glory, seems to be more or less dependent in part on the affliction we have endured with patient faith.

Jesus pointed in the same direction when he said, "Blessed are you when others revile you and persecute you and utter all kinds of evil against you falsely on my account. Rejoice and be glad, for *your reward is great in heaven*" (Matt. 5:11–12). This would carry the greatest encouragement to rejoice if Jesus meant that the more we endure suffering in faith, the greater will be our reward. If a Christian who suffers much for Jesus and one who does not suffer much experience God's final glory in exactly the same way and degree, it would seem strange to tell the suffering Christian to rejoice and be glad (in that very day; cf. Luke 6:23) because of the reward he would receive even if he did not suffer. The reward promised seems to be in response to the suffering and a specific recompense for it. If this is not explicit and certain here, it does seem to be implied in other passages of the New Testament. I will let Jonathan Edwards bring them out as we listen to one of the most profound reflections on this problem I have ever read. Here Edwards deals, in a breathtaking way, with the issue of how there can be degrees of happiness in a world of perfect joy.

> There are different degrees of happiness and glory in heaven. ... The glory of the saints above will be in some proportion to their eminency in holiness and good works here [and patience through suffering is one of the foremost good works, cf. Rom. 2:7]. Christ will reward all according to their works. He that gained ten pounds was made ruler over ten cities, and he that gained five pounds over five cities (Luke 19:17–19). "He that soweth sparingly, shall reap sparingly; and he that soweth bountifully shall reap also bountifully" (2 Cor. 9:6). And the apostle Paul tells us that, as one star differs from another star in glory, so also it shall be in the resurrection of the dead (1 Cor. 15:41). Christ tells us that he who gives a cup of cold water unto a disciple in the name of a disciple, shall in no wise lose his reward. But this could not be true, if a person should have no greater reward for doing many good works than if he did but few.
>
> It will be no damp to the happiness of those who have lower degrees of happiness and glory, that there are others advanced in glory above them: for all shall be perfectly happy, every one shall be perfectly satis-

fied. Every vessel that is cast into this ocean of happiness is full, though there are some vessels far larger than others; and there shall be no such thing as envy in heaven, but perfect love shall reign through the whole society. Those who are not so high in glory as others, will not envy those that are higher, but they will have so great, and strong, and pure love to them, that they will rejoice in their superior happiness; their love to them will be such that they will rejoice that they are happier than themselves; so that instead of having a damp to their own happiness, it will add to it.

And so, on the other hand, those that are highest in glory, as they will be the most lovely, so they will proportionally excel in divine benevolence and love to others, and will have more love to God and to the saints than those that are lower in holiness and happiness. And besides, those that will excel in glory will also excel in humility. Here in this world, those that are above others are the objects of envy, because . . . others conceive of them as being lifted up with it; but in heaven it will not be so, but those saints in heaven who excel in happiness will also [excel] in holiness, and consequently in humility. . . . The exaltation of some in heaven above the rest will be so far from diminishing the perfect happiness and joy of the rest who are inferior, that they will be the happier for it; such will be the union in their society that they will be partakers of each other's happiness. Then will be fulfilled in its perfections that which is declared in 1 Corinthians 12:22: "If one of the members be honored all the members rejoice with it."[12]

Thus, one of the aims of God in the suffering of the saints is to enlarge their capacity to enjoy his glory both here and in the age to come. When their cup is picked up, as it were, from the "refuse of the world" (1 Cor. 4:13) and tossed into the ocean of heaven's happiness, it will hold more happiness if they have been long weaned from the world and made to live on God alone.

12. Jonathan Edwards, *The Works of Jonathan Edwards*, vol. 2 (Edinburgh: Banner of Truth Trust, 1974), 902. The parable of the workers in the vineyard who all made the same wage (Matt. 20:1–16) need not be in conflict with what Edwards (and the texts he cites!) teaches here. What that text may imply is that all of us are thrown into the same ocean of happiness. Another point of that parable is that God is free to give anyone any degree of blessing more than he deserves, and if there is anyone who is self-pitying or proud about his endurance, God is indeed free to exalt a person even above him so as to humble him and make him realize all of heaven is all of grace. I think Jonathan Edwards effectively answers Craig Blomberg's question: "Is it not fundamentally self-contradictory to speak of degrees of perfection?" "Degrees of Reward in the Kingdom of Heaven," *Journal of the Evangelical Theological Society* 35, no. 2 (June 1992): 162–63. I do, however, want to side with Blomberg over against those who speak of "earning" rewards and who distort the conditional promises of heaven into promises of levels of reward in heaven.

3. Suffering Is the Price of Making Others Bold

God uses the suffering of his missionaries to awaken others out of their slumbers of indifference and make them bold. When Paul was imprisoned in Rome, he wrote of this to the church at Philippi. "Most of the brothers, having become confident in the Lord by my imprisonment, are much more bold to speak the word without fear" (Phil. 1:14). If he must, God will use the suffering of his devoted emissaries to make a sleeping church wake up and take risks for God.

The sufferings and dedication of young David Brainerd has had this effect on thousands. Henry Martyn recorded Brainerd's impact on his life again and again in his *Journal.*

> September 11, 1805: "What a quickening example has he often been to me, especially on this account, that he was of a weak and sickly constitution!"
>
> May 8, 1806: "Blessed be the memory of that holy man! I feel happy that I shall have his book with me in India, and thus enjoy, in a manner, the benefit of his company and example."
>
> May 12, 1806: "My soul was revived today through God's never-ceasing compassion, so that I found the refreshing presence of God in secret duties; especially was I most abundantly encouraged by reading D. Brainerd's account of the difficulties attending a mission to the heathen. Oh, blessed be the memory of that beloved saint! No uninspired writer ever did me so much good. I felt most sweetly joyful to labor amongst the poor natives here; and my willingness was, I think, more divested of those romantic notions, which have sometimes inflated me with false spirits."[13]

Five Inspiring Wives

In our own time, it is difficult to overstate the impact that the martyrdom of Jim Elliot, Nate Saint, Ed McCully, Pete Fleming, and Roger Youderian has had on generations of students.[14] The word that appeared again and again in the testimonies of those who heard the Huaorani[15] story was "dedication." But more than is often realized, it

13. *Journal and Letters of Henry Martyn,* 240, 326–28.

14. For their remarkable story, see the following resources: Elisabeth Elliot, *Through Gates of Splendor,* 40th ann. ed. (Wheaton: Tyndale, 1986); Elisabeth Elliot, *Shadow of the Almighty: The Life and Testament of Jim Elliot* (San Francisco: HarperSanFrancisco, 1989); Elisabeth Elliot, *The Savage My Kinsmen,* 40th ann. ed. (Ann Arbor, Mich.: Servant, 1996); Steve Saint, "Did They Have to Die?" *Christianity Today* 40, no. 10 (16 September 1996): 20–27; and Russell T. Hitt, *Jungle Pilot: The Gripping Story of the Life and Witness of Nate Saint, Martyred Missionary to Ecuador* (Grand Rapids: Discovery House, 1997).

15. This is the name of the tribe formerly known as "Auca" ["savage"] by outsiders.

was the strength of the wives of these men that made many of us feel a surge of desire to be dedicated like that.

Barbara Youderian, the wife of Roger, wrote in her diary that night in January 1956:

> Tonight the Captain told us of his finding four bodies in the river. One had tee-shirt and blue-jeans. Roj was the only one who wore them. . . . God gave me this verse two days ago, Psalm 48:14, "For this God is our God for ever and ever; He will be our Guide even unto death." As I came face to face with the news of Roj's death, my heart was filled with praise. He was worthy of his homegoing. Help me, Lord, to be both mummy and daddy.[16]

It is not difficult to feel the biblical point Paul was making. The suffering of the servants of God, borne with faith and even praise, is a shattering experience to apathetic saints whose lives are empty in the midst of countless comforts.

Applications Doubled at His Death

The execution of Wycliffe missionary Chet Bitterman by the Colombian guerrilla group M-19 on March 6, 1981, unleashed an amazing zeal for the cause of Christ. Chet had been in captivity for seven weeks while his wife, Brenda, and little daughters, Anna and Esther, waited in Bogotá. The demand of M-19 was that Wycliffe get out of Colombia.

They shot him just before dawn—a single bullet to the chest. Police found his body in the bus where he died, in a parking lot in the south of town. He was clean and shaven, his face relaxed. A guerrilla banner wrapped his remains. There were no signs of torture.

In the year following Chet's death, "applications for overseas service with Wycliffe Bible Translators doubled. This trend was continued."[17] It is not the kind of missionary mobilization that any of us would choose. But it is God's way. "Unless a grain of wheat falls into the earth and dies, it remains alone; but if it dies, it bears much fruit" (John 12:24).

4. Suffering Fills Up What Is Lacking in Christ's Afflictions

The suffering of Christ's messengers ministers to those they are trying to reach and may open them to the gospel. This was one of the ways Paul brought the gospel to bear on the people in Thessalonica.

16. Quoted in Elisabeth Elliot, *Through Gates of Splendor* (New York: Harper & Row, 1957), 235–36.
17. Steve Estes, *Called to Die* (Grand Rapids: Zondervan, 1986), 252.

"You know what kind of men we proved to be among you *for your sake*. And *you became imitators of us* and of the Lord, for *you received the word in much affliction*, with the joy of the Holy Spirit" (1 Thess. 1:5–6). The Thessalonians had imitated Paul by enduring much affliction with joy. And that is the kind of man Paul had proven to be among them. So it was his suffering that moved them and drew them to his authentic love and truth.

This is the kind of ministry Paul had in mind when he said, "As we share abundantly in Christ's sufferings, so through Christ we share abundantly in comfort too. If we are afflicted, it is for your comfort and salvation" (2 Cor. 1:5–6). His sufferings were the means God was using to bring salvation to the Corinthian church. They could see the suffering love of Christ in Paul. He was actually sharing in Christ's sufferings and making them real for the church.

This is part of what Paul meant in that amazing statement in Colossians 1:24: "I rejoice in my sufferings for your sake, and in my flesh I am *filling up what is lacking in Christ's afflictions for the sake of his body*, that is, the church." Christ's afflictions are not lacking in their atoning sufficiency. They are lacking in that they are not known and felt by people who were not at the cross. Paul dedicates himself not only to carry the message of those sufferings to the nations but also to suffer with Christ and for Christ in such a way so that what people see are "Christ's sufferings." In this way he follows the pattern of Christ by laying down his life for the life of the church. "I endure everything for the sake of the elect, that they also may obtain the salvation that is in Christ Jesus with eternal glory" (2 Tim. 2:10).

"When We Saw Your Blistered Feet"

In 1992, I had an opportunity to hear J. Oswald Sanders speak. His message touched deeply on suffering. He was eighty-nine years old at the time and still traveled and spoke around the world. He had written a book a year since turning seventy! I mention that only to exult in the utter dedication of a life poured out for the gospel without thought of coasting in self-indulgence from sixty-five to the grave.[18]

He told the story of an indigenous missionary who walked barefoot from village to village preaching the gospel in India. After a long day of many miles and much discouragement, he came to a certain village and tried to speak the gospel but was spurned. So he went to

18. See note 25 on the development of the Finishers Project devoted to helping people nearing retirement give their energy, skill, and heart to the cause of Christ. Part of their vision statement says, "We can either give them to Jesus to lay up as treasure in Heaven or lose them."

the edge of the village dejected and lay down under a tree and slept from exhaustion.

When he awoke, the whole town was gathered to hear him. The head man of the village explained that they had looked him over while he was sleeping. When they saw his blistered feet, they concluded that he must be a holy man and that they had been evil to reject him. They were sorry and wanted to hear the message for which he was willing to suffer so much to bring them.

At the Third Beating the Women Wept

One of the unlikeliest men to attend the Itinerant Evangelists' Conference in Amsterdam sponsored by the Billy Graham Association was a Masai Warrior named Joseph. But his story won him a hearing with Dr. Graham himself. The story is told by Michael Card.

> One day Joseph, who was walking along one of these hot, dirty African roads, met someone who shared the gospel of Jesus Christ with him. Then and there he accepted Jesus as his Lord and Savior. The power of the Spirit began transforming his life; he was filled with such excitement and joy that the first thing he wanted to do was return to his own village and share that same Good News with the members of his local tribe.
>
> Joseph began going from door-to-door, telling everyone he met about the Cross of Jesus and the salvation it offered, expecting to see their faces light up the way his had. To his amazement the villagers not only didn't care, they became violent. The men of the village seized him and held him to the ground while the women beat him with strands of barbed wire. He was dragged from the village and left to die alone in the bush.
>
> Joseph somehow managed to crawl to a waterhole, and there, after days of passing in and out of consciousness, found the strength to get up. He wondered about the hostile reception he had received from people he had known all his life. He decided he must have left something out or told the story of Jesus incorrectly. After rehearsing the message he had first heard, he decided to go back and share his faith once more.
>
> Joseph limped into the circle of huts and began to proclaim Jesus. "He died for you, so that you might find forgiveness and come to know the living God," he pleaded. Again he was grabbed by the men of the village and held while the women beat him, reopening wounds that had just begun to heal. Once more they dragged him unconscious from the village and left him to die.
>
> To have survived the first beating was truly remarkable. To live through the second was a miracle. Again, days later, Joseph awoke in the wilderness, bruised, scarred—and determined to go back.
>
> He returned to the small village and this time, they attacked him before he had a chance to open his mouth. As they flogged him for the third and probably the last time, he again spoke to them of Jesus Christ,

the Lord. Before he passed out, the last thing he saw was that the
women who were beating him began to weep.

This time he awoke in his own bed. The ones who had so severely
beaten him were now trying to save his life and nurse him back to
health. The entire village had come to Christ.[19]

Surely this is something of what Paul meant when he said, "I fill up
what is lacking in Christ's afflictions, for the sake of his body."

5. Suffering Enforces the Missionary Command to Go

The suffering of the church is used by God to reposition the missionary troops in places they might not have otherwise gone. This is
clearly the effect that Luke wants us to see in the story of the martyrdom of Stephen and the persecution that came after it. God spurs the
church into missionary service by the suffering she endures. Therefore, we must not judge too quickly the apparent setbacks and tactical
defeats of the church. If you see things with the eyes of God, the Master strategist, what you see in every setback is the positioning of
troops for a greater advance and a greater display of his wisdom,
power, and love.

Acts 8:1 charts the divine strategy for the persecution: "There arose
on that day [the day of Stephen's murder] a great persecution against
the church in Jerusalem, and they were all scattered throughout the
regions of *Judea and Samaria,* except the apostles." Up until now no
one had moved out to Judea and Samaria in spite of what Jesus had
said in Acts 1:8: "You will receive power when the Holy Spirit has
come upon you, and you will be my witnesses in Jerusalem and in all
Judea and Samaria." It is no accident that these were the very two regions to which the persecution sent the church. What obedience will
not achieve, persecution will.

To confirm this divine missionary purpose of the persecution, Luke
refers to it in Acts 11:19: "Now those who were scattered because of
the persecution that arose over Stephen traveled as far as Phoenicia
and Cyprus and Antioch, speaking the word to no one except Jews."
But in Antioch some spoke to Greeks also. In other words, the persecution sent the church not only to Judea and Samaria (Acts 8:1) but
also beyond to the nations (Acts 11:19).

The Inertia of Ease, the Apathy of Abundance

The lesson here is not just that God is sovereign and turns setbacks
into triumphs. The lesson is also that comfort and ease and affluence

19. Michael Card, "Wounded in the House of Friends," *Virtue* (March/April 1991):
28–29, 69.

and prosperity and safety and freedom often cause a tremendous inertia in the church. The very things that we think would produce personnel, energy, and creative investment of time and money for the missionary cause instead produce the exact opposite: weakness, apathy, lethargy, self-centeredness, preoccupation with security.

Studies have shown that the richer we are the smaller the percentage of our income we give to the church and its mission. The poorest fifth of the church gives 3.4 percent of its income to the church, and the richest fifth gives 1.6 percent—half as much as the poorer church members.[20] It is a strange principle that probably goes right to the heart of our sinfulness and Christ's sufficiency: Hard times, like persecution, often produce more personnel, more prayer, more power, and more open purses than do easy times.

It is difficult for a rich man to enter the kingdom of heaven, Jesus said (Matt. 19:23). It is also difficult for rich people to help others enter. Jesus said as much in the parable of the soils. "The cares of the world and *the deceitfulness of riches* and *the desires for other things* enter in and choke the word, and it proves unfruitful" (Mark 4:19)—unfruitful for missions and most every other good work.

Persecution can have harmful effects on the church, but prosperity it seems is even more devastating to the mission God calls us to. My point here is not that we should seek persecution. That would be presumption—like jumping off the temple. The point is that we should be wary of prosperity, excessive ease, comfort, and affluence. And we should not be disheartened but filled with hope if we are persecuted for righteousness' sake, because the point of Acts 8:1 is that God makes persecution serve the mission of the church.

We must not be glib about this. The price of missionary advance is immense. Stephen paid for it with his life. And Stephen was one of the brightest stars in the Jerusalem sky. His enemies "could not withstand the wisdom and the Spirit with which he was speaking" (Acts 6:10). Surely he was more valuable alive than dead, we would all reason. He was needed! There was no one like Stephen! But God saw it another way.

How Joseph Stalin Served the Cause

The way God brought entire Uzbek villages to Christ in the twentieth century is a great illustration of God's strange use of upheaval and displacement. Bill and Amy Stearns tell the story in their hope-filled book, *Catch the Vision 2000.*[21] The key player was Joseph Stalin.

---

20. The *Minneapolis Star Tribune* carried an article on Friday, 3 May 1991, from which these data are taken.
21. Bill and Amy Stearns, *Catch the Vision 2000* (Minneapolis: Bethany, 1991), 12–13.

Thousands of Koreans fled what is now North Korea in the 30's as the Japanese invaded. Many of these settled around Vladivostok. When Stalin in the late 30's and early 40's began developing Vladivostok as a weapons manufacturing center, he deemed the Koreans a security risk. So he relocated them in five areas around the Soviet Union. One of those areas was Tashkent, hub of the staunchly Muslim people called the Uzbeks. Twenty million strong, the Uzbeks had for hundreds of years violently resisted any Western efforts to introduce Christianity.

As the Koreans settled around Tashkent, the Uzbeks welcomed their industry and kindness. Within a few decades, the Koreans were included in nearly every facet of Uzbek cultural life.

As usual in God's orchestration of global events, He had planted within the relocated Koreans strong pockets of believers. Little did Stalin suspect that these Koreans would not only begin enjoying a wildfire revival among their own people, they would also begin bringing their Muslim, Uzbek and Kazak friends to Christ.

The first public sign of the Korean revival and its breakthrough effects on the Uzbeks and Kazaks came on June 2, 1990, when in the first open air Christian meeting in the history of Soviet Central Asia, a young Korean from America preached to a swelling crowd in the streets of Alma-Ata, capital of Kazakhstan.

The result of these roundabout, decade-long maneuverings by God to position his people in inaccessible places is that Muslims, who would not receive missionaries, are confessing that Isa (Jesus) is the way, the truth, and the life. This was a costly strategy for many believers. Being uprooted from their homeland in Korea, and then again from their new home near Vladivostok, must have been a severe test of the Koreans' faith that God is good and had a loving plan for their lives. The truth was that God did have a loving plan, and not only for them but also for many unreached Muslims among the Uzbek and Kazak peoples.

Going Forward by Getting Arrested

God's strange ways of guiding the missionary enterprise are also seen in the way Jesus told the disciples to expect arrest and imprisonment as God's deployment tactic to put them with people they would never otherwise reach. "They will lay their hands on you and persecute you, delivering you up to the synagogues and prisons, and you will be brought before kings and governors for my name's sake. *This will be your opportunity to bear witness*" (Luke 21:12–13; cf. Mark 13:9).

The June/July 1989 issue of *Mission Frontiers* carried an article signed with the pseudonym Frank Marshall. This missionary in a politically sensitive Latin American country told the story of his recent imprisonment. He and his coworkers had been beaten numerous times and thrown in jail before. This time federal agents accused him of fraud and bribery because they assumed he could not have gotten his official documents without lying. They did not believe that he had been born in the country.

In prison, the Lord spared him from sexual assault by a huge man wrapped in a towel with four gold chains around his neck and a ring on every finger. When put in the cell with this man, Frank began sharing the gospel with him and praying in his heart, "Lord, deliver me from this evil." The man changed color, shouted at Frank to shut up, and told him to leave him alone.

Frank began to tell others about Christ when the men had free time in the courtyard. One Muslim named Satawa confessed Christ within the first week and invited Frank to answer questions from a group of fifteen other Muslims. In two weeks, Frank finally was able to get a lawyer. He also asked for a box of Bibles. The next Sunday forty-five men gathered in the courtyard to hear Frank preach. He spoke about how difficult it was for him to be away from his family and about how much God loved his Son and yet gave him up for sinners so that we could believe and live. Thirty of these men stayed afterward to pray and ask the Lord to lead them and forgive them. Frank was soon released and deported to the United States, but he now knows firsthand the meaning of Jesus' words, "This will be your opportunity to bear witness."

Miracles in Mozambique

During the 1960s, the Lord raised up an indigenous leader named Martinho Campos in the church in Mozambique. The story of his ministry, *Life out of Death in Mozambique,* is a remarkable testimony to God's strange ways of missionary blessing.

Martinho was leading a series of meetings in the administrative area of Gurue sixty miles from his own area of Nauela. The police arrested him and put him in jail without a trial. The police chief, a European, assumed that the gatherings were related to the emerging guerrilla group Frelimo. But even when the Catholic priest told him that these men were just "a gathering of heretics," he took no concern for justice, though he wondered why the common people brought so much food to the prisoner, as though he were someone important.

One night he was driving his truck with half a dozen prisoners in it and saw "what appeared to be a man in gleaming white, standing in the road, facing him." He swerved so sharply that the truck rolled over, and he was trapped underneath. The prisoners themselves lifted the truck so that the police chief could get out.

After brief treatment in the hospital, he returned to talk to Martinho because he knew there was some connection between this vision and the prisoner. He entered Martinho's cell and asked for forgiveness. Martinho told him about his need for God's forgiveness and how to have it. The police chief said humbly, "Please pray for me." Immediately the chief called for hot water so that the prisoner could wash, took him out of solitary confinement, and saw to it that a fair trial was held. Martinho was released.

But the most remarkable thing was what followed: "Not only did the Chief of Police make plain his respect for what Martinho stood for, but granted him official permission to travel throughout the whole area under his jurisdiction, in order to preach and hold evangelical services."[22] Such permission would never have been given through the ordinary channels. But God had made a way through suffering. The imprisonment was for the advancement of the gospel.

God Was Better Served in Prison

On January 9, 1985, Pastor Hristo Kulichev, a Congregational pastor in Bulgaria, was arrested and put in prison. His crime was that he preached in his church even though the state had appointed another man as the pastor, whom the congregation had not elected. Kulichev's trial was a mockery of justice, and he was sentenced to eight months of imprisonment. During his time in prison, he made Christ known every way he could.

When he got out he wrote, "Both prisoners and jailers asked many questions, and it turned out that we had a more fruitful ministry there than we could have expected in church. God was better served by our presence in prison than if we had been free."[23] In many places in the world, the words of Jesus are as radically relevant as if they had been spoken yesterday. "They will lay their hands on you and persecute you, delivering you up to . . . prisons. . . . This will be your opportunity to bear witness" (Luke 21:12–13). The pain of our shattered plans is for the purpose of scattered grace.

6. The Supremacy of Christ Is Manifest in Suffering

The suffering of missionaries is meant by God to magnify the power and sufficiency of Christ. Suffering is finally to show the supremacy of God. When God declined to remove the suffering caused by Paul's "thorn in the flesh," he said to Paul, "My grace is sufficient

22. Phyllis Thompson, *Life out of Death in Mozambique* (London: Hodder & Stoughton, 1989), 111.
23. Herbert Schlossberg, *Called to Suffer, Called to Triumph* (Portland, Ore.: Multnomah, 1990), 230.

for you, for *my power is made perfect in weakness.*" To this Paul responded, "I will boast all the more gladly of my weaknesses, so that the power of Christ may rest upon me. For the sake of Christ, then, I am content with weaknesses, insults, hardships, persecutions, and calamities. For when I am weak, then I am strong" (2 Cor. 12:9–10).

Paul was strong in persecutions because "the power of Christ" rested upon him and was made perfect in him. In other words, Christ's power was Paul's only power when his sufferings brought him to the end of his resources and cast him wholly on Jesus. This was God's purpose in Paul's thorn, and it is his purpose in all our suffering. God means for us to rely wholly on him. "That was to make us rely not on ourselves but on God who raises the dead" (2 Cor. 1:9). The reason God wants such reliance is because this kind of trust shows his supreme power and love to sustain us when we can't do anything to sustain ourselves.

We began this chapter with this claim: Loss and suffering, joyfully accepted for the kingdom of God, show the supremacy of God's worth more clearly in the world than all worship and prayer. We have seen this truth implicit in looking at six reasons why God appoints suffering for the messengers of his grace. But now we need to make explicit that the supremacy of God is the reason for suffering running through and above all the other reasons. God ordains suffering because through all the other reasons it displays to the world the supremacy of his worth above all treasures.

Jesus makes crystal clear how we can rejoice in persecution. "Blessed are you when others revile you and persecute you and utter all kinds of evil against you falsely on my account. Rejoice and be glad, *for your reward is great in heaven*" (Matt. 5:11–12). The reason we can rejoice in persecution is that the worth of our reward in heaven is so much greater than the worth of all that we lose through suffering on earth. Therefore, suffering with joy proves to the world that our treasure is in heaven, not on earth, and that this treasure is greater than anything the world has to offer. The supremacy of God's worth shines through the pain that his people will gladly bear for his name.

Gladly Will I Boast of Weakness and Calamity

I use the word "gladly" because that is the way the saints speak of it. One example is Paul saying, "I will boast all the more gladly of my weaknesses . . . insults, hardships, persecutions, and calamities" (2 Cor. 12:9–10). He says the same thing in Romans 5:3: "We rejoice in our sufferings." And the reason he gives is that it produces patience and a tested quality of life and an unfailing hope (Rom. 5:3–4). In other words, his joy flowed from his hope just the way Jesus said it should. And Paul makes clear that the reward is the glory of God. "We rejoice in hope of the glory of God" (Rom. 5:2). And so it is the supremacy of God's worth that shines through Paul's joy in affliction.

The other apostles react the same way in Acts 5:41 after being beaten for their preaching: "Then they left the presence of the council, rejoicing that they were counted worthy to suffer dishonor for the name" (Acts 5:41). This fearless joy in spite of real danger and great pain is the display of God's superiority over all that the world has to offer.

You Joyfully Accepted the Plundering of Your Property

And then there were the early Christians who visited their friends in prison, rejoicing even though it cost them their possessions. "For you had compassion on those in prison, and you joyfully accepted the plundering of your property, since you knew that you yourselves had a better possession and an abiding one" (Heb. 10:34). Joy in suffering flows from hope in a great reward. Christians are not called to live morose lives of burdensome persecution. We are called to rejoice. "Rejoice insofar as you share Christ's sufferings" (1 Peter 4:13). "Count it all joy, my brothers, when you meet trials of various kinds" (James 1:2).

The Love of God Is Better than Life

The basis for this indomitable joy is the supremacy of God's love above life itself. The "steadfast love [of the Lord] is better than life" (Ps. 63:3). The pleasures in this life are "fleeting" (Heb. 11:25), and the afflictions are "light and momentary" (2 Cor. 4:17). But the steadfast love of the Lord is forever. All his pleasures are superior, and there will be no more pain. "In your presence there is fullness of joy; at your right hand are pleasures forevermore" (Ps. 16:11).

Glad Suffering Shines Brighter than Gratitude

It is true that we should bear testimony to the supremacy of God's goodness by receiving his good gifts with thanksgiving (1 Tim. 4:3). But for many Christians this has become the only way they see their lifestyles glorifying God. God has been good to them to give them so much. Therefore, the way to witness to the reality of God is to take and be thankful.

But even though it is true that we should thankfully enjoy what we have, there is a relentless call in the Bible not to accumulate more and more things but to give more and more and to be deprived of things if love demands it. There are no easy rules to tell us whether the call on our lives is the call of the rich young ruler to give away all that we have or the call of Zacchaeus to give away half of what we have. What is clear from the New Testament is that suffering with joy, not gratitude in wealth, is the way the worth of Jesus shines most brightly.

Who can doubt that the supremacy of Christ's worth shines brightest in a life such as this:

> But whatever gain I had, I counted as loss for the sake of Christ. Indeed, I count everything as loss because of the surpassing worth of knowing Christ Jesus my Lord. For his sake I have suffered the loss of all things and count them as rubbish, in order that I may gain Christ.
>
> Philippians 3:7–8

You cannot show the preciousness of a person by being happy with his gifts. Ingratitude will certainly prove that the giver is not loved, but gratitude for gifts does not prove that the giver is precious. What proves that the giver is precious is the glad-hearted readiness to leave all his gifts to be with him. This is why suffering is so central in the mission of the church. The goal of our mission is that people from all the nations worship the true God. But worship means cherishing the preciousness of God above all else, including life itself. It will be difficult to bring the nations to love God from a lifestyle that communicates a love of things. Therefore, God ordains in the lives of his messengers that suffering severs our bondage to the world. When joy and love survive this severing, we are fit to say to the nations with authenticity and power: Hope in God.

How Is Hope in God Made Visible?

Peter talks about the visibility of this hope: "In your hearts regard Christ the Lord as holy, always being prepared to make a defense to anyone who asks you for a reason for the hope that is in you" (1 Peter 3:15). Why would people ask about hope? What kind of life are we to live that would make people wonder about our hope? If our security and happiness in the future were manifestly secured the way the world secures its future, no one would ask us about it. There would be no unusual hope to see. What Peter is saying is that the world should see a different hope in the lives of Christians—not a hope in the security of money or the security of power or the security of houses or lands or portfolios but in the security of "the grace that will be brought to you at the revelation of Jesus Christ" (1 Peter 1:13).

Therefore, God ordains suffering to help us release our hold on worldly hopes and put our "hope in God" (1 Peter 1:21). The fiery trials are appointed to consume the earthly dependencies and leave only the refined gold of "genuine faith" (1 Peter 1:7). "Let those who suffer according to God's will entrust their souls to a faithful Creator while doing good" (1 Peter 4:19). It's the supremacy of God's great faithfulness above all other securities that frees us to "rejoice insofar as [we] share Christ's sufferings" (1 Peter 4:13). Therefore, joy in suffering for Christ's sake makes the supremacy of God shine more clearly than all our gratitude for wealth.

Wartime Austerity for the Cause of Missions

Jesus presses us toward a wartime lifestyle that does not value simplicity for simplicity's sake but values wartime austerity for what it can produce for the cause of world evangelization. He said, "Sell your possessions, and give to the needy. Provide yourselves with moneybags that do not grow old, with a treasure in the heavens that does not fail" (Luke 12:33). "Make friends for yourselves by means of unrighteous wealth, so that when it fails they may receive you into the eternal dwellings" (Luke 16:9). "Do not seek what you are to eat and what you are to drink, nor be worried. For all the nations of the world seek after these things, and your Father knows that you need them. Instead, seek his kingdom, and these things will be added to you" (Luke 12:29–31).

The point is that an $80,000 or a $180,000 salary does not have to be accompanied by an $80,000 or a $180,000 lifestyle. God is calling us to be conduits of his grace, not cul-de-sacs. Our great danger today is thinking that the conduit should be lined with gold. It shouldn't. Copper will do. No matter how grateful we are, gold will not make the world think that our God is good; it will make people think that our god is gold. That is no honor to the supremacy of his worth.

The Deadly Desire for Wealth

The desire for riches is deadly. Gehazi, Elisha's servant, was struck with Namaan's leprosy because he could not pass up a reward (2 Kings 5:26–27). Ananias dropped dead because desire for money prompted him to lie (Acts 5:5–6). The rich young ruler could not enter the kingdom of God (Mark 10:22–23). The rich man who feasted sumptuously and neglected Lazarus was tormented in Hades (Luke 16:23). Paul said that the desire to be rich plunges men into ruin and destruction (1 Tim. 6:9).

God tells us about these tragedies not to make us hate money but to make us love him. The severity of punishment for loving money is a sign of the supremacy of God. We scorn the infinite worth of God when we covet. That is why Paul calls covetousness idolatry and says that the wrath of God is coming against it (Col. 3:5–6).

"I Had No Shirt"

It is almost impossible for Americans to come to terms with Jesus' commendation of the widow who "out of her poverty put in all she had to live on" (Luke 21:4). To see this spirit fleshed out, we may have to leave America and go elsewhere. Stanford Kelly illustrates it from Haiti.

The church was having a Thanksgiving festival, and each Christian was invited to bring a love offering. One envelope from a Haitian man named Edmund held $13. That amount was three months' income for a working man there. Kelly was as surprised as those counting a Sunday offering in the United States might be to get a $6,000 cash gift. He looked around for Edmund but could not see him.

Later Kelly met him in the village and questioned him. He pressed him for an explanation and found that Edmund had sold his horse in order to give the $13 gift to God. But why hadn't he come to the festival? He hesitated and didn't want to answer.

Finally, Edmund said, "I had no shirt to wear."[24]

Retirement and the Unreached Peoples

Two phenomena in America are emerging together: One is the challenge to give our all to do our part in finishing the task of world missions, and the other is a huge baby-boom bulge in the population reaching peak earning years and heading toward "retirement."[25] How will the Christians in this group respond to the typical American dream? Is it a biblical dream?

24. Norm Lewis, *Priority One: What God Wants* (Orange, Calif.: Promise Publishing, 1988), 120.

25. Since the first edition of this book in 1993, one of the significant advances in Christian mission strategy has been the emergence of ministries focused on mobilizing people in midlife for the cause of finishing the Great Commission. Paul's words in Acts 20:24 have come alive for thousands as they contemplate a better way to finish their earthly lives than to throw them away golfing or fishing in the unbiblical dreamworld of wasted lives called "retirement." Paul said, "But I do not account my life of any value nor as precious to myself, if only I may finish my course and the ministry that I received from the Lord Jesus, to testify to the gospel of the grace of God." For information about this movement, see the web site of the Finishers Project: www.finishers.gospelcom.net/. The Finishers Project is a service designed to provide adult Christians with information and challenge for processing and discovering ministry opportunities in the missions enterprise—short term, part term, or as a second career. The vision statement

Ralph Winter asks, "Where in the Bible do they see [retirement]? Did Moses retire? Did Paul retire? Peter? John? Do military officers retire in the middle of a war?"[26] I mentioned earlier that Oswald Sanders ministered around the world until he died at ninety and that he wrote a book a year between the ages of seventy and eighty-nine.

Why Simeon's Strength Quadrupled at Sixty

Charles Simeon, the pastor of Trinity Church, Cambridge, two hundred years ago learned a very painful lesson about God's attitude toward his "retirement." In 1807, after twenty-five years of ministry at Trinity Church, his health broke. He became very weak and had to take an extended leave from his labor. Handley Moule recounts the fascinating story of what God was doing in Simeon's life.

> The broken condition lasted with variations for thirteen years, till he was just sixty, and then it passed away quite suddenly and without any evident physical cause. He was on his last visit to Scotland . . . in 1819, and found himself to his great surprise, just as he crossed the border, "almost as perceptibly renewed in strength as the woman was after she had touched the hem of our Lord's garment." He saw in this revival no miracle, in the common sense of the word, yet as a distinct providence.
>
> He says that he had been promising himself, before he began to break down, a very active life up to sixty, and then a Sabbath evening [retirement!]; and that now he seemed to hear his Master saying: "I laid you aside, because you entertained with satisfaction the thought of resting from your labour; but now you have arrived at the very period when you had promised yourself that satisfaction, and have determined instead to spend your strength for me to the latest hour of your life, I have doubled, trebled, quadrupled your strength, that you may execute your desire on a more extended plan."[27]

---

says, "The Finishers Project is a movement to provide information, challenge and pathways for people to join God in His passion for His glory among the nations. Boomers are and will be the healthiest and best educated generation of empty-nesters ever. This generation is skilled and resourced with a multitude of talents. We can either give them to Jesus to lay up as treasure in Heaven or lose them."

26. Ralph D. Winter, "The Retirement Booby Trap," *Missions Frontiers* 7 (July 1985): 25.

27. Handley C. G. Moule, *Charles Simeon* (1892; reprint, London: Inter-Varsity, 1948), 125. For a biographical sketch of Simeon's life, see "Charles Simeon: The Ballast of Humiliation and the Sails of Adoration," in John Piper, *The Roots of Endurance: Invincible Perseverance in the Lives of John Newton, Charles Simeon, and William Wilberforce* (Wheaton: Crossway, 2002). An earlier version of this essay is found at www.Desiring God.org.

How many Christians set their sights on a "Sabbath evening" of life—resting, playing, traveling, and so on—the world's substitute for heaven, because they do not believe that there will be one beyond the grave. The mind-set is that we must reward ourselves in this life for our long years of labor. Eternal rest and joy after death is an irrelevant consideration. What a strange reward for a Christian to set his sights on! Twenty years of leisure while living in the midst of the last days of infinite consequence for millions of unreached people. What a tragic way to finish the last lap before entering the presence of the King who finished his so differently!

Why Not Be like Raymond Lull?

Raymond Lull was born in 1235 to an illustrious family at Palma on the island of Majorca off the coast of Spain. His life as a youth was profligate. But all that changed as a result of five visions that compelled him to a life of devotion to Christ. He first entered monastic life but later became a missionary to Muslim countries in northern Africa. He learned Arabic, which at the age of seventy-nine he was teaching in Europe.

His pupils and friends naturally desired that he should end his days in the peaceful pursuit of learning and the comfort of companionship.

Such however was not Lull's wish. His ambition was to die as a missionary and not as a teacher of philosophy. Ever his favorite "Ars Major" had to give way to that *ars maxima* expressed in Lull's own motto, "He that lives by the life cannot die." . . .

In Lull's contemplations we read . . . "Men are wont to die, O Lord, from old age, the failure of natural warmth and excess of cold; but thus, if it be Thy will, Thy servant would not wish to die; he would prefer to die in the glow of love, even as Thou wast willing to die for him."

The dangers and difficulties that made Lull shrink back from his journey at Genoa in 1291 only urged him forward to North Africa once more in 1314. His love had not grown cold, but burned the brighter "with the failure of natural warmth and the weakness of old age." He longed not only for the martyr's crown, but also once more to see his little band of believers [in Africa]. Animated by these sentiments he crossed over to Bugia on August 14, and for nearly a whole year labored secretly among a little circle of converts, whom on his previous visits he had won over to the Christian faith. . . .

At length, weary of seclusion, and longing for martyrdom, he came forth into the open market and presented himself to the people as the same man whom they had once expelled from their town. It was Elijah showing himself to a mob of Ahabs! Lull stood before them and threatened them with divine wrath if they still persisted in their errors. He pleaded with love, but spoke plainly the whole truth. The consequences can be easily anticipated. Filled with fanatic fury at his boldness, and unable to reply to his arguments, the populace seized him, and dragged him out of the town; there by the command, or at least the connivance, of the king, he was stoned on the 30th of June 1315.[28]

Lull was eighty years old when he gave his life for the Muslims of North Africa. As a hart longs for the flowing streams—and longs the more as the brook approaches and the smell sweetens and the thirst deepens—so longs the soul of the saint to see Christ and to glorify him in his dying (cf. John 21:19). It is beyond comprehension that soldiers of the cross would be satisfied in retiring from the battle just before the trumpet blast of victory—or just before admission to the coronation ceremony.

"Senior Discounts" Are for Missionary Travel

I am not saying that we can make professions and businesses keep us employed beyond sixty-five or seventy. I am saying that a new chapter of life opens for most people at age sixty-five. And if we have armed ourselves with the "thought" of the suffering Savior and saturated our mind with the ways of the supremacy of God, we will invest our time and energy in this final chapter very differently than if we take our cues from the American dream. Millions of "retired" people should be engaged at all levels of intensity in hundreds of assignments around the world. Talk about travel! Park the RVs and use the senior discounts and "super savers" to fly wherever the agencies have need. Let the unreached peoples of the earth reap the benefits of a lifetime of earning. "You will be repaid at the resurrection of the just" (Luke 14:14).

"You'll Be Eaten by Cannibals"

An aging Christian once objected to John G. Paton's plan to go as a missionary to the South Sea Islands with the words, "You'll be eaten by Cannibals!" Paton responded:

Mr. Dickson, you are advanced in years now, and your own prospect is soon to be laid in the grave, there to be eaten by worms; I confess to you, that if I can but live and die serving and honoring the Lord Jesus, it

28. Samuel Zwemer, *Raymond Lull: First Missionary to the Moslems* (New York: Revell, 1902), 132–45.

will make no difference to me whether I am eaten by Cannibals or worms; and in the Great Day my resurrection body will arise as fair as yours in the likeness of our risen Redeemer.[29]

When the world sees millions of "retired" Christians pouring out the last drops of their lives with joy for the sake of the unreached peoples and with a view toward heaven, then the supremacy of God will shine. He does not shine as brightly in the posh, leisure-soaked luxury condos on the outer rings of our cities.

Let There Be No Talk of Ultimate Self-Denial

From the youngest to the oldest, Christ is calling his church to a radical, wartime engagement in world missions. He is making it plain that it will not happen without pain. But let there be no Christian self-pity, no talk of ultimate self-denial. It is simply amazing how consistent are the testimonies of missionaries who have suffered for the gospel. Virtually all of them bear witness of the abundant joy and overriding compensations. Those who have suffered most often speak in the most lavish terms of the supreme blessing and joy of giving their lives away for others.

Lottie Moon said, "Surely there is no greater joy than saving souls." Sherwood Eddy said of Amy Carmichael, "Her life was the most fragrant, the most joyfully sacrificial, that I ever knew." Samuel Zwemer, after fifty years of labor (and the loss of two young children), said "The sheer joy of it all comes back. Gladly would I do it all over again." And both Hudson Taylor and David Livingstone, after lives of extraordinary hardship and loss said, "I never made a sacrifice."[30]

From this discovery I have learned that the way of love is both the way of self-denial and the way of ultimate joy. We deny ourselves the fleeting pleasures of sin and luxury and self-absorption in order to seek the kingdom above all things. In doing so we bring the greatest good to others, we magnify the worth of Christ as a treasure chest of joy, and we find our greatest satisfaction.

God is most glorified in us when we are most satisfied in him. And the supremacy of that glory shines most brightly when the satisfaction that we have in him endures in spite of suffering and pain in the mission of love.

---

29. Paton, *John G. Paton*, 56.
30. See John Piper, "The Battle Cry of Christian Hedonism," in *Desiring God* (Sisters, Ore.: Multnomah, 1996), 189–211.

PART 2

Making God Supreme in Missions

*The Necessity
and Nature
of the Task*

4

The Supremacy of Christ as the Conscious Focus of All Saving Faith

The supremacy of God in missions is affirmed biblically by affirming the supremacy of his Son, Jesus Christ. It is a stunning New Testament truth that since the incarnation of the Son of God, all saving faith must henceforth fix on him. This was not always true, and those times were called the "times of ignorance" (Acts 17:30). But now it is true, and Christ is the conscious center of the mission of the church. The aim of missions is to "bring about the obedience of faith *for the sake of his name* among all the nations" (Rom. 1:5). This was a new thing with the coming of Christ. God's will is to glorify his Son by making him the conscious focus of all saving faith.

Posing the Question

The general question posed in this chapter is whether the supremacy of Christ means that he is the only way to salvation. But that general question really contains three questions, and they are crucial for the missionary task of the Christian church. The three questions emerge as different people answer and qualify the main question.

Will Anyone Experience Eternal Conscious Torment under God's Wrath?

Many people today affirm that Christ is man's only hope but deny that there is eternal punishment for not believing in him.[1] Some

1. For a thorough assessment of the recent departures from a historic belief in hell as eternal conscious torment of the ungodly, see Ajith Fernando, *Crucial Questions*

111

would say that everyone is going to be saved whether they hear about Christ in this life or not. For example, even though he has been dead since 1905, the preacher-novelist George MacDonald is being published and read as never before in America and is extending the influence of his brand of universalism. He makes hell into an extended means of self-atonement and sanctification. In hell, the justice of God will eventually destroy all sin in his creatures. In this way, God will bring everyone to glory.[2] Everyone will be saved. Hell is not eternal.

Others would say that while not everyone is saved, there is still no eternal punishment because the fire of judgment annihilates those who reject Christ. Thus, unbelievers cease to exist and experience no conscious punishment. Hell is not a place of eternal punishment but an event of annihilation. This is the direction that Clark Pinnock, John Stott, Edward Fudge, and others have chosen to go.[3]

Therefore, the question we must ask includes this one: Is eternal punishment at stake? That is, will anyone be eternally cut off from

---

about Hell (Wheaton: Crossway, 1994); Robert A. Peterson, Hell on Trial: The Case for Eternal Punishment (Phillipsburg, N.J.: Presbyterian & Reformed, 1995); D. A. Carson, The Gagging of God: Christianity Confronts Pluralism (Grand Rapids: Zondervan, 1996), 515–36; Larry Dixon, The Other Side of the Good News: Confronting the Contemporary Challenges to Jesus' Teaching on Hell (Ross-shire, Scotland: Christian Focus Publications, 2003); Robert A. Peterson and Edward William Fudge, Two Views on Hell: A Biblical and Theological Dialogue (Downers Grove, Ill.: InterVarsity, 2000); and Robert Peterson and Chris Morgan, eds., Hell under Fire (Grand Rapids: Zondervan, forthcoming).

2. See, for example, his sermon on "Justice" in Creation in Christ, ed. Rolland Hein (Wheaton: Shaw, 1976), 63–81, where he argues forcefully that "punishment is for the sake of amendment and atonement. God is bound by His love to punish sin in order to deliver His creature: He is bound by His justice to destroy sin in His creation" (72). I have given an extended critique of MacDonald's view of divine justice, self-atonement, and universalism in The Pleasures of God (Sisters, Ore.: Multnomah, 2000), 168–74.

3. Clark Pinnock and Delwin Brown, Theological Crossfire: An Evangelical/Liberal Dialogue (Grand Rapids: Zondervan, 1990), 226–27. "I was led to question the traditional belief in everlasting conscious torment because of moral revulsion and broader theological considerations, not first of all on scriptural grounds. It just does not make any sense to say that a God of love will torture people forever for sins done in the context of a finite life. . . . It's time for evangelicals to come out and say that the Biblical and morally appropriate doctrine of hell is annihilation, not everlasting torment." Cf. Clark H. Pinnock, "The Conditional View," in Four Views on Hell, ed. William Crockett (Grand Rapids: Zondervan, 1996), 135–66.

David Edwards, Evangelical Essentials, with a Response from John Stott (Downers Grove, Ill.: InterVarsity, 1988), 314–20. "Emotionally, I find the concept [of eternal conscious torment] intolerable and do not understand how people can live with it without either cauterizing their feelings or cracking under the strain." He gives four arguments that he says suggest that "Scripture points in the direction of annihilation, and that 'eternal conscious torment' is a tradition which has to yield to the supreme authority of Scripture. . . . I do not dogmatise about the position to which I have come. I hold it tentatively. But I do plead for frank dialogue among Evangelicals on the basis of Scripture."

Christ and experience eternal conscious torment under the wrath of God?

Is the Work of Christ Necessary?

Other people today would deny that Christ is man's only hope. They may believe that Christ is the provision that God has made for Christians, but for other religions, there are other ways of getting right with God and gaining eternal bliss. The work of Christ is useful for Christians but not necessary for non-Christians.

For example, British theologian John Hick argues that different religions are "equals, though they each may have different emphases." Christianity is not superior but merely one partner in the quest for salvation. We are not to seek one world religion but rather should look to the day when "the ecumenical spirit which has so largely transformed Christianity will increasingly affect relations between the world faiths."[4]

This means that the question we are asking must include: Is the work of Christ the necessary means provided by God for eternal salvation—not just for Christians, but for all people?

Is Conscious Faith in Christ Necessary?

Some evangelicals say they just don't know if conscious faith in Christ is necessary.[5] Others, without denying the reality of eternal

---

I also believe that the ultimate annihilation of the wicked should at least be accepted as a legitimate, Biblically founded alternative to their eternal conscious torment."

Edward William Fudge, *The Fire That Consumes: The Biblical Case for Conditional Immortality*, rev. ed. (Carlisle, U.K.: Paternoster, 1994).

4. John Hick, "Whatever Path Men Choose Is Mine," in *Christianity and Other Religions*, ed. John Hick and Brian Hebblethwaite (Philadelphia: Fortress, 1980), 188. Hick ends with a quote from the *Bhagavad Gita*, iv, 11: "Howsoever man may approach me, even so do I accept them; for, on all sides, whatever path they may choose is mine." For a survey of Hick's thoughts, as well as a compelling response, see Harold Netland, *Dissonant Voices: Religious Pluralism and the Question of Truth* (1991; reprint, Vancouver: Regent Publishers, 1998); idem, *Encountering Religious Pluralism: The Challenge to Christian Faith and Mission* (Downers Grove, Ill.: InterVarsity, 2001). Similarly, John Parry, the Other Faiths Secretary of the World Church and Mission Department of the United Reformed Church in London, wrote in 1985, "It is to the faith of Jesus Christ that we are called. The change of preposition from in to of is significant. It is a faith that is shown in one's trust in God, in surrender to God's purposes, in giving oneself. Such a response of faith I have witnessed among my friends of other faiths. I cannot believe they are far from the kingdom of heaven, what is more, as Dr. Starkey writes '. . . people will not be judged for correct doctrinal beliefs but for their faith. Those who will enter the kingdom on the day of judgment are those who in faith respond to God's love by loving others.'" "Exploring the Ways of God with Peoples of Faith," *International Review of Missions* 74, no. 296 (October 1985): 512.

5. Edwards, *Evangelical Essentials*, 327. For example, John Stott says, "I believe the most Christian stance is to remain agnostic on this question. . . . The fact is that God,

judgment or the necessity of Christ's saving work, would say, "Yes, Christ is man's only hope, but he saves some of those who never hear of him through faith that does not have Christ for its conscious object." For example, Millard Erickson represents some evangelicals[6] who argue that, similar to the saints in the Old Testament, some unevangelized persons today may "receive the benefit of Christ's death without conscious knowledge-belief in the name of Jesus."[7]

------

alongside the most solemn warnings about our responsibility to respond to the gospel, has not revealed how he will deal with those who have never heard it." In William V. Crockett and James G. Sigountos, eds., *Through No Fault of Their Own* (Grand Rapids: Baker, 1991), Timothy Phillips, Aida Besançon Spencer, and Tite Tienou "prefer to leave the matter in the hands of God" (259, n. 3).

6. Crockett and Sigountos *(Through No Fault of Their Own)* include some essays by evangelicals who take the view that those who have never heard are in fact led to salvation through general revelation. Their conclusion is, "Those who hear and reject the gospel are lost. And those who do embrace the light of general revelation must be willing to turn from their dead idols to serve the living God (1 Thessalonians 1:9). General revelation, then, creates in them a desire to reject their pagan religion; it does not help them see the saving significance of their own" (260). See a good response to this in Ajith Fernando, *Sharing the Truth in Love: How to Relate to People of Other Faiths* (Grand Rapids: Discovery House, 2001), 211–33.

7. Millard Erickson argues from the revelation available in nature according to Romans 1–2 and 10:18. The essential elements in the "gospel message" in nature are: "1) The belief in one good powerful God. 2) The belief that he (man) owes this God perfect obedience to his law. 3) The consciousness that he does not meet this standard, and therefore is guilty and condemned. 4) The realization that nothing he can offer God can compensate him (or atone) for this sin and guilt. 5) The belief that God is merciful, and will forgive and accept those who cast themselves on his mercy. May it not be that if a man believes and acts on this set of tenets he is redemptively related to God and receives the benefits of Christ's death, whether he consciously knows and understands the details of that provision or not? Presumably that was the case with the Old Testament believers. . . . If this is possible, if Jews possessed salvation in the Old Testament era simply by virtue of having the form of the Christian gospel without its content, can this principle be extended? Could it be that those who ever since the time of Christ have had no opportunity to hear the gospel, as it has come through the special revelation, participate in this salvation on the same basis? On what other grounds could they fairly be held responsible for having or not having salvation (or faith)?" But here he is very tentative, for he goes on to say, "What Paul is saying in the remainder of Romans is that very few, if any, actually come to such a saving knowledge of God on the basis of natural revelation alone." Millard Erickson, "Hope for Those Who Haven't Heard? Yes, But . . ." *Evangelical Missions Quarterly* 11, no. 2 (April 1975): 124–25. He is following here A. H. Strong: "Whoever among the heathen are saved must in like manner [i.e., like the patriarchs of the Old Testament] be saved by casting themselves as helpless sinners upon God's plan of mercy, dimly shadowed forth in nature and providence." *Systematic Theology* (Westwood, N.J.: Revell, 1907), 842. This view is different from that of the older Reformed theologian Charles Hodge, who argued that only through the Word of God heard or read does the effectual call to salvation come. *Systematic Theology*, vol. 2 (Grand Rapids: Eerdmans, 1952), 646.

So we must make clear what we are really asking: Is it necessary for people to hear of Christ in order to be eternally saved? That is, can a person today be saved by the work of Christ even if he does not have an opportunity to hear about it?

Therefore, when we ask, Is Jesus Christ man's only hope for salvation? we are really asking three questions:

1. Will anyone experience *eternal conscious torment* under God's wrath?
2. Is the work of Christ the *necessary* means provided by God for eternal salvation?
3. Is it necessary for people *to hear of Christ* in order to be eternally saved?

A Nerve of Urgency

Biblical answers to these three questions are crucial because in each case a negative answer would seem to cut a nerve of urgency in the missionary cause. Evangelicals such as Erickson do not intend to cut that nerve, and their view is certainly not in the same category as that of Hick or MacDonald. They insist that the salvation of anyone apart from the preaching of Christ is the exception rather than the rule and that preaching Christ to all is utterly important.

Nevertheless, there is a felt difference in the urgency when one believes that hearing the gospel is the only hope that anyone has of escaping the penalty of sin and living forever in happiness to the glory of God's grace. It does not ring true when William Crockett and James Sigountos argue that the existence of "implicit Christians" (saved through general revelation without hearing of Christ) actually "should increase motivation" for missions. They say that these unevangelized converts are "waiting eagerly to hear more about [God]." If we would reach them, "a strong church would spring to life, giving glory to God and evangelizing their pagan neighbors."[8] I cannot escape the impression that this is a futile attempt to make a weakness look like a strength. On the contrary, common sense presses another truth on us: The more likely it is that people can be saved without missions, the less urgency there is for missions.

So with regard to all three of these questions there is much at stake. Nevertheless, in the end, the most crucial thing is not our desire to maintain the urgency of the missionary cause but to answer, What do the Scriptures teach?

8. Crockett and Sigountos, *Through No Fault of Their Own*, 260.

My aim here is to provide the biblical data that, in my judgment, compel a positive answer to each of these three questions. I hope to demonstrate that in the fullest sense Jesus Christ is man's only hope for salvation. To do this I will gather into three groups the texts that relate most directly to the three questions we have posed. Some comment will be made along the way.

A Hell of Eternal Conscious Torment

> And many of those who sleep in the dust of the earth shall awake, some to everlasting life, and some to shame and *everlasting contempt*.
>
> Daniel 12:2

It is true that the Hebrew *'olam* does not always mean "everlasting," but in this context it seems to because it points to a decisive division into joy or misery after death and resurrection. As the *life* is everlasting, so the *shame and contempt* are everlasting.

"His winnowing fork is in his hand, and he will clear his threshing floor and gather his wheat into the barn, but the chaff he will burn with *unquenchable fire*" (Matt. 3:12; cf. Luke 3:17). This is John the Baptist's prediction of the judgment that Jesus will bring in the end. He pictures a decisive separation. The term "unquenchable fire" implies a fire that will not be extinguished and therefore a punishment that will not end. This is confirmed in Mark 9:43–48:

> And if your hand causes you to sin, cut it off. It is better for you to enter life crippled than with two hands to go to hell, to the *unquenchable fire*. And if your foot causes you to sin, cut it off. It is better for you to enter life lame than with two feet to be thrown into hell. And if your eye causes you to sin, tear it out. It is better for you to enter the kingdom of God with one eye than with two eyes to be thrown into hell, "*where their worm does not die and the fire is not quenched*."

Here the "unquenchable fire" is clearly hell, and the last line shows that the point is the unending misery of those who go there ("their worm does not die"). If annihilation (the teaching that some cease to exist after death or after a limited period of conscious punishment in hell)[9] were in view, why would the verse stress the fire never being

---

9. Clark Pinnock of McMaster Divinity College argues that "the 'fire' of God's judgment consumes the lost. . . . God does not raise the wicked in order to torture them consciously forever, but rather to declare his judgment upon the wicked and to condemn them to extinction, which is the second death." "Fire, Then Nothing," *Christianity Today* 44, no. 10 (20 March 1987): 49.

quenched and the worm never dying? John Stott struggles to escape this by saying that the worm will not die and the fire will not be quenched "until presumably their work of destruction is done."[10] That qualification is not in the text. On the contrary, the focus on eternal duration is confirmed in Matthew 18:8: "And if your hand or your foot causes you to sin, cut it off and throw it away. It is better for you to enter life crippled or lame than with two hands or two feet to be thrown into the *eternal fire.*"

Here the fire is not only unquenchable but more explicitly "eternal." The fact that this fire is not merely a purifying fire of the age to come (as some take *aiōnion* to mean) is shown in the subsequent sayings of Jesus, especially the one on the unforgivable sin (Matt. 12:31–32; Luke 12:10). "And do not fear those who kill the body but cannot kill the soul. Rather fear him who can destroy both soul and body in hell" (Matt. 10:28; cf. Luke 12:4–5). The "destruction" referred to here is decisive and final, but it does not have to mean obliterate or annihilate. The word *apollymi* frequently means "ruin" or "lose" or "perish" or "get rid of" (Matt. 8:25; 9:17; 10:6; 12:14). It does not imply annihilate. It is eternal ruin (see 2 Thess. 1:9).

"Then he will say to those on his left, 'Depart from me, you cursed, into the *eternal fire* prepared for the devil and his angels.' . . . And these will go away into *eternal punishment,* but the righteous into eternal life" (Matt. 25:41, 46). The eternal fire is explicitly "punishment," and its opposite is eternal life. It does not honor the full import of "eternal life" to say that it refers only to a quality of life without eternal connotations.[11] Therefore, it would fall short of truth to say that "eternal punishment" has no reference to eternal duration. As Leon Morris says, "It is not easy to see the fate of the wicked as anything less permanent than that of the believer."[12]

Not only that, but when we compare this text to Revelation 20:10, the case for conscious eternal torment is strengthened. Here in Matthew 25:41, the goats are sentenced to "eternal fire prepared *for the*

10. Edwards, *Evangelical Essentials,* 317.

11. Scot McKnight devotes extensive treatment to Matthew 25:46 in view of recent efforts (such as John Stott's) to see the eternal consequence of unrighteousness as annihilation. His conclusion is solid: "The terms for eternal in Matthew 25:46 pertain to the final age, and a distinguishing feature of the final age, in contrast to this age, is that it is eternal, endless, and temporally unlimited. It follows then that the most probable meaning of Matthew 25:46 is that just as life with God is temporally unlimited for the righteous, so punishment for sin and rejection of Christ is also temporally unlimited. . . . The final state of the wicked is conscious, eternal torment." "Eternal Consequences or Eternal Consciousness," in *Through No Fault of Their Own,* 157.

12. Leon Morris, "The Dreadful Harvest," *Christianity Today* 35, no. 6 (27 May 1991): 36.

devil and his angels." This is precisely what is described in Revelation 20:10, namely, the final destiny of the devil. The condition is clearly one of conscious torment (see below in this text).

"The Son of Man goes as it is written of him, but woe to that man by whom the Son of Man is betrayed! *It would have been better for that man if he had not been born"* (Matt. 26:24). If Judas were destined for glory eventually (as in universalism) or even destined for extinction (as in annihilationism), it is difficult to imagine why it would have been better for him not to have been born.[13] In John 17:12, he is called the "son of destruction"—a term related to the word for "destroy" in Matthew 10:28.

"Whoever blasphemes against the Holy Spirit never has forgiveness, but is guilty of an *eternal sin"* (Mark 3:29). "And whoever speaks a word against the Son of Man will be forgiven, but whoever speaks against the Holy Spirit will not be forgiven, either in this age *or in the age to come"* (Matt. 12:32). This rules out the idea that after a time of suffering in hell, sinners will then be forgiven and admitted to heaven. Matthew says that there will be no forgiveness in the age to come for the unforgivable sin, and so Mark calls it an *eternal* sin, which shows that the word "eternal" is indeed a temporal word of endless duration and not just a word referring to a limited period in the age to come.

"And besides all this, between us and you a great chasm has been fixed, in order that those who would pass from here to you may not be able, and *none may cross from there to us"* (Luke 16:26). These are the words of Abraham in heaven speaking to the rich man in Hades. The point is that the suffering there cannot be escaped. There is no way out.

> [God] will render to each one according to his works: to those who by patience in well-doing seek for glory and honor and immortality, he will give *eternal* life; but for those who are self-seeking and do not obey the truth, but obey unrighteousness, there will be wrath and fury.
>
> Romans 2:6–8

This text is significant because wrath and fury are the alternative to "eternal life." This seems to imply that the wrath and fury are experienced instead of life "eternally"—forever.

13. In Edwards, *Evangelical Essentials*, 314, John Stott tries to honor this text by saying, "We surely have to say that this banishment from God will be real, terrible (so that 'it would have been better for him if he had not been born,' Mark 14:21) and eternal." But he gives us no idea why a man who eats, drinks, and is merry for seventy years and then ceases to have any consciousness would have been better off not to have existed.

They will suffer the punishment of *eternal destruction,* away from the presence of the Lord and from the glory of his might, when he comes on that day to be glorified in his saints, and to be marveled at among all who have believed.

2 Thessalonians 1:9–10

The word for "destruction" *(olethros)* means "ruin" (1 Cor. 5:5; 1 Tim. 6:9). The picture is not of obliteration but of a ruin of human life out of God's presence forever.

Let us leave the elementary doctrine of Christ and go on to maturity, not laying again a foundation of repentance from dead works and of faith toward God, and of instruction about washings, the laying on of hands, the resurrection of the dead, and *eternal judgment.*

Hebrews 6:1–2

These are blemishes on your love feasts . . . wild waves of the sea, casting up the foam of their own shame; wandering stars, for whom the gloom of utter darkness has been reserved *forever.*

Jude 12–13

And the smoke of their torment goes up *forever and ever,* and *they have no rest,* day or night, these worshipers of the beast and its image, and whoever receives the mark of its name.

Revelation 14:11

There is no stronger Greek expression for eternity than this one: "unto ages of ages" *(eis aiōnas aiōnōn).* "Once more they cried out, 'Hallelujah! The smoke from her goes up *forever and ever'*" (Rev. 19:3). "And the devil who had deceived them was thrown into the lake of fire and sulfur where the beast and the false prophet were, and they will be tormented *day and night forever and ever*" (Rev. 20:10). Again the strongest of expressions are used for everlasting duration: "unto the ages of the ages" *(eis tous aiōnas tōn aiōnōn).* John Stott again struggles to escape the clear intent of the eternal torments of the lake of fire. He says that Revelation 20:10 refers to the beast and false prophet who "are not individual people but symbols of the world in its varied hostility to God. In the nature of the case they cannot experience pain."[14]

But Stott fails to mention Revelation 20:15, where it says that "if anyone's name [not just that of the beast and the false prophet] was not found written in the book of life, he was thrown into the lake of fire." Similarly, Revelation 21:8 says that it is *individual sinners* whose

14. Ibid., 318.

"portion will be in the lake that burns with fire and sulfur, which is the second death." And the torment that lasts "forever and ever" in Revelation 14:10 is precisely the torment of people "with fire and sulfur"— that is, the torment of "the lake that burns with fire and sulfur" (21:8). In other words, the "lake of fire" is in view not only, as Stott suggests, when the beast, the false prophet, death, and Hades (20:13) are cast out but also when individual unbelievers are finally condemned (14:10–11; 20:15; 21:8), and that shows decisively that individual unbelieving persons will experience eternal conscious torment.[15]

Hell is a dreadful reality. To speak of it lightly proves that we do not grasp its horror. I know of no one who has overstated the terrors of hell. We can scarcely surpass the horrid images Jesus used. We are meant to shudder.

Why? Because the infinite horrors of hell are intended by God to be a vivid demonstration of the infinite value of his glory, which sinners have belittled. The biblical assumption of the justice of hell[16] is the

15. John Stott has been gracious enough to correspond with me personally about this issue of the eternal fate of the lost. To be fair to one I count a brother and a theological and pastoral mentor for more than thirty years, I want to give his perspective on what I have written from a personal letter dated 1 March 1993. He writes: "I cannot honestly say that I think you have done justice to what I have written in *Evangelical Essentials.* . . . For example, I do strongly affirm all the 'eternal' and 'unquenchable' verses which you quote, and do believe in 'eternal punishment.' It is not the eternity but the nature of the punishment which is under discussion. You do not make this clear. I also believe in torment in the interim state (as the Dives and Lazarus story shows), and that there will be terrible 'weeping and gnashing of teeth' when the lost learn their fate. I think I believe as strongly as you do that 'it is a fearful thing to fall into the hands of the living God.' What troubles me is the way you tend to quote proof texts as knock-down arguments, when they are capable of alternative interpretations. I just find you over-dogmatic, as I wrote in my earlier letter, leaving no room for the humble agnosticism which allows that God has not revealed everything as plainly as you make out." I mentioned to Dr. Stott in an earlier letter that my less-than-positive attitude toward "agnosticism" and "tentativity" is probably influenced by the sea of relativism that I am trying to navigate, both inside and outside the church. I do not want to communicate an unwillingness to learn or to change as new light on the Scripture emerges. But my diagnosis of the sickness of our times inclines me less toward "humble agnosticism" and more toward (I hope) humble affirmation. Whether I have moved from warranted and well-grounded firmness of conviction into unwarranted and poorly argued dogmatism, I leave for others to judge.

16. One person who has wrestled with the justice of hell and moved toward a very unusual position on annihilationism and the traditional view of conscious eternal misery is Greg Boyd, who represents the view called Open Theism. In his *Satan and the Problem of Evil* (Downers Grove, Ill.: InterVarsity, 2001), Boyd attempts to handle the texts used to argue for the eternal conscious torment of hell and the texts used to argue for annihilationism by "affirming both views as essentially correct" (336). On the one hand, he says, "When all the Biblical evidence is viewed together, it must be admitted that the case for annihilationism is quite compelling" (336). But on the other hand, he

clearest testimony to the infiniteness of the sin of failing to glorify God. All of us have failed. All the nations have failed. Therefore, the weight of infinite guilt rests on every human head because of our failure to delight in God more than we delight in our own self-sufficiency.

The vision of God in Scripture is of a majestic and sovereign God who does all things to magnify the greatness of his glory for the everlasting enjoyment of his people. And the view of man in Scripture is that man suppresses this truth and finds more joy in his own glory than he does in God's.

When Clark Pinnock[17] and John Stott[18] repeat the centuries-old ob-

---

sees some texts on the other side that do not fit the simple annihilationist view (he mentions Rev. 14:10; 20:10; Matt. 25:34, 41; 2 Thess. 1:6–9 [336]). He asks, "Where does this leave us? For my part, it leaves me in a conundrum. I do not believe that either the traditional position or the annihilationists' position adequately accounts for all the Biblical evidence cited in support of the opposing side's position. Yet I do not believe that Scripture can contradict itself (John 10:35). This raises the question: Is there a logically consistent way of affirming both views as essentially correct?" (336–37). His answer is yes: "I will attempt to move beyond the impasse of the traditional and annihilationist understandings of eternal punishment and construct a model of hell that allows us to affirm the essence of both perspectives" (339). He attempts to show that "hell is the eternal suffering of agents who have been annihilated" (356). He states a crucial premise: "There can be no shared reality between those who say yes to God and those who say no, just as there can be no shared reality between the actuality that God affirms and the possibilities that God negates" (347). Here is the conclusion that follows: "Love is about relationships, and relationships are about sharing reality. Hence, when in the eschaton reality is exhaustively defined by God's love, the 'reality' of any agent who opposes love cannot be shared by anyone else and thus cannot be real to anyone else. It is experienced as real *from the inside* of the one who sustains it by his or her active willing it. But to all who participate in reality—that is, who are open to God and to each other through the medium of God's love—it is nothing. It is eternally willed nothingness" (350). "Hell is real only from the inside" (348). Thus, "we are able to affirm that in one sense the inhabitants of hell are annihilated, though they suffer eternally. From the perspective of all who share reality in the eschaton, the damned are no more (Obadiah 16). They exist only as utter negation. . . . They continue to experience torment, but it is a torment of their own pathetic choosing in an illusory reality of their own damned imagining" (350). "As Scripture says, they are extinct, reduced to ashes, forever forgotten. . . . But we may also accept the scriptural teaching regarding the eternity of the torment of the reprobates. . . . From the inside of the rebel experience, the nothingness that they have willed is experienced as a something. To all others, it is nothing" (353). I am not persuaded that Boyd's complex and paradoxical "model" can survive close scrutiny. An extended critique of this view exceeds the bounds of this book, but I have written a partial response titled "Greg Boyd on 'The Eternal Suffering of Agents Who Have Been Annihilated,'" available from Desiring God Ministries at www.DesiringGod.org or 1-888-346-4700.

17. "It just does not make sense to say that a God of love will torture people forever for sins done in the context of a finite life." Pinnock and Brown, *Theological Crossfire*, 226.

18. "Would there not be serious disproportion between sins consciously committed in time and torment consciously experienced throughout eternity?" Edwards, *Evangelical Essentials*, 318.

jection that an *eternal* punishment is disproportionate to a *finite* life of sinning, they disregard the essential thing that Jonathan Edwards saw so clearly: Degrees of blameworthiness come not from how long you offend dignity but from how high the dignity is that you offend.

> The crime of one being despising and casting contempt on another, is proportionably more or less heinous, as he was under greater or less obligations to obey him. And therefore if there be any being that we are under infinite obligation to love, and honor, and obey, the contrary towards him must be infinitely faulty.
>
> Our obligation to love, honor and obey any being is in proportion to his loveliness, honorableness, and authority. . . . But God is a being infinitely lovely, because he hath infinite excellency and beauty. . . .
>
> So sin against God, being a violation of infinite obligations, must be a crime infinitely heinous, and so deserving infinite punishment. . . . The eternity of the punishment of ungodly men renders it infinite . . . and therefore renders no more than proportionable to the heinousness of what they are guilty of.[19]

One key difference between Edwards and our contemporary spokesmen who abandon the historic biblical view of hell is that Edwards was radically committed to deriving his views of God's justice and love *from God*. But more and more it seems that contemporary evangelicals are submitting to what "makes sense" to their own moral sentiments.[20] This will not strengthen the church or its mission. What is needed is a radical commitment to the supremacy of God in determining what is real and what is not.

The Necessity of Christ's Atonement for Salvation

The second question we must ask as part of our inquiry is whether Christ's work of atonement is necessary for the salvation of whoever is

19. Jonathan Edwards, "The Justice of God in the Damnation of Sinners," in *The Works of Jonathan Edwards*, vol. 1 (Edinburgh: Banner of Truth Trust, 1974), 669. For expositions of Edwards's view on hell, see John Gerstner, *Jonathan Edwards on Heaven and Hell* (Morgan, Pa.: Soli Deo Gloria Publishers, 1999); and Chris Morgan, *Hell and Jonathan Edwards: Toward a God-Centered Theology of Hell* (Ross-shire, Scotland: Christian Focus Publications, 2003).

20. See Pinnock's quote and Stott's quote in note 3 above. Also see my critique of the way Pinnock follows the same procedure concerning the omniscience of God in my book *Pleasures of God*, 57–59, n. 6. Another thing overlooked is that in hell the sins of the unrepentant go on forever and ever. They do not become righteous in hell. They are given over to the corruption of their nature so that they continue rebelling and deserving eternal punishment eternally. This latter insight was suggested to me by my colleague Tom Steller.

saved. Can people be saved any way other than by the efficacy of Christ's work? Are other religions and the provisions they offer sufficient for bringing people to eternal happiness with God?

The following biblical texts lead us to believe that Christ's atonement is necessary for the salvation of everyone who is saved. There is no salvation apart from the salvation that Christ achieved in his death and resurrection.

> If, because of one man's trespass, death reigned through that one man, much more will those who receive the abundance of grace and the free gift of righteousness reign in life through the one man Jesus Christ. Therefore, as one trespass led to condemnation for all men, so one act of righteousness leads to justification and life for all men. For as by the one man's disobedience the many were made sinners, so by the one man's obedience the many will be made righteous.
>
> Romans 5:17–19

The crucial point here is *the universality of the work of Christ.* It is not done in a corner with reference merely to Jews. The work of Christ, the second Adam, corresponds to the work of the first Adam. As the sin of Adam leads to condemnation for all humanity that are united to him as their head, so the obedience of Christ leads to righteousness for all humanity that are united to Christ as their head—"those who receive the abundance of grace" (v. 17). The work of Christ in the obedience of the cross is pictured as the divine answer to the plight of the entire human race.

> For as by a man came death, by a man has come also the resurrection of the dead. For as in Adam all die, so also in Christ shall all be made alive. But each in his own order: Christ the firstfruits, then at his coming those who belong to Christ.
>
> 1 Corinthians 15:21–23

In this text, Christ's resurrection is the answer to the universal human misery of death. Adam is the head of the old humanity marked by death. Christ is the head of the new humanity marked by resurrection. The members of this new humanity are "those who belong to Christ" (v. 23).[21] Christ is not a tribal deity relating merely to the woes of one group. He is given as God's answer to the universal problem of

---

21. Note that it would be an incorrect, superficial reading of this text, as well as of Romans 5:17–19, to assume that it is teaching universalism in the sense that all human beings will be saved. The "all" who are acquitted in Romans 5 are defined in Romans 5:17 as "those who receive the abundance of grace." And the all who are made alive in 1 Corinthians 15:22 are defined as "those who belong to Christ." The term "justification

death. Those who attain to the resurrection of the dead attain it in Christ.

"There is one God, and there is one mediator between God and men, the man Christ Jesus, who gave himself as a ransom for all" (1 Tim. 2:5–6). The work of Christ corresponds to his role as sole Mediator in the universe between God and man.

> Worthy are you to take the scroll and to open its seals, for you were slain, and by your blood you ransomed people for God from every tribe and language and people and nation, and you have made them a kingdom and priests to our God, and they shall reign on the earth.
>
> Revelation 5:9–10

The entire Book of Revelation pictures Christ as the King of kings and Lord of lords (17:14; 19:16)—the universal ruler over all peoples and powers. Revelation 5:9 shows that he purchased a people for himself from all the tribes and languages of the world. His atonement is the means in every culture by which men and women become part of his kingdom. (See John 11:51–52.)

"And there is salvation in no one else, for there is no other name under heaven given among men by which we must be saved" (Acts 4:12). The work of Christ is not mentioned here explicitly, but the universality of his name as the only way to salvation would imply that whatever he did to win salvation for his people (namely, shed his blood [Acts 20:28])

---

and life for all men" in Romans 5:18 does not mean that every human being who is in Adam will also be justified so that no one will perish and that there is no such thing as eternal punishment for anyone. I say this for several reasons: (1) Verse 17 speaks of *receiving* the gift of righteousness as though some do and some don't. Verse 17: "For if by the transgression of the one, death reigned through the one, much more *those who receive the abundance of grace and of the gift of righteousness* will reign in life through the One, Jesus Christ." That does not sound as though everybody does receive it. (2) "Justification of life to all men" in Romans 5:18 does not mean that all humans are justified because Paul teaches in this very book that there is eternal punishment and that all humans are not justified. For example, in Romans 2:5 he says, "But because of your stubbornness and unrepentant heart you are storing up wrath for yourself in the day of wrath and revelation of the righteous judgment of God," and then in verses 7 and 8 he contrasts this wrath with "eternal life" and so shows that it is eternal wrath, not temporary wrath. So there will be some who are not justified but come under the wrath of God forever and others who have eternal life. (3) "Justification of life to all men" in Romans 5:18 does not mean that all humans are justified because in all of Romans up to this point, justification is not automatic, as if every human receives it, but it is "by faith." Romans 5:1: "Therefore, having been *justified by faith* . . ." Romans 3:28: "For we maintain that a man is *justified by faith* apart from works of the Law." Further, a universalistic reading of Paul's "all" statements renders Paul's intense grief (Rom. 9:3)—to the point of wishing he could perish, if possible, on their behalf—unintelligible.

has universal significance. There are no other ways that a person in another religion can be saved. If anyone would be saved, he must be saved by the name of Christ. "All have sinned and fall short of the glory of God, and are justified by his grace as a gift, through the redemption that is in Christ Jesus, whom God put forward as a propitiation by his blood, to be received by faith" (Rom. 3:23–25).

Romans 3:9–20 establishes that all humans—Jew and Gentile—are under the power of sin and are speechless before the judgment of God. Therefore, the death of Christ is set forth as an answer to this universal problem of sin. It is not one among many ways God deals with sin. It is the basis of the way God justifies any sinner.

In answer to the second question, then, the New Testament makes clear that the atoning work of Christ is not merely for Jews or merely for any one nation or tribe or language. It is the one and only way for anyone to get right with God. The problem of sin is universal, cutting people off from God. The solution to that problem is the atoning death of the Son of God offered once for all. This is the very foundation of missions. Since the work of Christ is the only basis for salvation,[22] it must be announced to all the nations, as Luke 24:46–47 says:

> Thus it is written, that the Christ should suffer and on the third day rise from the dead, and that repentance and forgiveness of sins should be proclaimed in his name to all nations, beginning from Jerusalem.

The Necessity for People to Hear of Christ in Order to Be Saved

The question that concerns us here is whether some (perhaps only a few) people are quickened by the Holy Spirit and saved by grace through faith in a merciful Creator even though they never hear of Jesus in this life. In other words, are there devout people in other religions who humbly rely on the grace of the God whom they know through nature (Rom. 1:19–21) and thus receive eternal salvation?[23]

22. For further study of the significance of Christ's death, consider the following texts: Matt. 26:28; Mark 10:45; John 1:29; 6:51; Rom. 4:25–5:1; 5:6, 8–10; 1 Cor. 15:3; 2 Cor. 5:18–21; Gal. 1:4; 4:4; Eph. 1:7; 2:1–5, 13, 16, 18; 5:2, 25; Col. 1:20; 1 Thess. 5:9; Titus 2:14; 1 Tim. 4:10; Heb. 1:3; 9:12, 22, 26; 10:14; 12:24; 13:12; 1 Peter 1:19; 2:24; 3:18; 1 John 2:2; Rev. 1:5.

23. See notes 6 and 7 above for representatives of this view. Clark Pinnock embraces the idea that people from other religions will be saved without knowing Christ. "We do not need to think of the church as the ark of salvation, leaving everyone else in hell; we can rather think of it as the chosen witness to the *fullness* of salvation that has come into the world through Jesus" (emphasis added). Clark Pinnock, "Acts 4:12—No Other Name Under Heaven," in *Through No Fault of Their Own*, 113. Also see Clark H. Pinnock, *A*

Something of immense historical significance happened with the coming of the Son of God into the world. So great was the significance of this event that the focus of saving faith was henceforth made to center on Jesus Christ alone. So fully does Christ sum up all the revelation of God and all the hopes of God's people that it would henceforth be a dishonor to him should saving faith repose on anyone but him.[24]

Before his coming a grand "mystery" was kept secret for ages. With the uncovering of this mystery, the "times of ignorance" ended, and the call to repentance now sounds forth with a new specificity: Jesus Christ has been appointed Judge of all peoples by virtue of his resurrection from the dead. All appeals for mercy and acquittal must now come through him and him alone. We turn now to the texts that lay this truth open for us.

The "Mystery of Christ"

When you read this, you can perceive my insight into the *mystery of Christ*, which was not made known to the sons of men in other generations as it has now been revealed to his holy apostles and prophets by the Spirit. This mystery is that the Gentiles are fellow heirs, members of the same body, and partakers of the promise in Christ Jesus *through the gospel.*

Wideness in God's Mercy: The Finality of Jesus Christ in a World of Religions (Grand Rapids: Zondervan, 1992); and idem, "An Inclusivist View," in *More Than One Way? Four Views on Salvation in a Pluralistic World,* ed. Dennis L. Okholm and Timothy R. Phillips (Grand Rapids: Zondervan, 1995), 95–123. He is following others with similar views: Charles Kraft, *Christianity in Culture* (Maryknoll, N.Y.: Orbis, 1979), 253–57; James N. D. Anderson, *Christianity and World Religions* (Downers Grove, Ill.: InterVarsity, 1984), chap. 5; John E. Sanders, "Is Belief in Christ Necessary for Salvation?" *Evangelical Quarterly* 60 (1988): 241–59; and John Sanders, *No Other Name: An Investigation into the Destiny of the Unevangelized* (Grand Rapids: Eerdmans, 1992). For a short survey of representatives on both sides of the question, see Malcolm J. McVeigh, "The Fate of Those Who've Never Heard? It Depends," *Evangelical Missions Quarterly* 21, no. 4 (October 1985): 370–79. For books with multiple views represented, see Gabriel Fackre, Ronald H. Nash, and John Sanders, *What about Those Who Have Never Heard? Three Views on the Destiny of the Unevangelized* (Grand Rapids: Zondervan, 1995); and Ockholm and Phillips, *More Than One Way?* For critiques of inclusivism, see Carson, *The Gagging of God,* 279–314; Dick Dowsett, *God, That's Not Fair!* (Sevenoaks, Kent: OMF Books, 1982); Ronald H. Nash, *Is Jesus the Only Savior?* (Grand Rapids: Zondervan, 1994); Richard Ramesh, *The Population of Heaven* (Chicago: Moody, 1994); Paul R. House and Gregory A. Thornbury, eds., *Who Will Be Saved? Defending the Biblical Understanding of God, Salvation, and Evangelism* (Wheaton: Crossway, 2000), 111–60; and the contributions of R. Douglas Geivett and W. Gary Phillips in *More Than One Way?*

24. There is a continuity between God's path to salvation in the Old Testament times and the path through faith in Jesus during the New Testament times. Even before Christ, people were not saved apart from special revelation given by God. See Fernando, *Sharing the Truth in Love,* 224–33. It is not as though general revelation through nature was effective in producing faith before Christ but ceased to be effective after Christ. According to Romans 1:18–23, general revelation through nature has always

Of this gospel I was made a minister according to the gift of God's grace, which was given me by the working of his power. To me, though I am the very least of all the saints, this grace was given, to preach to the Gentiles the unsearchable riches of Christ, and to bring to light for everyone what is the plan of the mystery hidden for ages in God who created all things, so that through the church the manifold wisdom of God might now be made known to the rulers and authorities in the heavenly places.

Ephesians 3:4–10

There was a truth that was not fully and clearly revealed before the coming of Christ. This truth, now revealed, is called the "mystery of Christ." It is the truth that *people from all the nations of the world would be full and complete partners with the chosen people of God* (Eph. 3:6). It is called the "mystery of Christ" because it is coming true "through the gospel" (3:6), which is about Christ.

Therefore, the gospel is not the revelation that the nations already belong to God. The gospel is the instrument for bringing the nations into this equal status of salvation. The mystery of Christ (drawing the nations into the inheritance of Abraham) is happening through the preaching of the gospel. Paul sees his own apostolic vocation as the means God is graciously using to declare the riches of the Messiah to the nations (3:8).

So a massive change has occurred in redemptive history. Before the coming of Christ, a truth was not fully revealed—namely, that the nations may enter with equal standing into the household of God (Eph. 2:19). The time was not "full" for this revelation because Christ had not been revealed from heaven. The glory and honor of uniting all the peoples was being reserved for him in his saving work. It is fitting then that the nations be gathered in only through the preaching of the message of Christ, whose cross is the peace that creates the worldwide church (Eph. 2:11–21).

In other words, there is a profound theological reason why salvation did not spread to the nations before the incarnation of the Son of God. The reason is that it would not have been clear that the nations were gathering for the glory of Christ. God means for his Son to be

---

been sufficient to make people accountable to glorify and thank God, but not efficient to do so. The reason given is that people in their natural condition suppress the truth. See note 40. Thus, special revelation has always been the path to salvation, and this special revelation was centered in Israel, the promise of a Redeemer, and the foreshadowings of this salvation in the sacrificial system of the Old Testament. Jesus is now the climax and fulfillment of that special revelation so that saving faith, which was always focused on special revelation, is now focused on him.

the center of worship as the nations receive the word of reconciliation. For this reason also, as we will see, the preaching of Christ is the means appointed by God for the ingathering of the nations.

> (25a) Now to him who is able to strengthen you (25b) according to my gospel and the preaching of Jesus Christ, (25c) according to the revelation of the mystery that was kept secret for long ages (26a) but has now been disclosed (26b) and through the prophetic writings has been made known to all nations, (26c) according to the command of the eternal God, (26d) to bring about the obedience of faith—(27) to the only wise God be glory forevermore through Jesus Christ! Amen.
>
> Romans 16:25–27

This is a very complex sentence. But if we patiently examine its parts and notice how they relate to one another, the crucial meaning for missions emerges.

The verses are a doxology: "Now to him who is able to strengthen you . . ." But Paul gets so caught up in God that he does not come down again to the words of the doxology until verse 27: "to the only wise God be glory forevermore through Jesus Christ! Amen."

Sandwiched between the two parts of the doxology is a massive statement about the meaning of Paul's gospel in relation to God's eternal purposes. The thought moves as follows. The strength that Paul prays will come to the Romans (25a) accords with his gospel and the preaching of Christ (25b). This means that God's power is revealed in the gospel Paul preaches, and that is the power he prays for them to be strengthened by.

Then he says that this gospel preaching is in accord with the revelation of a mystery kept secret for ages and now revealed (25c, 26a). In other words, what Paul preaches is not out of sync with God's purposes. It "accords" with them. It expresses and conforms to them. His preaching is a part of God's plan, which is now being revealed in history.

How is it being revealed? It is being disclosed through the prophetic writings (26c). This means that the mystery was not *totally* hidden in past ages. There were pointers in the prophetic writings, so much so that now these very Old Testament writings are used to make the mystery known. In Paul's preaching of the gospel, he uses the prophetic writings to help him make known the mystery. (See, for example, how Paul does this in Romans 15:9–13.)

What then is the mystery? Verses 26c–26d say that making known this mystery accords with "the command of the eternal God for the obedience of faith to all the nations" (author's translation). The most natural way to interpret this is to say that the mystery is the purpose of God to command all nations to obey him through faith.

But what makes this a mystery is that the command to the nations for the obedience of faith is specifically a command to have faith in Jesus, the Messiah of Israel, and thus become part of the people of God and heirs of Abraham (Eph. 2:19–3:6). In Romans 1:5, Paul describes his calling to the nations with these words: "We have received grace and apostleship to bring about the obedience of faith for the sake of [Christ's] name among all the nations." Here he makes plain that the term "obedience of faith" in Romans 16:26d is a call for the sake of Christ's name. It is thus a call to acknowledge and trust and obey Christ. This is the mystery hidden for ages—that all the nations would be commanded to trust in Israel's Messiah and be saved through him.

The word "now" in 26a is crucial. It refers to the fullness of time in redemptive history when God put Christ forward onto the center stage of history. From "now" on things are different. The time has come for the mystery to be revealed. The time has come to command all the nations to obey God through faith in Jesus the Messiah.

God is "now" doing a new thing. With the coming of Christ, God will no longer allow "the nations to walk in their own ways" (Acts 14:16, see below). The time has come for all nations to be called to repent and for the mystery to be fully revealed that through faith in Christ the nations are "fellow heirs, members of the same body, and partakers of the promise in Christ Jesus *through the gospel*" (Eph. 3:6). Not without the gospel! But *through* the gospel. This will become increasingly obvious and crucial as we move on.

"The Times of Ignorance"

The times of ignorance God overlooked, but now he commands all people everywhere to repent, because he has fixed a day on which he will judge the world in righteousness by a man whom he has appointed; and of this he has given assurance to all by raising him from the dead.

Acts 17:30–31

This text comes from Paul's sermon to the Greeks on the Areopagus in Athens. He had noticed an "altar . . . to the unknown god." In other words, just in case there was another god in the universe whom they did not know about, they had put up an altar, hoping that this "unknowing" act of homage would be acceptable to this deity. So Paul said, "What therefore you worship as unknown, this I proclaim to you" (17:23).

It would be going too far to say that Paul means that true esteeming of the true God was going on in the building of this altar. One cannot truly esteem what one knows nothing about. The worshiping of
the "unknown god" was simply a polytheistic admission that there
might be another deity, unknown to them, whose favor, if he exists,
they would like to have. This "ignorant" worship is one thing that
makes the past generations "times of ignorance" (v. 30). And we will
see that even when there is some knowledge of the true God (as in the
case of Cornelius), the worship of the true God "ignorantly" is *not* a
saving act.

The "times of ignorance" in Paul's sermon correspond to the ages in
which the "mystery of Christ" was kept secret (Rom. 16:25; Eph. 3:4–
5; Col. 1:26). These were the times in which, according to Acts 14:16,
God "allowed all the nations to walk in their own ways," or as Acts
17:30 says, the times that God "overlooked."

The fact that God *overlooked* the times of ignorance does not mean
that he ignored sins so as not to punish sinners. This would contradict
Romans 1:18 ("The wrath of God is revealed from heaven against all
ungodliness and unrighteousness of men") and Romans 2:12 ("All
who have sinned without the law will also perish without the law").
Rather, God's overlooking the "times of ignorance" refers to his giving
men over to their own ways. His "overlooking" was his sovereign decision to postpone an all-out pursuit of their repentance through the
mission of his people. "The reason why men have wandered from the
truth for so long is that God did not stretch forth his hand from
heaven to lead them back to the way. . . . Ignorance was in the world,
as long as it pleased God to take no notice of it."[25]

This does not mean that in the Old Testament there were no commands and instructions for Israel to bear witness to the nations of the
grace of God and invite their participation in that grace in ways appropriate to that time in redemptive history (e.g., Gen. 12:2–3; Psalm
67). It means rather that for generations God did not intervene to purify, empower, and commission his people with the incarnation, crucifixion, Great Commission, and outpouring of Pentecostal power to
fulfill it. Instead, for his own wise purposes, he "allowed all the nations to walk in their own ways"—and allowed his own nation to experience extended failures of reverence and holiness and love so that
other nations would come to see the full need of a Redeemer from the
corruption of sin and the curse of the law and the limitations of the
old covenant for world evangelization.

25. John Calvin, *The Acts of the Apostles, 14–28*, trans. John W. Fraser (Grand Rapids: Eerdmans, 1973), 123.

God's ways are not our ways. Even today we live in a similar time of "hardening"—only now the tables are turned, and it is Israel that is being passed over for a season.

> Lest you [Gentiles] be wise in your own conceits, I want you to understand this mystery, brothers: a partial hardening has come upon Israel, until the fullness of the Gentiles has come in. And in this way all Israel will be saved.
>
> Romans 11:25–26

There was a time when the Gentiles were passed over while God dealt with Israel, and now there is a time while Israel is largely passed over as God gathers the full number of his elect from the nations. In neither case are the people of God to neglect their saving mission toward Jew or Gentile "that they might save some" (Rom. 11:14; 1 Cor. 9:22). But God has his sovereign purposes in determining who actually hears and believes the gospel. And we may be sure that those purposes are wise and holy and will bring the greatest glory to his name.

We are given a glimpse in 1 Corinthians 1:21 of this divine wisdom: "Since, *in the wisdom of God, the world did not know God through wisdom,* it pleased God through the folly of what we preach to save those who believe." This says that it was God's wisdom that determined that men would not know him through their wisdom. In other words, this is an instance and illustration of how God overlooked (i.e., glanced over) the times of ignorance and allowed men to go their own ways.

Why? To make crystal clear that men on their own, by their own wisdom (religion!), will never truly know God. An extraordinary work of God would be required to bring people to a true and saving knowledge of God, namely, the preaching of Christ crucified: "It pleased God through the folly of what we preach to save those who believe." This is what Paul meant in Ephesians 3:6, when he said that the mystery of Christ is that the nations are becoming partakers of the promise *"through the gospel."* Thus, 1 Corinthians 1:21 and Ephesians 3:6 are parallel ideas and utterly crucial for seeing that in this "now" of redemptive history, knowing the gospel is the only way to become an heir of the promise.

All boasting is excluded by God's showing that man's own wisdom in all the nations—his own self-wrought religions—do not bring him to God. Rather, God saves now by means of preaching that is "a stumbling block to Jews and folly to Gentiles, but to those who are called, both Jews and Greeks, Christ the power of God and the wisdom of God" (1 Cor. 1:23–24). In this way, all boasting is excluded, for left to himself man does not come to God.

In his inspiring book, *A Vision for Missions*, Tom Wells tells the story of how William Carey illustrates this conviction in his own preaching. Carey was an English Baptist missionary who left for India in 1793. He never came home but persevered for forty years in the gospel ministry.

Once he was talking with a Brahman in 1797. The Brahman was defending idol worship, and Carey cited Acts 14:16 and 17:30. God formerly "suffered all nations to walk in their own ways," said Carey, "but now commandeth all men everywhere to repent."

"Indeed," said the native, "I think God ought to repent for not sending the Gospel sooner to us."

Carey was not without an answer. He said:

> Suppose a kingdom had been long overrun by the enemies of its true king, and he though possessed of sufficient power to conquer them, should yet suffer them to prevail, and establish themselves as much as they could desire, would not the valour and wisdom of that king be far more conspicuous in exterminating them, than it would have been if he had opposed them at first, and prevented their entering the country? Thus by the diffusion of Gospel light, the wisdom, power, and grace of God will be more conspicuous in overcoming such deep-rooted idolatries, and in destroying all that darkness and vice which have so universally prevailed in this country, than they would have been if all had not been suffered to walk in their own ways for so many ages past.[26]

Carey's answer to why God allowed nations to walk in their own ways is that in doing so the final victory of God will be all the more glorious. There is a divine wisdom in the timing of God's deliverances from darkness. We should humble ourselves to see it rather than presume to know better how God should deal with a rebellious world.

In Acts 17:30, how does Paul assess the ignorant worship of the unknown god (17:23)? He says that the time has come for repentance in view of the impending judgment of the world by Jesus Christ ("He has fixed a day on which he will judge the world in righteousness by a man whom he has appointed" [Acts 17:31]). In other words, Paul does not reveal to the worshipers in Athens that they are already prepared to meet their Judge because they render a kind of worship to the true God through their altar to the unknown god (17:23). They are not ready. They must repent.

As Jesus said in Luke 24:47, from the time of the resurrection onward, "repentance and forgiveness of sins should be proclaimed *in*

26. Tom Wells, *A Vision for Missions* (Edinburgh: Banner of Truth Trust, 1985), 12–13.

his name to all nations." What is to be preached is that through confessing the name of Jesus sins can be forgiven. This was not known before, because Jesus was not here before. But now the times of ignorance are over. Jesus has brought the purposes of God to fulfillment. "All the promises of God find their Yes in [Christ]" (2 Cor. 1:20). At his throne every knee will bow (Phil. 2:10). Therefore, henceforth he is the focus of saving faith. He is now openly installed and declared as Judge, and he alone can receive the appeals for acquittal.

What then are we saying so far? We are saying that the coming of Jesus Christ into the world is an event of such stupendous proportions that a change has occurred in the necessary focus of saving faith. Before Jesus' coming, saving faith reposed in the forgiving and helping mercy of God displayed in events such as the exodus and in the sacrificial offerings and in prophetic promises such as Isaiah 53. Jesus was not known. The mystery that the nations would be fully included through the preaching of *his name* was kept secret for ages. Those were times of ignorance. God let the nations go their own way.

But "now"—a key word in the turning of God's historic work of redemption—something new has happened. The Son of God has appeared. He has revealed the Father. He has atoned for sin. He has risen from the dead. His authority as universal Judge has been vindicated. And the message of his saving work is to be spread to all peoples. This turn in redemptive history is for the glory of Jesus Christ. Its aim is to put him at the center of all God's saving work. Therefore, it accords with this purpose that henceforth Christ be the sole and necessary focus of saving faith. Apart from a knowledge of him, none who has the physical ability to know him will be saved.[27]

---

27. I state it like this so as to leave open salvation for infants and the mentally handicapped who do not have the physical ability even to apprehend that there is any revelation available at all. The principle of accountability in Romans 1:20 (God makes knowledge available "in order that they might be without excuse") is the basis for this conviction. The Bible does not deal with this special case in any detail, and we are left to speculate that the fitness of the connection between faith in Christ and salvation will be preserved through the coming to faith of children whenever God brings them to maturity in heaven or in the age to come. For a defense of this view, see Ronald H. Nash, *When a Baby Dies: Answers to Comfort Grieving Parents* (Grand Rapids: Zondervan, 1999); and Albert Mohler, "The Salvation of the 'Little Ones': Do Infants Who Die Go to Heaven?" *Fidelitas: Commentary on Theology and Culture* (http://www.sbts.edu/mohler/fidelitas/littleones.html). Mohler points out that John Newton, Charles Spurgeon, Charles Hodge, and B. B. Warfield all held such a position. All these were strong believers in original sin, as I am, but also believed that God would provide a just way for the salvation of infants without compromising that doctrine or the doctrine of unconditional election.

This tremendously important turn in redemptive history from the times of ignorance and the hiddenness of the mystery of Christ is not taken seriously enough by those who say people can be saved *today* who do not know Christ because people were saved *in the Old Testament* who did not know Christ. For example, Millard Erickson argues this way but does not reckon seriously enough with the tremendous significance that the New Testament sees in the historical turning point of the incarnation, which ended the times of ignorance and manifested the mystery of Christ.

> If Jews possessed salvation in the Old Testament era simply by virtue of having the form of the Christian gospel without its content, can this principle be extended? Could it be that those who ever since the time of Christ have had no opportunity to hear the gospel, as it has come through the special revelation, participate in this salvation on the same basis?[28]

This would perhaps be a valid argument if the New Testament did not teach that the coming of Christ was a decisive turn in redemptive history that henceforth makes him the focus of all saving faith.

But is this conclusion supported by other New Testament teaching? What about the case of Cornelius? Was he not a Gentile, living after the resurrection of Christ and saved through his genuine piety without focusing his faith on Christ?

The Case of Cornelius, Acts 10:1–11:18

The story of Cornelius the Gentile centurion could lead some to believe that a man can be saved today apart from knowing the gospel and just by fearing God and doing the good that he can.

Cornelius is described as a "devout man who feared God with all his household, gave alms generously to the people, and prayed continually to God" (10:2). On one occasion an angel says to him, "Cornelius, your prayer has been heard and your alms have been remembered before God. Send therefore to Joppa and ask for Simon who is called Peter" (10:31–32).

Meanwhile, the apostle Peter has had a vision from the Lord designed to teach him that the ceremonial uncleanness of the Gentiles is not a hindrance to their acceptance by God. A voice said to Peter, "What God has made clean, do not call common" (10:15).

When Peter meets Cornelius, he says, "Truly I understand that God shows no partiality, but in every nation anyone who fears him and does what is right is acceptable to him" (10:34–35). This is the sen-

28. Erickson, "Hope for Those Who Haven't Heard?" 124–25.

tence that might lead some to think that Cornelius was already saved from his sin even before he heard and believed the gospel. But in fact Luke's point in telling the story seems to be just the opposite.

It will be helpful to ask two questions that are really pressing in this story. One is this: Was Cornelius already saved before Peter preached Christ to him? The reason this is pressing is that verses 34–35 have led many to say that he was. These verses are the beginning of Peter's sermon: "Truly I understand that God shows no partiality, but in every nation anyone who fears him and does what is right is acceptable to him."

You can see how readers would easily conclude that Cornelius was already accepted by God since verse 2 said that he indeed feared God and prayed and gave alms. Did Peter then just inform Cornelius about the acceptance and salvation that he already had? And can we draw the conclusion for missions that there are unreached people who already have a saving relationship with God before they hear the gospel of Christ?

So the first question is, Does verse 35 mean that Cornelius and people like him are already justified and reconciled to God and saved from wrath? Is that Peter's point in saying this and Luke's point in writing it?

Was Cornelius Already Saved?

Let me give you four reasons from the text for answering no.

1. Acts 11:14 says that the message Peter brought was the means by which Cornelius was saved. In Acts 11:13–14, Peter tells the story of the angel's appearance to Cornelius: "He told us how he had seen the angel stand in his house and say, 'Send to Joppa and bring Simon who is called Peter; he will declare to you *a message by which you will be saved,* you and all your household.'"

Notice two things. First, notice that the message itself is essential. The gospel is the power of God unto salvation. Then notice that the tense of the verb is future: "a message by which you *will* be saved." In other words, the message was not simply a way of informing Cornelius that he already was saved. If he sends for Peter and hears the message and believes on the Christ of that message, then he *will* be saved. And if he does not, he won't be. This surely is why the entire story is built around God's miraculous act of getting Cornelius and Peter together. There was a message that Cornelius needed to hear to be saved (10:22, 33).

So Acts 10:35 probably does not mean that Cornelius is already saved when it says that people in unreached ethnic groups who fear

God and do right are acceptable to God. Cornelius had to hear the gospel message to be saved.

2. Peter makes this point at the end of his sermon in 10:43. He brings the message to a close with these words: "To him [i.e., to Christ] all the prophets bear witness that *everyone who believes in him receives forgiveness of sins through his name.*" Forgiveness of sins is essential to salvation. No one is saved whose sins against God are not forgiven by God. And Peter says that forgiveness comes through believing in Christ, and it comes through the name of Christ.

He does not say, "I am here to announce to you that those of you who fear God and do right are already forgiven." He says, "I am here so that you may hear the gospel and receive forgiveness in the name of Christ by believing in him." So again it is unlikely that verse 35 means that Cornelius and his household were already forgiven for their sins before they heard the message of Christ.

3. Elsewhere in the Book of Acts, even those who are the most God-fearing and ethical, namely, the Jews, are told that they must repent and believe in order to be saved. The Jews at Pentecost were called "devout men" (2:5), as Cornelius was called a devout man (10:2). But Peter ended his message in Acts 2 by calling even devout Jews to repent and be baptized in the name of Jesus for the forgiveness of their sins (2:38). The same is true in Acts 3:19 and 13:38–39.

So Luke is not trying to tell us in this book that devout, God-fearing people who practice what is right the best they know how are already saved and do not need the gospel. The gospel got its start among the most devout people in the world, namely, the Jews. They had more advantages in knowing God than any of the other peoples of the earth. Yet they were told again and again that devoutness and works of righteousness and religious sincerity do not solve the problem of sin. The only hope is to believe on Jesus.

4. The fourth reason for saying that verse 35 does not mean that Cornelius and others like him are already saved is found in Acts 11:18. When the people hear Peter tell the story about Cornelius, their initial misgivings are silenced. Luke says, "And they glorified God, saying, 'Then to the Gentiles also God has granted *repentance that leads to life.*'" In other words, they did not already have eternal life. Repentance *leads to* eternal life (literally, it is "unto eternal life"). They received eternal life when they heard the message about Christ and turned to believe and follow him.

So Acts 10:35 does not mean that Cornelius was already saved because he was in some sense a God-fearer and did many right and noble things. That is the answer to the first question.

How Was Cornelius "Acceptable" to God?

The second is simply, What then does it mean when Peter says, "In every nation anyone who fears [God] and does what is right is acceptable to him" (10:35)? And what does this have to do with our commitment to world evangelization?

In trying to answer this question, my first thought was that what Peter means in verse 35 is what God meant in the vision about the unclean animals, namely, the lesson of verse 15: "What God has made clean, do not call common." But something stopped me and made me think again.

Consider verse 28. Peter is explaining to the Gentiles why he was willing to come and says, "You yourselves know how unlawful it is for a Jew to associate with or to visit anyone of another nation, but God has shown me that I should not call *any person* common or unclean." In other words, a Christian should never look down on people from any race or ethnic group and say that that they are unfit to hear the gospel from me. Or, they are too unclean for me to go into their house to share the gospel. Or, they are not worth evangelizing. Or, they have too many offensive habits for me even to get near them.

But the phrase that makes verse 28 so powerful is the phrase "any person" or "anyone": "God has shown me that I should not call any person common or unclean." In other words, Peter learned from his vision on the housetop in Joppa that God rules no one out of his favor on the basis of race or ethnic origin or mere cultural or physical distinctives. "Common and unclean" meant rejected, despised, taboo. It was like leprosy.

Peter's point in verse 28 is that there is not one human being on the face of the earth that we should think about in that way. Not one. Our hearts should go out to every single person whatever the color, whatever the ethnic origin, whatever the physical traits, whatever the cultural distinctives. We are not to write off anybody. "God has shown me that I should not call anyone—not one—common or unclean."

Now, that is *not* what Peter says in verse 35, which is what kept me from assuming that verse 35 simply means that all people are acceptable as candidates for salvation, no matter their ethnic background. In verse 35, Peter says, "*In* every nation anyone who fears him and does what is right is acceptable to him." He is not talking about every person as he was in verse 28. Here he is talking about some *in* every nation. "*In* every nation anyone who fears him and does what is right is acceptable to him." The acceptability Peter has in mind here is something more, it seems, than merely not being common or unclean. That's everybody. Peter said, Do not "call *any person* common or unclean." Here he says that only *some* in every nation fear God and do right, and these are acceptable to God.

Now we know two things that verse 35 does not mean. (1) It does not mean that these God-fearing doers of good are saved. We saw four reasons why it can't mean that. (2) It does not mean merely that they are acceptable candidates for evangelism (not common or unclean, not taboo), because verse 28 already said that's true of everybody, not just some. But verse 35 says that only some are God-fearing, doing what is right and thus acceptable. Therefore, the meaning probably lies somewhere between these two: between being saved and being a touchable, lovable human candidate for evangelism.

My suggestion is that Cornelius represents a kind of unsaved person among an unreached people group who is seeking God in an extraordinary way. Peter is saying that God *accepts* this search as genuine (hence "acceptable" in verse 35) and works wonders to bring that person the gospel of Jesus Christ the way he did through the visions of both Peter on the housetop and Cornelius in the hour of prayer.

A Modern Cornelius

This "extraordinary searching" still happens today. Don Richardson, in his book *Eternity in Their Hearts,* tells of a conversion very similar to that of Cornelius. The Gedeo people of south-central Ethiopia were a tribe of a half-million coffee-growing people who believed in a benevolent being called *Magano,* the omnipotent Creator of all that is. Few of the Gedeo people prayed to Magano, being concerned instead to appease an evil being they called *Sheit'an.* But one Gedeo man, Warrasa Wanga, from the town of Dilla on the edge of Gedeo tribal land, prayed to Magano to reveal himself to the Gedeo people.

Then Warrasa Wanga had a vision: Two white-skinned strangers came and built flimsy shelters for themselves under the shade of a sycamore tree near Dilla. Later they built more permanent shiny-roofed structures, which eventually dotted an entire hillside. Warrasa had never seen anything like these structures, since all of the Gedeo dwellings were grass-roofed. Then Warassa heard a voice say, "These men will bring you a message from Magano, the God you seek. Wait for them." In the last scene of his vision, Warrasa saw himself remove the center pole from his own house, carry it out of the town, and set it in the ground next to one of the shiny-roofed dwellings of the men. In Gedeo symbolism, the center pole of a man's house stands for his very life.

Eight years later, in December 1948, two Canadian missionaries, Albert Brant and Glen Cain, came to Ethiopia to begin a work among the Gedeo people. They intended to ask permission from Ethiopian officials to place their new mission in the center of the Gedeo region, but they were advised by other Ethiopians that their request would be refused because of the current political climate. The advisors told them to ask permission to go only as far as Dilla, on the extreme edge of Gedeo tribal land. Permission was granted, and when they reached Dilla, the missionaries set up their tents under an old sycamore tree.

Thirty years later there were more than two hundred churches among the Gedeo people, with each church averaging more than two hundred members.[29] Almost the entire Gedeo tribe has been influenced by the gospel. Warrasa was one of the first converts and the first to be imprisoned for his faith.[30]

The Fear of God That Is Acceptable to God

The main evidence that Luke is talking about this kind of "acceptable" unsaved person who seeks the true God and his messengers is found in Acts 10:31–32, where Cornelius says that the angel said to him, "Cornelius, *your prayer has been heard* and your alms have been remembered before God. Send *therefore* to Joppa and ask for Simon who is called Peter." Notice: Your prayers have been heard . . . *therefore* send for Peter. This implies that the prayers were for God to send him what he needed in order to be saved.

So the fear of God that is acceptable to God in verse 35 is a true sense that there is a holy God, that we have to meet him someday as desperate sinners, that we cannot save ourselves and need to know God's way of salvation, and that we have to pray for it day and night and seek to act on the light we have. This is what Cornelius was doing. And God accepted his prayer and his groping for truth in his life (Acts 17:27) and worked wonders to bring the saving message of the gospel to him. Cornelius would not have been saved if no one had taken him the gospel. And no one who can apprehend revelation (see note 29) will be saved today without the gospel.

Therefore, Cornelius does not represent persons who are saved without hearing and believing the gospel; rather, he illustrates God's intention to take out a people for his name from "every nation" (Acts 10:35) through the sending of gospel messengers across cultural lines, which had once been taboo.

29. Don Richardson, *Eternity in Their Hearts* (Ventura, Calif.: Regal, 1981), 56–58.
30. W. Harold Fuller, *Run While the Sun Is Hot* (London: Hazell Watson and Viney Ltd., n.d.), 183–84.

We should learn with the Jewish church in Jerusalem that "to the Gentiles also God has granted repentance that leads to life" (11:18). But we must be sure that we learn this the way they learned it: They inferred this from the fact that the Gentiles *believed the gospel that Peter preached* and received the Holy Spirit. They did not infer the acceptance of the Gentiles from their fear of God and their good deeds.

It appears therefore that Luke's intention in telling the Cornelius story is to show that Gentiles can become part of the chosen people of God through faith in Christ in spite of their ceremonial "uncleanness." The point is *not* that Gentiles are already part of God's chosen people because they fear God and do many good deeds. The key sentence is Acts 11:14: "He will declare to you a *message by which you will be saved.*"

"No Other Name under Heaven"—Acts 4:12

The reason this message saves is that it proclaims the name that saves—the name of Jesus. Peter said that God visited the Gentiles "to take from them a people *for his name*" (Acts 15:14). It stands to reason then that the proclamation by which God takes a people for his name would be a message that hinges on the name of his Son Jesus. This is, in fact, what we saw in Peter's preaching at the house of Cornelius. The sermon comes to its climax with these words about Jesus: "Everyone who believes in him receives forgiveness of sins *through his name*" (Acts 10:43).

The implicit necessity of hearing and embracing the name of Jesus, which we see in the story of Cornelius, is made explicit in Acts 4:12 in the climax of another sermon by Peter, this time before the Jewish rulers in Jerusalem: "And there is salvation in no one else, for there is no other name under heaven given among men by which we must be saved."

The situation behind this famous sentence is that the risen Jesus healed a man through Peter and John. The man had been lame from birth, but he got up and ran through the temple praising God. A crowd gathered and Peter preached. His message makes it obvious that what is at stake here is not merely a local religious phenomenon. It has to do with everybody in the world.

Then according to Acts 4:1, the priests and the captain of the temple and the Sadducees came and arrested Peter and John and put them in custody overnight. The next morning the rulers and elders and scribes gather and interrogate Peter and John. In the course of the interrogation, Peter draws out the implication of the universal lordship of Jesus: "There is salvation in no one else, for there is no other name under heaven given among men by which we must be saved" (4:12).

We need to feel the force of this universal claim by taking several phrases very seriously. The reason there is salvation in no one else is that "there is no other name *under heaven* [not just no other name in Israel but no other name under heaven, including the heaven over Greece and Rome and Spain, etc.] given *among men* [not just among Jews but among all humans everywhere] by which we must be saved." These two phrases, "under heaven" and "among men," press the claim of universality to its fullest extent.

But there is even more here that we need to see. Commentators usually interpret Acts 4:12 to mean that without believing in Jesus a person cannot be saved. In other words, Acts 4:12 is seen as a crucial text in answering the question whether those who have never heard the gospel of Jesus can be saved. But Clark Pinnock represents others who say that "Acts 4:12 does not say anything about [this question]. . . . It does not comment on the fate of the heathen. Although it is a question of great importance to us, it is not one on which Acts 4:12 renders a judgment, either positive or negative."[31] Rather, what Acts 4:12 says is that "salvation in its fullness is available to humankind only because God in the person of his Son Jesus provided it."[32] In other words, the verse says that salvation comes only through the *work* of Jesus but not only through faith in Jesus. His work can benefit those who relate to God properly without him, for example, on the basis of general revelation in nature.

The problem with Pinnock's interpretation is that it does not reckon with the true significance of Peter's focus on the *name* of Jesus. "There is no other *name* under heaven *by which* we must be saved." Peter is saying something more than that there is no other *source* of saving power that you can be saved by under some *other* name. The point of saying "There is no other *name*" is that we are saved by calling on the name of the Lord Jesus. Calling on his name is our entrance into fellowship with God. If one is saved by Jesus incognito, one does not speak of being saved *by his name.*

We noticed above that Peter said in Acts 10:43, "Everyone *who believes in him* receives forgiveness of sins *through his name.*" The name of Jesus is the focus of faith and repentance. In order to believe on Jesus for the forgiveness of sins, you must believe on his name, which

31. Pinnock, "Acts 4:12—No Other Name Under Heaven," 110. Pinnock acknowledges that the commentators (e.g., Bruce, Haenchen, Longenecker, Conzelmann) take Acts 4:12 to support the "exclusivist paradigm."
32. Ibid., 109.

means that you have to have heard of him and know who he is as a particular man who did a particular saving work and rose from the dead.

The point of Acts 4:12 for missions is made explicit in the way Paul picks up on this very issue of the name of the Lord Jesus in Romans 10:13–15. This passage shows that missions is essential precisely because "'Everyone who calls on *the name of the Lord* will be saved.' But how are they to call on him in whom they have not believed? And how are they to believe in him of whom they have never heard? And how are they to hear without someone preaching?"

"How Are They to Believe in Him of Whom They Have Never Heard?"

In Romans 10:13, Paul makes the great gospel declaration, quoting Joel 2:32, "Everyone who calls on the name of the Lord will be saved." He follows this with rhetorical questions: "But how are they to call on him in whom they have not believed? And how are they to believe in him of whom they have never heard?" These are extremely important words relating to the necessity of the missionary enterprise.

Consider the context of these words in Romans 9:30–10:21. Paul begins and ends this unit by saying that Gentiles, who never had the advantages of God's revealed law, have nevertheless attained a right standing with God through Christ, while Israel, with all her advantages, has not attained a right standing with God. Here is how he says it in Romans 9:30–31: "Gentiles who did not pursue righteousness have attained it, that is, a righteousness that is by faith; but . . . Israel who pursued a law that would lead to righteousness did not succeed in reaching that law." Here is how he says it in Romans 10:20–21: "Then Isaiah is so bold as to say, 'I have been found by those who did not seek me; I have shown myself to those who did not ask for me.' But of Israel he says, 'All day long I have held out my hands to a disobedient and contrary people.'"

Paul is burdened to show that the great reason for this strange reversal—Gentiles getting right with God and actually fulfilling the demands of the law of God, but Israel failing with their own law to get right with God—is that "the goal (or culmination) of the law is Christ for righteousness for everyone who believes" (Rom. 10:4, author's translation). Israel missed the point of her own law, namely, to point her to Christ and the way of justification by faith as the only hope of fulfilling the law (9:32). And then, when Christ appeared, she "stumbled over the stumbling stone" (9:32). The Israelites would not "submit to God's righteousness" (10:3). But Gentiles embraced the promise that "whoever believes in him will not be put to shame" (9:33).

Paul makes the transition to his own gospel and the missionary setting of his life in 10:8, where he says that the message of the Old Testament law, pointing to Christ the Redeemer, is "the word of faith that we proclaim." Then he says explicitly that this Redeemer is Jesus and that all salvation is now had by confessing him—just as salvation in the Old Testament was had by embracing the pointers to his coming, banking on God's grace that he would provide. Thus, verse 9 says, "If you confess with your mouth that *Jesus is Lord* and believe in your heart that God raised him from the dead, you will be saved."

Paul underlines that salvation through believing and confessing Jesus as Lord was the Old Testament hope. He does this by quoting Isaiah 28:16 in Romans 10:11, "For the Scripture says, 'Everyone who believes in him will not be put to shame,'" and by quoting Joel 2:32 in Romans 10:13, "Everyone who calls on the name of the Lord will be saved." So when Romans 10:11 quotes Isaiah 28:16, "Everyone who believes in him will not be put to shame," the reference is clearly to Jesus, the predicted cornerstone. And when 10:13 quotes Joel 2:32, "Everyone who calls on the name of the Lord will be saved," Jesus is the "Lord" referred to, even though in Joel 2:32 "Yahweh" is in view. The reason we know this is that 10:9 said, "If you confess with your mouth that Jesus is Lord . . . you will be saved."

Paul is making clear that in this new era of redemptive history, Jesus is the goal and climax of Old Testament teaching, and therefore, Jesus now stands as Mediator between man and Yahweh as the object of saving faith.

The flow of thought from Romans 10:14–21 is not easy to grasp. The sequence of questions in verses 14–15 are familiar and are often cited in relation to missionary work:

> [Therefore,] how are they to call on him in whom they have not believed? And how are they to believe in him of whom they have never heard?[33] And how are they to hear without someone preaching? And how are they to preach unless they are sent? As it is written, "How beautiful are the feet of those who preach the good news!"

But how do these verses fit into the flow of Paul's thought? Why do they begin with the word "therefore" *(oun)*? How does asking a series of questions communicate an inference? Why does the next verse

---

33. The Greek verb for "hear" *(akouō)* followed by a person in the genitive case means "hear the person," not merely hear about him. Most commentators are agreed on this (e.g., Murray, Cranfield, Moo).

(v. 16) begin with *"But* [or *nevertheless*] they have not all obeyed the gospel"?

The answer seems to be this: The "therefore" at the beginning of verse 14 and the "nevertheless" at the beginning of verse 16 point to the fact that the series of questions in verses 14–15 are really making a statement to the effect that God has already worked to bring about these conditions for calling on the Lord Jesus for salvation. We could paraphrase as follows:

> (10–13) Salvation is richly available to both Jews and Gentiles—to every-one who calls upon the name of the Lord Jesus. (14–15) *Therefore,* God has taken steps to provide the prerequisites for calling on the Lord. He is sending those who preach so that Christ can be heard and people can be-lieve and call on the Lord Jesus. (16) Nevertheless, this has not led to obedience, as Isaiah predicted: "Lord, who has believed our report?"

So far then, the main point of verses 14–16 would be that *even though* God has taken steps to provide the prerequisites for calling on the Lord, *nevertheless* most have not obeyed.

But who is in view here when Paul says they have not believed? Dif-fering answers to this question lead to two different ways of construing Paul's line of reasoning in the entire passage. John Murray and Charles Hodge represent these two lines.

Murray says, "At verse 16 the apostle returns to that subject which permeates this section of the epistle, the unbelief of Israel."[34] Simi-larly, Murray says the focus on Israel's unbelief continues to the end of the paragraph. So, for example, verse 18 also refers to Israel. "But I ask, have they not heard? Indeed they have, for 'Their voice has gone out to all the earth, and their words to the ends of the world.'" He says the quote from Psalm 19:4 (which originally referred to works of na-ture declaring God's glory) is used by Paul to describe the worldwide spread of the gospel of Jesus, and the point is that if the gospel is go-ing out to all the world, "it cannot then be objected that Israel did not hear."[35] So the focus stays on Israel. The point of Paul's thought throughout Romans 10 is that Israel knows the gospel and is never-theless rejecting it and is thus accountable.

Charles Hodge, on the other hand, sees the focus differently in verses 11–21. "Paul's object in the whole context is to vindicate the propriety of extending the gospel call to all nations." He sees both verses 16 and 18 as references not to Israel but to the nations. "The 16th verse refers to the Gentiles, 'They have not all obeyed the gospel,'

34. John Murray, *The Epistle to the Romans*, vol. 2 (Grand Rapids: Eerdmans, 1965), 60.
35. Ibid., 62.

and therefore this verse [18], 'Have they not heard?' cannot, without any intimation of change, be naturally referred to a different subject. . . . In the following verse [19], where the Jews are really intended, they are distinctly mentioned, 'Did not Israel know?'"[36]

In spite of this difference between Murray and Hodge, the important thing for our purpose remains fairly clear, and both agree. Whether Paul is focusing in a narrower way on the accountability of Israel or more broadly on the availability of the gospel to the nations (and therefore also to Israel), both agree that calling on the name of the Lord Jesus is necessary for salvation (v. 13).

So necessary is it that Paul feels compelled to show that all the necessary prerequisites for calling on the Lord are being put in place by God (vv. 14–15). Even more relevant for our immediate question is the implication that "calling on the Lord" in a saving way is not something that a person can do from a position of ignorance. One cannot do it from another religion. This is made plain in the questions of verses 14–15.

Each succeeding question rules out an argument from those who say that someone can be saved without hearing the gospel of Jesus. First, "How are they to call on him in whom they have not believed?" shows that effective calling presupposes faith in the one called. This rules out the argument that one might call on God savingly without faith in Christ.

Second, "And how are they to believe in him of whom they have never heard?" shows that faith presupposes hearing Christ in the message of the gospel. This rules out the argument that a person might have saving faith without really knowing or meeting Christ in the gospel.

Third, "And how are they to hear without someone preaching?" shows that hearing Christ in the gospel presupposes a proclaimer of the gospel. This rules out the argument that one might somehow meet Christ or hear Christ without a messenger to tell the gospel.

Millard Erickson does not seem to take the force of this sequence seriously enough when he suggests that the quotation from Psalm 19:4 in Romans 10:18 teaches that general revelation in nature is all that some need to receive salvation, apart from missionary proclamation.[37]

At first this suggestion may seem compelling. Paul says that people must hear in order to call on the Lord. Then he asks in verse 18, "Have they not heard?" And he answers with the words of Psalm 19:4 (18:4

---

36. Charles Hodge, *Commentary on the Epistle to the Romans* (New York: A. C. Armstrong and Son, 1893), 548.

37. See note 7.

LXX[38]): "Indeed they have, for 'Their voice has gone out to all the earth, and their words to the ends of the world.'"

In the original context of Psalm 19, "their voice" and "their words" refer to what is communicated through "night" and "day" and "heavens" and "firmament." So one might conclude that the "hearing" that is necessary for saving faith (v. 17) is effectively provided through natural revelation. This is what Erickson concludes.[39]

The problem with this view is that it creates an insurmountable tension with the point of verse 14. There Paul says, "How are they to hear without someone preaching?" If Erickson were correct that a hearing that is effective to save comes through nature, then Paul's question is misleading: "How are they to hear without someone preaching?" He clearly means that one cannot hear what one needs to hear for salvation unless a preacher is sent. He would contradict this if he meant in verse 18 that preachers are not essential for salvation, because an effective message of salvation comes through nature.

Therefore, as most commentators agree, it is unlikely that Paul intends for verse 18 to teach that natural revelation fulfills the saving role of the "word of Christ," which gives rise to faith (v. 17). Murray and Hodge agree that Paul uses the words of the psalm to draw a parallel between the universality of general revelation and the universal spread of the gospel.[40] The point is that God has set in

38. LXX is an abbreviation for the Greek translation of the Old Testament called the Septuagint. It comes from the tradition that the translation was made by seventy (LXX) scholars.

39. He finds support for this conclusion also in Romans 1:18–21. But the problem with this is that though these verses teach the reality of general revelation that is sufficient to hold humanity accountable to glorify God (v. 21), nevertheless, they also teach that men suppress this truth in unrighteousness (v. 18) and do *not* thank God or honor him the way they should (v. 21) and are therefore without excuse (v. 20). General revelation is sufficient to hold all men accountable to worship God but not efficient to bring about the faith that saves. That is why the gospel must be preached to all peoples. God wills to honor his Son by accompanying the preaching of his name with heart-awakening power.

40. Murray, *Epistle to the Romans*, 61: "Since the gospel proclamation is not to all without distinction, it is proper to see the parallel between the universality of general revelation and the universalism of the gospel. The former is the pattern now followed in the sounding forth of the gospel to the uttermost parts of the earth. The application which Paul makes of Psalm 19:4 can thus be seen to be eloquent not only of this parallel but also of that which is implicit in the parallel, namely, the widespread diffusion of the gospel of grace." Hodge, *Commentary on the Epistle to the Romans*, 549: "This verse, therefore is to be considered as a strong declaration that what Paul had proved ought to be done, had in fact been accomplished. The middle wall of partition had been broken down, the gospel of salvation, the religion of God, was free from its trammels, the offers of mercy were as wide and general as the proclamation of the heavens. . . . His object in

motion a missionary movement (the "sending" of v. 15) that will reach to all the peoples of the earth on the analogy of the universal spread of God's glory through natural revelation.[41]

To sum up these thoughts on Romans 10, the theological assumption behind Paul's missionary conviction is that Christ is the fulfillment of all that the Old Testament pointed toward. Before Christ, faith was focused on the mercy of God to forgive sins and to care for his people. As revelation progressed, faith could move more easily from the animal sacrifices to the promised sin-bearer of Isaiah 53. But when Christ came, all faith narrowed in its focus to him alone as the One who purchased and guaranteed all the hopes of the people of God. From the time of Christ onward, God wills to honor Christ by making him the sole focus of saving faith. Therefore, people must call on him and believe in him and hear him and be sent as messengers with the Word of Christ.

Paul's Conception of His Own Missionary Vocation

The indispensability of hearing the gospel for salvation is seen in the biblical texts that show how Paul conceived of his own missionary vocation.

At his conversion, Paul received a commission from the Lord that clarifies the condition of those without Christ. He refers to this in Acts 26:15–18.

> And I said, "Who are you, Lord?" And the Lord said, "I am Jesus whom you are persecuting. But rise and stand upon your feet, for I have ap-

---

using the words of the Psalmist was, no doubt, to convey more clearly and affectingly to the minds of his hearers the idea that the proclamation of the gospel was now as free from all nations or ecclesiastical restrictions, as the instructions shed down upon all people by the heavens under which they dwell. Paul, of course, is not to be understood as quoting the Psalmist as though the ancient prophet was speaking of the preaching of the gospel. He simply uses scriptural language to express his own ideas, as is done involuntarily almost by every preacher in every sermon."

41. The words "Their voice has gone out" does not have to mean that the spread of the message is finished. In Paul's context, the natural meaning is that the gospel has been propelled into the world to reach all peoples. Olshausen suggests that "their voice has gone out" is to be understood as prophetically spoken; that which is begun is viewed as if already completed, and therefore we need not seek for any further explanation how it is that St. Paul can represent Christ's messengers as spread all over the earth, whereas, when he wrote these words, they had not so much as carried the preaching of Christ through the whole of the Roman empire." Hermann Olshausen, *Studies in the Epistle to the Romans* (1849; reprint, Minneapolis: Klock and Klock Christian Publishers: 1983), 354.

peared to you for this purpose, to appoint you as a servant and witness to the things in which you have seen me and to those in which I will appear to you, delivering you from your people and from the Gentiles—to whom *I am sending you to open their eyes, so that they may turn from darkness to light and from the power of Satan to God, that they may receive forgiveness of sins* and a place among those who are sanctified by faith in me."

Here we see what was at stake in Paul's ministry. Without making any distinctions, the Lord says that those who do not yet have the gospel are in darkness and in the power of Satan and without the forgiveness of sins. Christ commissioned Paul with a word of power that actually opens the eyes of the spiritually blind, not so that they can see they are forgiven but so that they can be forgiven. His message delivers from the power of Satan. The picture of nations without the gospel is that they are blind and in the darkness and in bondage to Satan and without forgiveness of sins and unacceptable to God because they are unsanctified.

This accords with what Paul says elsewhere about the condition of man without the power of the gospel: All are under sin with their mouths stopped before God (Rom. 3:9–19); they are in the flesh and unable to submit to God or please God (Rom. 8:7–8); they are natural and not spiritual and therefore unable to receive the things of the Spirit (1 Cor. 2:14–16); they are dead in trespasses and children of wrath (Eph. 2:3–5); and they are darkened and alienated from God and hard in heart (Eph. 4:17–18).

With the coming of Christ came a message that has power to save (Rom. 1:16; 1 Cor. 15:2; 1 Thess. 2:16) and bear fruit (Col. 1:6) and triumph (2 Thess. 3:1), and it is the mission of Paul and all his heirs to preach that message to the nations. "Since, in the wisdom of God, the world did not know God through wisdom [or false religion], it pleased God through the folly of what we preach to save those who believe" (1 Cor. 1:21).

Salvation is at stake when Paul speaks to Jews in the synagogue as well. Paul does not assume that God-fearing Gentiles or Jews are saved by virtue of knowing the Old Testament Scriptures. What does he say in the synagogue at Antioch of Pisidia?

Let it be known to you therefore, brothers, that through this man forgiveness of sins is proclaimed to you, and by him everyone who believes is freed from everything from which you could not be freed by the law of Moses.

Acts 13:38–39

Paul does not tell them that even the best of them are already forgiven by virtue of their obedience to the law. He offers them forgiveness through Christ. And he makes "freeing" ("justification") from sin conditional on believing on Christ. When the synagogue later opposes this message, Paul says in Acts 13:46–48:

> It was necessary that the word of God be spoken first to you. Since you thrust it aside and judge yourselves unworthy of eternal life, behold, we are turning to the Gentiles. For so the Lord has commanded us, saying, "I have made you a light for the Gentiles, that you may bring salvation to the ends of the earth." And when the Gentiles heard this, they began rejoicing and glorifying the word of the Lord, and as many as were appointed to eternal life believed.

Paul's vocation is to bring salvation to the end of the earth. The assumption is that salvation is not already at the end of the earth. Paul is to take it there. Paul's message is the means of salvation. There is no salvation without it: "As many as were appointed to eternal life believed" Paul's message and were saved. God has ordained that salvation come to the nations through sent messengers whose obedient preaching of the gospel brings salvation to the nations.

Through Paul's preaching, God is now doing the sovereign work that he had overlooked for so long during the times of ignorance. He is bringing Gentiles to faith according to his preordained plan. He is opening their hearts to the gospel (Acts 16:14), granting them repentance (Acts 11:18), and cleansing their hearts by faith (Acts 15:9).

Before this time of gospel privilege, these things were not possible, for God was allowing the nations to go their own way (Acts 14:16). But now a great movement is under way to gather a people for his name from all the nations, and God himself is active in the ministry of his messengers to sanctify a people for himself. This becomes wonderfully clear in Romans 15, where Paul describes his own vocation in its relation to the work of Christ in and through him.

> But on some points I have written to you very boldly by way of reminder, because of the grace given me by God to be a minister of Christ Jesus to the Gentiles in the priestly service of the gospel of God, so that the offering of the Gentiles may be acceptable, sanctified by the Holy Spirit. In Christ Jesus, then, I have reason to be proud of my work for God. For I will not venture to speak of anything except what Christ has accomplished through me to bring the Gentiles to obedience—by word and deed.
>
> verses 15–18

Notice the initiative of God in these verses. First, God gave Paul the grace of apostleship and called him to the ministry of the gospel (vv. 15–16). Second, the Gentiles who believe Paul's message are acceptable to God because they are sanctified by the Holy Spirit (v. 16). Third, it is not Paul who has won obedience from the Gentiles; it is what Christ has accomplished through him (v. 18).

Therefore, the Gentile mission is the new work of God. It is the fulfillment of divine prophecy that once God allowed the nations to go their own way, but *now*

> God . . . visited the Gentiles, to take from them a people for his name. And with this the words of the prophets agree, just as it is written, "After this I will return, and I will rebuild the tent of David that has fallen; I will rebuild its ruins, and I will restore it, *that the remnant of mankind may seek the Lord*, and all the Gentiles who are called by my name, says the Lord, who makes these things known from of old."
>
> Acts 15:14–18

A new day has come with Jesus Christ. The people of God are being rebuilt in such a way that they will no longer fail in their task of reaching the nations. In this new day, God will not suffer his people to neglect their mission; he will no longer allow the nations to go their own way. He is establishing a church "that the remnant of mankind may seek the Lord."

And he will now gather in all those among the nations who are called by his name! It is *his* new work! All those who are predestined *will* be called (Rom. 8:30). All those who are foreordained to eternal life *will* believe (Acts 13:48). All those who are ransomed *will* be gathered from every people under heaven (Rev. 5:9). God himself is the chief agent in this new movement, and he *will* take out a people for his name among the nations (Acts 15:14).

The Writings of John

John's conception of the new missionary task parallels Paul's. Just as Paul said that no one could believe in a Christ of whom they had not heard (Rom. 10:14), so Jesus says in John 10:27, "My sheep hear my voice, and I know them, and they follow me" (cf. 10:4, 14). In other words, Jesus gathers his redeemed flock by calling them with his own voice. The true sheep hear his voice and follow, and he gives them eternal life (10:28).

Whom does Jesus have in mind when he speaks of those who will hear his voice and follow him? He is referring to more than the Jews who actually heard him on earth. He says, "I have *other sheep that are not of this fold. I must bring them also, and they will listen to my voice. So there will be one flock, one shepherd*" (10:16). "Other sheep that are not of this fold" refers to the Gentiles, who are not part of the Jewish fold.

But how will these Gentiles hear his voice? The answer is the same as with Paul: They hear the voice of Jesus, not in nature or in an alien religion but in the voice of Christ's messengers. We see this in the way Jesus prays for his future disciples in John 17:20–21: "I do not ask for these only, but also for those *who will believe in me through their word, that they may all be one.*" We infer from this then that the "sheep that are not of this fold" will hear the voice of the Shepherd through the voice of his messengers.

Eternal life, therefore, comes only to those who hear the voice of the Shepherd and follow him. "My sheep hear my voice, and I know them, and they follow me. I give them eternal life" (10:27–28). This hearing is through the messengers of the Shepherd. This is what Jesus means in John 14:6 when he says, "I am the way, and the truth, and the life. No one comes to the Father except through me." "Through me" does not mean that people in other religions can get to God because Jesus died for them, though they don't know about it. The "through me" must be defined in the context of John's Gospel as believing in Jesus through the word of his disciples (John 6:35; 7:38; 11:25; 12:46; 17:20).

Eternal life is owing to the death of Jesus for his sheep (10:15)—a death that atoned not for a few Jewish sheep only but for sheep from every nation. We see this in John 11:51–53, where John interprets the words of Caiaphas: "Being high priest that year he prophesied that Jesus would die for the nation, *and not for the nation only, but also to gather into one the children of God who are scattered abroad.*"

The "children of God scattered abroad" (11:52) are the "other sheep that are not of this fold" (10:16). And when we look at John's picture of the consummation of the missionary cause in Revelation, we see that these "sheep" and "children" are truly from all the nations.

And they sang a new song, saying, Worthy are you to take the scroll and to open its seals, for you were slain, and by your blood you ransomed people for God *from every tribe and language and people and nation*, and you have made them a kingdom and priests to our God, and they shall reign on the earth."

Revelation 5:9–10

Here we see the true extent of the word "scattered" in John 11:52. Jesus died to gather the "children of God" who are scattered among "every tribe and language and people and nation." The implication is that the messengers of the Shepherd must (Mark 13:10) and *will* (Matt. 24:14) reach every people under heaven with the message of the gospel and the voice of the Shepherd. The redeemed in heaven from all the peoples are not redeemed without knowing it. Rather, as Revelation 7:14 makes clear, those "from every nation, from all tribes and peoples and languages" (Rev. 7:9) are those who "have washed their robes and made them white in the blood of the Lamb" (Rev. 7:14; cf. 22:14). They are those who "keep the commandments of God and hold to the testimony of Jesus" (Rev. 12:17). The gospel of the blood of Christ crucified for sinners and risen in victory must be preached to all the nations so that they can believe and be saved.

Conclusion

The question we have been trying to answer in this section is whether some people are quickened by the Holy Spirit and saved by grace through faith in a merciful Creator even though they never hear of Jesus in this life. Are there devout people in religions other than Christianity who humbly rely on the grace of a God whom they know only through nature or non-Christian religious experience?

The answer of the New Testament is a clear and earnest no. Rather, the message throughout is that with the coming of Christ a major change occurred in redemptive history. Saving faith was once focused on the mercy of God known in his redemptive acts among the people of Israel and in the system of animal sacrifices and in the prophecies of coming redemption. Outside Israel we hear of Melchizedek (Genesis 14), who seems to know the true God apart from connection with special revelation in the line of Abraham.

But now the focus of faith has been narrowed down to one man, Jesus Christ, the fulfillment and guarantee of all redemption and all sacrifices and all prophecies. It is to his honor that henceforth all saving faith shall be directed to him.

Therefore, this great turn in redemptive history is accompanied by a new mission thrust ordained by God. God no longer allows the nations to walk their own way (Acts 14:16) but sends his messengers everywhere to call all to repent and believe the gospel (Acts 17:30).

God in Christ is himself the power behind this mission. He has ordained his people to life (Acts 13:48) and ransomed them by laying down his life for them (John 10:15; Rev. 5:9). Now he is commissioning Spirit-filled messengers to preach to them (Rom. 1:5; 10:15), and he is speaking through these messengers with power (Luke 12:12; 21:15; 1 Thess. 2:13) and calling the lost effectually to faith (Rom. 8:30; 1 Cor. 1:24) and keeping them by his almighty power (Jude 24).

Those who affirm that people who have no access to the gospel may nevertheless be saved without knowing Christ try to argue that this idea enhances the motivation to evangelize the lost. As we saw above, this is a futile effort. The arguments fall apart as you pick them up. For example, John Ellenberger cites four ways our motivation will be "enhanced."

1. Citing Acts 18:10 ("I have many in this city who are my people"), he says that "the knowledge that the Holy Spirit has been working in the hearts of people prior to hearing the good news should encourage us."[42] I agree. But that is not the issue. Working in people's hearts to prepare them to respond to the gospel is very different from working in their hearts so that they are saved apart from the gospel. The first motivates missions; the second does not.

2. He argues unintelligibly that "because the great majority have not responded to general revelation, they need to be confronted by the claims of Jesus."[43] This amounts to saying that if you believe some are saved without hearing the claims of Christ, you will be more motivated to share those claims because most are not saved that way. But that is *not* an argument that the view that some can be saved without the gospel "enhances" our motivation to evangelize the lost. On the contrary, it's an argument that the more needed the claims of Christ are, the greater the motivation to share them.

3. Third, he argues that believing that some are saved apart from the preaching of the gospel "broadens our understanding of the whole gospel."[44] In other words, if we are going to pursue missions with zeal, we need to do so for reasons other than merely providing escape from hell (which some already have before we get there). We need to desire to bring the blessings of salvation in this life. I suppose this is true. But why should we assume that the church will be more motivated to bring *these* blessings to people than it is to bring the blessing of eternal life? The risk I am willing to take to save a person from execution is not increased by telling me, "He is no longer on death row, but surely you will want to feel all the same urgency to help him find a good life."

42. John Ellenberger, "Is Hell a Proper Motivation for Missions?" in *Through No Fault of Their Own*, 225.
43. Ibid., 226.
44. Ibid.

4. Finally, Ellenberger argues that believing some are saved apart from the preaching of the gospel "reaffirms love as the primary motivation."[45] Again this is unintelligible to me, because it seems to assume that the urgency of missions driven by the desire to rescue people from eternal torment is not love. How does saying some are saved without the gospel make a greater appeal to love?

So I affirm again that the contemporary abandonment of the universal necessity of hearing the gospel for salvation does indeed cut a nerve in missionary motivation. I say *a* nerve rather than *the* nerve because I agree that the universal lostness of man is not the only focus for missionary motivation. Arching over it is the great goal of bringing glory to Christ.[46]

Therefore, the church is bound to engage with the Lord of glory in his cause. Charles Hodge is right that "the solemn question, implied in the language of the apostle, how can they believe without a preacher? should sound day and night in the ears of the churches."[47]

It is our unspeakable privilege to be caught up with him in the greatest movement in history—the ingathering of the elect "from all tribes and languages and peoples and nations" until the full number of the Gentiles comes in, all Israel is saved, the Son of Man descends with power and great glory as King of kings and Lord of lords, and the earth is full of the knowledge of his glory as the waters cover the sea forever and ever. Then the supremacy of Christ will be manifest to all, he will deliver the kingdom to God the Father, and God will be all in all.

45. Ibid.
46. For my understanding, following Jonathan Edwards, on the relationship between passion for the supremacy and compassion for the souls of men, see chapter 6.
47. Hodge, *Commentary on the Epistle to the Romans*, 553.

5

The Supremacy of God among "All the Nations"

Can Love Decide?

How do we decide what the task of missions is, or even if there should be such a thing as missions? One answer would be that love demands it and love defines it. If people all over the world are under condemnation for sin and cut off from eternal life (Eph. 2:2–3, 12; 4:17; 5:6), and if calling on Jesus is their only hope for eternal, joyful fellowship with God (as chap. 4 shows), then love demands missions.

But can love define missions? Not without consulting the strange ways of God. Sometimes the ways of God are not the way we would have done things with our limited views. But God is love, even when his ways are puzzling. It may not look like love for your life if you sold all that you had and bought a barren field. But it might in fact be love from another perspective, namely, that there is a treasure buried in the field. So, of course, love will consult God's perspective on missions. Love will refuse to define missions with a limited human perspective. Love will test its logic by the larger picture of God's ways.

Two Sinking Ocean Liners

The limits of love's wisdom become plain when we imagine missions as a rescue operation during a tragedy at sea.

Suppose there are two ocean liners on the sea, and both begin to sink at the same time with large numbers of people on board who do not know how to swim. There are some lifeboats but not enough. And suppose you are in charge of a team of ten rescuers in two large boats.

You arrive on the scene of the first sinking ship and find yourself surrounded by hundreds of screaming people, some going down before your eyes, some fighting over scraps of debris, others ready to jump into the water from the sinking ship. Several hundred yards away the very same thing is happening to the people on the other ship.

Your heart breaks for the dying people. You long to save as many as you can, so you cry out to your two crews to give every ounce of energy they have. There are five rescuers in each boat, and they are working with all their might. They are saving many. There is lots of room in the rescue boats.

Then someone cries out from the other ship, "Come over and help *us!*" What would love do? Would love go or stay?

I cannot think of any reason that love would leave its life-saving labor and go to the other ship. Love puts no higher value on distant souls than on nearer souls. In fact, love might well reason that in the time it would take to row across the several hundred yards to the other ship, an overall loss of total lives would result.

Love might also reason that the energy of the rescuers would be depleted by rowing between ships, which would possibly result in a smaller number of individuals being saved. Not only that, but from past experience you may know that the people on the other boat were probably all drunk at this time in the evening and would be less cooperative with your saving efforts. This too might mean fewer lives saved.

So love, by itself, may very well refuse to leave its present rescue operation. It may stay at its present work in order to save as many individuals as possible.

This imaginary scene on the sea is not, of course, a perfect picture of the church in the world, if for no other reason than that the rescue potential of the church is *not* fully engaged even where it is. But the point of the illustration still stands: Love alone (from our limited human perspective) may not see the missionary task the way God does.

God May Have Another View

God may have in mind that the aim of the rescue operation should be to gather saved sinners from every people in the world (from *both* ocean liners), even if some of the rescuers must leave a fruitful *reached* people (the first ocean liner) in order to labor among an (possibly less fruitful) *unreached* people (the second ocean liner).

In other words, the task of missions may not be merely to win[1] as many individuals as possible from the most responsive people groups of the world but rather to win individuals from *all* the people groups of the world. It may not be enough to define missions as leaving the safe shore of our own culture to conduct rescue operations on the strange seas of other languages and cultures. Something may need to be added to that definition that impels us to leave one rescue operation to take up another.

This chapter shows that God's call for missions in Scripture *cannot* be defined in terms of crossing cultures to maximize the total number of individuals saved. Rather, God's will for missions is that every people group be reached with the testimony of Christ and that a people be called out for his name from all the nations.[2]

I believe that this definition of missions will in fact result in the greatest possible number of white-hot worshipers for God's Son. But that remains for God to decide. Our responsibility is to define missions his way and then obey. That means we must conduct a careful investigation of how the New Testament portrays the special missionary task of the church. More specifically, we must assess biblically the widespread concept of "unreached peoples" as the focus of missionary activity.

The Indictment of 1974: People Blindness

Since 1974, the task of missions has increasingly focused on evangelizing[3] unreached peoples as opposed to evangelizing unreached territories. That year at the Lausanne Congress on World Evangelization, Ralph Winter shocked and indicted the Western missionary enterprise

---

1. I use the word "win" in the sense that Paul does in 1 Corinthians 9:19–22. The use of "save" in verse 22 shows that this is what he has in mind: to be used by God in love and witness to win people over to faith in Christ and so to save them from sin and condemnation. "For though I am free from all, I have made myself a servant to all, that I might *win* more of them. To the Jews I became as a Jew, in order to *win* Jews. To those under the law I became as one under the law (though not being myself under the law) that I might *win* those under the law. To those outside the law I became as one outside the law (not being outside the law of God but under the law of Christ) that I might *win* those outside the law. To the weak I became weak, that I might *win* the weak. I have become all things to all people, that by all means I might save some."

2. The word "nations" in this chapter does not refer to the modern political state as in the "United Nations" or the "nation" of England. We will see that its biblical meaning has to do with an ethnic group that may or may not have political dimensions.

3. I use the word "evangelize" in the broad New Testament sense of speaking the Good News of Christ and his saving work. The speaking is with a view of bringing about faith and establishing the church of Christ (Rom. 10:14–15; 15:20), but true evangelizing does not depend on a believing response (Heb. 4:6). For a remarkably thorough historical survey of the concept, see David B. Barrett, *Evangelize! A Historical Survey of the Concept* (Birmingham, Ala.: New Hope, 1987).

with what he called "people blindness." Since that time he and others
have relentlessly pressed the "people-group" focus onto the agenda of
most mission-minded churches and agencies. The "shattering truth"
that he revealed at Lausanne was this: In spite of the fact that every
country of the world has been penetrated with the gospel, four out of
five non-Christians are still cut off from the gospel because the barriers are cultural and linguistic, not geographic.

> Why is this fact not more widely known? I'm afraid that all our exulta-
> tion about the fact that every *country* of the world has been penetrated
> has allowed many to suppose that every *culture* has by now been pene-
> trated. This misunderstanding is a malady so widespread that it de-
> serves a special name. Let us call it "people blindness," that is, blindness
> to the existence of separate *peoples* within *countries*—a blindness, I
> might add, which seems more prevalent in the U.S. and among U.S.
> missionaries than anywhere else.[4]

Winter's message was a powerful call for the church of Christ to re-
orient its thinking so that missions would be seen as the task of evangelizing unreached *peoples*, not the task of merely evangelizing more
territories. In a most remarkable way, in the next fifteen years the missionary enterprise responded to this call. In 1989, Winter was able to
write, "Now that the concept of Unreached Peoples has taken hold
very widely, it is immediately possible to make plans . . . with far
greater confidence and precision."[5]

A Milestone Definition, 1982

Probably the most significant unified effort to define "people group"
came in March 1982 as a result of the work of the Lausanne Strategy
Working Group. This meeting defined a "people group" as:

> a significantly large grouping of individuals who perceive themselves to
> have a common affinity for one another because of their shared lan-
> guage, religion, ethnicity, residence, occupation, class or caste, situa-
> tion, etc. or combinations of these. . . . [It is] the largest group within
> which the Gospel can spread as a church planting movement without
> encountering barriers of understanding or acceptance.[6]

4. Ralph D. Winter, "The New Macedonia: A Revolutionary New Era in Mission Begins," in *Perspectives on the World Christian Movement: A Reader*, 3d ed., ed. Ralph D.
Winter and Steven C. Hawthorne (Pasadena, Calif.: William Carey Library, 1999), 346.
5. Ralph Winter, "Unreached Peoples: Recent Developments in the Concept," *Mission Frontiers* (August/September 1989): 18.
6. Ibid., 12.

We should be aware that this definition was developed not merely on the basis of biblical teaching about the specific nature of people groups but also on the basis of what would help missionaries identify and reach various groups. This is a legitimate method for advancing evangelistic strategy. But we need to distinguish it from the method I will use in this chapter.[7]

We also need to make clear at the outset that I am not going to use the term "people group" in a precise sociological way as distinct from "people." I agree with those who say that the biblical concept of "peoples" or "nations" cannot be stretched to include individuals grouped on the basis of things such as occupation, residence, or handicaps. These are sociological groupings that are very relevant for evangelistic strategy but do not figure into defining the *biblical* meaning of "peoples" or "nations." Harley Schreck and David Barrett have proposed distinguishing the sociological category "people group" from the ethnological category "peoples."[8] I agree with the category distinction but have found the terminology to be a linguistic straitjacket that I can't wear. The singular "people" in the English language does not clearly signify a distinctive grouping. Therefore, when I use "people group," I am only calling attention to the group concept over against individuals. The context will make clear the nature of the grouping.

"Test All Things"—Including People-Group Thinking

My aim is to test the people-group focus by the Scriptures. Is the missionary mandate of the Bible (1) a command to reach as many individuals as possible, or (2) a command to reach all the "fields," or (3) a command to reach all the "people groups" of the world, as the Bible defines people groups? Is the emphasis that has dominated discussion since 1974 a biblical teaching, or is it simply a strategic development that gives missions effort a sharper focus?

So we turn now to the basic question of this chapter: Is it biblical to define the missionary task of the church as reaching all the unreached[9] *peoples* of the world? Or is it sufficient to say that missions is simply the effort to reach as many individuals as possible in places different from our own?

7. See note 38 on this difference of perspective and its effects.
8. Harley Schreck and David Barrett, eds., *Unreached Peoples: Clarifying the Task* (Monrovia, Calif.: New Hope, 1987), 6–7.
9. See below in this chapter for a discussion of what reached and unreached means.

The Most Famous Commission

> And Jesus came and said to them, "All authority in heaven and on earth
> has been given to me. Go therefore and make disciples of all nations,
> baptizing them in the name of the Father and of the Son and of the
> Holy Spirit, teaching them to observe all that I have commanded you.
> And behold, I am with you always, to the end of the age."
>
> Matthew 28:18–20

This passage is often called the Great Commission. The first thing
to make clear about it is that it is still binding on the modern church.
It was given not only to the apostles for their ministry but also to the
church for its ministry as long as this age lasts.

The basis for saying this comes from the text itself. The undergird-
ing promise of verse 20 says, "And behold, I am with you always, to
the end of the age." The people referred to in the word "you" cannot
be limited to the apostles, because they died within one generation.
The promise extends to "the end of the age," that is, to the day of judgment at Christ's second coming (cf. Matt. 13:39–40, 49). Jesus is
speaking to the apostles as representatives of the church, which would
endure to the end of the age. He is assuring the church of his abiding
presence and help as long as this age lasts. This is significant because
the promise of verse 20 is given to sustain and encourage the command to make disciples of all nations. Therefore, if the sustaining
promise is expressed in terms that endure to the end of the age, we
may rightly assume that the command to make disciples also endures
to the end of the age.

I conclude then that the Great Commission was given not just to
the apostles but also to the church, which would endure to the end of
the age. This is further buttressed by the authority Jesus claims in
verse 18. He lays claim to "all authority in heaven and on earth." This
enables him to do what he had earlier promised in Matthew 16:18,
when he said, "I will build my church." So the abiding validity of the
Great Commission rests on the ongoing authority of Christ over all
things (Matt. 28:18) and on the purpose of Christ to build his church
(Matt. 16:18) and on his promise to be present and help in the mission
of the church to the end of the age (Matt. 28:20).

Therefore, these words of the Lord are crucial for deciding what the
missionary task of the church should be today. Specifically, the words
"make disciples of all nations" must be closely examined. They contain the very important phrase "all nations," which is often referred to
in the Greek form *panta ta ethnē* (*panta* = all, *ta* = the, *ethnē* = nations). The reason this is such an important phrase is that *ethnē*, when

translated as "nations," sounds like a political or geographic grouping. That is its most common English usage. But this is not what the Greek means, nor does the English always mean this. For example, we say the Cherokee nation or the Sioux nation, which means something like "people with a unifying ethnic identity." In fact, the word "ethnic" comes from the Greek word *ethnos* (singular of *ethnē*). Our inclination then might be to take *panta ta ethnē* as a reference to "all the ethnic groups." "Go and disciple all the ethnic groups."

But this is precisely what needs to be tested by a careful investigation of the wider biblical context and especially the use of *ethnos* in the New Testament and its Old Testament background.

The Singular Use of *Ethnos* in the New Testament

In the New Testament, the singular *ethnos* never refers to an individual.[10] This is a striking fact. Every time the singular *ethnos* does occur it refers to a people group or nation—often the Jewish nation, even though in the plural it is usually translated "Gentiles" in distinction from the Jewish people.[11]

Here are some examples to illustrate the corporate meaning of the singular use of *ethnos*.

Nation *[ethnos]* will rise against nation *[ethnos]*, and kingdom against kingdom, and there will be famines and earthquakes in various places.

Matthew 24:7

Now there were dwelling in Jerusalem Jews, devout men from every nation *[ethnous]* under heaven.

Acts 2:5

There was a man named Simon, who . . . amazed the people *[ethnos]* of Samaria.

Acts 8:9

10. Galatians 2:14 appears to be an exception in the English text ("If you, though a Jew, live like a Gentile and not like a Jew, how can you force the Gentiles to live like Jews?"). But the Greek word here is not *ethnos* but the adverb *ethnikōs*, which means to have the life patterns of Gentiles.

11. Following are all the singular uses in the New Testament: Matt. 21:43; 24:7 (= Mark 13:8 = Luke 21:10); Luke 7:5; 23:2 (both references to the Jewish nation); Acts 2:5 ("Jews from every nation"); 7:7; 8:9; 10:22 ("whole nation of the Jews"), 35; 17:26; 24:2, 10, 17; 26:4; 28:19 (the last five references are to the Jewish nation); John 11:48, 50, 51, 52; 18:35 (all in reference to the Jewish nation); Rev. 5:9; 13:7; 14:6; 1 Peter 2:9. Paul never uses the singular.

You are a chosen race, a royal priesthood, a holy nation [ethnos], a people for his own possession.

1 Peter 2:9

By your blood you ransomed people for God from every tribe and language and people and nation [ethnous].

Revelation 5:9

What this survey of the singular establishes is that the word *ethnos* very naturally and normally carried a corporate meaning in reference to people groups with a certain ethnic identity. In fact, the reference in Acts 2:5 to "every nation" is very close in form to "all the nations" in Matthew 28:19. And in Acts 2:5 it must refer to people groups of some kind. At this stage, therefore, we find ourselves leaning toward a corporate "people group" understanding of "all the nations" in the Great Commission of Matthew 28:19.

The Plural Use of *Ethnos* in the New Testament

Unlike the singular, the plural of *ethnos* does not always refer to people groups. It sometimes simply refers to Gentile individuals.[12] Many instances are ambiguous. What is important to see is that in the plural the word can refer either to an ethnic group or simply to Gentile individuals who may not make up an ethnic group. For example, consider the following texts, which illustrate the meaning of Gentile individuals.

> Acts 13:48—When Paul turns to the Gentiles in Antioch after being rejected by the Jews, Luke says, "And when *the Gentiles* heard this, they began rejoicing and glorifying the word of the Lord." This is a reference not to nations but to the group of Gentile individuals at the synagogue who heard Paul.
>
> 1 Corinthians 12:2—"You know that when you were *pagans*, you were led astray to mute idols." In this verse, "you" refers to the individual Gentile converts at Corinth. It would not make sense to say, "When you were nations . . ."

12. For example, Matt. 6:32; 10:5; 12:21; 20:25; Luke 2:32; 21:24; Acts 9:15; 13:46, 47; 15:7, 14, 23; 18:6; 21:11; 22:21; Rom. 3:29; 9:24; 15:9, 10, 11, 12, 16; 16:26; Gal. 2:9; 3:14; 2 Tim. 4:17; Rev. 14:18; 16:19; 19:15, 20:8; 21:24. When I use the term "Gentile individuals" in this chapter, I do not mean to focus undue attention on specific persons. Rather, I mean to speak of non-Jews in a comprehensive way without reference to their ethnic groupings.

Ephesians 3:6—Paul says that the mystery of Christ is "that *the Gentiles* are fellow heirs, members of the same body." It would not make sense to say that nations are fellow heirs and *members* (a definite reference to individuals) of the same body. Paul's conception is that the local body of Christ has many *individual* members who are *Gentiles*.

These are perhaps sufficient to show that the plural of *ethnos* does not have to mean nation or people group. On the other hand, the plural, like the singular, certainly can, and often does, refer to people groups. For example:

Acts 13:19—Referring to the taking of the Promised Land by Israel, Paul says, "After destroying seven nations *[ethnē]* in the land of Canaan, he gave them their land as an inheritance."

Romans 4:17—"As it is written, 'I have made you the father of many nations.'" Here Paul is quoting Genesis 17:4, where "father of a multitude of nations" does not refer to individuals but to people groups. *Ethnōn* is a Greek translation of the Hebrew *goyim*, which virtually always means nations or people groups. For example, in Deuteronomy 7:1, Moses says that God will clear "away many nations before you, the Hittites, the Girgashites, the Amorites, the Canaanites, the Perizzites, the Hivites, and the Jebusites." The word "nations" here is *goyim* in Hebrew and *ethnē* in Greek.

Revelation 11:9—"For three and a half days some from the peoples and tribes and languages and nations *[ethnōn]* will gaze at their dead bodies." In this sequence, it is clear that "nations" refers to some kind of ethnic grouping, not just to Gentile individuals.

What we have seen then is that in the plural *ethnē* can mean Gentile individuals who may not be part of a single people group, or it can mean (as it always does in the singular) a people group with ethnic identity. This means that we cannot yet be certain which meaning is intended in Matthew 28:19. We cannot yet answer whether the task of missions is merely reaching as many individuals as possible or reaching all the people groups of the world.

Nevertheless, the fact that in the New Testament the singular *ethnos* never refers to an individual but always to a people group should perhaps incline us toward the people-group meaning unless the context leads us to think otherwise. This will be all the more true when we consider the Old Testament context and the impact it had on the writings of John and Paul. But first we should examine the New Testament use of the crucial phrase *panta ta ethnē* ("all the nations").

The Use of *Panta ta Ethnē* in the New Testament

Our immediate concern is with the meaning of *panta ta ethnē* in Matthew 28:19: "Go and make disciples of all nations." Since this is such a crucial phrase in the understanding of missions, and since it is tossed about as a Greek phrase today even in nontechnical writings, it is important to make all the uses of it readily accessible for the non-Greek reader to consider. Therefore, the following discussion provides all the texts in which the combination of *pas* ("all") and *ethnos* ("nation/Gentile") occur in the New Testament, either in the singular ("every nation") or plural ("all nations/Gentiles"). The different forms of *pan, panta, pasin,* and *pantōn* are simply changes in the grammatical case of the same word to agree with the various forms of the noun *ethnos (ethnē, ethnesin).*

Matthew 24:9—"You will be hated by *pantōn tōn ethnōn* for my name's sake."

Matthew 24:14 (= Mark 13:10)—"This gospel of the kingdom will be proclaimed throughout the whole world as a testimony to *pasin tois ethnesin,* and then the end will come."

Matthew 25:32—"Before him will be gathered *panta ta ethnē,* and he will separate people one from another as a shepherd separates the sheep from the goats." (This context seems to demand the meaning "Gentile individuals," not people groups, because it says that Jesus will "separate people from one another as a shepherd separates the sheep from the goats." This is a reference to individuals who are being judged as the "cursed" and the "righteous" who enter hell or eternal life. Cf. verses 41, 46.)

Matthew 28:19—"Make disciples of *panta ta ethnē.*"

Mark 11:17—"My house shall be called a house of prayer for *pasin tois ethnesin.*" (This is a quote from Isaiah 56:7. The Hebrew phrase behind *pasin tois ethnesin* is *lekol ha'ammim,* which has to mean "all peoples" rather than "all people.")

Luke 12:29–30—"Do not seek what you are to eat and what you are to drink, nor be worried. For *panta ta ethnē* of the world seek after these things."

Luke 21:24—"They will fall by the edge of the sword and be led captive among *ta ethnē panta.*" (This warning echoes the words of Ezekiel 32:9, where the corresponding Hebrew word is *goyim,*

which means "nations" or "people groups." See also Deuteronomy 28:64.)

Luke 24:47—"Repentance and forgiveness of sins should be proclaimed in his name to *panta ta ethnē*, beginning from Jerusalem."

Acts 2:5—"Now there were dwelling in Jerusalem Jews, devout men
from *pantos ethnous* under heaven." (This must clearly refer to
people groups rather than individuals. The reference is to various ethnic or national groups from which the diaspora Jews had
come to Jerusalem.)

Acts 10:35—"In *panti ethnei* anyone who fears him and does what is
right is acceptable to him." (Again, this must be a reference to
people groups or nations, not to individual Gentiles, because the
individuals who fear God are "in every nation.")

Acts 14:16—"In past generations he allowed *panta ta ethnē* to walk
in their own ways."

Acts 15:16–17—"I will rebuild the tent of David that has fallen . . .
that the remnant of mankind may seek the Lord, and *panta ta
ethnē* upon whom is called my name upon them." (I render this
verse with this awkwardly literal translation simply to highlight
the fact that this is a quotation from Amos 9:12, which in Greek
follows the Hebrew with similar literalness. Again, the Hebrew
word behind *ethnē* is *goyim*, which means "nations" or "people
groups.")

Acts 17:26—"And he made from one man *pan ethnos* of mankind
to live on all the face of the earth." (As with Acts 2:5 and 10:35,
this is a reference to every people group rather than to individuals because it says that every nation is made up "of mankind." It
would not make sense to say that every individual Gentile was
made up "of mankind." Nor does the suggestion of some that it
means "the whole human race" fit the meaning of *ethnos* or the
context.)[13]

---

13. Following Dibelius this is suggested by F. F. Bruce, *Commentary on the Book of
Acts* (Grand Rapids: Eerdmans, 1954), 358. But Lenski is surely right that the very next
clause in Acts 17:26 militates against such a translation: ". . . having determined allotted periods and boundaries of their dwelling place." This naturally refers, as John Stott
also says, to various ethnic groups with "the epoches of their history and the limits of
their territory." R. C. H. Lenski, *The Interpretation of the Acts of the Apostles* (Minneapolis: Augsburg, 1934), 729; John Stott, *The Spirit, The Church, and the World* (Downers
Grove, Ill.: InterVarsity, 1990), 286. The point of the verse is to take the air out of the
sails of ethnic pride in Athens. All the other *ethnē* have descended from the same "one"
as the Greeks, and not only that, but whatever time and territory a people has, it is
God's sovereign doing and nothing to boast in. "Both the history and the geography of
each nation are ultimately under [God's] control" (Stott).

Romans 1:5—"We have received grace and apostleship to bring about the obedience of faith for the sake of his name among *pasin tois ethnesin.*"

Galatians 3:8—"And the Scripture, foreseeing that God would justify the Gentiles by faith, preached the gospel beforehand to Abraham, saying, 'In you shall *panta ta ethnē* be blessed.'" (This is a quote from Genesis 12:3 that clearly refers to people groups. The corresponding Hebrew phrase, *kol mishpehot*, means "all families." See discussion below on Genesis 12:3 for more concerning Paul's translation.)

2 Timothy 4:17—"But the Lord stood by me and strengthened me, so that through me the message might be fully proclaimed and *panta ta ethnē* might hear it."

Revelation 12:5—"She gave birth to a male child, one who is to rule *panta ta ethnē* with a rod of iron." (Cf. Ps. 2:9. The Old Testament allusion makes it likely that the Old Testament reference to nations in Psalm 2:8 is intended here as well.)

Revelation 15:4—"Who shall not fear, O Lord, and glorify your name? For you alone are holy. *Panta ta ethnē* will come and worship you, for your righteous acts have been revealed." (Cf. Ps. 86:9; 85:9 Lxx.[14] Again, the Old Testament allusion suggests a corporate understanding of nations coming to worship the Lord.)

Out of these eighteen uses of *panta ta ethnē* (or its variant), only the one in Matthew 25:32 seems to demand the meaning "Gentile individuals." (See the comments above on that verse.) Three others demand the people-group meaning on the basis of the context (Acts 2:5; 10:35; 17:26). Six others require the people-group meaning on the basis of the Old Testament connection (Mark 11:17; Luke 21:24; Acts 15:17; Gal. 3:8; Rev. 12:5; 15:4). The remaining eight uses (Matt. 24:9; 24:14; 28:19; Luke 12:30; 24:47; Acts 14:16; Rom. 1:5; 2 Tim. 4:17) could go either way.

What can we conclude so far concerning the meaning of *panta ta ethnē* in Matthew 28:19 and its wider missionary significance?

The singular use of *ethnos* in the New Testament always refers to a people group. The plural use of *ethnos* sometimes must be a people group and sometimes must refer to Gentile individuals but usually can go either way. The phrase *panta ta ethnē* must refer to Gentile individuals only once but must refer to people groups nine times. The remaining eight uses may refer to people groups. The combination of

14. See note 38 in chapter 4.

these results suggests that the meaning of *panta ta ethnē* leans heavily in the direction of "all the nations (people groups)." It cannot be said with certainty that this phrase always carries this meaning wherever it is used, but it is far more likely that it does in view of what we have seen so far.

This likelihood increases even more when we realize that the phrase *panta ta ethnē* occurs in the Greek Old Testament nearly one hundred times and virtually never carries the meaning "Gentile individuals" but always carries the meaning "all the nations" in the sense of people groups outside Israel.[15] That the New Testament vision for missions has this focus will appear even more probable when we examine the Old Testament background.

The Old Testament Hope

The Old Testament is replete with promises and expectations that God would one day be worshiped by people from all the nations of the world. These promises form the explicit foundation of New Testament missionary vision.

All the Families of the Earth Will Be Blessed

Foundational for the missionary vision of the New Testament was the promise that God made to Abram in Genesis 12:1–3:

> Now the LORD said to Abram, "Go from your country and your kindred and your father's house to the land that I will show you. And I will make of you a great nation and I will bless you and make your name great, so that you will be a blessing. I will bless those who bless you, and him who dishonors you I will curse, and in you all the families of the earth shall be blessed."

This promise for universal blessing to the "families" of the earth is essentially repeated in Genesis 18:18; 22:18; 26:4; 28:14.

15. My survey was done searching for all case variants of *panta ta ethnē* in the plural. The following texts are references to Greek Old Testament (LXX) verse and chapter divisions, which occasionally do not correspond to the Hebrew and English versions: Gen. 18:18; 22:18; 26:4; Exod. 19:5; 23:22; 23:27; 33:16; Lev. 20:24, 26; Deut. 2:25; 4:6, 19, 27; 7:6, 7, 14; 10:15; 11:23; 14:2; 26:19; 28:1, 10, 37, 64; 29:23; 30:1, 3; Josh. 4:24; 23:3, 4, 17, 18; 1 Sam. 8:20; 1 Chron. 14:17; 18:11; 2 Chron. 7:20; 32:23; 33:9; Ezra 25:8; 38:16; 39:21, 23; Neh. 6:16; Esth. 3:8; Pss. 9:8; 46:2; 48:2; 58:6, 9; 71:11, 17; 81:8; 85:9; 112:4; 116:1; 117:10; Isa. 2:2; 14:12, 26; 25:7; 29:8; 34:2; 36:20; 40:15, 17; 43:9; 52:10; 56:7; 61:11; 66:18, 20; Jer. 3:17; 9:25; 25:9; 32:13, 15; 33:6; 35:11, 14; 43:2; 51:8; Dan. 3:2, 7; 7:14; Joel 4:2, 11, 12; Amos 9:12; Obad. 1:15, 16; Hab. 2:5; Hag. 2:7; Zech. 7:14; 12:3, 9; 14:2, 16, 18, 19; Mal. 2:9; 3:12.

In 12:3 and 28:14, the Hebrew phrase for "all the families" *(kol mishpehot)* is rendered in the Greek Old Testament by *pasai hai phylai*. The word *phylai* means "tribes" in most contexts. But *mishpahah* can be and usually is smaller than a tribe.[16] For example, when Achan sinned, Israel is examined in decreasing order of size: first by tribe, then by *mishpahah* ("family"), then by household (Josh. 7:14).

So the blessing of Abraham is intended by God to reach to fairly small groupings of people. We need not define these groups with precision in order to feel the impact of this promise. The other three repetitions of this Abrahamic promise in Genesis use the phrase "all the nations" (Hebrew: *kol goye*), which the Septuagint translates with the familiar *panta ta ethnē* in each case (18:18; 22:18; 26:4). This again strongly suggests that the term *panta ta ethnē* in missionary contexts refers to people groups rather than to Gentile individuals.

The New Testament explicitly cites this particular Abrahamic promise twice. In Acts 3:25, Peter says to the Jewish crowd, "You are the sons of the prophets and of the covenant that God made with your fathers, saying to Abraham, 'And in your offspring shall all the families of the earth be blessed.'" The Greek phrase in Acts 3:25 for "all the families" is *pasai hai patriai*. This is an independent translation of Genesis 12:3, differing from both the Greek Old Testament *(pasai hai phylai)* and the way Paul translates it in Galatians 3:8 *(panta ta ethnē)*.[17] But by choosing another word that refers to people groups *(patriai)*, the writer confirms that the promise was understood in the early church in terms of people groups, not in terms of Gentile individuals. *Patria* can be a subgroup of a tribe or more generally a clan or tribe.

The other New Testament quotation of the Abrahamic promise is in Galatians 3:6–8:

> Just as Abraham "believed God, and it was counted to him as righteousness?" . . . Know then that it is those of faith who are the sons of Abraham. And the Scripture, foreseeing that God would justify the Gentiles

16. Karl Ludwig Schmidt argues that the *mishpehot* are "smaller clan-like societies within the main group or nation." Gerhard Kittle, ed., Geoffrey Bromiley, trans. *Theological Dictionary of the New Testament*, vol. 2 (Grand Rapids: Eerdmans, 1964), 365.

17. Paul may have chosen to use *panta ta ethnē* because this is how the Greek Old Testament translates the promise of God to Abraham in three of its five occurrences (Gen. 18:18; 22:18; 26:4; but not 12:3 and 28:14, which translate it *pasai hai phylai*). But Paul's words do not correspond exactly with any of these five texts, so he may well have been giving his own composite translation from the Hebrew.

[ta ethnē] by faith, preached the gospel beforehand to Abraham, saying, "In you shall all the nations *[panta ta ethnē]* be blessed."

Interestingly, all English versions translate the word *ethnē* differently in its two uses in verse 8: in the first case, "Gentiles," and in the next, "nations."

One could try to argue that Paul's use of the promise to support the justification of individual Gentiles means that he did not see people groups in the Abrahamic promise, since it is individuals who are justified. But that is not a necessary conclusion. More likely is the possibility that Paul recognized the Old Testament meaning of *panta ta ethnē* in Genesis 18:18 (the closest Old Testament parallel) and drew the inference that individual Gentiles are necessarily implied. So the English versions are correct to preserve the two meanings in the two uses of *ethnē* in Galatians 3:8.

Paul's use of the promise warns us not to get so swept up into people-group thinking that we forget that the "blessing of Abraham" is indeed experienced by *individuals,* or not at all.

What we may conclude from the wording of Genesis 12:3 and its use in the New Testament is that God's purpose for the world is that the blessing of Abraham, namely, the salvation achieved through Jesus Christ, the seed of Abraham, would reach to all the ethnic people groups of the world. This would happen as people in each group put their faith in Christ and thus become "sons of Abraham" (Gal. 3:7) and heirs of the promise (Gal. 3:29). This event of individual salvation as persons trust Christ will happen among "all the nations." The size and makeup of the nations or people groups referred to in this promise and its New Testament usage are not precise. But the words point to fairly small groupings, since the reference to "all the nations" in Genesis 18:18 (= Gal. 3:8) is an echo of "all the families" in Genesis 12:3.

The smallness of the people groups envisioned in the Old Testament hope is brought out again by the phrase "families of the nations" in Psalms 22:27 (21:28 LXX) and 96:7 (95:7 LXX).

All the ends of the earth shall remember and turn to the LORD, and *all the families of the nations* shall worship before you. For kingship belongs to the LORD, and he rules over the nations.

Psalm 22:27–28

The phrase "all the families of the nations" is *pasai hai patriai tōn ethnōn.* So the hope in view is not just that "all the nations" *(panta ta ethnē)* would respond to the truth and worship God but that even smaller groupings, "all the families of the nations," would. "Family" does not carry our modern meaning of nuclear family but something more like clan.[18] This will be confirmed when we look at the hope expressed in Revelation 5:9, where worshipers have been redeemed not only from every "nation" *(ethnous)* but also from every "tribe" *(phylēs)*.

The Hope of the Nations

One of the best ways to discern the scope of the Great Commission as Jesus gave it and the apostles pursued it is to immerse ourselves in the atmosphere of hope that they felt in reading their Bible, the Old Testament. One overwhelming aspect of this hope is its expectation that the truth of God would reach to all the people groups of the world and that these groups would come and worship the true God. This hope was expressed in people-group terminology again and again (peoples, nations, tribes, families, etc.). Here is a sampling from the Psalms and Isaiah of the kind of hope that set the stage for Jesus' Great Commission. The texts fall into four categories of exhortation, promise, prayers, and plans.

"Declare His Glory among the Nations!"

The first category of texts expressing the hope of the nations is a collection of *exhortations* that God's glory be declared and praised among the nations and by the nations.

Sing praises to the Lord, who sits enthroned in Zion! Tell among the *peoples* his deeds!

Psalm 9:11

Clap your hands, *all peoples!* Shout to God with loud songs of joy!

Psalm 47:1

Bless our God, O *peoples;* let the sound of his praise be heard.

Psalm 66:8

Declare his glory among the nations, his marvelous works among *all the peoples!*

Psalm 96:3

Ascribe to the Lord, *O families of the peoples,* ascribe to the Lord glory and strength! ... Say among the nations, "The Lord reigns! Yes, the

18. The evidence for this would be, for example, the repeated use in the Greek Old Testament of the phrase "houses (or households) of the families," which shows that the "family" *(patria)* is a larger grouping than a household. Cf. Exod. 6:17; Num. 1:44; 3:24; 18:1; 25:14–15; Josh. 22:14; 1 Chron. 23:11; 24:6; 2 Chron. 35:5; Ezra 2:59. See below on "How Small Is a Family?"

world is established; it shall never be moved; he will judge the *peoples* with equity."

Psalm 96:7, 10

Oh give thanks to the LORD; call upon his name; make known his deeds among the *peoples!*

Psalm 105:1

Praise the LORD, *all nations!* Extol him, *all peoples!*

Psalm 117:1

And you will say in that day: "Give thanks to the LORD, call upon his name, make known his deeds among the *peoples,* proclaim that his name is exalted.

Isaiah 12:4

Draw near, O *nations,* to hear, and give attention, O *peoples!* Let the earth hear, and all that fills it; the world, and all that comes from it.

Isaiah 34:1

"Nations Shall Come to Your Light!"

The second category of texts expressing the hope of the nations is a collection of *promises* that the nations will one day worship the true God.

I will make the *nations* your heritage.

Psalm 2:8; cf. 111:6

I will cause your name to be remembered in all generations; therefore *nations* will praise you[19] forever and ever.

Psalm 45:17

The *princes of the peoples* gather as the people of the God of Abraham. For the shields of the earth belong to God; he is highly exalted!

Psalm 47:9

All the nations you have made shall come and worship before you, O LORD, and shall glorify your name.

Psalm 86:9

The LORD records as he registers the *peoples,* "This one was born there."

Psalm 87:6

19. This is a psalm to the king and refers in its final application to Christ the Messiah, as is shown by the use made of verse 7 in Hebrews 1:9.

Nations will fear the name of the Lord, and all the kings of the earth will fear your glory.

> Psalm 102:15

Peoples gather together, and kingdoms, to worship the Lord.

> Psalm 102:22

He has shown his people the power of his works, in giving them the inheritance of the *nations*.

> Psalm 111:6

In that day the root of Jesse, who shall stand as a signal for the peoples— of him shall the *nations* inquire, and his resting place shall be glorious.

> Isaiah 11:10

On this mountain the Lord of hosts will make for *all peoples* a feast of rich foods, a feast of well-aged wine, of rich food full of marrow, of aged wine well refined. And he will swallow up on this mountain the covering that is cast over all peoples, the veil that is spread over all nations.

> Isaiah 25:6–7

[The Lord] says: "It is too light a thing that you should be my servant to raise up the tribes of Jacob and to bring back the preserved of Israel; I will make you as a light for the *nations*, that my salvation may reach to the end of the earth."

> Isaiah 49:6

My righteousness draws near, my salvation has gone out, and my arms will judge the *peoples;* the coastlands hope for me, and for my arm they wait.

> Isaiah 51:5

The Lord has bared his holy arm before the eyes of all the *nations*, and all the ends of the earth shall see the salvation of our God.

> Isaiah 52:10

So shall [my Servant] sprinkle many *nations;* kings shall shut their mouths because of him; for that which has not been told them they see, and that which they have not heard they understand.

> Isaiah 52:15

Behold, you shall call a *nation* that you do not know, and a *nation* that did not know you shall run to you, because of the Lord your God, and of the Holy One of Israel, for he has glorified you.

> Isaiah 55:5

These I will bring to my holy mountain, and make them joyful in my house of prayer; their burnt offerings and their sacrifices will be accepted on my altar; for my house shall be called a house of prayer for all *peoples*.

Isaiah 56:7

And *nations* shall come to your light, and kings to the brightness of your rising.

Isaiah 60:3

For I know their works and their thoughts, and the time is coming to gather *all nations and tongues*. And they shall come and shall see my glory.

Isaiah 66:18

The time is coming to gather *all nations and tongues*. And they shall come and shall see my glory, and I will set a sign among them. And from them I will send survivors to the nations, to Tarshish, Pul, and Lud, who draw the bow, to Tubal and Javan, to the coastlands afar off, that have not heard my fame or seen my glory. And they shall declare my glory among the nations.

Isaiah 66:18–19

"Let All the Peoples Praise You, O God!"

The third category of texts that express the hope of the nations does so with confident *prayers* that God be praised among the nations.

May God be gracious to us and bless us and make his face to shine upon us, that your way may be known on earth, your saving power among *all nations*. Let *the peoples* praise you, O God; let all the peoples praise you! Let the nations be glad and sing for joy, for you judge the peoples with equity and guide the nations upon earth. Let the peoples praise you, O God; let *all the peoples* praise you!

Psalm 67:1–5

May all kings fall down before him, *all nations* serve him!

Psalm 72:11

May his name endure forever, his fame continue as long as the sun! May people be blessed in him, *all nations* call him blessed!

Psalm 72:17

"I Will Sing Praises to You among the Nations"

The fourth category of texts that express the hope of the nations announces the *plans* of the psalmist to do his part in making God's greatness known among the nations.

For this I will praise you, O LORD, among the *nations,* and sing to your name.

Psalm 18:49

I will give thanks to you, O Lord, among the *peoples;* I will sing praises to you among the *nations.*

Psalm 57:9

I will give thanks to you, O LORD, among the *peoples;* I will sing praises to you among the *nations.*

Psalm 108:3

Blessed to Be a Blessing

What these texts demonstrate is that the blessing of forgiveness and salvation that God had granted to Israel was meant eventually to reach all the people groups of the world. Israel was blessed in order to be a blessing among the nations. This is expressed best in Psalm 67:1–2: "May God be gracious to us and bless us and make his face to shine upon us, [Why?] that your way may be known on earth, your saving power among *all nations.*" Blessing came to Israel as a means of reaching the nations. This is the hope of the Old Testament: The blessings of salvation are for the nations.

The Missionary God versus the Reluctant Prophet

One of the most vivid Old Testament confirmations and illustrations of God's saving purpose for the nations is found in the Book of Jonah. The prophet was commissioned to preach to the pagan city of Nineveh. He tried to run away because he knew God would be gracious to the people and forgive them. The point of the book is not the fish. It's about missions and racism and ethnocentrism. The point is: Be merciful like God, not miserly like Jonah.

Nineveh did in fact repent at the begrudging preaching of Jonah. When God saw the repentance of Nineveh, "God relented of the disaster that he had said he would do to them, and he did not do it" (Jonah 3:10). This is what Jonah was afraid of.

It displeased Jonah exceedingly, and he was angry. And he prayed to the LORD and said, "O LORD, is not this what I said when I was yet in my country? That is why I made haste to flee to Tarshish; for I knew that you are a gracious God and merciful, slow to anger and abounding in steadfast love, and relenting from disaster. Therefore now, O LORD, please take my life from me, for it is better for me to die than to live."

Jonah 4:1–3

Jonah is not the model missionary. His life is an example of how not to be. As he sulks on the outskirts of town, God appoints a plant to grow up over Jonah to give him shade. When the plant withers, Jonah pities the plant! So God comes to him with these words: "You pity the plant, for which you did not labor, nor did you make it grow, which came into being in a night and perished in a night. And should not I pity Nineveh, that great city, in which there are more than 120,000 persons who do not know their right hand from their left, and also much cattle?" (Jonah 4:10–11).

The missionary implications of Jonah are not merely that God is more ready to be merciful to the nations than his people are but also that Jesus identifies himself as "something greater than Jonah" (Matt. 12:39–41). He is greater not only because his resurrection is greater than surviving a fish's belly but also because he stands in harmony with the mercy of God and extends it now to *all the nations*. Thomas Carlisle's poem "You Jonah" closes with these lines:

> And Jonah stalked
> to his shaded seat
> and waited for God
> to come around
> to his way of thinking.
> And God is still waiting for a host of Jonahs
> in their comfortable houses
> to come around
> to his way of loving.[20]

To see what power this Old Testament hope had on the missionary vision of the New Testament, we turn now to the apostle Paul and his idea of the missionary task. The Old Testament hope is the explicit foundation of his life's work as a missionary.

Paul's Idea of the Missionary Task

We examined Paul's use of Genesis 12:3 (Gal. 3:8) earlier in this chapter. He saw the promise that in Abraham all the nations would be blessed, and he reasoned that Christ was the true offspring of Abraham and thus the heir of the promises (Gal. 3:16). Further, he reasoned that all who are united to Christ by faith also become sons of Abraham and heirs of the promise. "It is those of faith who are the sons of Abraham. . . . If you are Christ's, then you are Abraham's off-

---

20. Quoted in Johannes Verkuyl, "The Biblical Foundation of the Worldwide Mission Mandate," in *Perspectives on the World Christian Movement*, 33.

spring, heirs according to promise" (Gal. 3:7, 29). This is how Paul
saw Abraham's blessing coming to the nations. It came through
Christ, who was the seed of Abraham. By faith people are united to
Christ and inherit the blessing of Abraham. "Christ redeemed us from
the curse of the law . . . that in Christ Jesus the blessing of Abraham
might come to the Gentiles" (Gal. 3:13–14). So the promise of Genesis
12:3 comes true as the missionaries of the Christian church extend the
message of the gospel to all the families of the earth.

How Would Abraham Be the Father of Many Nations?

But Paul saw another connection between the promise to Abraham
and Paul's own calling to reach the nations. He read in Genesis 17:4–5
that God promised to make Abraham the father of a multitude of nations. "Behold, my covenant is with you, and you shall be *the father of
a multitude of nations*. No longer shall your name be called Abram,
but your name shall be Abraham, for I have made you *the father of a
multitude of nations*."

We saw earlier that "nations" here refers to people groups, not Gentile individuals. But how was this promise supposed to come true?
How could a Jew become the father of a multitude of nations? It
would not be enough to say that Abraham became the great-grandfa-
ther of the twelve tribes of Israel plus the father of Ishmael and his de-
scendants plus the grandfather of Esau and the Edomites. Fourteen
does not make a multitude.

Paul's answer to this was that all who believe in Christ become the
children of Abraham. In this way, Abraham becomes the father of a
multitude of nations, because believers will be found in every nation
as missionaries reach all the unreached people groups. Paul argues
like this: In Romans 4:11, he points out that Abraham received circumcision as the sign of righteousness which he had by faith before
he was circumcised. "The purpose was to make *him the father of all
who believe* without being circumcised, so that righteousness would
be counted to them as well." In other words, the decisive thing that
happened to Abraham in his relation to God happened before he received the distinguishing mark of the Jewish people, circumcision. So
true spiritual sonship to Abraham is to share his faith, not his Jewish
distinctives.

The way Abraham becomes the father of many nations is by those
nations coming to share his faith and being united to the same source
of blessing that flows through the covenant God made with him. So
Paul says in Romans 4:16–17, "That is why it depends on faith, in order that the promise may rest on grace and be guaranteed to all his
offspring—not only to the adherent of the law [that is, Jews] but also

to the one who shares the faith of Abraham [that is, the non-Jewish nations], who is the father of us all, as it is written, 'I have made you the father of many nations.'"

When Paul read that Abraham would be made "the father of many nations," he heard the Great Commission. These nations would come into their sonship and enjoy the blessing of Abraham only if missionaries reached them with the gospel of salvation by faith in Jesus Christ. It is not surprising then that Paul supports his own missionary calling with other Old Testament promises that predicted the reaching of the nations with God's light and salvation.

"I Have Set You to Be a Light to the Nations"

For example, in Acts 13:47, Paul's explanation of his ministry to the Gentile nations is rooted in the promise of Isaiah 49:6 that God would make his servant a light to the nations. As Paul preached in the synagogue of Antioch of Pisidia on his first missionary journey, the Jews "were filled with jealousy and began to contradict what was spoken by Paul, reviling him" (Acts 13:45). So Paul and Barnabas turned away from the synagogue and focused their ministry on the people from other people groups. To give an account of this decision, Paul cites Isaiah 49:6: "Since you thrust [the Word of God] aside and judge yourselves unworthy of eternal life, behold, we are turning to the Gentiles. For so the Lord has commanded us, saying, 'I have made you a light for the Gentiles [*ethnōn*, "nations"], that you may bring salvation to the ends of the earth'" (Acts 13:46–47).

It is difficult to know why the English versions do not preserve the Old Testament sense of Isaiah 49:6 and translate, "I have made you a light for the *nations*." The Hebrew word in Isaiah 49:6 is *goyim*, which means people groups, not Gentile individuals. Then Paul would be doing just what he apparently did in Galatians 3:8. He would be drawing a necessary inference about individual Gentiles from an Old Testament reference to nations. Thus, Paul's own missionary vision was guided by meditating not only on the promises to Abraham but also on the wider Old Testament hope that salvation would come to all the nations.

Paul's Passion for Unreached Peoples

This is remarkably confirmed in Romans 15. Here it becomes crystal clear that Paul saw his missionary calling as reaching more and more people groups, not just more and more Gentile individuals.

In Romans 15:8–9, Paul states the twofold purpose for Christ's coming. "For I tell you that Christ became a servant to the circumcised [that is, became incarnate as a Jew] to show God's truthfulness, in order [1] *to confirm the promises given to the patriarchs*, and in order [2] that *the Gentiles* [ta ethnē] *might glorify God for his mercy."* The first purpose for Christ's coming was to prove that God is truthful and faithful in keeping, for example, the promises made to Abraham. The second purpose for Christ's coming is that the nations might glorify God for his mercy.

These two purposes overlap since clearly one of the promises made to the patriarchs was that the blessing of Abraham would come to "all the families of the earth." This is in perfect harmony with what we saw of the Old Testament hope. *Israel* is blessed that the *nations* might be blessed (Psalm 67). In the same way, Christ comes to Israel so that the nations might receive mercy and give God glory.

Saturated with the Hope of the Nations

To support this claim of God's purpose for the nations, Paul gathers four Old Testament quotations about the *ethnē*, all of which in their Old Testament context refer to nations, not just to Gentile individuals.

As it is written, "Therefore I will praise you among the *nations [ethne-sin]* and sing to your name."

Romans 15:9 = Psalm 18:49,
author's translation

Rejoice, O *nations [ethnē]*, with his people.

Romans 15:10 = Deuteronomy 32:43,
author's translation

Praise the Lord, all you *nations [panta ta ethnē]*, and let all the peoples praise him.

Romans 15:11 = Psalm 117:1,
author's translation

The root of Jesse will come, even he who arises to rule the *nations [ethnōn]*; in him will the *nations [ethnē]* hope.

Romans 15:12 = Isaiah 11:10,
author's translation

What is so remarkable about this series of texts that Paul strings together is that Paul either had them memorized or took the trouble to find them in the Old Testament—without a concordance! Either way it shows that he was intent on seeing his missionary calling in the light of the Old Testament hope that all the nations would be reached with the gospel. The people-group focus of these texts is unmistakable from the Old Testament context.

From Jerusalem to Illyricum: The Work Is Finished!

What we see next, therefore, is how the people-group focus governed Paul's missionary practice. Was his aim to win as many Gentile individuals as possible or to reach as many people groups or nations as possible? Romans 15:18–21 gives a startling answer:

> For I will not venture to speak of anything except what Christ has accomplished through me to bring the Gentiles [ethnōn, "nations"], to obedience—by word and deed, by the power of signs and wonders, by the power of the Spirit of God—so that *from Jerusalem and all the way around to Illyricum I have fulfilled the ministry of the gospel of Christ;* and thus I make it my ambition to preach the gospel, *not where Christ has already been named,* lest I build on someone else's foundation, but as it is written, "Those who have never been told of him will see, and those who have never heard will understand."

Literally, Paul says, "From Jerusalem and around to Illyricum I have *fulfilled [peplērōkenai]* the gospel." What can that possibly mean? We know that there were thousands of souls yet to be saved in that region because this was Paul's and Peter's assumption when they wrote letters to the churches in those regions. It is a huge area that stretches from southern Palestine to northern Italy. Yet Paul says he has *fulfilled the gospel* in that whole region, even though his work of evangelism is only ten or fifteen years old.

We know that Paul believed work was still needed there because he left Timothy in Ephesus (1 Tim. 1:3) and Titus in Crete (Titus 1:5) to do the work. Nevertheless, he says he *has fulfilled the gospel* in the whole region. In fact, he goes so far as to say in Romans 15:23–24, "But now, since *I no longer have any room for work in these regions* . . . I hope to see you in passing as I go to Spain." This is astonishing! How can he say not only that he has fulfilled the gospel in that region but also that he has no more room for work? He is finished and going to Spain (Rom. 15:24). What does this mean?

It means that Paul's conception of the *missionary task* is not merely the winning of more and more people to Christ (which he could have done very efficiently in these familiar regions) but the reaching of more and more peoples or nations. His focus was not primarily on new geographic areas. Rather, he was gripped by the vision of unreached peoples. Romans 15:9–12 (just quoted) shows that his mind was saturated with Old Testament texts that relate to the hope of the nations.

Driven by Prophetic Vision of Hope

What was really driving Paul when he said in Romans 15:20 that his aim is to preach not where Christ has been named *"lest I build on someone else's foundation"*? One could uncharitably assume a kind of ego that likes to be able to take all the credit for a church-planting effort. But this is not the Paul we know from Scripture, nor is it what the context suggests.

The next verse (Rom. 15:21) shows what drives Paul. The Old Testament conception of God's worldwide purpose gives Paul his vision as a pioneer missionary. He is driven by a prophetic vision of hope. He quotes Isaiah 52:15: "Those who have never been told of him will see, and those who have never heard will understand."

In the Old Testament, these words are immediately preceded by, "So shall he sprinkle *many nations [ethnē polla]*; kings shall shut their mouths because of him" (Isa. 52:15). No doubt Paul reflected on the fact that his commission from the Lord came to him in similar words. In a close parallel to Isaiah 52:15, the risen Lord Jesus had said to Paul that he was "to carry [Christ's] name before the *Gentiles [ethnōn,* "nations"] and *kings*" (Acts 9:15).

In other words, Paul was driven by a personal commission from the Lord that was richly buttressed and filled out with a prophetic vision of hope. He was gripped by the Old Testament purpose of God to bless all the nations of the earth (Gal. 3:8), to be praised by all the peoples (Rom. 15:11), to send salvation to the end of the earth (Acts 13:47), to make Abraham the father of many nations (Rom. 4:17), and to be understood in every group where he is not known (Rom. 15:21).[21]

So Paul's conception of his specifically missionary task was that he must press on beyond the regions and peoples where Christ is now preached to places such as Spain and to peoples "who have never been told of him." God's missionary "grace" for Paul was that he be a foundation-layer in more and more places and peoples. His aim was not to reach as many Gentile individuals as he could but to reach as many unreached peoples as he could. This was Paul's specific missionary vision.

Obedience for the Sake of His Name among All the Nations

Against this backdrop, the missionary statements at the beginning and end of the Book of Romans take on a distinct people-group coloring. Earlier we said that *panta ta ethnē* in these two verses is ambiguous. But from

---

21. To these reflections could be added Paul's crucial words in Romans 10:14–15 concerning the necessity of people being sent so that they can preach so that people can hear so that they can believe so that they can call on the Lord so that they can be saved. See the discussion of these verses in chapter 4.

what we have seen now, from the phrase's use in the Old Testament and from Paul's dependence on that Old Testament hope, it is likely that Paul has in view nations or people groups and not just Gentile individuals.

> Through [Christ] we have received grace and apostleship to bring about the obedience of faith for the sake of his name among *all the nations [pasin tois ethnesin]*.
>
> Romans 1:5

> [The mystery] has now been disclosed and through the prophetic writings has been made known to *all nations [panta ta ethnē]*, according to the command of the eternal God, to bring about the obedience of faith.
>
> Romans 16:26

Paul saw his special missionary "grace and apostleship" as one of God's appointed means of fulfilling the "command" that the obedience of faith be pursued among all the nations. To this he gave his life.

John's Vision of the Missionary Task

The vision of the missionary task in the writings of the apostle John confirms that Paul's grasp of the Old Testament hope of reaching all the peoples was not unique among the apostles. What emerges from Revelation and the Gospel of John is a vision that assumes the central missionary task of reaching people groups, not just Gentile individuals.

The decisive text is Revelation 5:9–10. John is given a glimpse of the climax of redemption as redeemed people worship at the throne of God. The composition of that assembly is crucial.

> [The four living creatures and the twenty-four elders] sang a new song, saying, "Worthy are you to take the scroll and to open its seals, for you were slain, and by your blood you ransomed people for God *from every tribe and language and people and nation,* and you have made them a kingdom and priests to our God, and they shall reign on the earth."

The missionary vision behind this scene is that the task of the church is to gather the ransomed from all peoples, languages, tribes, and nations.[22] All peoples must be reached because God has appointed people

22. One cannot help but sense that John means for us to see a great reversal of the idolatry so prevalent on the earth, expressed, for example, in Daniel 3:7. Nebuchadnezzar had erected an idol and called everyone to worship it. The words used to describe the extent of that worship are almost identical to the words John uses in Revelation 5:9 to describe the extent of the true worship of God: "All the peoples, nations, and languages fell down and worshiped the golden image that King Nebuchadnezzar had set up."

to believe the gospel whom he has ransomed through the death of his Son. The design of the atonement prescribes the design of mission strategy. And the design of the atonement (Christ's ransom, verse 9) is *universal* in the sense that it extends to all peoples and *definite* in that it effectually ransoms some from each of those peoples. Therefore, the missionary task is to gather the ransomed from all the peoples through preaching the gospel.

Gathering the Scattered Children

This understanding of John's vision of missions is powerfully confirmed from his Gospel. In John 11:50–52, Caiaphas, the high priest, admonishes the irate Jewish council to get Jesus out of the way because "it is better for you that one man should die for the people, not that the whole nation should perish." Then John comments on this word from Caiaphas. His words are crucial for understanding John's missionary vision. John says:

> [Caiaphas] did not say this of his own accord, but being high priest that year he prophesied that Jesus would die for the nation, and not for the nation only, but also *to gather into one the children of God who are scattered abroad.*

This ties in remarkably well with John's conception of missions in Revelation 5:9. There it says that Christ's death ransomed men "from every tribe and language and people and nation." Here in John 11:52 it says that Christ's death gathers the children of God who are scattered among all those nations. In other words, both texts picture the missionary task as gathering in those who are ransomed by Christ. John calls them "the children of God."

Therefore, "scattered" (in John 11:52) is to be taken in its fullest sense: The "children of God" will be found as widely scattered as there are *peoples* of the earth. The missionary task is to reach them in every tribe, language, people, and nation. The way they are to be reached is by the preaching of missionaries. This is what Jesus implies when he says in John 17:20, "I do not ask for these only, but also for those who will believe in me through their word." This parallels John 11:52, which says that Jesus did not die for the nation only but to gather into one the children of God who are scattered abroad. The saving power of his death will extend to people in all the nations of the world, but it will do so only through the word of those whom he sends.

I Must Bring the Other Sheep Also!

The same conception also lies behind the missionary text in John 10:16. Jesus says, "I have other sheep that are not of this fold. I must bring them also, and they will listen to my voice." "This fold" refers to the people of Israel. The "other sheep" refers to the "children of God" who are scattered abroad (John 11:52). These are the "ransomed from every tribe" in Revelation 5:9. Therefore, the words "I *must* bring them also" are a very strong affirmation that the Lord *will* see his missionary purpose completed. He will gather his "sheep" or "the children of God" or the "ransomed" from all the peoples of the earth. As he says in Matthew 16:18, he will build his church.

Thus, the Gospel of John lends tremendous force to the missionary purpose and missionary certainty implied in Revelation 5:9. Jesus has *ransomed* persons in all the peoples of the world. He *died* to gather these "children of God" who are scattered among all the peoples. Therefore, he *must* bring all these wandering sheep into his fold! And they will be brought in through the Word preached by his messengers.

Again and Again: Nations, Tribes, Peoples, and Languages

Four other passages from Revelation confirm that John understands the task of missions as reaching all the people groups of the world so that the redeemed can be gathered in.

> After this I looked, and behold, a great multitude that no one could number, from every nation, from *all tribes and peoples and languages*, standing before the throne and before the Lamb, clothed in white robes, with palm branches in their hands, and crying out with a loud voice, "Salvation belongs to our God who sits on the throne, and to the Lamb!"
>
> 7:9–10

Unless we restrict this multitude to the converts of the great tribulation and say that God's missionary purpose at that time will be different from what it is now, the implication of God's worldwide purpose is clear: He aims to be worshiped by converts from all the nations, tribes, peoples, and languages.

> Then I saw another angel flying directly overhead, with an *eternal gospel to proclaim to those who dwell on earth, to every nation [pan ethnos] and tribe and language and people*. And he said with a loud voice, "Fear God and give him glory, because the hour of his judgment has come, and worship him who made heaven and earth, the sea and the springs of water."
>
> 14:6–7

Again the intention is that the gospel be proclaimed not just to more and more individuals but to "every nation, tribe, language, and people."

Who will not fear, O Lord, and glorify your name? For you alone are holy. *All nations [panta ta ethnē]* will come and worship you, for your righteous acts have been revealed.

15:4

In view of the Old Testament allusion here to Psalm 86:9,[23] and in view of the context of Revelation with its repeated use of *ethnos* in reference to "nations" (at least ten times) and not persons, *panta ta ethnē* in 15:4 no doubt refers to people groups and not merely to Gentile individuals. Therefore, what John foresees as the goal of missions is a worshiping multitude of saints from all the peoples of the world.

And I heard a loud voice from the throne saying, "Behold, the dwelling of God is with man. He will dwell with them, and they will be his peoples *[laoi]*, and God himself will be with them as their God."

21:3

This is a surprising and remarkable glimpse of the new heavens and the new earth. It pictures *peoples*, not just people, in the age to come. It seems that *laoi* ("peoples") and not *laos* ("people") is the genuine, original reading.[24] Therefore, John (recording the angelic voice) seems to make explicit (in distinction from Leviticus 26:12, *laos*) that the final goal of God in redemption is not to obliterate the distinctions of the peoples but to gather them all into one diverse but unified assembly of peoples.

We may conclude from this inquiry into John's writings that his conception of the unique task of missions is to reach more and more people groups until there are converts from "every tribe and language and people and nation." It is a task that he is utterly certain will be accomplished, for he sees it as already complete in the Lord's vision of the age to come.

Did Paul and John Get This Focus on Peoples from Jesus?

Was this focus on peoples the intention of Jesus as he gave his apostles their final commission? Paul's conception of his own mission-

23. Psalm 85:9 LXX. See a discussion of this text earlier in this chapter.

24. The United Bible Societies *Greek New Testament* (4th ed.) and the Nestle-Aland Greek New Testament (27th ed.) chose *laoi* as original. The NRSV reads "peoples," as do the commentaries by Heinrich Kraft, Leon Morris, Robert Mounce, and G. K. Beale.

ary task, which he received from the risen Lord, would certainly suggest that this is what the Lord commanded, not only to him but to all the apostles as the special missionary task of the church.

The Great Commission: It Was Written!

But there is also evidence of this intention in the context of Luke's record of the Lord's words in Luke 24:45–47:

> Then he opened their minds to understand the Scriptures, and said to them, "Thus it is written, that the Christ should suffer and on the third day rise from the dead, and that repentance and forgiveness of sins should be proclaimed in his name to all nations [panta ta ethnē], beginning from Jerusalem."

The context here is crucial. First, Jesus "opens their minds to understand the Scriptures." Then he says, "Thus it is written" (in the Old Testament), followed (in the original Greek) by three coordinate infinitive clauses that make explicit what is written in the Old Testament: first, that the Christ is to suffer; second, that he is to rise on the third day; and third, that repentance and forgiveness of sins are to be preached in his name to "all nations."

So Jesus is saying that his commission to take the message of repentance and forgiveness to all nations "is written" in the Old Testament "Scriptures." This is one of the things he opened their minds to understand. But what is the Old Testament conception of the worldwide purpose of God (which we saw above)? It is just what Paul saw: a purpose to bless all the families of the earth and win a worshiping people from "all nations."[25]

Therefore, we have strong evidence that the panta ta ethnē in Luke 24:47 was understood by Jesus not merely as Gentile individuals but also as an array of world peoples who must hear the message of repentance for the forgiveness of sin.

Luke's other account of Jesus' commission in Acts 1:8 points in the same direction. Jesus says to his apostles just before his ascension, "You will receive power when the Holy Spirit has come upon you, and you will be my witnesses in Jerusalem and in all Judea and Samaria, and to the end of the earth." This commission suggests that getting to all the unreached areas (if not explicitly people groups) is the special task of missions. There is a pressure to keep moving, not just to un-

---

25. From all the uses of panta ta ethnē in the Old Testament that Jesus may be alluding to, at least these relate to the missionary vision of the people of God: Gen. 18:18; 22:18; 26:4; Pss. 48:2; 71:11, 17; 81:8; 85:9; 116:1; Isa. 2:2; 25:7; 52:10; 56:7; 61:11; 66:18–20 (all references are to the LXX verse and chapter divisions).

converted individuals nearby but also to places beyond, even to the end of the world. Not only that, but the phrase "end of the earth" is sometimes in the Old Testament closely associated with all the peoples of the earth. For example, Psalm 22:27: "All the ends of the earth shall remember and turn to the LORD, and all the families of the nations shall worship before you."

This parallel shows that "end of the earth" sometimes carried the association of distant peoples.[26] The apostles would probably not have heard the commission of Acts 1:8 as significantly different from the commission of Luke 24:47.

A House of Prayer for All Nations

Another pointer to the way Jesus thought about the worldwide missionary purposes of God comes from Mark 11:17. When Jesus cleanses the temple, he quotes Isaiah 56:7: "Is it not written, 'My house shall be called a house of prayer for all the nations [pasin tois ethnesin]'"?

This is important because it shows Jesus reaching back to the Old Testament (just as he does in Luke 24:45–47) to interpret the worldwide purposes of God. He quotes Isaiah 56:7, which in Hebrew explicitly says, "My house shall be called a house of prayer for all peoples [kol ha'ammim]."

The people-group meaning is unmistakable. Isaiah's point is not that every individual Gentile will have a right to dwell in the presence of God but that there will be converts from "all peoples" who will enter the temple to worship. The fact that Jesus was familiar with this Old Testament hope, and that he based his worldwide expectations on references to it (Mark 11:17; Luke 24:45–47), suggests that we should interpret his Great Commission along this line—the very same line found in the writings of Paul and John.

Back to the Great Commission in Matthew

We come back now to our earlier effort to understand what Jesus meant in Matthew 28:19 when he said, "Go and make disciples of panta ta ethnē." This command has its corresponding promise of success in Matthew 24:14: "And this gospel of the kingdom will be proclaimed throughout the whole world as a testimony to all nations [pasin tois ethnesin], and then the end will come." The scope of the command and the scope of the promise hang on the meaning of panta ta ethnē.

My conclusion from what we have seen in this chapter is that one would have to go against the flow of the evidence to interpret the

26. Similar associations are found in Pss. 2:8; 67:5–7; 98:2–3; Isa. 52:10; Jer. 16:19; Zech. 9:10. But four different Greek expressions are used in these texts, only one of which (Jer. 16:19) is the exact wording of the phrase in Acts 1:8.

phrase *panta ta ethnē* as "all Gentile individuals" (or "all countries"). Rather, the focus of the command is the discipling of all the people groups of the world. This conclusion comes from the following summary of our biblical investigation:

1. In the New Testament, the singular use of *ethnos* never means Gentile individuals but always people group or nation.
2. The plural *ethnē* can mean either Gentile individuals or people groups. Sometimes the context demands that it mean one or the other, but in most instances it could carry either meaning.
3. The phrase *panta ta ethnē* occurs eighteen times in the New Testament. Only once must it mean Gentile individuals. Nine times it must mean people groups. The other eight times are ambiguous.
4. Virtually all of the nearly one hundred uses of *panta ta ethnē* in the Greek Old Testament refer to nations in distinction from the nation of Israel. See note 15.
5. The promise made to Abraham that in him "all the families of the earth" would be blessed and that he would be "the father of many nations" is taken up in the New Testament and gives the mission of the church a people-group focus because of this Old Testament emphasis.
6. The Old Testament missionary hope is expressed repeatedly as exhortations, promises, prayers, and plans for God's glory to be declared among the peoples and his salvation to be known by all the nations.
7. Paul understood his specifically missionary task in terms of this Old Testament hope and made the promises concerning peoples the foundation of his mission. He was devoted to reaching more and more people groups, not simply more and more individuals. He interpreted Christ's commission to him in these terms.
8. The apostle John envisioned the task of missions as the ingathering of "the children of God" or the "other sheep" out of "every tribe, tongue, people, and nation."
9. The Old Testament context of Jesus' missionary commission in Luke 24:46–47 shows that *panta ta ethnē* would most naturally mean all the peoples or nations.
10. Mark 11:17 shows that Jesus probably thinks in terms of people groups when he envisions the worldwide purpose of God.

Therefore, in all likelihood, Jesus did not send his apostles out with a general mission merely to win as many individuals as they could but rather to reach all the peoples of the world and thus to gather the "sons of God" who are scattered (John 11:52) and to call all the "ransomed from every tongue and tribe and people and nation" (Rev. 5:9), until redeemed persons from "all the peoples praise him" (Rom. 15:11).

Thus, when Jesus says in Mark 13:10 that "the gospel must first be proclaimed to all nations [panta ta ethnē]," there is no good reason for construing this to mean anything other than that the gospel must reach all the peoples of the world before the end comes. And when Jesus says, "Go and make disciples of all the nations [panta ta ethnē]," there is no good reason for construing this to mean anything other than that the missionary task of the church is to press on to all the unreached peoples until the Lord comes. Jesus commands it, and he assures us that it will be done before he comes again. He can make that promise because he himself is building his church from all the peoples. All authority in heaven and on earth has been given to him for this very thing (Matt. 28:18).

What Is a People Group?

We have tried to establish that the special missionary task of the New Testament is to reach all the people groups of the world. But we have not defined precisely what a people group is. What we have found, in fact, is that a precise definition is probably not possible to give on the basis of what God has chosen to reveal in the Bible. God probably did not intend for us to use a precise definition of people groups. That way we can never stop doing pioneer missionary work just because we conclude that all the groups with our definition have been reached.

For example, the point of Matthew 24:14 ("This gospel of the kingdom will be proclaimed throughout the whole world as a testimony to all nations, and then the end will come") is not that we should reach all the nations as we understand them and then stop. The point rather is that as long as the Lord has not returned, there must be more people groups to reach, and we should keep on reaching them.

There are biblical pointers to the nature of a people group. For example, Revelation 5:9 uses four terms to describe the people groups that will be represented at the throne of God: "By your blood you ransomed people for God from every tribe and language and people and nation." To these four the promise to Abraham adds another: "In you all the families[27] of the earth shall be blessed."

What Is a Language?

From this we can say, for example, that at least every *language group* ("language" in Rev. 5:9) should be sought out in the missionary task. But when does a dialect become so distinct that it is a different language? Questions such as this show why there is such difficulty and disagreement concerning the definition of a people group. For years, Ralph Winter put forward the number twenty-four thousand as the total number of people groups in the world. However, Patrick Johnstone observes in the 2001 edition of *Operation World:* "It was only during the 1990s that a reasonably complete listing of the world's peoples and languages was developed. For the first time in history we have a reasonably clear picture of the remaining task for us to disciple the nations."[28] He refers to a total of "the world's twelve thousand ethnolinguistic peoples."

In harmony with Johnstone, David Barrett, in his 2001 revision of the *World Christian Encyclopedia,* defines an ethnolinguistic people as follows: "A distinct homogenous ethnic or racial group within a single country, speaking its own language (one single mother tongue). A large people spread across two, three, four, or several countries is treated here as being two, three, four, or several distinct ethnolinguistic peoples."[29] The total number of ethnolinguistic peoples, as Barrett reckons it, is 12,600.[30]

There is good reason for the discrepancy between the Winter number and the Barrett/Johnstone number, and this reason highlights the difficulty of defining precisely the biblical meaning of "language" in Revelation 5:9. Winter illustrates the problem. He observes the difference between his 24,000 estimate and Barrett's earlier estimate of

27. The Greek Old Testament translates the Hebrew *mishpehot* (families or clans) with *phylai*, which is translated "tribes" in Revelation 5:9. So it may look as though this is not a different category of group. But in fact *phylai* is usually the translation of the Hebrew *shebet*, and the Hebrew *mishpehot* is usually translated *suggeneia*. Therefore, we should take seriously the difference between *mishpehot* and "tribe," especially since it is clearly a smaller unit according to Exodus 6:14f.

28. Patrick Johnstone and Jason Mandryk, *Operation World: When We Pray God Works* (Carlisle, Cumbria, England: Paternoster, 2001), 15.

29. David Barrett, George T. Kurian, and Todd M. Johnson, *World Christian Encyclopedia: A Comparative Survey of Churches and Religions—AD 30 to 2200*, vol. 2 (Oxford: Oxford University Press, 2001), 27–28.

30. Ibid., 16.

8,990 peoples in the 1982 edition of the *World Christian Encyclopedia.* Then he says:

> It is clear in [Barrett's] table that his listing is almost identical to the number of languages which in his opinion need translations [of the Bible]. Now let's see where that leads us. Wycliffe Bible Translators, for example, go into South Sudan and count how many languages there are into which the Bible must be translated, and presented in printed form, in order to reach everybody in that area. Wycliffe's answer is 50 distinct translations. What does "50" mean in this instance? Does it mean 50 groups of people? Certainly not, if we are speaking of unreached peoples, because in many cases quite alien groups can read the same translation.
>
> How do I know this? Gospel Recordings also goes into South Sudan and counts the number of languages. Their personnel, however, come up with 130. Why? Because they put the gospel out in cassette form, and those cassettes represent a more embarrassingly precise language communication than does the written language. Different authors for different reasons, and different organizations for different purposes, are counting different things.[31]

So we can see that the reference to "languages" in Revelation 5:9 will not yield a precise definition of people groups. Neither will the other designations for people groups in that verse.

"People" *(laou)* and "nation" *(ethnous)*, for example, are virtually synonymous and interchangeable in Genesis 25:23 ("Two nations are in your womb, and two peoples from within you shall be divided"). Sometimes Israel as a whole is called a "people," but in Acts 4:27 we read about the "peoples *(laois)* of Israel." Nevertheless, in Revelation 21:3, "peoples" *(laoi)*[32] refers to all the groups and individuals in the new earth. These facts prevent us from forming precise definitions of the people groups missionaries are to reach.

How Small Is a Family?

The fact that all the families of the earth will be blessed alerts us to the fact that the groupings God intends to reach with his gospel may be relatively small. The modern nuclear family is not in view but rather something like a clan. For example, Exodus 6:14–15 reveals the sort of grouping that is probably in mind:

31. Ralph Winter, "Unreached Peoples: What, Where, and Why?" in *New Frontiers in Mission,* ed. Patrick Sookhedeo (Grand Rapids: Baker, 1987), 154.
32. See note 24.

These are the heads of their fathers' houses: the sons of Reuben, the firstborn of Israel: Hanoch, Pallu, Hezron, and Carmi; these are the clans ["families" in RSV and NASB] of Reuben. The sons of Simeon: Jemuel, Jamin, Ohad, Jachin, Zohar, and Shaul, the son of a Canaanite woman; these are the *clans* ["families" in RSV and NASB] of Simeon.

Thus, "families" are smaller than the tribes of Israel (cf. also 1 Sam. 10:20–21). But they are not as small as households. The case of Achan in Joshua 7 shows this. After Achan had sinned and was to be found out, Joshua said that there would be a test of all the people to find out who the culprit was.

> In the morning therefore you shall be brought near *by your tribes*. And the tribe that the Lord takes by lot shall come near *by clans* [*mishpehot* ("families" in RSV and NASB)]. And the clan that the Lord takes shall come near *by households*. And the household that the Lord takes shall come near man by man.
>
> Joshua 7:14

What this shows is that the "family" of the Old Testament is better thought of as a "clan" (which is why the ESV has translated it this way). Its size is between the size of a tribe and a household.

Thus, the missionary task of the New Testament is to reach not only every people the size of Israel and every tribe the size of Reuben or Simeon or Judah but also all the clans, such as those of Hanoch, Pallu, Hezron, Carmi, and Achan.

The fact that *ethnē* is used so often in the Old Testament and the New Testament to designate the focus of missions should not limit our focus to the larger groupings. The word is flexible enough to provide an inclusive designation for groups of various sizes. In fact, Karl Ludwig Schmidt concludes his study of *ethnos* in the *Theological Dictionary of the New Testament* by contrasting it with *laos*, *glōssa*, and *phylē*: "*Ethnos* is the most general and therefore the weakest of these terms, having simply an ethnographical sense and denoting the natural cohesion of a people in general."[33] Thus, *panta ta ethnē* would be the most suitable term for including the others, which is in fact what we find in Revelation 22:2. Here *ethnē* refers to all the people in the new earth, including the "languages" and "peoples" and "tribes." So *panta ta ethnē* is probably the simplest way of giving a summary designation not only to the larger but also to the smaller groupings.

33. Kittle, *Theological Dictionary of the New Testament*, vol. 2, 369.

What Do "Reached" and "Unreached" Mean?

If the task of missions is to reach all the unreached people groups of the world,[34] we need to have some idea what "reached" means so that the people called to the missionary task of the church will know which people groups to enter and which to leave. Paul must have had some idea of what "reached" means when he said in Romans 15:23, "I no longer have any room for work in these regions." He must have known what it means to complete the missionary task when he said in Romans 15:19, "From Jerusalem and all the way around to Illyricum I have fulfilled the ministry of the gospel of Christ." He knew his work was done in that region. That is why he headed for Spain. The 1982 Unreached Peoples Meeting, referred to earlier, defined an "unreached" people group as "a people group within which there is no indigenous community of believing Christians able to evangelize this people group."[35] Thus, a group is reached when mission efforts have established an indigenous church that has the strength and resources to evangelize the rest of the group.

Patrick Johnstone points out that in a strict sense "reaching has nothing to do with response. . . . Reaching is really an indication of the quality and extent of the effort to evangelize a people or region,

34. I will deal with two problems only briefly here in a note because they are not part of biblical revelation and do not seem to have much bearing on the missionary task: (1) One is whether all the peoples will be represented at the throne of God even without missions because infants in each of these peoples have died and presumably will go to heaven and come to maturity for the praise of God. (2) The other problem is whether all clans and tribes will in fact be represented at the throne of God since many clans and tribes no doubt died out before they were evangelized. With regard to the first problem, I do believe that infants who die will be in the kingdom. I base this on the principle that we are judged according to the knowledge available to us (Rom. 1:19–20), and infants have no knowledge available to them since the faculty of knowing is not developed. However, God does not ever mention this or relate it in any way to the missionary enterprise or to the promise that all the families of the earth will be blessed. Rather, it appears to be his purpose to be glorified through the conversion of people who recognize his beauty and greatness and come to love him above all gods. God would not be honored so greatly if the only way he got worshipers from all the nations was by the natural mortality of infants. With regard to the other problem, it may be true that some clans and tribes disappear from history with none of their members being saved. The Bible does not reflect on this issue. We would be speculating beyond the warrant of Scripture if we said that there had to be another way of salvation for such tribes besides the way of hearing and believing the gospel of Jesus. (See the support for this in chapter 4.) Rather, we would do well to assume, in the absence of specific revelation, that the meaning of the promise and the command concerning the nations is that "all the nations" refers to all those who exist at the consummation of the age. When the end comes, there will be no existing people group that is left out of the blessing.

35. Winter, "Unreached Peoples," 12.

not of discipling and church planting." But he admits that "because of popular usage, we have to extend [the meaning of] reachedness."[36]

Both the narrow and broader meaning are warranted from Scripture. For example, Mark 16:15 renders the missions mandate as, "[Jesus] said to them, 'Go into all the world and proclaim the gospel to the whole creation.'"[37] This does not say anything about response. If we had only this word, the missions mandate would be fulfilled if the message were universally proclaimed. Similarly, Matthew 24:14 says, "And this gospel of the kingdom will be proclaimed throughout the whole world as a testimony to all nations, and then the end will come." Again, there is no mention of response (cf. Luke 24:47; Acts 1:8). In this limited sense, therefore, a people group is reached if the message is proclaimed in it as an understandable testimony.

But this is *not* the only way the missions mandate is expressed in Scripture. Matthew 28:19 says, "Go therefore and make disciples of all nations." Here the mandate clearly includes a response. The missions task is not complete until at least some individuals in a people group have become disciples.[38] This is also the implication of Revelation 5:9 and 7:9, which portray the final company of the redeemed as coming "from every tribe and language and people and nation." If there are converts from all the peoples, then the missions mandate must include making converts, not just proclamation.

36. "What Does Reached Mean? An EMQ Survey," *Evangelical Missions Quarterly* 26, no. 3 (July 1990): 316.

37. The KJV translates, "Go ye into all the world, and preach the gospel to every creature." But "the whole creation" is more likely. The closest parallel to this Greek expression (*pasē tē ktisei*) is found in Romans 8:22: "We know that the whole creation *[pasa hē ktisis]* has been groaning together in the pains of childbirth until now." The words and word order are identical; only the case is different, dative in Mark 16 and nominative in Romans 8. For my purposes here, we do not need to settle whether Mark 16:9ff. is an early addition to the Gospel of Mark. Verse 15 represents one biblical way of expressing the Great Commission.

38. "Make disciples of all nations" might be taken to mean: make the whole nation into disciples. But the wording of verses 19 and 20 points in another direction. The word "nations" *(ethnē)* is neuter in Greek. But the word for "them" in the following clauses is masculine: "baptizing them *[autous]* in the name of the Father and of the Son and of the Holy Spirit, teaching them *[autous]* to observe all that I have commanded you." This suggests that the discipling in view is the winning of individual disciples from the nations, rather than treating the nation as a whole as the object of conversion and discipleship. This was affirmed strongly by Karl Barth, who lamented that the interpretation that took *ethnē* in the sense of corporate discipling "once infested missionary thinking and was connected with the painful fantasies of the German Christians. It is worthless." Karl Barth, "An Exegetical Study of Matthew 28:16–20," in *Classics of Christian Missions*, ed. Francis M. DuBose (Nashville: Broadman, 1979), 46.

Most missions leaders define a people group as "reached" when there is an indigenous church able to evangelize the group. This is because the New Testament clearly teaches that a people must continue to be evangelized once the missions task is complete. For example, when Paul finished his missionary work among the peoples of Ephesus, he nevertheless left Timothy there and told him to "do the work of an evangelist" (2 Tim. 4:5). Paul's specific missionary task was evidently to plant the church, which would then be able to go on with the task of evangelism (cf. 1 Cor. 3:6–10). But the task of evangelism is not the same as missions. Missions is what moved Paul away from the peoples of Asia Minor and Greece (even from those who were still unconverted!) and pressed him toward the unreached peoples of Spain (Rom. 15:24, 28).

There is a difficulty with defining the specific task of missions as planting an indigenous church in every people group. The difficulty is that our *biblical* definition of people groups includes groups that may be so small and so closely related to another group that such a church would be unnecessary. How large was the family or clan of Carmi in the tribe of Reuben, or the family of Achan in the tribe of Judah? And are we sure that the families in Genesis 12:3 are so distinct that each must have its own church? When Paul said that his special missionary work was completed from Jerusalem to Illyricum, had he in fact planted a church in every family or clan?

These questions show that there will always be some ambiguity in the definition of "reached" and in the aim of missionary work.[39] For some families or clans, "reached" may mean that there are converts among them and that the church in an adjacent kindred clan suffices as an effective ministry of worship, fellowship, and equipping. The task of missions with regard to such near-kinship families may not be to plant a church among each one but to plant a

39. This problem, of course, does not exist by definition for Ralph Winter and other missiologists who define a people group as "the largest group within which the Gospel can spread as a church planting movement without encountering barriers of understanding or acceptance." Winter, "Unreached Peoples," 12. In other words, if an unevangelized "family" is culturally near enough to another evangelized "family" that the gospel can move without significant barriers, then by definition this unevangelized family, according to Winter, is not an "unreached people group." It is simply part of a larger reached group that needs to evangelize its members. The difference between Winter's approach and mine is that I am simply trying to come to terms with the *biblical* meaning of "families" in Genesis 12:3, while he is defining people groups in terms of what missionary efforts are needed. The two approaches are not at odds, but the difference may result in my calling a "family" or clan an unreached people group in biblical terms (one of the *panta ta ethnē* to be discipled), which Winter, however, would say is not "unreached" for specifically missionary purposes.

church close enough in culture and language that they can be effectively evangelized. It seems that this must have been what Paul had done when he said that he no longer had room for work in that vast territory. Surely there were some families or clans that had not yet been touched. He would probably have said, "This is the work of the nearby churches."

What this implies is that the dividing line between missionary tasks and the tasks of near-neighbor evangelism are sometimes unclear. This is why the terms "E-1," "E-2," and "E-3" evangelism have been invented.[40] They show that there are not two clearly distinct tasks (domestic evangelism vs. frontier missions) but rather gradations of cultural distance from the Christian community. Where that distance becomes so great that we start calling its penetration "missions" is not always clear.[41]

Implications

But the fact that there is a distinct calling on the church to do frontier missionary work among all the remaining unreached people groups is crystal clear from the New Testament. Our question today should be: What persons or agencies in the various churches and denominations should pick up this unique Paul-type mission? It is not the *only* work of the church. Timothy-type ministries are also important. He was a foreigner working at Ephesus, continuing what Paul had begun. But Paul had to move on because he was driven by a special commission[42] and by a grasp of God's worldwide mission purpose revealed in the Old Testament. There is no reason to think that God's purpose has changed today.

40. These terms are not as frequent in the literature as they were when the first edition of this book was published in 1993, but some churches (including the one I serve) and organizations still use them as helpful tactical guides. The "E" stands for evangelize: E-1—people basically "like us"; E-2—people who are not like us but speak the same language and overlap significantly in culture (e.g., a suburban white church in relation to a black urban center); E-3—people who speak a different language and have a very different culture (regardless of how near or far away they live).

41. *Biblically,* reaching every clan in a region is a missionary task regardless of its cultural nearness to other reached clans. But *missiologically,* this effort may not be seen as part of the missionary task. What is needed perhaps is more refined distinctions in our language. Paul certainly saw his missionary work as finished before every clan in Asia was evangelized. Yet if the Great Commission of Matthew 28:19 includes "all the families of the earth" in *panta ta ethnē,* then the missionary task *in that sense* is not complete until all the clans are represented in the kingdom. Practically, it is probably wise to emphasize the Pauline strategy as the essence of missions.

42. "Go, for I will send you far away to the *ethnē*" (Acts 22:21).

Who then is to pick up the mantle of the apostle's unique missionary task of reaching more and more peoples? Shouldn't every denomination and church have some vital group that is recruiting, equipping, sending, and supporting Paul-type missionaries to more and more unreached peoples? Shouldn't every church and denomination have a group of people (a missions agency or board) who sees its special and primary task as not merely to win as many individuals to Christ as possible but to win some individuals (i.e., plant a church) among all the unreached peoples of the earth?

The Supremacy of God in the Worship of the Nations

What does this chapter have to do with the supremacy of God? God's great goal in all of history is to uphold and display the glory of his name for the enjoyment of his people from all the nations.[43] The question now is: Why does God pursue the goal of displaying his glory by focusing the missionary task on *all the peoples* of the world? How does this missionary aim serve best to achieve God's goal?

The first thing we notice in pondering this question is how the ultimate goal of God's glory is confirmed in the cluster of texts that focus missionary attention on the people groups of the world. For example, Paul said that his apostleship was given "to bring about the obedience of faith *for the sake of [Christ's] name* among all the nations" (Rom. 1:5). Missions is for the glory of Christ. Its goal is to reestablish the supremacy of Christ among the peoples of the world. Similarly, in Romans 15:9, Paul says that Christ did his own missionary work and inspired Paul's "in order that the Gentiles [or nations] *might glorify God* for his mercy." The goal of Christ's mission and ours is that God might be glorified by the nations as they experience his mercy. Accordingly, the consummation of missions is described in Revelation 5:9 as persons from "every tribe and language and people and nation" worshiping the Lamb and declaring the infinite worth of his glory. All of this is in accord with the repeated Old Testament calls: "Declare his *glory* among the nations, his *marvelous works* among all the peoples!" (Ps. 96:3). The goal of missions is the glory of God.

43. I have labored to demonstrate this from Scripture in chapter 1 and in *Desiring God: Meditations of a Christian Hedonist* (Sisters, Ore.: Multnomah, 1996), 255–66; and *The Pleasures of God: Meditations on God's Delight in Being God* (Sisters, Ore.: Multnomah, 2000), 97–119.

Diversity: Intended and Eternal

Another thing we notice as we ponder this question is that the diversity of the nations has its creation and consummation in the will of God. Its origin was neither accidental nor evil.[44] And its future is eternal: The diversity will never be replaced by uniformity. The evidence for this is found in Acts 17:26 and Revelation 21:3.

To the Athenians Paul said, "[God] made from one man every nation of mankind to live on all the face of the earth, having determined allotted periods and the boundaries of their dwelling place" (Acts 17:26). This means that the origin of peoples is not in spite of but because of God's will and plan. He *made* the nations. He set them in their place. And he determines the duration of their existence. The diversity of the nations is God's idea. Therefore, for whatever reason, he focuses the missionary task on all the nations; it is not a response to an accident of history. It is rooted in the purpose he had when he determined to make the nations in the first place.

God's purpose to have diversity among nations is not a temporary one only for this age. In spite of the resistance of most English versions, the standard Greek texts of the New Testament[45] now agree that the original wording of Revelation 21:3 requires the translation: "And I heard a loud voice from the throne saying, 'Behold, the dwelling place of God is with man. He will dwell with them, and they will be his *peoples*.'" Most versions translate: "They will be his *people*." But what John is saying is that in the new heavens and the new earth the humanity described in Revelation 5:9 will be preserved: persons ransomed by the blood of Christ "from every tribe and language and people and nation." This diversity will not disappear in the new heavens

44. The story of the tower of Babel in Genesis 11 does not mean that God disapproves of the diversity of languages in the world. We are not told that apart from the tower of Babel God would not have created different languages in the world. Blocking an act of pride (Gen. 11:4) was the occasion when God initiated the diversity of languages in the world. But that does not mean that the diversity of languages was a curse that would need to be reversed in the age to come. In fact, the diversity of languages is reported in Genesis 10:5, 20, 31 before the tower of Babel is mentioned in Genesis 11. What we learn is that God's plan of a common origin for all peoples on the one hand and his plan for diversified languages on the other hand restrains the pride of man on two sides: Diversity restrains the temptation to unite against God (as at Babel), and unified origin restrains the temptation to boast in ethnic uniqueness (as, we will see, in Athens). The miracle and the blessing of "tongues" at Pentecost was not a declaration that in the age of promise the languages of the world would disappear but rather a declaration that in the age of promise every obstacle to humble, God-glorifying unity in faith would be overcome.

45. See note 24.

and the new earth. God willed it from the beginning. It has a permanent place in his plan.

How Diversity Magnifies the Glory of God

Now, we return to the question, How does God's focus on the diversity of the peoples advance his purpose to be glorified in his creation?[46] As I have tried to reflect biblically on this question, at least[47] four answers have emerged.

1. First, there is a beauty and power of praise that comes from unity in diversity that is greater than that which comes from unity alone. Psalm 96:3–4 connects the evangelizing of the peoples with the quality of praise that God deserves. "Declare his glory among the nations, his marvelous works among all the peoples! *For great is the* LORD, *and greatly to be praised; he is to be feared above all gods.*" Notice the word "for." The extraordinary greatness of the praise that the Lord should receive is the ground and impetus of our mission to the nations.

46. One of the questions raised by those of us who believe God means to pursue worshipers from all the peoples of the world is, "What about peoples who exist and then die out before any gospel witness comes? If you believe that these people are lost, as you have argued, then none of them will be represented in the worshiping host of heaven." I have three responses to this question: (1) I do not know for sure that the biblical assurance that Christ has "ransomed people for God from every tribe and language and people and nation" must include those who live and die out before any can believe. (2) While the biblical teaching on the final state of those who die in infancy is not explicit, I hold the view that infants who die do not perish but prove to be elect and are brought to faith in Christ and eternal life in a way we are not told. (See chapter 4, note 27.) Therefore, those who have died as infants in the vanishing tribes would be represented among the redeemed. (3) But the way I argue in this closing section as to *why* diversity glorifies God points in another direction for the decisive answer. Among the main reasons diversity glorifies God is that conscious allegiance to one leader from a greatly diverse group magnifies the unique glory of the leader. See below. But this would suggest then that perhaps the decisive aim of God in commanding our pursuit of *living* peoples is that only those who hear of Jesus and consciously follow him will glorify him in this way. This may suggest then that the issue of vanished peoples is simply not in view when the "every" of Revelation 5:9 is contemplated.

47. I omit discussing the real possibility that there are mysterious correlations between the numbers and the purposes of the peoples and the numbers of the saints or the angels. Deuteronomy 32:8 says, "When the Most High gave to the nations their inheritance, when He separated the sons of man, He set the boundaries of the peoples *according to the number of the sons of Israel*" (NASB). The Greek Old Testament contains the strange rendering: ". . . according to the number of the *angels of God*," which the ESV follows, by translating, ". . . according to the number of the sons of God." Making much of this would be speculation, but it does remind us that God has reasons that are often high and hidden.

I infer from this that the beauty and power of praise that will come to the Lord from the diversity of the nations are greater than the beauty and power that would come to him if the chorus of the redeemed were culturally uniform. The reason for this can be seen in the analogy of a choir. More depth of beauty is felt from a choir that sings in parts than from a choir that sings only in unison. Unity in diversity is more beautiful and more powerful than the unity of uniformity. This carries over to the untold differences that exist between the peoples of the world. When their diversity unites in worship to God, the beauty of their praise will echo the depth and greatness of God's beauty far more than if the redeemed were from only a few different people groups.

2. Second, the fame and greatness and worth of an object of beauty increases in proportion to the diversity of those who recognize its beauty. If a work of art is regarded as great among a small and like-minded group of people but not by anyone else, the art is probably not truly great. Its qualities are such that it does not appeal to the deep universals in our hearts but only to provincial biases. But if a work of art continues to win more and more admirers not only across cultures but also across decades and centuries, then its greatness is irresistibly manifested.

Thus, when Paul says, "Praise the Lord all you nations, and let all the peoples extol him" (Rom. 15:11, author's translation), he is saying that there is something about God that is so universally praiseworthy and so profoundly beautiful and so comprehensively worthy and so deeply satisfying that God will find passionate admirers in every diverse people group in the world. His true greatness will be manifest in the breadth of the diversity of those who perceive and cherish his beauty. His excellence will be shown to be higher and deeper than the parochial preferences that make us happy most of the time. His appeal will be to the deepest, highest, largest capacities of the human soul. Thus, the diversity of the source of admiration will testify to his incomparable glory.

3. Third, the strength and wisdom and love of a leader is magnified in proportion to the diversity of people he can inspire to follow him with joy. If you can lead only a small, uniform group of people, your leadership qualities are not as great as they would be if you could win a following from a large group of very diverse people.

Paul's understanding of what is happening in his missionary work among the nations is that Christ is demonstrating his greatness in winning obedience from all the peoples of the world: "I will not venture to speak of anything except what *Christ has accomplished through me to bring the Gentiles [or nations] to obedience* (Rom. 15:18). It is not Paul's missionary expertise that is being magnified as more and more diverse peoples choose to follow Christ. It is the greatness of Christ. He is showing himself superior to all other leaders.

The last phrase of Psalm 96:3–4 shows the leadership competition that is going on in world missions. "Declare his glory among the nations. . . . *He is to be feared above all gods.*" We should declare the glory of God among the nations because in this way he will show his superiority over all other gods that make pretentious claims to lead the peoples. The more diverse the people groups who forsake their gods to follow the true God, the more visible is God's superiority over all his competitors.

4. By focusing on all the people groups of the world, God undercuts ethnocentric pride and throws all peoples back upon his free grace rather than any distinctive of their own. This is what Paul emphasizes in Acts 17:26 when he says to the proud citizens of Athens, "[God] made from one man every nation of mankind to live on all the face of the earth, having determined allotted periods and the boundaries of their dwelling place." F. F. Bruce points out that "the Athenians . . . pride themselves on being . . . sprung from the soil of their native Attica. . . . They were the only Greeks on the European mainland who had no tradition of their ancestors coming into Greece; they belonged to the earliest wave of Greek immigration."[48]

Against this boast Paul countered: You and the Barbarians and the Jews and the Romans all came from the same origin. And you came by God's will, not your own; and the time and place of your existence is in God's hand. Every time God expresses his missionary focus for *all* the nations, he cuts the nerve of ethnocentric pride. It's a humbling thing to discover that God does not choose our people group because of any distinctives of worth but rather that we might double our joy in him by being a means of bringing all the other groups into the same joy.

Humility is the flip side of giving God all the glory. Humility means reveling in his grace, not our goodness. In pressing us on to all the peoples, God is pressing us further into the humblest and deepest experience of his grace and weaning us more and more from our ingrained pride. In doing this he is preparing for himself a people—from all the peoples—who will be able to worship him with free and white-hot admiration.

---

48. Bruce, *Commentary on the Book of Acts,* 357–58.

PART 3

Making God Supreme in Missions

The Practical Outworking of Compassion and Worship

6

A Passion for God's Supremacy and Compassion for Man's Soul

Jonathan Edwards on the Unity of Motives for World Missions

Missions is not the ultimate goal of the church. Worship is. Missions exists because worship doesn't. Worship is ultimate, not missions, because God is ultimate, not man. When this age is over, and the countless millions of the redeemed fall on their faces before the throne of God, missions will be no more. It is a temporary necessity. But worship abides forever.

With those words I began this book on the supremacy of God in missions. There are deep roots to those sentences, and I owe more debts than I can ever pay. The person most responsible for my views and for my articulation of those views (under God and after the Bible) is Jonathan Edwards, the eighteenth-century pastor and theologian whose God-entranced worldview sheds its light across all the pages of this book. The impact that Edwards has had on my thinking as it relates to worship and missions (and almost everything else) is incalculable. This chapter is another tribute that I pay to him and to his God on the occasion of this three-hundredth anniversary of his birth.

The Pervasive Influence of Jonathan Edwards

You can hear his influence in the questions behind the first sentence: What is the ultimate goal of the church? What is the ultimate

203

goal of redemption and of history and of creation? Edwards was always asking about the ultimate end of things, because once we know
and embrace the final and highest reason that we and the church and
the nations exist, then all our thinking and all our feeling and all our
acting will be governed by that aim. It continually amazes me how
few people ask and answer with conviction and passion the most important questions—the ultimate questions.

But that is what Edwards cared about most. Edwards was absolutely clear on the ultimate question of why all things exist, including
you and me and the church universal and the nations and history. He
was absolutely clear on it because God was absolutely clear on it. Edwards wrote a book called *The End for Which God Created the World*.[1]
In my own thinking, it is the most important thing he ever wrote. Once
we understand what he wrote there, everything—absolutely everything—changes. His answer to the question, What is the ultimate goal
of creation and history and redemption and your life and everything
else? is this: "All that is ever spoken of in the Scripture as an ultimate
end of God's works, is included in that one phrase, the glory of God."[2]

Edwards's Biblically Saturated Argumentation

Edwards is sure of this because the Bible is clear about this. For
nearly seventy pages[3] Edwards piles text upon text from the Scriptures to show the radical God-centeredness of God. He puts it like
this:

> God had respect to *himself*, as his highest end [or goal], in this work [of cre-
> ation]; because he is *worthy* in himself to be so, being infinitely the greatest
> and best of beings. All things else, with regard to worthiness, importance,
> and excellence, are perfectly as nothing in comparison [to] him."[4]

He cites Romans 11:36: "For from him and through him and *to him*
are all things. To him be glory forever." And Colossians 1:16: "All
things were created through him and *for him*." And Hebrews 2:10:
"For it was fitting that he, *for whom* and by whom all things exist, in
bringing many sons to glory, should make the founder of their salva-

1. Jonathan Edwards, *The End for Which God Created the World* is published in its
entirety in John Piper, *God's Passion for His Glory: Living the Vision of Jonathan Edwards* (Wheaton: Crossway, 1998).
2. Ibid., 242.
3. Ibid., 183–251.
4. Ibid., 140 (italics in original).

tion perfect through suffering." And Proverbs 16:4: "The Lord hath made all things *for himself*" (KJV).[5]

The point of these texts—and dozens more[6]—is not that God has deficiencies He is trying to remedy but that he has perfections he wants to display. God's aim in creation is to put himself on display. "The heavens declare the glory of God," Psalm 19:1 says. Who set it up that way? God did. This is *his* aim in creation. To make himself known as glorious. And the same thing is true of the history of redemption. Isaiah 48:9–11 is like a banner not just over God's rescue of Israel from exile but over all his acts of rescue, especially the cross:

> For my name's sake I defer my anger, for the sake of my praise I restrain it for you, that I may not cut you off. Behold, I have refined you. . . . I have tried you in the furnace of affliction. For my own sake, for my own sake, I do it, for how should my name be profaned? My glory I will not give to another.

All of creation, all of redemption, all of history is designed by God to display God. That is the ultimate goal of the church.

Why Did I Put "Worship" Where the Glory of God Belongs?

But that is not what I said in the first sentence of this book on missions. I said, "Missions is not the ultimate goal of the church. *Worship* is." Why the substitution of "worship" for "the glory of God"? Why not say, "Missions is not the ultimate goal of the church. The *glory of God* is"? The reason is that missions is demanded not by God's failure to show glory but by man's failure to savor the glory. Creation is telling the glory of God, but the peoples are not treasuring it.

> His invisible attributes, namely, his eternal power and divine nature, have been clearly perceived, ever since the creation of the world, in the things that have been made. So they are without excuse. For although they knew God, they did not honor him as God or give thanks to him.
>
> Romans 1:20–21

5. Emphasis added. Most modern versions translate this verse so that "for himself" is rendered "for its own purpose": "The Lord has made everything *for its own purpose, even the wicked for the day of evil*" (NASB). But this is a contextual judgment call, not a necessary grammatical feature of the text. The Hebrew *lamma'anehu* can be properly translated "for himself."

6. Some of these are gathered in chapter 1 of this book.

Natural revelation is not getting through. Honor and thanks to God are not welling up in the hearts of the peoples when they see his glory manifest in nature. They are not worshiping the true God. That's why missions is necessary.

Missions exists because *worship* doesn't. The ultimate issue addressed by missions is that God's glory is dishonored among the peoples of the world. When Paul brought his indictment of his own people to a climax in Romans 2:24, he said, "The name of God is blasphemed among the Gentiles because of you." That is the ultimate problem in the world. That is the ultimate outrage.

> The glory of God is not honored.
> The holiness of God is not reverenced.
> The greatness of God is not admired.
> The power of God is not praised.
> The truth of God is not sought.
> The wisdom of God is not esteemed.
> The beauty of God is not treasured.
> The goodness of God is not savored.
> The faithfulness of God is not trusted.
> The commandments of God are not obeyed.
> The justice of God is not respected.
> The wrath of God is not feared.
> The grace of God is not cherished.
> The presence of God is not prized.
> The person of God is not loved.

The infinite, all-glorious Creator of the universe, by whom and for whom all things exist—who holds every person's life in being at every moment (Acts 17:25)—is disregarded, disbelieved, disobeyed, and dishonored among the peoples of the world. That is the ultimate reason for missions.

The opposite of this disrespect is worship. Worship is not a gathering. It is not essentially a song service or sitting under preaching. Worship is not essentially any form of outward act. Worship is essentially an inner stirring of the heart to treasure God above all the treasures of the world—

> a valuing of God above all else that is valuable
> a loving of God above all else that is lovely
> a savoring of God above all else that is sweet
> an admiring of God above all else that is admirable

a fearing of God above all else that is fearful
a respecting of God above all else that is respectable
a prizing of God above all else that is precious

Worship from the Inside Out

In other words, worship is right affections in the heart toward God, rooted in right thoughts in the head about God, becoming visible in right actions of the body reflecting God. These three stages of worship from inner essence to outward display can be seen in three texts.

- First, Matthew 15:8–9: "This people honors me with their lips, but *their heart* is far from me; in vain do they worship me." So if worship is not from the heart, it is vain and empty, meaning it is *not* worship. That means the essence can't be outward. The essence of worship is affection, not action.
- Second, John 4:23: "The hour is coming, and is now here, when the true worshipers will worship the Father in spirit *and truth*, for the Father is seeking such people to worship him." Notice, the Father seeks worship in spirit *and* truth—right affections rising for God, rooted in right thinking about God.
- Third, Matthew 5:16: "Let your light shine before others, so that they may see your *good works* and give glory to your Father who is in heaven." God intends for his glory to be public. He did not create the world so that his glory would remain incognito. And he does not redeem people so that they will have merely private experiences of his preciousness. His aim is that his glory be openly reflected in the *deeds* of his people, whose *thoughts* reflect his truth and whose *affections* reflect his worth. Worship is seeing, savoring, and showing the glory of all that God is for us in Jesus Christ.

The first and ultimate goal of missions is that this worship happens among all the nations of the world—that God's glory and greatness find a fitting reflection among the peoples.

Not Just More People but People from All Peoples

Note that I said "peoples," not people. The aim of missions (as distinct from local evangelism where the church already exists) is that there be a church who worships God through Jesus Christ in all the peoples and tribes and languages and ethnic groups of the world. We have seen this goal of missions most clearly in the result of missions in Revelation 5:9. The song to Christ in heaven will be, "Worthy are you to take the scroll and to open its seals, for you were slain, and by your blood you ransomed people for God from every tribe and language and people and nation." Jesus Christ, the Son of God, died to redeem a worshiping people for his Father from all the peoples, tribes, languages, and nations. Missions exists to plant Christ-purchased, God-exalting worshiping communities of the redeemed in all the peoples of the world.

The passion of a missionary—as distinct from that of an evangelist—is to plant a worshiping community of Christians in a people group who has no access to the gospel because of language or cultural barriers. Paul was one of these "frontier" missionaries: "I make it my ambition to preach the gospel, not where Christ has already been named. . . . But now, since I no longer have any room for work in these regions . . . I go to Spain" (Rom. 15:20, 23–24).

The first great passion of missions, therefore, is to honor the glory of God by restoring the rightful place of God in the hearts of people who presently think, feel, and act in ways that dishonor God every day, and in particular, to do this by bringing forth a worshiping people from among all the unreached peoples of the world. If you love the glory of God, you cannot be indifferent to missions. This is the ultimate reason Jesus Christ came into the world. Romans 15:8–9 says, "Christ became a servant to the circumcised . . . *in order that the Gentiles might glorify God for his mercy.*" Christ came to get glory for his Father among the nations. If you love what Jesus Christ came to accomplish, you love missions.

Compassion for People, Not Just Passion for God

But now comes the question this chapter is mainly designed to answer: How does the motive of compassion for people relate to this primary motive of a passion for the glory of God? Most of us would agree that Jesus came not only to vindicate God's righteousness and uphold God's glory but also to rescue sinners from everlasting misery.

Alongside the truth that we are all guilty of treason and have dishonored our King, we must now put forward the truth that we are therefore worthy of execution and everlasting punishment. With mutiny comes misery. Unbelief not only dishonors God but also destroys the soul. Everything that discredits God damages man. Every assault on God's holiness is an assault on human happiness. Every thought or feeling or action that makes God look wrong or irrelevant increases man's ruin. Everything that decreases God's reputation increases man's suffering.

And so missions is driven by a passion not only to restore the glory of God to its rightful place in the worshiping soul but also to rescue sinners from everlasting pain. If there is one thing that almost everyone knows about Jonathan Edwards, it is that he believed in the reality and eternality of hell.

Edwards Wanted to Honor God *and* Rescue People from Hell

In his most famous sermon, "Sinners in the Hands of an Angry God," Edwards was not a cool, detached observer of perishing people. He was a passionate evangelist pleading for people to receive mercy while there was still time. After referring to Revelation 14:20, which speaks of "the winepress of the fierceness and wrath of Almighty God," he says:

> The words are exceeding terrible. . . . "The fierceness and wrath of God." The fury of God! The fierceness of Jehovah! O how dreadful must that be! Who can utter or conceive what such expressions carry in them? . . . Consider this, you who are here present, that yet remain in an unregenerate state. . . . Now God stands ready to pity you; this is a day of mercy.[7]

And Edwards believed not only that hell would be horrible and conscious but also that it would be never ending. He would have been appalled at the number of so-called evangelicals today who have abandoned the biblical teaching on hell as eternal, conscious torment in favor of a view of annihilation (Matt. 25:41, 46; Mark 9:42–48; 2 Thess. 1:5–10; Rev. 14:9–11; 20:10, 14–15).[8] In response to the annihilationists of his own day, Edwards preached a message on April 2, 1739, with the stated doctrine, "The misery of the wicked in hell will be absolutely eternal." In another sermon, he makes the point that annihilation is not the form of punishment that unbelievers receive but the relief from punishment that they desire and don't receive. "Wicked men will hereafter earnestly wish to be turned to nothing and forever cease to be that they may escape the wrath of God."[9] I believe Edwards is right, and we should tremble and fly to Christ, our only hope.[10]

7. Jonathan Edwards, "Sinners in the Hands of an Angry God," in *The Works of Jonathan Edwards*, vol. 2 (Edinburgh: Banner of Truth Trust, 1974), 10.

8. See my response to this abandonment in chapter 4.

9. Quoted in John Gerstner, *Jonathan Edwards on Heaven and Hell* (Grand Rapids: Baker, 1980), 75.

10. For a fuller treatment of Edwards's argument about the justice of hell, see chapter 4, note 19.

So I say again, missions is driven not only by a passion for the supremacy of God in all things but also by a compassion for perishing people, whom we all once were.

Edwards preached a series of fifteen sermons on the "love chapter," 1 Corinthians 13 ("Charity and Its Fruits") and said in sermon four, on verse 4 ("Love suffers long and is kind"), "A Christian spirit disposes persons meekly to bear ill that is received from others, and cheerfully and freely to do good to others."[11] One of his applications was:

> Men may do good to the souls of vicious persons by being the instruments of reclaiming them from their vicious courses. They may do good to the souls of secure and senseless sinners by putting them in mind of their misery and danger and so being the instruments of awakening them. And persons may be the instruments of others' conversion, of bringing them home to Christ. We read in Daniel 12:3 of those that turn many to righteousness.[12]

The motive of love toward sinners and the desire to do good to them are essential to the Christian spirit. It is the spirit of Christ himself. Mark 6:34 says, "When [Jesus] went ashore he saw a great crowd, and he had *compassion* on them, because they were like sheep without a shepherd. And he began to teach them many things." In Luke 15:20, in the parable of the prodigal son, Jesus portrays the heart of his Father in the same way: "[His son] arose and came to his father. But while he was still a long way off, his father saw him and felt *compassion*, and ran and embraced him and kissed him." "For God so loved the world, that he gave his only Son, that whoever believes in him should not perish but have eternal life" (John 3:16). The love of God for perishing sinners moved him to provide at great cost a way to rescue them from everlasting destruction, and missions is the extension of that love to the unreached peoples of the world.

How Does Compassion for People Relate to Passion for God?

Here is the main question I am pursuing: What is the relationship between our passion for the supremacy of God—the glory of God, the honor of God and of his Son among the nations—and our compassion for perishing sinners whose end is everlasting misery if they do not

11. Jonathan Edwards, "Charity and Its Fruits," in *The Works of Jonathan Edwards*, vol. 8, *Ethical Writings*, ed. Paul Ramsey (New Haven: Yale University Press, 1989), 185.

12. Ibid., 207–8. Daniel 12:3 says, "And those who are wise shall shine like the brightness of the sky above; and those who turn many to righteousness, like the stars forever and ever."

hear the gospel and believe? I wonder if you've ever experienced a tension in your own soul between these two motives. I have. That's why this question matters so much to me. I want to be utterly devoted to the cause of world evangelization, and I want it to be from God-exalting, person-loving motives. And these two do not always feel emotionally compatible. Are they? How are they? Does Jonathan Edwards provide a key? I will try to unfold the answer in five steps:

1. *Compassion pursues the rescue of perishing sinners.* Compassion moves us to work for the rescue of unbelievers from the coming wrath of God in hell (1 Thess. 1:10). The biggest problem in the world for every human being—from the poorest to the richest, from the sickest to the healthiest—is the same: how to escape the wrath of God that hangs over all humans because of our sin. Love demands that we work to rescue people from the wrath of God.

2. *Fear of hell by itself saves nobody.* Edwards never tired of warning people to flee from the wrath to come.[13] But he knew that mere fear of the consequences of sin is not a saving fear. People who love sin fear and sometimes weep over the consequences of sin.[14] It is natural to hate pain. It is supernatural to hate sin. It is natural to love sin and supernatural to love Christ.

What this implies is that you can scare people toward heaven, but you can't scare anybody into heaven. Saving faith means receiving Christ as your treasure, not just as a deliverer from pain. It is possible to claim faith in Christ as merely a rescuer from hell. Such faith saves no one. Jesus said, "I am the bread of life; whoever comes to me shall not hunger, and whoever believes in me shall never thirst" (John 6:35). Saving faith is a coming to Jesus for the satisfaction of your soul thirst.[15]

Until your soul has a thirst for Christ as the bread of life and the living water, you will use Christ for what your soul thirsts after. Many people who claim to have saving faith simply use Christ to get what they really want, which is not Christ but his gifts (escape from hell, peace of mind, health of body, a better marriage, a social network, etc.). We are saved by coming to Christ not only as our deliverer but

---

13. Gerstner, *Jonathan Edwards on Heaven and Hell.* See page 51 for a 1747 sermon in which he comments on how frequently he warned his people about the dangers of hell.

14. Note the contrast in 2 Corinthians 7:10 between "godly grief" and "worldly grief": "For *godly grief* produces a repentance that leads to salvation without regret, whereas *worldly grief* produces death."

15. For an extended exposition of this sentence, see John Piper, *The Purifying Power of Living by Faith in FUTURE GRACE* (Sisters, Ore.: Multnomah, 1995).

also as our treasure—coming for all that God is for us in Jesus. Test yourself: Would you want to go to heaven if Christ were not there? Is he or his gifts your treasure?

3. *Therefore, compassion must not merely warn people about the pains of going to hell but must also lure people to the pleasures of knowing Christ.* The only way to get to heaven is by wanting to be with Christ and by trusting his work to get you there. Wanting to avoid hell is not the same as wanting to be with Christ. And so it would not be compassionate merely to warn people about hell. We must display to them the beauties of Christ. Compassion does not merely warn people; it woos people. Compassion aims to awaken in people a delight in Christ, not just a dread of hell. No one goes to heaven who does not love Christ. Paul said, "If any one does not love the Lord, let him be accursed" (1 Cor. 16:22 NASB). Compassion seeks, with prayer and preaching and serving in the power of the Holy Spirit, to create joy in who Christ is. Compassion stirs up satisfaction in Christ. At its heart, that is what saving faith is: being satisfied with all that God is for us in Jesus.

4. *The key from Jonathan Edwards: It is precisely this satisfaction in Christ himself that magnifies Christ and glorifies God.* The key to the coherence between passion for God's glory and compassion for perishing man is that rejoicing in God himself, through Christ, glorifies God. The pleasure you take in God is the measure of the treasure you find in him. You make much of him and show him to be great when you find your joy in him, especially when the taste and lure of this joy enables you to leave comforts and risk your life in the cause of missions. Here is the key quotation from Edwards:

> So God glorifies Himself toward the creatures also in two ways: 1. By appearing to . . . their understanding. 2. In communicating Himself to their hearts, and in their rejoicing and delighting in, and enjoying, the manifestations which He makes of Himself. . . . *God is glorified not only by His glory's being seen, but by its being rejoiced in.* When those that see it delight in it, God is more glorified than if they only see it. His glory is then received by the whole soul, both by the understanding and by the heart. God made the world that He might communicate, and the creature receive, His glory; and that it might [be] received both by the mind and heart. He that testifies his idea of God's glory [doesn't] glorify God so much as he that testifies also his approbation of it and his delight in it.[16]

16. Jonathan Edwards, *The "Miscellanies,"* in *The Works of Jonathan Edwards*, vol. 13, ed. Thomas Schafer (New Haven: Yale University Press, 1994), 495, emphasis added. Miscellany #448; see also #87, 251–52; #332, 410; #679 (not in the New Haven volume).

My way of saying this is, "God is most glorified in us when we are most satisfied in him."[17]

With this profound insight from Jonathan Edwards into God's purpose in creation and redemption, we see the unity of our two motives in missions:

5. *The aim of compassion to rescue sinners from everlasting pain and the aim of passion to see God honored are not in conflict.* Sinners escape hell and honor God with the same act: treasuring all that God is for them in Christ, being satisfied with all that God is for them in Christ. God does not get the honor he should, and man does not escape the pain he would, if Christ himself is not our treasure. But if, by the mercy of God, Christ becomes the treasure of the nations and God becomes their delight, then he is honored and we are saved.

And that's the goal of missions. Therefore, the twofold motive of missions, mercy for man and glory for God, is one coherent goal. So let us take up our cross and, for the joy set before us, be willing to lay down our lives to make the nations glad in God.

> Let the peoples praise you, O God;
>   let all the peoples praise you!
> Let the nations be glad and sing for joy.
>
> Psalm 67:3–4

---

17. For an exposition of this statement, see John Piper, *Desiring God: Mediations of a Christian Hedonist* (Sisters, Ore.: Multnomah, 1996); and idem, *The Dangerous Duty of Delight: The Glorified God and the Satisfied Soul* (Sisters, Ore.: Multnomah, 2001).

7

The Inner Simplicity and Outer Freedom of Worldwide Worship

I write this final chapter[1] to clarify the first two sentences of chapter 1: "Missions is not the ultimate goal of the church. Worship is." I want to clarify what I mean by "worship," lest any take me to mean merely the gathering of Christians for corporate worship or (still more limiting) that part of the gathering for singing songs and hymns. I love those times and meet God powerfully in them. But to say that missions exists for *that* would be too narrow and far from my meaning. I mean something much more radical and soul-gripping and life-encompassing when I speak of worship as the goal of missions.

A Stunning Degree of Indifference to Outward Form

My thesis is that worship in the New Testament moved toward something radically simple and inward, with manifold external expressions in life and liturgy. One of the reasons for this is that the New Testament is a vision for missions that is usable across thousands of cultures and therefore could not be laden with externals. I would even dare to claim (not that every reader will be as excited about this as I am) that this radical simplification and internalization is in line with the Reformed tradition. In short, what we find in the New Testament is an utterly stunning degree of indifference to worship as an outward

1. This chapter is an adaptation of material first published in John Piper, *Brothers, We Are Not Professionals* (Nashville: Broadman & Holman, 2002), chap. 28.

form and an utterly radical intensification of worship as an inward experience of the heart.

Little Explicit Teaching in the New Testament about Corporate Worship

Let's begin with a startling fact, namely, that the epistles of the New Testament contain very little instruction that deals explicitly with corporate worship—what we call worship services. Not that there were no corporate gatherings for worship. First Corinthians 14:23 speaks of "the whole church" assembling together, Acts 2:46 speaks of the early church "attending the temple together and breaking bread in their homes," and Hebrews 10:25 speaks of "not neglecting to meet together." But this is not much, and the remarkable thing is that even when the gatherings are in view, the apostles do not speak of them explicitly as worship.

Let me illustrate this so we can feel its full force. In the Old Testament, the most common word for worship is the Hebrew word *hishtahavah* (or a related form of that word). Its basic meaning is "bow down," with the sense of reverence, respect, and honor. It occurs 171 times. In the Greek Old Testament, 164 of those instances of this Hebrew word are translated by the Greek *proskyneō*. In the Greek New Testament, this is the main word for worship. But when we look at its use, we notice something astonishing.[2] It is common in the Gospels (twenty-six times)—people would often bow down worshipfully before Jesus. And it is common in the Book of Revelation (twenty-one times) because the angels and elders in heaven often bow down before God. But in the epistles of Paul, it occurs only once, namely, in 1 Corinthians 14:25, where the unbeliever falls down at the power of prophecy and confesses that God is in the assembly. And it doesn't occur at all in the letters of Peter, James, or John.

2. Heinrich Greeven in *Theological Dictionary of the New Testament*, ed. Gerhard Friedrich, trans. Geoffrey Bromiley, vol. 6 (Grand Rapids: Eerdmans, 1968), 765, observes the "astonishing fact" that while *proskyneō* is abundant in the Gospels (twenty-six times) and Acts (four times) and Revelation (twenty-one times), it is almost completely absent in the epistles (Heb. 1:6 and 11:21 are Old Testament quotations). Apart from Acts 24:11, where *proskynein* is a technical term for worship in the temple, the only instance of *proskynēsis* in the primitive Christian community is in 1 Corinthians 14:25, where there appears to be an actual falling down. Elsewhere there is reference to kneeling in prayer (Acts 9:40; 20:36) and lifting the hands (1 Tim. 2:8), but the word *proskynein* is not used. Greeven concludes: "This is, however, a further proof of the concreteness of the term. *Proskynēsis* demands visible majesty before which the worshipper bows. The Son of God was visible to all on earth (the Gospels) and the exalted Lord will again be visible to His own when faith gives way to sight (Revelation)."

This is remarkable. The main word for worship in the Old Testament is virtually absent from the letters of the New Testament.[3] Why is this? Why are the very epistles that were written to help the church be what it ought to be in this age almost totally devoid of this word and of explicit teaching on the specifics of corporate worship?

Jesus Is the New "Place" of Worship

I think the reason is found in the way Jesus treated worship in his life and teaching. His main statement is found in John 4:20–24. But before we look at this text, consider a few other things he said. For example, his attitude toward the temple, the main place of Jewish worship, was not at all what the Jewish leaders thought it should be.

When he wove a whip and drove out the moneychangers, he said he did so not for the sake of proper sacrifices but for the sake of prayer—in fact, prayer for *all the nations*. "My house shall be called a house of prayer for all the nations" (Mark 11:17). In other words, he focused attention away from the outward acts of Jewish sacrifices to the personal act of communion with God for all peoples.

Then he said two other things about the temple that pointed to a radically altered view of worship. He said, "Something greater than the temple is here," referring to himself (Matt. 12:6), and, "Destroy this temple, and in three days I will raise it up" (John 2:19). This attitude toward the temple got not only him killed (Mark 14:58; 15:29) but also Stephen (Acts 6:14). That's how important it was.

Jesus identified himself as the true temple. "Something greater than the temple is here." In himself he would fulfill everything the temple stood for, especially the "place" where believers meet God. He diverted attention away from worship as a localized activity with outward forms and pointed toward a personal, spiritual experience with himself at the center. Worship does not have to have a building, a priesthood, and a sacrificial system. It has to have the risen Jesus.

Jesus Loosens Worship from Place and Form

What Jesus did to worship in the way he related to the temple is made explicit in John 4:20–24. Here he uses the word *proskyneō*—the dominant Old Testament word for worship—and shows that it is laden with outward and localized meaning. Then he transforms it into a concept that is mainly inward rather than outward and mainly pervasive rather than localized.

3. See note 2 for the few apparent exceptions in Hebrews.

The woman at the well said:

> Our fathers worshiped on this mountain, but you say that in Jerusalem is the place where people ought to worship." [The word for worship used here is the common Old Testament word *proskyneō*. Note the localized emphasis in her mind.] Jesus said to her, "Woman, believe me, an hour is coming when neither on this mountain nor in Jerusalem will you worship the Father."
>
> John 4:20–21

Here Jesus loosens worship from its outward and localized connotations. Place is not the issue: "neither on this mountain nor in Jerusalem." He goes on:

> But the hour is coming, and is now here, when the true worshipers will worship the Father in spirit and truth, for the Father is seeking such people to worship him. God is spirit, and those who worship him must worship in spirit and truth."
>
> John 4:23–24

Here is the key sentence: True worship, which was anticipated for the age to come, has arrived: "The hour *is coming* [in the age to come] and is *now* here [in me!]." What marks this true future worship, which has broken into the present from the glorious age to come, is that it is not bound by localized place or outward form. Instead of being on this mountain or in Jerusalem, it is "in spirit and truth."[4]

Jesus strips *proskyneō* of its last vestiges of localized and outward connotations.[5] It will not be wrong for worship to be in a place or to use outward forms, but he makes explicit and central that this is *not* what makes worship worship. What makes worship worship is what happens "in spirit and truth"—with or without a place and with or without outward forms.

What do those two phrases mean: "in spirit" and "in truth"?

4. In line with what we saw in note 2, Heinrich Greeven remarks that "if instead of naming a place to which the pilgrims should go to worship, Jesus says that the true place of worship is in the spirit and in truth: this is an oxymoron. Undiluted *proskynein*, the act of worship which is concrete in place and gesture, is lifted up to a new dimension: 'spirit and truth.'" *Theological Dictionary of the New Testament*, 6:764.

5. I am aware that Jesus may not have spoken Greek with this woman at the well and so may not have actually used the word *proskyneō*. But I take it that John's rendering of Jesus' intention is accurate and that John's use of *proskyneō* faithfully captures what Jesus wanted to communicate about the meaning of worship carried by that word.

I take "in spirit" to mean that this true worship is carried along by the Holy Spirit and is happening mainly as an inward, spiritual event, not mainly as an outward, bodily event. And I take "in truth" to mean that this true worship is a response to true views of God and is shaped and guided by true views of God.[6]

Jesus, therefore, broke decisively any necessary connection between worship and its outward and localized associations. It is mainly something inward and free from locality. This is what he meant when he said, "This people honors me with their lips, but their heart is far from me; in vain do they worship me" (Matt. 15:8–9). When the heart is far from God, worship is vain, empty, nonexistent. The experience of the heart is the defining, vital, indispensable essence of worship.

Why Is the Main Old Testament Word for Worship Boycotted?

Let's go back to our earlier question: Why is the central Old Testament word for worship, *proskyneō*, virtually boycotted by Peter, James, John, and Paul in the letters they write to the churches?[7] I think the reason is that the word did not make clear enough the inward, spiritual nature of true worship. It carried significant connotations of place and form. The word was associated with bodily bowing down and with the actual presence of a visible manifestation to bow down before.

In the Gospels, Jesus was present in *visible* form to fall before, so the word *proskyneō* is used often. In the Book of Revelation, the act of bowing down usually happens before God's manifestation in heaven or before false gods on the earth. Therefore, the word *proskyneō* is widely used in Revelation too. But in the epistles something very different is happening. Jesus is not present in visible glory to fall before. As a result, the tendency of the early church was to deal with worship as primarily inward and spiritual rather than outward and bodily, and primarily pervasive rather than localized.

6. See John Piper, *Desiring God: Meditations of a Christian Hedonist* (Sisters, Ore.: Multnomah, 1996), 73–95, for a fuller treatment of the context of John 4 and its relationship to worship in spirit and truth.

7. Another important word for worship, *sebomai*, is used twice in the Gospels ("In vain do they *worship* me" [Matt. 15:9 = Mark 7:7]) and eight times in Acts, always for God-fearing Gentiles except once for pagan worship (Acts 19:27). The absence of this word in the epistles is again remarkable. It is as if the apostles, in their letters, avoided words that were current for synagogue worship, both *proskyneō* and *sebomai*.

Unlocalizing and Unformalizing Words for Worship

To confirm this and to see even more clearly how radically non-place and non-event oriented the New Testament view of worship is, consider what Paul does to some of the other words related to Old Testament worship. For example, the next most frequent word for worship in the Greek translation of the Old Testament (after *proskyneō*) is the word *latreuō*[8] (over ninety times, almost always translating the Hebrew *'abad*), which is usually rendered "serve," as in Exodus 23:24: "You shall not bow to their gods or *serve [latreusēs]* them."

When Paul uses it for Christian worship, he goes out of his way to make sure that we know he does not mean a localized or outward form for worship practice but a nonlocalized, spiritual experience. In fact, he treats virtually all of life as worship when lived in the right spirit. For example, in Romans 1:9, he says, "I *serve* [or worship, *latreuō*] [God] *with my spirit* in the gospel of his Son." In Philippians 3:3, Paul says that true Christians "worship *by the Spirit* of God . . . and put no confidence in the flesh." And in Romans 12:1, Paul urges Christians, "Present your bodies as a living sacrifice, holy and acceptable to God, which is your *spiritual* worship."

Even when Paul uses an Old Testament word for worship, he takes pains to convey that what he has in mind is not mainly a localized or external event of worship but an internal, spiritual experience—so much so that he sees all of life and ministry as an expression of that inner experience of worship.

The same thing can be seen in the New Testament use of the Old Testament language for temple sacrifices and priestly service. The praise and thanks of the lips is called a sacrifice to God (Heb. 13:15). But so are the good works in everyday life (Heb. 13:16). Paul calls his own ministry a "priestly service [of worship]," and he calls the converts themselves an "acceptable offering [in worship]" to God (Rom. 15:16; see also Phil. 2:17). He even calls the money that the churches send him "a fragrant offering, a sacrifice acceptable and pleasing to God [in worship]" (Phil. 4:18). And his own death for Christ he calls a "drink offering" to God (2 Tim. 4:6).[9]

8. The noun of this verb is *latreia* and is used to translate the noun *'abodah* five times in the Greek Old Testament. Paul uses it twice, once for the Old Testament worship (Rom. 9:4) and once for the Christian life (Rom. 12:1).

9. The same thrust is seen in the imagery of the people of God (body of Christ) as the New Testament "temple" where spiritual sacrifices are offered (1 Peter 2:5), where God dwells by his Spirit (Eph. 2:21–22), and where all the people are seen as the holy priesthood (1 Peter 2:5, 9). Second Corinthians 6:16 shows that the New Covenant hope of God's presence is being fulfilled even now in the church as a people, not in

Making Worship Radically Inward So That It Permeates All of Life Outwardly

In the New Testament, worship is significantly de-institutionalized, de-localized, de-externalized. The entire thrust is taken off ceremony and seasons and places and forms and is shifted to what is happening in the heart—not just on Sunday but on every day, and all the time in all of life.

This is what is meant when we read things such as, "Whether you eat or drink, or whatever you do, do all to the glory of God" (1 Cor. 10:31). And "whatever you do, in word or deed, do everything in the name of the Lord Jesus, giving thanks to God the Father through him" (Col. 3:17). This is the essence of worship: to act in a way that reflects the heart's valuing of the glory of God. But the New Testament uses those greatest of all worship sentences without any reference to worship services. They describe life.

Even when Paul calls us to "be filled with the Spirit, addressing one another in psalms and hymns and spiritual songs, singing and making melody to the Lord with all your heart, giving thanks always and for everything to God the Father in the name of our Lord Jesus Christ" (Eph. 5:18–20), he makes no reference to a time or a place or a service. In fact, the keys words are "always" and "for everything"—"giving thanks *always* and for *everything*" (cf. Col. 3:16). This may in fact be what we should do in a worship service, but it is not Paul's burden to tell us that. His burden is to call for a radical, inward authenticity of worship and an all-encompassing pervasiveness of worship in all of life. Place and form are not of the essence. Spirit and truth are all-important.

The Reformed and Puritan Impulse

This is what gripped and shaped the Reformed tradition, especially the Puritans and their heirs. Worship is radically oriented on the experience of the heart and freed from form and place. John Calvin expresses the freedom of worship from traditional form in the following way:

> [The Master] did not will in outward discipline and ceremonies to prescribe in detail what we ought to do (because he foresaw that this depended on the state of the times, and he did not deem one form suitable

---

any particular service: "We are the temple of the living God; as God said, 'I will make my dwelling among them and walk among them, and I will be their God, and they shall be my people.'"

for all ages). . . . Because he has taught nothing specifically, and because these things are not necessary to salvation, and for the upbuilding of the church ought to be variously accommodated to the customs of each nation and age, it will be fitting (as the advantage of the church will require) to change and abrogate traditional practices and to establish new ones. Indeed, I admit that we ought not to charge into innovation rashly, suddenly, for insufficient cause. But love will best judge what may hurt or edify; and if we let love be our guide, all will be safe.[10]

Luther expresses the freedom of worship from place: "The worship of God . . . should be free at table, in private rooms, downstairs, upstairs, at home, abroad, in all places, by all people, at all times. Whoever tells you anything else is lying as badly as the pope and the devil himself."[11] The Puritans carried through the simplification and freedom of worship in music, liturgy, and architecture. Patrick Collinson summarizes Puritan theory and practice by saying that "the life of the Puritan was in one sense a continuous act of worship, pursued under an unremitting and lively sense of God's providential purposes and constantly refreshed by religious activity, personal, domestic and public."[12] One of the reasons Puritans called their churches "meeting houses" and kept them very simple was to divert attention from the physical place to the inward, spiritual nature of worship through the Word.

A Radical Intensification of Worship as Inward, Spiritual Experience

My conclusion, then, is that in the New Testament there is a stunning indifference to the outward forms and places of worship. At the same time, there is a radical intensification of worship as an inward, spiritual experience that has no bounds and pervades all of life. These emphases were recaptured in the Reformation and came to clear expression in the Puritan wing of the Reformed tradition. One of the reasons for this development in the New Testament is that the New Testament is not a manual for worship services. Rather, it is a vision for missions in thousands of diverse people groups around the world. In such groups, outward forms of worship will vary drastically, but the inner reality of treasuring Christ in spirit and truth is common ground.

10. John Calvin, *Institutes of the Christian Religion*, vol. 2 (Philadelphia: Westminster, 1960), IV, 10, 30, 1208.
11. Quoted in Ewald M. Plass, ed., *What Luther Says*, vol. 3 (St. Louis: Concordia, 1959), 1546.
12. Quoted in Leland Ryken, *Worldly Saints: The Puritans as They Really Were* (Grand Rapids: Zondervan, 1986), 116.

What Is the Essence of This Radical, Inward Experience of Worship?

What begs for attention now is the question, What is the essence of this radical, authentic, inward, unifying experience called worship, and how is it that this experience comes to expression in gathered congregations and in everyday life? My answer in advance is that the essential, vital, indispensable, defining heart of worship is the experience of *being satisfied with God*. And the reason this worship pervades all of life is that all Christian behavior is properly motivated by a thirst for more and more satisfaction in God.

In other words, the basic reason why the apostle Paul makes so little distinction between worship as a congregational service, on the one hand, and worship as a pattern of daily life, on the other hand, is that they are united with the same root—a radical valuing, cherishing, esteeming, treasuring of God in Christ and a passion for more of him. The impulse for singing a hymn and the impulse for visiting a prisoner are the same: a freeing contentment in God and a thirst for more of God—a desire to experience as much satisfaction in God as we can.

I have written for some years on these things and have tried to unfold them and defend them biblically, especially in *Desiring God*,[13] *Future Grace*,[14] *The Pleasures of God*,[15] and *God's Passion for His Glory*.[16] So here I will give just a brief explanation to show the biblical root of my thesis, which is so crucial for the missionary enterprise.

I start with God. The root of our passion and thirst for God is God's own infinite exuberance for God. The root of our quest for satisfaction in God's glory is God's jealousy that his own satisfaction in his own glory be known and shared by his people. God is infinitely committed to preserving and displaying his glory in all that he does from creation to consummation. And in this commitment, we see his zeal and love and satisfaction in his glory (as we saw in chapter 1 and chapter 6). God has purposed and worked so that predestination (Eph. 1:4–6), creation (Isa. 43:6–7), incarnation (Rom. 15:8–9), propitiation (Rom. 3:25–26), sanctification (Phil. 1:10–11), and consummation (2 Thess. 1:10) are all designed to magnify his own worth and glory in the world.

In other words, God is so overflowingly, unashamedly satisfied with his own glory that he devotes all his energies to making this glory

13. See note 6.

14. John Piper, *The Purifying Power of Living by Faith in FUTURE GRACE* (Sisters, Ore.: Multnomah, 1995).

15. John Piper, *The Pleasures of God: Meditations on God's Delight in Being God* (Sisters, Ore.: Multnomah, 2000).

16. John Piper, *God's Passion for His Glory: Living the Vision of Jonathan Edwards* (Wheaton: Crossway, 1998).

known. The creation of the universe, the history of redemption, and the consummation of all things are driven ultimately by this great passion in the heart of God—to exult fully in his own glory by making it known and praised among all the nations.

But if God is so satisfied with his glory that he makes its display the goal of all that he does, then is not his own satisfaction in himself the root of our satisfaction in him? But putting it that way doesn't quite get to the heart of the matter. To get to the heart of the matter we need to ask, Why is it a loving thing for God to be so self-exalting, and why, if we come to share his satisfaction in himself, is it the essence and heart of worship?

How C. S. Lewis Helped Me See the Obvious

The answer to the first question—Why is it loving of God to be so self-exalting that he does all that he does for his own glory?—came to me with the help of C. S. Lewis. When I was pondering the fact that in Ephesians 1:6, 12, 14 Paul says that God performs all the acts of redemption so that we might praise his glory, I discovered that in his early days as a Christian, Lewis was bothered by the commands of God to praise God. They seemed vain.

But then he discovered why this is not vain but profoundly loving of God to do. Here is his all-important insight:

> The most obvious fact about praise . . . strangely escaped me. . . . I had never noticed that all enjoyment spontaneously overflows into praise. . . . The world rings with praise—lovers praising their mistresses, readers their favorite poet, walkers praising the countryside, players praising their favorite game—praise of weather, wines, dishes, actors, horses, colleges, countries, historical personages, children, flowers, mountains, rare stamps, rare beetles, even sometimes politicians and scholars. . . . My whole, more general difficulty about praise of God depended on my absurdly denying to us, as regards the supremely Valuable, what we delight to do, what indeed we can't help doing, about everything else we value.
>
> I think we delight to praise what we enjoy because the praise not merely expresses but completes the enjoyment; it is its appointed consummation. It is not out of compliment that lovers keep on telling one another how beautiful they are, the delight is incomplete till it is expressed.[17]

17. C. S. Lewis, *Reflections on the Psalms* (New York: Harcourt Brace and World, 1958), 93–95.

In other words, genuine, heartfelt praise is not artificially tacked on to joy. It is the consummation of joy. Joy in some beauty or some value is not complete until it is expressed in a kind of praise.

Now, if God loves us the way the Bible says he does, then he would surely give us what is best for us. And what is best for us is *himself.* So if God loves us, God must give us God, for our enjoyment, and nothing less. But if our enjoyment—if our satisfaction in God—is incomplete until it comes to completion in praise, then God would not be loving if he were indifferent to our praise. If he didn't command us to praise him, he would not be commanding us to be as satisfied as we could be, and that would not be loving.

So what emerges on reflection is that God's self-exaltation—his doing everything to display his glory and to win our praise—is not unloving; it is the only way that an infinitely all-glorious God can love. His greatest gift of love is to give us a share in the very satisfaction that he has in himself and then to call that satisfaction to its fullest consummation in the expression of praise.

The love of God is expressed by the repeated biblical commands that we rejoice in the Lord (Phil. 4:4), that we delight ourselves in the Lord (Ps. 37:4), that we serve the Lord with gladness (Ps. 100:2), that we be glad in the Lord (Ps. 32:11) and by the manifold promise that "in your presence there is fullness of joy; at your right hand are pleasures forevermore" (Ps. 16:11).

Joy in God Is Itself a Tribute to His All-Satisfying Worth, Even before Praise

There is one more component of this argument, leading to the conclusion that overflowing satisfaction in God is the essence (not the entirety) of worship. I will state it logically and then exegetically. Logically, if our praise is the consummation of our joy in God and not a mere add-on, then our joy in God must itself be a tribute to God. This joy, even before it overflows in praise, is a reflection (if we could see into the heart) of God's all-satisfying worth. That is, he is honored by our delight in him. We know this from experience; to enjoy someone's presence is to honor that person. To feel constrained to be around someone out of duty does not honor the person very much. This, then, is our conclusion: God is glorified in us when we are satisfied in him. And since worship is essentially the experience of magnifying the glory of God, the essence of worship is being satisfied in God.

Now, we must see how this is rooted in Scripture. Consider Philippians 1:20–21. Paul says, "It is my eager expectation and hope that . . .

Christ will be honored in my body, whether by life or by death. For to me to live is Christ, and to die is gain." The issue is, How shall Christ be honored in Paul's body? That is a worship question. How shall Paul show the worth of Christ with his body? He says he wants to honor Christ "whether by life or by death," so there is a way to honor Christ in the body by dying. The question is, What is it? How do we honor Christ in death?

Paul answers in verse 21. He says in sum, "I expect and hope to honor Christ in my body in death . . . *for* to me to die is gain." In other words, if I can experience death as gain, my death will honor Christ. We can see here how Paul's mind is working. The honor and all-satisfying worth of Christ is reflected in my dying to the degree that in my soul I am not begrudging the loss of all my earthly things and relations but am counting Christ as so superior that death is all gain. The assumption—which he makes clear in verse 23—is that death means a closer intimacy with Christ. In verse 23, he says, "My desire is to depart and be with Christ, for that is far better." So the reason death is gain is that it brings a better experience of Christ. The exegetical conclusion then is that savoring Christ above all that we lose in death magnifies the worth of Christ. The degree to which we are satisfied in him as we die is the degree to which he is honored as we die. He is most glorified in us when we are most satisfied in him—in life and death.

What Then Is the Essence of Worship?

From all this I conclude (logically and exegetically) that the essential, vital, indispensable, defining heart of worship is the experience of *being satisfied with God in Christ.* This experience magnifies his worth, and such magnifying is what worship is. This is why Jesus and the apostles were so stunningly indifferent to external forms and so radically intent on inward, spiritual, authentic worship. Without the experience of heartfelt satisfaction in God, praises are vain. If genuine praise can flow from a heart without satisfaction in God, then the word "hypocrisy" has no meaning, and Jesus' words are pointless when he says, "This people honors me with their lips [that is, with verbal praises], but their heart [that is, their heartfelt treasuring and satisfaction] is far from me" (Matt. 15:8).

So when I say, "Missions is not the ultimate goal of the church. Worship is," I do not mean "worship services." I do not mean "worship singing." Those are part of the *expression* of the essence of worship, but those things can happen and *not* be worship. Worship is not first an outward act; it is an inner spiritual treasuring of the character and the ways of God in Christ. It is a cherishing of Christ, a being satisfied with all that God is for us in Christ. When these things are missing, there is no worship, no matter what forms or expressions are present.[18]

Implications

Now consider four implications of this for the experience of worship and its expression in worship services.

1. *The pursuit of joy in God is not optional. It is our highest duty.* Millions of Christians have absorbed a popular ethic that comes more from Immanuel Kant than from the Bible. Their assumption is that it is morally defective to seek happiness—to pursue joy, to crave satisfaction, and to devote ourselves to seeking it. This is absolutely deadly for authentic worship. The degree to which this Kantian ethic flourishes is the degree to which worship dies, for the essence of worship is satisfaction in God. To be indifferent to or even fearful of the pursuit[19] of what is essential to worship is to oppose worship—and the authenticity of worship services (in any culture or any form).

Not a few pastors foster this very thing by saying things such as, "The problem is that our people don't come on Sunday morning to give; they only come to get. If they came to give, we would have life." That is probably not a good diagnosis. People ought to come to get. They ought to come starved for *God*. They ought to come saying, "As a deer pants for flowing streams, so pants my soul for you, O God" (Ps. 42:1). God is mightily honored when a people know that they will die of hunger and thirst unless they have God. It is the job of pastors to

18. Don't take me to mean that the true Christian never struggles with low and almost dead and barren seasons of spiritual affections. We do. See especially the crucial discussion of three levels or stages of worship in Piper, *Desiring God,* 85–87. There can be faint echoes of the worth of God that shine through even when we are hanging on to hope in him by our fingernails. He is honored by the pitiful, dying woman who drowns in her own vomit (I speak from pastoral experience) and does not curse God but submits, if with screams, and hopes against hope that this horror is not wrath but the last ghoulish terror before everlasting dawn.

19. I am keenly aware of the criticism that the direct pursuit of joy by taking one's eyes off The Enjoyed is deadly. I am not commending that you go to the Grand Canyon of God's greatness and sit on the rim with your finger on your pulse and your mind on your inner condition. That would cancel out the Canyon. Give yourself up to the Canyon. See it. Revel in it. Absorb it. Ponder it. That is the kind of pursuit I have in mind. God's all-satisfying glory is not experienced by focusing on the experience but on the glory.

spread a banquet for them. Recovering the rightness and indispensability of pursuing our satisfaction *in God* will go a long way toward restoring the authenticity and power of worship—whether in solitude, in a group of six elders in Uzbekistan, in a rented garage in Liberia, in a megachurch in America, or on the scaffold in the last moment just before "gain."

2. *Another implication of saying that the essence of worship is satisfaction in God is that worship becomes radically God-centered.* Nothing makes God more supreme and more central than when people are utterly persuaded that nothing—not money or prestige or leisure or family or job or health or sports or toys or friends or ministry—is going to bring satisfaction to their aching hearts besides God. This conviction breeds a people who go hard after God on Sunday morning (or any other time). They are not confused about why they are there. They do not see songs and prayers and sermons as mere traditions or mere duties. They see them as means of getting to God or God getting to them for more of his fullness.

If the focus shifts to our giving to God, subtly it becomes not God at the center but the quality of our giving. Are we singing worthily of the Lord? Are our instrumentalists playing with quality fitting a gift to the Lord? Is the preaching a suitable offering to the Lord? And little by little the focus shifts from the utter indispensability of the Lord himself to the quality of our performances. We even start to define excellence and power in worship in terms of the technical distinction of our artistic acts.

Nothing keeps God at the center of worship like the biblical conviction that the essence of worship is deep, heartfelt satisfaction in him and the conviction that the expression and pursuit of that satisfaction are why we are together. No outward act can replace this. The act can only express it (which we call a service of worship) or substitute for it (which we call hypocrisy).

3. *A third implication of saying that the essence of worship is satisfaction in God is that this essence protects the primacy of worship by forcing us to come to terms with the fact that worship is an end in itself.* If the essence of worship is satisfaction in God, then worship can't be a means to anything else. We simply can't say to God, "I want to be satisfied in you so that I can have something else." Such an expression would mean that we are not really satisfied in God but in that something else, and that would dishonor God.

For thousands of people and pastors, however, the event of worship on Sunday morning (that is, the worship service) is conceived of as a means to accomplish something other than worship. We "worship" to raise money; we "worship" to attract crowds; we "worship" to heal human hurts; we "worship" to recruit workers; we "worship" to improve church morale. We "worship" to give talented musicians an opportunity to fulfill their calling; we "worship" to teach our children the way of righteousness; we "worship" to help marriages stay together; we "worship" to evangelize the lost among us; we "worship" to motivate people for service projects; we "worship" to give our churches a family feeling, and so on.

If we are not careful, when we speak of aiming at these things "through worship," we bear witness that we do not know what true worship is. Genuine affections for God (the essence of worship) are an end in themselves. I cannot say to my wife, "I feel a strong delight in you so that you will make me a nice meal." That is not the way delight works. Delight ends with her. It does not have a nice meal in view. I cannot say to my son, "I love playing ball with you . . . so that you will cut the grass." If your heart really delights in playing ball with him, that delight cannot be performed as a means of getting him to do something else.

I am not denying that worship (the essence and the service) may have a hundred good effects in the life of the church. It will, just as true affection in marriage makes everything better. My point is: The degree to which we "do worship" for these reasons is the degree to which worship ceases to be authentic. Keeping satisfaction in God at the center guards us from that tragedy.

4. *Finally, the last implication of saying that the essence of worship is being satisfied with God is that this definition accounts for the fact that Paul considers all of life an expression of worship.* All Christian behavior (in every culture at every level) is to be done out of satisfaction in God and with a view to preserving and increasing satisfaction in God. I devoted a chapter in *Desiring God* ("Love: The Labor of Christian Hedonism") to justifying that sentence, but let me commend it to you with one word from the Lord Jesus.

In Luke 12:33, Jesus says, "Sell your possessions, and give to the needy. [And thus] provide yourselves with moneybags that do not grow old, with a treasure in the heavens that does not fail." I understand the "treasure in the heavens" refers to increased measures of joy at God's right hand and pleasures in his fellowship in the age to come. Jesus says that we are to provide ourselves with that—in other words, make efforts to increase our joys with God in heaven. He says that the way to do so is by selling our possessions and giving alms. That is illustrative of all the ways we sacrifice and love in the Christian life. We are to live this way so as to provide ourselves with treasures in heaven.

In other words, we should aim in all we do to maximize our satisfaction in God—now and in the age to come. If someone asks, "Is it loving to give alms to others with a view to maximizing our own joy in God?" the answer is a resounding yes, because in giving up worldly things so that we can meet the needs of others, our aim is to persuade them that the treasure of God, which frees us to give in this way, is so valuable that they too should embrace it and live for it and so join us in the joys of heaven. Everyone who falls in love with God because they have seen in us that God is more precious than things will make our satisfaction in God all the sweeter. Which is one reason why missions is one of the most deeply satisfying callings in the world. "It is more blessed to give than to receive" (Acts 20:35).

So I believe it can be shown biblically that all our behavior should be motivated by a deeply freeing taste of God's goodness and a thirst for more and more satisfaction in God. Therefore, the root of Christian living and the root of congregational praise are the same, which is why for Paul worship simply cannot be merely or even mainly thought of in terms of Sunday services but of all of life. His is an absolutely God-saturated vision of Christian existence. When our whole life is consumed with pursuing satisfaction in God, everything we do highlights the value and worth of God, which simply means that everything becomes worship. May God make himself—manifest fully in Jesus Christ—that precious to us.

That is what I am referring to when I say, "Missions is not the ultimate goal of the church. Worship is." Our goal is to see that experience happen among all the peoples of the world. May the power of the gospel waken the dead, bring them from darkness to light and from the power of Satan to God, so that they see him and savor him with all their hearts. And may they be so radically satisfied in him that they are freed from the fears and pleasures of this world and follow Jesus on the Calvary road of love. Then others will see their good works and give glory to their Father in heaven—and the Word will go on from glory to glory.

Conclusion

The ultimate goal of God in all of history is to uphold and display his glory for the enjoyment of the redeemed from every tribe and tongue and people and nation. His goal is the gladness of his people, because God is most glorified in us when we are most satisfied in him. Delight is a higher tribute than duty. The chief end of God is to glorify God and enjoy his glory forever. Since his glory is magnified most in the God-centered passions of his joyful people, God's self-exaltation and our jubilation are one. The greatest news in all the world is that God's ultimate aim to be glorified and man's aim to be satisfied are not at odds.

Worship

The goal of missions, therefore, is the gladness of the peoples in the greatness of God. "The LORD reigns, let the earth rejoice; let the many coastlands *be glad!*" (Ps. 97:1). "Let the nations *be glad and sing for joy!*" (Ps. 67:4). The missionary command to be happy in God is simply a command for the consummation of praise. Professed praise of God without pleasure in God is hypocrisy.

Therefore, worship is the fuel and the goal of missions. Worship is the goal of missions because in missions we aim to bring the nations into the white-hot enjoyment of God's glory. It is the fuel of missions because we can't commend what we don't cherish. We can't call out, "Let the nations *be glad!*" until we say, "*I rejoice* in the Lord." Missions begins and ends in worship.

Prayer

This means that God is absolutely supreme in missions. He is the beginning and the end. He is also the one who sustains and empowers the entire process. "From him and through him and to him are all things. To him be glory forever" (Rom. 11:36). God's moment-by-moment sustaining of the Christian movement preserves his supremacy, because the one who gives the power gets the glory. Let him who serves serve "by the strength that God supplies—in order that in everything God may be glorified through Jesus Christ" (1 Peter 4:11).

This is why God has ordained prayer to have such a crucial place in the mission of the church. The purpose of prayer is to make clear to all the participants in missions that the victory belongs to the Lord. "The horse is made ready for the day of battle, but the victory belongs to the LORD" (Prov. 21:31). Prayer is God's appointed means of bringing grace to the world and glory to himself. "Call upon me in the day of trouble; I will deliver you, and *you shall glorify me*" (Ps. 50:15). "Whatever you ask in my name, this I will do, *that the Father may be glorified in the Son*" (John 14:13).

Prayer puts God in the place of the all-sufficient Benefactor and puts us in the place of needy beneficiaries. Therefore, when the mission of the church moves forward by prayer, the supremacy of God is manifest and the needs of Christian missionaries are met. In prayer, he is glorified and we are satisfied. "Until now you have asked nothing in my name. Ask, and you will receive, *that your joy may be full*" (John 16:24). The purpose of prayer is the Father's fame and the saints' fullness.

Suffering

God himself is the fullness we live on and the fountain of life that we commend in missions. He is our treasure. His "steadfast love is better than life" (Ps. 63:3). Therefore, the greatness of his worth is seen most clearly when we are willing to give up our lives for the sake of his love. We measure the worth of a treasure by what we will gladly give up in order to have it.

Suffering alone proves nothing, but suffering accepted because of the "surpassing worth of knowing Christ" and losses embraced in order to "gain Christ" (Phil. 3:8) prove that Christ is supremely valuable. "Blessed are you when others revile you and persecute you. . . . Rejoice and be glad, for your reward is great in heaven" (Matt. 5:11–12). The extent of our *sacrifice* coupled with the depth of our *joy* displays the worth we put on the reward of God. Loss and suffering, joyfully accepted for the kingdom of God, show the supremacy of God's glory more clearly in the world than all worship and prayer.

Therefore, God ordains that the mission of his church move forward not only by the fuel of worship and in the power of prayer but also at the price of suffering. "If anyone would come after me, let him deny himself and take up his cross and follow me" (Mark 8:34). "A servant is not greater than his master. If they persecuted me, they will also persecute you" (John 15:20). "If they have called the master of the house Beelzebul, how much more will they malign those of his household" (Matt. 10:25). "The Son of Man must suffer many things" (Mark 8:31). "As the Father has sent me, even so I am sending you" (John 20:21). "Behold, I am sending you out as sheep in the midst of wolves" (Matt. 10:16). "I will show him how much he must suffer for the sake of my name" (Acts 9:16).

Is Knowing Christ Crucial?

Because the price is so high, one may well ask, Is it really necessary? If the goal of God in history is to uphold and display his glory for the enjoyment of the redeemed, may it not be that he will redeem people without missions? Could people come to praise the true God from hearts of saving faith while still ignorant of Jesus and his saving work? Could nature or other religions lead people into eternal life and joy with God?

The biblical answer we have seen is no. It is a stunning New Testament truth that since the incarnation of the Son of God, all saving faith must henceforth fix on him. This was not always true. Before Christ, the people of Israel focused faith on the promises of God (Rom. 4:20) summed up in a coming Redeemer. And the nations were allowed to walk in their own ways (Acts 14:16). But those times were called the times of ignorance. With the coming of the Son of God into the world, Christ was made the conscious center of the mission of the church. The aim of missions is to "bring about the obedience of faith *for the sake of his*[1] *name* among all the nations" (Rom. 1:5). God's will is to be glorified in his Son by making him the center of all missionary proclamation. The supremacy of God in missions is affirmed biblically by affirming the supremacy of his Son as the focus of all saving faith.

People or Peoples?

Since the eternal destiny of every individual hangs on knowing Christ and embracing him gladly as the highest value of life, is then the task of missions to maximize the number of people redeemed or the number of peoples reached? The biblical answer is that God's call for missions in Scripture *cannot* be defined merely in terms of crossing cultures to maximize the total number of individuals

1. The context makes it crystal clear that "his" refers to Jesus Christ: "[He] was declared to be the Son of God in power according to the Spirit of holiness by his resurrection from the dead, Jesus Christ our Lord, through whom we have received grace and apostleship to bring about the obedience of faith for the sake of *his* name among all the nations" (Rom. 1:4–5).

saved.[2] Rather, God's will for missions is that every people group be reached with the testimony of Christ and that a people be called out for his name from among all the nations. It may be that this definition of missions will, in fact, result in the greatest possible number of white-hot worshipers for God's Son. But that remains for God to decide. Our responsibility is to define missions his way and then obey.

The ultimate goal of God in all of history is to uphold and display his glory for the enjoyment of the redeemed from every tribe and tongue and people and nation. The beauty of praise that will come to the Lord from the diversity of the nations is greater than the beauty that would come to him if the chorus of the redeemed were culturally uniform or limited. Moreover, there is something about God that is so universally praiseworthy and so profoundly beautiful and so comprehensively worthy and so deeply satisfying that God will find passionate admirers in every diverse people group in the world. His true greatness will be manifest in the breadth of the diversity of those who perceive and cherish his beauty. The more diverse the people groups who forsake their gods to follow the true God, the more visible God's superiority over all his competitors.

By focusing on all the people groups of the world, God undercuts ethnocentric pride and throws all peoples back upon his free grace rather than on any distinctive of their own. This humility is the flip side of giving God all the glory. Humility means reveling in his grace, not in our goodness. In pressing us on toward all the peoples, God is pressing us further into the humblest and deepest experience of his grace and weaning us more and more from our ingrained pride. In doing this, he is preparing for himself a people—from all the peoples—who will be able to worship him with free and white-hot admiration.

Therefore, the church is bound to engage with the Lord of glory in his cause. It is our unspeakable privilege to be caught up with him in the greatest movement in history—the ingathering of the elect from every tribe and language and people and nation until the full number of the Gentiles comes in and all Israel is saved and the Son of Man descends with power and great glory as King of kings and Lord of lords and the earth is full of the knowledge of his glory as the waters cover the sea forever and ever. Then the supremacy of Christ will be manifest to all, and he will deliver the kingdom to God the Father, and God will be all in all.

2. David Doran, in his book, *For the Sake of His Name: Challenging a New Generation for World Missions* (Allen Park, Mich.: Student Global Impact, 2002), 131–54, has written a chapter called "The Territory of the Great Commission." In it he gives a corrective to a lopsided emphasis on the people-group focus in missions at the expense of the geographic focus. In spite of our interaction, I do not think it necessary to change anything I have written. But I do alert the reader that Doran interacts with me in his book and so may provide a perspective that I am neglecting.

The Supremacy
of God
in Going
and Sending

by Tom Steller

There is a wonderful passage in the often neglected epistle of 3 John that sums up the burden of this book beautifully. We want to leave you with its truth ringing in your mind and heart. There are only two ways for us to respond to the truth we have been considering about the supremacy of God in missions. We must either go out for the sake of his name, or we must send and support such people who do, and do so in a manner worthy of God. Listen to the words of the apostle John, who heard the heartbeat of Jesus as he leaned on his breast and who listened with his own ears to the giving of the Great Commission.

> The elder to the beloved Gaius, whom I love in truth. Beloved, I pray that in all respects you may prosper and be in good health, just as your soul prospers. For I was very glad when brethren came and bore witness to your truth, that is, how you are walking in truth. I have no greater joy than this, to hear of my children walking in the truth. Beloved, you are acting faithfully in whatever you accomplish for the brethren, and especially when they are strangers; and they bear witness to your love before the church; and *you will do well to send them on their way in a manner worthy of God. For they went out for the sake of the Name, accepting nothing from the Gentiles. Therefore we ought to support such men, that we may be fellow-workers with the truth.*
>
> 3 John 1–8 NASB

235

It is worth noting what makes a godly old man happy. The apostle John, who refers to himself simply as "the elder," is overjoyed. He has just received word that Gaius, one of his spiritual children, is walking in the truth. There is no greater joy than this!

What evidence compels this old apostle to be convinced that Gaius's soul is prospering? What is the truth in which Gaius is walking? Apparently some itinerant evangelists/missionaries, whom John knew, had visited Gaius and were loved by him in a special way. They returned to the church of which John was a part and testified that Gaius treated them well, even though they were strangers to him. This so moved John that he wrote Gaius a letter to encourage him for walking in the truth and for acting faithfully. He wanted to urge Gaius to continue all the more. "You will do well to send them on their way in a manner worthy of God."

Gaius was admonished by the apostle to be a sender. This phrase, "to send on one's way," occurs nine times in the New Testament, and each one occurs in a missionary context.[1]

The most descriptive verse is found in Titus 3:13. In this verse, Paul writes to Titus, "Diligently help Zenas the lawyer and Apollos on their way so that nothing is lacking for them" (NASB). From this verse we can learn that sending is something to be done diligently and is all inclusive—"so that *nothing* is lacking for them."

In 3 John, this diligence and thoroughness is captured in the phrase "in a manner worthy of God" (v. 6). This elevates the importance of sending as high as can be imagined. It is a commandment of God (notice the "ought" of verse 8). The reason we must send them in a manner worthy of God is that they go out for the sake of the name. The name of God is at stake in how we treat our missionaries. God is glorified when we support them substantially with our prayers, our money, our time, and myriad other practical ways (notice the "whatever" in verse 5). God is not glorified when our missionaries are simply a name on the back of the church bulletin or a line item in the budget.

It is not of secondary importance to be engaged in this ministry of sending. It is a very high calling. It is walking in the truth. It is the manifestation of a healthy and prospering soul. Senders are fellow workers with the truth. To send in a manner worthy of God is a call to excellence in the support of missionaries. It is a direct participation in God's purpose. The cruciality of sending cannot be overemphasized. Therefore, it must not be done in a shoddy manner but in "a manner

1. See especially the uses of *propempō* in Acts 15:3; Rom. 15:24; 1 Cor. 16:6, 11; 2 Cor. 1:16; and Titus 3:15.

worthy of God."[2] There is a world of difference between a church "having" a missionary and a church "sending" a missionary. When we send missionaries in a manner worthy of God, God is glorified, our souls prosper, and we are fellow workers with the truth. We are in sync with God's heartbeat and his purpose to be glorified among all the peoples.

But just as there is a God-centeredness to sending, there is also a God-centeredness to going. In fact, the two are intimately related. Listen to the apostle John's flow of thought. "You will do well to send them on their way *in a manner worthy of God. For* they went out *for the sake of the Name,* accepting nothing from the Gentiles. *Therefore* we ought to support *such* men." According to this text, only a certain kind of person is to be supported and sent to the mission field (notice the word "such"). Only those who *go out for the sake of the name* ought to be supported.

Here is perhaps the best definition of a missionary in the New Testament. A missionary is someone who goes out for the sake of the name, accepting nothing from the Gentiles. Private material gain must not be the motive. Even genuine humanitarian concern, though crucial, must not be the driving motive. Rather, a missionary is propelled by a deep love for the name and glory of God. Like the apostle Paul, a missionary's aim is to "bring about the obedience of faith among all the Gentiles, *for His name's sake*" (Rom. 1:5 NASB).

The purpose of this book has not been merely to inform you of the supremacy of God in missions. Rather, from start to finish we have sought to invite you to become more personally engaged in the cause of missions with a heartfelt, God-centered passion. Our aim has not been to exalt the missionary but to exalt God and to exalt his mission. The precise nature of your engagement in the cause of missions will be different from that of any other person. Whether you go as a missionary or stay as a sender is a secondary issue. The primary issue is that whatever you do, you do it for the glory of God (1 Cor. 10:31) and for the advance of his kingdom (Matt. 6:33) and with a view to its consummation, which will embrace every tribe and tongue and people and nation (Matt. 24:14; Rev. 7:9).

2. John Stott, commenting on verse 6, says, "They are not just to be received when they arrive, but to be so refreshed and provided for (no doubt with supplies of food and money) as to be sent forward in a manner worthy of God. . . . Such thoughtful sending forth of missionaries on their journey is not only a 'loyal thing' (v. 5 RSV), but a 'beautiful' thing (v. 6, *kalōs poiēseis, you will do well*)." *The Letters of John: An Introduction and Commentary,* Tyndale New Testament Commentary, rev. ed. (Grand Rapids: Eerdmans, 1989), 225.

David Bryant calls one who has this mind-set a "world Christian."[3] Not every Christian is called to be a missionary, but every follower of Christ is called to be a world Christian. A world Christian is someone who is so gripped by the glory of God and the glory of his global purpose that he chooses to align himself with God's mission to fill the earth with the knowledge of his glory as the waters cover the sea (Hab. 2:14). Everything a world Christian does is with a view to the hallowing of God's name and the coming of God's kingdom among all the peoples of the earth. The burning prayer of the world Christian is, "Let the peoples praise you, O God; let all the peoples praise you!" (Ps. 67:3). So whether we are those who send or those who go, let us glory in the supremacy of God in missions, and let us link arms together as we join in the refrain of old, "Let the nations be glad!"

Tom Steller is Pastor for Leadership Development, Bethlehem Baptist Church, and Dean of the Bethlehem Institute, Minneapolis, Minnesota.

3. David Bryant has helped define and popularize the notion of "world Christian" in his book *In the Gap: What It Means to Be a World Christian* (Downers Grove, Ill.: Inter-Varsity, 1979).

Subject Index

amillennialism, 54 n. 5
annihilationism, 111–12, 120 nn. 15–16, 209
  texts against, 116–22
apathy, 94–95
atonement
  necessity for salvation, 122–25
  universality of, 123
austerity, 47–48

blessed to be a blessing, 174

China, 65
Christ
  came to glorify God, 24–25
  his name the only name, 33–34
  and missions for his name, 38–39, 127–28
  and necessity of his work, 113, 122–25
  as only hope for salvation, 116
  summary statement of his necessity, 233
  supremacy in missions, 111–54
  as true temple, 217
compassion
  not at odds with passion for God, 33–35, 210–13
  seeks to show people glory of Christ, 212
  and zeal for God, 42
Cornelius, not saved before hearing gospel, 134–38
covenant, new, 57

diversity
  how magnifies God, 198–200
  intended and eternal, 197–98

election
  focused now on Christ, 127–28
  for God's glory, 22
  see also predestination
eternal security, 46
ethnos, 161–64
evangelism
  E-1, E-2, E-3, 195
  see also missionary, missions

faith
  fight of, 46
  nature of, 211–12
  as necessary for salvation, 113–15, 125–52
  strengthened by suffering, 86–87
families of the earth, 167–70
  size of, 190–91

general revelation, as way of salvation, 114 nn. 6–7, 115
glory of God
  as chief end of God, 20–27, 28, 63, 204–5, 223
  as goal of prayer, 58–59
  relation to worship, 205–6
God
  commands joy, 36–38
  glorified in eternal diversity, 198–200
  and goal to glorify self, 20–27, 63, 204–5
  and hallowing his name, 39
  and his God-centeredness, 21–22
  and loving to seek his glory, 31–35
  make more of his glory, 40–41
  may do what we may not, 29–31
  not to be served, 36–37
  an overweening ego? 29

239

Person Index

Scripture Index

Desiring God Ministries

DesiringGod.org

Desiring God Ministries exists to spread a passion for the supremacy of God in all things for the joy of all peoples through Jesus Christ. We have hundreds of resources available for this purpose, most of which are books, sermons, and audio collections by John Piper. Visit our web site and discover:

- free access to over twenty years of printed sermons by John Piper
- new, free, downloadable audio sermons posted weekly
- many free articles and meditations
- a comprehensive online store where you can purchase John Piper's books and audio collections, as well as God-centered children's curricula published by DGM
- information about DGM's conferences and international offices

Designed for individuals with no available discretionary funds, DGM has a whatever-you-can-afford policy. Contact us at the addresses or phone numbers below if you would like more information about this policy.

Desiring God Ministries
720 Thirteenth Avenue South
Minneapolis, MN 55415-1793
Toll free in the USA: 1-888-346-4700
International calls: 612-373-0651
Fax: 612-338-4372
mail@desiringGOD.org
www.desiringGOD.org

Desiring God Ministries
United Kingdom
Unit 2B Spencer House
14-22 Spencer Road
Londonderry
Northern Ireland
BT47 6AA
United Kingdom
Tel/fax: 001 (02871) 342 907
dgm.uk@ntlworld.com
www.desiringGOD.org.uk

John Piper has been Pastor for Preaching at Bethlehem Baptist Church in Minneapolis since 1980. He has written over twenty books that call readers to a passion for the supremacy of God in all things for the joy of all peoples through Jesus Christ, including the best-seller *Desiring God: Meditations of a Christian Hedonist*. He has been married to Noël for more than thirty-four years and has five children and two grandchildren.

CATHOLIC HOME SCHOOLING

A HANDBOOK FOR PARENTS

By

Mary Kay Clark, Ph.D.

DIRECTOR OF SETON HOME STUDY SCHOOL

REVISED EDITION

*"Suffer the little children to come unto me,
and forbid them not."* —Mark 10:14

TAN BOOKS AND PUBLISHERS, INC.
Rockford, Illinois 61105

TAN BOOKS AND PUBLISHERS, INC.
P.O. Box 424
Rockford, Illinois 61105
1998

This book is dedicated to the Sacred Heart of Jesus,
and to His Blessed Mother under her title
"Our Mother of Good Counsel."

Contents

Acknowledgments

I wish to thank my parents, John and Jacqueline Lynch of Cleveland, Ohio, for my Catholic upbringing, which led me to teach my children at home and eventually to write this book.

I thank those who have helped me write this book, especially my son Kevin, who helped edit the manuscript, and my son John, who put it on Pagemaker.

In addition, I gratefully thank those who have donated chapters: Mr. Gerry Matatics, home schooling father of eight children, and director of Biblical Foundations; Dr. Mark Lowery, home schooling father and professor of Moral Theology at the University of Dallas; Ginny Seuffert, a home schooling mother of twelve children who has many years of home schooling experience; Mary Claire Robinson, a home schooling mother who also has many years experience; Kenneth Clark, my oldest son and Seton's home schooling attorney; Cathy Gould, a certified LD (learning disability) counselor for Seton; and Cathy Rich, a home schooling mother with an LD child.

I also thank my husband Bruce, and my seven sons, Kenneth, Kevin, Daniel, Paul, John, Jim, and Timothy, for their cooperation over the years which has helped me to grow spiritually, and allowed me to spend so much time working with home schooling families.

In addition, I thank Father John Hardon, Father Charles Fiore, Father Paul Marx, Father Robert Hermley, Father Robert Fox, and Father Matthew Habiger, all of whom have been so supportive of Catholic home schoolers and my work.

I thank all the staff at Seton Home Study School who work together so cooperatively to make home schooling possible for many Catholic families.

Finally, I thank all the Seton Home Study School families who have allowed me the privilege of being part of their home schooling experience.

Foreword
by Father Robert J. Fox

Parents, if any of you are inclined to think the content of this book, *Catholic Home Schooling,* is out of focus or extreme, let me, as a pastor, share some experiences with you.

I know what it is to serve the same parish as assistant priest and later as pastor, in both cases teaching grades one through twelve each week. I know what it is to teach in a Catholic school where children were taught the basics of the Catholic Faith, only to return years later after the Second Vatican Council and discover that children in the same school now knew almost nothing about Catholicism.

I know what it is to be assigned as pastor to a parish where, when I arrived, teenagers in the High School CCD program saw no difference between Catholicism and the "great world religions" of Muhammadanism, Buddhism, and Hinduism. I know what it is to be assigned to still another parish where the CCD teachers thought it was "ecumenism" not to teach that the Catholic Church is the True Church. I know what it is to give a two-day workshop to parish priests on the religious education of youth at one of the most prestigious Catholic universities in the United States and have someone from the University staff tell me I had no right to insist that young people be taught that the Catholic Church is the True Church.

Since ordination, I have taught in my parish grades one through twelve each week of the school year. As the bishop is the primary teacher of the Faith in the diocese, so as pastor I am the primary teacher in the total parish, and I want to know what is going on in our classrooms. I was ordained when everything was in place: Catholic schools were CATHOLIC schools. Children and teenagers knew the basics of the Faith.

Twelve years after being transferred from the parish where I first served, I was reassigned there as pastor. I discovered that the children in the full-time Catholic grade school now did not know the basics of the Faith. Catholic students in the local high school, most of whom had gone through the local parish grade school, had no idea that in Holy Communion we receive the Body, Blood, Soul and Divinity of Jesus Christ. They had no idea that the Mass re-enacts throughout all time the Sacrifice of the Cross. They had no concept of sin as mortal or venial or the obligation of Sunday Mass. What is more, their parents were ignorant of the fact that their children knew almost nothing about the Faith. They had completely entrusted their own primary duty as educators and formers of their children to others. They did not bother to check if their children were being taught the Faith. They assumed others were doing it for them.

When I was a newly ordained priest, my greatest love, after offering the Holy Sacrifice of the Mass and administering the Sacraments as acts of Jesus Christ extended in time and space, was the education and formation of children and teenagers. After 38 years in Christ's Holy Priesthood, my priorities remain the same. I consider my work in educating and forming children as auxiliary to the primary task of parents and as an extension of my duty to preach the Gospel of Jesus Christ.

Writing for the Catholic press, I know what it is to receive thousands of letters from Catholic parents in every part of the United States. During the past 25 years, these parents often discovered too late that their children were not being taught Catholicism, but were being taught heresy. To give a few examples:

"We have eight children. They robbed our first five children of the True Faith in Catholic grade and high school. They'll not get our remaining three. We are teaching them at home ourselves." Or, "Father, in our local school, children are being taught in the name of the Catholic Church things that we know are contrary to Catholicism. Will we be sinning if we take them out of that school?" My answer: "You are asking the wrong question. You should ask, 'What is my responsibility if I leave them in?'"

Often I have heard this in reply: "But the alternative in the public school is even worse. No discipline, no morals, etc....What can I possibly do?"

Now I can answer that question with, "Read the book *Catholic Home Schooling* by Dr. Mary Kay Clark, and you will know what you are seriously bound to do."

The Second Vatican Council was not responsible for the abuses so rampant today. An Ecumenical Council is guided by the Holy Spirit. Also, there are some notable exceptions to what I wrote above, concerning the failure to teach the Faith in Catholic schools. There are some good Catholic schools remaining. The number is not great. There are good informed pastors. There are also pastors who do not know what is going on in their CCD programs or local Catholic schools. They have too often entrusted everything to others, just as parents have.

Some pastors simply do not understand the obligations of parents to teach their children. "We don't want that magazine on our parish rack. It promotes home schooling." That is what one pastor said of the family magazine for which I am editor. "Those people are a bit odd. They home school their children. They are hindering development of their children by home schooling them."

These kinds of statements--made by laity, religious and priests--are contrary to authentic Catholic Faith. Even some pastors display their ignorance of Church teachings and the documents of the Second Vatican Council by failing to recognize the validity and importance of home schooling.

The Declaration on Christian Education of Vatican II makes it very clear:

> As it is parents who have given life to their children, on them lies the gravest obligation of education. They must therefore be recognized as being primarily and principally responsible for their education. The role of parents in education is of such importance that it is almost impossible to provide an adequate substitute.

When the present book, *Catholic Home Schooling*, fell into my hands, and after reading the Introduction, which I considered an accurate assessment of the problems we face today, the first chapter I looked at was "The Father's Role in Home Schooling." When I addressed the International

Symposium for the 75th anniversary of Fatima—where Our Lady came as a catechist and Mother of Evangelization—I laid much of the responsibility for the crisis in faith today on the fathers of our families. The crisis of faith is something that has been escalating for several centuries, reaching back to the Protestant Revolt and to the causes which led up to it. Catholic fathers have frequently relinquished their roles while mothers have all too often fallen for the Feminist Movement.

The next chapter I could not wait to get at was "The Socialization Issue." This is the first objection I hear to home schooling. Strange, in having led multiple hundreds of youth for many years from every part of the United States and Canada to Fatima for four weeks each summer, I have noticed no social problems with home schooled youth. I have found those who are home schooled possessing a maturity I have not witnessed in other youth.

Next my eyes fell on the chapter "Discipline in the Catholic Home Schooling Family." I have noticed on the youth pilgrimages to Europe that those best in possession of self-discipline, who immediately grasp why we are in Mary's land and what I am attempting to accomplish, are often those who are in home schooling. They are always (I say *"always"*) the youth who know their Faith in some depth and can discuss it intelligently. They are motivated youth from motivated parents. They come motivated to experience the Church as One, Holy, Universal and Apostolic.

Observing the modernists, the dissenters within the Church, and growing secularism invading our parish churches—having succeeded quite well in our schools—Fulton J. Sheen said, "It is the laity who will save the Church." I can say, in my own work as pastor and journalist these 25 years past, that what has helped me remain quite optimistic that truth will prevail and that the Sacred Heart of Jesus and the Immaculate Heart of Mary will triumph has been the thousands of good parents from coast to coast who have contacted me. They have been gravely concerned that their children be educated and formed in true Catholicism.

Young people on "Youth for Fatima" pilgrimages often

conclude their two weeks by saying, "Now I am not alone. Now I know there are many other youth across the United States whose parents are teaching them the same Catholic values of faith and morals as my parents have been doing for me."

Parents, in home schooling you are not alone! I have been writing for the last 30 years on Catholic education and formation, on the duty of parents as the primary educators of their children and on the need for faithfulness to the Magisterium. About a quarter of a century ago, a Catholic parent encouraged me to give up my apostolates in order to form Catholic home schooling programs. It would have meant giving up my assignment as pastor of a parish also. She and some other Catholic parents, in desperation because there were no good Catholic or public schools locally, were using home schooling programs such as those produced by Baptists. They attempted to supply the Catholic doctrine to the essentially Protestant programs. I thought this practice risky at best. But now we have our own Catholic home schooling. And it is logical that such came from the laity.

We are still in the infancy of home schooling for our modern times. But home schooling in itself is as old as the Church. There was a time when the Divine Liturgy and the home were the chief and only educators in the Faith. If our Catholic schools, which made such a noble contribution in the past, failed in any special area, it was the failure to communicate to parents that *they* are the primary educators and formers of their children in the fullness of True Faith and that it is virtually impossible to provide an adequate substitute.

Father Robert J. Fox
Fatima Family Messenger

Preface

by Thomas A. Nelson

"Does home schooling make sense academically?" And if so, *"Can I do it?"* These two questions are undoubtedly uppermost in the minds of many parents who are considering home schooling. Dr. Mary Kay Clark has written *Catholic Home Schooling* in large part to answer these two extremely important questions—as well as, of course, to give the spiritual reasons for home schooling.

The purpose of this Preface is to add an exclamation mark to what Dr. Clark says in her book and to answer a resounding, "Yes!" to both of the above questions.

First of all, why does it make excellent sense academically? As a former teacher with a Master's Degree in Education who has taught self-contained sixth grade twice (once in Catholic, once in public school), seventh and eighth grade junior high school (for two years each, in Catholic and public schools), public high school English for two years, and junior college philosophy for two years; as someone who has seen good, bad and mediocre teachers; who has seen good and bad things done in the name of education; who has enjoyed some remarkable successes as the fruit of hard work and intelligent planning; who has seen every mistake in the book committed and gotten away with by "state certified" teachers; who has had to mop up academically on students after they had spent years under poor instruction; having these credentials, I believe I can say—with a certain amount of authority—that home schooling makes excellent sense academically, and this for some eight basic reasons:

1. *You do not waste the students' time.* In a junior or senior high school setting, about one hour 40 minutes per day are spent among a) home room, b) travelling between classes and c) getting ready to leave class and settling down in the new class. Added to this, between one-half hour and one hour, average, are spent going to and coming from school. This amounts to more than two hours wasted during the day, not to mention classroom time ill-spent, wasted by an unpre-

pared or poor teacher or waiting for unprepared and/or poor students to respond or be dealt with by the teacher.

2. *You do not re-teach what the student already knows.* Since the parent-teacher knows intimately what has been covered in the previous days, weeks, months and years, she does not have to go back and cover that ground all over again, other than to make a general review. It is axiomatic academically that the larger the school, the less that gets taught. During the 1960's one of the last of the one-room schools in the United States closed. It was in Tennessee. Almost every student who attended eight years of school there went on to win a National Merit Scholarship after high school. The reason was simple: The school had an excellent teacher who knew all the children and did not re-teach them what they already knew, but kept them growing and growing. About the same time there was a study done on the schools of Finland which showed that those children who came from the northern hinterlands, where schools usually had only two teachers—one for the first four years of grade school and one for the second four years—did much better academically than children from the larger towns and cities, where there was a different teacher for every year. The reason deduced by those conducting the study was that the teachers in these small schools knew their students well and did not re-teach what had already been learned.

3. *You can give your own children more individualized attention.* Even if you are a mother with a large family, you can still give far more, and far faster, individual attention to each of your children than a teacher in a classroom with 25 to 30 students. You do not have to take attendance, deal as much with naughty children or handle administrative details. You can get right to work and your children are not waiting for help.

4. *You can gear the work speed to a pace your children can handle and that will keep them interested.* One of the chief reasons for failure in school, or failure of students to do well in school, is the slow (sometimes snail-paced) work speed of the class.

5. *You can, and SHOULD, eliminate the option to fail!* Not adopting this simple academic principle is the reason why public schools do not succeed academically with *all* students. After all, the opposite of failure is success. If the teachers in public schools, along with the administrators, all swore themselves not to fail with *any* child and to do whatever it takes to succeed with *every* child, then *every* child would go forth a success, academically speaking, even from our public schools. Despite lack of support from the administration, I was always able to achieve this objective in both public and Catholic schools. The idea is not hard. Applying it is. It means work—lots of it! Much of it after school! The school bus leaves, the children must be on it (or so everyone thinks), the teachers shrug their shoulders and mollify their consciences with, "If the parents don't care, what can I do?" and take their unearned paychecks and let tomorrow's generation slip through their academic fingers irreparably unprepared for life. And the country has another batch of empty heads to help after they leave school and to try to bootstrap up into something productive once they enter the work force. Or, it sends them on to college to learn finally what should have been taught in grade school and high school.

6. *You can build in automatic consequences for failure to perform.* This reason is actually an extension of number 5 above, but it is covered separately because of its importance. Building into your home school regimen automatic consequences for failure to perform a) on time, b) with work completely done, c) with work done correctly and d) with it executed well (i.e., neat, clean, well written and well punctuated) will ensure academic excellence. Because we are all subject to Original Sin, we tend not to want to do what we should, especially if it is hard. To inculcate a spirit of virtue in your children, therefore, it is imperative always "to hold the stick" as a consequence for failure to perform, to perform on time, to perform completely and well. If your children know that they will *automatically* receive extra schoolwork in those areas where they are weak, PLUS be assigned a nice little essay (well executed, now!) on why they

should have their work done properly and on time, every time they fail to perform, believe me, *they will start to perform!* It may take a week or two or three of this routine to break bad habits, but the extra work load, plus being deprived of some of their free time, will eventually send a message that the avenue of failure is no longer open. Within a short time you will, by this method, channel a balky student into the path of achievement, which is a pleasant experience, and he or she will then become self-motivated, and that battle is won.

7. *You can emphasize reading.* Ninety percent of academics hinges upon reading. I used to require a book a week, on top of all other English curriculum (or in self-contained sixth grade, on top of all other work). There were cries and moans the first two weeks or so, but because I would allow the students to read anything they wanted, so long as it was a decent book, the idea was easy to sell. Reporting also was easy, being done on 3 x 5 cards handed in at the end of each month. Occasionally, reports were given orally to others in the class, and about once a month a book report was given as the topic of the weekly essay. Extra credit was given for extra books read. The average student can easily read more than one book per week in addition to other work. The results of this practice are incredible: up goes vocabulary, up goes reading comprehension, up goes interest in school, up goes the ability to write good sentences, up goes the psychosomatic ability to read faster and faster with more and more understanding, up goes the fund of knowledge acquired, up goes the ability to spell, up goes interest in all sorts of things, up goes student confidence that they can achieve academically—and very possibly, *in* comes that lifetime interest which will lead them to the career they should enter. If you implement the "book a week" reading program, you can achieve amazing results with your children—even if you are the world's worst possible teacher, for your children will far out-pace whatever they could have achieved in the very best of formal schools. Make this simple reading program the "academic safety net" of your home schooling

effort and you simply cannot fail!

8. *Home schooling eliminates the silliness and nonsense picked up from peers.* Rather than your children modeling themselves on some cool goof, they will continue to model themselves on you, as they have since infancy, and their behavioral education will continue to be formed upon an adult as a role model. The net result is that you will have adult-acting children, especially if you continue to speak to them intelligently on intelligent topics and expect intelligent conversation from them in return.

Other reasons could be elicited, and Mary Kay Clark does so, but these eight reasons should be enough to convince you that home schooling is a sound concept academically. Now we must address the second important question: *"Can I do it?"*

Why not? You are presumably a person of at least reasonable intelligence, and certainly a person of uncommon common sense, if you have gone to the effort of beginning to read this book and possibly even to the expense of buying it. Just this much shows you realize something is very wrong with education today and you would like to do something about it for your children.

Let me assure you, as a former teacher who taught in six different situations—in grade school, junior high school, high school and college—teachers are human beings, just like you. There are good ones and bad ones, well educated ones and poorly educated ones, effective ones and ineffective ones, energetic ones and lazy ones—you name it. They come from a cross-section of our society, some with a sound philosophy and morality, but many without these essentials for a good teacher. Just keeping your children from the bad influence of bad teachers is a tremendous plus.

Probably what bothers you most is the nagging question: *"Can I teach?" "Can I actually do it?"* I answer again, "Why not?" Thousands of incompetents are teaching in our schools; are you going to do any worse? The old-time nuns that made the Catholic educational system the model and marvel of our country were basically high-school educated ladies. Granted, their orders helped them with instructions in how to teach, but you can get that sort of information in "how to" books and from other home schoolers. Plus, the course work from the home school suppliers—and even the textbooks themselves—hold your hand through the work. Teaching is largely a question of getting in and starting to do it.

In home schooling your own children, nobody is asking you to do anything horribly difficult. I learned how to teach under extremely adverse circumstances, with no formal background whatever, partially by doing and partially by the guidance of a fellow sixth-grade teacher. You too can call on others who are home schooling to help you, just as this teacher helped me.

A famous proverb from the Roman writer Tacitus reads, *Omne ignotum, pro magnifico,* which translates roughly, "Everything unknown (is taken) for wonderful." Right now, if you are apprehensive about home schooling, you are operating under the typical human syndrome of taking as wonderful that which is unknown. Let's face it, once you do it, it won't be unknown anymore, and your fear of teaching your children at home will disappear. All you have to do is get in and do it. If you get over your head in some area, call upon other home schoolers for help with your problems. And, of course, Dr. Clark solves a great many of the potential problems in this tremendous book.

If, in any way, I can be an added voice of encouragement to that of Dr. Clark, let me say that you do not need to have a college degree to become an excellent teacher, but you do have to work at it. You don't have to have extraordinary intelligence to teach your children; you mainly have to want them to excel. You do not need fancy courses in teaching to learn how to teach, but it does help to ask other teachers (home schoolers or others) for advice on particular points. In short, what I would like to say to you Mothers and Fathers is this: *"You CAN do it!"* Even if you have only a high school education (or less), still, *"You CAN do it!"*

A simple principle exists in all education. The teacher always learns more than the student. You are going to learn the subjects that you teach your children, and you will know them better than they do. That will make you a better you. It will also give you a great deal in common with your children. And it will help to make your home a little university of human knowledge. Rather than shirking the role of home-schooling teacher, you should embrace it as a wonderful learning experience. Not only can home schooling succeed academically for your children, it has a far better chance of working than any other alternative available today. So what are you waiting for?

Pray for guidance—especially to Our Lady of Good Counsel, through the Holy Rosary—read this book, talk with those who are home schooling, and then step out there with confidence.

Introduction

The story of how I came to be the Director of Seton Home Study School is, in many ways, the story of a typical Catholic family seeking the authentic Catholic family lifestyle in confusing times. In my travels to various cities, I have been surprised by the similarities of stories among Catholic families struggling to keep the Faith.

The oldest of a family of nine children, I grew up in the Forties and Fifties in Bethesda, Maryland, a suburb of Washington, D.C. My parents were active politically in the Republican Party and often campaigned for better legislation, usually concerning education and family issues. They were concerned about the local public schools and better education; once my father ran for the local school board. They were active in the Church and involved with the parish school. Mom and Dad fought against pornography in the Fifties, giving lectures to parent groups.

While in high school in Cleveland, Ohio, I met Bruce, my future husband, but went on to a Catholic college for four years. Bruce and I were married the month I graduated from college, but I continued my education at Western Reserve University and at Catholic University to obtain my Master's degree. My husband was in Vietnam while I was in college, and later, after we were married, he was recalled for the Berlin Crisis. My first baby, Kenneth, was born almost exactly a year after we were married.

During the early Sixties, though I was married, pregnant, working as a librarian and going to Western Reserve library graduate school, I was still involved with my mother in Church and political activities. The encyclical *Pacem in Terris* was published, and we both attended conferences to hear "Catholics" proclaim that we should accommodate Socialists and Communists. We attended lectures where "Catholic" women gave their own version of what it meant to be a modern Catholic woman.

In the Sixties, the first immediate disturbance to an ordinary family's faith came with the "new" religion texts in schools and parish programs. The publishers' names became household words, as parents across the country compared notes with relatives and friends. My mother started Concerned Catholic Parents of Cleveland, a group dedicated to fighting the new religion being promoted in the Catholic schools. During this battle, I moved to Columbus, Ohio, with Bruce and our three young children. I was asked by parents in Columbus to analyze a catechism series. I spent hours in a seminary library researching the teachings of the Church and became convinced that the "new" religion texts were not presenting Catholic truths.

The basic problem with the new religion texts back in the Sixties was their failure to teach the Ten Commandments, Original Sin, actual sin, Confession, the Holy Sacrifice of the Mass as a re-enactment of Christ's sacrifice on Calvary and so on.* The emphasis was on deciding for oneself what was best; truth was subjective. Children were not taught that the Catholic Church is the True Church, nor that the Pope is the vicar of Jesus Christ on earth. Church truths, if mentioned at all, were presented as just another viewpoint among many from which to choose.

Catholics United for the Faith was started during this turbulent period, evaluating religion texts being used around the country. *The Wanderer* became very popular as a support for all of us who thought we were alone.

The Catholic parents in Columbus, as in other cities nationwide, were not willing to sit by quietly. Our first enterprise was to print the questionable quotes from the new religion texts on flyers and distribute them to every Catholic church at all Masses on a particular weekend.

This activity caused quite a stir, which resulted in the formation of a city-wide organization, Catholic Parents of Columbus. Membership quickly included parents statewide. We printed a monthly newsletter and met with pastors and parish committees, with the Diocesan Board of Education,

---

*A 1997 report by the NCCB's Catechetical Committee headed by Archbishop Buechlein of Indianapolis stated that most catechisms in parish programs today are "seriously deficient."

and even with the bishop. We sponsored a weekly radio program to teach the truths of the Faith.

After a year or so, not only had no changes been made by the diocesan authorities or educators, but updated versions of the new religion texts were proceeding further from the official teachings. A second "parking-lot apostolate" project encompassed the whole Columbus area, extending well into the suburbs. After a couple of years, our parking-lot apostolate struck for a third time.

More years passed, and though parents continued to complain and actively tried to seek a return to the teachings of the Church, things became continually worse. In fact, by the late Sixties the first sex education program appeared in the Catholic schools: the "Becoming a Person" series from Benziger Publishers.

Our organization fought back again. We published a flyer with exact quotes from the "Becoming a Person" program and distributed it one weekend in every parish parking lot at every Mass in the greater Columbus area. The result? Complaints were made by parents about the pornography on the windshields, even though the explicit sexual quotes were directly from the textbooks their own children were using in the schools! Nearby Protestant churchgoers were terribly upset when their cars were accidentally covered with "Catholic" pornography.

Diocesan authorities were upset about the parents' movement against their new and "relevant" changes to make things better for children! We had a meeting with the diocesan school board to complain officially, but to no avail. We met with the Bishop, who questioned us about specific theologians we should be reading! We had meetings with pastors and with parents in various parishes. Besides our monthly newsletter, we continued our weekly radio program, pointing out the teachings of the Catholic Church which were no longer being taught correctly.

Like a steamroller, the Catholic schools continued to push toward a confused new religion which parents could not recognize, to implement secular humanism in other subject areas, especially social studies, and to teach explicit sexual material fraudulently titled "Family Life Education." We felt pulled into the sewer of discussing explicit sexual perversions.

By 1971, we in the Catholic Parents of Columbus organization felt our energies were being wasted in trying to change the schools and/or the educators. So the organization changed its approach completely. We decided to form our own Catholic school, Mater Dei Academy, in Columbus, Ohio.

Through the 1970's, Mater Dei was a tremendous success. It is still in existence. Parents in other cities around the country began similar schools. Philosophy professor Dr. William Marra founded "Holy Innocents" schools. Wanderer columnist Frank Morris began a school in Denver. Anne Carroll, wife of Dr. Warren Carroll, the founder of Christendom College, started Seton School outside Washington, D.C. Similar schools sprang up in Cincinnati, Cleveland, Detroit, Denver, New York City, Dallas, Los Angeles, and other areas around the country. Some are still going.

At one point there may have been about 200 small parent-operated schools in the country. After helping various parent groups in nearby states, a group of us sponsored a convention in Cleveland to help start parent-operated schools and to help with home schooling. These schools had names like Agnus Dei, Our Lady of Fatima, and Rosary Academy. The names reflected parents' love for the Blessed Mother, the Rosary, and the use of Latin in Catholic culture.

Though some of these schools continue to this day, by the 1980's most parents were overwhelmed by the tremendous difficulties of raising a family and running a school at the same time. By 1985, more and more Catholic families were starting to teach their children at home.

In 1982, Seton Home Study School was founded by Anne Carroll as a division of Seton School, a private parent-operated school in Manassas, Virginia. Our family moved to Front Royal, Virginia, to be near Christendom College, where my two oldest sons were attending college.

In 1983, I joined Seton Home Study as the assistant director. There were about 50 students in the home study division and about 100 students in the day school. Today the day school has about 175 students; whereas, the home study school has over 9,000 students. In 1982, the home study division was run from one room in the Seton School building. Today, we have a 25,000 square foot building for office and warehouses, with 130 employees. By January, 1991, the home study division had grown so large that Seton Home Study School officially separated as a legal entity from the day school.

Meeting with families around the country, I see a pattern repeated. Families first start complaining to Church authorities, hoping for understanding and a return to the teachings of the Church. Parents discover their complaints are not heeded. Then, after a few years, parents form a school or simply start schooling with another family or two— or start home schooling just one or two children or enroll in a home study school. The means may be different, but the emphasis is the same: parents become the teachers; students learn from parents.

What the new breed of Catholic educators and catechists did not count on is that today's parents are better informed and mothers are more sure of themselves and their ability to educate their own children. At first, Catholic educators were able to push parents around regarding the religion texts, making parents doubt their own understanding of their faith learned in childhood. But Catholic educators, especially priests and nuns, could not fool Catholic parents about sexual programs.

Some Church leaders minimize the abuses in Catholic education, and counsel patience, but parents cannot wait for a better day at the expense of their own children's souls. Children are being formed, one way or another, with every passing day, and parents rightly feel pressured to take action. The Church can wait decades to deal with issues, but children have only a few short years in which they will either become good Catholics or be lost to the Church, to the Faith, to eternal salvation.

When I speak with some older parents or with grandparents, tears come to their eyes as they admit they have lost their older children. "My children don't want children" is a fairly common remark.

Young parents, however, are discovering through the grace of God their deep privilege and grave obligation to be the primary educators of their children. Even parents who are not aware of the depth of the Catholic teachings are determined to keep their families strong in traditional values. They have a love for Jesus and Mary and refuse to keep their children in schools which reject the teachings of the Church, or even simple moral truths.

Parents are pulling their children out of Catholic schools because they cannot find a single Catholic textbook. They bring their children home because teachers say parents who say the Rosary are old fashioned. Mothers do not want their children subjected to laughter and verbal abuse from teachers and peers who think wearing a scapular is silly. Finally, parents do not want their children to experience the degradation of sex education programs.

Mothers who are home schooling are giving their children love and stability, a spiritual way of life, a habit of looking to Jesus and Mary for answers and of making the sacramental life real and active in the home.

Families who are home schooling are joining with other home schooling families whenever possible to attend Mass, to say the Rosary, to visit Marian shrines, to make Advent wreaths, to decorate May altars, and in general to make the traditional beliefs, faith, and customs of the Catholic heritage an integral part of their lifestyle. With their philosophy and activities, home schooling families are preserving the Catholic Faith and are becoming a faithful remnant in difficult times. Above all, however, they are planting the seeds--through the formation of their children--for a new springtime of the Catholic Faith.

Parents today realize they are living in a pagan society in which Christian values, particularly those related to family life, are being destroyed through the media and through government policies. They also realize our Catholic children are losing the Faith through the Catholic schools they once trusted and which were built through the sweat and money of their parents and grandparents.

Parents see that the time has come for them to stop depending on others to transmit the Faith to their children. The time has come to stop looking to priests and bishops for the solutions to their problems. They do not doubt that the Church will survive, as Christ promised. However, these parents are discovering that part of Our Lord's promise is the grace offered to revitalize the Church through strong Catholic families. These home schooling parents are responding to that grace.

Chapter 1:
Why Catholic Home Schooling?

Why do parents choose home schooling?

Ninety percent of home schooling Catholic parents choose it in order to protect their children from evil influences in the schools, Catholic and otherwise, which are pulling their children away from God, away from the Catholic Church, and away from their own family. This book could be filled with stories from heart-broken parents. The following are only a few typical examples.

One mother chose home schooling for her young kindergarten daughter after watching a child abuse film scheduled to be shown to her daughter's class in a Catholic school. It was so graphic this young mother said she blushed. In addition, the film was convincing young children to be frightened of their fathers, brothers, and uncles, presenting them as the ones most likely to abuse them sexually.

One father made the decision for home schooling after visiting his daughter's Catholic school. He noticed there was no crucifix in his daughter's classroom. When he asked the teacher why, she told him that it was too traumatic for young children to see a crucifix.

A mother from Michigan chose home schooling because of the reader in her local Catholic school. The book contained stories of witchcraft, and the young girls in the class were practicing some of the things they learned in the stories. The mother felt it was dangerous when the girls started laughing at her daughter because she wore a scapular.

The problems in schools, even Catholic schools, often are physical dangers. One mother decided to home school her daughter after two boys raped a girl in a bathroom. A father chose home schooling after a teacher was raped in the Catholic school. One mother enrolled her junior high son in Seton after the boys in his class tried to hang him. One mother enrolled her daughter after finding out that the man who pushed her daughter down in the school hallway was an undercover detective in the process of chasing a high school drug dealer.

In a junior high school, a mother volunteering in the nurse's room was shocked to discover the number of guns, knives, and razor blades carried by students. There were frequent fights in the halls, students even biting other students. She was warned to wear gloves whenever touching the students since so many had AIDS. After a few months, the mother quit and is now teaching her children at home.

Sex education

More and more parents are choosing home schooling because of the renewed push for explicit sex education. The new condom brigades have invaded practically every school in the country to peddle their wares. Even in Catholic schools, parents have discovered that teachers are instructing the students on how to use condoms because they assume that the kids are going to be sexually active. Priests, nuns, and Catholic teachers can cause parents to doubt themselves about the religion they grew up with, but they cannot cause parents to doubt themselves about proper sex education for their children. Many mothers have removed their children from Catholic high schools after Planned Parenthood was invited to speak to their children.

Some Catholic mothers learn about the sex education programs as they become involved in crisis pregnancy centers, in helping girls who have become pregnant, and being active in the Pro-Life Movement. Mothers have learned that public schools not only have "health clinics" which give the students condoms and abortifacients, but give the girls a day of the week in which they can obtain permission slips from the school nurse to visit the community health clinic for abortion referral service if they "need" it. And this without parents' knowledge or consent!

The AIDS crisis has brought into many schools demonic new curricula which include homosexuality. Under the guise of teaching non-violence, civil rights, and non-discrimination toward ethnic groups, the curriculums teach young children that homosexuality is a morally acceptable practice.

A mother writes from New Jersey:

> Most recently, the public school system in New Jersey, New York, and Connecticut, announced that they will be introducing three new books in the first grade: *Daddy's Roommate*, *Heather Has Two Mommies*, and *Gloria Goes to Gay Pride*. All these books deal with the topic of homosexuality and "alternative" lifestyles. In our opinion, this is immoral and blasphemous. We couldn't believe we were witnessing this. They removed prayer in the school, only to drill this kind of literature down the throats of our impressionable children.

In the FIRST GRADE! The more mothers learn about the sex education programs, the more likely they are to home school their children.

Character formation

Some parents have started home schooling because of the broad range of false and immoral ideas propagated by books, teachers, classroom discussions, and peer pressure in schools. Many parents first learn of these bad ideas through the books assigned to their children for book reports. The stories in these books often present young people involved in early sexual activities, with no comment that this is immoral conduct. The books teach the children that fornication is normal behavior, having sex on dates is routine, and that "taking the pill" is as common as wearing tight jeans.

An eighth grade girl was supposed to do a book report on a story about a woman who consulted a voodoo witch and whose husband had committed adultery with the witch. When the mother complained, the teacher declared that the children like reading these books. When the mother went to the principal, he told her that her concern was "just her opinion," and he did not think he could do anything even if she wrote a formal complaint.

Parents have asked that their children be allowed to read different books for their reports, but most teachers are very insistent that the children read these "X-rated" type books.

One mother pulled her high school daughter out of the Catholic high school in her junior year. She said that her daughter was daily arguing in class against the students and against the teacher, standing up for Pro-Life values mainly, as well as many other traditional Catholic doctrines. She felt her daughter was so upset all the time that she could not concentrate on her studies.

One father enrolled his daughter in home study after visiting her Catholic high school classroom when the students were having a debate about Clinton and Bush. When abortion was mentioned, the teacher said that was a subject which could not be part of the debate. Later, the debate teacher allowed the pro-Clinton students to chant "pro-choice" over and over while the pro-Bush students were speaking.

Academics

Some parents have chosen home education because of the lack of academics being taught in the schools. Parents are upset that their children receive A's on report cards, or are even classified as gifted, when they discover how little they have learned. One mother wrote us this:

> Time allotted for systematic instruction in basic subjects seems to be spent discussing strategies for achieving New Age goals, or personal "decision making" based on a poll of the peer group. "Creativity" is the current god of education, created to cover the glaring deficiencies of thirty years of mismanagement. On a general basis, the only area in which personal discipline and endeavor are demanded so to reach the highest standard of excellence is that of sports.

The main problem we hear from parents regarding academics is that children are not learning to read. Instead of phonics, a proven method of teaching people to read, most schools use the look-say method, or the current fad, the whole language method. No matter which method is currently in vogue, or what they call it, if it is not phonics, children will not learn to decode sounds to read words. While other methods may work for a few years, by the fifth or sixth grade, the method will break down. Of course, if a child cannot read, grades in all subjects will plummet quickly.

The United States is now 49th among the nations of the world in educational achievement, 39th in literacy. One out of every four students will never reach high school, one out of every four who reaches high school will never graduate. The United States has 50 million functional illiterates, and this figure grows by 2.2 million per year.

Weep for your children . . .

When Jesus spoke these words to mothers, He was not referring to children who lose their physical lives, but to those children who lose their spiritual lives, their souls.

Jesus once said to His Apostles, "Do not be afraid of those who kill the body, but cannot kill the soul. But rather be afraid of him who is able to destroy both soul and body in Hell."

The "him," dear friends, is the school.

The souls of children are being destroyed in the schools. This is worse than murder.

The public schools of this nation are the enemy of this nation, and the enemy of each American child. The schools and their promotion of drugs through the drug programs, their promotion of illiteracy through erroneous reading programs, their promotion of contraception, their promotion of homosexuality, their promotion of suicide and abortion, are leading us out of existence as a free nation. No longer a Christian nation, soon we will be no nation at all.

And many of the Catholic schools of this nation are the training camps of the enemies of the Catholic Church.

No longer do we find in the Catholic schools stalwart and unflinching defense of God's Truth. What we find more often is a tacit acceptance of contraception and other sexual evils, the denial of the existence of absolute truth, the acceptance of secular humanist ideas, along with a general contempt for and neglect of the doctrines of the Faith. Wishywashy Catholic schools can hardly produce a generation of saints. What they will be more likely to produce is a generation of wishy-washy Catholics.

The Charter of the Rights of the Family, issued by Pope John Paul II in 1982, declares that parents are not to send their children to any school which sets itself against their moral and religious convictions.

Well, what do you do when *every available school* goes against your religious convictions?

The answer is simple and yet difficult: a family catechetical program at home, teaching all subjects at home from the Catholic perspective.

We are in spiritual warfare. Our spiritual enemies, though we should love them as individuals created by God, do not recognize the Truth of Jesus Christ.

Give all the speeches you want, but children will not listen after being in the training camp of the enemy. Write all the books you want, but Catholics will not read them after being in the training camp of the enemy. Take to court all the constitutional cases you want, but the judges and juries will have been trained in the enemy's camp, and they will not understand the issues.

Our spiritual enemies are being trained in the schools! The future lies in the children, as our enemies well know. The children are being trained in the camp of the enemy!

As long as your children or your grandchildren, your nephews or nieces, or your neighbor's children, are being trained in the camp of the enemy, our spiritual enemies could not care less about your books and speeches. They have the children. They have the Future in their camp.

Unless we bring the children home to the family, and teach them the truths of the Catholic Faith, the leaders of tomorrow will not hear, they will not listen, they will not understand the Truth. They will be imbued with Secular Humanism. They will be deadened to the Truth.

Perhaps our situation has gone so far that there is little hope for change. Secular humanists sit as judges and jurists, as educators and school superintendents, as lawyers and as legislators, as textbook authors and teachers. The other side misses no chance to impose their values upon us, while judging our moral standards to be "un-Constitutional."

But there is hope in the next generation of home schooled adults. We can place hope in a generation trained and living the Catholic life, one which is better educated than those taught in the schools, not influenced by peers or perverse lifestyles, but a generation acting by God's Truths.

Home schoolers are independent thinkers. They are not pressured to agree with the group or with an authority other than God and His representatives, their parents.

Catholic children trained at home in a complete family catechetical program, can be, and will be, effective leaders in restoring the nation and the Catholic Church. It is not too late. With God, it is never too late for those who believe in Him.

Raising "Cradle Catholics"

What parents quickly discover once they start teaching their children is that home schooling is a very special way of living. Most of us have come to love this lifestyle so much that even if the best Catholic school were next door, we would not send our children to it.

To the casual observer, home schooling means teaching one's children all the academic subjects at home. To Catholic home schooling parents, it means teaching about God and His Word, teaching about living the Catholic life through example as well as books, and teaching the academic subjects through the perspective of the Truths of Jesus Christ.

The main purpose of Catholic home schooling is to raise saints, not scholars.

Catholic home schooling means raising cradle Catholics. A cradle Catholic is a person born into a Catholic family who is taught the culture, the traditions, and the faith of the Catholic Church by words, actions, songs, Sacraments, and sacramentals. This teaching is given primarily by parents, but also by other family members.

In this confused pagan society, we need to raise a generation of cradle Catholics. These children will be a small minority among many who have accepted the anti-Christian

teachings of our society. Our children will need the strength
and the graces which come from a lifetime of living the
Faith. Growing up Catholic—in an atmosphere of love as
well as sacrifice and reparation—is necessary in order to
defend loyally the Faith and to proclaim it courageously in
a post-Christian world.

Raising children as Catholics, in a strong and stable
Catholic home filled with Catholic culture and traditions,
should produce Catholics who both understand the Catholic
Faith and live the Catholic lifestyle. Historically, many born
and bred Cradle Catholics may not have been able to score
high on a theology quiz, but they knew in their hearts, in
their souls, and in their very bones, what *being Catholic* is
all about. They had a *sensus fidei*, a sense of the faith.
Their devotion to daily Mass, their love for the Blessed
Mother and the Rosary, their prayer and lighting of candles—
all these indicate the authentic Catholic lifestyle, a deep love
and understanding of Jesus and His Church.

Today, the best defense, and often the best offense,
against heresy and other deviations from Catholic truths, are
the common people—the laity—living the authentically Catholic lifestyle throughout the liturgical year.

It should come as no surprise that sacramentals and the
sacramental life have been systematically attacked by those
who would destroy the Church. The simple devotions of the
Catholic people—the Rosary, the scapular, the Stations of
the Cross, the Advent wreath—give structure and substance
to the Faith. The symbolism of these devotions helps the
faithful to understand the profound mysteries of life which
they represent.

In our current pagan society, where the Catholic schools
have been using secular textbooks since the 1960's, where
Catholic parents have trusted the Catholic schools to pass on
the Faith and the Culture, many of the Catholic treasures
have been lost to millions. The sacramental life in the home
carried the Irish through hundreds of years of persecutions,
and sacramentals carried Japanese Catholics through hundreds
of years, since they had no priests. But the sacramental life
and sacramentals are now completely unknown to a whole

generation of Catholics educated in the Catholic school system.

It is not an overstatement to say, as Catholic professor Dr. William Marra has said, that a generation of children today has been deprived of their Catholic inheritance, the treasures not only of the knowledge of the graces and supernatural helps of the Church, but of the Catholic cultural heritage. He feels a generation has been robbed by the "trustees" of the Church. And those who stood by and did nothing while it happened cannot escape blame, either.

Certainly the laity have reacted. The Traditional Mass Society, the Una Voce organization asking for a traditional ordinariate, Mother Angelica's Eternal Word Television Network, the parent-operated schools started in the Sixties (and some still going in the Nineties), Pro-Life organizations, Catholics United for the Faith, Christendom College, Magdalen College, Thomas Aquinas College, and Thomas More Institute, etc.—all these are among the innumerable organizations that have been started by the laity to restore the Church, defend the Faith, and protect the family and the unborn.

Catholic home schooling is a natural and logical part of the ongoing restoration of the Church. Catholic home schooling is a family apostolate in the forefront of the spiritual battle to preserve the Catholic Faith and the Catholic culture and traditions. Unless the changes occur within the basic unit of society, the family, changes will not happen in the Church and in the nation.

The continuing attacks on the family have been devastating to our Church and society. As always, it has been the children who have suffered the most from the breakdown of family bonds. The shattering of families has shattered the hearts of innumerable children.

It is precisely because the family has been so assaulted, and nearly destroyed, that the Catholic Church and our American society have lost Christian values. When homosexuality, a direct attack against family and children, is accepted as an alternative lifestyle in America, one no longer can pretend to live in a Christian nation. As of 1992, three states have mandated the teaching of homosexuality as an acceptable lifestyle to young children—as young as first grade—in the public schools.

The necessity of home schooling

The only answer for Catholic families is to bring the children home, keep them close, and teach them in the inner sanctum of the domestic church, our Catholic homes. Many of us Catholic home schooling parents have chosen to keep our children away from the influences of the pagan society right from the cradle. At the same time, we want to keep our children aware of society's problems, and prepare them for the fight ahead of them.

Some well-meaning Catholic parents believe that their children should be promoting good Catholic ideas in the public or Catholic schools. Some Pro-Lifers believe that other children need to hear the message of respect for life which their children bring to the school. While sympathizing with the concept and applauding the efforts their children are making, we home schoolers strongly disagree with the premise.

There is nothing Biblical or remotely Catholic in the idea that *children* should be placed for at least six hours a day, five days a week, in an environment which continually savages their beliefs. *All* the secular texts are permeated with anti-Christian values, New Age ideas, feminist views, one world government, or the "New World Order." But worst of all, they are permeated with a mentality that everything is relative, that truth is not absolute, that God may not exist, and that every idea is as good as every other.

Home schooling parents are disgusted at the horrors that are perpetrated on children in the name of education. Children are learning filthy language and filthy ideas from their textbooks! Children in schools are acquiring all kinds of sexual information, and consequently endorsing perverse activities as acceptable behavior. Little girls are encouraged by peers to have boyfriends, which, combined with sex education, has been devastating to some young children.

In such an environment, even children of committed Catholics will pick up some modern secular values and attitudes. It would be impossible not to! They are certainly learning terminology and information which is inappropriate, not only for their age level, but for any decent Christian.

Catholic children—even from the best of families—are human beings and likely to be influenced by the constant barrage of anti-Catholic and immoral ideas which are promulgated for hours and hours every day, by the textbooks, by the teachers, and by the other students. This is supplemented even more graphically by movies and television, by youth "music" and sports "heroes" championing immoral lifestyles.

What chance does a Catholic parent have, who spends perhaps a few minutes a day talking about the Catholic position on population control, on true compassion, or on the gift of life? Generally the school supervises the children for more hours than the parent. How is the parent to undo, in a short time in the evening, all the damage that has been done by the school for the whole day?

Why not send children to a parent-operated school?

The time, money, and energy involved in running a parent-operated school is great. I helped to establish one in Columbus, Ohio, and was the principal during the 1970's.

A parent-operated school needs to be run by someone whose children are grown, or by someone whose career is taking care of the school. Mothers who are having children are the ones who want such a school, but they cannot give the proper amount of time to their own children and families if they run a school.

The constant problem of raising enough money to pay the rent and the salaries can be emotionally and physically draining. In addition, there is a problem finding good Catholic textbooks. Most Catholic parent-operated schools do not have Catholic textbooks.

Some parent-operated schools are successful, but most are not. Most parent-operated schools have a short life span.

Many do not make it through the first year due to financial
pressures, leadership problems, personality differences of the
board members, children with learning problems, and parents
whose ideas about various aspects of the school differ.

But, just for the sake of argument, let's assume that you
could find a Catholic school that is run by totally committed
lay Catholics, that enforces good Christian discipline, that
uses Catholic textbooks. Perhaps the teachers even take the
children to Mass every week, and encourage frequent confession. And, as an added bonus, the tuition is reasonable.

In my view, however, even this kind of school takes children away from the parents and out of the home. Even this
kind of school may take away from the stability and strength
of the family. It sets up an outside authority as someone with
"credentials" who may oppose parental values.

Can a school ever be better?

Pope Pius XI in his encyclical *Christian Education of Youth*
(1929) had high praise for good Catholic schools. Today, however, schools which meet the requirements of the Church for
being Catholic are very few. And because of the consistent
teachings of the Church, Catholic children should never be in
a public school today. So a public school can never be better
than any other option.

If the family for some reason cannot home school, some
families have chosen to have a relative, or a close friend, or
a home schooling mother, or a former teacher who is home
schooling, teach the child. In these cases, the mothers work
with their children in the evening, or in the early morning. In
addition, they constantly talk with their "partner in home
schooling," so it is a joint working relationship.

From my phone calls, I have found that there are many
home schooling parents who are temporarily teaching other
children along with their own until things are smoothed out
in the children's family. They so much believe in home
schooling that they are generously willing to help out on a
temporary basis.

Some families have joined together and are home schooling as a group. This is not unusual and works well as long as parents are actually involved in the teaching. These groups sometimes accept one or two children from families who want to home school but are not able to do so.

If parents are going to put their children in a school, they need to look for Catholic parent-operated schools. These are schools started by parents who are rejecting the secular humanism of most curriculums. There are a number of these around the country.

In addition, some religious, such as the Legionaries of Christ, recently have started Catholic schools based on the traditional teachings of the Church. These are certainly a viable option, though I continue to believe that the best choice for Catholic families is home schooling and that there is simply no better place for children than at home with their parents.

Other benefits of home schooling for the Catholic family

There are many, many benefits of home schooling for the Catholic family. There are benefits to each individual member as well as to the whole family, the Church, and the nation.

For the student

The benefits to the individual student are obvious. The spiritual and moral development which the parents can shape according to Catholic values is the most important and long-lasting benefit.

In the home environment, there is no challenge to the parental influence, either by peers, textbooks, modern nuns or secular-thinking teachers. Home schooled children tend to be innocent and retain their childhood at a natural pace without being thrown into conversations and discussions beyond their natural interests and maturity level.

Personal development is natural, not adversely affected, as children grow up in a stable family situation. The home schooler's personality is shaped by the family, the basic and natural unit of society, rather than by hours of interaction with others at the same level of immaturity. Because of the breakup of so many families, children from original-parents families are in a minority in the classroom. Children from families living the Christian lifestyle of sacrifice rather than materialistic pursuit find themselves an oddity in the classroom.

Academic development is decidedly superior for the home schooled student. It has become almost a self-evident proposition in America that the school is not a place for learning. When the U.S. Department of Education researched the academic situation in the nation's schools in 1983, they wrote the pamphlet "A Nation at Risk." They pointed out that such a terrible disaster has happened in America that our nation is at risk of losing its freedom. The authors, educational bureaucrats who believe in the system after all, went so far as to say that if a foreign power had done to this country what the educational establishment has done, we Americans would consider it an act of war!

Another benefit for the home schooled student is social development. The papal documents repeatedly stress the value and importance of children learning at home, from parents and other members of the family. One pope pointed out that each member of the family represents a microcosm of different groups in society. Thus children learn about the needs and interests of the elderly from grandparents. They learn about the helplessness of babies and their need for protection. They learn to forgive those who disregard their possessions as they deal patiently with little brothers and sisters. Home schooled children learn to serve others as they help younger siblings with their studies. Obedience and respect for authority are learned as parents respect grandparents, as children respect and serve parents.

The interaction of children with members of the family at different stages of maturity is far more beneficial to healthy social development than the interaction with children in the same grade level in the schools. In most schools, there is an almost visible line separating the students by grade level.

Many children in the schools, often from broken homes, have parents whom they see so seldom that they have little opportunity to learn from adult role models. School children tend to follow their peers, other children at the same level of immaturity. Classroom teachers are so dedicated to promoting individual "freedom" that they do not provide the moral, social, or personal leadership they once did.

For the mother

Besides benefits to the individual student, Catholic home schooling provides benefits for the Catholic mother. First, it provides the opportunity to fulfill her responsibility in the marriage vocation to educate her children. It provides a maturing process for a young woman as she dedicates herself in service to youngsters who look up to her with loving eyes for direction. It causes the young mother to want to learn Truth, and to pass it on to those trusting souls who have full confidence in her ability and knowledge.

When a young lady marries, she often may be inexperienced in matters of sacrificing for others. But as the children arrive, as she takes the responsibility to get up in the middle of the night to care for crying babies or sick children, as she surrenders her own self to serve the helpless, a young mother's maturing process is obvious. Home schooling provides a continuation of that maturing process, a process that encompasses academic development, social development, personal development, and spiritual development.

But if Catholic women could express their emotions in earthly words, feminists would be surprised at the ultimate pleasure and joy mothers experience as they teach their children. Home schooling mothers know in their hearts the inexpressible personal reward of working, teaching, learning, and praying with their own children.

Many a mother cries in happiness as her baby gives her his first smile, his first word, his first laugh. Such inexpressible moments happen as she nurses her baby, as she teaches him to take his first steps, as she teaches him the Sign of the Cross. This continues as she teaches him the catechism, his addition and subtraction, his geography and his Catholic history, his spelling words and his essay writing.

When her baby becomes a teenager, she finds joy in his ability to discuss ideas, in his ability to stretch his mind to understand the Faith, in his ability to take pleasure in a twist of words in a poem. She sees her youngster reading a novel for the first time, and takes delight in having a good discussion with him about the characters in the story!

How many home schooling mothers have told me that their education was wasted on them when they were young, but now they are enjoying relearning everything from how to diagram a sentence to learning about the earth to discussing the French Revolution!

For the father

There are also benefits for the father in the Catholic home schooling family. Father can see, provide, and protect his family in his home. They are not scattered around in different schools during the day, scattered at dinnertime at different school-sponsored sports events, scattered after dinner with school friends or social activities away from home.

Fathers work hard these days to provide for their family, yet they are often deprived of the joy of time spent with the children. In the home schooling family, the father can share in the very joys for which he is providing. In a way, it seems cruel for dads to miss that joy because of school-related activities. While fathers who have their children in school may be able to spend time with their children, home schooling fathers have many more opportunities since the children's schedule can be adapted so easily.

When the children are at home in the evening with the father, or if the children are engaged in activities with father, he is establishing and living out the concept that family and children are important. Somehow children have a built-in respect for the authority of Father. If Father thinks that being at home with the children is important, that value will be conveyed in the living of it. You can bet that these children will be at-home fathers with their children.

Fathers in the home schooling family are likely to become more deeply aware of their responsibilities as head of the family as they are surrounded with their "responsibilities" almost continually. And they will become more aware of the consequences of their decisions and how they affect individual members of the family as well as the family as a whole. Father will lead, but also respect, and even depend on the support of his own children, especially as they grow into young adults.

The Catholic father will grow in his own understanding of what fatherhood means as he sees the dependency of his home schooled children who look to him for guidance, rather than to peers or teachers. The Catholic home schooling father is likely to grow in his own spiritual life. Many mothers have phoned to tell me that when their husbands become involved in the home schooling lessons, which are permeated with Catholic beliefs, and when they hear their children asking questions about the Catholic Faith, they themselves begin to study and learn more about the Faith. Several mothers have told me that their non-Catholic husbands converted after being involved in Catholic home schooling. They credit the Catholic home schooling as being important in their husband's conversion.

About ten years ago, a priest who had been visiting in Rome told me that Pope John Paul II favors home schooling because he believes that it will benefit the whole family to learn more about their faith. The Pope believes that home schooling would be of special benefit for parents to learn more about their faith as they teach it to their children. When I first heard the Pope's remark, I did not take it too seriously, but as the years go by, more and more parents call and tell me that they have learned more about their faith, and have grown in their faith through teaching their own children.

For the family

In addition to the benefits of home schooling for individual members of the family, there are benefits to the family as a whole. Home schooling can strengthen internal family relationships as members help each other in the learn-

ing process. As members of the family work and learn together, and come to understand the strengths and weaknesses
of each other, they can develop Christian virtues which help
them to live together peaceably. They learn to work out
problems together, and to stand as a unit against outside
influences or pressures.

Some have advised me not to idealize the home schooling situation so greatly, and not to criticize those families
not home schooling. Consequently, I will say this: not every
home schooling family is perfectly happy. Like all families,
we have our struggles also. At the same time, I believe it is
possible for a family with children in school to be a healthy,
united family. However, from all the phone calls I have received over the past fifteen years, my conclusion is that families teaching children at home are much happier, in spite of
the struggles, than families with children in schools, even
"good" schools.

For the community

Home schooled children benefit the community because
they are not shaped by peers but by parents who teach their
children about the current problems in our society. These
young people grow up being activists on social issues, especially family issues such as abortion. Home schoolers are
more likely to picket clinics and attend Pro-Life rallies. This
"hands-on" Catholic social action will result ultimately in a
generation of Catholic leaders, educated and dedicated, willing and anxious to be involved in changing our society for the
better.

These observations are based on my experiences attending Human Life International conferences, and other Pro-
Family or Pro-Life conferences. Home schooled students are
often present. Students attending schools are not only absent,
but parents even remark to me that their children do not
agree with them and have been influenced by the schools to
reject their Pro-Life values.

For the Church

The Catholic Church should reap the benefits of home schooling families because they will swell its numbers. As parents teach their children at home, many come to a greater understanding and realization of the joy of children. Home schooling families are responding to God's will to be open and charitable regarding having children. And their children and their children's children are likely to do the same.

The Pope is constantly encouraging evangelization. But the most effective evangelization is from parents to children. When I was growing up, it was considered important to convert at least one person to the Catholic Faith. Every Catholic parent has the opportunity to convert his children to the Catholic Faith. Just as in converting friends and neighbors, good example is the best means for the conversion of our children. As home schooling parents, we have more opportunities to give good example in living the authentic Catholic life.

The Catholic home schooling family benefits the local Catholic parish community, especially other home schooling families, or families struggling to maintain traditional Catholic values. The Catholic home schooling family gives witness to Catholic truths, the main truth being that, with God's grace, the authentic Catholic family life *can* be lived.

Seeing the potential vocations from home schooling families, one Midwest bishop has made a special invitation for home schooled young men to visit his diocese and attend his seminary. He understands that the home schooling family is supportive of vocations. We have heard this from vocations directors from the Legionaries of Christ and other growing seminaries. They say that home schooled young seminarians know their catechism and respect the special vocation of the priesthood. It is no coincidence that the Arlington Diocese, one of the focal points for Catholic home schooling in the United States, also has a remarkable number of vocations to the priesthood.

For the nation

For those of us who love our country and want to restore it to Christ, we see our home schooling family as a
tool to help our nation grow in the love of God. Our Catholic home schooling families are training leaders dedicated to
Christian moral values, who will help return the nation to
Christ. Our home schooling families, now and in the future,
will help our nation to find itself, to understand its purpose,
to seek Christian heroes, and to take direction from Christian
precepts. The specific moral virtues which Catholic home
schooling families are developing, and which will benefit
our nation, are loyalty, patriotism, obedience to authority,
respect for the law, respect for life, respect for the elderly,
responsibility, dedication to work and the value of work,
self-discipline, justice, charitable works, and mercy. These
are virtues without which no nation can long survive. Most
importantly, Catholic home schooling families are passing on
the true Catholic Faith, which will be crucial to any true
Christian restoration of our beloved country.

With so many benefits from home schooling to children
and parents, to families, to the Church, and to the nation, I
hope parents soon realize that the reason they should teach
their children at home is not because of the problems in our
society and in our schools, but because it is the best way to
live the authentic Catholic family life.

Chapter 2:
What Is Catholic Home Schooling?

As I travel around the country to home schooling conventions, meeting parents and priests, I have come to realize that most people don't know what is meant by Catholic Home Schooling. Catholic Home Schooling means that the entire curriculum is permeated with the teachings of Christ, that is, with Catholic doctrine and values. At the same time, the family is living the Catholic family life as the "domestic church," the church of the home. This involves living a truly Catholic life in the home all year round, including during summer vacations.

Actually, according to the Bible and according to Church documents, "education" means, first of all, formation in the Catholic Faith by parents in the home.

Fr. Joseph Fessio, S.J. of Ignatius Press remarked at a Catholic home schooling conference in Santa Clara, California in February of 1998 that the Catholic home schools today are doing something that the monasteries did in the "Dark Ages." Catholic home schooling families have become little centers of the Catholic Faith. They are preserving the Catholic Faith and Catholic culture in a very hostile environment.

What is a *Catholic curriculum?*

A Catholic curriculum is one in which every subject taught is permeated with the truths of the Catholic Faith. A Catholic curriculum is not a standard curriculum that simply includes a religion class. Every class is to incorporate Christ's teachings. How else can we follow the direction of St. Paul to "restore all things in Christ"?

Let me explain how we accomplish this at Seton.

Arithmetic

People laugh when we speak about making our math courses Catholic. But we are in the process of doing it anyway. No subject can be divorced from God because God is Truth, indeed the Creator of Truth. Therefore He is the Creator of Math. We need to make this clear to our children on a frequent basis.

When we started Seton Home Study School, we started with a Protestant series since no Catholic series was available. In addition, for the past few years, we have had an alternative math series, the Saxon series, which has been acclaimed nationally for helping students to dramatically improve their math scores.

However, our goal is to have a Catholic math series. If we use math in our daily life, and if our daily life is to be lived with Jesus Christ, then our math must somehow be affected. And it can be and should be. For instance, we need to be honest and accurate in our financial dealings with others.

In schools, students are given math word problems so that they may learn to apply abstract concepts to real situations. In the secular texts, the real-life situations involve classroom or school situations, and kids doing things together, often without family members. In the Catholic home schooling families, the real-life situations involve visiting shrines as a family, going to Mass, playing with other home schoolers, enjoying family activities, field trips with home school support groups, and picketing abortion clinics. Consequently, our aim is to produce a math series reflecting the real-life situations of a Catholic home schooling family.

We have begun using a secular, formerly Catholic, text-workbook math series. For this series, Seton is producing a supplement, *Solving Word Problems*, for each chapter. Problems relate to real-life Catholic family situations, involving real people. Problems relate to gas mileage on the way to a rosary rally, or measuring a floor width at the parish church, working in a Catholic bookstore, and so on. We hope these math word problems help our children to realize the importance of honest and accurate math in the Christian life.

Some may say that it is "overkill" to try to Catholicize even math word problems. I am reminded, however, of a math workbook produced by the Communist Sandanistas in

Nicaragua in the 1980's. Among the word problems were topics involving machine guns and hand grenades, to prepare the children for warfare. The Communists in Nicaragua understood and made use of math to further their atheistic regime. The enemies of the Catholic Church understand the purpose of education to further their ideas among the next generation. The secular humanists promote their agenda in all subject areas in the public schools and textbooks. We Catholics, as directed by our Church, must promote Jesus Christ in all subject areas.

Art

There is no reason why the majority, if not all, of the art projects in the Catholic home cannot be related to our Faith and the Liturgical Year. Even simple drawings of trees and flowers remind us of God's goodness and generosity. The liturgical year is so rich in the celebration of saints and religious events, that there are almost unlimited possibilities.

Reed and Roxalana Armstrong, both internationally recognized Catholic artists, are writing the new Seton art program. Several grades are available. A Catholic art appreciation course has been added to the eighth grade program. In addition, we give ideas and some directions for arts and crafts projects, but if you search Catholic bookstores or St. Vincent de Paul shops, you can find further ideas. In addition, many projects from secular arts and crafts books can be adapted to a feastday.

Here is one example. On the feast of the Sacred Heart, help your child to make a stuffed red velvet heart. Draw a heart on a piece of construction paper, and then use it as a pattern to cut the heart out of velvet. Using red thread, help your child to sew up the heart. The heart could be attached to a piece of construction paper and hung on the wall. If you want to be more elaborate, wire or twigs can be encircled around the heart. Gold-colored construction paper could be added to represent the fire from the Sacred Heart. As the heart is being made, there can be discussion about the Sacred Heart. It could be followed by a Litany to the Sacred Heart. Place the red velvet heart on the family altar.

English

Seton is now producing a Catholic English series since the famous Loyola University series, *Voyages in English,* has now removed all Catholic references. Several grades are already available, with the others in production.

Seton's English series is being written in compliance with the directives from Rome to permeate the curriculum with Catholic values. Unquestionably, these books will be excellent teaching tools for grammar and composition. Catholics have always stressed these areas, because we recognize their importance to our spiritual goals. Consequently God has blessed Catholic graduates with an unusual ability not only to write concisely and accurately, but also to think logically.

This series will take students beyond the basics, challenging them to think and analyze their thinking and their presentation of thoughts.

Sentences to be analyzed for parts of speech or punctuation teach Catholic Faith and attitudes at the same time. For example, sentences from the sixth grade text have included: "Prayer brings peace to the soul....The early missionaries helped the natives in many ways....The angel Gabriel brought a message to Mary."

In addition to sentences, composition exercises give wonderful opportunities for the children to express their Catholic faith.

Many assignments ask the children to write about saints or other Catholic topics. Here is a beginning sentence our sixth graders have used in writing a paragraph: "The sanctuary lamp is only a little lamp, but it keeps God company day and night."

English should teach our children an appreciation for Catholic Culture as well as high standards in grammar and composition.

Handwriting

In the secular handwriting texts, the students practice their letters by writing paragraphs which often promote secular humanist values.

In Seton's Catholic handwriting textbooks, writing selections are taken from the Psalms and other books of the Bible. Other selections are on such topics as saints and Catholic sacramentals. For example, in grade four, for the practice of the capital *A* and capital *E*, the students are to practice their cursive letters by writing: "St. Anthony the Abbot lived in Egypt in the third century."

In grade five, for the practice of the capital *N* and *M*, students write: "Merciful and gracious is the Lord, slow to anger and abounding in kindness. Not according to our sins does He deal with us."

History

Our history books recognize that the central event in history is the Incarnation of Jesus Christ. In first grade, children learn about immigrant priests and color a picture of a priest saying Mass. In second grade, the children learn about patron saints of countries around the world. In third grade, our children read biographies of the Catholic heroes of America. In fourth and fifth grades, the children use history texts produced for Catholic schools, teaching American history with an emphasis on Catholics who played an important role in our country's history.

In sixth grade, using Catholic history books, the children come to understand world history, the Crusades, and the Middle Ages. Students learn that Western Civilization was shaped by the Catholic Church. In seventh grade, the children are presented with more advanced concepts about America and the importance of Catholics and Catholic concepts in American life and government. A chapter in this text is dedicated to the spiritual leadership of the Catholic Church.

In eighth grade, our own Seton *Catholic World Culture* text presents Catholic culture through the lives and contributions of Catholic musicians, artists, architects, kings, and queens.

We consider history to be one of the most important

subjects for home schooling families. Living in a post-Christian society, our children need to learn from the past in order to make the necessary changes in the future to bring Christ back to the center of life in our nation, and in the world.

Music

Music is important for children as a means of learning the Christian message, as well as giving children the opportunity to express Catholic beliefs in song.

Our texts follow the liturgical year, offering songs not only for Christmas and Easter, but also for St. Patrick's Day, St. Joseph's feastday, and other special days. Books at the older grade levels teach Gregorian Chant.

Catholic culture is rich in art and music. We need to teach our children about these spiritual treasures. Much of the art and music of our modern society is without beauty. Our children should have the opportunity to learn about, see, and hear great art and music.

Phonics

Seton is producing a Catholic phonics series, and several grades are now available. For the other grades, supplemental Catholic exercises are introduced through the lesson plans. For instance, in grade two, children are learning the sounds *ch*, *sh*, and *wh*. The children are to include them in sentences such as these:

Jonah spent three days in a whale.
On Sunday, we go to church to worship God.
Jesus tells us, "I know My sheep and they know Me."

Physical Education

This is another area where people get a laugh at the idea that sports could be "Catholic." Actually, the popes have written fairly often about sports and how such activities can have spiritual lessons for us. The popes often compare the self-discipline in sports with the self-discipline required in the spiritual life. In fact, St. Paul compared the spiritual life to running a race.

So while we give lessons for specific individual exercises, we relate these to the spiritual life, following the direction of St. Paul and the popes. In grade two, the children are told after an exercise that "This should help you to stand straight the way God wants you to stand." And again: "This will help strengthen the stomach muscles God gave you." And again: "Even while having fun, we must thank Jesus for giving us good health so we can exercise."

Reading

Obviously, in the area of reading, there are almost no limits to the amount of Catholic materials we can give our children to read if we can find something in print at their reading level. The regular curriculum at Seton consists of mainly the *Faith and Freedom* readers, which emphasize Catholic family life. In the upper grades, the stories teach the children about the values of Catholic immigrant families in the various parts of the new American nation. In sixth grade, the stories are about Catholic people in Europe in times past, relating it to the study of Old World History.

At least two book reports a year are to be on biographies of saints. Many parents obtain books about saints from older relatives and friends, as well as from Catholic publishers and used book stores, though we send one saint's biography for each grade level.

In addition to readers, Seton has written *Reading for Comprehension* workbooks which support Catholic values. Many selections are about Catholic saints, while others are from the writings of saints, such as the words of Our Lord to St. Bridget.

The fifth grade *Reading for Comprehension* workbook consists of a long story about a Jewish boy and an Egyptian boy during the time of Moses. The student learns about life during that period and how the Jews lived in Old Testament times. Here is a selection from the book as the Jewish people follow Moses in the desert:

> They drove their animals down onto the dry bed of the sea. They stared nervously at the rippling walls of water, at the same time marveling at the works of the Lord God. The waves of the sea high above their heads clashed like cymbals as they hurled themselves together, loudly objecting to their strange displacement.
>
> Jacob and Seti kept their families near the watery walls, fearing the press of anxious people in the middle of the great throng. The two fathers kept themselves between their families and the hastening people, the mothers and small children being between the fathers and the big boys. Thus, Joe and Pepi found themselves moving fast next to the wall of water on the right side.
>
> Joe and Pepi were not the only ones to find it irresistible to stick their hands into the water of the walls! Joe put his hand into the water up to his elbow, splashing himself all over as he moved along—and so did Pepi! The wall kept its vertical position. The boys showed their fathers their wet hands.
>
> Jacob said, "The Lord God is mighty—His strength past our comprehension—keeping the sea away from us!"
>
> "Amen!" said Seti.

In grade eight, students learn about different saints and often read the words of the saints themselves in the *Reading for Comprehension* workbooks. Here is a selection from Lesson 44: The Stigmata of St. Francis:

> "Do you know," said Christ, "what I have done to you? I have given you the Stigmata, which are the marks of My Passion, so that you may be My Standard-Bearer. And as I descended into Limbo on the day of My death, and delivered all the souls there by the merits of My Stigmata, so do I grant you each year on the anniversary of your death, to visit Purgatory, and by the virtue of your Stigmata, you shall release all the souls whom you shall find there belonging to your three Orders—namely Friars Minor, Sisters, and Penitents—as well as others who have had great devotion to you, and you

shall lead them to the glory of Paradise."

Questions which follow the *Reading for Comprehension* selections are of three kinds: some are objective questions, some are interpretive, and some are application questions. These latter questions are to help the children to think about the application of the ideas, such as a particular virtue of a saint, and how they might apply the virtue in their own lives.

Religion

This is the heart of the matter of Catholic education. Our core text is the *Baltimore Catechism*, which, as Father Bourque declared on Eternal Word Television Network, is contained within the pages of the new *Catechism of the Catholic Church*. The *Baltimore Catechism*, St. Joseph edition, covers all the basic Catholic doctrines: the Creed, the Ten Commandments, the Sacraments, and the Prayers. It includes questions and answers for study, fill-in Exercises, and Bible references.

Bible story books are included for each grade except eighth, where we have a Church history text. An additional textbook series gives the children more explanation of the questions and answers in the *Baltimore Catechism*.

Seton is producing a catechism series specifically geared for home schoolers to supplement the Baltimore Catechism. Several grade levels are now available, and others are in preparation or are awaiting ecclesiastical approval.

Science

Catholic science textbooks in the past were very minimally Catholic. Sometimes the only thing "Catholic" was the author's name. We have produced several Catholic science textbooks which truly reflect Catholic thinking.

In grade one, for example, we teach the children about the heart and blood. We conclude the chapter with information about the Eucharistic miracle of Lanciano.

The blood is real blood. The flesh is real flesh. The
flesh is muscular tissue from the heart. The blood is
type AB. There is no explanation as to how flesh could
be kept without decaying for 1200 years. What we know
by faith, science has also found!

In grade two, in learning about multi-colored butterfly
wings, children read, "It is amazing how God makes the
patterns on butterflies' wings so colorful and so varied." In
discussing the compass, our science book declares that "This
is another example of God's goodness. Without the compass,
sailors in the past could never have found their way through
the oceans."

In the fourth grade Catholic science text, students read,

The wind reminds us of the Holy Spirit, the third
Person of the Blessed Trinity. Remember the wind blow-
ing on Pentecost Sunday? Remember it was the way
God chose to reveal Himself to the Prophet Elijah in
the Old Testament? Can you find the story in your
Bible?

The books are filled with science. But they are also filled
with the Author of science.

A new grade eight life science text is Pro-Life. In an
explanation of cells, the author writes in our supplemental
material in the lesson plans:

The entire body is much more than any one cell or
group of cells. In a parallel, consider that we, as members of the Roman Catholic Church, are members of
the Body of Christ. Some are called to be ordained as
priests, some as religious, some as husband or wife,
and some are called to be single. For the Body of Christ
to grow on earth, we must each carry out our vocation
to our best ability.

Spelling

The secular spellers include the words to be studied, the
spelling rule, and a selection to be read in which the spell-

ing words are used. The selections may be paragraphs which promote a politically correct agenda item.

The Catholic spellers composed by Seton teach the same spelling words plus some words from our catechism, but include selections which promote Catholic values.

In grade two, for example, while children learn to spell words with the sounds of long "A," they read about a little girl named Molly who always complained. One day, she decided to run away from home and met Mrs. Henry, her neighbor. Her neighbor explained the Commandments and concluded by saying,

> When I have a dirty job to do, I don't ask, "Why should I do it?" I simply tell myself, "Nobody likes doing it, but it has to be done by someone, and why not me? God has put me in this place at this time. So I must try to do a good job." I try to make my job like a little prayer for Him.

The speller in grade four includes stories from the Bible about Abraham, the Ark and the Tabernacle, King Saul, David, and Solomon. The speller for grade five includes stories about St. Nicholas of Tolentino, St. Edward the Confessor, St. Isidore the Farmer, St. Hugh of Lincoln, St. Mary Magdalen de Pazzi, Blessed Margaret of Castello, St. Clare of Montefalco, St. Zita, St. Rita, and many more.

The speller in grade eight teaches the students about St. Joan of Arc, Cardinal John Henry Newman, The Black Madonna of Czestochowa, The University of Paris, St. Lawrence, The Venerable Bede, Good King Edward, Michelangelo, the Cure of Ars, Our Lady of Fatima, and the apparitions of Mary at Lourdes.

Vocabulary

The vocabulary series at Seton is secular since there is no Catholic series available. We don't anticipate writing one very soon since our resources are going into other areas at this time. However, we have written weekly Catholic tests in which the vocabulary words are to be used. These tests are

sentences based on the catechism, Bible stories, sacramentals, lives of the saints, and general Catholic culture.

In grade four, for example, some of the vocabulary sentences are "The apostles *scattered* when Our Lord was arrested in the Garden of Gethsemane." "One of the jobs of
the angels is to be a *messenger* for God." "St. Stephen as
King of Hungary was not *stingy* with his gifts of money to
beggars." "While the apostles were working miracles and
curing the sick, the fake magicians such as Simon could not
peddle their tricks."

In the seventh grade, our students learn, "Except in Faith
and Morals, the church can *adapt* herself to the customs of
the people." "When we think about God's goodness and
mercy, it should *evoke* from us prayers of praise and thanksgiving."

Conclusion

In summary, a totally Catholic curriculum is possible.
Not only is it possible, but it is also necessary if we want
to be thoroughly and authentically Catholic. Catholic home
schooling is for all families who want to live the Faith every
day as Jesus has instructed us.

Chapter 3:
Church Teachings on
Marriage and Education

Since the education of children is an essential part of the vocation of marriage, it is important to understand the official Catholic Church teachings regarding marriage and education.

The clear and absolute teaching of the Catholic Church is that marriage was raised to the level of a Sacrament by Jesus Christ. This is based on the Gospel of St. Matthew, Chapter 19, Verses 4 to 9:

> Have ye not read that he who made man from the beginning, made them male and female? And he said: For this cause shall a man leave father and mother, and shall cleave to his wife, and they two shall be in one flesh. Therefore now they are not two, but one flesh. What therefore God hath joined together, let no man put asunder.

The exact same words by Jesus were repeated in Mark's Gospel, Chapter 10, verses 2 to 12. Interestingly, in both Gospels, these words of Jesus are followed by the incident of little children gathering around Jesus. "Little children were presented to Him...and the disciples rebuked them that brought them." It is not a coincidence that children, the primary purpose of marriage, were presented to Jesus immediately following His teachings on marriage. Nor does it seem coincidental that parents, in the process of bringing their children to Jesus for His blessing, are hindered by the Apostles. Jesus must reprimand the Apostles, in fact.

In our current American society, we are sorry that our Catholic children are being hindered from coming to know Jesus, sometimes even by Catholic religious or clergy.

It is obvious that Jesus wants parents to have children, and to bring them TO Him not just physically, but also spiritually—which is where our Marriage vocation to educate our children has its foundation.

33

It was not a coincidence that Jesus scheduled His first public miracle at a wedding ceremony, nor that the miracle was specifically requested by His own Mother! Jesus wants us to understand that marriage is a sacred vocation and a Sacrament, and if we fulfill His will regarding the responsibilities of marriage, we will receive an abundance of graces and blessings, many through the intercession of His Blessed Mother.

According to the Catholic Church, the primary purpose of marriage consists of two co-equal responsibilities: the procreation of children and the education of children.

They are co-equal responsibilities.

They are equally important.

The educating of children by parents is a duty, a serious responsibility of the vocation of the Sacrament of Matrimony. From the many statements of the popes we know that this education includes the daily "formation" of children by their parents to be good Catholics, but with parents also bound to make sure that in their children's academic schooling, either at home or in a school, the Catholic Faith "permeates every branch of knowledge." This is what home schooling is all about.

Home schooling is a re-affirmation of the marriage of the husband and wife. Indeed, home schooling can bring about many changes for the better in marriages where the spouses have drifted apart.

This seems like an incredible statement, but it is absolutely true. It is true because as husbands and wives use their sacramental graces to fulfill their marriage vocation to teach their children, they obtain more graces, both sanctifying grace and actual graces. These graces enable a husband and a wife to understand and to live out an authentic Catholic marriage and authentic Catholic family life. They come to better understand their own Catholic beliefs and values as they home school.

The commitment and daily sacrifice on the part of parents as they home school their children can help them to grow spiritually as well as in the practice of the authentically Catholic family lifestyle. Educating one's children is intimately entwined with the purposes of marriage, with the vocation of marriage. The more we teach our children, the more we understand our vocation. The more we understand our vocation, the more successful will be the results of home schooling our children.

A public statement

Every Catholic marriage is a public statement that we are called to obey Christ's commands concerning marriage. Each baby born into a Catholic family is a public statement to our pagan society that we are obeying God's command to increase and multiply, to provide souls for His kingdom. Every Catholic home schooling family is making a statement that we are going to take the responsibility given to us by God, and we are going to take it seriously.

Just as Jesus is faithful to His Church, His bride, and will be faithful to each one of us as members of His Church, so we are to be faithful to Him by being obedient to His commands. Consequently, following Christ means being faithful to our spouse in marriage, and being faithful to our children in their Catholic education.

Sadly today, affected by our over-materialistic society, young-adult Catholics often look on love and marriage with a humanistic view. Even the Pre-Cana conferences deal more with how the prospective spouses can get along together and with how to prevent babies rather than with the Church teachings about the responsibilities of the vocation of marriage.

In the current American society, most parents, Catholic and non-Catholic, will never learn about the vocation and responsibilities of the Sacrament of Matrimony. If families become involved with home schooling or Pro-Life activities, they may find Catholics who will give them a good example. Hopefully, this will propel them to read and learn about their vocation of marriage.

For those who want to learn the teachings of the Catholic Church about marriage, there is no lack of material. The Catholic Church, knowing the importance of marriage and family, has constantly given her children guidance in this

area. Perhaps the most important encyclical written for
married Catholics is *Casti Connubii*, or, *On Christian Marriage* in English. It is the basic document all married Catholics and Catholics considering marriage should read and study.

Casti Connubii

In this encyclical, Pope Pius XI, inspired by the Holy
Spirit, instructed Christian couples about the graces which
we receive from the Sacrament of Matrimony to help us
live out our duties in the vocation of marriage.

These graces help us to fulfill the duties of the married
state, the first duty to cooperate with God in having children, and the second duty to educate our children in the
Christian virtuous life.

Pope Pius XI declared that

> ...the faithful can...open up for themselves a treasury of
> sacramental grace from which they draw supernatural
> power for the fulfilling of their rights and duties faith-
> fully, holily, perseveringly, even unto death. Hence this
> sacrament not only increases sanctifying grace...but also
> adds particular gifts, dispositions, seeds of grace, by
> elevating and perfecting the natural powers.

Thus the Catholic Church teaches that we can have a
treasury of sacramental grace from the Sacrament of Matrimony. From this treasury, we can draw *supernatural power*.
This power will help us to fulfill the *rights and duties* of the
married state. We will be able to fulfill them faithfully. We
can fulfill them in a holy manner. We will be able to persevere as we fulfill our duties. With our matrimonial graces,
we will be able to persevere even unto death!

The Catholic Church teaches that we merit more sanctifying grace as we fulfill our duties, and can merit even extra
gifts, such as certain dispositions or graces, to elevate and
perfect some natural powers we already have. The natural
abilities, in every area, seem to increase as home schooling
mothers and fathers dedicate themselves to their children in
fulfilling these responsibilities.

Pius XI continues:

> By these gifts the parties are assisted not only in under-
> standing, but in knowing intimately, in adhering to firmly,
> in willing effectively, and in successfully putting into prac-
> tice, those things which pertain to the marriage state, its
> aims and *duties*, giving them a right to the actual assis-
> tance of grace, whensoever they need it for fulfilling the
> *duties* of their state. (Emphasis added)

The Catholic Church declares that we will obtain the
grace from God *whenever* we need it for fulfilling the duties
of the married state. If we believe Jesus, if we believe in
His Church, if we believe in the infallibility of the Pope as
the Vicar of Jesus Christ, how can we doubt for a minute
that we will have the graces and ability to educate our own
children?

Some parents say they lack confidence in their ability to
teach their children. But we are not supposed to have
confidence in our own ability. We are supposed to have confidence in Jesus Christ! We are supposed to have confidence
in His Word in the Bible and in the documents of the Church
as proclaimed by the Vicar of Christ. We are supposed to have
confidence in the graces which He has given us and continues to give us as we teach our children, as we fulfill the duties
of the vocation of the Sacrament of Matrimony.

Why some parents are not successful

Pius XI goes on to explain why some parents may not be
successful in fulfilling their responsibilities:

> Nevertheless, since it is a law of Divine Providence in
> the supernatural order that men do not reap the full fruit
> of the sacraments...*unless they cooperate with grace*, the
> grace of matrimony will remain for the most part an
> unused talent, hidden in the field, unless the parties exer-
> cise these supernatural powers, and cultivate and develop
> the seeds of grace they have received.

> If however, doing all that lies within their power,
> they cooperate diligently, they will be able with ease to
> bear the burdens of their state and to fulfill their duties.
> By such a sacrament, they will be strengthened, sancti-
> fied, and, in a manner, consecrated. (Emphasis added)

The power to educate

Continuing in the encyclical letter, *On Christian Marriage*, Pope Pius XI repeats the long-standing teaching of the
Church:

> The blessing of offspring, however, is not completed
> by the mere begetting of them, but something else must
> be added, namely the proper education of the offspring.
> For the wise God would have failed to make sufficient
> provision for children that had been born...if He had
> not given to those to whom He had entrusted the power
> and right to beget them, the power also and the right to
> educate them.
>   Now it is certain that both by the law of nature and
> of God, this right and duty of educating their offspring
> belongs in the first place to those who began the work
> of nature by giving them birth, and they are indeed
> forbidden to leave unfinished this work....In matrimony,
> provision has been made in the best possible way for
> this education of children.

And then Pius XI quotes again from the Code of Canon
Law of 1917, "The primary end of marriage is the procreation and the education of children."

Education: the long-term duty

In our child-abusing and pro-abortion society, it is important that the emphasis today among good Catholics be on
recognizing that children are a gift from God, and that we
remain open to life in the marriage union. The fact is that
the long-term obligation for parents, the day-to-day, minute-
by-minute obligation over a period of many, many years is
not procreating, but educating!

For some reason, Pre-Cana conferences spend much of the class time on the physical aspects of marriage, and whether this or that birth control method is okay or not. It is a serious omission in these classes that the graces of the Sacrament, as well as the long-term process of spiritual growth of the family members through home education, is ignored.

Father Hardon on marriage

In the summer of 1991, Father John Hardon, an outstanding Catholic theologian, gave a summer course at Christendom College on the Sacrament of Matrimony. He taught the basic principles of Christ concerning marriage. His exposition on the Sacrament was so beautiful that all those hearing it were filled with gratitude to God for this great gift.

Father Hardon's first message was that it is a Divine Law that every marriage must be monogamous, that a man may have only one wife, and a woman only one husband, until one of them dies. And every marriage between baptized persons is intrinsically indissoluble. No matter what non-Christians, Eastern Orthodox, Protestants, or Catholic writers urge, there cannot and will not ever be a change in this Divine Law. The Unity and the Indissolubility of marriage has always been the universal teaching of the Church of Jesus Christ.

This foundation for marriage means that parents need to work out their family problems, seek solutions together, and not run from their spouses. This means the family will be stable for the children, and will provide a solid environment for educating them at home.

A mother unhappy with her marriage can and will find solace in the daily teaching interaction with her children. She cannot dwell on her personal problems as she daily teaches her children, by prayer and good example as well as by more formal methods.

Graces

Especially interesting for home schoolers was Father Hardon's lesson on Graces of Christian Marriage. We know from our catechism that we receive sanctifying grace as well as a sacramental grace when we receive each Sacrament.

What most of us did not realize is that this single one-syllable word, grace, has so much meaning to our vocation of marriage. The special sacramental grace of each sacrament, as the catechism teaches, helps our intellects to know what is God's Will, and to understand better how to carry out God's Will in responding to certain events in our lives. It helps our will to carry out God's Will. The sacramental grace of Matrimony helps us to apply our intellect and will to the situations related to our vocation of marriage.

Father pointed out that while we need these graces to help our intellect and will, the primary purpose of these graces is to help each spouse to be an instrument of grace to the other spouse! The husband's primary duty as husband is to be a channel of grace to his wife, to help sanctify her; the wife's primary duty as wife is to be a channel of grace to her husband, to help sanctify him.

In addition, parents have special sacramental graces from the Sacrament of Matrimony by which they are to serve as channels of grace to their children. And from experience, many of us have come to realize that our children serve as channels of grace to us parents.

Certainly the directives of God to Moses, that parents are to teach their children, and be an example to their children, sitting and walking, rising and resting, clearly show us that we are to be "channels" for teaching the Ten Commandments. With the institution of the Sacrament of Matrimony by Jesus, this responsibility can be more easily fulfilled because of the special sacramental graces. And the responsibility extends beyond the Ten Commandments, to an authentic Catholic family lifestyle.

The responsibility to help save the souls of our family members is an awesome responsibility. It is an overwhelming responsibility. Obviously, without the abundance of sacramental graces, this would be impossible.

The bottom line is that we must be good, we must be obedient, not only because we love God, not only to save our own soul, but also because we need to serve as an example for our spouse and for our children.

> Then after he had washed their feet, and taken his garments, being set down again, he said to them: "Know you what I have done to you? You call me Master, and Lord; and you say well, for so I am. If then I being your Lord and Master, have washed your feet; you also ought to wash one another's feet. For I have given you an example, that as I have done to you, so you do also." (John 13:12-15)

Cooperate with grace

While we received these graces at the Sacrament of Matrimony, we must constantly work to use these graces. Nothing beats that combination for personal fortification against the continual daily onslaughts of the spiritual enemy: daily prayer, especially the Rosary, daily Mass if possible, and confession at least once a month.

As we cooperate with grace, we will be able to go beyond the strict duties of our vocation, not only to recognize what else we must do, but to carry out these responsibilities beyond the strict duty. Grace helps us to "be apostolic," says Father Hardon, to our spouse, to our children, and even to other families.

Edouard Cardinal Gagnon from the Pontifical Council on the Family told me at a Philadelphia conference that American parents need to evangelize in their own families. The Cardinal believes that home schooling is vital for evangelizing from one generation to the next generation. It is because parents neglected their duties in the past to educate their children themselves and relied on the schools that we have suffered the loss of faith among Catholics today, the Cardinal stated.

Marriage is permanent

No human authority can dissolve a valid, sacramental, consummated marriage. This principle deserves special attention, due to the almost universal breakdown of marriage and the family in "materially superdeveloped countries," as Father Hardon says. Current attitudes about individual freedom have made many people think that marriage should last only as long as it is convenient. Consequently, there is a loss of commitment by millions of people to their marriage and to their families.

Home schooling is a complete reversal of these modern trends. Home schooling parents are willing to make God-ordained commitments, commitments to family, commitments to the spouse as they teach together, and commitments to their children, serious commitments involving time and energy and sacrifice.

Marriage strengthens society

Many home schooling parents understand that strengthening marriage and family also strengthens society. Home schooling parents' commitment to raise Catholic children means their Catholic values will ultimately "rule the world." Home schooling parents see clearly that the eternal rewards offer ultimate freedom for themselves and for their children. With the home schooling families, the national trend toward divorce and remarriage will be considerably slowed down, in this generation and in the generation to come.

Jesus became Man to redeem the human race, not only individual persons but also human societies, especially the basic unit of human society, the family. As Father Hardon teaches, families are called to become holy as families, and Jesus "merited the graces they need to become holy in this life." It is a "theme running through the New Testament that Christ has redeemed the human race, not only individually but collectively, not only personally but socially."

It is part of our Catholic tradition that God has ordained certain angels as guardians of cities and towns, of churches and city halls, of nations and peoples. Consequently it is not too difficult to imagine that if families are called to be holy, if Christ died to redeem families as families, each family must have a family guardian angel.

In the Catholic Byzantine Rite marriage ceremony, the bride and groom each wear a crown, symbolizing the beginning of a new "kingdom" for God. From each family, living the Christian life, not only will their children come to populate Christ's kingdom, but a second generation will come to Christ, and a third. This reflects the instructions in *Exodus,* in which Moses told the people to teach God's Commandments to their children, and their children's children.

My parents, still living, have nine living children. Eight are married, and there are 49 living grandchildren and 19 living great-grandchildren. Now that's what I call a family kingdom!

Superhuman charity

Jesus makes "superhuman demands" of married people and their families, especially demanding a superhuman charity towards one another, says Father Hardon. It is superhuman to day after day put up with the faults of your spouse. It is superhuman especially in today's secular humanist society when all of us are so influenced by the media propaganda telling us to "do your own thing," to "be yourself," and to do everything "MY way."

"Be true to yourself" has a new meaning today. It means "Me first!" So to remain faithful to someone for a lifetime, to put up with another's faults for a lifetime, to give up our own personal wants and desires for the good of the spouse, for the good of the family, for the glory of God, demands superhuman effort. These superhuman demands by God can be met only with the "superhuman light and strength made available by Christ's redemptive death on Calvary." These superhuman personal sacrifices of self can be met only with sanctifying grace and actual graces, with the sacramental grace coming to us from the Sacrament of Matrimony and the other Sacraments.

In practical terms

Married people thoroughly understand the tremendous difficulty in obeying Christ's command to "turn the other cheek." It is not our enemies who are so difficult to forgive. It is our spouse who is so difficult to forgive! And sometimes our children!

Father Hardon declared that the secret for a peaceful and happy marriage and family life is to realize that our spouses, our children, our parents, and our other family members are all potential vehicles of grace for us. No other creatures are as close, as constant, as providential. No matter how difficult or demanding, our family members are a gift from God, a gift of His loving providence, an opportunity for us to grow spiritually.

However, to see what God wants us to do, for us to choose what God wants, requires constant daily prayer.

Father Hardon reminded us that in addition to living a holy lifestyle in our vocation of Catholic marriage and family, our family is to be a witness in our pagan society to Christ and to His teachings. In a world that has "abandoned Christ, ignores Him, and even openly opposes Him," we and our family must be a source of grace in our society which is "literally struggling for survival." We must have a family-to-family evangelizing apostolate.

Humanae Vitae

In the encyclical letter of Pope Paul VI, *Humanae Vitae* or *Of Human Life*, the teachings of the Catholic Church regarding marriage and the procreation of children are carefully explained. In this encyclical, the Pope repeats the teachings of the Church regarding the importance of education as essential to the vocation of marriage. He writes about collaborating with God "in the generation and education of new lives." And again, "Marriage and conjugal love are by their nature ordained toward the begetting and educating of children."

Pope Paul VI declared that

> Christian married couples...must remember that their Christian vocation...is reinforced by the sacrament of matrimony. By it, husband and wife are strengthened and as it were consecrated for the faithful accomplishment of their proper duties, for the carrying out of their proper vocation even to perfection, and the Christian witness which is proper to them before the whole world.

Notice again that the Pope is stressing that husbands and wives who have received the Sacrament of Matrimony are consecrated in order for them to accomplish the proper purposes of the married state.

The vocation of parents to educate

In the 1960's and 1970's, Catholic parents started home schooling because they believed it was the only option to protect their children. Parents began to investigate the Scriptures and the teachings of the Church to determine if home schooling is approved by the Church. Not only do the Scriptures and the Catholic teachings support home schooling, in many situations they seem to command home schooling.

Historically, traditionally, and doctrinally, the Catholic Church strongly promotes, not just supports, parents teaching their own children.

In 1875, the Vatican sent "Instructions" to the bishops of the United States in regard to Catholic children attending the public schools. Since today the Catholic schools are in many ways very similar to public schools (they have no Catholic textbooks), these instructions could most certainly apply to them.

Instructions of the Holy Office to the Bishops of the U.S., November 24, 1875.

> To the Sacred Congregation, this method (of public education) has appeared intrinsically dangerous and absolutely contrary to Catholicism. Indeed because the

special program adopted by these schools excludes all religious instruction, the pupils cannot grasp the elements of the faith, nor are they instructed in the precepts of the Church, and therefore they are deprived of that which is most essential for man to know and without which it is impossible to live in a Christian manner.

The fact that in these schools, or at least in the majority of them, the adolescents of both sexes are grouped together in the same classrooms to attend lessons, and boys and girls must sit together on the same benches, exposes them to corruption to a certain extent. The result of all this is that youth is unfortunately in danger of losing its faith, while its good morals are threatened.

(Note: The Catholic Church has always, even to the present day, opposed co-education in the schools. The latest letter—to my knowledge—from the Vatican to the United States religious teaching congregations forbidding co-education in the Catholic schools was issued on December 8, 1955, entitled *Instruction of the Sacred Congregation of Religious on Co-Education*.)

The Instructions continue:

If this danger, which borders on perversion, is not averted, these schools cannot be attended with peace of mind. The divine and natural laws themselves proclaim it.

This was clearly defined by the Holy Father when on July 14, 1864, he wrote to the Archbishop of Fribourg: "In all places, in every country where this pernicious plan to deprive the Church of its authority over schools is formulated, and worse still, put into effect, with the result that the young will be exposed to the danger of losing their faith, it is the duty of the Church to make every effort not only to take steps to obtain the essential instruction and religious training for youth, but even more so to warn the faithful, and to make it clear to them that they cannot frequent such schools which are set up against the Catholic Church."

These words, founded on the natural and divine law, state definitely a general principle, have a universal bearing, and apply to all countries where this injurious method of instructing youth will unfortunately be introduced.

It is, therefore, absolutely necessary that all bishops should make every effort to see to it that the flock entrusted to them may avoid every contact with the public schools.

It is clear from the above that Catholic parents are prohibited from using public schools. And if the public schools of the last century were morally unacceptable, how much more so does this condemnation apply to today's schools?

The question in the minds of many parents is that if a Catholic school is following the same pattern, excluding authentic religious instruction, how can we entrust our children to that "Catholic" school?

The Instruction goes on:

This instruction and this necessary Christian education of their children is often neglected by those parents who allow their children to frequent schools where it is impossible to avoid the loss of souls or who, notwithstanding the existence of a well-organized neighboring Catholic school or the possibility of having their children educated elsewhere in a Catholic school, entrust them to the public schools without sufficient reason and without having taken the necessary precautions to avoid the danger of perversion; it is a well-known fact that, according to Catholic moral teaching, such parents, should they persist in their attitude, cannot receive absolution in the Sacrament of Penance.

Many parents today believe that if they send their children to the local Catholic school, the children will reject the teachings of the Church, as so many are currently doing. Therefore, before God, we must avoid the danger of perversion for our children. It would be a sin, many of us believe, to put our children in either public or some so-called "Catholic" schools.

If it had not been for the problems in the schools, Catholic parents would probably not have even thought about teach-

ing their children at home, and would not have discovered
the joys of the authentic Catholic family lifestyle. They would
not have realized the blessings of living the Catholic Faith
daily in every aspect of their lives.

Government schools

When the government public schools began after the Civil
War, there was no Protestant "religion" class in these government schools.   But the Protestant philosophy or values
permeated the textbooks and curriculum, teachers were Protestant, and Catholic children were being influenced by them.

In the *Blumenfeld Education Letter* of September, 1990,
Mr. Blumenfeld quoted a Catholic of the 1800's regarding
the American public schools:

> So far as Catholics are concerned, the system of Com-
> mon Schools in this country is a monstrous engine of
> injustice and tyranny. Practically, it operates a gigantic
> scheme for proselytism....the faith of our children is
> gradually undermined....In general, so far as it professes
> to be religious, it is anti-Catholic, and so far as it is
> secular, it is pagan.

Today, many Catholic children attend the government
schools or "Catholic" schools and imbibe the secular values.
So far as they profess to be religious, they are anti-Catholic;
and so far as they profess to be secular, they are pagan.

The traditional parish one-hour-a-week CCD program,
even if it presents traditional Catholic ideas (like Jesus is
the Son of God, for instance), cannot compete with the seven
hours a day, five days a week the Catholic children spend in
the camp of the enemy of the Catholic Church. The schools
are turning the souls of the children away from love of God,
away from love of family, away from love of country, away
from the love of our Catholic Faith.

In the following encyclical, Pope Leo XIII declared that
the heads of families are commanded to keep their children
away from schools where there is a lack of devotion and
reverence for God.

Encyclical *Sapientiae Christianae*, January 10, 1890

This is a suitable moment for Us to exhort especially heads of families to govern their households according to these precepts, and to educate their children from their earliest years. The family may be regarded as the cradle of civil society, and it is in great measure within the circle of family life that the destiny of the State is fostered. Consequently they who would break away from Christian discipline are working to corrupt family life and to destroy it utterly, root and branch. From such an unholy purpose they are not deterred by the fact that they are inflicting a cruel outrage on parents, who have the right from nature to educate those whom they begot, a right to which is joined the duty of harmonizing instruction and education with the end for which they were given their children by the goodness of God.

It is then incumbent upon parents to make every effort to resist attacks on this point and to vindicate at any cost the right to direct the education of their offspring, as it is fitting, in a Christian manner; and first and foremost to keep them away from schools where there is risk of their being imbued with the poison of impiety.

Where the right education of youth is concerned, no amount of trouble and labor is too much. In this matter there are many Catholics of various nations who deserve to be praised and who incur great expense and exhibit much zeal in opening schools for the education of children. It is desirable that this noble example be followed according to the needs of the times.

However, let everyone be firmly convinced, first of all, that the minds of children are best trained above all by the teaching they receive at home. If in their growing years they find in their homes the rule of an upright life and the exercise of Christian virtue, the salvation of society will be in great part assured.

The total curriculum must be Godly

In 1897, in the encyclical *Militantis Ecclesiae*, by Pope Leo XIII, the Catholic Church teaches that the total educational program is to be permeated with "the sense of Christian piety," with the sense of devotion and reverence toward God and the doctrines taught by Jesus Christ.

Encyclical *Militantis Ecclesiae*, August 1, 1897

In this matter special care must be paid to these points. First of all, Catholics should not frequent "mixed" schools [those for Catholics and non-Catholics], especially those for little children. They should everywhere have their own schools and should choose excellent, trustworthy teachers. An education which contains religious errors or which bans all religion, is full of dangers: and this often happens in the schools we have called "mixed." Let nobody easily persuade himself that piety can be separated from instruction with impunity.

In fact, in no period of life, whether in public or in private affairs, can religion be dispensed with, much less can that inexperienced age, full of life, yet surrounded by so many corrupt temptations, be excused from religious obligations.

Whosoever, therefore, organizes education so as to neglect any point of contact with religion is destroying beauty and honesty at their very roots, and instead of helping the country, is preparing for the deterioration and destruction of the human race. For, once God is eliminated, who can make young people realize their duties or redeem those who have deviated from the right path of virtue and fallen into the abyss of vice?

Religion must not be taught to youth only during certain hours, but the entire system of education must be permeated with the sense of Christian piety. If this is lacking, if this holy spirit does not penetrate and inflame the souls of teacher and pupil, small benefit will be derived from any other sort of education; instead damage will be done.

Almost every sort of training has its dangers, and only with difficulty will these be averted from growing youth, especially if the divine controls are lacking which restrain their minds and wills. Great care must therefore be taken so that what is essential, namely, the pursuit of justice and piety, may not be relegated to a second place, confining youth to the visible world and thus leaving their vital potentiality for virtue to rot; so that, again, while teachers, with painful exertion, drill on boring subjects and analyze syllable and accent, they may not neglect that true wisdom, whose beginning is the fear of the Lord and whose precepts demand obedience in every circumstance of life.

A wide knowledge should go hand in hand with care for spiritual progress; *religion must permeate and direct every branch of knowledge* whatever be its nature, and by its sweetness and majesty must make so great an impression on the minds of youth as to be an incitement to better things.

Since it has always been the Church's intention that *every branch of study be of great service in the religious formation of youth,* this particular subject matter not only must have its place, and the principal place at that, but nobody should be entrusted with so important a teaching role who has not first been declared suitable for the purpose in the judgment and by the authority of the Church. (Pope Leo XIII)

Christian Education of Youth

Another great Catholic encyclical on education is called *Christian Education of Youth* or, in Latin, *Divini Illius Magistri,* published in 1929, by Pope Pius XI.

This encyclical letter is the most powerful Catholic Church document commanding parental responsibility in the education of children. Pius XI quotes the Code of Canon Law of 1917, Canon 1113:

Parents are under a grave obligation to see to the religious and moral education of their children, as well as to their physical and civic training, as far as they can, and moreover to provide for their temporal well-being.

Leo XIII is quoted extensively in this encyclical:

By nature, parents have a right to the training of their children, but with the added *duty* that the educa-

tion and instruction of the child be in accord with the
end for which by God's blessing it was begotten. Therefore, it is the *duty* of parents to make every effort to
prevent any invasion of their rights in this matter, and
to make absolutely sure that the education of their children remains under their own control in keeping with
their Christian *duty*, and above all to refuse to send
them to those schools in which there is danger of imbibing the deadly poison of impiety. (Emphasis added)

Pope Pius XI continues to quote Pope Leo XIII: "...the
obligation of the family to bring up children includes not
only religious and moral education, but physical and civic
education as well, principally insofar as it touches upon
religion and morality." This is an important quote for parents to remember, for it reminds us that the sacramental
graces will help parent-teachers in all academic areas.

Family education

Pope Pius XI continues in *Christian Education of Youth*:

We wish to call your attention in a special manner to
the present-day lamentable decline in family education...
for the fundamental *duty* and *obligation* of educating
their children, many parents have little or no preparation, immersed as they are in temporal cares. The de-
clining influence of domestic environment is further
weakened by another tendency...which...causes children
to be more and more frequently sent away from home,
even in their tenderest years. And there is a country
where the children are actually being torn from the bo-
som of the family to be formed (or to speak more
accurately, to be deformed and depraved), in godless
schools and associations, to irreligion and hatred...thus
is renewed in a real and more terrible manner the slaughter of the Innocents. (Emphasis added)

These were strong words from the Pope. When children
are deformed and depraved in godless schools, this is a more
real and more terrible slaughter of the Innocents than in the

Biblical slaughter of the Innocents, says the Pope. And this was long before children were being taught in 5th grade to practice putting condoms on bananas in the classroom.

The next several pages of quotes are from the encyclical *Christian Education of Youth* by Pope Pius XI.

It is therefore as important to make no mistake in education, as it is to make no mistake in the pursuit of the last goal with which the whole work of education is intimately and necessarily connected. In fact, since education consists essentially in preparing man for what he must be and for what he must do here below in order to attain the sublime goal for which he was created, it is clear that there can be no true education which is not wholly directed to man's last end, and that in the present order of Providence, since God has revealed Himself to us in the Person of His only-begotten Son, who alone is "the Way, the Truth and the Life," there can be no ideally perfect education which is not Christian education.

Education belongs to Family, Church, Civil Society

Education is essentially a social and not merely an individual activity. Now there are three essential societies, distinct one from the other and yet harmoniously combined by God, into which man is born: of these, two, namely the family and civil society, belong to the natural order; the third, the Church, to the supernatural order.

In the first place comes the family, instituted directly by God for its particular purpose, the procreation and the formation of offspring; for this reason it has priority of nature, and therefore of rights, over civil society. Nevertheless, the family is an imperfect society, since it has not in itself all the means for its own complete development...

Consequently, education, which is concerned with man as a whole, individually and socially, in the order of nature and in the order of grace, necessarily belongs to all these three societies, in due proportion, corresponding, according to the disposition of Divine Providence, to the coordination of their respective ends.

Extent of the rights of the Church

And first of all, education belongs preeminently to the
Church by reason of a' double title in the supernatural
order, conferred exclusively on her by God Himself;
absolutely superior therefore to any other title in the natural order....

Therefore with full right the Church promotes letters,
science, art, insofar as necessary or helpful to Christian
education, in addition to her work for the salvation
of souls; founding and maintaining schools and institutions adapted to every branch of learning and degree of
culture....

Again, it is the inalienable right as well as the indispensable duty of the Church to watch over the entire education of her children, in all institutions, public or private,
not merely in regard to the religious instruction there
given, but in regard to every other branch of learning and
every regulation insofar as religion and morality are
concerned.

All actions must be done in light of the supernatural

This is clearly set forth by Pius X, of saintly memory:
"Whatever a Christian does, even in the order of things
of earth, he may not overlook the supernatural; indeed he
must, according to the teaching of Christian wisdom, direct
all things towards the supreme good as to his last end;
all his actions, besides, insofar as good or evil in the order
of morality, that is, in keeping or not with natural and
Divine law, fall under the judgment and jurisdiction of
the Church."

Family rights in education cannot be violated

In the first place the Church's mission of education is
in wonderful agreement with that of the family, for both
proceed from God, and in a remarkably similar manner...

The family holds, therefore, directly from the Creator
the mission, and hence the right, to educate the young,
a right inalienable because inseparably joined to a strict
obligation, a right anterior to any right whatever of civil

society and of the State, and therefore inviolable on the part of any power on earth.

That this right is inviolable St. Thomas proves as follows: "The child is naturally something of the father... so by natural right the child, before reaching the use of reason, is under the father's care. Hence it would be contrary to natural justice if the child, before arriving at the use of reason, were removed from the care of its parents, or if any arrangement were made concerning him against the will of the parents." And as this duty on the part of the parents continues up to the time when the child is in a position to provide for itself, this same inviolable parental right of education also endures. "Nature intends not merely the generation of offspring, but also its development and advancement to the perfection of man considered as man, that is, to the state of virtue," as St. Thomas himself says.

Parental obligation

The wisdom of the Church in this matter is expressed with precision and clearness in the Code of Canon Law, canon 1113: "Parents are under a grave obligation to see to the religious and moral education of their children, as well as to their physical and civic training, as far as they can, and moreover to provide for their temporal well-being."

Children belong to the family

On this point the common sense of mankind is in such complete accord, that they would be in open contradiction with it who dared to maintain that the children belong to the State before they belong to the family, and that the State has an absolute right over their children. Untenable is the reason they adduce, namely, that man is born a citizen and hence belongs primarily to the State, not bearing in mind that before being a citizen, man must exist; and existence does not come from the State, but from the parents, as Leo XIII wisely declared: "The children are something of the father, and as it were an extension of the person of the

father; and, to be perfectly accurate, they enter into and
become part of civil society, not directly by themselves,
but through the family in which they were born."

"And therefore," says the same Leo XIII, "the father's
power is of such a nature that it cannot be destroyed or
absorbed by the State; for it has the same origin as
human life itself."

Education must be in accord with the purpose of man's existence

It does not, however, follow from this that the parents' right to educate their children is absolute and des-
potic; for it is necessarily subordinated to the last end,
and to natural and divine law, as Leo XIII declares in
another memorable encyclical, where he sums up the
rights and duties of parents: "By nature parents have a
right to the training of their children, but with this added
duty: that the education and instruction of the child be
in accord with the end for which, by God's blessing, it
was begotten."

Education must remain under parents' control

Therefore it is the duty of parents to make every effort
to prevent any invasion of their rights in this matter, and
to make absolutely sure that the education of their children remain under their own control in keeping with their
Christian duty, and above all to refuse to send them to
those schools in which there is danger of imbibing the
deadly poison of impiety.

Obligation for religious, moral, physical, & civic education

It must be borne in mind also that the obligation of
the family to educate children includes not only religious
and moral education, but physical and civic education as
well, principally insofar as it touches upon religion and
morality.

State laws should protect family educational rights

Consequently, in the matter of education, it is the right, or to speak more correctly, it is the duty of the State to protect by means of its legislation, the prior rights, already described, of the family as regards the Christian education of its offspring, and consequently also to respect the supernatural rights of the Church in this same realm of Christian education.

Christian education concerns the whole man

It should never be forgotten that the subject of Christian education concerns man as a whole, soul united to body by nature, together with all his faculties, natural and supernatural, such as right reason and revelation show him to be; man, therefore, fallen from his original estate, but redeemed by Christ and restored to the supernatural condition of adopted son of God, though without the preternatural privileges of bodily immortality or perfect control of appetite. There remain, therefore, in human nature the effects of original sin, the chief of which are weakness of will and disorderly inclinations.

The mind must be enlightened, the will strengthened

"Folly is bound up in the heart of a child and the rod of correction shall drive it away." Disorderly inclinations then must be corrected, good tendencies encouraged and regulated from the tender age of childhood, and above all the mind must be enlightened and the will strengthened by supernatural truth and by the means of grace, without which it is impossible to control evil impulse, impossible to attain the complete and full perfection of education intended by the Church, which Christ has endowed so richly with divine doctrine and with the Sacraments, the efficacious means of grace.

Sex education in the schools a grave danger

Another very grave danger is that naturalism which nowadays invades the field of education in that most delicate matter of purity of morals. Far too common is the error of those who with dangerous assurance and under an ugly term propagate a so-called sex-education, erroneously imagining that they can arm youths against the dangers of sensuality by purely natural means, such as foolhardy initiation and precautionary instruction for all indiscriminately, even in public; and, worse still, by exposing them at an early age to the opportunity, in order to accustom them, so it is argued, and as it were to harden them against such dangers.

Evil results from weakness of the will

Such persons grievously err in refusing to recognize the inborn weakness of human nature, and the law of which the Apostle speaks, warring against the law of the mind; and also in ignoring what is taught by facts, from which it is clear that, particularly in young people, evil practices are the effect not so much of ignorance of intellect as of weakness of a will exposed to dangerous occasions, and deprived of the means of grace.

Good example in the family

The first natural and necessary element in this environment, as regards education, is the family, and this precisely because it is so ordained by the Creator Himself. Accordingly, that education received in a well-ordered and well-disciplined Christian family will, as a rule, be more effective and lasting, and more efficacious in proportion to the clear and constant good example set, first by the parents, and then by the other household members.

The lamentable decline in family education

Nevertheless, Venerable Brethren, and beloved children, We wish to call your attention in a special manner to the present-day lamentable decline in family education. The offices and professions of a transitory and earthly life, which are certainly of far less importance, are prepared for by long and careful study; whereas for the fundamental duty and obligation of educating their children, many parents have little or no preparation, immersed as they are in earthly cares.

Pastors to warn parents of their obligations

For the love of Our Savior Jesus Christ, therefore, We implore pastors of souls, by every means in their power, by instructions and by catechisms, by word of mouth and by widely distributed written articles, to warn Christian parents of their grave obligations. And this should be done not merely in a theoretical and general way, but with practical and specific application to the various responsibilities of parents touching the religious, moral and civil training of their children, and with an indication of the methods best adapted to make their training most effective, in addition to the influence of their own exemplary lives.

Parents are vicars, or representatives, of God

Parents, therefore, and all who take their place in the work of education, should be careful to make right use of the authority given them by God, whose vicars in a true sense they are. This authority is not given for their own advantage, but for the proper upbringing of their children in a holy and filial "fear of God, the beginning of wisdom," on which foundation alone all respect for authority can rest securely; and without which, order, tranquillity and prosperity, whether in the family or in society, will be impossible.

The school is complementary to family and Church

Since however the younger generation must be trained in the arts and sciences for the advantage and prosperity of civil society, and since the family of itself is unequal

to this task, it was necessary to create that social institution, the school. But let it be borne in mind that this
institution owes its existence to the initiative of the family and of the Church, long before it was undertaken by
the State. Hence, considered in its historical origin, the
school is by its very nature an institution subsidiary and
complementary to the family and to the Church.

Parents are forbidden to send their children to non-Catholic schools

From this it follows that the so-called "neutral" or
"lay" school, from which religion is excluded, is contrary to the fundamental principles of education. Such a
school, moreover, cannot exist in practice; it is bound to
become irreligious. There is no need to repeat what Our
Predecessors have declared on this point, especially Pius
IX and Leo XIII, at times when laicism was beginning
in a special manner to infest public schools.

We renew and confirm their declarations [in 1864,
1880, 1884, 1886, 1887, 1894, etc.], as well as the Sacred
Canons [1917 Code] in which the frequenting of non-
Catholic schools, whether neutral or mixed, those namely
which are open to Catholics and non-Catholics alike, is
forbidden to Catholic children, or at the most is tolerated,
on the approval of the Ordinary [bishop] alone, under determined circumstances of place and time, and with special precautions [Canon 1374]. Neither can Catholics
allow that other type of mixed school...where the students
are provided with separate religious instruction, but receive
other lessons in common with non-Catholic pupils from
non-Catholic teachers.

The definition of an authentic Catholic school

The mere fact that a school gives some religious instruction (often extremely stinted), does not bring it into
line with the rights of the Church and of the Christian
family, or make it a fit place for Catholic students. To be
this, it is necessary that all the teaching and the
whole organization of the school, its teachers, syllabus

and textbooks of every kind, be regulated by the Christian spirit, under the direction and maternal supervision of the Church; so that religion may be in very truth the foundation and crown of the youth's entire training; and this applies to every grade of school, not only the elementary, but the intermediate and the higher institutions of learning as well.

To use the words of Leo XIII: "It is necessary not only that religious instruction be given to the young at certain fixed times, but also that every other subject taught be permeated with Christian piety. If this be wanting, if this sacred atmosphere does not pervade and warm the hearts of masters and scholars alike, little good can be expected from any kind of learning, and considerable harm will often be the consequence."

What makes a perfect Catholic school

For whatever Catholics do in promoting and defending the Catholic school for their children is a genuinely religious work and therefore an important task of "Catholic Action."...

Perfect schools are the result not so much of good methods as of good teachers, teachers who are thoroughly prepared and well-grounded in the matter they have to teach; who possess the intellectual and moral qualifications required by their important office; who cherish a pure and holy love for the youths confided to them, because they love Jesus Christ and His Church, of which these are the children of predilection; and who have therefore sincerely at heart the true good of family and country. Indeed it fills Our soul with consolation and gratitude towards the Divine Goodness to see, side by side with Religious men and women engaged in teaching, such a large number of excellent lay teachers...

The supernatural man is the product of Christian education

The proper and immediate aim of Christian education is to cooperate with divine grace in forming the true and perfect Christian... For the true Christian must live a supernatural life in Christ: "Christ who is your life," and display it in all his actions... For precisely this reason, Christian education takes in the whole of human life, physical and spiritual, intellectual and moral, individual, domestic, and social...

Hence the true Christian, a product of Christian education, is the supernatural man who thinks, judges, and acts constantly and consistently in accordance with right reason illumined by the supernatural light of the example and teaching of Christ....

The authentic Christian does not renounce the activities of this life, he does not stunt his natural faculties; but he develops and perfects them, by coordinating them with the supernatural. He thus ennobles what is merely natural in life...

Institutions of Christian education have benefited families and nations

What...of the vast numbers of saintly educators, men and women, who have perpetuated and multiplied their life work by leaving behind them prolific institutions of Christian education, in aid of families and for the inestimable advantage of nations?

Such are the fruits of Christian education. Their price and value are derived from the supernatural virtue and life in Christ which Christian education forms and develops in man. Of this life and virtue Christ Our Lord and Master is the source and dispenser. By His example, He is at the same time the universal model, accessible to all, especially to the young, in the period of His hidden life, a life of labor and obedience, adorned with all virtues, personal, domestic and social, before God and men. *(Christian Education of Youth)*

The teachings still stand

The content of the encyclical *Christian Education of Youth* has been taught over and over in encyclicals and papal documents, right up to the present time. In 1955, in a papal letter to the Cardinal of Malines, Pope Pius XII wrote about this encyclical:

The inviolable principles which this document lays down regarding the Church, family, and State in the matter of education, are based on the very nature of things and on revealed truth. They cannot be shaken by the ebb and flow of events. As for the fundamental rules which it prescribes, these too are not subject to the wear and tear of time, since they are only the faithful echo of the Divine Master, Whose words shall never pass away. The encyclical is a real Magna Carta of Christian education, "outside which no education is complete and perfect."

Later in the same letter, the Pope repeated the teaching that the family has a "priority of right over the State in the matter of education." But the Church has the right and duty to teach "the highest truths and laws of the religious and moral life." And the Pope concludes that

The State therefore has the duty to respect the prior rights of the family and of the church in the matter of education, and even protect these rights. If the State were to "monopolize education," this would violate the rights of individuals, of the family, and of the Church.

The divine responsibility

In the encyclical *Mit Brennender Sorge* in 1937, Pope Pius XI wrote strong words for those pretending to have Catholic schools:

The formal preservation of religious instruction, especially when controlled and shackled by incompetent people, in the atmosphere of a school which, in the teaching of other subjects, works systematically and invidiously against religion, can never be a justification for a believing Christian to give his free approval to such a school that aims at destroying religion.

...keep this in mind: no earthly power can release you from the divine responsibility which unites you to your children. None of those who today are suppressing your right in the matter of education, and pretending to free you from your duty in this matter, will be able to

reply for you to God Almighty when He asks: "Where
are those whom I have entrusted to you?" Let each one
of you be able to reply: "I have not lost any of those
whom You have entrusted to me." [John 18:9]

Summi Pontificatus, **October 20, 1939**

The charge laid by God on parents, to provide for
the material and spiritual well-being of their offspring
and to procure for them a suitable training, imbued with
the true spirit of religion, cannot be wrested from them
without grave violation of their rights.

Undoubtedly, that formation should aim as well at
preparing youth to fulfill with intelligence, conscien-
tiousness, and pride those duties of noble patriotism,
which gives to one's earthly fatherland all due measure
of love, self-devotion, and service. On the other hand,
a formation which forgets, or worse still, deliberately
fails to direct the gaze and desire of youth to their
heavenly fatherland, would be an injustice to youth, an
injustice to the inalienable duties and rights of the
Christian family...

The souls of children, given to their parents by God
and consecrated in Baptism with the royal character of
Christ, are a sacred charge over which the jealous love
of God watches. The same Christ Who pronounced the
words "Suffer the little children to come unto Me" has,
for all His mercy and goodness, threatened with fearful
evils those who offend the ones so dear to His Heart.

Of all that exists on the face of the earth, only the
soul is immortal. A system of education that did not
respect the sacred precincts of the Christian family pro-
tected by God's holy law, that attacked its foundations,
barred to the young the way to Christ...that considered
apostasy from Christ and the Church as a proof of fi-
delity to the people or to a particular class, would pro-
nounce its own condemnation...

Speech to teachers

In a speech to secondary teachers in 1949, Pope Pius
XII declared that the "Chair of Peter" has always dedicated

itself to standing for parental rights. The Chair of Peter

> will never consent to let the Church, which received
> this right [to guard the welfare of souls] by divine man-
> date, or the family, which claims it through natural jus-
> tice, be deprived of the effective exercise of the natural
> right.

Second Vatican Council

In the Declaration on Christian Education of the Second Vatican Council, October, 1965, many of the above quotes are repeated, re-emphasizing and supporting the traditional teachings of the Church. In fact, the words of this Council are even stronger than previous documents:

> Since parents have given life to their children, they
> are bound by a *grave obligation* to educate their off-
> spring, and so must be regarded as their primary and
> principal educators. Their role in education is of such
> importance that where it is missing, its place can
> scarcely be supplied. For it is the parents' task to cre-
> ate the kind of family atmosphere, inspired by love,
> and by devotion toward God and men, that is favorable
> to the complete personal and social education of their
> children.
> The family is therefore, the principal school of the
> social virtues which are necessary to every society. It is
> therefore above all in the Christian family, inspired by
> the grace and the responsibility of the sacrament of
> matrimony that children should be taught to know and
> worship God, and to love their neighbor...In the family,
> they will have their first experience of a well-balanced
> human society....Parents should appreciate how impor-
> tant a role the truly Christian family plays in the life
> and progress of the whole people of God. (Emphasis
> added)

In the Decree on the Apostolate of Lay People, the pope and bishops teach, in Paragraph 11, that Christian parents

> ...are the first to pass on the Faith to their children and

to educate them in it. By word and example they form
them to a Christian and apostolic life....[they] assert with
vigor the right and duty of parents and guardians to
give their children a Christian upbringing.

The mission of being the primary vital cell of society
has been given to the family by God Himself. This
mission will be accomplished if the family, by the mutual affection of its members and by family prayer,
presents itself as a domestic sanctuary of the Church
["domestic church" is another translation]; if the whole
family takes its part in the Church's liturgical worship;
if it offers active hospitality and practices justice and
other good works for the benefit of all those suffering
from want.

Christian families bear a very valuable witness to
Christ before the world when all their life they remain
attached to the Gospel and hold up the example of
Christian marriage.

In the decree, "Pastoral Constitution on the Church," the
Council declared,

> ...by its very nature the institution of marriage and mar-
> ried love is ordered to the procreation and education of
> the offspring...When they are given the dignity and role
> of fatherhood and motherhood, [parents] will eagerly
> carry out their duties of education, especially religious
> education, which devolves primarily on them.
> (No. 48)

> Marriage and married love are by nature ordered to the
> procreation and education of children...Married couples
> should regard it as their proper mission to transmit
> human life and to educate their children. (No. 50)

Pope Paul VI, in an address before the Committee for
the Family in 1974, spoke about the virtues which the family should be promoting.

> ...the home is the privileged place of love, of the deep
> communion of persons, of apprenticeship in the con-
> tinual and progressive self-giving of husband and wife

> to each other....This love necessarily presupposes tenderness, self-control, patient understanding, faithfulness and generosity...

And again: "...conjugal love must not only master instinct, but it must overcome selfishness incessantly."

Catechesi Tradendae

In *Catechesi Tradendae*, or *Catechesis in Our Time*, Pope John Paul II reminds us of the traditional teachings of the Church regarding teaching of the catechism:

> The family's catechetical activity has a special character, which is in a sense irreplaceable. This special character has been rightly stressed by the Church, particularly by the Second Vatican Council.

The footnotes to this statement point out that councils of the Church have "insisted on the responsibility of parents in regard to education in the faith." Cited is the Sixth Council of Arles, Council of Mainz, Sixth Council of Paris, documents of Pius XI, the "many discourses and messages of Pius XII," and several documents of the Second Vatican Council.

Here is the quote from *Catechesi Tradendae* which explains why Catholic home schooling works:

> Education in the faith by parents, which should begin from the children's tenderest age, is already being given when the members of a family help each other to grow in faith through the witness of their Christian lives, a witness that is often without words but which perseveres throughout a day-to-day life lived in accordance with the Gospel. This catechesis is more incisive when, in the course of family events (such as the reception of the sacraments, the celebration of great liturgical feasts, the birth of a child, a bereavement) care is taken to explain in the home the Christian or religious content of these events.

Pope John Paul II goes on to say that in some places,

> ...where widespread unbelief or invasive secularism
> makes real religious growth practically impossible, "the
> church of the home" remains the one place where chil-
> dren and young people can receive an authentic
> catechesis. Thus there cannot be too great an effort on
> the part of Christian parents to prepare for this ministry
> of being their own children's catechists, and to carry it
> out with tireless zeal.

Notice the phrase "church of the home," which is somewhat similar to the previous papal phrases "domestic church"
and "sanctuary of the home."

Code of Canon Law

The 1983 Code of Canon Law speaks strongly about
parents' rights and responsibilities in the education of their
children, in all subjects, and even especially in religious education and in the preparation of their children for the reception of the Sacraments.
Canon 226.2:

> Parents, because they have given life to their children,
> are bound by the most grave obligation and enjoy the
> right of educating them; therefore, it is first for the
> Christian parents to take care for the Christian educa-
> tion of their children according to the teaching handed
> on by the Church.

Canon 774.2:

> Before all others, parents are bound by the obligation
> of forming their children by word and example in the
> faith and the practice of the Christian life...

Canon 776 proclaims: "The pastor is to promote and foster the role of parents in the family catechesis mentioned in
Canon 774.2."

Canon 793.1 states:

> Parents and those who hold their place (such as guard-
> ians) are *bound by the obligation* and enjoy the right of
> educating their children; Catholic parents also have the
> *duty* and the right of selecting those means and insti-
> tutes by which, in the light of local circumstances, they
> can better provide for the Catholic education of their
> children. (Emphasis added)

Canon 835.4:

> ...parents share in a special way in this office of
> sanctification through their conjugal life in the Chris-
> tian spirit, and in taking care for the Christian educa-
> tion of their children.

Canon 1055.1 declares: "The matrimonial covenant... is
by its nature ordered toward the good of the spouses and the
procreation and education of children..."

Canon 1134 declares: "...in Christian marriage, moreover,
spouses are strengthened and, as it were, consecrated by this
special sacrament for the duties and dignity of their state."

Canon 1136, from the section "The Effects of Marriage":

> Parents have a most grave *duty* and enjoy the primary
> right of educating to the very best of their ability, their
> children physically, socially, and culturally and morally
> and religiously as well. (Emphasis added)

Canon 1366 declares: "Parents, or those holding the place
of parents, who hand over their children to be baptized or
educated in a non-Catholic religion are to be punished by
censure or other just penalty."

In *Home Schooling and the New Code of Canon Law,*
canon lawyer Edward N. Peters writes:

> The canonical rights of parents over the education of
> their children are strongly affirmed in the 1983 Code of
> Canon Law. Therefore, any attempt, whether by proper
> ecclesiastical authorities or otherwise, to restrict the

prudent exercise of these educational rights (including, as we shall argue shortly, the parental decision to home-school a child) must by canon law be strictly scruti-nized lest the exercise of those rights be unjustly impeded....What is important to realize, however, is that questions concerning the practice of home schooling affect not just the child's right to an education, but ultimately the sacramental identity and mission of the family and each of its respective members.

Pope John Paul II's *Familiaris Consortio*

Perhaps the most important modern document for home schooling families is the apostolic exhortation *The Role of the Christian Family in the Modern World*, or *Familiaris Consortio*, published in 1981. This encyclical should serve as a basis for greater study by Catholic home schooling par-ents as we grow in a deeper understanding of the Sacrament of Matrimony and the graces and duties of the married state.

Pope John Paul II proclaims that

> The task of giving education is rooted in the primary vocation of married couples to participate in God's cre-ative activity: by begetting in love and for love a new person who has within himself or herself the vocation to growth and development, parents by that very fact take on the task of helping that person effectively to live a fully human life....the family is the first school of those social virtues which every society needs. The right and duty of parents to give education is essential, since it is connected with the transmission of human life; it is original and primary with regard to the edu-cational role of others...it is irreplaceable and inalien-able, and therefore incapable of being entirely delegated to others or usurped by others. In addition to these characteristics, it cannot be forgotten that the most basic element, so basic that it qualifies the educational role of parents, is parental love, which finds fulfillment in the task of education...as well as being a source, the parents' love is also the animating principle and there-fore the norm inspiring and guiding all concrete educa-tional activity, enriching it with the values of kindness,

constancy, goodness, service, disinterestedness and self-sacrifice that are the most precious fruit of love.

It is obvious that home schooling parents need to be sure that they themselves are developing these Christian virtues, and that their children are developing them also. In this way, we can bring these virtues to our society as well. Pope John Paul II continued in this encyclical to emphasize the educational priority of the parents by calling it a "mission."

> For Christian parents the mission to educate...has a new specific source in the sacrament of marriage, which consecrates them for the strictly Christian education of their children....it enriches them with wisdom, counsel, fortitude, and all the other gifts of the Holy Spirit in order to help the children in their growth as human beings and as Christians.
>
> The sacrament of marriage gives to the educational role the dignity and vocation of being really and truly a "ministry" of the Church, at the service of building up her members. So great and splendid is the educational ministry of Christian parents that Saint Thomas [Aquinas] has no hesitation in comparing it with the ministry of priests.
>
> A vivid and attentive awareness of the *mission* that they have received with the sacrament of marriage will help Christian parents to place themselves at the service of their children's education with great serenity and trustfulness, and also with a sense of responsibility before God.

Charter of the Rights of the Family

In 1983, Pope John Paul II published the *Charter of the Rights of the Family*, mainly to support parents in their right to oppose Sex Education programs in the schools. The Pope re-emphasizes the irreplaceable role of the family as having primary rights in the education of children.

> The family constitutes much more than a mere juridical, social, and economic unit, a community of love

and solidarity which is uniquely suited to teach and
transmit cultural, ethical, social, spiritual, and religious
values, essential for the development and well-being of
its own members and of society.

The family is the place where different generations
come together and help one another to grow in human
wisdom and to harmonize the right of individuals with
other demands of social life.

...Since they [parents] have conferred life on their
children, parents have the original, primary, and inalienable right to educate them; hence they must be acknowledged as the first and foremost educators of their
children.

Parents have the right to educate their children in
conformity with their moral and religious convictions,
taking into account the cultural traditions of the family....

Parents have the right to choose freely schools or
other means necessary to educate their children in keeping with their convictions.

Parents have the right to ensure that their children
are not compelled to attend classes which are not in
agreement with their own moral and religious convictions.

The rights of parents are violated when a compulsory
system of education is imposed by the state from which
all religious formation is excluded.

It is obvious that God's plan for Christian families is for
parents to dedicate themselves to educating their children.
This is not a haphazard mission, but a full-time mission, a
duty and a command, to be fulfilled on a daily basis. It
encompasses primarily religious education and preparation for
the Sacraments, but it includes making sure that all education is from a Catholic perspective.

Some parents decide to home school for academic reasons, and often find the struggle too difficult. But those who
are committed to the Faith and to authentic Catholic family
values are able to undergo tremendous pressures and crosses,
even from family members.

Pastors, bishops, and other religious should encourage
parents who are willing to make the difficult sacrifices to

fulfill their mission and duty by teaching their children at home. Pope John Paul I, in September of 1978, when speaking to a group of U.S. archbishops and bishops, remarked about the importance of family prayer. He declared that the church of the home, through family prayer, could bring about a renewal of the Church and a transformation of the world. "A most relevant apostolate" for the twentieth century, he believed, is parental teaching of God's love and parental support of the Faith by good example.

In conclusion, Pope John Paul I pleaded with the American bishops:

> Dear brothers, we want you to know where our priorities lie. Let us do everything we can for the Christian family, so that our people may fulfill their great vocation in Christian joy and share intimately and effectively in the Church's mission—Christ's mission—of salvation.

Chapter 4:
Biblical Foundations of Home Schooling
by Gerry Matatics

Gerry Matatics is a Catholic home schooling father and former Presbyterian minister who now heads Biblical Foundations and teaches Sacred Scripture at the Fraternity of St. Peter's seminary in Scranton, Pennsylvania.

One of the factors fueling the modern home-schooling movement is parents' traumatic realization that, as our culture collapses all around us, we can no longer assume that our community, state, and national leaders are committed to promoting or protecting traditional values in our children.

If anything is going to save our country from utter chaos during the remaining years of this decadent decade, it will be home schooling and similar grassroots movements, rather than the bewilderingly slow-to-die delusion that politicians in power are really able or even willing to support our family life and values. For this reason, and many others, my wife and I have been passionate about promoting home schooling since before our first child was born.

I am convinced, however, that even we committed home schoolers need to have our understanding of our task deepened and enlarged, and that Sacred Scripture has much to say about home schooling beyond the few frequently cited prooftexts. The Bible abounds with passages stressing that instructing our children—especially in our values and beliefs —is an essential and inescapable part of our parental role.

As I look at Sacred Scripture, I find that from cover to cover, from Genesis to Revelation, the writers of Scripture, and more importantly, Almighty God Himself, presuppose that His covenant children, you and I, will understand that He lays upon us a solemn covenant obligation to be the primary educators of our offspring. As always, God never commands anything from us that He Himself does not set the pattern for, of which He does not provide the perfect model. So we can begin the biblical basis for home schooling by going back into the opening chapters of the book of *Genesis*.

The book of *Genesis* is my favorite book of the Old Testament because it is so foundational, so fundamental to our faith. "Genesis" means, of course, the beginning, the origin. We find the origins of so many things there — of the family, of worship, of parentage, and of home education. Adam and Eve had a very unique relationship in a very unique situation. They were the only human beings, apart from Our Blessed Lady, who had the privilege of coming into the world as unfallen human beings. They are in a class by themselves. We see already that they must have been home schooling parents. They could not delegate the education of their children to anyone else, because they themselves were the only adults around.

God as Teacher

But Adam and Eve are not the starting point, but the first recipients of home schooling. The Bible is very clear that God designed all human beings to be, by grace, His sons and daughters. We are made not just for a natural, but for a supernatural destiny. The Bible teaches that Adam and Eve were made to be the first son and first daughter of the ever-living God by supernatural grace.

We read in *Genesis* 1 that God said, "Let us make man to our image and likeness." That phrase means that this image of God resides primarily in the soul, that the soul is like God, and it too is a spiritual being possessed of personhood, intellect and will. This enables man to have "dominion" over the other creatures of this world, as God sets forth in *Genesis* 1:26: "And let him have dominion over the fishes of the sea, and the fowls of the air, and the beasts, and the whole earth, and every creeping creature that moveth upon the earth." This was a tremendous responsibility, so we know that God imparted to Adam the knowledge necessary for carrying it out. But there is more than just that philosophical sense to that phrase that we are made in the image of God. The greatest image and likeness of God

in man is the divine sonship of sanctifying grace which Adam
received at his creation and which we receive in Baptism.
This supernatural gift, infinitely surpassing the gifts of nature, fitted Adam for a supernatural destiny. It was a sharing in the life of God. So we know that God imparted to
Adam the knowledge he needed in order to understand and
to live a life in accord with this supernatural destiny.

God created Adam with infused knowledge, but He also
instructed him. He gave him information about who he was
and his calling in life. He gave him what we call a kingly
task to perform in the world: to guard the garden against
any intruder, such as Satan. He taught Adam about his
duties, and He told him to stay away from this particular
tree, with this forbidden fruit.

The first example of home schooling in the Bible is the
example provided by the perfect teacher, God Himself, who
condescended to fellowship with the first man, Adam, and to
actually teach him, in the classroom of Paradise, how he
should walk in a manner pleasing and acceptable to Almighty
God.

The first teacher, the first classroom, the first pupil, the
first curriculum of character building, was that which was
administered by Almighty God Himself.

Adam and Eve followed that example. They taught their
children. In *Genesis* 4, we read that God accepted Abel's
sacrifice but rejected Cain's. There was something wrong
with Cain's sacrifice. He had imbibed the heretical theology
that so many people, even many Catholics today, have imbibed: that basically there is nothing wrong with human
nature. So Cain simply brought a grain offering that God
had to reject, because Cain had not admitted that he was a
fallen human being, a sinner who deserved to die. He did
not offer a substitutionary sacrifice, a blood sacrifice. Abel
did. He brought the firstlings of his flock.

He thus performed a priestly task. A grain offering is
acceptable in biblical theology, but only on the foundation
of an animal sacrifice, where you admit that a life must be
given in place of your life. Cain did not do that. He was
saying, "I'm not cursed, the earth isn't cursed. My works

and the works of the earth are acceptable to God." God rejected this. It would be unfair for God to do that unless Adam and Eve had taught their children the necessity of blood atonement sacrifice. We do not hear that recorded in Scripture. There is no story about how Adam and Eve taught their children. But we must assume that it occurred, because God holds Cain responsible for rejecting what his parents must have taught him.

This reminds us that if we want our children to grow up to be like Abel, faithful witnesses to the true faith, people who know how to worship God, we must teach them. In this age that is very hard. Probably the hardest thing that you and I have in all of our educational responsibilities is to teach our children how to worship God with reverence, dignity, and holiness of mind, heart and body. They will grow up to be like Cain if we do not teach them well. We see here at the outset of Scripture the necessity for parents to teach their children the importance of worship. That is part of our home schooling responsibility.

The example of Abraham

If we go on in the book of *Genesis*, we see that all the great covenant leaders — Noe, Abraham, Isaac, Jacob, Joseph — take seriously the responsibility to teach their children. I will only mention one of them here, and that is Abraham. This is an enormously important passage for us today, because here we have a situation very similar to our own. This is a great home schooling text in *Genesis* 18, when God is on His way to Sodom and Gomorrha to destroy them. This is relevant today because we are seeing a Sodom and Gomorrha politically established all around us. In Abraham's day, as God sent those two angels to bring about Sodom and Gomorrha's discipline, God said:

> Can I hide from Abraham what I am about to do, seeing that he shall become a great and mighty nation, and in him all the nations of the earth shall be blessed? For I know that he [Abraham] will command his children and his household after him, to keep the ways of

> the Lord, and do judgment and justice: that for
> Abraham's sake, the Lord may bring to effect all the
> things he hath spoken unto him. (*Genesis* 18:17-19)

That is a powerful passage for many reasons, because it teaches us the centrality of home schooling. God basically says to Abraham, "I have a plan for the world. You are a part of that plan. Through the seed that I have promised you will come the Messias and the blessings for all the nations. And I can bring this salvation about because I know that you are going to play your necessary, instrumental part by teaching your children everything that I have taught you." Abraham did not hold back anything. Every instruction that God gave him, Abraham diligently taught his children. God knew that Abraham's family would stand firm when the storm of judgment came.

As we go on in the Old Testament to the laws that God gave to Moses, and through Moses to His covenant people, we see that over and over again, this parental obligation to teach children is underscored. In *Exodus* 12, God gives them their great Passover, and He says, "In the days to come, every time you celebrate this feast every year, your children will ask you why you eat this unleavened bread and slaughter this Passover lamb. You must tell them about that great deliverance that I effected for you on that first Passover." God says parents must teach their children what the feast means, and explain all the details of it.

The application for us is to teach our children the Mass. Do not delegate that to anybody else. That is our parental responsibility—to teach our children how to worship God. It is not enough to simply attend Mass. The Sunday obligation is to assist at Mass, to join our hearts and minds (at least implicitly) with that of the priest so that we are actually praying through the prayers of the Mass, and offering God that adoration to which He is entitled. Many of our children have not been taught that, and as a result they are not doing these things. We must teach our children what Mass is all about, and how they must participate, as the Jews were told to instruct their children in *Exodus* 12.

Teaching at all times

In *Deuteronomy* 6:1-7, one of the most famous passages about the importance of teaching our children, God has this to say,

> These are the precepts, the ceremonies, and the judgments which the Lord your God commanded that I [Moses] should teach you, so that you should perform them in the land which you pass over to possess. That thou mayst fear the Lord thy God, and keep all His commandments and precepts which I command thee, and thy sons, and thy grandsons, all the days of thy life, that thy days may be prolonged. Hear, O Israel, and observe to do the things which the Lord hath commanded thee, that it may be well with thee, that thou mayst be greatly multiplied, as the Lord the God of thy fathers hath promised thee, a land flowing with milk and honey ... and these words which I command thee this day shall be in thy heart, and thou shalt teach them to thy children. Thou shalt reflect upon them when thou sittest down in thy house, when thou risest up to walk, when thou sleep in the evening and rise up in the morning.

All through the day, parents should be teaching their children the law of God. When you get up in the morning, join them in an act of family worship. Make a Morning Offering together as a family. Open the Bible, fathers, and teach your children the Bible on a daily basis. Teach them to sing the Psalms, those mighty battle hymns of the true kingdom, the kingdom of God. Be a spiritual director to your child. Know the state of their hearts. Do not allow them to go for days while wondering what is going on with them spiritually. Know your child's heart, know the Word of God, and bring the two together, so your child has an indelible impression upon his or her conscience of the full body of truth that we find in Sacred Scripture. That is our obligation as parents, as God tells us in *Deuteronomy* 6.

The Law of Moses not only tells us positively that we must educate our children, it also gives us very strong negative warnings not to allow them to be catechized by a culture that is pagan and lawless. Socialization is not paganization. I always tell people who ask me about my children's socialization that they are not going to learn bad language, or how to use condoms, or any of the other things that kids are taught in the great public schools of this land. They will not acquire the skill to sneer at sacred things. Of course our kids will not get socialized, if by socialization you mean forming their minds and hearts to take on the same values of the society in which we live. God have mercy on us if we allow our children to be socialized by our essentially pagan society! The law of God commands us not to let our kids be socialized by that, but to be positively socialized by a Christian society. I would encourage you to take seriously passages such as *Leviticus* 20:22-26, *Josue* 23:11-12, *Psalms* 105:35-43, *2 Corinthians* 6:14-7:1. All of these have the same basic point, that God has given us a certain measure of freedom—the freedom to worship Him, the freedom to raise our children. But if we do not make sure that our children are not influenced by society and the culture around them, we will lose our freedoms, our families, our faith, our lives and everything that is near and dear to us.

In Psalm 105, David tells what the Israelites did:

> And they were mingled among the heathens, and learned their works: and served their idols, and it became a stumblingblock to them. And they sacrificed their sons, and their daughters to devils. And they shed innocent blood: the blood of their sons and of their daughters which they sacrificed to the idols of Chanaan. And the land was polluted with blood, and was defiled with their works: and they went aside after their own inventions.

And this is exactly what is happening to America. We are sacrificing our sons and daughters. We are staining and soaking this land with the blood of innocent children. We will share their fate unless we repent. God has not mellowed or changed. He has the same standards of justice and righteousness He has always had. Soon blood builds up, and cries out like the blood of Abel and the martyrs, and

God says "Enough!" We alone can hold that off from happening, by our standing in the gap, by our Masses, by our prayers. It is part of our responsibility to teach our children that. But when our children are taught values by the world instead of by their parents, the parents aid and abet in the American way of life that will bring about America's ultimate doom.

Psalm 77:1-7 mentions that the memory of God's works and faithfulness to His commandments will only continue if parents take the responsibility to teach them to their children. All the wisdom literature of the Old Testament is a blueprint for how parents can train their children. The whole Book of *Proverbs* is addressed by a father to his children. "My son, listen to the words of your father, and do not despise the instruction of your mother" is a recurring refrain in the Book of *Proverbs*. Look at *Proverbs* 4:3-5, *Proverbs* 22:6: "Train up a child in the way he should go, and even when he is old he will not depart from it."

Machabees

The book of *Second Machabees* gives us two beautiful examples of the power of parental instruction to preserve children's faith in the midst of a very wicked and hostile environment. There is the story of the imposition of a heretical faith upon the Jews by Antiochus Epiphanes. Most of the Jews compromised and changed their faith. But there was a man named Mattathias who had trained his children well. They led the resistance against the false faith that was duping and deceiving so many people. There is the story in *2 Machabees* 7 about that marvelous mother with seven sons. Each one of them is tortured by Antiochus Epiphanes for not renouncing his faith. These were children, tortured in a very painful and frightening fashion, and every one of them had been so instructed by his mother that he refused to renounce his faith. That mother stood there and saw the spectacle of her children being put to death. She was allowed to talk to the last one, whom Antiochus Epiphanes thought would break. She told him to stand fast, to hold firm, not to give in. Her last son goes to a glorious martyrdom.

I do not want to be melodramatic or sensationalistic, but I believe that an essential part of home schooling today is that parents teach their children about the martyrs. We need to teach our children about the grace and glory of martyrdom, because God may require that of many of us. The only way He can right the wrongs of our land is to take many of us through a period of great martyrdom that will liberate us, spiritually speaking, from the bondage we are in. I believe that we are called, as the Holy Father has been reminding us repeatedly, to be ready to give our lives, if need be, for the Catholic Faith. Take the example of Daniel, taught by his parents for just a few years, going off to a pagan empire, and in three years of intensive instruction by the pagan Babylonians, he did not once lose his Faith. He remained steadfast. What a credit to his parents!

Learning from Our Lord

The greatest example of home schooling in the whole Bible, of course, is Our Lord Jesus Christ Himself. He was taught the true faith in His own unimpeachable, orthodox and godly home, by His parents, Joseph and Mary. None of us can do the job they did, but the Holy Family is given to us as an ideal, to approximate, by the grace of God, as much as we can.

Unfortunately, our children cannot claim the same immunity from error which Jesus had. That makes it all the more incumbent upon us that we teach them, and not allow this to be done by some delegate who might be well-intentioned and sincere, but may not know the Faith. You never know what your kids are being taught. I could not have my children being taught their faith by someone else, because I would only make them tell it to me all over again. Why go through the whole process twice? Home schooling is a much more efficient and time-saving way to do it. If you do it yourself, you know it is being done correctly. Of course, this points out the necessity of knowing the Faith ourselves.

Jesus is the great model of home schooling, and the Holy

Family, our model as a home school. Jesus conquered the world in the first century by home schooling His twelve Apostles. He called them away from their homes. He did not set up a classroom and have them come for a few hours a day so He could teach them. He called them to leave father, mother, sister and brother, and even spouses (and God must obviously have done something to provide for those families), and they lived with Jesus as family for those three years. They were with Him twenty-four hours a day. Jesus home schooled them, and that is why the Apostles, energized by the Holy Spirit at Pentecost, were able to conquer their world, because they knew the Faith intimately.

Parental obligation

St. Paul commands us to do the same with our children. He says in *Ephesians* 6:4, "Fathers, do not provoke your children to anger, but bring them up in the discipline and correction of the Lord." We are commanded as fathers to teach our children. St. Paul says in *1 Thessalonians* 2:11-12 that, when he was among the Thessalonians, he was like a parent with his children, entreating and comforting them. He gives us a beautiful description of what a parent should do. We are told in *2 Timothy* 3:15 that Timothy, from infancy, was taught the Sacred Scriptures, and that he was reared in the holy Faith. We are told that the elders of the Church were largely married men who had raised their own children well.

St. Paul says to Timothy in *1 Timothy* 3:2-4 and to Titus in *Titus 1*, that no family man should be ordained to the priesthood unless he has raised his own children to be respectful, godly and obedient. If he could not even instruct his own children, how can he catechize, preach, and lead the larger household of faith, the Church?

The Bible does not promote no-fault child rearing. It holds us responsible if our children grow up to be wild, reckless and disobedient. Remember, though, that even one of Our Lord's twelve Apostles betrayed Him. Judas preferred thirty pieces of silver to loving his Lord. What does that tell us about Jesus? Does it mean that Jesus was not the perfect teacher; that if He had only spent one more hour with Judas, given him another example, had a better lesson for this or that, Judas would not have betrayed Him? Obviously not. There was nothing wrong with the perfection of Christ's teaching, yet even He lost one. There will always be that Judas factor, and we should not berate or flagellate ourselves unnecessarily if perhaps one of our children grows up and does not follow in the footsteps of our faith. But if all of them live their adult lives in total confusion as to what their conscience requires of them as Catholics, if they have all fallen away, then we need to take a good hard look at whether we are doing home schooling with the effectiveness that the Bible can make possible.

We can all see that the Bible has much to say about the importance of home schooling. Families especially need this today, when the whole concept of the family is questioned. Raising a family is difficult today, but we in home schooling can maximize the unity and the unanimity of our family. Do not worry about the mistakes that you make. We all fall, pick ourselves up, and learn through trial and error. You are giving your children an incredible blessing, because it is a biblical blessing. Despite our many flaws and imperfections, we are doing for them something that no one else can do.

Chapter 5:
How To Begin Catholic Home Schooling

Before you begin home schooling, you must be convinced that it is something to which you are truly committed. Home schooling is not like buying a new coat. Catholic home schooling is a way of life. It should be something you have already attempted in some small way with your children, by teaching religion, by teaching about the Sacraments, by turning off the TV once in a while, and trying to be an authentic Catholic family.

Catholic home schooling is not easy or simple. It is primarily a commitment to God, and secondarily a commitment to family. Once you have decided you want to make this commitment, you should try to prepare yourself.

Make a novena. Start by going to Confession. Take nine days to pray to the Blessed Mother or to the Sacred Heart. Go to Mass each day. Pray to your guardian angel and to the children's guardian angels, asking them to pray for you. Ask your patron saint to help you. Say the Rosary every day if possible. Ask for the grace to know what you should do, for the courage to make the right decision, for the strength to carry it out. Have your spouse join you as much as possible in these nine days of prayer. You will need at least a minimum of support from him or her. This is, after all, a responsibility of the vocation of marriage.

If you finally decide after nine days of prayer that you should home school, but your spouse remains against it, ask if he or she would allow you just one year as a trial. After all, considering the reputation of the schools these days, it might be seen that the children would not lose out academically by staying out of school for a year, even if they did not learn *anything* in that time.

How to tell your husband

Since ninety percent of the time, it is mothers who want to teach their children at home, this section is directed to mothers. However, if you are a father who wants to home school your children, these ideas will help you also.

Some husbands think that home schooling is some sort of underground movement, a kind of "mother earth" fad. Show him as much home schooling literature as possible. Seton has a video produced by the Home School Legal Defense Association called "Home Schooling: A Foundation for Excellence." This has been produced primarily for husbands or wives and other relatives who think that children will "suffer" academically if they do not attend a "regular" school. Many husbands, after seeing the film, and after a wife's prayers, will agree to a trial of one year.

If you are considering Seton, tell your husband that Seton is accredited. Accreditation is important in many professional organizations, and husbands understand that.

If more is needed, there are other videos, cassette tapes, and books available. Ask him to read this book. Other materials are available from us or from your local or state home schooling organization. If you can take your husband to one of the Catholic or state home schooling conventions, he will see hundreds (and in some states thousands) of people who are home schooling or who are considering home schooling. It will not seem like such a strange idea when he sees good Christian people who teach their children at home.

Consider taking your husband to your local support group meetings, particularly when you know that other fathers will be present. This will be an opportunity for him to ask questions of other fathers.

Visit your local library or Christian bookstore and look over the home schooling books available. Many more, of course, are available at the state home schooling conventions. Encourage your husband to read a few books and become more informed about this "new" idea called home schooling. If he refuses to read them, then you should read them and discuss the ideas with him at the dinner table or whenever you can.

The chapter in this book by Dr. Mark Lowery might also help your husband.

Statement of philosophy

Before you start, put in writing the reasons why you want to teach your children at home. This will help you to clarify your own goals. Try to express yourself clearly, as this will strengthen your thinking and your resolve. You need to understand yourself and your own reasons for making this decision which, after all, you may have to defend to relatives, in-laws, fellow parishioners, and friends, eventually.

Be sure to discuss this thoroughly with your spouse if possible. He (or she) should completely understand your perspective. Take the time, if your children are older, to have a family conference. You and your spouse should explain to your children exactly why you believe so strongly that you should teach them at home. Including the children early in the discussions may head off complaining and bitterness later.

Once you have a statement of philosophy about your reasons for home schooling, and what you want to accomplish with your home schooling, post this in a prominent place in your home. You will need to refer to this on the days the going "gets tough." It will serve as a frequent reminder to everyone in the house.

Statement of goals

In addition to your statement of philosophy, list specific goals or objectives. For instance, some religious goals might be that everyone goes to Mass every day, that you and the family go to Confession once a month, that at least once a week certain activities should relate to the liturgical calendar. Character-building goals might be that little Susie learns to say "please" and "thank you," that Johnny might learn to be gentle and not irritate his younger brother, that George might begin to appreciate his parents, and so on.

Academic goals might be, if you are in an enrolled program, that the children finish a grade in nine months, or that no matter what, little Sally is going to learn her multiplication tables this summer. Seton has produced a "Scope and Sequence" series, available for our families, which sets out academic curriculum goals for each subject in each grade level. While you may want to reshape this, it can give you an idea about writing your own. In some states, parents are asked to submit a Curriculum Guide every year for each child they are homeschooling.

Having specific goals keeps you and your children on track. Even if you do not accomplish your goals exactly as planned, unless you have written goals, you will never reach any goals. With more and more parents turning to home schooling, we are starting to see some parents allowing too much to "fall through the cracks." Unless you write down your goals, then, like an unwritten budget, the daily steps toward the goal are forgotten, and soon lessons are not accomplished. Then you feel frustrated and wonder why you ever started this anyway! Or you feel guilty, or lose confidence in yourself.

Post a reminder

Make a list of the disadvantages of having your children in school. This can be a list of just phrases, but it is important because the disadvantages you list are personal and meaningful to *you*. You do not need this as much for the children as for yourself. You can work with the children and have them make a list for themselves, assuming they are old enough to understand.

Some mothers seem to forget after a couple of years exactly what the problems were. They begin to think that maybe it was not really that bad in the first place. Some children are returned to school, only to return home again after a semester of misery.

Sometimes mothers will call Seton Home Study School with the most terrible stories of emotional and psychological abuse of their children. After a year or two at home, they think maybe the next year will not be so bad. So little Susie goes back to school. Within two weeks, little Susie is listening to bad language and repeating sleeping-around stories, and wants to wear short skirts and makeup to match the girls at school. Hopefully, as often happens, Susie will cry and plead and beg mom to let her come home again.

The stories we hear are so outrageous that we think most parents do not hear about them or do not believe them because they are so incredible. It is like abortion. It is so evil that our minds cannot comprehend the horror of it!

Keep some of these true stories in a book in your bedroom in your bedside table or dresser. It can serve as a reminder of how bad the alternative is, no matter what happens at home. Parents who are home schooling their last children should make notes about the effects of school on their older children. Even good parents have had children who have left the Church, who have married outside the Church, who have divorced, who have had children out of wedlock, or who have lived with boyfriends or girlfriends without the benefit of marriage. Remind yourself of these problems from which you want to spare your remaining children.

We need to face hard facts. We are living in a pagan society. As the well-known moral theologian Father John Hardon says, the schools are "dangerous" places for our children. Recently, in northern Virginia, an eleven-year boy was picked up by police for having a loaded gun in school. In fact, in a study done by the Department of Health and Human Services, it was estimated that *1 of every 20 students carries a gun to school at least once a month.* Having guns and knives in the public schools has become so common, that one of the debates among administrators these days is which is the most effective machine to detect the weapons as children enter the building!

Of course, Father Hardon means that the schools are spiritually dangerous. He points out that when you have educators who are supportive of mothers' "rights" in the killing of innocent unborn babies, or who even think that abortion, fornication, or homosexuality can be justified alternatives, how can you morally allow these people to teach your children about anything at all, spiritually or academically?

Grandparents

One of the problems you need to face before you begin home schooling is what your own parents or in-laws will think. What will they say? Will they support you or oppose you? Will they criticize you to the children?

Try to do your best to explain to them why you are home schooling, since they do have a legitimate interest in your children.

Most grandparents are not aware of just how bad the schools have become but they should be aware of the low academic standards since the television and newspaper reporters, as well as the governors and President of the United States have acknowledged it. You can certainly point out to them that most schools do not offer children a quality education. That will be hard to dispute.

Besides offering the negatives about schools, explain the positive reasons why you are home schooling. Explain the teachings of the Church, and that you believe you have the graces to make this decision, and that God will give you the graces to carry out this responsibility. Let them understand your spiritual reasons. They should respect you for that.

If possible, consider asking your parents or in-laws to help. Some families have reported that grandparents make wonderful teachers. They love their grandchildren, are patient, and many have the time.

When grandparents are opposed to home schooling, it is because they think the children will not be properly socialized. Give them the information as contained in our chapter on *Socialization*. Also, point out the many opportunities for socialization which your children will have through home schooling groups, through sports, and through church or other clubs or activities to which they belong.

Some grandparents think that home schooled children will not be able to go to college. Such thinking is certainly not keeping up with the times. Hundreds of thousands of people have been attending correspondence schools for years. Private colleges are looking for high SAT or ACT test scores. Most are not concerned about where or how the students obtained their knowledge. State colleges usually require only the G.E.D. test by home schoolers.

Catholic colleges have been very pleased with the Catholic home schooled students. Seton graduates are usually offered scholarships every year from several Catholic colleges, such as Christendom, Magdalen, Thomas Aquinas, St. Vincent's, and Franciscan University. After all, home schooled students are self-motivated, self-disciplined, are not on drugs, and tend to have traditional Catholic and family values. They are exactly what good Catholic colleges want.

Relatives worried about acceptance by colleges should read the book *School's Out,* by Lewis Perelman. This author contends that with all the problems in the schools today, and with all the technology which can make learning at home so successful, there is simply no reason to keep the outdated and unsuccessful government school system alive. Also, many colleges themselves have correspondence programs. These have become very successful and well-attended, especially with the use of computer modems, interactive media, and CD-ROM, not to mention educational stations by satellite television offering many courses for credit. Besides the Discovery Channel and the Learning Channel, secondary and college students can tune in Mind Extension University and Oklahoma State courses.

If grandparents remain opposed, tell them you would like to try home schooling for a year and see how it works. During the year, have them visit occasionally while you teach, or have your children read for them, or recite their multiplication tables for them.

Sometimes, however, grandparents actually work to turn the children against the home schooling and cause a serious problem for the family. Some have gone so far as to call local authorities and complain that their grandchildren are not being educated. This is a difficult situation, but we need to remember that they are being sincere in their beliefs, even if they are inaccurate. Parents may need to make grandparents realize that the family will not be able to visit them if the problem continues. Some parents believe the grandparents cannot be told because of the potentially very unpleas-

ant situation. This decision needs to be prayed about. Please
be cautious, wise as serpents, gentle as doves.

The pastor

After you have firmed up your commitment to home
schooling, after you have had some discussions and come to
an agreement with your spouse, after you have talked with
your parents and in-laws and other relatives, the next concern is your pastor and the parishioners.

Of course, you are under no obligation to inform your
pastor of what you are doing. However, it does tend to
come up, especially if you take the children to weekday
Masses. In such cases, the pastor is going to ask you why
the children are not in school. You also may want to prepare your children for the Sacraments yourself, rather than
have them attend the parish classes. In such a case, you
will have to explain to the pastor that you are home schooling and are teaching religion at home.

From the documents of the Catholic Church, many quotes
of which are contained in this book, you should have a
pretty good grasp of Church teachings, knowing that it is
not only your right but your responsibility to teach your
children.

However, many pastors are not aware of the Catholic
Church's teachings in these documents which apply to the
rights and responsibility of parents in the matter of educating their children. In seminaries, home schooling is not even
being discussed. So your approach needs to be cautious. If
you and the pastor have had previous disagreements, it is
probably best not to bring it up. You may wish to send him
a letter, or you may just forget the whole thing.

If your pastor has been neutral about home schooling,
you may choose to go to him or not. If you do, be very
confident, and explain your positive reasons for home schooling. He should not object on any grounds, but if he does,
remain respectful of his office as pastor.

You may offer to explain that you have been doing research on the Church's teachings, and are convinced that

this is what you believe God wants you to do. If he appears interested, you could send him some materials (or give him a gift subscription to a home schooling periodical). Whatever you do, do not get into a discussion or debate about Church teachings. After all, he will not be willing to listen to *you* about the teachings of the Church!

Dr. Ed Peters, a canon lawyer, has written an excellent pamphlet titled, "Home Schooling and the Code of Canon Law," which explains the strong Church teachings through Canon Law regarding the rights and responsibilities of parents to teach their own children. It also deals specifically with parental rights and responsibilities in preparing your children for receiving the Sacraments. It is available from Seton, and would be a good document for your pastor. Send it to him in the mail, however, as you want to avoid direct confrontation.

Fellow parishioners and neighbors

The most common reason why home schooling families have problems with local school authorities is because of unfriendly neighbors. Before you begin home schooling, contact your local support group. Find out how neighbors are reacting to home schooling. If they are not friendly, you have two choices. You can stay in the neighborhood and try to work to establish understanding or tolerance, or you can move. Both options need to be seriously considered.

If you have a chance, read *The Child Abuse Industry*, by Mary Pride, a home schooling mother and author. We are living in a strange period of American history in which child abuse has become a big business! People are aware that they can make anonymous phone calls to local social service agencies and complain about people they do not like without any possible recriminations. The cry "Child abuse!" can begin a terrible series of events for a family. Be aware of the dangers, and keep alert. Also, keep in touch with other home-schooling families. Don't ostracize yourself from friends.

If you live in a neighborhood or town rather than in a rural or farm area, you might find it a good idea to keep your children in the house during school hours. Many home schoolers argue against keeping the children inside for the school hours, so you need to consider both advantages and disadvantages. It is not a matter of hiding as much as a matter of not causing your neighbors to be reminded every day of what you are doing. To many, home schooling is just not American!

Consider choosing your neighbors. There are areas where home schooling is strong. You should be looking for Catholic people who want to strengthen family values. Hopefully, you can find a location where other Catholic home schoolers are situated. Many of us had ancestors who moved because of religious intolerance. It is because of our religious and family values that we have decided to teach our children at home. If your neighbors are deep-down intolerant, see if you have some of that determination from your ancestors to make a move for your family.

State home schooling association

Join your state home schooling association. They publish a monthly or bi-monthly newsletter, which keeps you informed about proposed state legislation which can affect home schooling families. They announce statewide or regional home schooling meetings or conventions. They keep you informed about activities which are of interest to home schooling families. Though these organizations tend to be mainly Protestant, the mutual interest is in pro-Life and pro-Family values. Most organizations are not anti-Catholic, at least overtly.

Join your local home schooling support group. If a Catholic one is available, you should join that. If only a Protestant one is available, join that one until enough Catholics start home schooling in your area to start a Catholic group. After all, you might even make some converts.

Home School Legal Defense Association

Many home schoolers enroll in the Home School Legal Defense Association. This is a legal insurance corporation which, for a reasonable yearly fee of $100 ($85 for Seton families), will give you legal counseling if you have any problems with your local or state authorities. HSLDA works with lawyers in each state who are familiar with your state laws and with how the local school districts are interpreting state legislation. Many of the local educational bureaucrats are not aware of the state regulations.

We recommend that Catholic home schooling families join HSLDA each year, even if the home schooling situation is running smoothly in your state. If you do not use the services, your fee will be put to good use defending the rights of home-schooling families across the nation.

There has been some controversy in recent years about HSLDA and its work regarding state legislation. Most home schoolers follow HSLDA's advice concerning pending legislation. Other home schoolers believe that HSLDA has sometimes taken it upon themselves to negotiate laws with state officials without sufficiently consulting the home schoolers in that particular state.

Historically, home schoolers could not be where they are today if it had not been for HSLDA working to defend home schoolers and working for better legislation. What we are seeing today is more home schoolers becoming involved in the state lobbying activity, and more home schoolers who are well educated themselves. Consequently more home schoolers, exhibiting the independence and leadership we should expect from those going against the bureaucratic educational system, want to "do it themselves."

We still encourage Catholic home schoolers to take advantage of the legal expertise and insurance of having attorneys in their own state who are knowledgeable about the state laws. However, we highly recommend that Catholic parents keep informed about current laws and pending legislation.

State regulations

Learn about the home schooling laws and regulations in your state. While home schooling is legal in every state, you will want to be familiar with your own particular state laws and regulations. You can obtain them from your state home schooling association. Seton has a full time attorney who is ready to answer questions regarding state home schooling regulations or to address inquiries if you have questions about your particular situation.

We home schoolers are concerned about education for our children. It is appropriate that we are concerned about educating ourselves about the state and local laws and regulations. If you really want to delve into it, read the home schooling court cases in your state. It is interesting material!

We highly recommend that you do not follow any regulations which go against your conscience. If you feel uncomfortable about any regulations, call an attorney at your state home schooling association, or call a Catholic attorney. Also, if your superintendent asks for any information beyond the state requirements, please call a home schooling attorney. This subject is discussed in greater detail in a later chapter.

If you want to be independent of a program

Decide if you want to enroll in a Catholic home study program, or if you want to try to do it yourself. If you are an experienced teacher, you probably have more self-confidence, have an idea about where to obtain materials, and possibly have a good grasp of the scope of the concepts which should be learned at various grade levels.

If you want to hear about the advantages of not being enrolled in a program, contact families who are doing it on their own. Each family has its own unique goals, ideas, methods, and materials, so you should talk to several home schooling families, and take the ideas which you like best.

If you are not enrolled in a program, your first major objective will be to find Catholic textbooks. Twenty-five or even fifteen years ago you could go to a St. Vincent de Paul shop or local garage sale and purchase used Catholic textbooks. Now they are practically non-existent. If you are not living in a predominantly Catholic community, it will be nearly impossible to locate old Catholic textbooks.

Catholic publishers

When the Catholic schools decided to take state and/or federal funds, they were not allowed to use these funds for anything religious. As a consequence, the publishers of Catholic materials stopped publishing. This has been true now for over twenty-five years.

There are some publishers of Catholic books for children but it is difficult to recommend most of them as textbooks. The old Vision books, a series of saints' biographies, are still around. These are good reading for book reports. Nevertheless, it would take a mother a good deal of time to use something like this for vocabulary development, reading comprehension, and analytical thinking skills, skills which should be included in a good educational curriculum.

There are still some small Catholic publishers. Daughters of St. Paul has books for children, but does not have textbooks. TAN has published four Catholic history texts (world and U.S.), two Church history texts, several religion texts, saints' biographies for children and Catholic coloring books. Ignatius Press has published a Catholic catechism series for children, written by Catholics United for the Faith.

I foresee a long time before Catholic textbooks come back into print, except by the Catholic home study schools. To keep the price of an individual book reasonable, a publisher needs to go to press with 5,000 copies. It is not likely that 5,000 Catholic home schooling mothers of third graders would all know about and agree to buy a particular third grade speller or history book.

You can find Christian texts at Book Fairs sponsored by your local or state home schooling association. Please be sure to read the books to check for any anti-Catholic bias before giving them to your children.

Not too many years ago, home schooling parents could purchase used, older Catholic texts from secular used-books companies, but these are all gone now, and the companies will no longer service home schoolers. The companies sell the books for so little per copy that they want large orders and will not take single-book orders any longer. I have noticed a few Protestant used-book companies popping up, home schooling families with a cottage industry to help other home schooling families. These will be growing, I am sure, but they surely will not offer anything Catholic!

While it is sometimes possible to order directly from publishers, many publishers will not sell one book at a time to a home schooler. You will find better prices and more appropriate books for home schoolers at the home-schooling Book Fairs or conventions. Some home schoolers are starting to trade or sell their used textbooks. Catholic books will not be found, however.

Protestant publishers vary in quality and outlook. The Rod and Staff books are Mennonite and have no anti-Catholic bias. The fundamentalist A Beka and Bob Jones books are of high academic quality, but you need to read them to check for anti-Catholic bias. It is not in every text. Huge numbers of Christian books are being sold at the state home-schooling conventions, but they are of various quality and Christian perspective. You must look them over carefully.

Be aware that at the state conventions some "publishers" might be home schooling mothers themselves who have produced a book or two. This makes it difficult if you want to use one series through many grades. The books may be excellent for you, and they may not be. Just go through as much as you can before purchasing.

A common pitfall at large conventions is to buy too much. Parents often spend several hundred dollars buying textbooks for the whole school year. As they go through the year, they discover problems of one sort or another, and end up using only a percentage of the books they purchased. So shop cautiously or be prepared to build a large home schooling library (which is not a bad idea, either).

As the home-schooling market becomes larger, and thousands instead of hundreds are attending conventions, the sheer number of exhibits is becoming almost overwhelming for the home schooling family. I am now seeing private firms getting into the business of presenting state conventions. Exhibitors are being charged between $150 to $350 to exhibit. When you see 100 to 200 exhibitors at a convention, you need to realize that someone is making big money ($350 x 200 is $70,000). Please be cautious and remember that while there are probably some things which will be good for you and your children, there is probably a great deal which is not.

The big controversy

If you are going independent and not enrolling in a program, there is a controversy among Catholic home schoolers about whether it is better to have fundamentalist or secular texts when no Catholic texts are available.

There are Christian books, such as the *Rod and Staff,* which are not fundamentalist. But if you can find a fundamentalist text with only a sprinkling of anti-Catholic bias, you can work around it. After all, you are the teacher, you can choose the assignments, and you can explain the Catholic position to your child regarding, for instance, Galileo. The problem is that there may be anti-Catholic or non-Catholic positions on topics about which you may not be familiar.

If you absolutely cannot find a Christian textbook to your satisfaction, then you need to turn to a secular text. This should be your last resort, however. The reason is that not only is God totally ignored, but all the modern secular attitudes and values, and current politically correct ideas, are usually presented throughout the text, even if they do not relate to the topic. The secular textbooks today are literally filled with un-Christian ideas, and some of them are difficult to recognize because we have all become somewhat affected by the pagan society in which we live. Many of these un-Christian ideas relate to social values, economic justice, government principles, and so on.

At Seton, we reluctantly use a few secular texts along with Catholic and Christian textbooks, but our teachers present the Catholic viewpoint in the lesson plans and tests. For instance, in the elementary grades, our vocabulary workbook is secular, but the weekly tests include sentences which teach about the Bible or saints, or about Jesus or catechism lessons. In the high school Geography text, which contains "politically correct" ideas, our teachers use this as an opportunity to state the accurate, Catholic position.

Some Catholics believe they should not give money to a fundamentalist publisher. Please remember that the Christian fundamentalists believe in the Bible, do not have abortions, are not practicing homosexuals, and do not practice witch-craft or engage in other occult activities. At secular publish-ing houses, in which the employees are likely to be a reflec-tion of the community in general, you can find all these things being practiced.

In our pagan society, I can guarantee you that when you go shopping for anything any place, some of your money is going for the support of persons who do not agree with you on abortion and other basic anti-Christian practices. I would rather my money go to a fundamentalist Christian publisher than to any secular publisher, but each of us has to make his own decision.

Catholic home study schools

There are many advantages and benefits to having chil-dren enrolled in a program. If you are not an experienced teacher, or if you have been a teacher but do not have the time to work on all the details of setting up daily lessons, you will probably want to enroll in a program. If you want Catholic textbooks, you need to enroll in a Catholic home study school. If you want counseling and other school ser-vices, you will want to enroll in a program.

Most home study schools will help prospective families to contact other home-schooling families who live in the same region. It helps to discuss the program as well as the whole concept of home schooling with another Catholic fam-ily before you begin.

Just as there is no single car that is best for everyone, just as people have different needs and are looking for dif-ferent qualities in a car, the same is true of a home study school. There is no one home study school that is best for everyone. A family needs to look at what each home study school offers to decide which is best for them and their children's needs.

Remember that none of the Catholic home study programs will be detrimental or dangerous to your child, as are regular schools. You are in control each minute of each day. You can make changes as you go along. If you start with one program, and it does not quite meet your needs, you can change the following year. While it is an important decision, do not feel that you are locked into it permanently.

Flexibility

Some home schooling parents believe that if they enroll in a program, they will not have the flexibility they could have otherwise. This depends on how much flexibility you want, versus a certain amount of structure to help keep you on schedule. I assume all programs encourage flexibility. Our motto at Seton is "Adjust the program to fit the child, not the child to fit the program."

In home study schools, parents are required to submit tests for their children if they want a report card. If they do not want records, they are free not to submit tests. At Seton, no matter what the lessons suggest or recommend, parents are entirely free to teach as they wish. Home school programs give report cards based on the tests. What parents teach to prepare for the tests, or how they teach, or at what pace they teach, is entirely up to them.

Some home study programs have a calendar, some do not. At Seton, there is no calendar, so parents and students are not under pressure to submit tests by a certain date. Also, some home study programs like Seton are happy to customize the materials, sending higher level books in one or more subjects, or sending lower level books when a student needs more remedial work.

Lesson plans

Enrollment in a Catholic program is the easiest way to home school. Many home schooling counselors strongly recommend enrollment at least for one year. A program usually contains complete materials and ready-to-go daily lesson plans. In addition, a home schooling mother has the advantage of having an objective person helping to evaluate the schoolwork and/or tests. The teachers do not simply grade the student's work, but add comments to help the student as well as give encouragement. Stickers and stamps, many religious, are given for work well done. Certificates of Achievement for excellent work are offered to encourage children. The children themselves can benefit from the knowledge that their family is part of a larger school—and that their work is evaluated by a teacher familiar with the same grade level.

Another advantage of enrollment is the counseling service by teachers. Catholic counseling service is and should be an integral part of the home schooling service. Some schools, such as Seton, have specialists in learning disabilities, as well as high school teachers certified in particular subject areas. Seton has a full time home schooling attorney on duty to answer questions regarding state regulations or other related questions. Our computer programmer answers questions as well as evaluates and provides educational software. Other schools may offer similar services.

Enrollment in a program, especially for parents without college degrees, often helps in keeping local school authorities such as school boards, superintendents, or principals, from being troublesome. Seton, following its policy of being service-oriented, has obtained accreditation for the purpose of providing protection for our families. Our accreditation is from the Northwest Association of Schools and Colleges. Accreditation has meant almost trouble-free home schooling for our enrolled families as far as local authorities are concerned.

Accreditation

There is some confusion in the home schooling community regarding accreditation. Accreditation means that an objective body has looked over your business and declared that it has kept certain standard objectives.

Seton was accredited for five years by the National Home Study Council. Then Seton was approved for accreditation a second time, but we chose to be accredited by the Northwest

Association of Schools and Colleges instead, mainly because it was much less expensive.

To confer accreditation, the NWASC reviews the curriculum materials to see if there are sufficient daily lessons or guidelines for a student to learn on his own. There are no "philosophy of content" guidelines. They evaluate home study programs on business methods, efficiency, and staff qualifications. In addition, they survey the "client families" to see if there are any problems. After a year's study and visits by the accreditation committee, if the school meets the standards, the accreditation certificate is granted. The school is then reviewed for renewal every five years.

Accreditation helps public school superintendents to know that a home school program has been objectively evaluated by professionals and has passed certain criteria. They can be assured that it is in fact a business operation, using professional business methods, and not a fly-by-night organization.

The only other comprehensive home study program for children which has accreditation is Home Study International, which is run by Seventh-Day Adventists. There are several accredited schools, not Catholic, which serve high school and college level students. Most of the schools tend to specialize in engineering, art, electronics, radio & television broadcasting, paralegal training, tax training, and so on.

To give some idea of the standards by which these educational accrediting associations evaluate a school, the following is from a 240-page book, *Home Study School Accreditation: Policies, Procedures, and Standards,* published by the former National Home Study Council, now called the Distance Education and Training Council.

* It has a competent faculty.
* It offers educationally sound and up-to-date courses.
* It carefully screens students for admission.
* It provides satisfactory educational services.
* It has demonstrated ample student success & satisfaction.
* It advertises its courses truthfully.
* It is financially able to deliver high-quality educational service.

To become accredited, each school must have made an intensive study of its own operations, opened its door to a thorough inspection by an outside examining committee, supplied all information required by the Accrediting Commission, and submitted its instructional materials for a thorough review by competent subject matter specialists. The process is repeated every five years.

The NHSC has been in existence for nearly 70 years, and employs standards and procedures similar to those of other recognized educational accrediting associations. It establishes educational and ethical business standards. It examines and evaluates home study schools in terms of these standards, and it accredits those which qualify.

The independent Accrediting Commission of the National Home Study Council is listed by the United States Department of Education as a "nationally recognized accrediting agency." The Accrediting Commission is also a recognized member of the Council on Postsecondary Accreditation (COPA).

Withdrawing from the local school

When you decide to home school, if your child has been attending a local school, try to make the change at the beginning of a school year, or at the semester break, or during a long vacation, such as at Christmas or Easter vacation. It makes no difference for children in the elementary grades to change schools at any time of the year. However, for the high school level, a student could lose credits by withdrawing before the semester ends. Nevertheless, often a situation is so serious that parents must pull their children out of school immediately.

It is best not to have your children talk about leaving a school while they are still attending. Teachers, principals, parents, and students sometimes react in unpleasant ways when they know a student is leaving to be home schooled.

Once you have received the books for home schooling, notify your school principal in writing, unless you have good personal relations with the school personnel. A short letter, sent by certified mail, should state simply that you have decided to enroll your child in a private Catholic school, and the request for records will be sent to them shortly from the new school. This last statement is important because it signifies to them that, in fact, you are enrolling in a school. The former school is less likely to contact you if they expect a request for school records.

The home study school should send parents a form, such as a "Request for Transfer of Records," which needs to be signed by parents and returned to the home study school. This is then mailed to the previous school. Most schools do not like parents to personally bring in the Request form, but want to receive it from the new school, thus giving evidence of being enrolled somewhere.

If home schooling parents do not want the student records requested, or want a delay on the request, that should be no problem. At Seton, parents may request that such forms not be sent to the previous school. In fact, only the high school records are absolutely necessary for transferral. However, the former school will be less concerned about a student's whereabouts if the student's record is out of their filing cabinet, so seriously consider requesting the transcript file be sent to the home school.

Questions from the previous school

Keep in mind that a) home schooling is legal in every state but b) local school authorities do not like home schoolers, who mean less money in their yearly budget. School principals or superintendents have a tendency to harass home schooling parents whenever they can get away with it. They usually do get away with it when parents are uninformed and want to avoid confrontation or unpleasantness.

Whenever the local school principal or teachers ask why you are home schooling, be sure to present the positive reasons. Talk about the benefits of your family learning together, individualized instruction, the flexibility, unifying family experiences, and that you want to do more with teaching your children your Catholic values. If local Catholic school teachers are upset, simply say that you are going to try this home schooling "alternative" for a year and see how it works out.

It is important to stress the positive benefits of home schooling for your family and your child, and not to mention any negatives regarding the former school.

Whenever possible, avoid unpleasant discussions with public or Catholic school personnel. Unexpected and unpredictable repercussions may hurt your child, your husband and his job, your family, and/or your home schooling.

Placement tests

Most home study programs have an evaluation or "screening" procedure for grade placement. Placement Tests are sent to the parents to administer to the children. While the scores will present an objective picture of a student's achievement level, it is only one factor. Parents' observation and evaluation are more important in determining the grade level. The home study program always should defer to the parents' decision in this matter.

The curriculum

Obviously, if you are Catholic, you want a Catholic curriculum. If possible, every course should reflect the Catholic perspective. This follows the directives of Rome, which are contained in many encyclicals and other documents. The Church clearly states that the curriculum should be permeated with Catholic values.

The Catholic home study programs have a basic problem. Catholic textbooks have been out of print for more than twenty years. The Catholic home study programs are doing their best, but none of them can offer 100% Catholic texts. In fact, the Catholic schools in America even in the 1950's did not have Catholic textbooks in every subject.

The Catholic home study programs are using older Catholic textbooks, or reprinting older texts, or writing new Catholic books. This last takes a long time and a large amount of money, which makes publishing difficult.

At the moment, the Catholic home study programs are able to provide a majority of Catholic texts. However, the main area of difficulty is in the science area. As the years go by, older books become outdated very quickly. Seton is writing a Catholic science series now; several grades are currently available.

Protestant home study schools

Despite the fact that Protestant home study programs reflect Protestant perspectives, many Catholic families have enrolled their children in Protestant home study programs. This can be dangerous because Catholic parents and children may not recognize some of the differences in the teachings between Catholicism and Protestantism, though we admit there are many similarities also.

Some basic errors which sometimes occur in various Protestant textbooks include editorial slants regarding historical events, or mis-translations or mis-interpretations of the Bible. Certainly anything regarding the Blessed Mother, the Spanish Inquisition, Christopher Columbus, Galileo, Catholic saints, and the Rosary, is going to be presented in an unfavorable light. In addition, sometimes there is outward prejudice expressed in words such as "Romanism" or "papists."

Catholic home schooling parents should obtain at least one of two books explaining the most common doctrinal errors in Protestantism. *Catholicism and Fundamentalism* by Karl Keating is available from Ignatius Press. *Protestant Fundamentalism and the Born Again Catholic* by Father Robert Fox is available from the Fatima Family Apostolate. If you are using Protestant texts, these will alert you to the typical errors in Protestant thinking.

Secular books are not good for Catholic children either. In fact, secular books are worse than Protestant texts because there is no attempt at being Christian. Secular authors simply ignore the fact that God exists and that there are moral values. Many secular books can be seriously harmful.

Nevertheless, Catholic home study programs are forced

to use a few Protestant and secular texts. We are not happy
about this, and are writing Catholic books as fast as we can.
The non-Catholic texts we use have been carefully evaluated, however, and are used mostly at the high school level.
At this date, there are simply not enough Catholic textbooks
to provide a total Catholic program.

Other materials and services

Seton can serve as an example of the materials and services offered by the Catholic home study programs. Along
with textbooks and workbooks, Seton sends daily lesson plans
for a year, quarterly report forms, tests, answer keys, and a
teacher plan book. At the end of each quarter's work, certain
end-of-chapter or end-of-quarter tests are sent to the home
study school for the teachers to grade. The Seton teachers
write comments for support as well as to explain concepts.
Religious stickers or stamps are added to the papers for the
children to enjoy. For straight A's, Achievement Certificates
are awarded.

Recent studies have indicated that only about one-third
of home schooling families in America are using a program.
We hope that if Catholics are not using a program, they are
doing their best to obtain Catholic materials.

How much time?

One of the most common questions mothers ask before
they start home schooling is "How much time will it take?"

There is no simple answer. A little girl in first grade
who is anxious to learn is obviously going to take less time
than a little boy who is not interested in school and wants
to spend his day playing outdoors. A boy starting in sixth
grade who cannot read is going to take longer than a boy
who started home schooling in first grade. Students with less
motivation and fewer study skills will take longer than those
who have them. Children with learning problems will take
longer to learn.

Your philosophy has a great deal to do with how much

time you will be teaching. For instance, many parents feel that the important subjects can be finished up by noon, with some fun activities scheduled in the afternoon. Catholics who intend for their children to go on to college, on the other hand, often insist on extra activities and fill out a regular school day to three o'clock, and often have their children do extra reading in the evening.

Our Seton program gives a suggested time for each subject, but that obviously would vary from child to child. A boy usually needs to study his spelling longer than a girl; a girl often needs to spend more time on math than a boy. Math and reading should usually take about an hour a day, while spelling and vocabulary can usually be done in 20 minutes. English, religion, history, and science are usually 30 to 40 minute classes. High school classes are 50 minutes each, for most students.

With this said, we could state that most children in the primary grades (one to three) could probably finish most of their work in three or four hours, though those hours should be broken up throughout the day and early evening. Students in the intermediate grades could finish the major work in four hours, but extra reading for book reports, for instance, might take another hour in the evening.

Students in the junior high grades could be done in four hours, but for the college-bound, we would recommend another hour, and sometimes an additional hour in the evening. High school students should plan on an hour a day per subject, with perhaps an extra hour in the evenings or weekends for extra reading or research.

While we have talked about the time involved for the teaching or learning periods, there is also a certain amount of time parents need for preparation. This also varies. Usually with the primary grades, no preparation is necessary, as you can usually just move along with the lessons as the child learns. However, with the other grades, a certain amount of preparation is necessary as you may need to do more teaching. You should figure an hour to two hours a week to look over what you need to do for the following week.

At the high school level, the time required to help your

children depends on whether they have been home schooling in the earlier grades. Most students coming out of schools do not have good study skills and they need parental help. Students who have been home schooling for several years can do practically all their high school assignments without help. However, it is important for parents to involve their high schoolers in discussions about their schoolwork, especially religion, literature, and history, in order to convey the proper Catholic perspective.

Arranging the home

Home schooling is a full time job, involving all members of the family, and probably involving most of the living space. If at all possible, Dad should help with building an extra room or shaping an extra room out of some area of the house. Some families create a classroom in the basement, putting in colorful panels and bookcases for all the schoolbooks, with lots of good lighting. In some homes, the family room is the classroom. Some families convert the garage into the classroom. One family has converted a small building on the property into a classroom.

It is difficult to use the dining room or the living room as the main classroom. There needs to be a permanent place where books, globes, encyclopedias, and desks can be kept.

Because your time will be spent teaching, you will be spending less time doing housework, cooking, and cleaning. We advise having a gigantic spring cleaning before you begin to home school. Throw out everything you possibly can. Limit the number of items, especially dishes and glasses, in the kitchen. You will need room for books and other learning materials, for such things as science projects and art projects. In another chapter, we will deal more specifically with the housework. We know that this is a real sacrifice for those women who want to keep their homes in "apple pie" order, but we also know that these lovely ladies are willing to make this sacrifice to give their children the time they need.

Home schooling is a lifestyle. The home will be redecorated eventually. Maps will be put up on the walls, and a globe or telescope or a model of a heart will appear. If presently there is no altar or place for prayer, this should be added. Also prepare places to post drawings and samples of schoolwork well done.

You should decide whether it would be easier to teach the children all together in one room, or have the children working in different rooms. Most families end up with a combination, with children doing math and English, for instance, in separate rooms, but coming together for other classes, such as religion and music. This can be changed back and forth as you proceed through the year. More details about grouping the children for learning are contained in the chapter "Home Schooling in the Large Family."

When the materials arrive

Children usually do not like school, but they like learning. What comes as a surprise to most parents is how eagerly the children look through the box of books as soon as it arrives. Sometimes the kids just start going through the materials, reading the stories and filling in the first few pages of workbooks.

Parents and children need to take time to look over the school materials, locate the answer keys, see the pattern of the assignments in each subject, notice the schedule and kinds of tests, and in general become familiar with the overall program.

It is important to involve the children in some of the decision-making. Work with the children, for instance, on the schedule. Most children like the most difficult subjects in the morning, with the easier subjects in the afternoon. Ask the children to use colored pencils or pens and outline their weekly schedule, and to post it near their desks.

The family should discuss the fire exits, and practice fire drills. It is a good beginning-of-the-year project for the children to chart a diagram for a fire exit for each room. They should draw the room, and, in a colored pen, trace the exit route. This is posted in each room. One year we had our classroom on the third floor. We purchased a heavy rope, and kept it near the window. We had regular fire drill practice. My only problem, with seven sons, was they wanted to practice every day. I know they practiced when I was not looking! They became regular monkeys as their mother's hair turned gray!

By the way, do not forget to purchase several fire extinguishers! Show the children how they work. Also, have a field trip to the fire station, and ask a fireman to demonstrate the different kinds of extinguishers. He can explain when you need a new one. Encourage your children later in the year to submit a poster for the local fire safety contest.

Other supplies

Before you begin to home school, purchase whatever you need to set up a schooling or learning area. Purchase not only the normal school supplies, such as notebooks, pens and pencils, and a pencil sharpener, but other supplies which give you and your children a psychological help to prepare yourself for the job ahead. For instance, buy a chalkboard or find a piece of plywood and help your children paint it with special chalkboard paint. Having the children help with the school equipment encourages them and motivates them toward doing the work, toward writing on the board they helped to paint!

Consider repainting or repapering the walls for the "classroom." Locate a special table or desks at a garage sale. Some children want a school desk; it just seems more like school! Of course, if you prefer *not* to have a classroom atmosphere, that is up to you. Try to be creative to obtain an environment which helps you and your children to become motivated and excited about learning at home.

Visit other home schooling families in your area and see how they decorate their "classroom" to give you some ideas. Do not hesitate to emphasize those hobbies or special gifts or talents which predominate in your family.

Conclusion

Many home schooling families have found that the special times we have with our children as we pray, work, and learn together can never be equalled for the joy they bring us. Though there are quite a few things which must be accomplished even before you begin, once you do begin you will believe it was all worth it!

Beginning is a big first step toward trusting in Jesus to provide you with the graces to fulfill His commandment to teach your children.

Remember that as a member of the Mystical Body of Christ, you are entitled to many graces. Ask for them.

Chapter 6:
Home Schooling in the Large Family

Most people become a little overwhelmed at the idea of teaching a large number of children at home. Home schooling in a large family, however, is not more difficult—it is less difficult. Still difficult, but less difficult.

Anything we want to do, or need to do, that is important or valuable, is not easy. Father John Hardon, when speaking to a group of home schooling families, said that home schooling is difficult.

The basic reason why home schooling in a large family is less difficult is that there are so many people to help you do the chores around the house, to help with the schoolwork, to help even with disciplining. In addition, older children who have been trained in the past now can set a standard or pattern for the younger ones to follow.

God's overall plan

Home schooling will be easier if we understand how important our home schooling family is in God's overall plan for our society. It will be easier to persevere in spite of difficulties if we realize that the final goal or victory is so great!

We may think our own life and the lives of our particular family members are not important in God's overall total plan for humanity. But each one of us is vital in God's plan.

In the encyclical *Humanae Vitae*, Pope Paul VI asks that Catholic married couples evangelize other married couples about God's teachings regarding birth control. Our very lifestyle, our daily example, is a kind of evangelizing. Because we are following God's commands, representing something unusual in our society, we are going to cause other parents to investigate, and perhaps convert to living the authentic Catholic family life. One of the best examples we can give in today's pagan society is to have children and to take on personally the responsibility to educate our children rather than hand them over to government schools.

Furthermore, our home schooling is important as we learn and practice our Catholic faith, not only for our own salvation, and for the salvation of our immediate family, but also for the salvation of our future grandchildren, and great grandchildren.

In addition, our home schooling family can have many consequences in God's overall plan for the salvation of souls in our parish, in our neighborhood, and extending beyond that as God wills. Like St. Francis, we home schoolers are called not simply to repair our local church, or in this case, our own domestic church. We are called to evangelize all of Christendom by giving an example of the authentic Catholic family life.

The secular society encourages people to practice perversions openly, to "come out of the closet." We Catholics need to be open ourselves, perhaps not aggressively promoting home schooling, but certainly not being fearful to tell others about home schooling in response to inquiries.

The large family promotes the virtuous life

The large family is especially important in God's plan for the fullest development of a virtuous individual, a virtuous family, and a virtuous society. The Catholic family, whatever size, is, as the Catholic Church teaches, a domestic church. But the large family provides the opportunities for training children in practicing more virtues more often and more deeply.

The larger the family, the more aspects of the general society the family members tend to represent. In a large family, children have more opportunities for interrelating, and thus the members of the family have more opportunities to practice Christian virtues, such as kindness, patience, generosity, sharing with others, doing things for others before being asked, sympathizing with members of the family who are sick or elderly, and taking care of babies.

In general, the larger the family, the more demands there

are for the individual child. For instance, most large families today will not be wealthy. Now, while this may be simply an external fact, it can also be an internalized virtue as parents and children grow in understanding how unimportant material things are in comparison to people and values. As Catholic parents "choose life" for the sixth, seventh, eighth, and more times, the message is clear to the children as they sacrifice to make room for one more.

The virtue of quick obedience is vital to sanity and order in a large family. The large family needs to have obedience and respect for authority, or, when times of crisis arise, the members of the family will not remain steady but will go in too many different directions for the good of the whole family. A large family, where children are required to be obedient not only to parents but often to older children in the family, provides more opportunities to explain and live the Fourth Commandment, which directs us to obey all proper authority.

Unacceptable behavior cannot continue long in a large family because so many people in the family will not put up with it. Pressure would be on Mom and Dad from other siblings if parents put up with misbehavior by a single child, or if parents did not sufficiently punish disobedience. In fact, older children will mete out the punishment if parents do not.

It is readily recognized in a large family how the practice of virtue is necessary for the good of each member of the family as well as of the family as a whole. Individual members learn in the family how to practice virtue in the larger society, such as at the workplace, in the marketplace, in the parish, in the neighborhood, in civic and political life.

We all realize the necessity of living the virtuous life for the purpose of saving our immortal souls. But it is also part of God's plan for us to evangelize others in our society. Catholic home schooling families are part of that plan. We need to humbly accept the fact that God has chosen our own family to fit into that plan by performing an important task in evangelization. This should inspire us to be the very best Catholic family we can be.

Recently, Steve Wood, a former Protestant minister who has been active in the Pro-Life movement for several years, visited Front Royal. He has seven children. He made the remark, which all of us can testify to, that whenever the whole family goes anywhere, their very presence is a witness to Christian values. People know that this family has given up material things for the sake of having a large family. Once they were in a restaurant with all the children, and a woman came up to his wife and said, "You are religious, aren't you?" His wife answered, "Yes." Then the lady said, "Catholic, right?" And, though they had been converts only three days, his wife answered, "Yes, Catholic."

The large family is a symbol of the internal life of faith, a symbol recognized even by those who have rejected such a life. The large family is a public rejection of the prevailing secular values of materialism and the self-fulfillment goals without personal sacrifice promoted by the contraceptive mentality, the feminists and homosexuals, and abortionists.

So the first tip for home schooling successfully in the large family is understanding what we are about...and why. Then, write it down and tape it on the back of your bedroom door and refer to it often, on good days as well as bad.

The second tip for home schooling successfully in the large family is for the teaching mother to evaluate herself, her own emotional and spiritual life, to understand herself and her strengths and weaknesses, and to discipline herself to be an authentic Catholic wife and mother.

The teaching mother

There is no question about the importance of disciplining our children, but what about our own self-discipline? Home schooling mothers must have self-discipline. We need to ask ourselves questions, such as "Am I able to control myself so I don't use angry words with the children? Or with my husband in front of the children? Do I discipline the children when I should, or is it just too difficult to bother with it?"

We should pray to Our Mother of Good Counsel to give

us the virtues of patience and understanding, as well as good judgment and perseverance. We need to be consistent in administering punishment, yet be sensitive to special needs. We must pray for the courage and emotional strength to train our children to choose to be obedient.

In the first year of home schooling, our household routine will be changed, to put it mildly. We need to be ready to accept these changes and to learn to accept sacrifices related to material things.

Discipline yourself to keep going. Do not hesitate to enlist the help of other good Catholic home schooling mothers who will certainly be happy to help you with your current problem. Seeing how other home schooling Catholics resolved a problem often makes a seemingly intractable situation become simple. And, of course, depend on the Blessed Mother—the best of all home schooling mothers—to bring you through the tough times, as well as those blessed moments of smooth sailing.

Many saints are examples for us. St. Elizabeth Ann Seton continued to teach her own children through many difficulties. She taught while her husband was extremely ill and needed her attention. She taught after her husband died, while she was in Italy. She taught her own and other children in Emmitsburg, Maryland, when she established a little school there. Through it all she kept her children with her, even after she became a nun. The first convent was very cold and primitive, and she became sick with tuberculosis, but she kept her children around her. Home schooling means keeping your children around you, no matter what.

Discipline yourself to keep going when the problems seem overwhelming: an alcoholic spouse, an unfaithful spouse, death or serious illness, too small a house, an uncontrollable budget, living with in-laws. These are situations when children need you more than ever; in school, children turn to drugs, sex, and immature peers for answers to these problems. Be there for your children.

The times of trouble are exactly the times to keep your children close to you, to Jesus, to the stable Catholic family home schooling lifestyle. In times of trouble, your children will be channels of grace to you, and you will be channels of grace to your spouse and your children. Home schooling provides the opportunity and time for this flow of grace. Trust in God to provide you with the time and space through Catholic home schooling.

God gave you the graces to understand the need for home schooling, now have faith He will give the graces to help you continue. He *will* give you the graces to discipline yourself, and to consistently discipline your children.

Remember that the highest manifestation of love is giving and sacrificing, as Jesus did by suffering and dying for us. Home schooling is a continuing act of giving and sacrificing, for the best people in the world, your own children. Train yourself, discipline yourself, to give and to sacrifice. Be the extraordinary mother that Father John Hardon has said we must be to survive as a Catholic family.

When suffering comes, we must remember that suffering is a gift from God. It teaches us humility, it teaches us the true meaning of love as we sacrifice and give for others though we may seem unappreciated. God permits us suffering so that we draw closer to Him. He told this to Sister Josefa, as explained in *The Way of Divine Love*. He told her that He must allow illness and problems so that people will turn to Him in their distress because so many of us completely forget about Him when things are going well.

On Eternal Word Television Network, Mother Angelica often interviews people with problems—medical problems or problems with children on drugs, an alcoholic spouse, or teens as unwed mothers, and so on. Their stories are ones of spiritual growth! That is why God allows suffering.

We need to understand that home schooling—especially in a large family where the trials and tribulations, the aggravations and frustrations continue for many years—is a special blessing! What you will discover is that you can be truly happy, even with daily frustrations.

St. Paul gives us encouragement in the first letter to the Corinthians: "My beloved brethren, be ye steadfast and unmovable, always abounding in the work of the Lord, knowing that your labor is not in vain." Again, St. Paul wrote to the Philippians: "I can do all things in Him Who strengthens me."

We must be like the Blessed Mother, who had faith and trust in Him. At Cana, she said to the waiters, "Do as He tells you!" She had faith that He would provide what was needed, because He had already demonstrated it at their home.

Trust in Jesus and His Blessed Mother. Whether you have a large family or a small family, whether you have a single parent or a two-parent family, be motivated, be disciplined, trust in His word, and believe: "I can do all things in Him Who strengthens me."

Group teaching

To be successful in home schooling, especially in the large family, parents need to group the children according to subject matter or ability. The general principle is to combine the children in classes whenever possible. And secondly, to remember that the greatest "educational resource" in your family is the other members of the family.

Let us use these principles in a typical large family. The Kelly family has a baby, a toddler, and children in kindergarten, second grade, fifth grade, sixth grade, ninth and tenth grade.

Art, Music, Physical Education

In general, all the children, except the baby, may take art, music, and physical education together. In art, the children's work may be at different levels, but the children certainly can all be assigned to, for instance, make Easter cards. One child may be cutting and pasting, another may be drawing an original, another may concentrate on an Easter poem for his card.

In music, the family may sing together, listen to liturgical chants, visit a music store and learn about musical instruments, attend a local high school or church musical production, or even join a local musical dramatic group.

Physical education is certainly easy. In my family of

seven boys, they all played baseball, football, and other sports together. Children about the same age may join a gymnastic class or fencing class, as my boys did, or other local sports activities.

If you enroll your children in any art, music, or sports activity, be sure to monitor at least the first three or four classes or practices, and more if you have time.

Fifth and sixth graders

Looking at the grade levels of the Kelly family, it is obvious that the fifth and sixth graders could easily be combined in some classes. Mothers have found that, in general, girls often can be moved up in reading, spelling, and vocabulary, while boys can be moved up in math and science. (Of course, this is a general rule open to variation.)

The easiest classes for group teaching are Religion, Science, and History. The lower-level child could move up with the older, but it would not hurt an older child to review or work on the same topic as the younger child's assignments. After working with the children for a couple of weeks, a mother can usually evaluate which child should be moved up or down a level, subject by subject.

With both children reading the assignments by alternating paragraphs, the younger child should be able to keep up. In addition, the children learn to work together, hopefully to become friends, and to come to some understanding about God's various gifts to each individual person. They are learning also to practice the virtues of charity, patience, and understanding as they work and learn together.

In a large family, when you may not be able to give as much time to each child, be sure each one is at the level where he feels comfortable. Be sure each child is not needing a great deal of help. Better to start a little lower and have your child be able to do the work rather than starting a little higher, where he would need more daily help and you and he both may feel frustrated.

Another advantage to children working together is that they will tend to keep each other progressing in their work

so mother does not have to supervise them as closely. She
will, of course, need to be available to explain new concepts, to explain instructions if necessary, to listen to reading pronunciation at least twice a week, and to discuss the
studies in Religion. At the fifth grade level and above, the
students can help grade each other's daily work.

Kindergarten and second grader

The kindergarten child and the second grader will take
more of a parent's time since they are just beginning their
schooling. However, if mother assigns the second grader to
be a "teacher's aide" sometimes for the kindergarten child,
she will find it not only gives her more time, it strengthens
the phonics or math skills for the older child.

When a child is having difficulty in a subject area, he
could become a teacher's aide in the same subject with a
younger child. Teaching the lower level skills or concepts
will reinforce the foundation and thus strengthen the subject
area for the child.

In addition, the older child learns to be patient and kind
to his younger brother or sister, thus practicing the greatest
of the virtues, charity. The younger child learns (eventually)
to appreciate help from a family member, learns to be humble
in receiving, and learns the value of older brothers and sisters. The virtues of humility and trust are thus learned early.

Both the kindergarten child and the second grader can
help with the toddler, perhaps playing "school" and teaching
letters and numbers to the toddler. Emphasis on service starting with young children will result in charitable acts of mercy
later on in life. Remind your children of the words of Christ
when He washed the feet of the Apostles, "I have given you
an example, that as I have done to you, so you do also."

Some mothers like to teach a young child to read during
the summer. By concentrating on the child's reading during
the summer, less time needs to be spent during the regular
year when there are more demands from other children as
well.

Sometimes mothers would like to move a younger child

up with an older child, but believe it is too much of a jump. Consider working over the summer with a child in a lower grade, such as in reading, spelling, or vocabulary, so in the fall, the child may be able to move up with an older sibling. At these lowest levels, children may need much more than a summer, however, to absorb abstract concepts, such as in math or grammar.

High school

Some parents are nervous about teaching high school subjects because they are concerned that they may not be qualified. They sometimes ask, "How can I teach Geometry or Chemistry when I do not understand these subjects myself?"

There are several answers to this problem. First, if you have access to a computer, consider buying educational software for the particular subject. There are so many excellent programs available now for such a wide variety of topics, you should have no problem finding one that fits your child's needs.

Second, many families find relatives who can help or a college student in the neighborhood who is willing to tutor once a week, at very reasonable fees.

Third, teachers at local Christian schools are always anxious to help highly motivated students and earn a little extra tutoring money on the side. One year, a Catholic high school teacher at a local public school tutored my sons in math occasionally as the need arose.

Fourth, several of our students, with permission from Seton, have enrolled in community college courses for advanced math, advanced science, and advanced foreign languages. Taking only a single course limits social interaction with the other students.

Fifth, some home schooling families pool their resources and meet together with someone in the community who has expertise in a particular subject area. For instance, one group of students on the Seton program meets together and has a class with a research chemist. Another group is meeting

with a teacher from France who enjoys helping home schooling children learn French.   There are many other examples.
   If your child is enrolled at Seton, and none of these
options is available to you, call us and we will help to find
a solution to your problem.
   The important thing to remember is that Catholic home
schooling is not primarily about geometry or chemistry; it is
about living the virtuous Catholic life.   It is primarily about
raising saints, not scholars.
   If the choice is between my child never learning geometry because I cannot teach it and my child being daily
taught to accept pagan values, such as homosexuality, have
I a choice?

Ninth and tenth graders

   The ninth grader in our imaginary Kelly family should
be able to do a good amount of work on his own. If students are home schooled for the elementary years, they are
usually independent learners at the high school level. Mine
kept saying, "Mom, I can do it myself." I would have to
say, "But I want to have a little fun out of this home schooling too!"
   At the high school level, mothers need to keep aware of
the progress, and to be involved in discussions of religion,
and of other subjects if necessary. Subjects which would
require more discussion would be English, in relation to the
books read and analyzed, history, and sometimes geography.
Algebra and geometry are usually not difficult if children
have been home schooled previously. Otherwise, we encourage fathers or older brothers to help out. Most of the time,
however, high schoolers are able to move ahead with their
assignments without too much supervision.
   However, if the child is *starting* home school in ninth
grade, problems sometimes arise because the student does
not have the academic background, study skills, or motivation. In addition, school teachers may not have demanded
that he work up to his potential.
   Some children in the schools are pressured by their peers

not to appear to be bright or to do well. In these cases, Mother may have to work with the ninth grader more than she anticipated.

The home schooling mother must keep in mind that one of her aims is to teach the student to develop study skills so that he may continue his schooling more on his own. At Seton, we have written a mini-study skills course which we send to our students in grades seven through twelve. We give advice about setting up a place and time to study, having books and other study materials at hand, how to avoid distractions, and so on.

The mini-study skills course explains about taking notes, outlining a chapter, studying important details, and remembering facts. Once these skills are mastered, a student will learn more easily.

Hopefully by 10th grade, Mother needs only to supervise in a few subjects, though we encourage parents to be involved in discussions relating to religion, history, and literature selections.

Ninth and tenth continued

The ninth and tenth grade students should be able to take several courses together, especially courses that need not be taken in any order. History or geography, religion, literature survey courses, and science courses usually can be taken by students at different grade levels because they do not build on concepts from the previous year. A foreign language could be started early by the younger student in order to work with an older brother or sister.

Obviously, the ninth grader will not be able to take Algebra 2 or Geometry with the older student. It is likely that the English course will not be able to be taken together because certain rules of writing, analysis, composition, and grammar are assumed to have been learned in ninth. However, if a student is ambitious, a younger student could take one subject, such as Algebra I, over the summer, intensively, in order to take a more advanced course with an older brother or sister during the regular school year.

A rebellious teenager

One of the banes of modern existence is the rebellious teenager. If parents start a teenager in home schooling, there may be some problems. If a teenager is rebellious, the first year of home schooling may be mainly a program to teach Catholic family values and attitudes, and self-discipline. It may take up to two years to finish the academics.

Some parents pull their children out of the public or Catholic high school as late as twelfth grade. We know it is difficult, but the idea of "better late than never" is an important admonition here.   Even at this late date, if parents realize the dangers of the school environment to their child's soul, they have an obligation before God to take these last months to teach as much as they can as fast as they can.

Some parents, when realizing the dangers to their children, as well as their child's lack of good Catholic values, will start their children over with the high school subjects, with religion, history, and literature especially. Some students start the whole high school curriculum over again to obtain the Catholic perspective. Much of the material can be learned quickly because it is review, yet much of it has an entirely different perspective. The politically correct concepts learned in geography classes, for instance, can be corrected through a Catholic perspective.   Catholic lesson plans for Geography might include a variety of topics presented with the Catholic viewpoint—topics such as multi-culturalism and globalism, population growth and communism.

Part time grouping

We have discussed grouping two children together in a class, moving an older down or a younger up in a subject where they can both benefit from taking a single class together.   But there is another kind of grouping which can work also, called part time grouping.

For instance, suppose you have children in grades four, five, and seven, and you do not want to teach three different levels of religion, science, or history, but you feel the ability differences are such that you cannot combine them in their daily work assignments. A way to handle this would be to group all the children together for a discussion or explanation of a particular topic. Your presentation would be geared to the middle child most likely, using the middle child's textbook or lessons. But later, or the next day, each child could do his own textbook assignment at his own level. Thus the fourth grader may be working on memorizing the catechism facts on the Fourth Commandment, the fifth grader may be answering factual questions, and the seventh grader may be writing a paragraph on a more complex situation of a young teen who is disobedient to his parents or another authority figure. Thus our Kelly family is able to teach mainly by grouping and part-time grouping.

Other family members

While the family members you most rely on to help teach the children are usually the other children themselves, your husband should be helping in some way also. (This is covered more specifically in the chapter on the father's role.)

Other family members who might help are grandparents. They often have the time and energy to help by baby-sitting or by teaching. Encourage even reluctant grandparents to help because, in most cases, the more they learn about home schooling, the more supportive they become.

Grandparents can be really great teachers for your children. First, they have so much experience, knowledge, and wisdom about living the Catholic life, they are a veritable treasure for your children. Second, they tend to be very patient, sensitive, understanding, and loving toward their grandchildren. This wonderful, often cuddly, security for your children is a healthy environment for growing spiritually as well as intellectually. Thirdly, grandparents tell the most wonderful stories!

Grandparents are wonderful teachers for the younger children, but their wisdom and experience can be a deep learning experience for teenagers, who tend to think they know everything. In a pagan society which is accepting euthanasia and promoting the value of usefulness over the value of living a holy life, grandparents in the home schooling family teach priceless lessons. This multi-generational teaching is something which children in schools never experience.

Also, high school and college level children are great at helping younger siblings, especially in math and English. Another favorite helper among home schoolers is a retired teacher or a retired nun, who might help on a once-a-week basis to review math or English work.

Consider having older children spend time, taking turns, maybe one-half hour per day with your preschoolers. They can play with them or baby-sit, or teach them their letters or numbers. This is important interaction among the children, benefiting both the younger and the older child.

Do not neglect allowing the preschoolers to be involved in the home schooling situation. They should not feel left out. They can be playing on the floor or sitting in someone's lap, or have their own "schoolbook" or be writing with chalk on a blackboard. Involving pre-schoolers will mean fewer discipline problems. In addition, these children start picking up the lessons early, are better students as they unconsciously adopt learning skills, and anticipate their home schooling with eagerness as a sign of growing up.

Flexibility

To be successful in your home schooling in the large family, you must be flexible. That's a terrific understatement! The biggest academic benefit in home schooling is the individualized curriculum. If you do not gear the material and pace to your child's individual learning strengths and weaknesses, you are missing out on a great benefit which home schooling offers.

At Seton, we always encourage flexibility. Our motto is: "Adjust the program to fit the child, not the child to fit the program." This means that while there might be specific mathematical facts which need to be learned in a particular grade level, we recommend that you teach the daily lessons at a pace and with a method that is best for the student.

An individual child may be able to do two lessons in one day, or at another time, he may need to take two days to do one lesson. Some young boys and girls in the warm months will need to have several short lessons so they can go outside and play more often.

At Seton, while we provide day-to-day lessons and recommendations, these are to serve as a guideline. If you want to follow them exactly, you certainly may. And many parents do. On the other hand, if you wish, you may adjust them, giving more oral assignments rather than written, or shortening an assignment because your child learned the concepts quickly. You might want to enrich a lesson in reading, for instance, by doing more research in an encyclopedia about an artist mentioned in a reader.

Enrichment

Be flexible in your daily lessons whenever possible by utilizing supplemental materials to enrich the lessons. Read the lessons for the following week on the previous weekend, and visit the library for books, pamphlets, audio tapes, videos, and reference books which relate to the upcoming lessons. Ask the librarian for an explanation of all the features or materials they offer. Ask about borrowing books from other libraries through inter-library loan. Most libraries have circulating reference books, usually older editions of encyclopedias. Also, ask your librarian if she might be selling the library's older copy of the encyclopedia. You should be able to purchase the whole set for about $25. Ask them to call you when they will be selling it. Also, CD-based encyclopedias are now easily available.

Ask the librarian about other sources where you can obtain information and study materials. Local and state governments offer loads of free materials. Check garage sales for used encyclopedias and other reference books, such as illustrated science encyclopedias. The Internet provides almost limitless educational resources.

School teachers, limited because of space, time, location, and overload of student problems, cannot begin to offer children the almost unlimited resources available to the home schooling family.

Scheduling

Scheduling can be very tricky for the large family. Some mothers like all the children to be taking the same subject at the same time. Thus all the children have math from 9:00 to 10:00. The advantage to this is that as you travel from child to child, you may find it easier yourself in your teaching. Also, if a child needs to help another child, their brains are on the same subject at the same time.

On the other hand, some mothers need to hear the children read their stories every day, so they stagger the reading classes. Some mothers find that they can concentrate on the older children and their assignments in the early morning, while helping the younger children later in the day. Some mothers schedule working with a child on his weak subject at the same time another child is working on a subject in which he needs no help.

Most mothers try to cover the more difficult subjects in the morning, when the children are fresh, with workbook-type assignments in the afternoon. Of course, if you have a baby who naps in the afternoon, that is a good time to listen to reading or to help a child on a more complex subject like English. Many mothers prefer the children to take one subject with Dad in the evening or on Saturdays.

While it is important to be prepared to be flexible in case something changes, it is better to start the year with a definite schedule and to try to stick with it for a few weeks before making changes. Structure provides stability and discipline, which children want and need.

Children like routine. They want to know when it is time for dinner, when it is time to go to bed, when they can play, when they have to do the math or English, when it is time to pray or go to Mass. Routine gives them security, and they are more willing to do WHAT they should do WHEN they should do it. In a large family, things can easily become chaotic without a schedule.

Children often are more motivated to keep to a schedule if they have some input in making out the schedule. Ask them if they want their easiest subject first or their most difficult subject first. You may not always be able to accommodate, but try to whenever possible.

When you have worked out the schedule together, have each child write out his schedule, and then decorate it artistically with colored pens or crayons. The schedules can be put on the wall of the room where they do most of their school work. With this kind of personal attention to their schedule, they are more likely to follow it.

At Seton, daily lessons are written for parents, subject by subject. While parents are encouraged to adjust these to the needs and abilities of their children, having a written schedule as a guideline makes them and their children feel better. They have a road map. They know where they are going, even if they do not keep the exact pace, or even if they make changes now and then.

Starting the year

With a large family, it is important to start the school year a little slowly. The public schools schedule 180 days of school, but not all the children are actually in attendance 180 days. They are out sick, or have field trips, or there are training days for teachers. Many times children have little schooling when they have substitute teachers or when some all-school event is going on. Schools have an abundance of study halls and movies. So do not worry if you do not have exactly 180 days of school. It is better to start slowly and establish good procedures for the year.

Start the oldest child, or if you are grouping, the oldest two children, for the first week, but do not teach the other children that week. Take that first week to make the schedule, locate the answer keys, see how often tests are scheduled, become familiar with the pattern of the assignments, and so on. If the child is in high school, be sure he becomes familiar with the materials and how to use them. During that week, the pattern can be set for the weeks to come.

In the second week, teach the next oldest, or two, and work without interruptions from the other children as much as possible. You can teach all the children this way when you start each year. Some mothers like to do this before the Labor Day weekend so the full-fledged program can begin in September.

Be sure each child knows what to do if Mother is not available at the time needed. He may be told to a) continue with the current assignment as best as possible by going on to other problems; or b) read for a book report; or c) do an assignment for another course. Do not allow your children to waste time waiting for you to be available. You may need to institute a "wait and waste" punishment until they understand the value of time.

Fridays

Some large families find it very difficult to have home schooling for five days a week because they need a day for other things. Consequently, many of our Seton courses are scheduled for only four days a week. This gives a fifth day for catching up with anything not finished on the first four days, or for doing housework, or scheduling doctor appointments. When there is a Holy Day during the week, some families like to have either no classes or fewer classes. In my family, we always omitted math and science on Holy Days to give us extra Mass and prayer time.

Some families use Friday primarily for the whole family to clean up the house. In a large family, have teams for the chores, with one older child working with a younger child. That way, the younger one is learning from the older, and the older one cannot daydream because he is in charge of supervising the younger one. The chore is done faster and more thoroughly.

Unique but typical day

Prospective home-schooling mothers often call and ask what a typical home schooling day is like. They are worried about just how much demand there is going to be on their time.

As most of us have learned, there is no typical home schooling schedule. It is unique for each family because each family is unique. How much "demand" on the mother is unpredictable. Boys are often more demanding. Younger children are more demanding than older ones. Older children just starting are more demanding than younger ones just starting. In some families, English takes more time and in other families math takes more time. In some families, science goes quickly and composition takes forever.

In one family, the mother is totally devoted to her family and their needs. Everything is organized down to the last cup. She has her children trained to work in certain places, to study at certain times, to do each day's work exactly as written in their lesson plans. The girls read and read, and obtain very high scores on tests. They love learning, and eat it up like candy as Mother devotes each minute of the school day to making the lessons exciting.

In another family, Mother does not have time to take off her bathrobe. She is on the phone with the needs of the pregnancy center, but she keeps the lessons going as her children work in the living room. She checks on their lessons between her calls. She has a large family, and the older children often help the younger ones. She gives help when it is needed. She and her husband are professionals and the house is like a library. The children spend much time reading many books.

Another Mother has several children but only one child old enough for formal schooling. She sits the baby on her lap while her boy reads and the toddlers play on the floor. Sometimes she listens to the math facts while she puts the clothes in the washing machine. Sometimes her son goes to his room where it is quieter to study his phonics. Her husband teaches new math concepts to her son every morning before he goes to work.

One family lives on a farm and the children need to help Dad during certain seasons of the year. During the off season, the children work hard on their schooling, and Dad helps them. During the farming season, the children do not do as much schoolwork except in the evening, as they are busy helping Dad during the day. The children have projects of their own with 4-H. They even raise their own crop, and market it.

Another family does their home schooling between their music lessons, since Dad is a professional musician and wants them to practice often. They love to play in the local orchestra. They really do not like math and have a tutor come once a week to help out.

A family with several children in high school has joined with two other home schooling families with high school students. They hired a tutor to review the high school science and math assignments, while Mother continues to teach the younger children.

One family has high school children active in drama, and the lessons are often done in the theater. In another family, the high school girls are active in being "Candy Stripers," volunteers in a local hospital, and schoolwork is arranged around their schedule. In many families, picketing abortion clinics and participating in Rescues is an important part of the Catholic social work.

In another family, two high schoolers are being paid as they serve as apprentices, the girl in office and bookkeeping, the boy in welding and machine work.

In one family, the boys work several hours a week with the local priest, helping around the church and rectory. A high school boy in another family helps out as a teacher's aide at a local school for children with special problems.

In most families, home schooling methods change as children grow older. Methods and scheduling change with different children. While one child did well working in his own bedroom in quiet, another child seems to work better at the dining room table with sounds all around him.

Time causes us to change, and time causes our children to change. Dads may be more or less available for helping with the home schooling as they change jobs.

As is obvious, a typical day for any one family is not a typical day with any other family. As each family is unique in its gifts and talents, in its weaknesses and interests, so is the home schooling schedule for that family shaped. It is also shaped by the occupations of the parents, some children learning farming and animal husbandry, others learning programs on the computer, while still others learn to knit sweaters and sew beautiful dresses.

My own family

People often ask me how my seven boys were home schooled. So here is my typical but unique story. This is presented only as an example of what one family has done. It may give you some thoughts about your own situation, but it is certainly not presented as an ideal for you or any other family.

When I first started home schooling, I was working as an elementary school principal for a private parent-operated Catholic school which I founded along with some other Catholic parents. My younger children attended. (Later, I home schooled all my children.) My three oldest boys were in high school at this time. They worked at their studies, each on his own grade level, while I was away. When I came home at four o'clock, I looked over their work, asked them questions, or they asked me questions. On Sundays, I would spend the afternoon grading and writing out their assignments for the week.

My sons did a great deal of school work. They worked the regular school hours, and were able to read extra books from the library or do extra reading in the encyclopedia. They read a great deal of literature and political works since these are my main interests. We went to the library every week.

A few years later, in another house, I had left my job as principal and was home schooling full time with all my children, except for my oldest who was in college. We had one large room where most of the boys had their own tables and scheduled assignments. They worked on their own grade levels, and I would rotate my time with them.

A younger boy was in a separate room with a neighbor

boy in the same grade level. I taught them both, with some help from a friend on occasion. My youngest simply played wherever I was.

In a third house, the boys were older and helped a great deal with household chores. I was going back to work, by this time, on a limited basis. Two, and then three of the boys were in college. Much of my professional work was done at home in the evenings. I continued to have each boy work on his own grade level most of the time, but did have them work together on science projects.

My husband up to this point had helped only occasionally, but now he began to spend more time helping the boys in math and history. The older boys began to help the younger boys, especially in math.

The schooling schedule was very similar in all three situations. We started the day with prayer: Morning Offering, Litany of the Sacred Heart, and a reading of the life of the saint for the day. Our first class was always religion, with math always the second subject. Subjects the children needed me for, such as English and Reading, always followed in the morning. For English, I often used a blackboard for diagramming, which made it more fun for my boys. I listened to the boys read each day, if only for 15 minutes, up to eighth grade. Proper pronunciation and inflection seems important to determine a degree of comprehension. The assignments in the readers at the end of the selections I considered very important.

Phonics, spelling, and vocabulary were done in the late morning or early afternoon. My boys tended to do these easily, though they were often careless with spelling. They needed more practice with their handwriting, so the spelling and vocabulary were handwriting lessons also.

In the early years, we said the daily Rosary in the evening, but I realized the children were too tired. So we decided to say the Rosary at 11:00 AM, and whoever was home (from college) would join in. After lunch, we would say more prayers, the Angelus and the Act of Contrition especially. While we tried to say prayers at the end of the school day, this did not work out as the children often finished at different times.

The boys did science and history on their own in the afternoon, though further supplemental reading was done regularly in the encyclopedia and with library books. Dad would occasionally take the children to a museum or historical area.

When I lived near a library with films, we would obtain films every week, mostly on science topics. I really missed this once we moved to a small town.

Afternoon was spent doing easy workbook-type assignments. Physical education was a subject integrated throughout the day, since my boys were active between classes, jumping rope being a favorite. My boys became experts at jump rope tricks. Though the boys went outdoors during lunchtime, they otherwise were not allowed in the yard until after three o'clock. I felt more comfortable without questions being asked by neighbors.

Some of my children had piano lessons, which was the music curriculum. Otherwise, it was not regular, though my husband is a semi-professional musician. They daily heard good music on the piano. Art was more of an inspirational topic; they did it when they or we were inspired. We always did projects related to the important holidays and liturgical feasts: Thanksgiving hats, Christmas decorations, Easter posters.

No matter what the arrangement for the home school assignments, we always had daily prayer, scheduled at regular times of the day. I myself attended Mass frequently, almost daily. My boys did not attend daily Mass with me, though they went on occasion. This was because the Mass was fairly late and caused too much disruption with the home schooling, and because I did not want my children being outside during school hours.

My last situation was unusual. My two youngest children did their home schooling work in my office for the last few years.

One year, some of us local parents taught our high schoolers together for some subjects. I taught American literature, a father taught math and science, my husband taught history, a relative taught Latin, and a priest taught religion. In a couple of classes, it was mostly a supervisory situation. In other classes, we did more teaching.

It is obvious from my own experience, and from the many experiences that have been shared with me by home schooling mothers, that there are many ways to home school successfully. There is no typical home schooling situation, or even best home schooling situation. It is important that parents work out the schedule, methods, or programs that are best for their children.

As the year progresses

In some subjects, the children can quickly learn the pattern for a week, which remains the same for every week of the year. This is true for the Seton courses in Vocabulary, Spelling, and Handwriting. After a couple of weeks, the child knows the daily assignments, and should not need too much help. This is a help for the mother in the large family.

After you have been home schooling for a while, if you have a child who seems to dawdle or fool around or dreams away the time, you might consider scheduling the classes around meals and snacks. This is especially effective with boys. For instance, you can schedule a one-half hour math class before breakfast, two or three classes before a morning snack, two or three classes before lunch, and so on. Meals or snacks are not eaten until the assignment is done.

Of course, whether you have a small or large family, when you are making out your schedule, plan morning and afternoon prayer, the Rosary, and whatever other religious activities are appropriate according to the liturgical year. Daily Mass attendance is something we should all try to do.

Short classes

It is best for younger children to keep lessons short. Usually, more math will be learned in three 20-minute classes than a one hour class. Reading class can be divided up into a reading session, then a workbook or written assignment.

Do not have too long a school day. Home schooling is

far more intensive learning than in a classroom, so do not go past five or six hours total. For primary age children, many can do the work in three to four hours. It would be better to work on a Saturday morning, or to make your school year longer, than to have children work a very long day. After a certain amount of formal class time, children simply cannot absorb any more, so continuing becomes pointless. You certainly might include more hands-on learning to add variety. Using kitchen measurements, for instance, will help diversify the learning process for math, as a child helps with cooking a meal.

Integrate your housework

When you are making out your schedule, consider doing housework and home schooling at the same time. For instance, I used to listen to my children read or listen to their math facts while I washed the dishes or wiped off the kitchen counters. I would have the children working in the kitchen while I cooked. Admittedly, I have never been much of a housekeeper, but the boys helped with the housework.

By the way, after having my babies, I would often help my older children with their studies while I lay in bed nursing my baby. Just think of home schooling as an integral part of the normal Catholic family life.

Integrate their chores

Include household chores for the children in the daily home school schedule. This is especially important in the large family where there is so much to do and mothers will become exhausted if they try to do all the housework. Even a two-year-old child can feel important by doing some sort of job.

In my family, I found that my boys did not like chores after school hours. They preferred chores along with the schoolwork, between the subjects to break up their schoolwork, and also because when the school day was done, their chores were finished.

Another reason for having chores between classes is that studies have shown that children perform better mentally when physical exercise is interspersed with the lessons. A study reported in *Prevention* magazine showed that children's grades improved when short daily exercises were included between classes right in the classroom.

Potential interruptions

Many mothers of large families are very busy, and working Pro-Life activities into the busy schedule is fairly common. However, work outside the home should be kept to a minimum until the children are older. Of course, activities *with* the children, such as picketing abortion clinics, are important to teach Catholic values by example.

Do not let phone calls and other people's problems keep you from fulfilling your own priorities with your own children. Too many mothers spend so much time helping others that their own children suffer. Charity DOES begin at home!

Married children return home

Another situation happening with large families is that older children in their twenties, some even older and married with children, tend to come back home when they have problems. While this is fine, they must understand that you have responsibilities first with the younger children still needing guidance. If older children come back home and move in, they should be helping the whole family situation, not making more demands on you. Schedule them to help, either with classes or errands or housework, which is really a minimal request.

Location, location, location

Some families add an extra room to the house, or make a classroom from a family room, a garage, or a basement room. Some families use another building on the property, such as a garage or tool house. A large farming family in

New York use a barn. The children along with the parents can work to make this their special place for home schooling. It is very motivational for the children to do their schoolwork in the room or building which they worked so hard to make their own by decorating it themselves.

In locations such as a barn or family room, the children often work together; but keep in mind that children do need quiet time for some of their courses. For the large family, a basement recreation room or something similar is ideal, a room where the formal schoolwork is done during the day.

As many families have told us, home schooling is very adaptable to changes in location. Many families take the children with their books and lessons on vacations, or visits to elderly or sick family members, or on business trips. Lessons can be done while waiting in a doctor's office.

Grading

Parents sometimes complain about the time it takes to grade their children's work. A way to cut down on this time is to encourage your children to grade their own papers immediately after they have done their assignment. The advantage to this is that children can recall their thought processes when they answered their questions or problems, and thus can learn from their grading. In addition, self-grading develops honesty and usually accuracy. For the mother in a large family, it really cuts down on paperwork time.

A tip for saving time is for the children to mark off assignments in their plan book after they are done, corrected from the answer key, and then graded. This does not mean that Mother should not check the work, but answers can be spot-checked or randomly double-checked.

Home library

For the large family, it is especially useful to build up a family library, especially of Catholic books. With a large family and the many varied interests and demands, you will need your own library sooner or later. Purchase used books from the public library book sales, even encyclopedias and other reference books. Check for used books at thrift shops, at home schooling conventions, and at St. Vincent de Paul shops. Also, especially in Catholic areas, comb the garage sales for old but good Catholic books. Sometimes you can even find old textbooks, as well as saints' biographies.

Retired nuns may have old textbooks and other Catholic books hidden away. They may be willing to give them up to a good Catholic family. Contact local nursing homes for the retired or aged nuns.

Dictionaries are very important for children to learn to use at a very young age. You can buy Beginning Dictionaries, Intermediate, and Advanced Dictionaries, often used, at libraries and garage sales. Be sure there are plenty of dictionaries in the house. Insist that the children use them. Sometimes I think we should give prizes to the child who uses the dictionary the most often. (Of course, then you might have to deal with children saying, "Mother, the infant is ululating. Can someone placate him?")

Look for other used items, such as globes, atlases, microscopes, aquariums, bird cages, book cases, historical photographs or paintings, any educational equipment or games. Buy lamps, desks, and study tables at thrift stores.

A large family may want to invest in hobby shop projects, such as building a replica of a heart or an eye, or of the development of an unborn baby.

Local activities

Do not rush to enroll children in local activities. Some are fine, but many families register children in too many, to the point where the activities control family life. In a large family especially, formal outside social activities are not as necessary, or not necessary at all.

Further enrichment

In a large family, where Mother cannot listen to all the children read every day, or hear the answers for all the questions, have children use the tape recorder for reading, for proper inflection and pronunciation, for recording words for future tests in spelling and vocabulary, and for answering questions.

If parents attend home schooling conferences, usually tapes are made of the speeches or workshops. It may be helpful for children to listen to some of these tapes, especially if they cover ideas about learning subject matter, such as science.

In a large family, when you cannot spend the money for music lessons for everyone, spend the money to teach one child a musical instrument, then have that child teach some of the younger children. You could have one child take an arts and crafts class, and then come home and teach the other children his lessons.

If your children watch a television show, ask them to look up at least one thing in the encyclopedia which relates to the TV program, and share it with the family at dinnertime. This encourages the children to analyze the programs they watch for educational content.

A television show which is great for the home schooling family is *Mr. Wizard*. I myself never could get enthusiastic about science, so this program really filled a need. My boys loved it. They would watch the science projects and then try to do them. It was not unusual to have various projects either strewn about the house or hanging overhead!

A large family often does not have the money for field trips, or because of the busy schedule, it is seldom possible to find the time. In that case, consider mini-field trips to local businesses in town, such as to the bakery, print shop, or welding shop. Take the children to visit the post office when you need to purchase stamps, or the local upholstery shop when you buy fabric, or have the children watch the mechanics as you wait to have your car repaired. Look for local, no-cost, but educational field trips just in your regular trips around town.

Consider everything you do as a possible opportunity to teach your children.

And then there is the computer

For the large or small home schooling family, there is nothing like a computer to make home schooling easier. Purchase a computer, even if old and used. These are wonderful helps for the children. Word processing is valuable especially for boys who think faster than they can write. Boys will see better results and be happier to do schoolwork when they see good work on paper. (Using computers in home schooling is discussed at length in a later chapter.)

Structure versus non-structure

One of the topics buzzing around home schooling groups is the issue of structure versus non-structure in home schooling families. Looking through the home schooling literature, it seems that some programs advertise freedom and independence, others advertise high academics, some advertise character education, some the unit approach, some basic skills and content.

The programs which are unstructured, or using the unit approach, claim that structured programs are trying to bring the classroom into the living room. Those promoting programs which are structured are heard to say that the lack of structure could result in the possibility of basic skills or areas of knowledge "falling through the cracks."

Often, the unstructured programs or unit approach programs revolve the various subject lessons around an idea or concept. Christian programs, for instance, will take a concept of a virtue, such as patriotism or loyalty, and start with characters from the Bible who practice this virtue. Historical characters are studied who may demonstrate this virtue. Spelling words, vocabulary words, and historical readings may be taken from the Bible. Grammar lessons, such as the study of nouns, would be based on sentences from the Bible or historical readings.

Some unstructured programs tend to emphasize hands-on experiences, field trips, and "child-initiated" lessons. Sometimes the children pick their own "unit" to study, such as the Revolutionary War. Mother and children work together to plan lessons in other subject areas which can be derived from the Revolutionary War studies.

Proponents of this approach believe that children's interest level and motivation is high because the program is more child-directed. Because the motivation is high, even the spelling, vocabulary, and English are learned more thoroughly, they say, than in a structured approach.

Most of the well-known curriculum programs are structured, such as Pensacola Christian, Christian Liberty, Calvert, Home Study International, and Seton. These schools all have certain guidelines for study, require tests periodically, provide report cards and standardized testing, and offer teacher counseling services. Seton and Home Study International, which is a Seventh Day Adventist school, are accredited.

Obviously, in an unstructured program in which the studies are more child-directed or child-initiated, the child will be more motivated because he is more interested. The conclusion is that a consequence of the high motivation is a good education. If mothers are highly involved to make sure that all the skills are covered, this could be true. However, there is no question that many children have received excellent educations through the structured programs as well.

Certain home schoolers and home school leaders believe that the "burnout" experienced by some home schooling mothers is due to structured programs or the structured classroom approach. This is too simplistic. Burnout can be caused by lack of organization, lack of discipline, lack of support by the spouse, antagonism by family and friends, and personal and family problems. It also can be caused by the amount of work required by parents for an unstructured program.

We have had several families begin on a structured program, then go off the structure for a year, then return to the structure because they felt it was too difficult without the daily lessons. One mother, a well-educated professional, admitted she liked the accountability aspect of a structured program, which helped her to keep on track. She also found that her children were more motivated, especially the junior high and high school students, when they received papers back from Seton with grades and comments from a teacher.

It is my contention, however, that there is no one curriculum or method of curriculum for every student, for every family, or for every mother. If I were to claim there is a best answer for most home schooling families, it would be a balance between the structured and the non-structured approach. But, again, a basic premise of home education is that the best education is one tailored to the needs and abilities of the child. So the structure or no structure debate must be resolved by the parents.

Catholic educational history

There are advantages to both the structured and unstructured approaches that we Catholics should not forget. Formalized Catholic education was begun by the Catholic Church with the cathedral schools in Europe. From those schools came such great scholars as St. Albert and St. Thomas Aquinas. Down through the centuries, we can list thousands of highly educated Catholics, many Doctors of the Church as well as professional and scientific geniuses who were taught by the formal and structured Catholic schools.

It would be a denial of history, a denial of the achievements of the Western World, in fact, to deny the great education provided by the structured curricula of the Catholic schools and universities.

However, within the structure of the programs was an encouragement of creativity, creative thinking, and flexibility of methods.

Consider the *Summa Theologica* of St. Thomas Aquinas. St. Thomas had certain truths to teach, but he encouraged his students to ask questions. He first restated the questions, then he gave his basic teaching, such as the proofs for the existence of God, then he answered the questions. He encouraged questions and discussion among the students.

Think about the excellent convent schools in the United States. From the convent schools came great Catholic women leaders, women who volunteered their services for the community, in schools and hospitals, established Catholic charities for the poor, the sick, the elderly. Some became doctors and lawyers. The schools which taught them facts also taught them thinking skills, how to be creative, how to initiate projects, and perhaps most important, how to serve their neighbor.

Patrick Buchanan and William Bennett, two well-known Catholic political thinkers, are products of the superior Catholic school system. They attended structured Catholic schools. In fact, they both attended Gonzaga High School in Washington, D.C. Neither friend nor enemy could say that they are not thinkers, are not creative, are not well-educated and articulate speakers and writers. Yet they learned English using Loyola University's structured *Voyages in English* series, which promotes a high understanding of the English language as well as composition exercises. Within the composition exercises, creativity and original thought are fostered.

So what is the answer?

The answer is a balance between structure and non-structure. But this balance must be reached after a consideration of various factors. These factors include the age of the student, the learning ability, the best learning style for the student, the teacher-mother's ability, and the subject matter itself.

For instance, a kindergarten child does not need formal structure at all, unless kindergarten is required in a state. If so, probably there would need to be some structure in math and phonics, though the structure might consist of only 20 minutes a day in the morning for each subject, and perhaps 20 minutes in the afternoon.

Older children need more structure because certain skills and basic content should be learned. Every day the student should be reading, practicing his handwriting, phonics, and math drills, and nearly every day spelling and vocabulary. English Grammar needs to proceed more cautiously according to the maturity of the student, since this involves a higher degree of logical thinking. Composition exercises, however, should be started as early as first grade, with creative sentences and even short creative paragraphs. The structure involved would be the daily formal practice: the amount of time would tend to be regular, and the time of day should be regular.

Children want a certain amount of structure. It gives them stability and a sense of things being in order. How would we feel if some days Father had Mass at 8:00, sometimes 9:00, sometimes 10:00. We would quickly become frustrated and stop attending Mass! In the same way, children need to get up at a certain time, to eat at a certain time, to rest at a certain time. This promotes mental and physical health.

Structure regarding the time *of* a class, the amount of time *for* the class, and possibly even a routine for the class, such as for the study of spelling and vocabulary, will result in security and healthy progress in learning the material.

On the other hand, some classes lend themselves naturally to flexibility, such as science and history. In these subjects, the lessons may be closely followed, or there may be more creativity and ingenuity.

Science

The science program at Seton, for instance, has daily and weekly lessons with the textbook, but projects and experiments are encouraged. Some families do not use the textbook at all. We have farm families whose children become involved in 4-H projects which are their science class for the year. Some raise animals, some grow experimental vegetables, some work with Dad on educational projects, such as photography. My own children, due to my working-mother hours, have watched the *Mr. Wizard* programs and have done many of the science experiments from that program.

While our history courses include a textbook and daily lesson assignments, field trips to historical museums or famous battlefields are encouraged. Historical or biographical films or videos are available. Such activities can enrich the courses, can supplement the courses, and sometimes actually replace lessons or chapters in a text.

In religion, especially with the large family, we encourage flexibility by having two or more children learn the same subject matter at the same time, but do individual assignments at their own level, or do a project together as the parent decides is best. The children may all discuss the Eighth Commandment with Mother or Father, but perhaps the older children should read more details in their text, the youngest may draw a colorful picture of a child returning his library book on time, and the middle child may need to work on memorizing a catechism answer.

Most parents, on a structured or unstructured program, group the children for art, music, and physical education classes. Some home schooling support groups are working toward joint arts and crafts classes, or physical education activities, or even a joint science class.

At Seton, while we have a structured program, if parents want a grade on the report card, and their child is involved in a support group class, we ask that a description of the course is sent to us, along with evidence of work done, the average number of hours per week, and a grade based on the teacher's evaluation. The above flexible arrangements offer our families the benefits of the structured program as well as the advantages of the unstructured courses.

Testing and grades

One aspect which parents do not like about a structured program is what they consider an emphasis on testing and grades. There are advantages and disadvantages with testing and grades. Advantages include helping mothers and students stay on a fairly regular schedule, and having a "proof" of consistent progress. In some states, formal testing and a report card are either required, or serve as a protection against hassling by local or state education authorities. The advantage of no testing and grades is a lack of pressure on mothers and students to perform in a certain way or by a certain time. Of course, families at Seton who choose not to test or to have grades on a report card are free to choose this option.

After high school

If a parent chooses not to enroll in a program for the high school years, the parent should become fully informed about what is expected by the college or vocational school which the student is likely to attend. The college should be asked what they expect, not only in the way of curriculum, but also for report cards and standardized testing. The military and military academies are very difficult to enter at this time without being enrolled in an accredited program.

It is most important for all of us to remember that, especially in these difficult times, God gives each parent the graces to make the decisions for his or her own children. It is not for us to judge an individual parent's decision about the methods chosen.

Eternal Word Television Network

Many families do not have televisions, but I do recommend it if you can get a Catholic station, such as EWTN, Mother Angelica's station. Some of these programs can be scheduled into your home schooling day. If you cannot obtain this Catholic cable station in your area by cable, you may wish to purchase a satellite dish. The station is on 24 hours a day, seven days a week. You can have your satellite fixed so that only EWTN will come in. It brings into your home fine Catholic people to encourage you and your children to live the Catholic life.

EWTN presents a beautiful sung Mass four times a day, the Divine Mercy Chaplet every day at 3 P.M., the Holy Rosary three times a day, Stations of the Cross, Benediction, the Sacred Heart Litany, the Litany of the Blessed Virgin Mary, and various meditations throughout the day.

Priests presenting fine programs for the different members of the family are Father Brian Mullady (excellent for understanding the nature of Jesus Christ and the complexities of the Ten Commandments); Father Benedict Groeschel from the Bronx, who tells how to be holy in down-to-earth terms; Father George Rutler, another Bishop Sheen; Father

Kenneth Roberts, who talks to today's teenagers about being young and holy; Father Matthew Habiger, a former college professor currently with Human Life International who presents difficult topics in easy language; Father Ray Bourque, who conducts us on trips to places in the Holy Land; Archbishop Hannan, whose show presents the latest political and social news involving Catholics around the world; and Father Mitch Pacwa on the New Age movement.

In addition, there are many fine Catholic laymen who have valuable shows.

For the home schooling family, these people make the Catholic Faith alive and vibrant and meaningful for our children. They support the very ideas of faith and culture which we are trying to convey, but which often seem foreign or "weird" in the midst of a pagan society.

Conclusion

If I could say that anything is typical about home schooling families, it is that most are doing their best to keep up a strong prayer life. Most have scheduled prayer, many attend Mass during the week. As I visit families in my travels, I am impressed by the humble lifestyles and fervent dedication to their children, to God, and to their church.

We all need to respect other families and their methods. At the same time, in our own family, we need to adjust to the different personalities as well as the needs and abilities of each child. Ultimately this will result in a generation of Catholic adults who see the value of individualizing the learning process, and the value of each individual as a child of God. Ultimately it will result in a better Christian society, both academically and spiritually.

Chapter 7:
The Sacramental Life

The most important key for success in home schooling is living the authentic Catholic sacramental life in the family. The sacramental life means not only the regular reception of the Sacraments of the Holy Eucharist and Penance, but also the daily practice of using sacramentals to help us to live the life of prayer and to celebrate the feasts of the liturgical year.

The Catholic home has been termed the "domestic church" by the Second Vatican Council, in some previous church documents, and in later church documents. If our home is to be truly a "domestic church," then using sacramentals and revolving our family activities around the liturgical year is not only appropriate but the best plan for a family to live the authentic Catholic family life.

The Church dispenses the seven Sacraments as a direct means for its individual members to receive sanctifying grace from God. This Sanctifying Grace, as well as sacramental graces, are necessary for each member of the home schooling family. We can receive graces also through the sacramentals, which are approved by the Church, but which we can use in our own home.

The Holy Eucharist

Daily reception of Jesus in the Sacrament of the Holy Eucharist is most important for the Catholic home schooling family. Receiving the sacrament of the Holy Eucharist can guarantee successful Catholic home schooling. To repeat, if you want to be successful in your Catholic home schooling, attend Mass every day, and receive the Holy Eucharist, preferably with your children.

If you cannot attend Mass, say the Mass prayers at home with your children. Ask Our Lord to come to you and your children in a Spiritual Communion. This is an official teaching of the Church, based on Galatians 5:6, "Faith that worketh by charity," that those who greatly desire to receive Jesus in the Holy Eucharist do benefit and profit to some degree by the Sacrament. The Council of Trent declared that the Faithful can receive from a Spiritual Communion "if not the entire, at least very great benefits." On Eternal Word Television Network, when the Mass from the Monastery of the Angels is televised every day, Sister encourages the viewers to receive Jesus spiritually, and leads the viewers in a special Spiritual Communion prayer.

We Catholic home schooling families are in the forefront of the spiritual battle to save souls, the Church, and the nation. We need Jesus with us every day in this battle against the spiritual forces of evil.

The graces from the sacrament of the Holy Eucharist help us deal with the daily worries and frustrations of every family. Many of us have learned that it is not so much the big crisis that wears us down but the constant little aggravations. Many of us are called to be Saints by dealing with small but constant daily problems.

Jesus wants us to show our love for Him by visiting Him and having Him come to us every day. Jesus did not establish the sacrament of the Holy Eucharist only to have His friends ignore Him in this sacrament He has so lovingly given us. Coming to us in Holy Communion, Jesus shows His extreme love for us as He wants to be with us, as He wants to give Himself to us, and we should show Him our gratitude by receiving Him.

The most important event that is happening in your town each day is the coming of the Son of God, Jesus Christ in the Blessed Sacrament. How can we not be there? How can we not be there to receive Him?

For those of us who are able to attend Mass every day, we need to pray for all our fellow home schooling families. As members of the Mystical Body of Christ, they can utilize our prayers and the resulting graces. This kind of charity on our part will obtain great favors from Jesus and Mary for our own home schooling.

With our society drowning in its own immorality, the command by Jesus to be a light and leaven in society takes on new meaning. We simply cannot survive and promote the Faith without the DAILY help of Jesus Christ Himself present within us. As Father John Hardon so often remarks, for Catholic families to survive as authentic Catholic families, we need to make extraordinary efforts to live holy lives.

We must take our children to daily Mass, and teach them about the meaning of Mass. The closer we bring our children to Jesus, and teach them about His death for our sake, the more they will love Him and obey His commands, and obey our commands. With obedient and respectful children, we will have successful home schooling.

Home schooling burnout, much talked about at state home schooling conferences, results when children are difficult, either in the training of the will or the teaching of the academics. It also occurs because mothers struggle to meet the many demands of home schooling, housework, cooking, and taking care of the needs of their husbands. But if the home schooling mother can develop her spiritual life by receiving Jesus daily, and the home schooling children can come to know and to love Jesus more by receiving Him in the Blessed Sacrament, burnout is much less likely to happen.

As we teach our children about the Sacrament of the Holy Eucharist, we need to relate it to their home schooling. We can better understand Jesus and the world which God created as we study our books and become educated. The more we know about God, the more we can love Him and serve Him properly. Once our children understand the relationship between learning from our Catholic books and learning about God, there should be fewer conflicts in the home schooling family.

The more we love Jesus, the more worthily we can receive Him in Holy Communion. As we receive Him more worthily, He will give us the graces to learn even more about Him, to love Him more deeply, and thus to do better in our schoolwork, in our chores, and in our relationship with the other members of the family.

It is a theological principle that the more we utilize the graces we receive, the more graces we will be given. So the more graces we receive from the daily reception of the Holy

Eucharist, the more graces we will obtain to fulfill our teaching duties. The more graces our children receive, the more graces they will obtain to be good students and good children, thus ensuring successful home schooling.

Home schooling for the Catholic family is most successful through the reception of the Holy Eucharist by parents and children. In the Catholic home filled with Jesus daily, the atmosphere of love and spiritual growth will permeate both home schooling and the whole domestic environment.

Penance

The Sacrament of Penance is one of our biggest helps in living the Catholic life on a daily basis. Some people want to do only the minimum required by the Church, going to Confession once a year if one is in mortal sin. Some Catholics try to follow the recommendation of going to Confession at least once a month.

Many years ago, I decided to go to Confession every week during Lent. It changed my life. I discovered how many imperfections I had been overlooking. When you examine your conscience each night, and add them up each Saturday, you really have a pretty good list of careless faults. You begin to realize your unkind and unnecessary remarks, unkind thoughts, and moments of impatience. With only a monthly Confession, you tend to overlook the little remarks, thoughts, and faults, and remember only the unkind acts. The bottom line is that we are all called to be Saints, to be perfect, as Our Lord Himself commanded. Weekly or bi-weekly Confession is almost a requirement according to many Saints if we want to be serious about trying to live the perfect life.

If we are really aiming to be the best possible Catholic family, it is important that we try to go to Confession each week, all year long. Because of the paganism of our environment, we are likely to become desensitized to sin. Receiving the Sacrament of Penance every week will help us and our children to concentrate on strengthening our virtues and ultimately on improving our Catholic family life. As everyone in the family is working together to improve, as we discuss the imperfections with the children at bedtime, or in the car on the way to Confession, we help each other in a calm way to become Saints.

St. Francis de Sales taught that if you are trying to rid yourself of a fault, you need to practice the opposite virtue, and in an extraordinary way. For instance, if your fault is that you tend to say unkind things about a person, then you should make a point first, not to say unkind things, but second, to say especially kind things even when it is not necessary.

In a way, home schooling is following the directive of St. Francis de Sales. When we know that what our children are learning in school is detrimental to their spiritual welfare, it is not sufficient to simply take them out of the sex education class. We need to do everything we possibly can to give our children the very best Catholic education. We know it is a matter of sin to expose our children to anti-Catholic values five days a week. But it is a matter of heroic virtue to take on the total responsibility of teaching our children at home to be sure that they receive the very best Catholic education we can provide.

We need to relate our home schooling to the Sacrament of Penance. Our children need to understand first, that it is our duty as parents to teach them, and second, that it is their duty as children to obey us and learn more about obeying God. If the children do not obey us in their studies or in their daily chores, then they have committed a sin. When you help your children review their sins for Confession, help them see that refusing to do their work, complaining or whining while doing their work, doing their work in a sloppy or careless manner, not applying themselves, and daydreaming do not please God and are a shirking of their responsibility.

As we proceed through each day, we should be reminding our children when they commit a sin to be sorry and to tell it in Confession. When a child hits a brother, we must remind him to be sorry and confess it. When a child is disobedient about doing a chore, we need to remind him to be sorry and to confess it. When a child refuses to do his math, we need to remind him to be sorry and to confess it. In the evening at prayer time, sins could be reviewed with each child, appropriate to his age, and there could be a discussion about how to avoid the same sin again. This should not be a constant nagging, but a spiritual uplift.

Some parents believe that while the child should be corrected at the time of the offense, a discussion about the religious implications should take place later when the child is not upset about the wrongdoing. Whenever the discussion seems suitable, spiritual writers have always encouraged a nightly examination of conscience and Act of Contrition. This is a good habit for all of us, adults and children.

Home schooling will be successful in a Catholic family pursuing the virtuous life through a daily examination of conscience and weekly or bi-weekly Confession.

Baptism

If you are having babies every other year, your children should be attending the rite of the Sacrament of Baptism fairly often. If not, be sure to take your children to the parish church when a Baptism is scheduled, and teach them about this essential Sacrament. Explain the Sacrament, going over the words of the rite:

> You have asked to have your child baptized. In doing so, you are accepting the responsibility of training him (her) in the practice of the Faith. It will be your duty to bring him (her) up to keep God's Commandments as Christ taught us, by loving God and our neighbor.

It is clear that home schooling is an acceptance in the deepest way of the responsibility given to parents at the baptism of their children. If you read these words of the Sacrament and explain this to your children, they are more likely to be obedient children.

The priest in the Sacrament of Baptism prays that the parents and godparents serve as good examples of faith for the child being baptized. Explain to your children that the best way for parents to serve as good examples is to spend time with their children. Home schooling is the best method of education because it gives parents the most time to be good examples to their children. A Baptism is an excellent time to review the Catholic truths on Adam and Eve and on Original Sin, which is now to be washed off the soul of the little brother or sister. Teach your children about their godparents and their important role in your family.

After reading about the various times when God used water for the benefit of His people, the priest continues the Rite of Baptism with the Renunciation of Sin and Profession of Faith. The parents and godparents are told:

> You must make it your *constant* care to bring him (her) up in the practice of the Faith. See that the divine life which God gives him (her) is kept safe from the poison of sin, to grow always stronger in his (her) heart.

It strikes me that constant care means home schooling. There is little opportunity for constant care if a child leaves the house on a school bus at 7:30 in the morning and returns at 4:00 o'clock in the afternoon, too tired to discuss anything at all, least of all religion.

Certainly one has only to turn on the television or visit a school to see the nearby "poison of sin." Notice that we parents are admonished not only to keep our child away from sin, but, in agreement with St. Francis de Sales, we are to do something positively good to make the practice of the Faith as well as divine life "grow always stronger." This is the purpose of Catholic home schooling.

After you have discussed all this with your children, the whole family can participate in a special ceremony, either on a birthday, or on an anniversary of a Baptism, or at a Baptism of a baby, or whenever it seems appropriate, to have a Renewal of Baptismal Vows. Father could repeat the questions and the rest of the family could answer.

> Do you reject Satan?
> *I do.*
> And all his works?
> *I do.*

And all his empty promises?
I do.
Do you believe in God, the Father almighty,Creator of
Heaven and earth?
I do.
Do you believe in Jesus Christ, His only Son, Our Lord,
Who was born of the Virgin Mary, was crucified, died,
and was buried, rose from the dead, and is now seated
at the right hand of the Father?
I do.
Do you believe in the Holy Spirit, the holy Catholic
Church, the communion of Saints, the forgiveness of
sins, the resurrection of the body, and life everlasting?
I do.

As you go over the words of the Sacrament, explain how
Baptism, Catholic family life, and home schooling are related. For instance, if we Catholics renounce the devil and
enter God's family at Baptism, then we must avoid sin and
perform virtuous acts as we grow up, and, as our catechism
says, live according to the teachings of the Church. As our
children see their admission into the Church family through
the Sacrament of Baptism, they more clearly understand their
role and obligation in regard to learning more about their
Catholic Faith through home schooling.

Confirmation

In Confirmation, the baptized young person receives the
Holy Spirit in a deeper way, is strengthened in grace, and
"sealed" or marked as a soldier of Jesus Christ. Most children respond eagerly to the idea that they are made soldiers
of Christ at Confirmation. Teach your children about St.
Francis of Assisi, who thought he wanted to be a soldier of
his city, but soon learned how to be a soldier of Christ.
Teach your children about St. Ignatius of Loyola, who was
a soldier until he was thirty years old and then put on the
armor of poverty and humility. Teach your children about
St. George, a young soldier who advanced in the army but
who rebuked the Emperor for persecuting the Christians, and

then became a soldier of Christ.

Explain that Confirmation strengthens virtues that help youth become soldiers of Christ, such as courage, loyalty, moral strength, and strength against temptations. Use a catechism and explain how each virtue can help in their studies and how they can grow in each one through their studies.

Teach your children that while the seeds of the Seven Gifts of the Holy Spirit are infused at Baptism, they are made fully operative in the Sacrament of Confirmation with their cooperation. These gifts are wisdom, understanding, counsel, fortitude, knowledge, piety, and fear of the Lord. If these gifts are explained to your children each year, and how they relate to home schooling, the children will be more inclined toward home schooling.

Point out that home schooling is in some respects like boot camp, employing weapons both for the mind to learn about God and the will to love and obey God. My boys took this very seriously. One of my boys investigated the possibility of joining one of the orders of Knighthood. He thought there should still be an order of Knights to fight evil around the world, and was disappointed to discover that none still exists which actually does battle!

Another one of my sons became a Marine because of his concern to fight for Christian values and against atheistic Communism. He lobbied for the Afghan freedom fighters, and on his own, visited them on the front line of war in Afghanistan. He discussed with them the concept of hating the sin but loving the sinner, or at least praying for the sinner's conversion. They were sure he was crazy! Later, he served in Desert Storm, and took part in the ground assault and the battle for the airport in Kuwait City. Then, while working on a Doctorate in Philosophy, he was a lobbyist for the Bosnians in Washington, D.C. He saw all these activities as being a Soldier of Christ.

One of the favorite movies around my house was *Cyrano de Bergerac*. It is the story of a soldier who fights for honor, an actor and writer who defends virtue and traditional values, a man who sacrifices his own happiness for the happiness of the girl he loves and a friend he cares about. Cyrano is a Christian gentleman, whose white plume represents his desire to live the highest standards of the virtuous life. A movie like this is great for discussing Confirmation.

Take the children to see a Confirmation at your church. Explain that at one time, the bishop gave a symbolic slap on the cheek as a reminder that we Soldiers of Christ must expect to suffer for Christ as we fight for His truths. This can be related to any current Pro-Life efforts which you and your family may be undertaking, as well as to our home schooling as a preparation for life as a Soldier of Christ.

Marriage

Explain the Sacrament of Matrimony to your children. In accord with its primary purpose, marriage gives a couple two equal responsibilities: to accept children and to educate their children. Explain to your children that if they are disobedient or do not do their home schooling, it is difficult for you to fulfill your marriage duty. Some of the papal documents on marriage could be explained to the children which faithfully expound on the responsibilities of teaching and training children.

Take the children to see a wedding at the parish church at a time when you can explain the ceremony. Impress on them the formality and seriousness of the Sacrament. Let them understand the duty you have before God, from the Sacrament of Matrimony, to educate them: that you have made a solemn promise before God and the Church to be responsible for educating the children whom God gives you.

If children realize that you have a command from God through the sacrament of Matrimony to teach them, and they have a consequent responsibility to learn from you, they are not as likely to be disobedient or rebellious. And you will have successful Catholic home schooling.

Extreme Unction, or Anointing of the Sick

Extreme Unction or Anointing of the Sick should be explained to your children for many reasons, but each year it should be related to the home schooling effort. This sacrament helps us to focus on eternity. This is a good time to discuss the shortness of life and this temporal abode. Emphasize that our ultimate aim is to be happy with Jesus in Heaven.   Such a discussion can easily be led into home schooling and our emphasis on the eternal truths, versus the schools, whose usual and main emphasis is on this world and *its measures* of success.

Once children understand these differences in the schools' this-world view versus Catholic home schooling's eternal-world view, the likelihood of rebelliousness and disobedience is lessened.

Holy Orders

Home schooling gives children the opportunity to grow spiritually in the Faith without being pressured by teachers or fellow students to conform to current social values. More than one mother has told me that because of the home schooling, a very young son, still in primary grades, began to talk about becoming a priest. More than one parent has told me about a son who wants to learn Latin, or who practices saying the Mass, or who wants to dress like a priest. It is not unusual in a Catholic home schooling family for boys in elementary or junior high levels to avidly read biographies of saints.

Boys and girls can be taught the value of the priesthood and religious life. The best way is to read about and discuss the lives of the Saints. Even while they are growing up, our children should be concerned about bringing the knowledge of Jesus Christ to others. Our home schooling way of life can help each family member to grow spiritually so that whether or not a child enters religious life, he or she can still help others to come to know and love Jesus, and even convert to the Catholic Faith.

Catholic home schooling families are to build up Christ in the domestic church and bring Him to society through their children. Therefore we parents need to discuss the catechism and the Bible with our children to emphasize that only priests can offer the Mass and administer the wonderful gifts of the Sacrament of Penance and the Holy Eucharist.

As we highlight the value of service to others in the priesthood and religious life, our high school children should be encouraged to help at local rest homes for the aged and other similar places. Home schooling gives the flexibility for our children to choose these special valuable works.

There is no question that all seven Sacraments should be meaningful in the lives of our children. As they understand the responsibilities of each of these Sacraments, as they regularly attend Mass, receive Holy Communion daily or frequently, and go to Confession each week or every other week, such good families, struggling to be authentically Catholic, will not be disappointed in the abundant graces bestowed by God.

The Sacramentals

While the sacramental life means ideally the daily reception of the Holy Eucharist and weekly Confession, the sacramental life also means the daily use of sacramentals.

Sacramentals are a part of our authentically Catholic cultural heritage which have, unfortunately, fallen out of favor in the modern world. Yet sacramentals are an important supplement for the practice of our daily Catholic life, and, in some cases, may be the only way for some families to maintain the sacramental life during the week between Sunday Masses.

Our catechism concentrates on the doctrines and morals of the Church, but also includes a brief chapter on sacramentals. We are taught that "Sacramentals are holy things or actions of which the Church makes use to obtain for us from God, through her intercession, spiritual and temporal favors."

The catechism teaches us that sacramentals are signs reminding us of God, of the Saints, and of Catholic truths. While Sacraments were instituted by Jesus Christ as a direct means of obtaining sanctifying and sacramental graces, sacramentals were instituted by the Church to obtain graces for us indirectly. The chief benefits from the sacramentals are actual graces, the forgiveness of venial sins, the remission of temporal punishment, health of body and material blessings, and protection from evil spirits.

Catholic home schooling parents should begin using sacramentals with their children if they are not using them now. It is humbling to realize that God, standing behind the declarations of His Church, is willing to forgive venial sins and remit temporal punishment due to sin through the use of sacramentals. This is a fantastic gift which needs to be taught to our children and used by them for their own spiritual benefit.

The catechism explains that the chief sacramentals are blessings by priests and bishops, exorcisms, and blessed objects of devotion. The most popular blessed objects of devotion are the Rosary and the Scapular. Other blessed objects are holy water, candles, ashes, palms, crucifixes, medals, relics, images or statues of Our Lord, the Blessed Mother, and the Saints. A church building, Benediction, novenas, and the Stations of the Cross are also considered sacramentals. The catechism concludes by encouraging us to use these sacramentals with faith and devotion.

Take the time to read about these blessed objects in the *The Catholic Encyclopedia* or books available from TAN publishers. The history of the Rosary, the Blessed Mother's appearances, and the many miraculous events in history due to the Rosary are all fantastic teaching opportunities to impress on our children the value of an authentic Catholic sacramental life. *The Catholic Encyclopedia* lists all the various types of scapulars, with their many colors and associations with various religious orders, not to mention the miraculous events that have occurred as a result of people wearing scapulars.

No one can guarantee that Catholic home schooled children will be perfect because they say a daily Rosary and wear a Scapular. However, from my own experience and from what I hear from parents on the phone, children living the sacramental life are more likely to be good and obedient children. In fact, several parents have admitted to me that the spiritual growth of their innocent young children has been a humbling experience. Some of us Catholic home schooling parents have come to a new understanding, though admittedly inadequate, of the spiritual life of very young Saints, such as St. Therese, the Little Flower.

Sacramentals help us to create the domestic church in our home as the Church has always asked Catholic families to do. We need to redecorate our home with sacramentals to make it a Catholic home. The Catholic Church has traditionally wanted families to surround themselves with reminders of the Faith. This goes back to the time when Moses spoke to the Jewish people about obeying the Ten Commandments. Moses said that God wanted signs of their faith on the doorposts, on the doors, on the entrances to the house. They were to wear signs on their foreheads and on their wrists. These physical signs were to be not only a witness to belief in His truths, they also served as a moment-to-moment reminder of God and that He belongs in our moment-to-moment household activities and thoughts.

Our Seton chaplain, Father Robert Hermley, said that when he was growing up, they had so many religious items in the house that the non-Catholic children in the neighborhood called their home "the holy store." It is not a coincidence that Father and his brother both became priests.

Living the authentic Catholic life means not only receiving the Sacraments, but surrounding ourselves in our homes with sacramentals as reminders of our Faith, as continual opportunities to immerse ourselves in Jesus and His Blessed Mother, in His Saints, and in His doctrinal and moral truths. St. Francis de Sales said that if one wishes to lead a devout life, things and events of our daily life should lead us to think about God and His attributes. If our surroundings encourage us, we and our children will more easily be led to such admirable thoughts.

An example

Let me briefly mention my own home as an example, since I am sometimes asked, of a home with religious articles. In the living room, I have used the fireplace mantle as our "altar" where I have two sculptured Stations of the

Cross which were removed from a parish church that was being remodeled. Relics and holy pictures are there also, including a cross, the type to be used when someone needs to receive Extreme Unction or Anointing of the Sick. An original painting of the Blessed Mother, a large antique painting of St. Rita, and a three-paneled painting of Our Lady of Perpetual Help are on my living room walls.

Every room in my home has religious statues, photographs, and relics. Both my "china" cabinets are filled with religious statues, primarily of the Blessed Mother. The dining room table centerpiece is a statue of the Baby Jesus with an angel kneeling over Him. An angel sits over my stove, and a statue of the Sacred Heart on my kitchen sink.

My collection is the result of years of visiting garage sales, St. Vincent de Paul shops, parish church sales, religious goods stores, and every conceivable place to purchase religious items. My mother always has had her home filled with religious statues, pictures, and relics, and continues to have an elaborate altar. Now my sons bring me religious items. My son Paul brought religious statues from Spain. Friends and Seton families send religious gifts from around the country; these are placed around the Seton offices.

All my children, seven sons, are practicing Catholics who go to Mass frequently. I have never had a rebellious son. It is a miracle, of course, the kind of miracle that comes to almost every Catholic family who daily works to live the Catholic life by receiving the Sacraments frequently as a family and by spending time in family prayers. We are not a perfect family, by any means, but we know what we are about and work to stay on the narrow road.

If our homes are not clearly identifiable as Catholic to anyone walking into the living room, we are not following the directives of God to His people, nor the will of the Church. The Catholic environment of our home will help all the family members to be good and virtuous. On more than one occasion I can remember saying something like, "Don't say that in front of the picture of the Blessed Mother. Do you want her to feel bad?"

Father John Hardon, who often speaks about Catholic

family life, encourages our families to have statues, pictures, and medals of the Blessed Mother in our homes. He also recommends that family members join the Association of the Miraculous Medal. The Miraculous Medal received its name because so many miracles have happened for those who wear the medal. The design of the medal was given by the Blessed Mother to St. Catherine Laboure in 1830 in France. The medal reads, "O Mary, conceived without sin, pray for us who have recourse to thee."

The Enthronement

Catholic home schooling families are rediscovering an old tradition: Consecration of the Family to the Sacred Heart through an Enthronement ceremony. This is a family devotion and ceremony growing out of the Promises of the Sacred Heart of Jesus to St. Margaret Mary. The purpose is to have the family recognize the reign of the Sacred Heart in their home, to be detached from worldly goods, and to try to imitate the virtues of the Holy Family. A picture or a statue of the Sacred Heart is to have a special place of honor. A priest usually comes to the home, and blesses the statue or picture as the Sacred Heart is officially enthroned as King of the family. The words of consecration and the ceremony are approved by the popes, who have granted a partial indulgence, with a plenary indulgence under the usual conditions of having been to Confession and Holy Communion and prayed for the intentions of the Holy Father (at least one Our Father and one Hail Mary) within several days, before or after the Enthronement.

Usually the Enthronement ceremony is done on the Feast of the Sacred Heart or of Christ the King, or on a First Friday, or on the occasion of a First Communion. It is usually done after a Mass at the parish church, though sometimes Mass is said at the home before the ceremony. While the Act of Consecration is the required part of the ceremony, families often say the Litany of the Sacred Heart and sing appropriate hymns. Some families invite relatives and friends, and have a little social gathering afterwards.

The liturgical year

Many sacramentals with appropriate prayers should be used in conjunction with the liturgical year. The liturgical year, starting with Advent, takes us through the history of mankind awaiting Jesus our Redeemer, and then through the life of Jesus Christ. This is a wonderful way for us to grow spiritually, but best of all, a joyful way to teach our children how to live and practice the authentic Catholic family life through the year.

In our Seton lesson plans for Art classes, we suggest many arts and crafts activities through the liturgical year which relate to the feast days. We especially encourage murals or mobiles or other arts and crafts projects which all the children can work on together. One project, for instance, is to obtain different-colored felt and to construct a banner with symbols of each Apostle.

Advent

Certain traditional Catholic practices can be started and maintained over the years to help us better understand and love our Catholic Faith. During Advent, the making of the Advent wreath is a very special event. It can be made one year, and simply added to or refreshed in the following years. Making these traditional items as a family, and then using them the following years brings back memories, and is a unique treasure for *our* family. You can start out with something simple, but as the years go by, add more purple velvet ribbons, and bunches of wheat and grapes, real or otherwise to the wreath.

The nightly lighting of the candles on the wreath and saying the Advent prayers make our home seem more like the domestic church! If you miss Mass any of the days, you may want to recite the appropriate Mass prayers for the day. In addition, the Daughters of St. Paul sell Advent calendars which include daily Bible readings or illustrations. These little calendars, with doors which are to be opened each day of Advent, are especially exciting for the little children.

Many families start a Christmas Crib for Baby Jesus, which is empty at the beginning of Advent, but every day each member of the family adds a piece of straw, representing a very small secret sacrifice, a gift which the person makes in preparation for Christmas. By Christmas morning the Crib is filled with straw and ready for the Baby Jesus.

Father Charles Fiore, who often speaks at home schooling conferences, told us about a family which takes the statue of the Baby Jesus at the beginning of Advent and puts it at a distance, outside the house. Each day of Advent, the Baby Jesus is moved a little closer to the Christmas Crib by one of the children until on Christmas morning, He reaches the Crib. These projects are hands-on learning experiences to help the children understand the real meaning of Advent and Christmas.

Shortly after Advent starts, the Feast of St. Nicholas is celebrated. In the Byzantine Rite, this feast is celebrated with a party for the children at the parish hall, with "St. Nicholas" giving out gifts to the children. In our domestic church, it needs to be a meaningful occasion, emphasizing the joy of giving of which St. Nicholas was such a good example. It can be a time for each member of the family to exchange a very small gift, or donate to the parish poor box.

Similar creative activities may be done for the Feast of the Immaculate Conception, and the Feast of Our Lady of Guadalupe. These feasts can be preceded by a novena, as well as by the Litany of the Blessed Virgin Mary. Eternal Word Television Network broadcasts the Mass on December 8th from the National Shrine of the Immaculate Conception.

Be sure to impress on your children the meaning of the Feast of the Immaculate Conception. The current popular reference to an unborn baby as a "fetus" may be "politically correct" terminology but should not be accepted by us. Our babies are babies from the moment they are conceived. The use of the word "fetus" is an attempt to dehumanize our babies. A "morning-after" pill kills a baby if one has come into existence by the will of God.

Visit shrines on the feast days. The *Catholic Almanac* lists the Catholic shrines by states. Find out which ones are near enough to visit, and take the whole family. If a shrine is not nearby, visit a parish church which is unfamiliar to the children. Teach your children about the Faith from the statues, pictures, and stained glass windows. Take a camera so you can remember your visit later and discuss the events depicted in the windows. A video camera would be great because it can adjust to the light coming through the stained glass. Unfortunately, most of these churches do not offer postcards. When you go on vacations or travel to other cities, visit shrines and historic churches.

As you celebrate liturgical feasts, precede them with a novena. A novena is nine days of prayer, usually specific prayers said in relation to a Saint or feast day. Sometimes these can be found at shrine bookstores or in older prayer books, but they also can be original prayers. TAN publishes an inexpensive booklet called *30 Favorite Novenas*. This includes novenas to the Blessed Mother, St. Joseph, St. Michael, and St. Anne.

A novena in preparation for Christmas should be started on December 16th. At the start of the nine days, you could put up a Jesse Tree, or a Christmas tree. On this tree, for nine days, the children can hang items to represent symbolically various Old Testament characters or events preceding the birth of Jesus. For instance, a fragment of an apple may represent Adam and Eve's Original Sin, which eventually led to the Incarnation. The slingshot of the boy David as he fought and killed Goliath, and the burning bush which Moses saw are favorite themes for children to draw for the tree.

After Christmas

Other days which can be celebrated with religious activities or projects are the Twelve Days after Christmas, the Feasts of St. Stephen, of the Holy Family, of Good King Wenceslaus, of St. John the Evangelist, of the Holy Innocents, and of St. Elizabeth Ann Seton. While you want to celebrate the major liturgical feasts every year, some of the smaller feast days could be celebrated every few years.

There are some specific things the family can do in relation to each feast, but the family may celebrate all of them with the reading of the Biblical event or of the biography of the Saint. The family can act out scenes from a Saint's life, or write a play, or put on a puppet show. Asking a religious sister for dinner, or a priest to come for a special blessing adds to the reverence of the celebration. Include the Rosary, the use of holy water, singing or listening to some hymns, or watching a video of the Saint's life.

Epiphany

The Feast of the Epiphany is a high holy day, especially in the Byzantine Rite. On the days from Christmas to the Epiphany, the Three Kings, plus their camels, slowly make the trip around the base of the Christmas tree, approaching the stable in which resides the Holy Family.

On the Feast of the Epiphany, some traditional Catholic families exchange one small gift with another member of the family, to represent the gift giving of the three kings. Gifts could be given to a poor family with a new baby, or to the elderly at a nursing home. Other families celebrate by having the children dress like the Kings and act out the journey. Each year, as the family grows, the costumes become more elaborate.

This feast day would be an opportune time to discuss with your older children the reign of Christ the King, not only in our home but also in our country. Teach your children that just as the Three Kings bowed down to Christ the King, so the leaders of our country, and of all countries, need to bow down and obey the laws of God. Explain to your children that unless laws are in conformity to God's laws, they are not just, even if the majority of the people vote for them.

The Presentation

If your parish church does not have a Candlemas Procession on February 2, the Feast of the Presentation of Our Lord in the Temple, have one in your domestic church.

Candlemas Day, as this is often called, should include the blessing of candles, but you may obtain previously blessed candles. Read the Bible story of the Presentation. If you can obtain a meditation or reading on the Presentation from a book about the mysteries of the Rosary, this would be worth reading or retelling for your children.

The Blessing of Throats with crossed blessed candles on the Feast of St. Blaise, February 3, is a beautiful sacramental for Catholics and non-Catholics in order to obtain good health and relief from sore throats or other throat problems and protection from evils. Mothers have traditionally considered this blessing important for their babies.

On February 11, the Feast of Our Lady of Lourdes, Catholic families should try to visit a Lourdes shrine or write a shrine and ask how they celebrate the feast day. Some of the prayers and activities could be re-enacted in your domestic church. By the way, many Marian shrines have replicas of the Lourdes shrine or of St. Bernadette, though it may not be advertised. Devotion to Our Lady of Lourdes was once very popular in this country. Encourage your children to read the biography of St. Bernadette and to see the movie, which is available on video for rent. After Fatima, this was Our Blessed Mother's greatest and most miraculous appearance.

Ash Wednesday

Ash Wednesday is the first day of Lent. Everyone should attend Mass on Ash Wednesday. Explain the meaning of Father's words as he blesses foreheads with the ashes: "Remember, man, that thou art dust, and unto dust thou shalt return." Be sure to discuss the rules of fast and abstinence with your children. In our home, we have stressed the meaning of abstaining from meat on Fridays, but we also have abstained from meat on Wednesdays of Lent which is additionally recommended in the Byzantine Rite. In the Byzantine Rite, no meat or dairy products may be taken on the day of the Great Fast, the first Monday of Lent, or on Good Friday.

The Mass on Ash Wednesday sets the tone for Lent, and graphically illustrates the meaning of life and death. The family should discuss the lesson of Ash Wednesday and the Lenten sacrifices each member of the family intends to make. In addition to small daily sacrifices, we need to encourage our children in positive acts of prayer or generosity or instant obedience. I tell my kids, "What's the point of giving up candy for Lent if you have arguments or tease a brother or say something unkind?"

Fasting has become unpopular in America, but the meaning and value of fasting needs to be taught to our children. Lent is a reminder of the forty days of the fast of Jesus in the desert. While Mother and Father may restrict their diet considerably, children should be encouraged to "fast" from desserts or sweets.

Various references to fasts in the Bible could be explained several times during Lent. The Bible Concordance lists the words "fast," "fasts," and "fasting" 143 times! During Lent, Bible stories about events involving fasting should be discussed. It was fasting which caused Nineve to be saved from the wrath of God, a lesson we in America need to remember. Do not let anyone tell you fasting is not an integral part of the practice of our Catholic Faith. Like the Bible itself, fasting will never be outdated!

Lent

During Lent, explain the sacrifices we need to make, why they are so important, and how we are joined with Christ and others in the Mystical Body of Christ to make reparation for sin. Read about how Saints celebrated Lent. Read the fantastic words of Jesus to Sister Josefa in *The Way of Divine Love* (available from TAN), as He relates His thoughts during the events leading up to His Crucifixion.

Lent in the Liturgical Year is a time when families could look into the Catholic customs of their ethnic culture. The Catholic cultural traditions, especially in the type of foods for Lent and for Easter, can become a cultural religious experience for the family, which can be handed on to future generations. We may develop a new appreciation for our Faith as we look into our own and other cultural Catholic traditions in our community.

In the past, all the statues, Stations, and paintings in the churches were covered with purple cloth during Passion Week and Holy Week. This was a sign of penance. It was a time when feasting and enjoying beautiful things were put aside. In some families, this tradition is kept alive, not by totally covering the statues in the domestic church, but by placing purple ribbons at the foot of each statue or holy picture. Sometimes a purple shawl or cloth is hung over the top and down the sides of religious paintings.

Feasts of March

On March 17, try to attend a St. Patrick's Day parade with your children, or have your own parade with another home schooling family. Help your children to make shamrocks, and relate the story of St. Patrick and his explanation of the Trinity. Be sure to discuss the tremendous sacrifices and efforts of St. Patrick to convert the Irish. Try to develop a sensitivity in your children for the Irish Catholics who have suffered so much from the English Protestant government. Your children may not only wear green, but hand out little holy cards to friends in the neighborhood or home schooling group, explaining who St. Patrick is. This is a form of witnessing or evangelizing to our society, such as what St. Patrick did himself!

St. Joseph's feast day, on March 19, could be celebrated over several days, with stories about him read each day. Since he is the special protector of the home and family, Catholic home schooling families will want to have an annual novena to him, including the Litany to St. Joseph. In these days of economic problems, St. Joseph needs to be called on to help Father in his job situation. Some home schooling families pray to St. Joseph every day, and keep a candle lighted for him in the parish church representing a daily reminder of our petitions to him. St. Joseph is considered the most powerful intercessor with Jesus next to the

Blessed Virgin Mary.

On March 25th, for the Feast of the Annunciation, help your children to collect famous paintings of this marvelous event! Write to art galleries and obtain photographs. Take photographs or video pictures of stained glass windows which depict the Annunciation in your area churches. Consider visiting a Marian shrine on this feast day, and praying the Litany of the Blessed Virgin Mary.

Stations of the Cross

Lent is the most appropriate time to teach your children about the meaning and ritual of the Stations of the Cross. Prayers have been composed by several Saints for meditation on the Stations, the most popular being "The Way of the Cross" by St. Alphonsus Liguori and "The Way of the Cross" by St. Francis of Assisi, who originated the devotion of the Stations. Both are available from TAN.

While the Stations of the Cross can be made all year long, consider making them with your family every Friday in Lent. A Plenary Indulgence is given to anyone making the Stations in church, with meditation, on the same day on which the Holy Eucharist is received. This is a wonderful way to obtain relief or release for the souls in Purgatory.

The Plenary Indulgence is granted only if the person making the Stations (or, in a large group, at least the leader) walks around to each Station. Remember that for a Plenary Indulgence, one must go to Confession within several days, before or after, plus pray for the Holy Father's intentions.

To make the Stations more varied for the children, use several different meditations. If you are in a hurry, simply walk around to each Station, genuflect, and say, "We adore Thee, O Christ, and we bless Thee, because by Thy holy Cross Thou hast redeemed the world." Teach your children the *Stabat Mater* song to be sung with the Stations: "At the cross her station keeping, stood the mournful Mother weeping, close to Jesus to the last," and all the following verses.

Since the Stations can be said at any time of day, you could take your children to the local Catholic church and say them every Friday afternoon. Some Catholic families make it a practice to visit a Marian shrine on First Fridays, and make the Stations there. When you visit shrines, see if you can obtain a Plenary Indulgence for visiting and praying there, as many popes have given such blessings.

If you cannot say the Stations at a church or shrine, consider purchasing pictures of the Stations and putting them up in a room where you and your family can say them. If you cannot find any pictures, you can purchase a coloring book, *I Follow Jesus*, from the Mother of Our Savior Catholic supply company, or from Seton. Your children may color the illustrations of the Stations and then you can use them for making the Stations.

Palm Sunday

On Palm Sunday, explain the meaning of palms and then put them around the house, on your family altar, and around holy pictures and statues. Some children like to make crosses out of the palms, often braiding them, in order to put them up on the wall. Remind your children that palms are a blessed sacramental. If your parish church does not have a procession, you may want to find a Byzantine Church which does, or have one in your domestic church or with your local Catholic home schooling support group. Read to your children the Bible account of the triumphal entry of Jesus into Jerusalem.

Holy Week

Holy Week should be a time for serious reflection on the meaning of Christ's suffering and death. The week can be filled with both liturgical prayer and private prayer. Attend Mass each day if possible, as well as all the church services for the week. Teach your children the Lenten songs, such as "O Sacred Head Surrounded." For older children and parents, a book could be chosen to meditate on Jesus and His sufferings, such as *The Way of Divine Love, Revelations of St. Bridget,* or *The Sermons of St. Francis de Sales for Lent* (all available from TAN publishers).

The Catholic and Protestant television stations during Holy Week often feature visits to the Holy Land or documentaries about the Crucifixion or the miraculous Shroud in which Jesus was buried. You can rent videos about the life of Christ or other appropriate movies.

Look for a parish which includes the traditional Holy Week ceremonies. The Byzantine Rite is very elaborate and inspiring. Holy Week ceremonies will be remembered for a lifetime by your children. Consider that, if in the future they cannot attend such ceremonies, they will be able to carry them on in somewhat the same fashion in their own homes.

On Holy Thursday, explain the meaning of the services before the children attend so they can understand how the services relate to the first Holy Week events. For Good Friday, try to go to a parish church which has the Stations and services in the afternoon. Not only are children too tired to appreciate the service in the evening, but since Jesus hung on the cross in the afternoon, an afternoon service is more appropriate and accurate.

If your family is in the house, rather than in your parish church, after twelve noon on Good Friday, you may want to follow the tradition of keeping silence between noon and 3 o'clock. With young children, this may not be completely possible, but certainly some attempt at this is possible. Children should be encouraged to meditate or to say private prayers. Consider showing a video on the Stations of the Cross or on the Sorrowful Mysteries of the Rosary, and having the family pray along.

Church services usually start at 2 o'clock. Some families try to spend some time in church beforehand, or go to Confession later in the afternoon. The Church requires fasting on Good Friday (ages 18-59) and abstaining from meat (from age 14). In some families, almost no food is eaten by teenagers and adults. In the Byzantine Rite, "The Great Fast" means abstaining from meat and also from dairy products. Many continue the fast on Holy Saturday, until after the Easter Mass.

Holy Saturday

If the children decorate Easter eggs, teach them the various Catholic symbols, such as the symbol of the Paschal Lamb for Christ. These Catholic symbols can be taught to very young children to help them understand the proper meaning of Easter. In the Byzantine Rite, the parish churches usually have classes to teach adults and children how to make pysanky eggs, which are eggs decorated with religious symbols and elaborate designs.

If your children attend the Holy Saturday or Easter Vigil services, they will come to love them, and to look forward to them each year as they grow up. The lighting of the candles in the darkened church gives vivid meaning to "The Light of the World." The ceremony of the Lighting of the New Fire and the Easter candle should be read and explained to the children before attending at church.

Some families attend the Easter Vigil services in order to be present at the Resurrection, but attend Mass again on Easter Sunday morning to celebrate the events surrounding the finding of the empty tomb as Mary Magdalen meets the angel and then Jesus, as St. John and St. Peter run to the tomb, and as the two disciples meet Jesus on the road to Emmaus. Both at the Easter Vigil and during the Mass on Easter morning, Baptism promises are renewed. Review their importance in the home schooling family.

In Byzantine Rite churches, parishioners bring homemade breads and baked goods to be blessed after the services. You and your children might make bread to be blessed.

Holy Communion may be received both at the Easter Vigil Mass as well as on Easter morning. In fact, the new regulations allow the reception of Holy Communion twice a day, any day of the year, as long as Mass is attended both times.

Easter

Make sure the excitement of the Resurrection is conveyed in your home. You might rent a video about the first

Easter Sunday. Tell the story of Peter and John as they ran to the Tomb and later to the Upper Room. Read the different accounts of the Resurrection from the four Gospels.

The message of the Resurrection is the center of our Faith. As Christ's apostles today, we want to spread the message. Have your children write "He is Risen" on different colored sheets of construction paper, and tape them all over the doors of your domestic church. Greet each other with "He is Risen! " answered by "Indeed, He is Risen." Teach your children some of the Easter hymns, or listen to them on tapes.

In many Catholic cultures, a Lamb cake is made for Easter dinner dessert. This is a beautiful cake shaped like a lamb, with white frosting and covered with coconut. You might want to buy one the first year to get an idea of how to make one the following year. Usually around Easter time you can buy the special lamb-shaped pans. Ask at bakery shops if you cannot find one.

During the forty days between Easter and Ascension, try to convey the happiness of the Apostles as Our risen Lord appears again and again in His risen Body. This is an opportunity for the children to display their best artwork as they draw pictures of the glorified and risen Lord. If you are not on the Seton program, study arts and crafts books for methods and materials, but encourage your children to colorfully illustrate or represent the glorious event of the Resurrection.

During this time, discuss Our Lord's institution of the Sacrament of Penance. Notice how many times Our Lord says, "It is I. Do not be afraid." Present the Sacrament of Penance as a calm, loving Sacrament. When I take my boys to Confession on Saturday, it is a happy occasion. We try to take their friends with us when we go, and sometimes have a treat on the way home.

Ascension

Ascension Thursday! What an event to celebrate! Jesus leaves us, rising on a cloud as the Apostles stand looking up. But we have the promise that He will return! How we look forward to that now.

Review the Apostles' Creed with your children, and explain "He ascended into heaven, sits at the right hand of God the Father Almighty; from thence He shall come to judge the living and the dead." Read the Gospel story of the Ascension.

If you read some of the accounts of the Ascension by Saints, Doctors of the Church, or Catholic writers, you might retell some of the surrounding events. Teach your children about the angels and the Blessed Mother, about the sorrow and regret of the Apostles as He was about to leave them, the gathering of the one-hundred-twenty persons to be witnesses, the many risen Saints who must have accompanied Him, the joyful yet sorrowful singing that must have come from His Apostles. Retell the story of the procession walking up the mountainside of Mount Olivet, the message of Jesus to His apostles, His prediction of the coming of the Holy Ghost, the likelihood that the risen Saints ascended with Him, the questions of the two angels standing by and their assurance that He would return, and the Apostles being filled with joy and returning home, constantly speaking the praises of God.

Your Catholic home schooling support group could gather on Ascension Thursday and have a re-enactment of the Ascension procession, with prayers, a reading of the event, and the singing of hymns. Since there were several occasions when Jesus ate fish with His Apostles during the forty days before He ascended to Heaven, perhaps this event could be concluded with a picnic with tuna-fish sandwiches or tuna salad. Remind your children about the symbol of the Fish as a secret sign for Christians for many years to come. Perhaps children could draw or cut out fish designs at the Ascension picnic.

Pentecost

Between Ascension Thursday and Pentecost, your family could say a novena to the Holy Spirit. During this time, the catechism questions about the Holy Spirit could be reviewed, especially the virtues, the gifts, and the fruits of the Holy Spirit. During the novena, the family could pray for one gift of the Holy Spirit each day.

On the Feast of Pentecost, the readings from the Bible as well as from meditations about the descent of the Holy Spirit could be read as a family. Like the disciples, Apostles, and the Blessed Mother, the family could be gathered around the family table, waiting in expectation. The imagination of the children might be encouraged to imitate the thunder and the wind and bright light filling the house.

Remind the children that this event is considered the Birthday of the Church, as well as the institution of the Sacrament of Confirmation. Parents could review again the virtues, the gifts, and the fruits of the Holy Ghost.

Three thousand persons were baptized after St. Peter gave his sermon on Pentecost. Some of your children might want to represent different cultures by wearing a hat or other clothing to signify a nationality. After the readings, and perhaps a song or two, the family can celebrate with a Holy Spirit cake, with white frosting and bright red tongues of fire. Place settings or coasters could be made by the children, each one shaped like a red tongue of fire.

If there is a Holy Spirit parish in your area, check to see if any particular celebrations will be going on there for your family to attend. Also, if you receive Eternal Word Television Network, your family might watch the Mass for Pentecost Sunday from the National Shrine of the Immaculate Conception.

The month of May

The Feast of St. Joseph the Worker, on May 1, should have special meaning for our home schooling children as we emphasize the importance and joy of work in our lives. The Feast could be preceded by a novena to St. Joseph. It is common tradition that we ask for our intentions carefully as St. Joseph is well-known for fulfilling requests. Besides their regular work, this would be a good day to have the children do some woodworking project around the house, such as fixing the wooden railings, or building that much-needed bookcase for the "classroom," or perhaps repairing the wooden screen door. Discuss these carpentry projects and tell the children to ask St. Joseph to pray for them as they do their work, especially their school work. Special prayers to St. Joseph should be included for Father and his work.

During the month of May, the month to honor the Blessed Virgin Mary, a few churches still have May processions. Perhaps your local home schooling support group could persuade a pastor to have one. If not, have one in someone's yard for the Catholic home schoolers in your area.

Traditionally, the May procession is composed of children dressed in their Sunday best, processing toward a statue of the Blessed Mother while singing a Marian hymn. The procession is led by a young girl, usually dressed in white, carrying a crown of flowers to be placed on the statue. She is accompanied by two little girls, usually in white, carrying flowers. When the statue is reached, the Blessed Mother is crowned to the singing of

> Bring Flowers of the Fairest, Bring Flowers of the Rarest,
> From gardens and woodlands and hillsides and dale.
> Our full hearts are swelling, our glad voices telling,
> The praise of the loveliest Rose of the Vale.
> O Mary we crown thee with blossoms today,
> Queen of the Angels, Queen of the May.
> O Mary we crown thee with blossoms today,
> Queen of the Angels, Queen of the May.

After the May crowning, the Litany of the Blessed Mother may be said, followed by Benediction if possible. Two or three Marian songs may be sung during the program. Afterwards there can be a small social gathering.

June and July

On the Feasts of the Sacred Heart of Jesus and the Immaculate Heart of Mary, Father Robert Fox sponsors an annual Marian Congress in South Dakota, in special honor of the apparitions of Fatima. If your family cannot make that, then consider having a mini-Marian Congress with other home schooling families in your area. Have a speaker on the Blessed Mother, and a Rosary procession, followed by a social for the families.

There are some wonderful Saints' feast days we celebrate in July which can lead to art and music projects, such as those of Blessed Junipero Serra, Blessed Kateri Tekakwitha, Our Lady of Mt. Carmel, St. Bridget, St. Maria Goretti and Sts. Joachim and Anne. Use your creativity to help celebrate these feasts. Ask the children to read the lives of these Saints and then ask them for creative ideas for the family to celebrate the feast day.

Starting the school year

As the school year starts, be sure to have a home schooling event in relation to a feast day. In Front Royal, Virginia, last year, the home schoolers started the year with a Dedication for School Children to the Infant of Prague in the parish church. It included Benediction, prayers, the sprinkling of Holy Water, and songs in Latin. The children decorated a little program book for each person which included the prayers and a drawing of the crown of the Infant Jesus, decorated with sequins. After the ceremony, the families enjoyed a party with an appropriately decorated cake.

Eternal Word Television Network

Eternal Word Television Network, the national Catholic television station, brings you events appropriate for the liturgical year and can help you and your family celebrate each feast day. EWTN is available on cable or by satellite. If you cannot access it by cable, you might buy a satellite dish. One home schooling family said they were able to purchase a used dish, from a reputable dealer, and were able to buy it so it focused in on EWTN and did not receive other satellites. Their total cost was $600!

Conclusion

If your family life revolves around the annual feasts and seasons of the liturgical year, each member of the family should increase in prayer, in study of the Bible, in the knowledge and love of Jesus and Mary and the Church. Each member of the family can grow in understanding the importance of living the virtuous life. For more ideas about how to celebrate the various feast days, look for books which give you information about the Saint or the event, and then try to devise creative ideas with the children. Be alert for Saints who were taught at home (most of them were) and to Saints who taught their children at home (most of them did).

Catholic home schooling is almost guaranteed to be successful if you and your family live the sacramental life. The key to successful Catholic home schooling is living the sacramental life. Utilize some of these ideas in your home schooling family. Trust in Jesus and Mary to help you in your home schooling undertaking, in your home schooling apostolate. As Cardinal Gagnon, former head of the Pontifical Council for the Family stated to me, home schooling is simply evangelizing at home, which is where evangelizing should start.

Chapter 8:
The Father's Role in Home Schooling

The following are reflections by Dr. Mark Lowery, a professor of Theology at the University of Dallas and a home schooling father.

Introduction

My wife, Madeleine, and I have seven children ranging from 12 years old to a few months old (as of 1993). When we moved to Texas in 1988, we began home schooling, having been disappointed in the parochial school where our eldest son, David, had attended kindergarten and first grade. We are presently home schooling our four oldest children: David in 7th grade, Daniel in 5th, Benjamin in 2nd, Elizabeth in 1st. We are now using our own curriculum, assembled over the last several years from a variety of sources, but we must credit Seton Home School for helping us get organized and bolstering our confidence when we first started. We had made a rather uneven start, and without Seton it probably would have been a disaster.

As a father, I have learned only gradually the things I wish to talk about in this chapter, and I am sure a wealth of insight still awaits my discovery. The most important thing for home schooling families—and the father therein— is to be patient. You will not "get it right" instantly; indeed, you will never have everything perfect. Be patient, and be open to new insights and suggestions, a few of which I will offer here. One important caveat, though: the fact that I have some suggestions, some of which may be helpful to you, does not mean that my family and I carry these out to perfection. Much of what I present here consists of ideals for which we strive, and only attain imperfectly. We have our fair share of blundering, frustration and failure. Just as in living out our Catholic faith, we all must be patient. "For us there is only the trying." (T. S. Eliot).

While we must be patient, we must be constant in our

efforts because so much is at stake; the family is *the* essential bedrock of society. According to the fathers of the Second Vatican Council, in the document *The Church in the Modern World,*

> The family is a kind of school of deeper humanity. But if it is to achieve the full flowering of its life and its mission, it needs the kindly communion of minds and the joint deliberation of spouses, as well as the painstaking cooperation of parents in the education of their children. (#52)

The very next line of the document says: "The active presence of the father is highly beneficial to their formation." This chapter, as a reflection on that line, is organized around six key themes that should be of special interest to fathers: conversion to his family, attitude toward his spouse, discipline in the family, discipline in his home school, his practical contribution to the home school, and his role in teaching religion.

Conversion to the family

The most important skill needed for home schooling has nothing to do in particular with intelligence or teaching skills, the things that first come to mind when a father contemplates the task of home schooling. Rather, success at home schooling is integrally related with his understanding of what it means to be a father. While he of course *is* a father at the conception of the first child, he must work to *become* who he is—just as a person baptized into the Christian community must work to become who he is. In each case, he must work at being faithful to his new kind of life now possessed.

Many people who were raised as Catholics experience, as adults, a kind of conversion to the Faith they already possess, a whole-hearted affirmation of the Church and the sacramental life. A similar conversion occurs for many fathers. They, of course, are committed to their family, but a part of their heart—often a significant part—lies elsewhere. Writer George Gilder has described how men have a natural impulse to be free and unfettered, a tendency to be "barbarians," and how they must sacrifice this impulse to hearth and home—to the values of the family.

This task is made especially difficult in our own society for a whole host of reasons. Pope John Paul II, in *The Role of the Family in the Modern World (Familiaris Consortio,* hereafter *FC*), devotes a special section to fathers, in which he says:

> Above all, where social and cultural conditioning so easily encourage a father to be less concerned with his family, or at any rate less involved in the work of education, efforts must be made to restore socially the conviction that the place and task of the father in and for the family is of unique and irreplaceable importance. (*FC*, #25)

Fathers need to convert fully to the gift they possess; as Pope John Paul II says, "the man is called upon to live his gift and role as husband and father" (*FC*, #25).

I remember a precise moment at which such a conversion happened in my own life. We had two children at the time. I have always enjoyed bicycling, and had spent considerable time on various bicycling adventures. Now, I had installed a child carrier on my 10-speed and enjoyed taking my two children on short rides around town. But I would still go on longer rides by myself, and I distinctly recall on the morning of one such ride being irritated that I had a childseat attached to my bike which would take some minutes to remove. I decided to just leave it on, even though it would cause wind resistance. About half-way through my ride, it suddenly occurred to me that I was only half-way dedicated to my family. It was with a real reluctance that I had been making the necessary sacrifices mandated by family life. I was quite attached to the part of myself represented by a childseat-free ten speed!

Before this experience, I simply had not thought seriously about the *need* to shift my attitude. Just the awareness of it had a powerful impact on me and I must honestly say that I returned home that morning a new man—con-

verted to what I already possessed.   In the years that followed, I still enjoyed my own interests but I developed much
more of a proclivity to sub-order them to my primary task
of being a husband and father.   This included not feeling
sorry for myself when my commitment to the family pre-
cluded some interest of my own.   And on the positive side,
it included developing new interests directly related to the
needs of my family.   For instance, I developed a fascination
for playground equipment, and it became somewhat of a
hobby to visit every playground in the surrounding area, and
then to return to the ones the children loved best.

What impact does this idea of "conversion to the family"
have on education?   The education of one's children is no
longer just one more item in a long string of exhausting
duties.   Education is so essential a part of the child's life
that, regardless of what kind of schooling is chosen by the
parents, the father becomes integrally involved in the whole
process.   As Pope John Paul II says,

> ...a man is called upon to ensure the harmonious and
> united development of all the members of the family;
> he will perform this task by exercising generous re-
> sponsibility for the life conceived under the heart of the
> mother, by a more solicitous commitment to education,
> a task he shares with his wife.... (*FC*, #25)

If parents have chosen a public or parochial school, it is
essential for both parents—not just the mother—to be integrally involved with the educational process. Parents we know
who get the most out of a school system are the ones who
are constantly involved in the whole process, both at home
and at the school. (And it often occurs to such parents that
if they are already so involved in education, why not home
school and reap the additional benefits?)

The breadwinner's attitude toward the mother

Fathers—even those really committed to their families—
may easily suppose that it is the wife's task to be most
involved in the educational process of the children.   Of

course, she is going to be more involved as regards amount of time spent. But, I submit, both father and mother must be equally involved in the task itself.

Consider this analogy. In pregnancy and childbirth, the mother obviously spends the greatest *quantity* of time. But the *qualitative* aspect of the project itself requires an equal donation of energy and commitment from both parents. So too with education. It must be a primary commitment for both, even though that commitment will be lived out in different ways that involve different quantities of time. The father should never have to say, "My wife does most of the work when it comes to the education of the children."

Indeed, it is extraordinarily easy for the husband to fall into the mistaken way of thinking in which he considers himself to have the really important and challenging work and his wife who stays at home to have the easier job— even if home schooling. Husbands need to reverse this way of thinking! Wives and mothers have the more important role, as well as the more difficult role. As George Gilder has put it,

> The woman assumes charge of what may be described as the domestic values of the community—its moral, aesthetic, religious, nurturant, social, and sexual concerns. In these values consist the ultimate goals of human life—all those matters that we consider of such extreme importance that we do not ascribe financial worth to them. Paramount is the worth of the human individual life, enshrined in the home, and in the connection between woman and child. These values transcend the marketplace. (*Men and Marriage*, p. 168)

Likewise, Pope John Paul II recognizes that "The true advancement of women requires that clear recognition be given to the value of their maternal and family role, by comparison with all other public roles and all other professions," and speaks of the "original and irreplaceable meaning of work in the home and in rearing children." (*FC*, #23) Add to this the task of being the primary moderator of the home school! In a word, a crucial contribution to the home school on the part of the father is his attitude toward his wife. Needless to say, children pick up very quickly on the quality of relationship between their two parents and are profoundly influenced by it.

Discipline in the family

Just as it is easy for the father to relegate much of the "schoolwork" to his spouse, so too with discipline. The old caricature of the heavy-handed and much-feared father had its obvious problems, but today I see all too many fathers, including very sincere and dedicated fathers, taking too laid-back an approach to discipline. This is dangerous enough in the family where children attend school outside the home, and it becomes all the more dangerous in a home-schooled family. I have worked in various classroom settings for many years and have become somewhat of a fanatic about a well-ordered, disciplined classroom. It makes for a happier and more effective teacher, and it is what children really do want even though they appear to want just the opposite. That appearance is deceptive—they are begging for order. One of my main frustrations with various schools we tried was the kind (or better, the lack) of discipline used. All too often the classroom was inundated by unruly children, who then commanded most of the teacher's energy. Even an exceptionally competent and ordered teacher will soon become frustrated because classroom discipline problems are so deeply rooted in the uneven discipline of home life.

Hence, in the home school, as well as in the home in general, humane but solid discipline is essential. During the day the mother will be disciplinarian from a quantitative point of view, but the father, once again, must be thoroughly involved in the unending, demanding, but very rewarding project of raising well-mannered children.

Perhaps the most important aspect of a good system of discipline is knowing what to expect from a child. Generally the expectations of parents today are far too low (though ironically the expectations in terms of achievement, at ever earlier ages, are often far too high). Children are *capable* of

being well-mannered. One ought never to look upon his
children misbehaving in church, in a restaurant, or at the
shopping center, and say "They're just kids."

The child's capacity to be well-mannered is analogous to
a key feature in the Catholic moral life. As an abiding
result of the Fall, we all have a tendency to misuse our
freedom (to sin), a tendency called concupiscence. But we
have a capacity to resist this tendency. As moral theologian
William May has put it, "We can do as we ought." Similarly, children have a capacity to resist the tendency to be
unruly. In both cases, we are happier when we rise above
our lower appetites. And interestingly, these two areas of
our lives—manners and morals—affect and mutually condition one another. Of course, there can be well-mannered
thieves just as there can be (perhaps) ill-mannered saints,
but in general a well-mannered person has conquered the
lower appetites and developed good habits, and hence is well-
practiced when it comes to doing the same in a moral situation.

One particular method I have found quite effective—and
an easy entrance into this area for fathers—is to develop
very concrete and clearly written out sets of standards for
various situations. For example, some standards one might
put forth for one's children while attending Mass are: stand
straight; do not fidget; fold your hands when kneeling—and
the like. The father should remind the children of these
standards on the way to church, and let the children know
precisely the consequences of breaking the standards. I call
this the "method of pre-emption." It anticipates problems in
advance, which goes a long way toward avoiding them in
the first place. Most parents work the other way around.
They are not consistently clear about the standards to which
they wish to hold their children, and then throw somewhat
of a tantrum of their own when they see their children following their natural tendencies!

Other situations for which concrete standards can be
developed are shopping, eating, and, of course, home schooling. One of the reasons I wish to stress these other areas,
however, is that home schoolers need to portray themselves

very attractively in public (and with extended family). A home schooling family must go the extra mile to demonstrate to skeptics that they really "have their act together"— which might make skeptics wonder whether home schooling might not be so bad after all. So fathers, take charge! Make your family the kind to which others will be attracted and will wish to emulate.

Perhaps the greatest threat to a good system of discipline is a noxious idea that has run rampant in our culture: that self-esteem is the most important goal to strive for in raising children. This is a rather deadly idea because it gets right in the way of discipline. When you must be firm with children, you simply do not feel as though you are helping their self-esteem, and so you will draw back (and be quite ineffective). Self-esteem is obviously an absolutely crucial component of a healthy human being, but here is the catch: it is not an end in itself. If you try hard to help someone (or to help yourself) have self-esteem, you will probably fail. Self-esteem is an *end-product*, something that comes about as a result of having done other things—like discipline—well. It is very much like happiness. Most people who try hard to be happy fail. Happiness comes about as the *result* of a well-lived life. It cannot be pursued in and of itself. Rather, if you lead an ordered life, you will simply find yourself to be happy. Likewise, if children are properly raised, which especially means being challenged to live up to good objective standards of conduct, they will simply find themselves to have high self-esteem. Another catch: they often will not tell you how happy they are!

Discipline in the home school

If the father is away most of the school day, how can he possibly play a major role in building a well-ordered home school? Again, although he is not present quantitatively, he can be qualitatively. The children need to know that Dad is behind Mom. Some possible methods: Have a list of very clear rules for the home school. The father can read these at the beginning of the day if possible, or the evening before the school day. I myself have found it helpful to call home at mid-day, when possible, and talk briefly with each home schooler. If discipline problems have arisen, they can at least be discussed on the phone. This method is a great preventative—the home schooler knows Dad will call, or can be called.

Each family, of course, has to work out their own system of consequences for misbehavior. There is a lot of trial and error involved. The important thing is not having a perfect system, but rather that a consistent program exists and is in a constant state of upgrading. Part of the constant upgrading in our family is the "family council meeting," held every Saturday after breakfast. This is a time when all the older children along with Mom and Dad can vent their complaints and problems (regarding the home school as well as any other facet of family life). Such a meeting serves the purpose of a "mini-retreat" where everyone can stand back and look at difficulties a bit more objectively. It is most helpful for children to know that they can voice a complaint, and that the complaint can be intelligently discussed (outside the context within which the complaint arose). When complaints arise during the week, we have our children write them out and put them in a special jar for the upcoming family council meeting.

The actual task of home schooling

Throughout the years that we have home schooled our children, I have discovered that I thoroughly enjoy teaching my own children. In teaching, you become "grafted" into your children's lives in a special way. Being integrally involved with one's children is immensely enriching, for a reason that Pope John Paul II has hit upon perfectly:

> Concern for the child, even before birth, from the first moment of conception and then throughout the years of infancy and youth, is the primary and fundamental test of the relationship between one human being and another. (FC, #26)

As parents work to "pass" this test, they are rewarded in turn, for the children "offer their own precious contribution to building up the family community and even to the sanctification of their parents." (*FC*, #26)

The father should not just "help out" with the teaching work of the mother; he should have several subjects that are his own, that he teaches to the children. What subjects ought he to choose? The usual reply is, whatever subjects he is especially competent in. Certainly that is a good criterion, but I think that, especially in grade school, the criteria can be much broader, and can extend to whatever subjects he is *interested* in. One of my friends tells the story of being hired to teach English in a high school. When the freshman physics teacher was on extended sick leave, he was asked if he would fill in. He knew little about physics, but was interested in the subject. He did a fine job, keeping just ahead of the students. College students will report that some of their best classes are from new professors who have a great deal of energy and enthusiasm even though, being just out of school, they feel barely competent. So as long as you are motivated and willing to think, you will do fine and will enjoy expanding your own horizons alongside those of your children.

How can a father fit several subjects into an already crowded day? For one, you can give assignments for each day (write them out in an assignment book for the students to check off), but only do formal work with the children every other day. I have been able to arrange my schedule so as to spend several hours at home two mornings a week. When this is not possible, I reserve evening or weekend time. I use this special time to work on areas that require intensive one-on-one instruction.

Other areas require less intensive work. All sorts of techniques can be used to allow for quick daily accountability. For science, we recently had the two oldest boys read chapters from a book of "fascinating facts" (*The Big Book of Amazing Knowledge*, Creative Child Press) and report on their findings at dinner each night. With mathematics, they do their daily assignment on their own each day, getting help from Mom if necessary, and usually I quickly correct their work soon after coming home. When they were mastering the catechism, I had them greet me upon my return home each evening with the answer to the assigned question for the day— they would beam with pride, and my own home-coming was combined with an enjoyable method of account-ability.

I have often been asked whether the task of being both a father and a teacher to my children causes conflict. I think it is far more difficult for a mother to keep her roles as mother and teacher distinct, and this makes it all the more important for the father to be closely involved in the actual task of home schooling. I have found it relatively easy to keep the roles distinct, partly because I outrightly tell the children that they must view me and treat me as a teacher during school time.

One of the best parts of home schooling is that you yourself learn a lot. This is a real blessing because it feeds your enthusiasm, thereby making it easier for the student as well. Permit me to wax enthusiastic about my own involve-ment for a moment. I have (gradually) taken on five sub-jects in our home school. While teaching music, I have mastered parts of music theory I never had understood be-fore. I have been motivated to improve my own technical skills. I have learned those obscure third and fourth verses of various songs we are learning as a family. While teach-ing Latin, I have mastered various paradigms — especially for irregular verbs — that I had never quite mastered before. I have not learned much new in mathematics yet— though I'm sure that will come— but I have greatly enjoyed trying to explain aspects like fractions or the decimal system. It is especially fun to find aspects of practical life for the chil-dren to practice with. My son Daniel and I are fanatics over the game Yahtzee; having kept track of our scores, we average them monthly and graph our averages. And what could be better than teaching math vis-a-vis baseball statis-tics! Physical education — for this, my role as father and teacher merge completely! We have a special "sports ban-quet" every year where the students are rewarded for their accomplishments with a prize of some sort. And finally, I teach religion, a topic to which I wish to give special attention.

The Father's role in teaching Religion

Religion is my most difficult subject, which is ironic because I teach religion and theology as a profession. But my own difficulties aside, I think it is essential for the father to teach, or at least co-teach, this topic. Due to the inherent differences between male and female, women have a more natural proclivity to enter into an attitude of worship before their God. Men have to surrender a hefty portion of their ego to do so—and this is no easy task. But it is absolutely crucial that the children see their father doing this. They must see their father pray and they must hear their father speak and teach with pride about that noblest possession of the Catholic home school—the one, holy, Catholic, and apostolic Faith. As Pope John Paul II says:

> The concrete example and living witness of parents is fundamental and irreplaceable in educating their children to pray. Only by praying together with their children can a father and mother—exercising their royal priesthood—penetrate the innermost depths of their children's hearts and leave an impression that the future events in their lives will not be able to efface. (*FC*, #60)

The Pope then quotes Pope Paul VI's appeal to mothers, and then to fathers:

> And you, fathers, do you pray with your children, with the whole domestic community, at least sometimes? Your example of honesty in thought and action, joined to some common prayer, is a lesson for life, an act of worship of singular value. In this way you bring peace to your homes: *Pax huic domui* [Peace be to this house]. Remember, it is thus that you build up the Church. (*FC*, #60)

(In this last sentence, we find a cardinal tenet of Catholic social thought: that the proper role of the laity is to build up the Church, not chiefly by doing "churchly" things in the parish, though in this regard the donations of those who have time are of inestimable value; rather, their role is to bring transcendent truths to bear in the home and in society at large.)

When children see their father taking his religion seriously, they learn that religion is not in "the woman's sphere" —it is in the sphere of all who acknowledge themselves to be *creatures* rather than their own gods. They learn that freedom is not "doing your own thing," being autonomous, but rather a gracious surrender to a higher truth. We are most free when we are bound to the truth.

On the practical side, as regards religion, I would suggest combining the catechism, the Bible, and good biographies of the Saints. When my children learned the catechism, they memorized one or two questions per day. As noted above, they would greet me when I came home with the answer to their assigned question—a most successful technique. And an added bonus: the answers to the catechism are in finely crafted sentences, the memorization of which facilitates the child's knowledge of grammar and composition as well as of the Faith.

In the context of teaching religion, it is important to note the father's irreplaceable role in educating toward chastity. Pope John Paul II connects this role to one of the principles of Catholic social thought, the principle of subsidiarity, which, among other things, asks that tasks which belong to a particular rung of the societal ladder, such as at the family level, ought not be taken over by higher levels, such as the State. Rather, the higher levels should serve the family and give them help (*subsidium*) in carrying out their appointed task.

> Sex education, which is a basic right and duty of parents, must always be carried out under their attentive guidance, whether at home or in educational centers chosen and controlled by them. In this regard, the Church reaffirms the law of subsidiarity, which the

school is bound to observe when it cooperates in sex education, by entering into the same spirit that animates the parents. (*FC*, #37)

This quote all by itself is a fine argument for the home school! The Pope goes on to note the central role of chastity in such formation:

> In this context *education for chastity* is absolutely essential, for it is a virtue that develops a person's authentic maturity and makes him or her capable of respecting and fostering the "nuptial meaning" of the body. Indeed, Christian parents, discerning the signs of God's call, will devote special attention and care to education in virginity or celibacy as the supreme form of that self-giving that constitutes the very meaning of human sexuality. (*FC*, #37, emphasis added)

What practical steps can the father take in his children's education to chastity? First, be a real man and "toss" the TV. Do this literally if you can, but if you are like me, at least put it on wheels and keep it in the closet most of the time (baseball is better on radio anyway). If there were only one thing you were allowed to do for your family, this would be the optimal choice. It will educate to chastity and to many other virtues as well.

More directly, talk to your children about the virtues, and keep chastity and purity in the front line. When teaching the Sixth Commandment, explain its meaning *for them*, namely, that God wants them to respect their bodies and to respect their sexual organs in a special way. You must be very concrete with your sons as they grow toward and through puberty. Define purity in clear terms. Talk about how to refrain from playing with themselves, with a language that is humane and that will not produce excessive guilt should they fail. Ask them at regular intervals, "How are you doing with purity?" Do not get mad at them if they are struggling with it, but encourage them, letting them know that God will be patient with them but also that God wants them to master their desires. No doubt this is a challenging task—but keep the lines of communication open. They will know that you are there, willing to answer big questions when they arise. In all of this, you will find yourself strengthened in chastity as well. Stress to your children (and to yourself) that being chaste is a truly heroic activity.

When your children become adolescents and start paying attention to members of the opposite sex, some have suggested that, after appropriate discussion, you give your sons (Mom can work with your daughters) a special ring—a ring of purity—as a sign or reminder that they have pledged to God that they will remain chaste.

Conclusion

I hope you have taken my suggestions just as that—mere suggestions. As long as you completely embrace the one *non*-negotiable central idea—being integrally involved—the rest will flow from there as you develop your own distinctive methods. Fathers, as heads of your families, you are performing the most important of all tasks in your life. For as the Holy Father tells us, "The future of humanity passes by way of the family." (*FC*, #86) And you may be sure that God will give you all the grace and strength necessary to carry through.

The End.

Dr. Lowery presents a wonderful picture for us of a home schooling father.

What Mothers think

A friend of mine, a home schooling father who gave a talk for our Home Educators Association of Virginia a few years ago, took a survey of the home schooling mothers in his very large northern Virginia home schooling support group. His question in the survey was "What do home schooling mothers see as the role of their husbands in the home schooling family?"

The Number One overwhelming answer by home schooling mothers was that the husband be committed to home schooling and be supportive of it by giving encouragement—encouragement to their wives and encouragement to their children. It surprised everyone—including the home schooling fathers—to discover that the wives were asking for a supportive attitude and encouragement rather than asking them to take over some of the teaching.

Mothers made statements about the importance of fathers being patient when they get home in the evening, showing interest in the children's work, praising the home schooling commitment, and believing that it is God's will that the family be home schooling.

The second point most often mentioned by home schooling mothers was that the fathers be willing to accept a different kind of lifestyle. Mothers simply cannot keep up the housework and the cooking as they did before home schooling, especially if the children are still too young to help out.

Third, fathers need to understand that home schooling is difficult for mothers. It takes a great deal of time and energy, especially if the mother is home schooling a strong-willed child or a child with a learning problem. Mothers would like their husbands to attend local support group meetings once in a while to hear others talking about their home schooling situations.

Fourth, mothers surveyed said that fathers should have a high vision for their children. Fathers need to believe in their children and in their ability to do their best. Children need to feel the support and encouragement from their fathers to do their best. Fathers should praise the children's success and minimize their failures.

Fifth, mothers would like fathers to be available by phone during the day so that on occasion, when a child needs some verbal disciplining, Father is ready and available to do it. It is usually not the length of the call that is important, but for children to know that Father is concerned that children do their work and that he is only a phone call away from keeping informed about what is going on at home.

Some Seton mothers, by the way, have told me that being

able to call their husbands when there is a discipline problem has kept the problems to a minimum. Steve Wood, a Catholic home schooling father of eight children who gives talks on discipline, says that when the school year starts, if he gets a "discipline" call from his wife while at work, he goes home to administer the discipline. This sets the tone for the school year, and the children know their dad is serious about obedience to their mother.

Fathers must realize that home schooling mothers have some additional needs for the home. For instance, fathers should provide a room to be used for study purposes. It helps mothers to keep order and discipline to have a special place for home schooling, especially as the school materials increase over the years.

Fathers as well as mothers need to talk with the children about why the family is home schooling and to show support for the purpose. They should discuss the fact that home schooling is the family's way of living out the kind of Christian life that Jesus wants.

Fathers should be concerned about the proper socialization of the junior high and high school children, especially for the boys. They need to take time with their children, take them to controlled activities, or be involved with them in church activities.

In this survey, the majority of mothers did not ask for fathers to teach any subject! As you can see, with Father's support, these Mothers feel they can handle the teaching themselves.

Discipline

We have another chapter on discipline, but when the focus is on the father's role, disciplining the children always comes into the picture. It is natural that the father should discipline the children since he is the head of the family.

Steve Wood, mentioned above, is an active leader in the Florida Pro-Life Movement. The more he became involved in Pro-Life, the more he realized that even good people did not want to have more children because they could not discipline those they already had. Mr. Wood believes that if we hope to "sell" people on the idea of having as many children as God wants to send them, and to stop practicing contraception, then we need to help these parents solve the problems they have with their present children. And the biggest problem is discipline.

He believes the same is true about home schooling. Many of us in the home schooling movement believe that problems with disciplining children are one of the most common reasons why parents either do not home school or cease to home school.

The *Book of Proverbs* is a wonderful guide for parents to study, especially for fathers. It is a God-given guide for the training and disciplining of children. In fact, many of the verses refer to a son taking instruction from his father.

"A wise son heareth the doctrine of his father." 13:1

"He that spareth the rod hateth his son; but he that loveth him corrects him betimes." 13:24

"A fool laughs at the instruction of his father; but he that regardeth reproofs shall become prudent." 15:5

"A foolish son is the grief of his father." 19:13

"Folly is bound up in the heart of a child, and the rod of correction shall drive it away." 22:15

St. Paul reminds the Hebrews in Chapter 12 about the commands in *Proverbs*. He says that God, like all good fathers who love their children, disciplines us, His children. If children are without chastisement, then they are not treated as true sons, but as illegitimate children. St. Paul says that the "fathers of our flesh" are our instructors, "and we reverenced them."

In *Ephesians*, Chapter 6, verses 1 to 4, St. Paul instructs fathers and sons:

> Children, obey your parents in the Lord, for this is just. Honor thy father and thy mother, which is the first commandment with a promise: That it may be well with thee, and thou mayest be long lived upon earth. And you, fathers, provoke not your children to anger, but

bring them up in the discipline and correction of the Lord.

Some years ago, our Home Educators Association of Virginia convention focused on the role of the father in the home schooling family. We took as our theme *Malachias* 4:6: "And he shall turn the hearts of the fathers to the children, and the hearts of the children to their fathers." We truly believe that as fathers become more involved with their children, they will come to know them better and to love them more, and the children will respond in kind. And the children will be motivated to do well in their schoolwork.

One of the points that Steve Wood makes in the training and disciplining of children is the vital necessity for fathers to spend time with them. Children are made in the image and likeness of their fathers, just as we are made in the image and likeness of God. Children tend to imitate their fathers. If fathers give good examples of living the authentic Catholic family lifestyle, children will not be the discipline problems that so many are today. Most children today take their "instructions" from their peers, not their parents, because they spend so much time with their peers, and not with their families. One of Steve Wood's favorite comments is "Love is spelled T-I-M-E."

Additional helps

While it is clear about the father's role in many areas, nevertheless, we need to discuss some other ways fathers can be of help in the home schooling family. Mainly, fathers can help in the area of housekeeping. Mothers do the vast majority of the housework, and this responsibility is primarily theirs. Nevertheless, we encourage fathers to help whenever possible. While children usually help their mother, it is certainly a good example for children to see that housework is not just "women's work," but that good housekeeping is in the best interest of the whole family.

Daily school reports

Many home schooling mothers believe in the importance of Father asking for daily school reports from Mother and the children. This is the best technique for keeping the children on track and focused on their daily work, because they know they will be reporting to Dad when he comes home.

In addition, Dad needs to ask for a daily report about the chores. Mother needs her children to help with the housework, but they often will not do so unless they know that Dad has a serious interest in their performance, and will inflict due punishment on the unwilling if necessary.

Fathers could work with the children to arrange a chore schedule just like a job supervisor would, as he could explain. The children will better understand the importance of work and being part of the household team when Dad is in charge.

Building projects

The physical needs of the home school are Dad's domain. Money is needed for books and supplemental materials. Additional bookshelves are required on a regular basis. Fathers, in conjunction with children, should plan on building new shelves as Mother adds to the family library. Dad should keep aware of sales of used books, computers, and other equipment. This will be of great help to Mom, who spends her days teaching.

It should be Dad's responsibility to help develop a classroom or space for home schooling—sometimes a recreation room or a garage or study, or a room in the basement. One family converted an attic room into a classroom. This can be an all-family project sometimes, but Father needs to provide the supervision. And the money!

Teaching

Teaching is usually the toughest part for most fathers to adjust to doing, but it is truly the most wonderful experience. We especially encourage fathers to teach math to their sons. Even if a class is only fifteen minutes each day or every other day, just to teach new concepts, it gives the children time with Dad. Children come to understand how smart Dad is! They develop a real respect for Dad as an authority in certain academic areas, or in all areas, as the case may be.

Fathers should consider teaching science, or at least helping the children in weekly science projects, perhaps on Saturdays or Sunday afternoons. Trips could be taken to museums or local conservation parks or special exhibits. A father could become an authority on educational resource opportunities, such as historical statues or underground caverns or old Catholic churches in the state.

In most families, since fathers are away from the home during the day, no one expects them to be greatly involved with the day-to-day teaching. But this is the fault of our society. Fathers should be involved on a daily basis with the teaching. We encourage families to consider, if possible, changing their lifestyle so that Father can be home more often to spend more time with the family. No matter what career Father has, it eventually will come to an end. However, raising children has eternal consequences, and ultimately fathers understand, often too late, that this is their primary job in life.

Home schooling has been causing conversions among fathers, and, as Mark Lowery reports above, conversions to the family. Many fathers are looking for jobs closer to home, or for homes which are less expensive. Some families are trying to find jobs for Father, or for both Father and Mother, which can be done at home. In addition, cottage industries are starting to become popular among home schooling families, in which the whole family, including the children, develop a family business. Like the Holy Family, parents and children can learn together, work together, and pray together.

And play together.

And sacrifice together.

And grow together.

And love together.

Babysitting

Some fathers do not like babysitting, but it really helps the overworked home schooling mother to have perhaps a Saturday afternoon free to do something with her friends. Some mothers may not need it, but other mothers would certainly appreciate it.

Learning about home schooling

The American home schooling movement is a gentle and growing revolution, impacting both American family life and education. The reasons for home schooling, the teachings of the Church, Biblical passages relating to education and parents, the many ideas about individualized learning and how children learn, stimulating ideas in relation to developments in religion, history, science—all these things offer intriguing topics for reading, learning, studying, and discussing. Fathers should be challenged to learn more about home schooling and to become involved in this movement which is in the forefront of the educational revolution in this country.

The home schooling movement, as it grows and expands, as it matures among Catholics, is going to offer interesting and professional work, intellectually stimulating work, for home schooling fathers.

As Catholic home schooling support groups grow, as regional and statewide groups develop, as lobbying efforts progress, there is going to be room, even a need, for home schooling fathers to be involved.

St. Joseph

No discussion of the role of the father in the home schooling family would be complete without mention of St. Joseph. After all, Jesus was at home for thirty years before He entered public life, meaning that His relationship with Mary and Joseph was certainly continual and close.

Jesus made the statement in *John* 5:19-20 that

the Son cannot do anything of himself, but what he
seeth the Father doing; for what things soever he doth,
these the Son also doth in like manner. For the Father
loveth the Son, and sheweth him all things which himself doth.

Jesus is clear that because God the Father loves God the
Son, God the Father shows Him all things which He does,
and then God the Son does them also, imitating His Father.

Since that is true, it would seem logical that St. Joseph
gave Jesus a good example, showing Him all the good things
he did, and in regard to human things, Jesus imitated St.
Joseph.

Though Jesus is the Second Person of the Blessed Trinity, nevertheless, God wanted to emphasize the importance
of Joseph as head of the Holy Family. God sent an angel to
Joseph in a dream to tell him that "that which is conceived
in her is of the Holy Ghost." God sent an angel to Joseph
to tell him to "fly into Egypt" to protect Jesus from Herod's
soldiers. It was Joseph to whom the angel appeared to tell
him to return the family to Nazareth. It would seem that
God the Father was careful that the head of the Holy Family
was being notified from Heaven, instead of Jesus giving His
foster-father instructions. This demonstrates the profound
respect which God wants wives and children to have for the
head of the family.

St. Joseph, as head of the family, was responsible for
taking Jesus and Mary to Jerusalem for Jewish feast days.
Thus the importance of fathers being responsible for leading
the family to religious services is clearly evident.

At the finding in the Temple, when Jesus answered, "Did
you not know I must be about My Father's business," it
would seem He might be starting His public life. But, on the
contrary, He voluntarily, immediately, and completely subjected Himself to the authority of Joseph and Mary for the
next eighteen years.

The very fact that Jesus subjected Himself to Mary and
Joseph, though He certainly was not required to, showed He
wants us, parents and children, to respect the authority of
parents over children. More than that, He was declaring to

all of us the importance of obedience on the part of children and of authority on the part of parents. It is a strong message, delivered in an extraordinary way. God subjects Himself to the authority of human parents. And He does it for a long time—thirty years, as if to doubly emphasize the importance of obedience of children to the authority of parents. Jesus is really teaching us that a father's authority in the family is of supreme importance, of supreme value, and of supreme dignity.

The Holy Family in Nazareth can teach us another lesson, that while fathers need to provide good example, religious education, and honest work, fathers should not worry about providing more than is necessary.

We can be sure that St. Joseph led the family in prayer as well as in reverence to God, their heavenly Father, in self-sacrifice, in humility, in purity, and in holiness. We pray that our Catholic home schooling fathers will look to St. Joseph for guidance in leading their families to live the authentic Catholic family life.

Chapter 9:
Discipline in the Catholic
Home Schooling Family

"Discipline" must be one of the most rejected words in our society. With the advent of the "Do your own thing!" generation, the very concept of restraint seems a quaint, old-fashioned idea. For those wishing to live the Catholic life, however, discipline is paramount. "Discipline" and "disciple" come from the same root.

The discipline drift has affected even orthodox Catholic families. The most common reason why Catholic families are afraid to start home schooling or do not succeed with their home schooling is lack of discipline.

This is a pretty tough indictment of the Catholic family, which, even while rejecting the prevailing cultural attitudes, is still affected by them. Without even realizing it, many Catholic parents have lost control of their own children.

Definition

What do we mean by discipline? Basically, discipline means training—training of the will. Before we can hope to teach the minds of our children academic subjects or even the Faith, we need to train ourselves and our children to do the will of God.

Discipline is a way of life with rules. It means self-control. It means, for the Catholic family, obedience to God's rules.

One of the definitions in the dictionary for the word discipline is "a system of practice or rules for members of a church." In the Second Vatican Council documents, the Catholic home is called a "domestic church," so it is appropriate that a home should be ruled by discipline.

Another definition of the word "discipline," found in *The Catholic Encyclopedia*, is the whip or cord which the monks used in the monasteries for self-flagellation as a means of mortification. A mortification is an act of self-discipline.

These are acts done to lessen our love for self and to increase our love for God and others, to increase our willingness to suffer in reparation for our own sins as well as for the sins of others.

Before we can expect our children's obedience in relation to schoolwork assignments, we need to teach our children obedience first to God's rules, and second to ourselves as God's representatives. Our children need to understand the positive reasons why Catholics believe in discipline.

In addition to training our children, we need to think about disciplining ourselves as mothers and fathers. If our children understand that we ourselves are striving for discipline, then they will be more likely to make such an effort.

Catholic philosophy as basis of discipline

The Catholic Church teaches that because of Original Sin, the individual's intellect, even after Baptism, is darkened and needs guidance to attain the truth. Man's will also has been weakened, and thus has an inclination to evil. Divine Grace enlightens the intellect to know the good and guides the will to choose good through the use of the Sacraments and prayer.

In the Old Testament, God directed His chosen people through the Jewish leaders, who represented God's authority. In the New Testament, Christ established His Church, the Catholic Church, as our authority in this world. By following the teachings of the Church on doctrine and morality, we can have the sure and certain knowledge of Truth.

All Catholics have the responsibility to recognize and be obedient to our rightful authority on earth, the Catholic Church. Catholic parents have the further responsibility to teach their children to obey *them* as the rightful authority delegated by God until they are old enough to follow the authority of the Church directly.

So the goal of parental discipline in the Catholic family is to bring children to understand the will of God and to do His will. God has given parents, as well as the Catholic Church, the necessary authority to command obedience from children. The ultimate goal is to help the individual child to act always in accordance with the will of God, and thus become holy as God calls us to be.

While most parents find that there often must be an external compulsion for the child to do what he is told, the goal should always be to obtain an internal change or self-discipline in the mind and will. The child must recognize the authority of the parent, and ultimately recognize God as the Source of all authority.

Discipline in the Catholic family aims for all members to act constantly in accordance with the will of God. But at the same time there is a recognition that there is a constant interior battle due to the darkened intellect and weakened will. Each member of the family, as an outside influence, needs to help the other members to see the truth more clearly and to do the right thing more faithfully.

Discipline: training of the will

For us Catholics, the training of the will to do good is more important than the training of the mind to know. It is useless for the mind to know, if the will chooses to act in an evil fashion. Those running our schools believe that the more children know about things, such as sex and drugs, the better it is for the children. But if the will is not trained to act correctly on knowledge, to pursue the good, what is the point of knowing?

In the schools, children are taught to choose to do whatever they want, after they supposedly are "informed" about their choices. The children in America know everything there is to know about sex and drugs, but they continue to make bad choices. The school policy is to give no training in doing good and avoiding evil. Children in the schools have no discipline because the schools have given them no training in choosing good.

In the encyclical *Christian Education of Youth*, Pope Pius XI wrote that the "subject of Christian education concerns man as a whole, soul united to body." Man fallen from his original state has problems in learning as well as in controlling his passions. The chief effects of Original Sin, in fact, are a weakness of the will and "disorderly inclinations."

These disorderly inclinations, according to the Pope, must be corrected. "Good tendencies" must be encouraged and "regulated from the tender age of childhood." The will must be strengthened by supernatural truths and by grace. This is the kind of discipline we need in our Catholic families. Without it, there can be no real learning or true education.

The Bible on discipline

The Bible has a great deal to say to parents regarding the education and disciplining of children. God spoke to Moses about how the Commandments are to be taught to children by parents. This theme continues throughout the Old and New Testaments.

For instance, the Book of *Proverbs* begins:

> The parables of Solomon, the son of David, king of Israel. To know wisdom, and instruction: to understand the words of prudence: and to receive the instruction of doctrine, justice, and judgment, and equity: to give subtilty to little ones, to the young man knowledge and understanding. A wise man shall hear and shall be wiser: and he that understandeth, shall possess governments...The fear of the Lord is the beginning of wisdom. Fools despise wisdom and instruction. My son, hear the instruction of thy father, and forsake not the law of thy mother: that grace may be added to thy head, and a chain of gold to thy neck.

Some of the statements from the Book of *Proverbs* upon which we parents should reflect are the following:

"Instruct thy son, and he shall refresh thee, and shall give delight to thy soul."

"The rod and reproof give wisdom, but the child that is left to his own will bringeth his mother to shame."

"It is a proverb: 'A young man according to his way, even when he is old he will not depart from it.'"

"He that spareth the rod hateth his son; but he that loveth

him correcteth him betimes [speedily]."

"Chasten thy son while there is hope, and let not thy soul spare for his crying."

"Folly is bound up in the heart of a child, and the rod of correction shall drive it away."

Other Biblical quotes we should consider are *Ephesians* 6:4: "And you fathers, provoke not your children to anger, but bring them up in the discipline and correction of the Lord."

Exodus 20:12, *Matthew* 15:4, and *Ephesians* 6:2: "Honor thy father and thy mother."

Colossians 3:20: "Children, obey your parents in all things."

Deuteronomy 27:16: "Cursed be he that honoreth not his father and mother."

1 Kings 3:13: "For I have foretold unto him, that I will judge his house forever, for iniquity, because he knew that his sons did wickedly, and did not chastise them."

We need to remember the words of Jesus which point out the necessary spiritual emphasis in our disciplining: "Let the little children come unto Me, and forbid them not, for of such is the kingdom of God."

Infants

The disciplining of infants is especially difficult for us Catholic parents in this period of American history. We are living in times when infants are murdered, before birth and after birth, and each precious innocent baby has an extra special meaning for God and for us. But it is important that we protect not only the sweet little bodies of our babies, but also that we protect their souls from evil inclinations. In fact, protecting their souls is the graver responsibility. The best way to protect our babies from physical and spiritual harm is to train them, to teach them, and to discipline them

These sweet precious babies have a way of ruling a household. That is fine up to a point. But mothers can become exhausted to the point where they cannot fulfill their duties to their spouse and other children. Mothers need to have a break from the constant demands of a baby. It will not hurt the baby, in fact it can help the baby, to have a playpen in which he can have space to play but also limits on his freedom for his own protection and safety.

When a nursing baby bites, a mother will discipline her baby immediately, usually with a little slap on the cheek. Hopefully this is done not only because biting hurts the mother at the moment, but also because the mother understands she needs to train her baby not to bite again.

Another common problem with infants is sleep patterns. While a baby should set his own schedule the first six months, after that, Mother needs to train her baby. Mom and Dad should not have to be up all night taking care of a crying baby who just wants attention or is restless. Some of us mothers have found that if a baby is put down in the evening and not picked up while he fusses, after three or four nights the baby will stop and either play by himself or go to sleep. Babies also can be trained to take a nap in the afternoon after lunch. Even if the baby plays quietly, he is obtaining the needed rest.

Because each mother must find her own solutions to each situation, I will not go into more details, but do consider the fact that it is not good infant training for mothers never to say "no" to a child, even to a baby.

You know the phrase, "The hand that rocks the cradle rules the world." We should be sure that as we rock our babies, we are concerned about training them so that someday when they "rule" the world, it will be with justice and self-discipline.

Toddlers

The toddler years are the most important time to train your child, probably the most important period in your child's life. It is said that a child learns more during these years than during all the rest of his life put together. Although I would question that, certainly attitudes about love, obedience, and respect for authority are learned at this stage.

This is a time when a child, for his own physical safety,

needs to learn to be instantly obedient to his parents. He must recognize their rightful authority, as well as accept the fact that his parents know what is best for him, and that obeying instantly, without question, is important.

Young parents should understand that it is their responsibility as parents to train their young child, even if they are tired or exhausted. Sometimes it is a matter of persistence and a battle of wills, but parents must persevere.

We parents should study the Church teaching about the Sacrament of Matrimony, which tells us that we parents have the graces from the Sacrament of Matrimony to know what is best for our own children. We have the command from God in our vocation as parents to demand respect and obedience from our children, just as God demands respect and obedience from us, His children.

We parents need to have confidence in ourselves, confidence in the graces which God gave us, and confidence from our own life experiences and knowledge. We can know and must demand what is best for our children.

We parents should be convinced, in spite of the television, modern psychologists, and social service workers, that children absolutely do not know what is best for themselves. We parents do. Many Catholic documents teach that parents, under the Natural Law, have the *responsibility* to demand respect and obedience from their children.

Tough love

Training young children is very difficult. Training young children can be a daily conflict of wills. Our parental will is often in conflict with the will of a sweet little precious toddler whom we love more than we love ourselves. We would give our lives for our precious toddler, but what our toddler needs now, at this stage in his life, is not our life, but our own personal sacrifice to demand obedience. In the short run, demanding obedience is arduous, but in the long run, it will save untold trouble and heartbreak. Once, I met with a group of older ladies who were not Catholic. When a young mother stated she was holding her eighth child, one mother said, "I had only one child, and that was enough for me." Another mother said, "Two was all I could handle." Discipline is a key to managing children.

This is no time for a soft personality. This is no time to say, "Well, Mary never spanked Jesus." True. He never defied her, either. Or scratched her coffee table on purpose. Or kept banging the glass on her counter after she told Him ten times not to do it!

Parenthood is a tough vocation! It demands a strong parent to say, "Stop that, or you will get a spanking!" It demands a tough mother to get up off the couch when she is two months pregnant, and spank that plump little two-year-old leg! This is no time for Mom to whine, "Sweetheart, won't you please stop that constant banging?"

Pray daily with your children, including your toddler, for the necessary graces, the strength, the energy to train them, and to give them the necessary discipline and self-control so that eventually they will be obedient to their heavenly Father. This is a primary duty in the vocation of motherhood.

House rules for toddlers

Determine your house rules and post them on the refrigerator or in an appropriate room. Verbally explain them to your toddler. Even though your toddler cannot read them, he can understand that you read rules and that reading rules leads you to follow rules. Show your young child how you read labels on the cans in the kitchen and recipes in the cookbook, and then act on what you read. Show him that if you follow the directions correctly, measuring the ingredients carefully, setting the oven the correct number of degrees, the result will be a successful meal.

Teach your child that you read signs when you drive the car, and by following the signs and directions, you can arrive safely at your destination. Toddlers can understand that the rules on your refrigerator are for him to obey, that you are reading them to him and telling him to obey them. Teach him that by obeying rules, the family can reach a goal: a nice pleasant home. Teach that, by learning to follow the rules of God, we can all obtain the ultimate goal: happiness in Heaven with Jesus.

Your house rules could include putting toys away after playing with them, picking up clothes, helping Mother to pick up at the end of the day, using a napkin to wipe up spills, eating at the dining table and not in the living room, not going into the bathroom without Mother, not banging on the table, playing the piano gently, wearing a hat outside, and so on. Needless to say, you cannot have an endless list, but a few for each room or occasion would not be too much.

Toddler psychology

The inclinations left from Original Sin are very obvious in young children. Many toddlers will purposefully, every day, test Mother to see how far they can go before she will actually punish them. Mothers can become tired of this daily conflict, this daily training period for toddlers. Toddlers can and often do outlast mothers. That is why we mothers need to ask for the daily graces to persevere and to be consistent.

Boys and girls who are disobedient, disrespectful and who talk back to their mothers at thirteen are boys and girls who were not trained to be obedient and respectful toddlers.

Be obedient to God yourself. Train your children.

Give your toddler a certain period of the day to sit still, at least for a few minutes, perhaps 15 minutes in the morning, and later in the afternoon. Give your toddler a book or a toy, but explain that this is sit-still time. When you take your toddler to church, insist on his sitting still for Mass.

When your toddler is sitting at the table for meals, insist that he not jump up and down, or get out of his chair. Teach him to sit for a reasonable time, fifteen minutes or so, during the meal.

Take the time and effort to have a practice session with your toddler about the rules. For instance, if you have a rule that your toddler is to come into the house immediately when you call him, practice it. Send him outside, and call him in. Do this several times to make him understand and remember the rule.

Pre-School catechism

When children are very young, even before they begin to talk, parents should begin teaching about Jesus, about His love for all of us, and about the importance of pleasing Jesus by being obedient. Show your child holy pictures. Teach him to pray. Teach your child about the Child Jesus and how He obeyed His parents. Read stories about Jesus and other Bible stories.

Explain over and over to your child that you love him, no matter what he does wrong, but that because you love him, because you must be obedient in training him as God has commanded you, you must punish him whenever he behaves with disrespect or disobedience.

Have regular prayer times when all the children, including your toddler, are required to join in saying the Rosary and other prayers. Schedule these times when the children are refreshed, not after the evening meal when the children are too tired. Children—whether toddlers or teens—should not be excused from the family prayer time. Adapt the prayers and participation according to the child's age. However, even very young children can learn the Rosary quickly, and soon can be leading the prayers.

Pre-School home schooling

For the sake of discipline in the family, allow toddlers and pre-schoolers to be part of the home schooling program. If you use desks for the older children, obtain a small desk for your toddler so he can feel like a part of the family home schooling activities. Give your toddler coloring books and crayons, or a small chalkboard with colored chalk. Allow a toddler or pre-schooler to sit on your lap while you are teaching. Let him turn the pages of the book for you.

Try to have a little "formal" home schooling with your toddler, even for just a few minutes each day, if he or she appears interested. Girls are interested even at two or three years old. Toddlers can learn their letters and their numbers. You want to develop a good attitude toward learning, and during the toddler years is the best time to start. The more a toddler feels involved in the family activities, the fewer discipline problems you will have.

Usually toddlers pick up the memory work from their older brothers and sisters even while they are playing on the floor. They may not understand everything they have memorized just from hearing it, but they have memorized it nevertheless. When it comes time for them to understand concepts, such as two plus two is four, or "The Saviour of all men is Jesus Christ," they already have many of the facts memorized and can easily apply understanding. Discipline problems lessen as concepts are learned quickly and easily.

If a toddler becomes cranky, an older brother or sister might like to help him learn his letters or numbers or preschool catechism; or the brother or sister might like to read stories to the toddler. This is a good experience for children to help each other, and for the toddler to accept help from an older sibling. Often spoiled children will insist on only Mother teaching. Encourage the development of a good attitude on the part of the toddler to accept learning from an older sister or brother.

Children in the elementary levels

If your children have been enrolled in a school before you decide to bring them home, you have your work cut out for you as you try to discipline. Our society is selling children the idea that each person, young or old, male or female, husband or wife, infectious disease carrier or abortionist, has the right to choose whatever he wants for himself. No one, not parents or friends or society, has any authority over anyone else. This secular teaching of "liberty," which many children have accepted, makes it very difficult for parents to discipline their children.

Equality

The idea of individual freedom has become so perverted that many elementary children believe that their decisions are of the same value with any their parents might make, and consequently they have equal rights and authority. Modern family counselors have sold young parents on the idea that they should have family meetings where each child may express his or her own ideas. This is fine if children realize Dad and Mom have the final say as heads of the family. Many parents are literally bullied, sometimes even frightened, first by family counselors, and then by their children.

Television programs portray families with children having equal decision-making authority in the family. Those with Cable TV have it better by being able to tune in the older shows which portray Mother and Father "knowing best." The whole concept of family is being portrayed perversely today. Situation comedies portray several men raising children, or simply groups of people of different ages living together.

Textbooks, especially in the anti-family "family life" programs, consistently describe families only as a group of people living together. Regulations in some cities give paid leave time to an employee to attend a funeral of a homosexual partner. Courts, employers, and insurance companies are being forced to accept "alternative life styles" and "alternative families." This kind of "thinking" in our society damages the lines of authority and the interpersonal relationships which exist in the natural, traditional family. Everyone is affected in some way.

A line of authority

The Catholic Church has a line of authority which was established by Jesus Christ Himself when He named St. Peter as the first Pope. When the Pope speaks on Faith and Morals, there is no vote taken among the bishops (except at Church councils). The Pope speaks with divine authority, directed by the Holy Spirit. Bishops are to obey the Pope, priests are to obey bishops, lay people are to obey the priests. Of course, all of this assumes a faithfulness to the truths of the Church. This line of authority must continue in the Catholic family. Father is the head of the family, Mother is the heart of the family. Children are to obey their parents.

Parents who do not enforce respect and authority from their children are not following Catholic teachings, and their children are not being obedient to the Commandment of God that children must honor and obey parents. This particular Commandment was repeated strongly and frequently in the Old Testament. Parents who do not demand respect and authority from their children are committing a sin, even a grave sin in some cases, because this is directly related to their vocation of marriage: to educate their children, which means the training of the will as well as the training of the mind.

Do not accept the world's view that children are normal if they insist on making all their own decisions or go through periods of being rebellious. Do not accept disrespect as a "sign of growing up." Do not accept back talk as normal. Do not accept freaky popular haircuts and strange or immodest clothes as normal. These outward signs are evidence of an inner acceptance of the values of the world.

It is SO hard to be consistently strong. But do it while they are young and little. It can just about kill you if you wait until they are teenagers!

The Catholic Church is like a loving mother. Her directives will give you strength and courage for the discipline work ahead. Read works from Pope Pius XII on discipline.

Excerpts from Pope Pius XII

Children are like the "reed shaken by the wind." They are delicate flowers whose petals fall with the slightest breeze. They are virgin soil on which God has sown the seeds of goodness but which are stifled by...the "concupiscence of the flesh and the concupiscence of the eyes, and the pride of life."

Who will straighten the reed? Who is to protect these flowers? Who will cultivate this soil and make the seeds of goodness bear fruit against the snares of evil? In the first place, it will be the authority which governs the family and the children: namely, parental authority.

Fathers and mothers today often bewail the fact that they can no longer get their children to obey them.

Stubborn little children listen to nobody; growing children spurn all guidance; young men and women are exasperated by any advice given, are deaf to all warnings, and insist on following their own ideas because they are convinced that they alone are fully in a position to appreciate the needs of the modern way of life....

And what is the cause of this insubordination? The reason generally given is that the children of today no longer possess the sense of submission and respect due to the commands of their parents....Everything they perceive around them serves the sole purpose of increasing, exciting, and setting fire to their natural, untamed passion for independence, for mocking the past, and thirsting avidly for the future....

The normal exercising of authority depends not only on those who have to obey, but also, and in large measure, on those who have to command. To put it more clearly: We must distinguish between the right to possess authority and give orders on the one hand, and, on the other, that moral excellence which is the essence and spirit of an effective...authority, which is able to impose itself on others and to exact obedience.

The former right is conferred on you by God in the very act of your parentage. The latter privilege must be acquired and preserved; it can be lost and it can be strengthened. Now the right to command your children will not be worth much if it is not accompanied by that control and personal authority over them which ensures that they really obey you....

This authority must be tempered...with loving kindness and patient encouragement.

To temper authority with kindness is to triumph in the struggle which belongs to your duty as parents....All those who would advantageously rule over others, must, as an essential element, first dominate themselves, their passions, their impressions. There is no real submission to and respect for any authority, unless those who obey feel that this authority is exercised with reason, faith, and a sense of duty, because then only do they realize that a similar duty binds them to obey.

If the orders you give your children and the punishment you inflict proceed from the impulse of the moment, or from outbursts of impatience or imagination or blind ill-considered sentiment, they will mostly be arbitrary or inconsistent, and perhaps even unjust and ill-suited.

But how are you going to rule over your children, when you do not know how to conquer your moods, to control your imagination, and to dominate yourselves? If on occasions you feel that you are not completely master of your feelings, then put off to a later and better time the correction you want to make or the punishment you think you must inflict. This quiet dignity with which you speak and correct will be far more effective, far more educative and authoritative...

Do not forget that children, no matter how small they may be, have a very observant eye and will immediately be aware of the changes in your moods. From the cradle itself...they soon become aware of the power their childish whims and fits of crying have over weak parents, and with innocent cunning, will not hesitate to exploit it to the full.

Avoid everything that may lessen your authority with them. Beware against ruining this authority by a nonstop series of recommendations and criticisms...Avoid deceiving your children with fake reasons....Never falsify the truth. It is far better to keep silent....Take care that no sign of disagreement appear between you [parents]....Do not make the mistake of waiting till your children are grown up in order to make them feel the calm weight of your authority...

Your authority must be devoid of weakness, yet it must be an authority which stems from love, and is steeped in love, and sustained by love....If you really have this parental love...in the commands you give your children, these commands will find an echo in the intimate depths of the hearts of your children, without there being need to say very much.

The language of love is more eloquent in the silence of labor than in much speech. A thousand little signs, an inflection of the voice, an almost imperceptible gesture, an expression of the face, a little hint of approval... all these tell them, more than any protestations, how much affection there is in the prohibition that annoys them, how much kindness is hidden in the order they find troublesome. Then only will authority appear to them, not as a heavy weight, a hateful yoke to be cast off...but as the supreme manifestation of your love.

Must not example go hand in hand with love? How can children, who, after all, are naturally inclined to imitate, learn to obey, if they see the mother paying no heed to the order of the father, or worse, quarreling with him; if the home is full of continual criticism of all forms of authority; if they see their parents are the first not to obey the commands of God and the Church?

You must give your children the example of parents whose manner of speaking and acting serves as a model of respect for legitimate authority, of faithfulness to duty. From this edifying sight, they will learn the true nature of Christian obedience and how they should practice it towards their parents, in a far more convincing manner than any sermon to that effect. Be firmly convinced that good example is the most precious heritage you can leave your children.

Pius XII, 1941, *Speech to Newlyweds*

Explanation of philosophy

Children of school age can understand your explanation of why you are home schooling. The children need to understand. Understanding motivates them to be obedient, to do the schoolwork, and to help with the housework.

Take the time, perhaps at the beginning of each quarter of the school year, to explain again why you are home-schooling. Take a whole day and help the children to write it down for themselves, in their own words. Let them post it up in their study area. They can decorate it with crayons or colored pens around the margins, perhaps even frame it.

"I am home schooling because I love Jesus and want to learn more about Him from my parents." Let them phrase it for themselves, but the spiritual motivation is important.

Emphasize the spiritual reasons you are homeschooling, the positive reasons and not the negative problems in the local schools. Do not talk about drugs or sex education or lack of discipline or poor academics. Talk about living the Catholic Faith, being able to say family prayers together during the day, and using sacramentals for liturgical feasts.

Talk about the virtues to your children, that you want your Catholic family to live the virtuous life. Explain to your children that after faith, hope, and charity, the most important virtue is obedience. Have the children look up the virtues in their catechism. Let them write down and discuss the theological virtues of Faith, Hope, and Charity. Let them write down the moral virtues of prudence, justice, fortitude, and temperance. Let them write down and discuss the other virtues listed in their catechism: piety, patriotism, patience, humility. Let them discuss other virtues they can think of.

You *can* discipline your children, that is, train them to be obedient and follow rules and regulations. They need to understand the higher goal, what the "big picture" is, what the mission of the Catholic individual and the Catholic family is about.

Explain again and again to your children that if parents love God, they must obey Him. In obeying Him, you yourself must teach your children to behave according to His rules, to practice the virtues. In order to properly train children, parents often must use punishment as a consequence of disobedience to the rules.

Explain Purgatory and why God requires justice in reparation for sin, either in this world or in Purgatory. Bring stories of saints into your explanation. Many young saints prayed and offered their sacrifices and sufferings to Jesus in reparation for sin. Relate stories of young saints to your children as you explain the purpose of discipline, or submitting one's will as an act of reparation for sin.

Teach your children about Hell. For almost two thousand years, parents have taught their children about Hell and about the Last Judgment. We should not hide the existence of Hell from our children due to some modern psychological opinion. Children need to know the consequence of sin, especially of mortal sin. After all, Jesus died on the Cross as a consequence of sin and the need to repair for such offenses to God the Father. Your discussion of Hell, and its horrors, can be shaped by your child's degree of maturity. The Blessed Mother revealed a vision of Hell to the three children at Fatima.

A benevolent dictatorship

Do not run your family like a democracy. Run your family like a benevolent dictatorship. Parents are the loving "dictators" because they are given the graces to know what is best for their children. One problem that parents often have is that they try to explain to their children over and over why they should not do something. Explain to your children once or twice why they should not do something. Do not continue the conversation endlessly. Try not to argue or raise your voice, try not to keep talking, try not to become emotional or upset as a child persists in asking the same question over and over again.

Practical rules

For children at the elementary level, it is important to be very clear about the rules and regulations you expect for your home and family. Take a day about four times a year to discuss these and help your children write them down and memorize them. If you do this at the beginning of each quarter of the school year, they can be revised as necessary. Have the children post them at their study area, in the bedroom, or in the kitchen.

Some of the rules might be: to rise at a specific time, to make the bed, no running in the house, and to keep the clothes off the floor. "Keeping the room clean" is not specific enough for children. Other rules or goals, based on the Commandments, would be: no talking back disrespectfully, no temper tantrums, no throwing things at people, and no teasing brothers and sisters. Some positive rules might be doing the schoolwork when it is assigned, doing it neatly, reviewing the work, and correcting the errors before handing it in to Mom. Of course, do not overwhelm your children with rules. You can work on a few at a time. Discussing these rules when everyone is calm will result in better understanding and a better attitude toward obeying.

One note of hope for young families who are having problems disciplining their three or four young ones: as your family grows, believe it or not, the disciplining becomes easier. This is because once the older children have learned your rules and are obeying them, they will not allow the younger ones to break them. Often older children will do some disciplining themselves, keeping the young ones in line when Mother is absent or busy with the baby. Have courage. It does get easier!

Some references

There are many books on disciplining children, but choose ones which are written by Christians. One of the best is Dr. James Dobson's *The Strong-Willed Child*. His basic point is that there are consequences to be paid for disobedience, which is of course in line with Christ's message. Dr. Dobson has also published *Discipline with Love* and *Temper Your Child's Tantrums*. His latest book is *Dare to Discipline, Revised*.

There are a few books by Catholics on disciplining children. One I would recommend is by a Catholic father of twelve children, Marion Michael Walsh, called *The Christian Family Coping*. It covers more than discipline. It is divided into four sections: The Early Years of Marriage, Having Children, Keeping the Faith, and Living the Faith.

Steve Wood, a Catholic home schooling father of eight children, gives excellent talks on discipline based on Biblical principles. His audio tapes are available from Family Life Center (P.O. Box 6060, Port Charlotte, FL 33949).

Punishment

One Christian child psychologist believes that when children do something they should not, or refuse to do something you have told them to do, you should count to three and then the child must go to his room for five minutes. If you tell your child to stop teasing his little brother, and he continues to do so, you tell him, "That's one." If he continues, the parent does not shout or argue, but says, "That's two." If the action still continues, the parent says, "That's three. Take five." Taking five means the child must go to his room for five minutes. Sometimes, of course, the child must be dragged to his room, but after about a week, the child understands that when you start the counting, if he does not stop his unacceptable behavior, he will end up in his room.

If you try this, you might want to choose another place than the bedroom. Some parents choose a place without distractions or toys available. Some suggestions are a basement or an area in the hallway or a walk-in closet. Some parents have a younger child stand in a corner, or sit by himself in a chair away from others in the family. The amount of time should be adjusted according to the age of the child and the seriousness of the misbehavior. This type of punishment is to make the child aware that since he or she is not acting in an acceptable Christian manner, he has temporarily lost the privilege of being part of the family activities.

The key to success in disciplining your children is to explain the rules first, then to explain the punishment (counting and then a time away from the family, or a spanking), and then to keep control by not talking, not arguing, not becoming upset yourself. *It is important to be consistent in your punishments*, giving them when they are needed.

Marion Walsh in *The Christian Family Coping* states that he and his wife started moral training in obedience as soon as a child could walk. In a chapter on punishment, Mr. Walsh discusses various types of punishment: rebuking, humiliation, deprivation, exaction, restitution, and corporal punishment.

Mr. Walsh defines a rebuke as "any word or action which condemns or rejects another's conduct." Humiliation is a method to make the action look ridiculous; deprivation is depriving the child of such things as a meal, sweets, toys, books, or some activity. Exaction means to require the child to do some work as a punishment, such as cleaning the basement. Restitution means paying for any loss or damage due to the child's fault or carelessness. While he includes corporal punishment, he warns against using it in public. He himself spanks his children, but warns that it should never be done in anger, nor should it be done often, and it should be on the buttocks or legs.

Some families believe in using a switch, similar to the "rod" mentioned in the Bible. A switch can be used on the leg of a child, causing a sting, but not any injury. The advantage of a switch is: first, the parent is not using his hands, which should be used for hugging and affection; second, since a parent cannot use the hands as a threat, simply picking up a switch can serve as a threat for a switching. Usually children quickly change their behavior at the *sight* of the switch.

Give children some decisions in home schooling

Older children will need less discipline and will be more motivated in their home schooling if they are allowed to have participation in some of the decisions regarding their home schooling. Let them help decide their schedule for chores and when they want to work on each school subject for the day. Let them write their daily schedule and post it on the wall where they study. Ask them for their ideas concerning projects for the science class, and creative ideas for history lessons.

Meals, study, and chores

Little tricks can help older children learn self-discipline. Relate the schoolwork schedule to meals and chores for the day. For instance, schedule a certain number of school work assignments before meals are allowed. Perhaps a math assignment would need to be finished before breakfast. Certain classes would have to be finished before lunch, and three or four more classes before dinner. This should be only for older children, about 10 or older. This emphasizes the relation of work to eating, which is Biblical, and teaches the child in a dramatic way the value of Dad's work for the family. Household chores could be scheduled in the same manner. This should cut down on the necessity of Mother constantly nagging at the children to keep working.

The trick is for Mother to remain firm. It will not hurt a child to miss a meal or two; results will be achieved by the third meal. Be realistic, of course, especially when you start. Require less work rather than more. For instance, you actually want little Joey in fifth grade to do two math pages in the half hour before breakfast. However, require only one page the day you start the new "Math Before Breakfast" program. In a couple of days, require one and a half pages. A few days later, require two.

In addition, chores should be scheduled between classes. This gives your children an opportunity to be active periodically throughout the day. It will help in the area of discipline if children can have frequent but brief physically active periods throughout the school day. If chores are left to the end of the day, after classes, parents will find children resistant and difficult to discipline.

Time

Some children lack self-discipline because they have no concept of time. They seem to dawdle over their assignments and let their minds wander. Obtain an alarm clock for such a child to place on his desk. Set the time and the alarm for the amount of time needed to do an assignment. As the child works each day with his clock, he begins to realize how much time a particular subject takes him. He is able to pace his work. This teaches discipline, self-control, and responsibility—and keeps Mom from nagging!

The "I'm Dumb" syndrome

In a large family, you are likely to have one! He may be very bright, but with all the family activity going on all around him, and his attraction for the outdoors, he cannot seem to keep pace academically, especially as compared with his siblings. So he complains and whines, "I'm dumb." He resists doing his work because the others are doing so well or moving along more quickly.

Emphasize the different gifts which each family member has been given by God. Talk about the gifts of Mother and Father, as well as the gifts of grandfathers and grandmothers. Talk to him about the gifts your child inherited from Mother or Father. Explain that God decided that in an efficient society, everything could not run smoothly unless each person has different strengths and gifts, and consequently can do different jobs.

Give this child an opportunity to spend more time on assignments at which he can feel successful. Emphasize the spiritual aspect. Tell him to ask his guardian angel to help him to do his best for his patron saint and for the Baby Jesus. Give him more assignments at which he can feel successful. If he loves drawing, give him an opportunity to make birthday cards for cousins. If he has great coordination at basketball shots, see if other home schooling families might like to start a basketball team.

Learn how your children learn

Sometimes discipline problems arise because children are frustrated with the learning process. Young boys, for example, often learn better orally, by hearing stories read to them. Obviously they need to learn to read eventually, but some may not be ready for reading until they are seven or eight. So be sensitive to how each child learns best, and be sure that the classes are geared to the appropriate learning style. Using the proper method for the child, subject by subject, will increase learning success, and decrease behavior problems.

Handwriting

Discipline problems sometimes arise because of assignments related to writing. Most boys have a problem with handwriting because their small muscle development is slow. They can swing a bat, toss basketballs into a hoop, and bang a volleyball over the net, but putting little lines down in a tiny space between parallel lines on a piece of paper just does not come naturally to the young male.

Consider doing the assignments with your boys orally. They can record some assignments onto a tape recorder. They love hearing their own voice! Another popular option is for them to type assignments on a word processor. Boys do extremely well on these because they can make corrections without rewriting the whole book report or assignment.

Do not give up teaching your boys handwriting, but for longer essay-type assignments, or when the boys are frustrated and are on the verge of becoming a discipline problem, parents should consider the word processor. The final product will even be legible!

Work too hard

Discipline problems often arise if the schoolwork is too difficult, or too easy, or too boring, or too repetitious. In the home schooling situation, even with a program, materials should be adjusted to the abilities of the child. Most school programs will customize the materials, so that a student may be in fifth grade, but be taking fourth grade Math and sixth grade Spelling.

Home school programs will send placement tests which will help parents and the school to identify the proper grade level for their children in each individual subject. However, placement tests are just one factor. The best evaluation is really done by the parents as they work on a day-to-day basis with the children.

Memory work

Discipline problems can arise when children do not have basic concepts memorized. Children become frustrated as they work long hours over math problems because they never memorized their multiplication tables. They become frustrated over catechism memory work in Book Two when they never mastered the questions and answers in Book One.

One of the attitudes in today's society is that nothing needs to be memorized. "Everything is going to change anyway, so why bother memorizing anything today?" But many things do not change. Our Catholic teachings will not change, the Bible will not change. Mathematical concepts will not change; addition and subtraction facts will not change. It is important to memorize basic facts in each area of knowledge.

Most important to the present discussion of discipline is this: children are more disciplined about their studies if they have basic facts memorized. In addition, memory work itself is a discipline. It forces the mind to focus on learning facts in a logical manner.

If your child has been in a school

There is no question about it. Many home schooling mothers can testify to it. The longer a child has been in a school situation, the more difficult the disciplining and home schooling are, especially during the first year.

Not only are the children usually behind academically, but their attitudes and behavior, in regard to schoolwork and to parents and family, often have been shaped negatively by the school environment, by schoolmates, by the secular textbooks, and by their teachers.

In addition, school principals and teachers sometimes become nasty when they lose a good student. One mother with a large family enrolled several children in our program. The oldest girl was in eighth grade, and was an honor student at the previous Catholic school. One of the teachers at the school was upset that she was losing an honor student. Without the mother's knowledge, this teacher would phone the young girl, talk against home schooling, speak disparagingly about the Catholic textbooks, and criticize the girl's mother. The teacher so influenced the girl that she soon refused to open her books.

Eventually, the girl became convinced by the teacher to go to a social worker to claim her "right" to be educated in a school. The father, who was not Catholic and was away from the home much of the time, could not give the mother the support she needed. Eventually the mother was emotionally drained by the pressure of social workers and the threat of a court situation. She gave all her children back to the "Catholic" school system.

Your Catholic philosophy, your attitude about the Catholic lifestyle, probably is contrary to what your child has been learning from the secular, politically-correct textbooks that are used in both public and Catholic schools. Your values are in conflict with what the children have learned from many of their classmates, who are often children emotionally disturbed or feeling unwanted by their own parents or legal guardians.

Your values about family are often in conflict with those of teachers who are promoting their own ideas or the National Education Association's ideas of a new world order where "family" is being redefined, a world in which homosexual fathers are given custody of their children in divorce cases, and lesbian women are allowed to adopt children with their female "lovers."

The less time your children have attended school, the fewer discipline problems you will have.

Some rules to help you keep control

Exclude anti-Christian worldly influences, such as rock music, playmates with conflicting values, certain styles of clothes and haircuts, vulgar words, phrases, or conversation. Encourage pictures or illustrations of teen saints. Do not allow posters of secular "heroes" on bedroom walls. Show videos of good Catholic or moral stories rather than allowing the children to attend movies. Do not allow your children to attend any local classes, such as sports or arts and crafts, unless you monitor them for a while.

It is surely unnecessary to say anything here about television. Many home schooling families do not have a television. If you do, be sure you monitor what the children watch. Most of the shows reflect the pagan values of our society. Even television cartoon shows portray sex and violence and promote occult and criminal activities. This is very specifically documented in a book titled *Saturday Morning Mind Control* by Phil Phillips.

Mr. Phillips has studied toys which generally promote aggression. He has researched the electronic video games, which portray blowing up people, places, and things as the goal. Heroes and villains act violently with maces and swords; they mug their enemies, throw people onto subway tracks, and invent horrible death traps. Computer games commonly portray evil spirits, demonic characters, and witchcraft. Many advertise they are for "those interested in astrology, magic, fortune telling, and ancient mysteries." (p. 151, Phillips)

Mr. Phillips continued his research to include comic books.

> Many comic books have viciously anti-Christian themes and plots. Some blatantly present reincarnation, spirit channeling, and the use of psychic powers and even crystals as means of gaining and exercising power. (p. 155, Phillips)

In his research on specific PG-rated movies for children, Mr. Phillips writes

> In *Care Bear Movie II*, an evil spirit occupies the body of a fourteen-year-old boy. *Rainbow Brite and the Star Stealer* was a children's movie with almost everything in it that a parent doesn't want to teach children: greed, self-centeredness, violence, sexism, and all-around evil. (p. 159, Phillips)

Many more children's movies are documented by Mr. Phillips.

We are living in a pagan society, and the only way to raise our children as Christians is to keep them from these anti-Catholic, anti-family, anti-life influences. It is almost a guarantee that if children are constantly exposed to these influences, there will be a discipline problem at home.

Confraternity of Christian Doctrine (CCD) classes

Some home schooling parents ask about whether their children should attend CCD classes at their parish church. Many CCD teachers are influenced by the world, and are not necessarily Catholic in their beliefs. Some CCD teachers do not even pretend to be Catholic. There have been cases of non-Catholics hired as CCD teachers and even as directors of religious education for parish programs.

The students in CCD classes are from public schools and are very affected by the pagan school curriculum and environment. The CCD program was set up specifically for children in non-Catholic schools, not for children being taught daily by their own Catholic parents, using a Catholic curriculum and forming them in the Faith by their own daily good example and good works. Often CCD classes present values conflicting with authentic Catholic teaching because of the values of the teacher, the fellow students, or the text-books. Let's not forget than an American bishops' committee studying the American catechisms announced in 1997 that most catechisms being used in parish programs are "seriously deficient."

Some dioceses are drafting guidelines to pressure home schooling families to enroll their children in parish CCD classes. Up until 1997, most home schooling parents did not object to their children attending the CCD classes because they believed that in seven days a week, they could correct "deficiencies" of one-hour-a-week parish programs.

However, about 1996 and 1997, many CCD classes began presenting Catholic children with information regarding AIDS, homosexuality, masturbation, the use of condoms, and so on, as early as fifth grade, to counteract what is being taught in the public schools. While the parents, clergy, and CCD educators of the public school children may see such a need for public school children, home schooled children have not been exposed to such teachings and remain, for the most part, innocent.

In fact, it is precisely the sex education being presented in the Catholic schools, and now in the CCD programs, which undermines the innocence of children and has been the main force for parents to teach their children at home.

Home schooling parents will never allow their children in CCD programs which present sex education, even under the name of "family life" or "chastity" education, because it is an occasion of sin, it deprives them of their innocence and it often causes spiritual and emotional disturbance. If pastors insist that home schooled children may not receive the Sacraments unless they attend the CCD classes, home schoolers will do without the Sacraments until their children are 18 and can enter adult classes.

Some pastors who are using good catechisms, such as the Faith and Life series, and do not include sex education in their programs, ask why some home schoolers do not send their children to the parish CCD classes. I believe that the teaching of the Church, and especially of Pope John Paul II, is clear: parents have the right and responsibility, and the graces from the Sacrament of Matrimony, to choose the means and methods which they believe are appropriate to teach the Faith to their children. Not attending even a good program is a matter of choice.

Parents must make their own decisions with the sacramental vocational graces they have been given. Whatever the decision, parents should make it clear that they recognize the right and responsibility of the Church to offer religious education programs and to evaluate the readiness of the child to receive the Sacraments. In fact, home schooling parents should consider becoming CCD teachers so as to teach the Faith, omitting lessons dangerous to the faith and morals of children, especially during the years in which their own children are preparing for the Sacrament of Confirmation.

Integrate Catholicism

The very best way to maintain discipline in your home is to integrate the Catholic sacramental life into your family life. If you and your children are daily living the Catholic life by saying the Rosary, wearing the scapular, making Advent wreaths, decorating a May altar, and all the other year-round liturgical observances, your children are more likely to be good children. They will respond to your directions and instructions. The spiritual bond and the respect based on their understanding of spiritual authority will keep them from exhibiting discipline problems.

Just because neighbors are having such terrible discipline problems with their children does not mean that we will have terrible problems. It does not mean that we should expect discipline problems, nor accept discipline problems as normal.

Catholic families should not have serious discipline problems with their children. It is a matter of taking control when children are young, and keeping control. Discipline is not easy, but it is important in preventing rebellious children, and in home schooling successfully.

Junior high and high school levels

Discipline must be started with babies, or as the papal directives put it, from the cradle. It must be done consistently during the toddler stage, and continued up to about age twelve. By age twelve or thirteen, the children should be well-disciplined.

Some parents might laugh at the idea that teens can be self-disciplined, because the teenagers of today seem to be the worst discipline problem of all. They talk back, wear outlandish clothes and haircuts, spend money foolishly, spend too much time with their friends, talk on the phone too much (even insist on their own phone), and are generally out of the control of their parents. Some parents think this is just part of growing up, the generation gap, or some other secular modern excuse.

In a Catholic home schooling family, where discipline starts when the children are young, we can almost guarantee that the common teenage problems will not exist. In fact, many home schooling parents can say that the teen years are the best age for home schooling because their teens are self-disciplined, self-motivated, and have their study skills developed. In addition, the teens help the younger children with their studies and with baby-sitting, help with taking care of the house, and also assist Father with his business. In addition, they are interesting people who have thoughtful discussions about important matters with Mom and Dad. Many start taking vocational courses or college courses early; they become involved in church activities, or begin helping at the local pregnancy center.

Home schooling parents who have teenagers taught and

trained at home since they were babies will tell you that
one of their greatest joys is their teenagers. These young
adults are happy, they are mature, they are good students,
they are good Catholics, they are good citizens, they are
concerned about the basic issues of our society. Unlike many
teens, they are socially well-adjusted.

In the biographies of successful people, whether saints
or American heroes, we read that most matured at a rather
young age. Our schools today are keeping young people from
maturing, mostly from maturing spiritually. That is the key.
With spiritual maturity comes maturity in many other ways.
Mature home schooled teens are a great blessing for parents.

Discipline for the young adult

For the home schooling teenager who has not had the
benefit of home schooling in the earlier grades, learning at
home can be a difficult adjustment. Since many teenagers
are not happy in a school where values conflict with their
own family's values, parents will find they are anxious but
willing to come home to learn. Though the academics may
be difficult, they are willing to work hard to remain at home
away from the environment they have experienced at school.

Some teens, of course, resist home schooling. For some
families, bringing the teens home can be a terrible experience. Some teens are resentful and rebellious, and cause
serious family disruptions.

Nevertheless, parents should persist in the struggle to teach
obedience to their teens. In fact, for the first year a teen is
home for schooling, it may be necessary to give the teen
only two or three academic courses. The main thrust of the
first year at home will be to teach discipline, that is, respect
for authority, the meaning of obedience, the virtues of charity, kindness, and humility. The teen needs to discover Jesus
and Mary, to pray every day, to go to daily Mass if possible, to get back to regular Confession, and so on.

Do you remember the movie *The Miracle Worker*, about
Helen Keller and her teacher Anne Sullivan? Anne literally
fought with Helen to make her change. Mothers of autistic

children have to physically keep touching, pulling and pushing their children to come out of themselves into reality.
When mothers love their children, they can go to great lengths
to help them overcome terrible handicaps. If a teenager has
been in a school and has accepted many of the attitudes and
behaviors typical of the schools, home schooling parents will
need to take drastic action, requiring great physical and emotional perseverance, to save their children's souls.

When a teenager is brought home, the training of the
will must take priority over the academics. With the grace
of God and the love and patience of parents, a young person can be turned around to accept and live the authentic
Catholic family life.

Father can help

For the best help in discipline, enlist Dad. We can almost
guarantee success in disciplining children when Dad becomes
involved with them. God gave fathers a certain authoritative
manner in their voices which seems to elicit quick obedience from their children. A father's interest and concern in
the disciplining and home schooling is a strong factor in
motivating children. Father is especially important in the
disciplining of teens.

On the other hand, if Dad is non-supportive or openly
critical of the home schooling, it will be most difficult to be
successful. Children, though often innocently, try to widen
the conflict between parents, usually as a gesture of unhap-
piness more than any personal pleasure in fomenting trouble.

Dad needs to teach and to reinforce certain attitudes
about work: that work is important, that work is commanded
by God, that we can gain graces by doing our school work
well, and that God teaches us through the Bible that if we
do not work, we do not eat! The children need to see that
work provides the food and shelter for the family, and that
a job well done is a source of human happiness.

In the encyclical *Christian Education of Youth*, Pope Pius
XI quotes the practical instruction of St. Paul to the Ephesians: "And you, fathers, provoke not your children to

anger." The Pope explains that this fault of provoking the children to anger is the result

> not so much of excessive severity as of impatience and ignorance of the means best calculated to effect the desired correction. It is also due to the all-too-common relaxation of parental discipline which fails to check the growth of evil passions in the hearts of the younger generation.

Disciplining ourselves

We home schooling mothers and fathers need to learn how to discipline ourselves as well as our children. Mary Kay Ash, of Mary Kay Cosmetics, in her autobiography, explains her very disciplined life. She writes about getting up before the rest of the family, saying her prayers, and doing an hour of work in the quiet of the morning. Of course, she takes the time to put on her Mary Kay Cosmetics, making herself look and feel beautiful.

We need to do the same in a Catholic way.

The best way to keep yourself disciplined is to have a schedule or plan for each day, written down. A teacher's plan book, such as we use for our children's lessons, makes a great personal plan book. For many years I have been using these to record what needs to be done day by day. Obtain one large enough to record everything you want. Keep it in the kitchen or wherever you can get to it easily and frequently throughout the day. It may be near your telephone or on your dresser. Attach a pen so you never are looking for something with which to write.

Start each day by referring to your plan book. Write in it as the day goes along, recording appointments set up, calls you need to make, special times with the children, times for Mass or other church events, and so on. You may want to put some home-schooling related items, but those may be recorded sufficiently in the children's plan books. Before you retire at night, check off what you accomplished, and move into the next day what you did not accomplish.

If you do not set daily goals for yourself, you will never accomplish very much, and you will feel distressed that you did not do anything. Do you frequently say to yourself, "Where did the day go?" With a plan book, you know beforehand where you are going, and at the end of the day you know where you have been.

Good example

In a speech (1941), Pius XII told parents that good example is the primary means of disciplining their children:

> Would it be consistent to correct a child for the same faults that you commit daily in his presence? To want him to be obedient and submissive if, in his presence, you criticize ecclesiastical or civil superiors, if you disobey the commandments of God or the just laws?
> Would it be reasonable to want your children to be loyal when you are untruthful, patient if you are violent and ill-tempered? Example is always the best teacher.
> With love, guided by reason, and reason guided by faith, home education will not be subject to those deplorable extremes that so often imperil it: alternating weak indulgence with sharp severity, going from culpable acquiescence which leaves the child unguided, to severe correction that leaves him helpless. On the other hand, the affection shown by parents...distributes due praise and merited correction with equal moderation, because it is master of itself, and with complete success, because it has the child's love.

Our primary goal in home schooling is presenting our children to God, teaching them the Faith, the prayers and celebrations of the Liturgical feasts, teaching our children to be obedient to us as parents because we are the representatives of God while they are growing up. Finally, we must discipline ourselves by following God's commands and by giving good example.

Chapter 10:
Home Management in the
Catholic Home Schooling Family

Mrs. Ginny Seuffert, the mother of eleven children, has been home schooling for many years. She has been active in the Pro-Life movement for many years, and has home schooled her children for several years. She often speaks at home-schooling conferences. Following are some of her thoughts on Home Management.

I have a dear elderly friend, in poor health, who becomes frustrated when she is unable to remember some event that happened recently, or when she must search for a word she needs to express a thought. Yet she can remember, in vivid detail, events from her childhood in a loving home. These memories are fresh and alive eighty years later. What a gift her parents gave to her!

No matter what sadness our children may encounter later in life, memories of a happy, loving, well-ordered home will sustain them. It is the ideal setting to pass on to them our beautiful Catholic beliefs. Armed with the true Faith and their parents' values, our children will never be alone with the troubles that come in every person's life. They will always have their faith in Christ, their Guardian Angels, and the comfort of the Blessed Mother. A dependable schedule will allow little ones the time and opportunity to develop a regular prayer life. Finally, a smooth, well-run household fosters attitudes of serenity and confidence which aid our children in their educational development.

In light of all this, isn't it sad that modern American society seems to save its recognition and support for professional accomplishments which occur outside the home? We devalue the irreplaceable role of parents, mostly Mother, in making homes places where the next generation of good citizens and holy saints will come from. Should we not devote to our homes the energy and innovation we now reserve for the workplace?

The key to successful home management, then, is to restore each Catholic household, the domestic church, to its
rightful place as the building block of society. We must
apply the same goal-oriented principles and professional attitudes to the running of our homes that a CEO gives to
directing a Fortune 500 company.

A typical routine

Treating our housework as valued professional work
means thinking about how we do our work, not just carrying
on the same routine that Mother or Grandmother may have
had. The following daily routine, which I generally follow
for our family of ten, is offered as a starting point to get
you and other members of your family thinking about how
to operate your home in an efficient, thrifty, cheerful
manner.

A good day actually has its start before evening prayers
the night before. Take a few moments and straighten the
bedrooms. Have the children pick up any toys, put away any
laundry, and clear the tops of their dressers. Have them lay
out their clothes for the next day. This way you can approve
of their choices and deal with any problem ("Mom! I don't
have clean socks!") before it becomes an emergency. You
probably will not have to dust and vacuum, and this should
take no more than ten minutes per room.

The next day, try to get up at least 30 minutes before
the rest of the family. This will allow you to say a good
Morning Offering and plan for the school day without having every thought interrupted by a child's voice. Get dressed
and complete your grooming for the day (even if you're
wearing sweat pants and a ponytail) right away. Try to make
your bed before heading out to the kitchen.

I start home schooling with the younger children as soon
as the breakfast dishes are cleared. Math or Phonics is usually assigned so they can work, more or less on their own,
at the kitchen table, while I wash up. My two older pupils
work independently in other rooms. My four-year-old plays
with the toddler.

After dishes, the rest of the morning is spent home schooling. I usually sit down and work on Religion, Reading, and English, subjects which the younger children may need help with. After the second and third graders have completed most of their work, they take a turn with the baby so I can give my preschooler a reading lesson. My two older daughters, seventh and fourth grade, pop in and out as they need help with something.

We usually take a long lunch break, an hour or more. The older girls make lunch for the younger children while I fold a load of laundry and pop another one in the washer. The students have play time while I eat and then wash another set of dishes. Sometimes I go to noon Mass.

Before the children begin schoolwork again, I plan my supper. Anything that can be prepared in advance is begun now. A little thought will show that almost any meal can be started hours before. For example, you can mix and shape a meatloaf and wash baking potatoes at noon. It will be easy to put them in the oven at 4:30 for a 6:00 dinner. Salad greens can be washed and cut in the middle of the day, allowed to drain in a colander, and refrigerated until mealtime. This planning and preparation will really pay off as dinnertime approaches and Mom is running kids to after school activities, Dad is coming in, the baby is fussing and the phone is ringing off the wall.

We start school again around 1:00. The younger children might color a map or write their spelling words. Sometimes they do an art or science project. I give more attention to the older girls, correcting their morning work, drilling their spelling or vocabulary, or proofreading a writing assignment on the word processor. Hopefully the baby is napping now.

Around 3:00 school is over. Now is the time to clean the main living area of your home. Have the children pick up the mess they made while you were teaching. Make sure the bathrooms, especially the sink and toilet, are cleaned, run the vacuum, sweep the floors and generally straighten the living room or den and the kitchen. Fold the last of the laundry and distribute it to the appropriate bedrooms.

Next, have a child set the table. This is a great job for

a pre-schooler because you are in the room to supervise, and once the dinner plates are set, it is easy to add the silverware, napkins, and drinking glasses. As you finish with a pot, pan or utensil, wash it right away. Dinner will be more enjoyable if you do not have to look at a sinkful of dirty pots. After dinner, clean-up will be quicker, too.

In our house, Mom and Dad usually do the dishes with the oldest son while the two older girls give baths and get the preschoolers ready for bed. The middle children take care of themselves.

As the children prepare for bed, your home should be reasonably straightened, the kitchen and bathrooms clean, and the laundry done.

Weekend work

A daily routine, similar to the one I just outlined, will keep your home tidy, decent meals on the table, and clean clothes in the dresser. At the same time, your children will be receiving the best education available in America today. In most cases, however, especially with a large family, you will still have to catch up on weekends.

I use weekends to correct assignments, prepare lesson plans and organize the children's work for the following week. This is especially important for the older students who complete much of their work on their own. Even self-motivated, experienced home-educated pupils need to have their assignments reviewed and their progress monitored. This weekly overview makes the end of each quarter less stressful.

Saturday is also the time to tackle more time-consuming chores such as washing windows, mopping floors, scrubbing the tiles around the tub, ironing, and grocery shopping. Reserve Sunday as a day of worship and visiting with family and friends. It is crucial that home educated children be allowed to socialize with children from other observant Catholic families. Memories of these happy times, and even many friendships made, will last a lifetime.

This is also the time to point out a fact that many hard-working Christian women are hesitant to admit: there is no disgrace in hiring domestic help. The year I began home schooling, I used the money we had been spending on tuition and had a cleaning lady come in two or three times each week. I no longer have any cleaning help, but that got me over the "hump" and allowed me some time to gain confidence in my ability to teach my own children and develop my daily routine.

Home teaching, especially if you have several children or students in the upper grades, is not something that can be done in your spare time. I believe many families send the children back to institutional schools when it seems as though the burden is overwhelming, as can happen when a new baby arrives. Domestic help might get you over a rough spot. Before you pay to send your children to parochial schools, where they may lose their Faith, try getting a cleaning service in. Even once a month service (getting the webs down before the place looks haunted) will be a real help.

If you cannot afford a cleaning service, be creative. Maybe you can swing getting your husband's shirts professionally laundered. You can probably hire neighborhood kids to shovel walks or mow the lawn. Sometimes you can get a local teenager to watch the children for a few hours each week, freeing you up for household chores. Ask relatives to give you a one-shot cleaning service as a Christmas, birthday, or anniversary gift.

If none of this works for your situation, do not put the kids in school yet! Roll up your sleeves and begin the difficult task of training your children to help you around the house.

Motivating the children

The keys to training your children to be responsible for household chores are starting early and being consistent. Pray to their Guardian Angels for help in this important task. Give them the example of the Holy Family and add the ejaculation, "Jesus, Mary and Joseph, pray for us now and at the hour of our death, Amen," to your Morning Offering.

One home school leader suggests you keep a basket in the corner of your toddler's crib and have the baby put stuffed animals and other crib toys into it before you pick him up. That is about as early as anyone could hope to start! Certainly, sometime between the ages of one and two years, all children can be trained to follow simple instructions. "Get me your diaper" and "Put this in the hamper" are just two examples.

Most three-year-olds are anxious to please Mommy and are capable of performing many simple tasks. They can empty wastebaskets with help, wipe down the kitchen table and the seats of the chairs, and pick up laundry.

Four-year-olds should be responsible for putting their own clothes into the proper dresser drawer, setting the table for dinner, and feeding the family pet.

By five, most children can sweep or vacuum a floor (well, maybe not the best job!), dust furniture, and even fold laundry. As soon as you are sure your child will not try to taste a dangerous substance and can learn safety rules, he can be taught to clean the bathroom.

Now most parents will claim that the problem is not that their children are unable to help with chores, it is that they are unwilling. I would like to see them be cheerful as they work, but my husband claims that is impossible, and if they were that good at this age, they would not need parents at all. Still, I will pass on a few tips that might prove useful in your situation.

1. Do not allow your children to argue with you. Complaints like, "Why do I have to do this all the time?" should be met with, "The only answer I expect to hear is, 'Yes, Mom.'"

2. Give your children the good example of hard-working adults. I am grateful to my own parents who instilled this value in their children, mostly through their own actions. All of my siblings are hard workers who are not afraid to tackle any new job. My husband gives great example to our own children.

3. Remind a child to do a job, even if it is for the fifth time, in the same tone of voice that you used the first time.

Comments like "How many times do I have to tell you...?" delivered in a high-pitched screech are understandable but ineffective. A courteous and reasonably quiet atmosphere is more difficult to maintain in a large family, but just as important.

4. Remember that your children owe you respect and prompt obedience. Remind them that deliberate disobedience is a sin against the Fourth Commandment and should be confessed.

5. Thank your children when they do a good job, and brag about them, in their hearing, to Daddy and others.

An efficient laundry routine

I have been attending a series of lectures given by a woman who directs a school for those entering the field of hotel and hospital management. After twenty-one years of marriage and eleven children, I can finally clean up my act in the laundry room. As with everything else, thinking about how to do the job will allow you to streamline the operation. Here are some simple ideas that have worked for me.

1. Have your husband hang a clothes bar next to the washer so shirts and dress pants can be hung up as soon as they have dried.

2. Buy a package of large safety pins and have family members pin their socks together before they are put into the hampers.

3. Invest in three hampers and write one word, either "light," "dark" or "white," on the tops. The wearer places the garments in the appropriate bin. You will be able to put a load of wash on much more quickly if it has already been sorted.

4. Fold each individual load as it is finished. Do not let it pile up!

Not all of the ideas in this chapter can be applied to every situation, but a little thought will allow you to come up with your own solutions. Pray to the Blessed Mother for help in modeling your home after hers.

Successful Home Management

Ginny Seuffert's ideas for home management are certainly good ones, and you would do well to implement many of them. As you continue home schooling, you will, of course, make adjustments and find your own ways of doing things.

Successful home schooling is dependent on successful home management. If a mother feels she cannot keep her house decent, her frustration will be reflected in her home teaching. Or lack of home teaching.

Mothers often call me to say they are afraid to start home schooling because they are so disorganized. They believe they cannot manage both the housework and the schoolwork. We need to establish priorities here. Are we going to allow our kids to have sinful exposure to sex education classes, or to have peers laugh at them because they wear a scapular, or to have teachers tell them that their parents are "old-fashioned" and that they can choose their own values? Are we going to allow this because we are disorganized, or because we are afraid we will not have time for housekeeping? Let's get control of ourselves and our lives!

To organize means to put parts together so that they work as a whole. For us home schooling mothers, it means to be efficient enough in the parts, the day-to-day tasks, so that our home schooling works overall, and is successful in training our children to be educated Catholics living the Catholic lifestyle.

Home schooling mothers need organization for their home management for several reasons: for themselves to have control over their own lives; to be a good example to their children; to bring calm and stability to the household; to accomplish goals and not feel frustrated and unhappy; and to give their children the best Catholic environment for learning and living their Faith.

Scheduling

The home schooling mother is a manager of a small business. She needs to keep control of what is happening in her little home schooling household. The first thing I recommend is that you obtain your own Plan Book. You can purchase a Teacher's Plan Book from Seton or an office supply store, or even a businessman's Plan Book in the stationery section of a department store.

Before we can achieve order, we need to define order. Some mothers feel that order means that everything is in its proper place, things are done at certain times, and the house is straightened up daily. But order, like so many other things, can be an attitude more in the mind than in the things around you.

A busy executive has a desk piled high with work. To a stranger, his desk is disorderly. But if his wife comes along and straightens up his desk, he has a fit. He has certain piles in certain places, certain types of things in certain piles, and he is familiar with the order in the "disorder." He is mentally comfortable with his desk situation.

We mothers need to pray for a proper understanding of what an orderly home means. We should be able to function, but that may not mean the floor needs to be mopped every day or that everything needs to be in its place every day. We need to come to an emotional peace within ourselves, accept a certain amount of imperfection, and realize that the daily home schooling lessons, encompassing spiritual values, are much more important than perfect physical order in the house.

This is not to say that we cannot do better with putting things in their place, and keeping the house clean and straightened. We need to keep trying, and as our family grows, we need to teach these values to our children. In fact, they need "hands on" practice in this area!

Clean rooms

I have worked to keep the major areas of my house under control. Thus if someone walks into my home, he will see that the living room, the dining room, and the front hall are clean. It makes me feel better to have the major living areas kept clean and orderly.

Up until a few years ago, when I began working full time, I would make the boys clean their rooms weekly. But I seldom got upset about their rooms. There were too many other important things, such as saying the daily Rosary.

I have kept an extra closet for kitchen utensils. There is nothing more wonderful than a whole closet with lots of shelves to put away the mixing bowls and extra pans, the sifter and the mixer. In a small house, you can keep these things on a shelf in the laundry room. This is something you need to have your husband build for you if necessary.

Here is a trick one mother gave me to keep shoes and boots for her large family: her husband built shelves in an entryway by the back door. All the shoes and boots are kept there and do not cause a constant mess by being all over the house or under beds.

In addition, I have a place to put things which are out of season, or which I just want out of sight for a while. This is usually a place in the basement, but could be an extra small bedroom, or large walk-in closet.

Cleaning a room

When cleaning a room, have your child carry a trash bag and pick up things to throw away. Items to go in other areas of the house should be put in a pile according to the area. Once the room is picked up, others can pick up a pile and deliver it to the proper room.

Scheduling the cleaning

We busy home-schooling mothers need to see ourselves as managers of a small home business. We need to develop a strong managerial personality as we train our children to be the helpers necessary to maintain our home. Dad should be involved to make sure, each evening, that the children have done their daily household chores as well as their schoolwork.

Schedule what you are going to do each hour, each day, each week. This can be done for your home schooling, for housework, for Mass, *and for prayer*. (Prayer will often, almost inevitably, take a back seat unless it is scheduled— but it has to be given the front seat!) Schedule chores for each child in your plan book. This should be written in your child's lesson plan book as well, or posted in the kitchen.

Keep everything on a schedule as closely as possible: meals, chores, bedtime, rising, school work. You and your children need a regular schedule. You will feel better emotionally and even physically if you eat, work, and sleep on a regular schedule.

Get the kids to help with housework. Schedule household chores within the schoolday schedule, between classes. Making their beds or putting on a load of laundry can be scheduled between history and science. Other chores are taking out the trash, sweeping the floor, vacuuming the carpet, dusting, mowing the lawn, bringing in the wood (if you have a wood stove), straightening up the classroom or recreation room, and so on.

One successful home schooling mother of ten children said her success was due in large part to the fact that she had a daily schedule and "stuck to it religiously." She told me her schedule was never off "by even five minutes."

The meals

Keep your meals organized. The regularity of family meals is very important to children. Give children different responsibilities for setting the table or helping prepare the meals. Establish regular times and regular procedures for meals: prayer before meals, rules of courtesy, proper dress at the table, and so on.

There are many little tricks for preparing meals. When making dinner, make enough for at least two nights. I always make two meatloaves, or a double recipe of chicken, or enough stew for two nights. I have a friend, a home schooling mother, who is also a midwife, with a large family of eight children, who takes one day each month and cooks, with her children helping, THIRTY meals! She freezes them, and, for the next four weeks, has the basic main meal ready in minutes. This gives *"Semper Paratus!"* (always prepared) a new meaning!

Reduce the number of things you have in the kitchen or pantry. Give away extra glasses, or dishes (as gifts!). Keep only what you actually want to wash. When I moved the last time, I evaluated each kitchen item as to how much I really needed it. I gave away tons of things. I really like having less to clean. I am a big believer in paper plates for breakfast and lunch, and for dinner during the week.

Your greatest help, your children

It is important to teach your children to help with the housework. A home schooling mother cannot do the home schooling properly and still do all the housework. Children should not only help because mothers need the help, but also because it is morally a matter of justice that children learn to work as part of the family team. In addition, God made us so that we need to work to be happy, and children should learn that.

Many teenagers and adults have not learned the joy and happiness that work can bring. Since Jesus was "subject" to His parents, we know that Joseph taught Him his trade of carpentry, the normal procedure at that time in Jewish history. We need to remind our children that Jesus was thirty years old before He started His public preaching, and St. Joseph had died before that. So we know that Jesus worked to help His foster father, and later to provide for Himself and Mary. He was known as "the carpenter's Son."

It has been discovered that men who have problems with keeping jobs often did not work when they were young. They either came from wealthy families, or were spoiled, or no one really cared whether they worked or not. When children are not required to do work around the home, it is difficult to have them do their schoolwork as well. They are being pampered.

Schoolwork is important for children, but housework is for the benefit of the whole family. Housework promotes team effort. If we are home schooling to strengthen our family life, or family bonds, we need to realize that housework actually helps more in this area than schoolwork.

Some jobs for personal care should be routinely done, such as taking care of one's own bedroom. Extra jobs could receive some small allowance if the parents wish, such as washing the kitchen floor, cleaning the basement, or doing extra yardwork.

Teaching the chore

When teaching children to do a chore, you need to help the child with the work the first few times. That is the only way the child will do the job the way you want, or nearly the way you want. I have found that working alongside my children on a big cleaning project helps keep them moving and doing the work the way I want.

It is important to show your children very clearly how to do a job. Instead of just handing a child the cleanser and a rag, show him how you clean the sink. Explain as you go, pointing out the necessity of getting behind the faucet, and so on. When you check his work at first, and later randomly, check all those points you spoke about when you taught him.

My boys have been doing their laundry since they could reach the dials on the washing machine! They can sew and iron and take care of themselves and their clothes.

Older children can help teach younger children to do chores. If a younger child and an older child are a team, the older will keep doing the work as he teaches, and the younger one will be kept moving by the older one. The two children should not be close in age as they will end up teasing each other. There should be several years age difference in the children on a work team.

Just as you encourage your children in the schoolwork, encourage them in their house chores. One of the things I tell my children is that they should clean as if Jesus Himself were going to visit that particular room. It is important that our children understand that they must do their very best even in seemingly small and unimportant things. I remind my sons that when the Challenger exploded in the sky and several people were killed, it was because someone was careless in regard to the formation of ice on an "O ring." Little things can mean life and death in some cases!

Just as it is a serious responsibility to teach our children their reading and their math, so it is a serious responsibility to teach them to do household chores. There is nothing worse than adults who cannot take care of themselves or their homes in an orderly and reasonably clean fashion. And if a child does not do his chores, or his schoolwork, to the best of his ability, he will probably not do his best at his job or career later on.

Teaching children to work, both physically, as in doing household chores, and intellectually, as in doing schoolwork, is a serious parental responsibility.

Learn from others

Locate books at the library or Christian bookstore on home management and chores for children, such as: *401 Ways to Get Your Kids to Work at Home.* This book has "Techniques, tips, tricks, and strategies on how to get your kids to share the housework...and in the process become self-reliant, responsible adults." There are several books in Christian bookstores which can help you in home management also. The home schooling associations promote the books by Don Aslett: *Is There Life After Housework?*, *Clutter's Last Stand*, *It's Not Just a Woman's Job to Clean*, and *Make Your House Do the Housework.* Another book presenting interesting and time-saving ideas is *Once-a-Month Cooking* by Mini Wilson.

A Caution

One word of caution. Church activities are wonderful, but do not allow them, even though they are good religious activities, to cause you to neglect your home and children. Your first duty is to raise your children in the Catholic family lifestyle. Limit your church activities or charitable works to those in which your children can participate with you.

Conclusion

Adjust your lifestyle and your home for home education. Make your home a haven, a stable, comfortable orderly place, not like the frantic, stress-filled, disorderly, chaotic and confused outside world. Make your home a refuge, a protection from the outside problems; make it a pleasant, loving, prayerful home. When God told Moses that our homes were to be decorated with the Ten Commandments on our doors and doorposts, on our entryways inside our homes, I believe He meant that our home environment should reflect our Faith. Keeping an orderly home should reflect our Faith in a God of order and harmony.

Chapter 11:
Home Schooling in the
Single-Parent Family
by a Home Schooling Single Mother

"Suffer the little children to come unto me, and *forbid them not....*" (*Mark* 10:14) These words of Christ, the greatest Teacher that ever was or ever will be, show the enormous responsibility that parents have of teaching their children about God from infancy, developing in them a steady, ever-increasing knowledge, love, and service of Our Lord.

The Catholic position is, and has always been, that "Parents have the most *grave* obligation and the *primary* duty to do *all* in their power to ensure their children's physical, social, cultural, moral, and religious upbringing." (1983 Code of Canon Law, 1136, emphasis added)

Pope Leo XIII in *Sapientiae Christianae* states that

> By nature parents have a right to the training of their children, but with this added duty: that the education and instruction of the child be in accord with the end for which by God's blessing it was begotten. Therefore it is the duty of the parents to make every effort to prevent any invasion of their rights in this matter, and to make absolutely sure that the education of their children *remain under their own control,* in keeping with their Christian duty, and above all to *refuse* to send them to those schools in which there is danger of imbibing the deadly poison of impiety.

The Catholic Encyclopedia further informs us that "Catholic parents are *bound in conscience* to provide for the education of their children, either at home, or at schools of the right sort." (Vol. V, p. 304, 1909 Ed.)

The Second Vatican Council also reiterated this statement in its document, *Declaration on Christian Education,* 1965. In fact, the primary and *co-equal* purposes of the Sacrament of Matrimony are the procreation *and* education of children. Our Creator Himself has ordained that for this divine purpose of marriage to be a success, it is essential that the order and structure of a solid family life be preserved.

What can be done, though, when you find that the sacred structure is missing a key component—when one parent is no longer part of the picture? Is it possible for the remaining members to survive? Can a broken home go beyond mere survival and elevate itself to becoming a healed, stable, happy, and God-centered family? Yes, if the children are home schooled.

Does home schooling under these circumstances seem unrealistic—perhaps impossible? Well, the Church informs us that as parents we have "the right," "the duty," and "the grave obligation" to provide for our children's education.

In his encyclical, *Christian Education of Youth*, Pope Pius XI tells us,

> Since education consists essentially in preparing man for what he must be and for what he must do here below, in order to attain the sublime end for which he was created, it is clear that there can be no true education which is not wholly directed to man's last end.

With this in mind, there is no way that a true educational system can include sex education, drug awareness, death awareness, AIDS education, values clarification, or any other topic of instruction of the humanist agenda. Clearly, this is not what Our Lord intended when He gave the command, "Go forth and teach ye all nations."

A further view into the history of Christian education will be enlightening and surprising to many. The Holy See back in 1875 issued an "Instruction to the Bishops of the United States Concerning Public Schools" in which it pointed out that the public schools as conducted involved grave danger to the faith and morals of Catholic children, and that "consequently both the natural and the Divine law forbade the attendance of Catholic children at such schools, unless the proximate danger could be removed." In many dioceses this meant the exclusion from the Sacraments for parents who sent their children to public schools. (*Catholic Encyclopedia*, Vol. XIII, p. 580, 1912)

In 1929, Pius XI, in his encyclical, *Christian Education of Youth*, wrote,

> We renew and confirm [the teachings of Pius IX and Leo XIII that]...the frequenting of non-Catholic schools...is forbidden for Catholic children, and can at most be tolerated, on the approval of the Ordinary alone, under determined circumstances of place and time, and with special precautions.

If the public schools of 1929 constituted grave occasions of sin and were considered so dangerous to the faith of a child as to necessitate such a papal statement, what conclusions can one draw from the school systems of today, both public *and even* Catholic schools, many of which do not teach the authentic Faith.

Let us recall Our Lord's stern warning:

> But he that shall scandalize one of these little ones that believe in me, it were better for him that a millstone should be hanged about his neck, and that he should be drowned in the depth of the sea. (*Matt.* 18:6)

If the Church's position on the importance of a truly Christian education is not a convincing factor to home school, perhaps the concerns for the mental stability of a child coming from a broken home environment will be. The emotional jarring that these children undergo during the breakup of their families is something they will carry with them for the rest of their lives. Do you want to further scar them by separating them from the family they have left—sending them to a school outside of the home six to eight hours each day? They will not find the security and stability they need so desperately there. Do you place the younger ones in a day care center, or perhaps an after-hours school program, so much the trend now, if the parent must seek outside employment? What about the adolescents or teenagers who must come home to an empty house? It will not be long before trouble finds them. Will any of these solutions help them?

We have already experienced a generation of children being raised by strangers: the baby-sitter or day-care provider is the one who discovers the first tooth or witnesses the first step, and sadly, the one who is very often even called "Mama." Will these children become the well-adjusted, family-oriented adults of tomorrow? How could they when there was no one around *just* for them, who would love them as no "care-giver" ever would, because no one can take the place of a parent. That was the way God intended it to be, and without either the order of a stable family life or the hierarchical structure of parenthood, children will lack the proper nurturing. Sadly, the child of today's broken marriage often loses not one, but both parents.

During such an emotional upheaval as the loss of a parent, would not the best place for these children be in their homes? Is it not important for them to be able to cry when they feel like it, to scream when they have to, to act out in any other way that they need to, but most importantly, to know that one parent is *still there* for them?

In the face of a broken family, which is better: to leave your children at the school bus stop each morning, or to pack them all up in the car, drive down to the parish church, and begin each and every day with the Holy Sacrifice of the Mass? Without doubt, neither you nor your children could possibly get through such a trial without God's *constant* grace and the nourishment and strength of His Precious Body and Blood.

Will the school day go smoothly? Probably not, especially in the beginning. But think of the alternative. In any event, it is far better to endure whatever comes, together, *as a family*, rather than each one suffering alone.

Trust and pray to the Holy Family often; never permit a day to go by without the family Rosary being said. Entrust your children to Our Lady's care, being confident that the Blessed Mother will guard them as her very own. Do this and Our Lord will be ever present in your home as King and Head of your family and your home school.

The Teaching

How does a single parent go about teaching the children without the benefit of a partner? Actually, in this regard, things are virtually the same as for home schools having both parents. In most households, it is the father who is the breadwinner, leaving the majority if not the entirety of the schooling up to the mother. There are also many families whose circumstances require that both parents be employed, and yet home schooling is still an integral part of their life. In this respect the situations are similar because the schooling is usually one parent's job, and so the same standards for successful home schooling apply to all.

First, be organized. Have a schedule and streamline your day. Eliminate all the unnecessary errands, visits, and events that take up your precious time. Set a timetable for getting up, Mass, breakfast, and the beginning of class, and stick to it. Do not answer the phone during school hours. Set a certain time for ending the school day and do not go beyond it, especially if you must then prepare for an outside job. If something in class is unfinished, it can hold until the next day.

Next, be flexible. If your situation requires you to work outside the house for two days, then teach on the other three days. Teach on the weekends. Homeschooling easily adjusts to a working schedule.

Third, be motivated. Home schooling is *good* for your family. Look upon it as such, each and every day.

Fourth, acknowledge that it is a sacrifice and a commitment, but no different, really, from the entire sacrifice that responsible parenting requires.

Fifth, enlist the help of others. The children, however young, should have their share of responsibilities: one washes dishes, the other sweeps the floor, the little one can put away clothes, pick up toys, etc. They must understand that you cannot do it all. If relatives approve of what you are doing, then have them help in whatever way they can. If they are not supportive, however, it is usually best to stay clear of them.

Finally, and most importantly, we must be virtuous. Patience must be cultivated as well as self-discipline, which also means self-denial. Perseverance also is vital. Do not be so discouraged that you want to give up! If the day becomes impossible, then let your child read a book on the life of a saint. Fill your children's bookshelves with wholesome, entertaining books: classics and good spiritual reading. (TAN Publishers is an excellent source.) Or let them watch a good video: *The Song of Bernadette, A Man for All Seasons, The Day the Sun Danced.* The children *will learn* from these.

Console yourself with the knowledge that as long as your children are home with you, their souls are safe. Teach them their prayers, the Ten Commandments, prepare them for the Sacraments, have them examine their conscience each and every night. In the end, being a computer expert will be of little consequence. What Our Lord wants to see in our children is a pure heart.

One of the things you must come to understand to successfully raise well-adjusted, spiritually healthy, *good* children without the benefit of a traditional family unit is that it cannot be done without traditional family routines and values. It is especially important that meals be taken with all family members present. These should be quiet, relaxed, sit-down-at-the-table times, where "company" manners are always observed and the TV is *never* on. This ought to be a time for discussion of the day's events, telling jokes, in all, pleasant communication among the family members. Cook their favorites. Avoid the temptation to think it is too much trouble to make that special dish just because there is only one adult around now.

Make a big deal of special occasions, especially those holidays that are traditionally family oriented. Go out together as a family often. Splurge when you can for a breakfast out. A dish of ice cream at the local shop is always a treat and is one of those few extravagances that will not do too much damage (hopefully) to a single parent's budget. Make Sundays special by packing a lunch and visiting a museum (or other free place of interest). The goal is to make life at home happy and memorable despite the circumstances.

How do you go about all this if you need to earn money as well as home school your children? Ideally, try to find employment that can be done at home. The fact that you will always be there for your children will be a far greater wealth than any you could amass at an office. But if this just is not feasible, then work out of the house in the evenings or at nights. The thing to strive for is to be home for your children during the day, when they need you most.

Remind yourself of the words of the great Doctor of the Church, St. John Chrysostom, "What greater work is there than training the mind and forming the habits of the young?" Be sure that the children are under the care of a trusted relative or conscientious baby-sitter. Have the sitter come to your home. This, too, builds stability in the child. It is never fun to sleep in an unfamiliar place only to be roused out of a deep slumber a few hours later, brought out into the cold night air and have to face another car ride before being in the comfort of your own bed.

Again, pray for a solution. This is one area where if you storm Heaven, Our Lord will provide in great measure. Teaching your children at home is what God *wills* for you to do and if He sees that you are determined to overcome the obstacles, He will reward you abundantly by removing whatever stands in your way.

The main objective is to minimize the loss, as far as possible, of the missing parent. You have been given the graces through the Sacrament of Matrimony to raise and *educate* your children properly, even if it means you must do so alone.

Our Lord has blessed nature with a wonderful capacity for resiliency and adaptability. If one should have the great misfortune to lose something so necessary as an eye, the tragedy does lessen to some extent because the surviving eye grows stronger *primarily because of the loss* and so begins to compensate and take over for that member which is no longer there.

A true follower of Christ knows that in being less we

are capable of more. When we recognize our nothingness, Christ will use us to accomplish great things. For the sake of our children, we must go to Him each day acknowledging our weaknesses, our limitations, our mistakes, our uncertainties as single parents and ask Him to do for us and through us all that we are incapable of doing ourselves.

An anonymous Seton single home schooling mother of several children wrote the previous article. We have several single parents who are home schooling their children on the Seton program.

How do they manage work and home schooling? Most have jobs they can do at home. This is usually typing or computer work, or editing, or proofreading. Some work for a relative who is understanding of the situation and is willing to allow the mother to be flexible in her hours.

Some are nurses or work in nursing homes, or work as private duty nurses at night. Others work at night-time jobs, such as with the phone company. Some arrange for another home schooling mother to take their children in the afternoon. Some live with or nearby their mother or a sister so they have a built-in baby-sitter when they need to work in the afternoon or evening.

Some single mothers take their children to work. One works at a bookstore and the children sit in the back room. One is a secretary and the child has a desk next to hers. One mother cleans homes and takes her children with her.

There are a few single fathers teaching their children. Most work at home. One is a writer, one is retired. One teaches in the morning, then goes to work in the afternoon. One lives with relatives who help.

We need to commend, and pray for, single parents who recognize their grave responsibility and are willing to make extra sacrifices for the sake of their children.

Chapter 12:
Teaching Children Who Learn Differently
by Cathy Gould

Mrs. Cathy Gould is Seton's learning disability special-
ist. She earned her B.A. in Education from James Madison
University in 1977, and her M.A. in Education with endorse-
ments in Learning Disabilities and Emotional Disturbance
from George Mason University in 1981. Cathy is fully cer-
tified for teaching L.D. children. She has been teaching L.D.
children and advising parent groups for the past sixteen years.
She has been working with Seton families, full time, for the
past eight years. Cathy is the mother of three young children.

Learning Disabilities (LD), Hyperactivity Disorder, and
Attention Deficit Disorder (ADD) are often referred to as
the hidden handicaps. Identifying educational handicaps early
may alleviate some problems that are typically seen in children with learning disabilities, such as low self-esteem, failure syndrome, and depression.

When parents school their children at home, they notice
at an early age when a particular child is not progressing
using the traditional methods. Then the search begins to
discover exactly how the child learns differently.

Just what is a learning disability? There are four points
that most professionals will accept as true of all individuals with learning disabilities:

1. The learning disabled individual does not learn satis-
   factorily with standard methods of instruction.
2. The basic cause of failure to learn is not a lack of
   normal intelligence.
3. The basic cause is not a psychological problem.
4. The basic cause is not a physical handicap.

The Education for All Handicapped Children Act defines
a learning disability as a disorder in one or more of the
basic psychological processes involved in understanding or
using language, spoken or written, which may manifest itself
in an imperfect ability to listen, think, speak, read, write,
spell, or do mathematical calculations. Learning disabilities

include perceptual handicaps, minimal brain dysfunction, brain injury, dyslexia, and developmental aphasia, but they do not include disabilities due to vision, hearing, or motor handicaps, or to mental retardation, or to cultural or economic deprivation.

Identifying

In assessing a child to determine if a learning disability exists, the professionals look for a discrepancy between a child's potential, or IQ, and performance or achievement. Children with a learning disability must have an average to above-average IQ. Listed below are characteristics that occur in individuals with learning disabilities. They can occur also in young children under 10.

1. *Mixed dominance and directional confusion.* Past the age of five or six, a child still seems confused about whether to use his right and/or his left hand for writing, picking up objects, and eating. Some children may have difficulty crossing the midline of the body. They may have a hard time picking up an object to the left of their body using their right hand.

2. *Poor concept of time.* They do not have that internal sense of time. They have difficulty staying on a schedule, or with scheduling projects. An example of this may be that when you give your child ten minutes to play outside, ten minutes come and go. In 30 minutes, you must find your child, who is totally oblivious to the amount of time which has passed.

3. *Unusual powers of observation.* Nothing escapes their view. They have a difficult time filtering out unnecessary things and focusing on what is important.

4. *Unusual creativeness.* They are able to see things very differently from others, and to approach problems in a very unique way. They can be very mechanical, take things apart, and eventually put them back together. Often these individuals can be very gifted artists.

5. *Appear to be "misfits and loners."* They are often called "dumb" by the other students; the teachers often call

them lazy; they may not pick up on body language or jokes, and they may have difficulty knowing what is acceptable behavior.

6. *Mental retrieval problems.* They may know the word "red," and may have known it for a long time, but when you are talking to them in a conversation, suddenly they cannot pull that word out of their repertoire of vocabulary.

7. *Memory problems.* Many children with learning disabilities have a terrible time memorizing the addition, subtraction, multiplication and division facts—the basic tables. They also may have difficulty memorizing lists of information, such as names of the planets, or names of bones.

8. *Reversals.* While this is normal in young children, it should not be continuing past age 10. Reversals are evident in the writing of words and numbers. The frequently reversed letters are b and d, p and q; sometimes numbers are reversed, such as 3, 7, and 9 being written backwards; sometimes 6 and 9 are reversed.

9. *Fine-motor problems.* This may be displayed through shaky writing, inappropriate formation of letters, difficulty finding the space on a paper, difficulty with spacing letters and words, or difficulty staying between the lines.

10. *Attention problems.* They may have difficulty focusing their attention on the task at hand, or they may be able to stay on task only for very short periods of time.

11. *Sequencing.* Many of these individuals have difficulty retelling something that happened to them in the correct sequence. They may go to a party, and come back and tell you everything that happened at the party; however, the sequence of events may be all out of order. They also may have difficulty sequencing information that is told to them. Consequently, they may find it difficult to follow directions in order. They may have difficulty with mathematical problems which require a sequence of steps.

Attention Deficit Disorder

In 1982, the American Psychiatric Association defined Attention Deficit Disorder as a biological disorder. Their definition is as follows: The child displays, for his/her mental chronological age, signs of developmental inappropriateness, inattention, impulsivity, and hyperactivity.

In 1987, the name of the disorder was changed from Attention Deficit Disorder to Attention Deficit and Hyperactivity Disorder. According to Dr. Craig Lidden, this is a collection of biologically based characteristics, as follows:

1. low arousal — These individuals show sleepiness during times that require focused attention. They may be less alert, less awake, or fidgety.
2. impulsivity
3. distractibility
4. short attention span
5. difficulty concentrating
6. poor monitoring — This is failure to critically evaluate behavior, which often makes them unaware of consequences of their actions.

General characteristics that seem to be accepted by professionals dealing with ADHD are:
1. inattention
2. impulsivity
3. difficulty delaying gratification
4. hyperactivity
5. emotional over-arousal — These individuals feel things more intensely than other people.

Please remember that such children demonstrate these characteristics, or behaviors, in a variety of situations over a long period of time.

Learning materials

Developing a curriculum for a child with LD or ADHD provides a unique challenge for parents. With the one-on-one approach in home schooling, many children with LD or ADHD are able to use a standard grade-appropriate curriculum. Of course, modifications may be necessary.

Other children may need a curriculum totally adapted to their needs. They may need books with shorter chapters, though basically the material is grade-appropriate. Some children need materials with more pictures and color. Some children may need to respond more frequently, meaning every paragraph or every few pages, rather than at the end of a chapter.

Several publishing companies carry materials that have been designed specifically for the learning disabled or the attention deficit hyperactivity disordered child. There are other companies that have designed "remedial" textbooks which may be appropriate also.

Globe Publishers produces a series of textbooks for the junior high student in Science, American History, and Geography. Steck-Vaughn publishes an appropriate Science and Social Studies series for the elementary level. Educators Publishing Service offers quality materials in spelling, vocabulary, phonics, and primary language arts in general. None of these are Catholic, but they are seldom anti-Catholic or anti-family, though parents should be sure to read the books before giving them to their children.

The questions to ask when you are looking for materials for your child are: what is your child's basic learning style, and what is the teaching style of the material? For example, if your child is an auditory learner, he or she may do very well with a sing-song kind of approach to phonics, whereas, if your child is a visual learner, that approach, no matter how catchy it might be, may not work for your child.

There are some key points to consider when you are establishing a curriculum for your child. The most important aspect to look at is your child's strengths and weaknesses. You want to develop a program that is based on your child's strengths, and using those strengths, you can reinforce the weaker areas.

If your child has a particular weakness, the most important thing to do is to find a way to deal with the material successfully. For example, if you have a child who has memory problems with math, work on the memorization of facts through using a variety of other materials, such as hands-on items. At the same time, you could take a few minutes each day and teach other math concepts, such as time or measurement.

If your child does not know the multiplication facts (tables), but you are letting him go on to the three-digit by three-digit multiplication problems using a calculator, such as 324 X 436, instead of having your child punch in each entire number and multiplying, have your child do the problem step by step, so that he is actually multiplying as he would on paper. The only need he has for a calculator is for the basic multiplication facts. When your child learns the facts, he is still able to do that particular type of multiplication problem. If you let him punch in the entire three-digit number times the entire three-digit number, your child is not learning how to multiply such numbers manually.

Memory problems

For children who have memory problems, a good technique is to develop a cue card system. Purchase spiral-bound index cards that are 5 X 8 or 4 X 6, or you can punch holes in the individual index cards and hook them together with a single notebook ring. Present the lesson, then have your child repeat the lesson back to you in his own words. As he repeats it, put the key points on a piece of paper or a chalkboard, and color code the different parts of whatever it is he is working with. For example, when presenting the three-digit by three-digit multiplication problem 324 x 436, color code the "6" in one color; use arrows drawn in the same color to indicate what to multiply (6 x 4; 6 x 2; 6 x 3), and use the same color when writing out the directions for these steps. Next, write the "3" in another color and draw arrows using the same color to designate what to multiply: (3 x 4; 3 x 2; 3 x 3). Write any instructions pertaining to the "3" in the same color. Use the same process when multiplying by the "4." Remember to write the addition sign in yet a different color.

In division problems, have your child use colored pencils for the different operations. Thus, the result of division would be in one color, the result of multiplying in another color, the result of subtraction in a third color. The words telling what to do for each step would correspond in each color. You can use this for math, spelling words, grammar, or anything else. Some parents use cue cards in Science or History, to help the child memorize lists of information.

Writing problems

The computer is a valuable asset for students with written language and fine-motor problems. Some students have difficulty forming letters, or spacing letters and words on the paper. Most children enjoy working on the computer, and children who have fine motor problems find that it helps them to avoid something that is just inherently difficult for them. The computer has wonderful modes on it; the edit mode allows children to move and rearrange information without rewriting it. Spellchecker helps children who have spelling problems.

A tape recorder is another asset for children with written-language types of problems. Some children just cannot use the paper and pencil to write their words on paper. If you ask them to tell you a story, they are beautifully creative; they can give you imaginative stories, long, in-depth, with a wonderful vocabulary. However, put a pencil in their hands, and they cannot do it. For these children, giving them a tape recorder is a terrific way to get around the negative feelings associated with trying to write. Once a child puts his thoughts on a tape recorder, he can go back and put those thoughts on a computer.

Learning styles

One of the most important things to keep in mind when you are designing your curriculum for your LD child is what his best learning style may be. For example, if a child is mainly an auditory learner, rather than visual or tactile, he learns best by hearing. So use materials with which you can do more auditory teaching. Most people learn best through a multi-modality presentation, combining auditory, visual, and tactile.

Children with learning problems need repetition. Be repetitive. If a child is having trouble with his multiplication facts, go over and over his multiplication facts, a few minutes every day, maybe several times a day, using different techniques. Use flash cards one time, drill sheets another time, a game another time.

When I talk about being repetitive, I'm also talking about spiraling. If something has been presented previously in the year, and the child has shown mastery, do not drop it. Try to incorporate that information in future lessons, either as part of the lesson, or as a review. For example, if you have taught addition, subtraction, and multiplication facts and now you are working on division, each of those skills is included in division. You would not really have to do a specific review, so you move past the division to fractions, then you might want to have one, two or three problems a day that would be considered review. Do not overdo the review problems; keep it limited to three to five problems, depending on the child's comfortable working time-frame.

Children who have LD or ADHD need structure. Many of these children, as mentioned before, have no concept of time, and usually need to be put on a schedule, and sometimes even on a timer. One of the benefits of home schooling is the ability to have flexibility. So when I say "Structure, structure, structure," some parents are going to grimace; however, that is what these children need. They need to wake up at the same time every morning, and have the same morning routine. They should start their school work at the same time every day, and should be expected to do the same subjects first, second, and third.

For the child who has difficulty staying on task for any length of time, you may need to try a timer for a while. Find your child's comfortable working range. If your child stays on task comfortably for seven minutes, then set the timer for seven minutes. Most children need concrete reinforcement, so a good thing to do would be to make a chart and break the school day down into seven-minute increments, and give a sticker or star for each seven minutes that your child stays on task. Let the child get up at the end of seven minutes and put a sticker on the chart, come back and start again. Generally, that is enough of a little break to allow the child to start back to work without getting too distracted.

Set your child up for success. Make sure that your child understands what you expect. When you give a presentation, have the child repeat back to you in his own words a summary of what he believes he is supposed to know. If you give directions, have the child repeat the directions back to you. If your child is supposed to do math problems, show an example, and then have him work one while you are watching. Make sure that your child can succeed independently at the task you are setting him up to do.

For a child who may have difficulty with writing, consider having your child do the work orally. This will get the work completed and have your child feel successful, and you will still be getting a response to the material. If you need a written response, you can write what your child answers.

Testing

Testing can be a difficult area for children with special needs. As a home schooling parent, you can be more flexible than the teacher in a classroom. Testing may be done with audio tapes, video tapes, singing, or dramatic presentation. Use any way you believe will show your child has mastered the material.

If you are in a situation where you need to have traditional testing done, either to submit to your school system or because you are with a home school that asks for testing, adapt the testing environment. Waive time limits. Take short periods of testing time over several days.

Read the test and the answers to your child, when you are testing the skills presented in the test, and not the ability to read and to figure out what is being asked for in the question. If necessary, allow your child to give answers orally, then write the answers yourself.

Another way that you can change the testing format is to change the test from a short answer, or a fill-in-the-blank or an essay, to multiple choice. Many times children do well with multiple choice; they see the answer, and they know it. Then there are children who do not do well with multiple choice at all because there are too many choices. If your child is in that category, I would keep the choices down to two. Maybe your child does better with an essay; let him tell you what he learned in the chapter. You may find that he actually gives you more information than the test asks for.

Having a child privately evaluated for learning disabilities is very expensive; therefore, you may want to go through your school system. Just keep in mind, if you do go through your school system, it will be a good idea to check with other local home schooling families to see what their experience has been with exposing themselves to the school system. Some of the school systems across the country feel that if you have a handicapped child, they have a right to educate that child because they are the professionals. So, if you are going to pursue testing, just make sure that you check with other home schoolers as to the local school's philosophy about home schooling special-needs children.

Home schooling

Basically, there are several good reasons why you should home school a child with special needs. The schools TRY to give your children individualized instruction; you CAN give your child individualized instruction. You can set up a curriculum that is designed to meet your child's specific needs, and you can be there, one on one, to give your child the attention and help that he needs.

There are many resources out there that are available for you and your child. Sometimes it is to your advantage to have your child formally tested so you can have access to those resources. Some of these resources are tape recorded textbooks for the blind. Some school systems will allow children to attend speech and language resource classes, or

learning disabilities resource classes, if they have been formally identified as having a learning problem.

There are laws to protect the special-needs child, such as
Public Law 94-142, and more recently 504, which might
make it possible for home schooling parents to place the
special-needs child in a school for one or two special services, such as occupational therapy, speech therapy, and
resource classes. Of course, the decision to make any use
of the public school should be approached with caution and
prayer.

Home schooling releases your child from peer pressure.
Many times children in schools are teased and made fun of
because they cannot follow directions, or they do not follow
conversations. They often look socially different. By taking
the child out of the school, you may be able to provide him
more suitable socialization in other situations, like Boy Scouts,
4-H clubs, a choir, or music lessons.

Research shows that a substantial proportion of delin-
quency or juvenile crime that is committed in America is
done by children with learning disabilities. The last thing
you need is for a child who already has problems to become
involved in a drug situation. Illegal drug use can destroy
the child who has perceptual and attention problems.

You may want to keep a child at home to give him the
incentive to learn. Children in a school situation often acquire a failure syndrome, but at home you can give positive
reinforcement and provide successful learning situations.

Your child does have special needs, and you know your
child better than anyone else. You have more invested in
your child being successful and feeling good about himself
than anyone else. You have the love and patience to be
successful. It may not be the easiest job in the world, but
you *can* home school a special-needs child. And your special-needs child needs the love and patience that only you,
as a parent, can give.

Chapter 13:
Home Schooling the Catholic LD Child

by Cathy Rich

There are many dimensions involved in raising, as well as teaching, the child with special needs. These include spiritual, parenting, sibling, and teaching issues.

I am the mother of five children. The boys are 12, 8, and almost 4. The girls are 10 and 2. My 12-year-old has Attention Deficit Disorder (ADD) without hyperactivity. The eight-year-old has Attention Deficit with Hyperactivity Disorder (ADHD), temporal lobe syndrome, visual/auditory perceptual problems, speech, and fine/gross motor difficulties. The four-year-old is delayed on speech. I suspect ADD, but it is not certain. My ten-year-old girl has processing and memory difficulties. The two-year-old so far appears to be "normal."

I have been home schooling for five years after finding out the hard way with my oldest that private education does not work educationally or spiritually with these children. Obviously, it is challenging educating these children. This is in addition to managing the extraordinary family dynamics that occur. Attention deficit impacts on every aspect of our lives.

Spiritual life

The first, and by far the most important, topic to address is spiritual. The children's spiritual life must take precedence over everything else. These children are especially vulnerable to temptation because of their difficulties with self-control and their tendency to manipulate others. We must provide them with every spiritual aid available in their battle against their disorders. When their spiritual life is in order, they are better equipped to be successful in their school work. Faith should be your child's fortress. Surround him with it.

The day should begin with prayer. When the children

first wake up, we make the Morning Offering and say the Angel of God prayer. This is followed by an Our Father, Hail Mary and seven Glory Be's. We try to see who the Saint for the day is the night before so we can begin knowing what virtues to concentrate on the next morning. Otherwise, the next morning or at the 12 noon Angelus we read about that Saint. We often make novenas in honor of special Saints, and practice monthly devotions such as to the Sacred Heart in June, and to Mary in May.

It is imperative that the Rosary is part of each day. My eight-year-old's attention span cannot handle a five-decade Rosary yet, so we have him join in for one decade each day. Before that, we would have him do the Our Father's and/or Glory Be's at the end of each decade. He started by doing the beginning and ending prayers to the Rosary. When it comes to long prayers such as the Rosary, we must remember that our goal is to cultivate their relationships with God, not turn them off to the Faith by overwhelming them.

Finally, each day should end with an examination of conscience, no matter how brief, and an act of contrition with a prayer for penance afterwards. How often, outside of Confession, do we make our acts of contrition without assigning a penance to ourselves afterwards? Children pick up on these omissions.

This may seem like a lot, but it actually goes fairly quickly. Depending on the age of your child, you may want to use some of the morning prayers as a mid-morning break. But the Morning Offering, Angel of God and Hail Mary at the beginning of each day, before breakfast, are a must.

The Sacraments are very important to these children. Because of their strong temptations, I have my children go to Confession at least every two weeks. Daily Mass is also very important. I realize managing these children in Mass can be very stressful. I bring along plastic statues of religious figures, or religious coloring books to keep their hands occupied. My rule is to make it religious, whatever they are playing with. This seems to work fairly well. I have noticed that my children do better in churches that have a lot of statues to look at. In fact, if you dare to do it, sometimes they are the most quiet in the front pew because they have a statue staring them in the face to absorb their interest. Up front they can follow the movements of the priest more closely. I encourage the children to light candles at church. Anything you can do to give them a more active part in the Mass will help. The less often we go to Mass during the week the harder it is to control the children on Sundays. Consistency is very important in learning proper behavior.

In preparing my eight-year-old for his first Confession and first Holy Communion, I had to keep his uniqueness in mind and avoid the temptation about when he would "normally" be receiving these Sacraments. He must be mature enough to understand the gravity of these Sacraments, not just know his catechism and be physically capable of going through the motions. This is an area in which the parents and priest must look at each child individually. The child needs to have a good idea of what sin is in his own life first and want to eliminate it. Right now he is not aware enough of what it is in his own life due to his attention problem. The other problem is understanding what Holy Communion means. It is very hard to feel comfortable with your child receiving Holy Communion when he cannot keep still at Mass. Again, you have to decide which of these behaviors are intentional, and which they honestly cannot control and be held accountable for. There are no easy answers.

The blessings of establishing in your children a devotion to their Guardian Angel are without end. I have just finished reading a book called *All About the Angels* (from TAN) by Fr. Paul O'Sullivan, O.P. I encourage everyone to read it. My children have so much more confidence knowing their angel is with them. It also helps them to avoid sin when they realize that their angels as well as they themselves suffer when they sin.

We do our children a supreme injustice when we do not help them foster a devotion to their guardian angels. They *must* have every advantage possible if they are to succeed in learning and in serving God.

After all of these everyday devotions comes your

children's catechism. It must come second to their daily
prayer life because actions speak louder than words. You
can teach them all the catechism in the world, but they must
see you practicing it, and you need to make them practice it.
If not, first, it becomes a burdensome subject because of the
memorization. Second, they will resist learning it. Third, they
are going to resent you for making them learn it. Logically,
why should they learn something that their parents do not
even feel is important enough to use? To put catechism before their daily living of the Faith would, in fact, ultimately
turn them away from God.

In teaching the young LD child the Faith, use as many
hands-on teaching tools as you can. A felt board with Bible
figures for teaching them Bible stories is a great tool. Do
role playing of different situations for teaching the Ten Commandments. Use your imagination and be creative. Encourage your child to work on a religious project for the topic
you are teaching. For instance, if you are teaching about the
Sacrament of Penance, let him make a poster showing how
to examine his conscience. Talk to him about the different
steps while you and he are working. Seton sells an explanation of the Baltimore Catechism on videocassette. This is
a jewel to have, particularly on a busy day. Seton also has
catechism songs on cassette. These include the articles of
the Apostles' Creed, the Sacraments and more. Keep your
eyes open for new resources to assist you in teaching the
Faith.

The older child needs a slightly different approach. When
teaching the Baltimore Catechism questions, decide which
ones are the most important. Which ones will assist him the
most in life? Have him memorize these. Discuss all of
them with your child, however. Keep reviewing these questions each week. Do not just drop them as soon as he
passes the test on them. Keep it up. You can rotate around
different ones so he does not end up with 100 questions
every week by the end of the year. An alternative to the
fill-in-the-blank study helps would be discussions with your
LD child. Fill-in-the-blanks and other types of quizzes can
tend to reassure the parent that learning has taken place

more than the actual learning that has occurred. They can also be an exercise in frustration for children who cannot find answers in texts easily because of a learning disorder. Discussions catch the child's interest and make him want to learn more. Go over the chapter narratives with your child. Explore them from all sides. Be a devil's advocate to show him how worldly values do not make sense. Point out the differences between today's secular values and Christ's teachings. Show them the fallacy in humanism. If we do not help our children think of arguments against Catholicism and then think of the rebuttal to these arguments, you can be sure that they will have a hard time when someone challenges them. We must prepare them for these attacks. Also, children naturally question their Faith as they reach puberty. If we can work with them now to reason these questions out, their faith will be strengthened. If we are not intimidated by these challenges, they will also realize how strong our faith is and that we are not afraid of these questions. It will give the Faith credibility. Go through this challenging phase hand in hand with your child. It will strengthen everyone's faith and relationships.

Parental humility

The next topic I want to address is the spiritual lives of the parents of an LD child. There are many facets to this. They include the Sacraments, forgetting self and being God's instrument, suffering, and our obligation to God.

We must keep our Faith central in our own lives as much as we do with our children. God must be our "rock" as well as theirs. Let us remember to pray to their guardian angels as well as Mary and St. Joseph. Only with God's help will the negative aspects of learning disorders be overcome, and the family remain intact spiritually.

Frequent reception of the Sacraments is one of my "rocks" in avoiding sin and keeping my sanity. The frequent reception of Penance has more blessings than I can describe. Penance helps me to avoid the many temptations I have to become angry when things get crazy, or to see only myself when I am frustrated with a child's lack of understanding or compliance. It is easy to feel sorry for ourselves when we see others having such an easy time of teaching their children, or managing them so well. I think one of our strongest temptations is comparing our children to others. This Sacrament helps me to die to myself, and become God's instrument. How easy it is just to think of how the day is going for ourselves with our daily tasks instead of what our children are feeling about the day.

Daily Mass is one of my biggest blessings. It gives my day order and meaning. Sometimes I become frustrated in Mass because of the children's behaviors and wonder why I bothered going. It is then that I remember that the Holy Sacrifice of the Mass is to God the Father, for Jesus's death on the cross. It is not just for us.

One of my most difficult crosses used to be public humiliation. But I remember that humility is a virtue. My children make sure I get a good dose of it! How many times I have wished I could crawl under a table (or a pew) at some of their behaviors. Or when you get the "What kind of mother are you that you can't control your child?" look. I would have an even greater problem with pride if it were not for these times.

I sometimes feel guilty because home schooled children on the whole are supposed to be so much better behaved than those in a private or public school. We are supposed to be the shining example for everyone else; yet here we are with the worst of them. This is when it hurts the most. Only those of us with these special children can appreciate what our days are like. Yet, we can take solace in the fact that we are very blessed to have these children. What an honor to know that Our Lord would not have given them to us if He thought we could not handle them with His grace. All things are possible with God on our side.

Teaching Methods

Let us now consider teaching the other subjects in the curriculum. First, no two children are the same, and each child's curriculum and management may vary even within the same household, from year to year and sometimes week to week. We must always be flexible. The only given is that a problem exists and what the general nature of that problem is. My eight-year-old is very cyclic in his degree of disability. We have never been able to figure out why or control it. Consequently, he has shorter lesson plans in the fall and spring until he is over this difficult phase.

Another problem involves retention. A child may spend weeks learning a concept, get it down, and then one morning wake up and have forgotten it all. We know how frustrating this is for us. Can you imagine how frustrating it is for a child? Try to have different ways of learning the same concept planned. This increases understanding of the concept, alleviates boredom, and fosters cooperation. Their learning must be in short sessions, concise, and interesting. In teaching your child, remember to stop before your child gets frustrated. Frustration impedes learning. Take a break and come back to the problem later.

In selecting your texts, try to choose ones that are both cumulative and sequential. This is an absolute must for my children. By cumulative I mean that one concept builds on another and there is a review of previously learned concepts. Saxon Math does this with their series. By sequential I mean that there is a logical order to the concepts. English texts that jump around have no place in your child's work. It is better to explore each topic thoroughly before starting a new one. My daughter was thoroughly confused and had almost no retention with a text that jumped around. As with religion, review of previously learned concepts is essential for long term retention, particularly if you have to worry about standardized tests at the end of each year.

As you plan your day, you must decide what is the absolute minimum that you wish to accomplish. What are your "core" subjects? Mine are religion, math, phonics/reading, English and handwriting. Handwriting may be incorporated into either my first grader's English or reading/phonics. Any other subjects are extras. If you do not set a minimum, you are going to be more frustrated at the end of the day if you do not accomplish your goals. Some days we only do math, reading and religion. This is particularly true during my son's difficult seasons.

Be sure to allow time for fun learning, like art projects and science experiments. These can be done after your core subjects. If your child is having a rough day, provide art projects that are simpler or have relay races or some activity outside.   Take a nature walk.

In teaching your child history, I encourage you to be as creative as you can.   Look at the suggested activities at the end of each chapter.   Have him do the map skill assignments.   End of chapter questions turn my children completely off to history. There is simply too much work involved in finding the answers and it is an exercise in frustration for them.   Discuss the chapters with your child.

Another teaching tool I use involves my two oldest making diagrams.   The chapters are usually divided into sections marked with boldface print.   For each section they must put the main ideas in the center of a circle. What is the main point?   In rays going out from this circle are pertinent supporting details. All of the information in their diagram must be in words or phrases. No complete sentences are allowed. It takes away from the exercise.   Discuss the diagram with them afterwards. They like doing this.   It also makes them think and increases their reading comprehension.   This is active learning vs. passive learning.

As I have mentioned previously, learning must be fun, interesting and concise. It should be in short sessions. Stop a session at the first sign of frustration. Little, if any, learning takes place when we are frustrated. It turns children off to the task at hand. If you are becoming frustrated, think of what your child is feeling! I know of an adult with ADD who turns away from any learning because of frustrations as a child. It has given him a distaste for reading anything, even religious stories or novels for enjoyment. Is this what we want for our children? Find out what your child's interests are and develop them. For instance, if your son is a baseball card collector, have him find out what was happening in history during the life of his favorite players. Were the players Catholic? What saints or holy people lived in their day? All of these things will foster their desire to learn.

Try to be flexible with how assignments are done. With a young child, you could have your child use stickers to mark answers instead of drawing circles or making x's. This is particularly helpful for the child with fine motor problems. For some of the phonics work, can your child draw lines to the correct answer instead of writing all the words? How about doing them orally or into a tape recorder? Be creative to accommodate their frustration levels and their disabilities.

Scheduling and spontaneity are both important for learning with ADD children. They must have structure in their lives. Usually we have several short sessions, or small doses of each subject, no more than 30 minutes long. My pre-K to first graders achieve most of their learning in impromptu settings. These include cereal box labels, clothing labels, signposts, license plates, etc. Anything that catches their attention, we try to turn into a learning experience. Try to make the most of every learning situation during the day. This is especially true with impulsive children. Either initiate the learning as the opportunity arises, or pick up on your child's most subtle cues.

I usually start my older two children on their assignments before beginning with my eight-year-old. I may give him a learning toy to play with while I get the others started. Then I switch back and forth with the children as the day progresses. Having several activities ready for him to switch to is important in keeping his attention. Organization is vital for success when teaching this many and tending toddlers at the same time. We do not have short days of school in our home; but, though we may go to late afternoon, our learning is not compacted and intense. There are many breaks for various reasons. This is not the norm, but it works for us.

Managing

One of my greatest trials is managing to teach and take care of my other children while keeping my hyperactive child occupied or teaching him. Many home schooling families enjoy the luxury of having the older children teach the younger to some extent. This is not possible for me. Either the child needs me there with him or he resists their efforts entirely.

Pacing yourself and the child so that he does not fall behind in the year is an area of concern. This is particularly true where standardized testing is concerned.

The first step is looking at your state's Standard of Learning Objectives. Devise your core curriculum to meet these goals. Keep in mind that the history and science tests are not usually required, depending on the age of your child and state you live in. Difficult as it sounds, religion class must come before meeting the SOL's. We answer first to God.

Decide on your goals for the year, then supplement as you are able. Please do not get hung up on completing one grade a year, or having your child in the same grade for each subject. This totally negates one of home schooling's main advantages, that is, learning well and at the child's own pace. What is more important: quality learning at a slower-than-average pace, or staying on schedule? Staying on schedule just leads to anger and resentment for both parent and child. It makes learning very difficult and will eventually lead to burn-out. Do not even concern yourself about what point in the school year he is in for different subjects. What is important is that he is learning at his pace and that you are working with him.

If your state allows, I would highly recommend that you use portfolios instead of the standardized tests to submit to your school board or for your own records. They are more accurate in evaluating your child's progress. Many of these children who learn differently simply do not do well on formal tests by the very nature of their disability, not because they do not know the answer. If you must use testing, be sure it is done in your own home, and ideally by you. Just as school children take their tests in a familiar school environment for accurate results, your children deserve the same allowance by taking tests in *their* own familiar environment.

Diagnosis

Diagnosing learning disorders is often a serious difficulty. ADD without hyperactivity is particularly hard to diagnose, as we found out. Our oldest was able to outsmart all the pen/pencil tests, yet we knew a problem existed. He simply could not get his work done in a reasonable amount of time. We thought it was just that he hated doing school work. It was not. The disorder caused the dislike of the work. We finally ended up with an accurate diagnosis through brain mapping. This showed an obvious problem. After that we had him undergo biofeedback treatments, using his textbooks to literally teach his brain how to concentrate again. Be very careful in selecting a doctor who has expertise in this. Make sure he is supportive of home schooling, will let you sit in on the sessions, and will use *your* books to retrain the child's brain. (Caution: this is expensive, but insurance may cover some of the cost.)

We recently found out about another tool in the treatment of complex cases of ADHD such as our first grader has. We knew that his was more than simple ADD. He was unresponsive to ritalin (which we hated anyway), and was simply out of control. A very kind soul wrote me a letter, after reading an article of mine, informing me about SPECT scans with Triple-Headed Cameras. Apparently, temporal lobe syndrome is not unheard-of in complex cases and can cause similar symptoms. However, it will not necessarily show up with just an ordinary SPECT scan, nor an EEG, or MRI. I would encourage you to seek one out if you are in a similar predicament. Our son's was positive. He is now on anticonvulsants and doing phenomenally better. Our physician is a neuro-psychiatrist, which is a specialty in how neurological disorders affect mood, attention, and other areas. You may have to do some hunting to find either of these two specialties. I know they are in California and in the Northern Virginia/DC areas. Please tell others about this test. If this woman had not taken the time to write me, our son would still be unmanageable.

On the subject of medication, I have mixed feelings.

Home schooling children with learning disabilities is a distinct advantage because we can manage and monitor their behaviors readily. However, there are a few instances where medication is appropriate. Pray for guidance, try first not to use medication, and then use it discreetly if you feel that it is appropriate for your child in your situation. As a priest told me when I was battling this decision: "You would not withhold insulin from your child, you have tried everything else, obviously he needs help, it is wrong to withhold it in certain circumstances. It is also wrong to give it needlessly."

Sometimes there is a question of whether or not to go through testing when ADD is suspected. We knew that our first grader was a candidate by the time he was two. We saw no value in testing then. In retrospect, a positive diagnosis might have been helpful, because we could have learned management techniques sooner, and had more realistic expectations of him. Testing at age five helped us because we finally knew what we were up against. We did not feel quite so much like failures, because we knew that there was a medical reason for the problem. We are more confident in our roles, though still overwhelmed. We are able to learn more about this disorder instead of searching in the dark.

Discipline

Misbehaviors are very common in ADD/ADHD children. A psychologist gave me a couple of excellent ideas in this area. First, she advised me to be exaggerated in my praise and correction. This does not mean severe punishments. ADD children have a hard time keeping messages straight. Give him 100% of your attention. PRAISE each accomplishment. Make a BIG DEAL of it. Stop what you are doing to let him know. Hug him. On the other hand, be equally clear when correcting him. Look STERN. Let him know you mean business and are upset with him. Equally important when doing this is not to mince words. Do not take this time for lengthy talks or explanations. The time for talks is after the appropriate consequence.

Social skills are usually an area of difficulty for children with learning problems. Large group settings should be postponed with these children until they can handle small group situations. Professionals have told me that my children need *more* social interaction than most so that they can develop their skills. I disagree. This simply overwhelms and frustrates them. Family life teaches these skills the best, and field trips, story hours at the library, and sports activities take care of the rest. Other home schoolers can provide small group interaction also. Surely Our Lord will give us parents the grace to teach these social skills without putting our children in a large classroom situation which encourages acting out misbehaviors by its sheer size and abundance of distractions!

Special joys

One of the many blessings we receive in raising our special children is the joy we experience over their accomplishments. What is an ordinary accomplishment for many children is frequently a struggle for ours. What a reward it is then, to see our children's faces when they have finally mastered something. It is a joy that parents of "normal" children can never fully appreciate.

Having a special child is hard on brothers and sisters as well as parents. Imagine having to love your brother, but hating his unpredictable behavior at the same time. Siblings are subject to the same emotions as we are in living with ADHD. It is not easy for them. I cannot emphasize enough the importance of accepting their feelings without judging them. Feelings are neither right nor wrong. It is what we do with them that may be sinful. We must teach them how to turn to God, the saints, and their guardian angels with their problems so that they, too, may be comforted and gain insight. We need to foster open communication with them so that they may understand why parenting techniques are modified and expectations are different with different children. Otherwise they will easily assume that favoritism is present, with subsequent anger and resentment.

Raising an ADD child is a formidable task. However,

with God's grace, particularly with the help of the Sacraments and prayer, it can be done. God has honored us by giving us special children to raise. We are truly blessed to have been exposed to home schooling so that our children will not have to suffer the humiliation and abuse they would receive in any school system. This knowledge is what keeps me going at the most trying times. There is no acceptable alternative. We and God know what is best for our children. Trust Him.

Chapter 14:
The Socialization Issue

Once all the positive reasons for home schooling have been explained, once the explanations about the family benefits have been made, both the educational benefits and the spiritual benefits, one question always remains:

"But what about socialization?"

It is a sad commentary on our times, not to mention on our educational institutions, that many people, even professionals, even Catholics, are more concerned about the socialization of children than they are about their academic or religious education.

The reason educators have invented this new word, "socialization," is because they can no longer "sell" the schools for academic reasons. They have had to invent a different reason for the schools to exist.

But, if the truth be told, the main purpose behind public schools has never been education. Writings of the fathers of the modern school system in America make it clear that what we are seeing today is the fulfillment of the plan they had from the beginning. "Mere learning" was never considered the goal, but rather "social efficiency, civic virtue, and character." (Ellwood P. Cubberley, *The History of Education*, p. 690. Also, Rousas John Rushdoony, *The Messianic Character of American Education*, passim.)

Of course, if schools were using the Bible as the guideline for social efficiency, civic virtue, and character development, we could not complain too much. Instead, since the 1960's, prayer is not allowed, religious books and materials may not be used, and now books such as *Gloria Goes to Gay Pride* and *Heather Has Two Mommies* are being mandated in the schools of New York, New Jersey, and Connecticut.

Wherever people congregate, there is going to be interaction, or socialization. What Catholic parents need to consider is what kind of socialization do we want for our children? Do we want our children socializing with classmates who are involved in the drug culture, in the free sex culture, in the "Me First" culture? Do we want our children to be indoctrinated with the politically correct New Age culture? Do we want the "Up with Owls and Down with Babies" culture propagandized to our children by many school teachers and brainwashed classmates?

How many times on the phone I hear from parents about the ridiculing by classmates of Catholic students who wear scapulars or who stand up against the pro-death teacher in defense of unborn life! Father Kenneth Roberts recounts the time when he visited a Catholic school where students laughed when he said that the Holy Eucharist is Jesus Christ, the Son of God. And there is Donna Steichen's experience (author of *Ungodly Rage*) when a student in her CCD class exclaimed, "Gosh, Mrs. Steichen, you talk about Jesus like He was God or something!"

What kind of companions do we want our children to socialize with? Do we want to teach them to "get along" with those who have anti-Catholic values, with those who would push our kids into early sex and use of condoms? Do we want to teach them to spend their childhood schooldays in misery, being always the one who is different, always the one who is ridiculed by peers and teachers alike? How much daily attack on Christian values can a child take, day after day, week after week, month after month, year after year.

"He that walketh with the wise, shall be wise; a friend of fools shall become like to them." *Proverbs* 13:20

Socialization in schools

I receive calls from heartbroken parents all the time. They want to try home schooling not because their children are receiving a poor education, but because their children have had terrible "socializing" experiences in the school. Parents call because their children's classmates, after reading stories in their readers, are actually practicing witchcraft on the other children. Some children have been abused by other children, physically, verbally, or sexually. In one school, two boys sexually attacked a girl in a restroom. In another school, classmates tried to hang a boy in seventh grade. The stories are endless. There is certainly little evidence of healthy socializing in the schools of America.

In April, 1992, ABC News aired a ten-minute story on sex education in the classroom. A group of fifth graders, with playful childish faces, were shown laughing and grinning as they literally frolicked, throwing around condoms and teasing each other with the birth control devices handed to them by their teachers supposedly to teach them "safe sex." Socialization, á la paganese!

The U.S. Department of Education published a report in the late seventies on violence in the schools, giving statistics on how many rapes, personal attacks, and robberies occur in the schools. It was surprising that they would put it in print, but the report declared that a school was one of the most dangerous places to be in America!

The television graphically demonstrated recently how wonderful is the socialization at schools as educators debated about which is better: a hand-held metal detector or a more expensive detector built into the door frame, to detect the guns and knives being brought into the school buildings.

In February of 1993, an eleven-year-old boy was found with a loaded gun in an upper-class school in northern Virginia. In an interview with the police who arrested the boy, the police reported that children are taking guns to school to protect themselves from other children with guns. *In fact, a recent study by the Department of Health and Human Services found that one in twenty public school students carries a firearm to school at least once a month!*

The school children and parents of America are quite aware of peer pressure to use drugs and begin sexual activity. AIDS is now the sixth largest cause of death among teens. Two girls in a small rural Catholic high school in the Midwest told me they were the only virgins in their class. Mary Elizabeth Podles, in the April, 1993 issue of *Crisis*, writes that her confidence in her local Catholic school was shaken when the eighth-grade class was assigned to write to *Catholic Review* asserting that the students should be given condoms to prevent AIDS.

There are so many children who have serious problems in the schools today that normal children think they are abnormal. Schools are conducting classes or classroom clinics designed for children's problems. After a suicide in a school, teachers will conduct clinical-type classes dealing with suicide. If a student's parent dies suddenly, the school faculty decides to conduct all-school classes on death and dying. Schools have regular classes dealing with drugs and early sex experiences. There are classes to help children with single-parent families, children with "a live-in roommate" for a parent, and children of one or more remarriages.

There are so many non-academic but clinical-type classes going on in the schools today that it affects normal, healthy children. It can actually cause stable Christian children to become disturbed, to wonder if maybe they are not normal because they are not having these problems! One mother called me and decided to pull her young son out of school when he was laughed at because he had only two parents, the same two he started with!

A recently published book exposes the terrible hypocrisy of socialization in schools. *Family Matters*, by public high school teacher David Guterson, who is also a home schooling father, tells about the obsession among high school students to be accepted by their peers. There is a constant battle for group status, and peer cliques keep teens from integrating into multi-age groups in the community. Their obsession to conform to the group regarding clothes, hair styles, values, and attitudes keeps them from emotional growth and adult socialization.

Some child psychologists are recognizing the social damage being done to children because of the schools. Dr. Raymond Moore reported in *Home Grown Kids* that Dr. Urie Bronfenbrenner of Cornell University conducted a study of 766 sixth graders, and concluded that most children are not carriers of sound social values. Dr. Moore believes that peer dependency is a social cancer of our times.

In this day and age, when children are spending more time with their peers than with their parents, both of whom are working outside the home for long hours, the children adopt the values of the peer group. Hence, we end up with the so-called "generation gap." This "gap" is being caused by the schools, and it is certainly not healthy socialization.

Catholic schools

Many Catholic parents are aware of these situations but hope that Catholic schools are morally safer. These Catholics are simply ignoring the facts. Problems may not be as common in the Catholic schools, but Catholic schools today rarely employ firm discipline and teach positive Catholic values; rather, there is clear evidence that the level of immorality and loss of Faith is steadily climbing.

In January, 1993, Father Kevin McBrien of the Brooklyn, New York Office of Catholic Education was interviewed by Mother Angelica on EWTN. When asked why there is a need for the new Universal Catholic Catechism, he declared that each year for the past eleven years, 100,000 eighth graders were surveyed about their knowledge of Catholic Faith and morality. Father McBrien said that the results had grown more appalling year after year. The Universal Catholic Catechism is an attempt to pressure schools to teach the Faith to Catholic children. It is an official declaration of the Church teachings of doctrines and morality which must be taught to the children. The Vatican hopes this Catechism will stop the terrible loss of faith and stop the practice of immorality among young people, said Father McBrien.

Healthy "socialization" means practicing Christian virtues. It means loving our neighbors as ourselves. It means wanting what is best for others, especially desiring their salvation. But if children are not reading the lives of the Saints, they do not have the heroes or the saintly role models they need. If children are not taught the Ten Commandments, or the Beatitudes, and do not understand the principles that they imply, they cannot practice the selfless love with others which is the basis of all true and great friendships. They need to learn about Jesus and His self-sacrifice and love for us, so they will practice good socialization habits of kindness, generosity, and charity.

Would we do it?

Sometimes parents claim that they want to keep their children in a school in order to help the other children. They feel that the good example their children give will show others how one ought to behave. Perhaps in this way, they think, the other children will change.

What such parents fail to realize is that it may be their own children who will change for the worse. Evil is often well disguised and holds a certain temptation. That is why good companions are so important and bad companions are so dangerous. In fact, our catechism teaches that after receiving the Sacrament of Penance, we should have a firm resolve of sinning no more, which means "not only to avoid sin but to avoid as far as possible the near occasions of sin." The Church requires us to avoid persons who are likely to lead us into sin.

Is it emotionally or spiritually good for children to be trying to convert their classmates, especially when the authority figures are themselves promoting anti-Catholic values or attitudes? How long can children stand against books put in front of them, which they are required to read, yet which attack the Catholic values they have learned from their parents? How long can children stand against teachers in positions over them, people to whom they should be "obedient," who laugh at and ridicule their Catholic beliefs?

Can we expect our children to stand firm for THIRTEEN years? And keep their Catholic Faith? And continue to live the Catholic life? Yet is not that what we expect our children to do, from Kindergarten through grade twelve, when we send them to schools which actively, daily, promote an anti-Catholic world view?

Much is made in the news media these days about sexual harassment on the job. It is said that sexual harassment creates a "hostile environment" in which women cannot be expected to function. Well, if a few lewd comments here and there constitute a hostile environment, then we would have to conclude that, to the average Christian child, a public school is a war zone. And, sorry to say, many Catholic schools as well.

The premise put forward by the educators is that somehow socialization with classmates is going to help children "fit in" to society. Of course, the irony is that they are right! After thirteen years of morally pluralistic indoctrination and socialization, they will be properly accepting of the society's pagan values, properly socialized into being passive adult citizens of our American society. It is questionable, after such socialization, however, whether they will ever be fine mature citizens of the heavenly society!

The Catholic perspective

As Catholics, we need to approach the socialization issue from a Catholic perspective. "Socialization" is a word and concept invented by our modern educators. There is no mention in any good Catholic catechism, or the Bible, about "socialization." In the 1989 Webster's dictionary, "socialization" is defined as "socializing or being socialized." Socialize means "to be active in social affairs." Probably educators mean children should be able to adjust or to relate to others, usually peers of the same age, in various social situations.

If more Christians were not practicing birth control, and were completely open to having children according to God's will, most families would have a good many more children. Historically, in times past, ten or more children was not unusual for Christian families. And grandparents used to live with the family. In times past, an argument for "socialization" outside the family would have been ridiculous. It is largely because families have become so small that American parents have been so easily brainwashed into thinking that "socialization" in the school is so important.

Many educators, of course, are concerned about maintaining the school community, over which they have strong control in forming children's values. Many educators want our children to be accepting of modern secular ideas which they present in the classroom. They want to shape the attitudes and values of children in a way they think is best for society. The Catholic children who are socialized in public schools, and in many Catholic schools, end up rejecting Catholic attitudes and values.

Teachings from Jesus

Catholic parents need to ask, "What has Jesus taught in the Bible? Is there any indication that we are to learn social virtues from a peer group situation?"

Jesus speaks often about how to treat others. Basically, he repeats the Ten Commandments, the last seven giving us specifics about how to act towards others: to be obedient and respect parents and those in authority; to not commit adultery; to not kill; to not steal; to not tell lies or bear false witness; to not covet another's goods; to not covet another's wife. These Commandments seem simple enough to state in a paragraph, but unless they are taught in the first place, backed up by the example of parents, teachers, and other role models, they will surely not be followed.

Jesus taught that Charity is the most important "social" virtue. He told the rich young man to go and sell what he had and give to the poor. Jesus told the parable of the man who lay hurt in the road while passersby ignored him. The "majority" did not choose to help the victim. The Good Samaritan who finally did help him was the true neighbor. Jesus teaches that true socialization often means going against the crowd, thinking not of our own business first, but of helping another individual. Christ's teaching is unflinching in calling us to self-sacrifice for Him and others.

An important command was given to us by Jesus after He washed the feet of the Apostles:

> You call me Master and Lord. And you say well, for so I am. If then I being your Lord and Master have washed your feet, you also ought to wash one another's feet. For I have given you an example, that as I have done to you, so you do also.

While we have constant teachings from Our Lord concerning how we should treat other people, the Bible is also clear that *children* are to be *taught* Christian values. We should not hinder children from learning of Him, Jesus explained to His Apostles on a particular occasion as the children crowded around Him. Yet in a school, public or state-funded Catholic, directives from the State Department of Education forbid the teaching of "religion." Children are not allowed to learn about Jesus and His "religious" teachings.

There is no indication in the Bible that Jesus attended a school. In fact, when He was twelve years old and visited the Temple in Jerusalem, the Jewish priests did not know Him, and were amazed at His understanding of the Scriptures. When Jesus went back home with Joseph and Mary, He was subject to them. During the time He was subject to them, He grew in wisdom and age and grace. There is no indication elsewhere in the gospels that He received schooling from anywhere other than at home, nor could I find in the writings of any of the Church Fathers that Christ attended a school of any kind.

Church documents

When looking over the Catholic Church documents on education, we cannot find the word "socialization." Obviously the Catholic Church does not agree that being "active in social affairs" is a goal in itself. In fact, the Church has declared many hermits saints!

In *Familiaris Consortio*, The Role of the Christian Family in the Modern World, paragraph 37, Pope John Paul II states the following:

> In a society shaken and split by tensions and conflicts caused by the violent clash of various kinds of individualism and selfishness, children must be enriched not only with a sense of true justice, which alone leads to respect for the personal dignity of each individual, but also and more powerfully by a sense of true love, understood as sincere solicitude and disinterested service with regard to others, especially the poorest and those in most need.
>
> The family is the first and fundamental school of social living: as a community of love, it finds in self-

giving the law that guides it and makes it grow.

The self-giving that inspires the love of husband and wife for each other is the model and norm for the self-giving that must be practiced in relationships between brothers and sisters, and the different generations living together in the family.

And the communion and sharing that are part of everyday life in the home, at times of joy and at times of difficulty, are the most concrete and effective pedagogy for the active, responsible, and fruitful inclusion of children in the wider horizon of society.

Lives of the saints

In reading the lives of the saints, I cannot recall a single saint who benefited by going along with the crowd, or who became a saint because he was so adept at his socializing skills. On the contrary, if there is one thing in common among the saints it would seem to be their lack of acceptance of the values of their society.

In the study of any saint, we find that he or she stood against the values of the society. They refused to be "socialized" to accept the current social norms. It was by teaching and living the values of God rather than of men, that they became saints.

Many of the saints lived as hermits or semi-hermits. St. Anthony of Egypt visited various holy men, learned about the virtuous life, then lived as a hermit for twenty years. However, several men visited him to learn more about living the holy life, and he eventually started a monastery, the first one in existence. Christ appeared to him, and he worked many miracles. In Butler's *Lives of the Saints*, it is stated that St. Athanasius, his biographer, says that "the mere knowledge of how St. Anthony lived is a good guide to virtue."

Other saints spent long hours or even days alone. St. Catherine of Siena spent several years in prayer before she worked in the hospitals and visited the Pope. St. Jerome lived as a hermit for thirty years and produced the Latin Bible. St. Rose of Lima prayed daily in her little hermitage, but came out to help at the hospital or to lead her town in prayer against an impending enemy.

Our Lord did not start His public life until He was thirty. Even then, after being baptized, He took time away from people and made a forty-day retreat in the desert for prayer and fasting. On several occasions during the next three years, He retreated from the crowds and even from the Apostles to spend time in prayer. Certainly we Christians can find many examples showing that in silence, in solitude, away from social situations, we can more easily find God. As is often said, God speaks in silence.

The lives of many saints give us and our children specific ways to carry out the social virtues in practice. The Saints helped out their friends and those around them in need. They worked in hospitals, caring for the sick and the poor. They aided minorities and those suffering from diseases. They cared for babies and the elderly. In short, they sacrificed themselves for others.

If we are truly called to holiness, and to be saints, how can we be so concerned about socializing with our peers? Are we not rather called to evangelize our society with Christ's values? Are we not called to be Christian witnesses to others who have been "socialized" to accept society's values? Are we not called to live the authentically Christian lifestyle, and show our pagan society that such a lifestyle can lead to eternal happiness?

Home schooling

Home schooling children can practice social virtues in their own homes while relating to others in their family community. They can practice social virtues when helping out at church or at the youth center, at local homes for the aged, at the local pregnancy center, at day-care centers for children or for the elderly or for the mentally handicapped. They can help elderly neighbors who cannot go out, or visit families in spiritual or physical need due to a death or illness in the family, or read to the blind, or visit old retired nuns.

The opportunities for Catholic children to develop "social" virtues are almost limitless. It takes little time to think of opportunities with the family, with the church, and with community activities. There are always people around us who are in need. Socialization does not need to be in the institution called school.

So the question comes up: Do we not socialize with others from our parish who think differently than we do? Should we not allow our children to attend the parish school so they can be witnesses to the Catholic Faith and lifestyle?

There are two different issues here. One is regarding our children, the other is regarding ourselves. Young children do not yet have the foundation to be doing battle against the complex, sometimes subtle, ideas being promoted in our society, on TV, in the textbooks, by teachers, and by peers. We cannot expose our children daily to anti-Catholic and anti-family values, for hours each day, and expect them to remain true to Catholic values. Can any parent take the equal amount of time after school and refute what is being taught each day in school? Even to know the issues which come up each day would be impossible. The children are not even necessarily aware that Mother and Dad would like to know what teacher said about overpopulation! Children need to be nurtured carefully, consistently, in a Christian fashion in the security and stability of the home.

Parents, on the other hand, firm in their Catholic Faith and in their beliefs, MAY expose themselves to the evils of our society, for the purpose of witnessing or evangelizing. However, even parents need to be careful lest they fall. Exposing ourselves to evil ideas or practices on a regular basis can lead to subtle acceptance of such ideas. Many a mother working in the battle against pornography or sex education has found herself becoming desensitized to the evils herself!

What about socializing with the local parishioners? It depends on the parish. As I travel around the country, the differences in the churches are like night and day. One usher explained that while the church and Mass did not look Catholic, "because we do things differently here," he was quick to reassure visitors that it was indeed a Catholic church!

Several mothers have called to tell me that after every Mass, they have a long discussion with their children to explain that various aberrations are not permitted, but they cannot explain why Father is doing them anyway. Sometimes parents even succumb to social pressure themselves and allow their children to participate in liturgical innovations that are forbidden by the Church, since they see so many others doing the same thing.

In some situations, parents could choose to attend a good church at some distance, taking their children with them, and pointing out the blessings of the Mass. (This has the added benefit of bringing parents into contact with like-minded Catholics.) Perhaps at a later Mass, a parent could attend the local parish, without the children, and do a certain amount of witnessing or evangelizing.

Socialization, or destruction of personality?

Dr. Damian Fedoryka, former president of Christendom College and home schooling father of ten children, declared at a home schooling conference:

> I really didn't consider it proper for my child to spend a year of her life learning how to be an eleven-year-old, then another year of her life learning how to be a twelve-year-old, another year learning how to be a thirteen-year-old....She has a mother at home. I'd rather she learn to be like her mother, and have plenty of time to do it.

Dr. Fedoryka is pointing out that the so-called social values being learned by children in school are constantly shifting values based on the collective immaturity of the group. On the other hand, the values learned from the mother are stable values which will be of use to the child all through life.

Instead of school socialization being simply an innocuous waste of time, Dr. Fedoryka claims that the kind of socialization which children are encountering in schools today is destructive of the child's personality, and consequently destructive of genuine society.

The child is like a precious, uncut, raw gem, Dr. Fedoryka

says. The parent has the task of turning the gem into

> a brilliant diamond with facets that reflect the light of
> eternal values of truth and goodness. In contrast, today's
> system insists on grinding these stones smooth in such
> a way that each one is uniformly similar to the other.

Dr. Fedoryka warns us that educators use words such as freedom, responsibility, and morality, but that these have entirely different meanings outside of the Christian perspective. Freedom, to the educational secular humanists, means

> the loosening of all the moral and sexual inhibitions.
> Responsibility means making sure that you use a con-
> traceptive. Morality means that you do not impose your
> opinions on somebody else.
>   What is commonly called socialization is, in fact, a
> process which destroys the child's personal center, his
> capacity to be a free individual who is truly responsible
> for his character and destiny. It promotes the child's
> centering or focusing on satisfaction or on what is often
> called the human need, and teaches him to function
> effectively in whatever system of values his society
> holds.

The social behavior being promoted in the schools involves "a non-judgmental acceptance of the rights of others to their values, and an ability to function in a pluralistic values system," said Dr. Fedoryka. To be socially correct, children are taught that everyone has a right to his own values, and one set of values is as good as another.

Simultaneously, children are taught that their own opinions, their own values, are of primary importance. "Your parents have values, and they are fine values for them. But you are developing your own values. You are not bound by the values of your parents, or by the values of the past, or by the values of a church." In their interaction or socialization with state-certified teachers, with counselors or "agents of social change," with state-approved textbook authors, with inexperienced but easily manipulated peers, children are to develop their own set of values.

No matter what Hillary Rodham Clinton says about the "rights of children" and their "emancipation," the teachers, textbook authors, and counselors are pushing aggressively to manipulate children to make decisions according to THEIR values. The issue is not about children's choices, but about who chooses for them.

The current self-esteem programs teach children to focus on themselves, and their own desires and wants. At the same time, they are taught not to be critical of others who focus on *themselves* and do whatever *they* want in order to obtain *their* wants and desires. With its emphasis on personal wants and desires, the whole public school system is an exercise in the destruction of true society.

Objective truth versus personal opinion

Dr. Fedoryka believes that a parent should be concerned

> with bringing the child out into the world of *objective* values. He should be concerned with the moral and religious perfection of his child, with the crystallization of his personality in light of the eternal and absolute values. And secondly concerned with the eventual communion of his child with another human being [such as in marriage], but in all cases with the ultimate communion with God. These should be the basic concerns of education.

If you deny a child guidance or education in the world of objective values, the child soon centers only upon himself.

"Modern philosophy of education," declares Dr. Fedoryka,

> in insisting that the child becomes self-centered, teaches the child to focus on what is peripheral and superficial in his experience: on the satisfaction of his needs....There is a loss of a sense of identity of who one is....The modern school system panders to that, teaches the child to turn inwards and, because of this, it is anti-personal. Because of this, every true communion is impossible, a genuine society is impossible.

Dr. Fedoryka's main thesis is that the modern secular humanist philosophy dominating the schools and seducing a nation of children rejects God as an authority, rejects God as our destiny, and sets up the individual person as a god.

> The philosophy of self-realization, self-affirmation, self-fulfillment, self-esteem is the dominant philosophy today, not only of our society and culture as a whole, but specifically of the schools. This is the predominant evil.

Once I attended a state Catholic Teacher's Association conference. As the teachers sat in an auditorium, they were told to beat their breasts with a clenched fist and yell out in unison like Tarzan, "I Am Great!" For several minutes, these adult teachers repeatedly beat their breasts with a clenched fist, yelling, "I Am Great! I Am Great!"

"Modern man is not atheistic by accident," continued Dr. Fedoryka.

> Modern man rejects God as an obstacle to his own satisfaction. He must prove that he is superior to God. He does that by seducing the child, by getting, first of all, the child to deny God, and not give himself to God.
>
> Then modern man can show himself greater than God by saying, "God...to whom does this child belong? Over whose heart are You Sovereign and Lord? Certainly not over the child's, because the child belongs to me, not to the parent." It belongs to Modern Man, the State, who cultivates a systematic warfare on innocence.
>
> In claiming possession of the child, Modern Man thinks he is superior to God. The modern school system is essentially hostile to God.

Catholics believe, of course, that we are to reform and change society, to bring the Gospel of Christ to society. Why should we have our children spend thirteen years learning "how to fit into something which is not fitting," as Dr. Fedoryka puts it.

Two world views

We are living in a society with two world views. The schools hold one world view, as promoted by the National Education Association, and we Catholics hold another world view, as promoted by Jesus Christ in the Bible and in His Catholic Church.

In our world view, socialization means that we must try to be good, kind, loyal, truthful, obedient to authority, diligent, faithful, just, humble, and generous to others for love of God. Our idea of community or society is based on the fact that God is our Creator, the Creator of each individual human being, and that we are all called to be brothers and sisters in Christ.

In the secular humanist world view, students are encouraged to do whatever makes them feel good. The world persuades children to do "good" by saying, "You will feel better if you give to the poor." Or, "If it makes you feel better to help the poor rather than go to Mass, then you must do what makes you feel better." In *our* world, we have a Father in Heaven. In *their* world, Heather has two Mommies.

So the question your friends and relatives should be asking is not "What about Socialization?" but "In whose world will your child be socialized—in the secular humanist world where personal satisfaction, personal values, and personal choice is primary, or in the Christian world, where serving others and ultimately serving God is the purpose of our existence?"

Service

The children in the schools today are not learning the basic Christian vocation which calls them to serve God and neighbor. Jesus said, "I am in the midst of you as He who serves." And again, "I have given you an example, that as I have done to you, so you do also."

According to Dr. Fedoryka, the schools give evidence of

...betrayal of the basic vocation of man as being created

to serve another. That is, I claim, the crisis in our culture, the crisis in our educational system, and the most important reason to take your children out of a school, public or private, which betrays this basic destiny or vocation of man.

A genuine bond between people, genuine socialization, depends on giving of oneself. "If anyone wishes to come after Me, let him deny himself, and take up his cross, and follow Me." This does not sound like the current philosophy of self-esteem being sold to our schoolchildren! "For he who would save his life will lose it; but he who loses his life for My sake will find it."

We know that it is required of us as Catholics to give up our lives in service to God and to God's children. In the past, we have considered as heroes those who have risked their lives in rescuing others from danger, and those who over several years have given their lives in service to others. Even post-Christian society still admires those who follow this ideal. Thus, Bob Hope has been recognized and respected because he has given up his time every Christmas to uplift the morale of our servicemen. His priority was to serve the soldiers rather than to look for his own personal satisfaction.

Dr. Fedoryka believes that a genuine socialization, a genuine bond between people can only arise

...when one individual gives himself, surrenders himself, submits himself to the other. This will make a tremendous difference in the way we educate our children. If we recognize that each one of us has a destiny to forget about ourself and to serve the other, we also will recognize that the children who have been given to us must be shaped and educated in this attitude.

The primary reason I am educating my children at home is that they learn to surrender to others, even if it costs them their happiness. They must be ready to give up, to negate themselves, in order to serve others. This should be the core, the heart, the spirit of Christian education.

Since our primary responsibility to our children is to direct them to Heaven, we need to have control over their social contacts, insisting that they be Christian and positive. The many deep and complex problems which children and young adults have today are, in part, the result of lack of parental control over their social contacts.

Social virtues are taught effectively primarily at home, within the family, as directed by the papal documents. Additional social contacts can be with Christian or Catholic home schooling support groups, where families come together as families rather than children of just one age group, where older children learn to care for younger children and where younger children learn Christian values from older children and adults.

When parents take children to local clubs, such as Boy Scouts, or local sports activities or supplemental classes such as drama or ballet, they should keep a watchful eye for lack of discipline, cursing, drinking, drugs, sexual aggressiveness, and so on. This is parent-controlled social activity, protecting the child from spiritually dangerous situations.

During children's formative years, parental control is a serious responsibility. Once the solid foundation is laid during childhood, like the house built upon the rock, the winds of society's pagan values may blow, but our children will be able to stand firm in the wake of the hurricanes to come. They will choose a spouse of like formation, they will choose self-sacrifice for the sake of their spouse and children, and will raise another generation of virtuous Catholic children.

The pagan agenda for schools

Some educators are promoting specific agendas which ruin social relations between people. One of the most common agendas currently being promoted is that of the homosexuals, which is guaranteed to warp a child's view of sexuality.

In December, 1992, when the city of New York decided to implement the *Children of the Rainbow* program to teach children to respect homosexuality as an alternative life style, many parents objected. The program was to begin in first grade, and the little ones were to be given books with illustrations, one depicting two men in bed. The children were to learn to respect "families" with "parents" who were homosexual or lesbian. Of course, in the process, children are being taught that such "families" are morally acceptable.

The agenda is being promoted by the National Education Association and other liberal groups. These groups supposedly support the ideals of democracy. However, when a majority of parents, who, through taxes, pay the salaries of these school educators, objected to the agenda, democratic ideals were thrown out.

In Virginia, meetings for a proposed sex education program were held around the state. Large groups of parents showed up at meeting after meeting to object, but the program was adopted anyway.

The same situation happened in Michigan. Interestingly, the Michigan Senate held hearings with parents who complained about the situation. The Senate reported:

> Listening to hundreds of parents testify at our hearings, it became obvious that the desires of the curriculum writers in the Departments of Education, Public Health, and Mental Health rode roughshod over the wants and wishes of families....Communities around the state were forced into accepting the state of Michigan's view of how and what their children should be taught about some of the most important and most intimate questions they will ever face.

In New York City, after a local school board supported the parents in their objection to the proposed homosexual-lesbian alternative lifestyle program, the duly elected school board was dismissed by the Central School Board. The local board was later re-instated, and this time the city school Chancellor, Joseph Fernandez, was dismissed.

How long Mr. Fernandez will be out of a job is anyone's guess. But he was not dismissed because anyone in the New York State bureaucracy thought he was wrong. He was dismissed because of the way he handled the situation. In February, 1993, ABC News "honored" Mr. Fernandez by featuring him in most laudable terms on their Person of the Week segment. He will be bringing his pro-death, anti-family, homosexual message to another school system shortly. You can bet on it!

Right here in rural Front Royal, Virginia, 240 parents petitioned the school board to choose other books for the Reading List which would not present children with street language, vulgarity, and violence, nor with the idea that they should develop their own moral values. The school board rejected the parents' pleas. The board members are sure they know what is best for other people's children.

The fact is that Christian parents believing in absolute values cannot win this battle because the idea of absolute values is so unacceptable to the school boards and educators. We cannot win this battle based on democratic values, such as that majority opinion should rule, because their demonic agenda is of more concern than "democracy."

Catholics need to face the fact that good, healthy Christian socialization can be found only in good, healthy, authentically Christian homes.

A Pro-Life view

In the Christian world view, each person has dignity. This includes both the unborn and the elderly. It also includes each child of school age. As we teach each of our children how important he or she is in God's eyes, and how each of our actions has importance to God, we are teaching the dignity of the individual.

In the secular humanist world view, which the children are learning at school, the group is what is important. While each child supposedly is to develop his own personal value system, if it does not fit into the group's values, the child is ostracized. Children in the schools often measure their worth by their acceptance by the group.

The reason why home schooling parents have difficulties teaching children at home when they pull them out of school in the later grades is that the children have replaced their parental image of themselves with the peer-group image of themselves. They miss the security and approval of their classmates. They have become peer-dependent.

Other home schoolers

Healthy socialization is a matter of importance to many home schooling parents. Much has been written about healthy socialization in many home schooling magazines. The following are a few points made by home schooling parents:

1. While many people seem to think that interacting with peers will help develop confidence and self-esteem, exactly the opposite is true. With stress, rivalry, competition, and comparison with peers, children come to view themselves as their peers see them. They are not able to evaluate themselves fairly, and are often convinced they are inadequate in some way.

2. Mass education is proving that children are not learning good positive social behavior in school. Children need personal, close associations with individuals, persons who love them and who can teach and train positive behavior, mainly through good example.

3. Children are too immature to have strong convictions and moral strength to develop positive social relationships when daily pressured by negative or immature social behavior. Children need to develop strong self-discipline, character, and strength before they can develop true friendships. This cannot be left to the result of interaction among others at the same level of immaturity, but should be directed by loving adults through daily good example.

4. The effects of peer group evaluation may inhibit creative expression and attempts to develop intellectually. In many schools, children purposely do not achieve because it is "cool" to be average with the group and not to appear "smart" (although in some schools the reverse could be true).

Peer-group evaluation is especially detrimental to girls of junior and high school levels in co-educational schools, as they want to be attractive to boys and so often purposely do not work to their full potential. Research and experience have shown that at these levels, girls achieve much higher when in all-girl classes.

Boys, who are not as mature as girls in the younger grades, tend to ask fewer questions or work less, since girls are more aggressive in achieving academically. (By the way, as more girls become altar girls, boys will stop trying to compete in an area where girls seem to perform better. And the fewer altar boys we have, the fewer boys will be inclined to consider the priesthood as a vocation.)

5. The peer group is becoming a replacement provider of family security for the individual child. The peer group, however, can offer neither the stability nor the love a child needs to grow emotionally and spiritually.

The "generation gap" has been a phrase used to show the incompatibility of values between the peer group and the family. Children end up leaving the family at some point, but they usually carry away peer group values and not family values.

6. Children do not need to experience the teasing and cruelty of other children to learn about "the real world." There is a certain amount of give and take in a family, whose members ultimately care about the individual. And in a neighborhood, a child can walk away. In a school situation, where children are forced to interact with their classmates day after day, week after week, month after month, year after year, personalities can be almost totally destroyed.

Parents should realize simply by reading the newspaper, by seeing what is on television, and by talking with other parents that the schools are not doing a good job of teaching proper social attitudes and behavior. They should rely on their own common sense in raising their own children.

7. We need to remember that having a large number of friends is not a measure of a person's worth. Most adults have only one or two good friends, while most other people are acquaintances. Parents will find that, if they concentrate on their children's development, encouraging each child daily, their children will be independent and self-confident.

8. Schools, run by professional educators with higher degrees, tend to set up a class status in the high schools, probably unconsciously. But as a result, those going into

vocational areas are really looked down upon as not fully making it. Interestingly enough, even years later, while someone with a vocational degree or business degree might be very successful in various areas of leadership, he continues to believe he is of a lower status than the professional educator with loads of degrees and years of schooling but few Christian values.

9. While there are many positive reasons for home schooling, many parents who turn to home schooling are doing so precisely because of the problems related to socializing with children at school. Most parents want to keep their children away from the many, many social problems in the schools, most related to sex, drugs, and violence. Parents also want to be involved in selecting good companions for their children.

Some believe that children should be exposed to evil in order to make them grow stronger as they mature. Experience shows exactly the opposite. And in fact, our Catholic catechism says we should avoid the occasions of sin, such as people or places which tempt us. In the schools today, it is not unusual for teachers, peers, textbooks, movies, school bathrooms, school "playgrounds," school health clinics, school counselors, and school bus rides to be daily occasions of sin for children. In fact, the public school system, *per se*, is an occasion of sin, because it is constantly pressuring children to rid themselves of their Christian values.

Some think that children should learn to live with different people in the world because for the rest of their lives they will have to live with people with different values. The fact is that as adults, we can control where we live and work and with whom we socialize. We can associate with good Catholic people if we try. Children should not be forced to associate with people who do not reflect Catholic values. After thirteen years, they will be so desensitized to the evil around them that they will accept this kind of living as part of their own lives.

There is a prevalent attitude that children should not be sheltered, but need to be out in the "real world." Well, what is the real world? Is the real world the world in which people know, love and serve God, and acknowledge the permanent truths of the universe? Or is the real world the world in which everyone denies the reality of God and of moral responsibility? Clearly, the loving Catholic home is the real world, the world in touch with reality. The world in which children are taught they can indulge in every vice without consequence is a fantasy world.

Ostracism

On December 19, 1985, there appeared an article in the *Chicago Tribune* by columnist Bob Greene. It was entitled "Successful Adults Haunted by Ostracism." It is a real eye-opener for some of us, and perhaps it is not surprising for some others. Every parent who is afraid his child might miss out on socialization in school should read it.

Bob Greene starts his article by saying, "There seem to be so many grown people walking around still feeling the hurts inflicted upon them when they were children." In a previous article, Mr. Greene had written the story of a boy who was devastated when his fellow classmates gave him a "Most Unpopular Student Award." After the article was published, Mr. Greene received many letters from adults who related their personal stories of ostracism by classmates.

"What I'm hearing," wrote Mr. Greene,

> ...is that this never really goes away. A man may be a successful executive now; a woman may be a well-paid attorney. But if, in their youth, they were picked on and put down because they weren't as popular as their classmates, this sticks with them.

One man wrote:

> I feel for that boy in your column. I know exactly what he's going through. It has been 35 years since I was in his position, but I remember clearly sitting home all by myself after school and on weekends, because no one wanted to be my friend. It hurt so deeply that I never even talked to my parents about it, although I'm sure

that they knew. It didn't seem like life was even worth
living.

And another man wrote:

That boy could be me when I was a child. It's the
most intense pain in the world—knowing that even
though it's not your fault, the other children don't want
you to be part of what they're doing. There's no one to
blame, so you end up blaming yourself. You even end
up believing that the other children must be right—that
there must be something wrong with you. Why else
would you be treated that way?

Bob Greene quoted other letters, and concluded:

I am finding that there are so many who went through
it, and who remember. The hurt never seems to completely go away....From what I can tell, there are so
many people who will never forget what it felt like to
be left out, and to be told that they weren't wanted.

When parents talk about the positive values of socialization in the schools, they never think about the anti-social
activities that hurt many children. I have spoken with parents whose children hated school because of the way they
were treated, because they did not "fit in," or because they
were afraid of others who bullied them. Other mothers complain that their children are so determined to fit in with a
group that they turn to bad influences. Several mothers have
called with pregnant daughters. Another mother told of her
boy who used foul language because he wanted to fit in.
One junior high girl actually told her mother she was turning bad because of her peer group and begged her mother to
teach her at home. These stories could go on endlessly.

Home schooling support

Home schooled children associate with all age groups,
within their family mainly, and within the home schooling

support groups. If Catholic parents are having large families, or if they have extended families with grandparents and uncles and aunts and cousins, the children will be interacting and socializing with all ages.

Home school support groups plan family activities, not just activities for a certain age level. This encourages healthy social development among all age groups. Home schooled children mature faster, though they are not as "street wise" as public or parochial school children.

Home schooled children are better able to relate to all age groups because they are not limited to several hours a day in a closed environment with children the same age. Nor are they pressured by textbooks, school movies, teachers, and peers to conform to the peer group. Their best friends are family members, brothers and sisters who are loyal, supportive, and not viciously competitive.

Because of better self-esteem based on a daily caring and loving family support system, a home schooled child is better able to deal with social setbacks or the group pressures of later life. A home schooled student tends to be a leader rather than a follower, more able to make decisions based on what *he* believes or what he has been taught by his family rather than on what social change agents want him to think. Since a home schooled student is better educated and more secure in his value system, in a peer group he is generally admired and respected by those looking for answers in their lives.

In the home schooling situation, families are encouraged to join their local home schooling support group. These groups sponsor social activities as families, rather than activities geared to a particular age. Natural social development occurs as children adapt to children and adults of all ages. Grandparents often join the families on these outings.

When home schooled children meet other children, they are not tense or afraid of being called names or labeled. They do not feel pressured to dress in the same name-brand jeans, or wear the latest hair style. They are not pressured into wearing make-up or having a boyfriend by fourth grade! Home schooled students are free to be involved in community activities or to be active in hobbies or sports. Seton has students who are semi-professional ballet dancers, ice skaters, actors, musicians, models, tennis players, gymnasts, and so on.

Home schooled students are not affected by the confused role-models being presented in the secular textbooks and classrooms of America. With the feminist ideology now infiltrating the schools, young people are being taught to reject their traditional Christian roles as mothers and fathers.

In *Familiaris Consortio*, His Holiness Pope John Paul II repeats earlier Catholic Church teachings when he declares in paragraph 36: "Social virtues are best learned in the home."

Why are social virtues best learned at home?

Mother stays home and home schools. She protects the children, says the prayers with the children, teaches them the Faith and tries to be like Mary, the Blessed Mother.

The socializing which children need today is with their parents and others who hold good Christian values. Their parents need to be role models, need to instruct both by words and by example, to follow the authentic Catholic lifestyle. All the negatives which we hear about the schools, all the positives which we see in the lives of the Saints, the teachings of the Catholic Church and the Biblical teachings point to the fact that, as Pope John Paul II said, "The social virtues are best learned in the home."

According to the Second Vatican Council,

> The family then is the first school of those social virtues that every society needs. But it is most important in the Christian family, enriched by the grace and the *obligations* of the sacrament of matrimony, that children must be taught right from infancy to know and worship God. (emphasis added)

If we are really followers of Jesus Christ, we should not overly concern ourselves with "socialization" or the need for our children to socialize with other children their age. This has never been mentioned in the Bible, in the Church documents, in our catechisms, nor in the lives of the Saints.

When it comes to relating to other people, this is what we Catholics are directed to do:

To feed the hungry.
To give drink to the thirsty.
To clothe the naked.
To visit the imprisoned.
To shelter the homeless.
To visit the sick.
To bury the dead.
To admonish the sinner.
To instruct the ignorant.
To counsel the doubtful.
To comfort the sorrowful.
To bear wrongs patiently.
To forgive all injuries.
To pray for the living and the dead.

Chapter 15:
Using Computer Technology

by Kevin Clark

Kevin Clark is computer operations manager for Seton Home Study School, as well as president of BC Enterprises Software, Inc.

When most home schooling parents were in school themselves, they probably never used a computer terminal or other interactive technology. Fifteen years ago personal computers were exorbitantly expensive and way beyond the price range of the average person.

Today, the latest in computer technology is cheap. A computer system that cost $10,000 fifteen years ago would cost about $500 now. State of the art computers can be purchased for well under $1,500.

This drastic decline in the price of technology is one of the most exciting developments in home schooling. It opens up a whole new world of information, as well as new teaching methods, to the home schooling family.

The benefits of computerization to the home schooling family are basically three. First, the home schooling family can use a computer as an interactive teaching tool. Second, they can use the computer as an information resource. Third, they can use the computer to enhance the smooth operation of the home school.

Computers as teaching tools

By now we have all seen some type of educational software, at least in stores. Educational software (that is, computer disks containing the programs) used to be quite expensive (and the software sold for school use still is), but prices have been coming down to the point where many programs can be purchased for under $30. In fact, one of the recent trends in software sales is to package multiple complete programs together at a very low price.

Computer software as a learning aid offers several advantages over traditional methods. First, the computer can continually furnish new material (such as math problems), unlike a workbook, which eventually runs out. Second, the computer is never tired (unlike parents), and is available for the student to use anytime. Third, computer software is often just plain fun and children like to learn using it because it offers a variety of approaches to learning concepts.

As a general rule, educational software either teaches new concepts or reinforces concepts already learned. An example of the former might be an algebra tutor program which takes the students through ten or twelve lessons which build upon each other. The student will be periodically tested on what is learned, so that mastery can be demonstrated before going on to the next lesson.

A reinforcement type of program would be a vocabulary or math drill type program. With these programs, the student has presumably already been taught the words or math concepts which are being used. For example, this type of math program does not teach a student how to multiply, but will drill the student on the multiplication tables.

Both these types of programs are worthwhile and should be considered when building a software library. Whether you need a drill program or a teaching program will vary from subject to subject.

Computer software also varies substantially based upon the age range it is meant for. Obviously, software for younger children needs to be more colorful and graphically oriented than software for high school students. Most programs for young children seem to be modeled on the lesson/reward pattern. The students do a lesson, then are rewarded by being able to play a game related to the lesson.

A lot of educational software is presented primarily as a game. To complete the game, however, the child must master facts or concepts. This type of software is often quite effective, although it is usually not in any sense meant to be a comprehensive treatment of a subject. For example, in the software package *Madeline's European Adventure,* children will pick up some French words, but will not learn French.

Another popular type of software is what might be called "unstructured." This type of software has several different activities which the student can pick at random and which have no particular plan. For example, a program called *Play Room* has pictures of several toys and games around a room. When the child clicks the "mouse" (a directional pointer) on a certain part of the room, that activity starts.

Another software category now developing is interactive stories. This is similar to the books in which the reader can decide what to do, then go to a certain page in the book to continue along that line. Interactive story software, though, is much more complex, with many more possibilities.

Almost all software, of whatever type, now comes on CD-ROM. CD-ROM disks hold vastly more data than floppy disks, which makes possible such features as speech and full-motion video in programs.

Computer as information resource

Besides being used as a tutor, the computer also can be used as an expert on any topic. This is achieved in two ways. First, the computer can call out over phone lines to access the Internet. Second, a CD-ROM player can bring a whole library of information to the computer user.

An exciting aspect of a personal computer is its ability to link itself with other computers over phone lines. It used to be that people called in to information services such as America Online (AOL) or CompuServe and could only access information on one service at a time. However, the Internet has changed all that.

The Internet must be the most exciting development in computing in the last five years. The Internet is a huge network of computers which are all linked together. Thus, if you want information on fishing in Pennsylvania or John Brown's raid on Harper's Ferry, or the writings of the early Fathers, you can find hundreds of computer systems with the information.

In its early days, the Internet was meant as a link among universities, military installations, and government agencies.

And, it still functions as such. However, it has grown to the point where just about every business and organization has its own web site. This means that the amount of information on the Internet is staggering.

There is so much on the Internet that you need to use special software called a "search engine" to help you find what you want. On the Internet, each document is called a "page." A search for the term "home education" may bring up over 10,000 pages that contain those words. A search simply on education may bring up over 1 million pages.

Getting on the Internet is quite easy. Windows 95 (and probably any later Windows version) contains all the software that you need. You will also need what is called an Internet Service Provider (ISP), which is a service that you call into that connects you with the Internet. Nearly all areas of the country are served by local ISP's, so you will probably not have to make a long-distance call to get on-line. If you do not have a local ISP, there are several national ISP's, such as AT&T.

Unfortunately, the Internet has a bad side as well as a good side. If there are 10,000 pages on home education, there are probably twice that many pages devoted to pornography. Besides that problem, you also have cults, Nazis, and all kinds of other undesirables on the Internet. There have even been a couple of cases of people using the Internet to lure unsuspecting children or adults to meetings which have resulted in murder.

Just as you would supervise any other information source for your children, you have to supervise the Internet. You may want your children to use the Internet only with you around. Or, you might want to invest in "screening" software which will prevent access to pornography and other objectionable materials.

The Internet will certainly grow and change a great deal in the next few years. New technologies coming along, such as cable modems, satellite uplinks, etc., will greatly increase the speed of the Internet, which will permit realtime good quality audio and video. This will open up a host of new uses for an already very useful network.

Another method of obtaining low-cost information is CD-ROM. CD-ROM used to be a luxury, but now that a CD-ROM player costs as little as $39 and virtually all software is distributed on CD, it is a necessity.

CD-ROM's can hold a great wealth of information. A single CD can hold the text of hundreds of books. Also very popular are the many encyclopedia CD's, which hold the entire contents of an encyclopedia, including many pictures. Some CD's contain a large number of reference works on a certain subject, such as U.S. History or marine mammals. Whatever is your area of interest, you are likely to find a CD devoted to the topic.

Having a CD with the text of a book is sometimes even better than having a copy of the book itself. With a CD, you can search for information on whatever topic you want, which is not always easy with a book. If you want to find a certain Shakespeare quote, it may take you hours searching through books, but only a second or two using a CD. But if you do want a paper copy of what you are studying, you can easily print it if you have a printer.

A vast range of CD's is currently available. If you want software, you can buy CD' s packed with thousands of shareware (try before you buy) and public domain (free) software programs. If you want art to use in documents, there are CD's filled with pictures. There are even sets of CD's with phone numbers and addresses for every listed number in the country!

We are seeing now some movement toward putting entire courses on CD-ROM. This is good up to a point, but it is hard to believe that CD could ever completely replace books. It is simply too hard to read extensive text on a computer screen.

Computer as home tool

Besides being used for educational purposes, the computer is a great tool for home management. Considering how hectic home schooling can be, a few minutes saved here or there can really make a difference.

One area in which computers are being used more and more is home finance. Several low-cost checkbook programs are available which let you keep better track of where your money goes. It is very nice at the end of the month to have the computer add up what you spent in each category, such as food, gas, repairs. If you are on a budget, you can easily see where you are succeeding or failing. And, when tax time rolls around, it is a lot easier to have the computer count up your charitable donations rather than sitting down with your check stubs!

If you want to save even more time, enroll in Checkfree (Internet address: www.checkfree.com), which is a checkwriting program that actually writes checks for you. You simply tell the computer whom you are paying, and how much, then you upload the information to a central computer. That computer then prints and mails the checks for you—all this for a small monthly fee.

A word processor and printer also can save a lot of time. Homeschooling students will be able to produce better work in shorter time with a word processor (and you, or anyone else reading their work, will avoid eye strain). A word processor is also much faster for writing letters to the editor, or legislators, or your friends. A word processor is especially helpful for political action, since you can easily write one letter and send a copy to your two senators and one representative. If you have a typewriter now and have been retyping, you will be amazed at the time saved.

There are lots of other home uses for the computer as well. For example, you can use the computer to keep your Christmas card list, or your shopping list, or lists of valuables around your house for insurance purposes. Just about any information you need to keep can be kept on the computer.

Buying a computer

To the uninitiated, a computer can be a fearful thing. People talking about computers use words like "random access memory," and "megabyte," and "local area bus video."

And, other than the military, nobody can use acronyms the way computer users do. You've got your VGA, your VLSI, your OS/2, your MCA, and your PCMCIA.

But, in reality, there is not much you need to know to buy a good computer. You really only need to know four things: what kind of monitor (screen) you want, how large a hard drive you want, what processor you want, and how much memory you want.

Before deciding on the components you want, though, you should decide what type of computer you want. The "type" of computer that you buy really means "what it is compatible with." The type of computer you buy will determine what software you can use with it. Software is written for a specific kind of computer, and is not interchangeable.

There are many types of computers, but for home use you should narrow the choice to two: Apple and IBM-compatible. Apple computers are fine for home use, and there is a lot of educational software available in Apple format. The only problem with Apples is that they are very expensive. For years, Apple worked very hard to make sure that people could not clone (make similar copies) of their computers, which means that if you wanted an Apple computer, you had to buy it from Apple. When you buy name-brand from a dealer, you always pay more.

In recent years, however, Apple has made some move to license their technology to other manufacturers. They seem, however, not to be able to make up their minds about what they want to do. So, at any given time, it may be possible to buy Apple-compatible clones from a few manufacturers.

IBM-compatibles (sometimes called PC's), on the other hand, are made by hundreds of different manufacturers, and hence are less expensive. An IBM-compatible computer will generally cost about half as much as a similarly configured Apple computer. For this reason, and because the trend in the marketplace seems to be away from Apple and toward IBM-compatibles, in my opinion you are probably better off with an IBM-compatible.

Should you buy a brand-name IBM, rather than a compatible computer from a different manufacturer? In my opinion, there is little reason to buy brand-name IBM, since you will tend to pay about 50% more. However, when you buy IBM, you can feel confident the company will be around for a good long time in case your computer ever needs repairs. But there are other large computer makers, such as Dell and Gateway 2000, who are also likely to be around for a long time and are cheaper than IBM.

One thing you will have to decide is whether you want to spend a lot of money on a very top-of-the-line computer or if you want a more moderately-priced model. Prices on different computer components are always coming down, but a good rule of thumb is that a very good computer system can always be purchased for under $1,500. A top-of-the-line system will always cost about $2,500. Computer prices are constantly falling, but what this really means is that you are going to get a much better computer for your money, not that you are actually going to spend less money.

Once you choose the type of computer, you are ready to pick the components. The monitor might be the most important decision of all because it is the part of the computer that you are going to spend a lot of time looking at. You want to get the best monitor you can afford. The two main things to be concerned about are the size of the monitor and the dot pitch. The size of the monitor is measured in the diagonal size of the picture tube. However, the rated size of the picture tube is larger than the actual viewing area. For example, a 17" monitor may have a viewing size between 15.8" and 16.1", so the actual viewing area is more important that the nominal size. The dot pitch is the size of each individual dot (or "pixel") on the monitor. Generally speaking, the lower the dot pitch the better quality (and the more expensive) the monitor is. Common dot pitches vary from a high of .31 to a low of .24. Before you buy, it is good if you can actually see a monitor's display; but this is not always possible, especially if you buy mail order.

When choosing a hard drive, bear in mind that you will probably always underestimate what you need. A hard drive stores programs and information on your computer. It is a common saying that what you want to store on a hard drive always expands to fill the available space. A good rule of thumb in choosing hard drives is to get one or two sizes higher than the standard that comes with the computer. For example, if a computer comes standard with a 1.2 gigabyte hard drive, you might ask for a 1.5 or 1.7 gigabyte drive. Going up a couple of steps like this will usually add almost nothing to the cost of the computer, but the extra space will eventually come in handy.

There are several different types of processors to choose from. The processor is the central "brain" of the computer that runs your programs. The basic difference between processors is the speed at which they run. A new generation of processors is released every year or two by Intel, the largest of the chip manufacturers. After Intel creates their chip, it is then duplicated by other manufacturers, such as AMD and Cyrix. Non-Intel chips are usually significantly cheaper and can offer a good price/performance ratio.

It is usually not a good idea for a home user to buy a computer with the most advanced processor. A better strategy is to buy a computer with the second newest processor type. For example, when Intel released the Pentium processor, prices on its predecessor, the 486 chip, fell drastically. When Pentium II processors were released, Pentium prices dropped. The slightly older technology is still very good and yields the best price/performance value.

Deciding how much memory (RAM) you will need depends largely on price. If memory is expensive at the time you buy your computer, you will want to minimize how much you get. If memory is cheap, then maximize it. In general, the more memory you have, the faster and more capable the computer will be. However, there is a point at which the computer simply cannot use any more memory and adding memory will not do anything.

Most of the other parts of the computer keyboard, power supply, case, input/output cards will not vary much from one computer to the next, and you do not need to worry about them. Standard items on a computer should include a CD-ROM player, modem (for connecting to other computers over phone lines), and sound card. These items are very necessary for almost everybody, so if the computer you are looking at does not include them, then you will end up buying and installing them yourself, which means that a "bargain" computer without these items may not turn out to be such a bargain.

If you are going to use your computer for schoolwork, you will want to purchase a printer. Fortunately, prices of good quality printers have been going down, and are now around $200-$300. You could also look through the classified ads in the newspaper and buy a cheap printer second hand.

There are three basic types of printers: dot-matrix, inkjet and laser. Dot-matrix printers are good for many business tasks, such as printing a large number of labels, but there is little reason to buy a dot-matrix printer for home use. Laser printers have the virtue of printing pages quickly and with very good quality, but they are generally limited to black and white. Inkjet printers, however, print with quite good quality and print in color, making them really ideal for home use, especially for children to use.

When looking at what printer to purchase, it is usually a good idea to look at the cost of operation as well as the purchase price. Some printers are markedly more expensive to use than others because of the cost of the toner (laser printers) or the ink cartridges (inkjet printers). Magazine reviews of different printers, or manufacturer Internet sites, will give their average cost per page.

The only decision left is where you will buy. If you live in a large city, you will probably be able to find a good deal locally. The good thing about buying locally is that you can always take the computer back if it does not work.

On the other hand, you can almost always find a better price buying mail order. When buying mail order, though, you should consider that if it breaks, you may have to pack the whole thing up and ship it across the country. Many mail order firms are now offering on-site service, which means that a technician will come out to your house to fix the computer. That is definitely a good service to have, although it might mean a slightly more expensive computer.

But wherever you buy your computer, make sure to pay by credit card. This protects you in case the company you buy from goes out of business, or otherwise does not live up to their end of the bargain. Computer companies tend to go out of business with great regularity, so you never want to take a chance by sending a check to someone. If you do not have a credit card to use, tell the company to send the computer COD. If they insist on prepayment by check, go somewhere else.

Many mail order companies are now selling computers over the Internet. There are several good sites which compare prices on components sold by many distributors. One of the best sites is a service from Ziff-Davis that you can find at www.netbuyer.com.

Buying Software

As confusing as buying a computer can be, it is not as confusing as buying software. The sheer volume of software available makes it difficult to pick the best package.

One suggestion is to attempt to see the software in operation before buying. Often a software store will demonstrate the software for you in the store. If the software is an education program for your children, bring a child along. See if it looks interesting and can hold a child's attention. Since most computer stores do not let you return opened software, you are unlikely to receive a refund for software you do not like.

A cheaper way to test software is to use "shareware." Shareware is software that you can try for free, but are asked to pay for if you like it. You can download shareware from the Internet or order shareware CD's, which are a very cheap way to purchase a lot of software. Shareware typically is also lower-priced than commercial software, generally in the $15 to $30 range.

As mentioned above, a trend in software is to bundle multiple CD's together. This is often a good value, assuming that the programs themselves are good. It is tempting to think that if you can buy 10 CD's for $29, you are getting a good deal. But if none of the CD's are good programs, or programs that you would use, the deal is not so good after all.

Internet Sites for Shareware:

C/Net
www.download.com

Shareware Shop
www.bsoftware.com

Ziff-Davis Shareware Library
www.hotfiles.com

TuCows
www.tucows.com

Internet Search Engines:

Excite
www.excite.com

InfoSeek
www.infoseek.com

Webcrawler
www.webcrawler.com

Outlet for CD-ROM software:

Walnut Creek CD-ROM
4041 Pike Lane, Suite E
Concord, CA 94520
(800) 786-9907
www.simtel.com

Seton Educational Media, a division of Seton Home Study School, also offers computer systems, software, etc. Free catalog available.

Seton Educational Media
P.O. Box 396
Front Royal, VA 22630
(703) 636-9996

Chapter 16:
Catholic Support Groups

Why do home schooling parents need Catholic support groups? Most of our home schooling mothers can answer that quickly—because they desire the moral support of other Catholic mothers who are facing the same stresses and who can share their home schooling experience. It is clear from the writings of the Pope and from many outstanding priests, such as Father Robert Fox and Father John Hardon, that Catholic families should join together to help each other persevere in virtue, particularly in a hostile anti-Christian culture.

We Catholics approach our problems and find our solutions through the Catholic Church, through our Catholic Faith, through our Catholic culture. Our Catholic philosophy of reparation for sin, of suffering and sacrifice, is distinctly Catholic. Our attitude about children, contraception, and marriage is distinctly Catholic. Most of us are Marian Mothers, who want to be Marian in our approach to marriage, family, and home schooling. Therefore, when we Catholic home schooling mothers approach any kind of marriage, family, or home schooling problems, we want to confer with other Catholics.

When Father John Hardon gave a seminar on marriage at Christendom College, he concluded his presentation by reminding us that "No less than the members of a family are to be channels of grace to one another, so Catholic marriages and families are to be the means of grace to the world in which we live." While we want to evangelize others to be Christ-like, we need to associate frequently with those who help us become stronger in our faith. A Catholic home schooling support group can help mothers, fathers, and children to better understand and live the authentic Catholic life.

Women whose children are grown and who are no longer home schooling should continue to take seriously the call to evangelize. While their primary obligation as mothers at this point is to serve their children and grandchildren, they should be willing to help the young mothers coming along who yearn to hear the words of experienced Catholic mothers.

Reaching out

Once we decide that having a local Catholic home schooling support group is important, we need to reach out to find other Catholic home schoolers. Some of the following suggestions you may feel shy to undertake. Have trust in God, not yourself. Look to Him to help you to be an instrument of grace to others. Do not worry about what you will say or how you will do. God will give the graces to others as they seek Him.

Attend your local home schooling support group, which is probably formally or de facto Protestant. Let it be known that you are Catholic and would like to share ideas with other Catholics. Ask the members if any of them are Catholic or if they know any Catholics who are home schooling or who might be interested in home schooling. Give out a "business" card or 3 by 5 card with your name, address, and phone number, and ask them to pass it along to someone Catholic. Put on your "business" card: "Looking for Catholic home schoolers to form a Catholic support group." If you feel there might be some antagonism, simply put on the card: "Catholic Home Schoolers Network."

Pass around your cards at the regional and state conventions you attend. If there is a possibility of having a table at a regional or state convention, have a "Catholic Home Schooling" table. Your books and lesson plans or other Catholic books should be available. See if you can purchase some coloring books or saints' biographies from TAN Catholic publishers, at booksellers' prices, and sell them to pay for your table!

Go to your pastor and ask if you could have a display on Sunday morning between Masses in the cafeteria. One mother in California gave us this idea. The pastor put it in his bulletin and it was announced at Mass that Mrs. Smith was a home schooling mother who was displaying materials and would answer questions between Masses about Catholic home schooling. Be sure to bring your husband and children (assuming the children are well behaved). Do not worry if you do not know all the answers to all the questions. Tell them you will find out. Take down names and addresses. This personal approach goes a long way. It gives you an opportunity to be an instrument of grace to others, and it gives others a chance to respond to God's grace.

Consider putting an ad in your small weekly community newspaper; or ask for a notice under "Community Events." You may not wish to use the diocesan newspaper or the large city daily paper. You want the people to be local. And you want just a few people at first. An advertisement could read: "Catholic home schoolers meeting on First Friday after 9 A.M. Mass on June 7 at St. Matthew's Catholic Church. Catholic home schoolers and Catholics interested in home schooling are invited." Ask Father to let you serve tea and doughnuts in the recreation room.

Consider renting the library meeting room, usually available free of charge. Post a notice stating that you will display Catholic home schooling materials and will answer questions. If the library will not do it because it is a religious meeting, ask a Protestant friend, and the two of you could do it together as a general home schooling meeting. Advertise in your community newspaper that you both will answer questions and display materials. It need not last more than an hour or so.

If you have a Catholic bookstore in your area, ask if you can put your 3 x 5 cards on their counter. You may want to put out a nice flyer instead, inviting them to a Mass and meeting for Catholic home schoolers, or those interested in home schooling. The Daughters of St. Paul sisters are very supportive, as will be most bookstores.

Forming the support group

Once you have made contact with Catholic families who would like to join your support group, you have a variety of things to consider. If you have only one or two other families, keep it simple, meet once or twice a month, let the kids play while you discuss home schooling and mutual family situations in a Catholic framework. Try to attend Mass together before your meeting. Continue with the reaching out activities at your local parish and local home schooling support group.

If you become a larger group of more than five families, you may wish to have a once a month meeting of just mothers, or mothers and fathers, for the purpose of adult discussion of home schooling and Catholic family life. This could be in the morning after First Friday Mass, or in the evening. In addition, mothers and children may want to meet once a week for a Play Day. This gives children a regular weekly time with other Catholic home schooling children, but should not be a time for mothers to conduct serious discussions.

You may be fortunate enough to have a sympathetic priest. If so, ask him to be the chaplain for your group. When you have your adult discussion meetings, he can help to present the authentic teachings of the Church. He need not come to every meeting, especially meetings which may be sharing ideas about disciplining and home management.

Maintaining

Some support groups start a monthly newsletter. This can be a simple list of upcoming local Catholic events and home schooling events, with perhaps a paragraph of commentary. Pro-Life and Marian events could be featured. It could be a longer newsletter, with one or more articles, but this takes precious time and money away from family and home schooling.

Catholic home school support groups begin meetings with prayer. Many start with Mass, others with the Rosary. Whatever it is, it should be done regularly. There is a real advantage for the group if it is general knowledge that on the First Friday of each month, you can find a group of home schoolers at the 9 AM Mass at St. Mary's. Some home schooling groups are having Confessions before their Mass on First Fridays.

In some support groups, mothers bring curricula or home school materials to the meetings in case prospective home schooling mothers want to look at materials. Home schooling mothers should allow prospective home schooling mothers to decide what is best for their children without undue pressure.

Catholic Action or acts of charity should be encouraged as activities by the children in the Catholic Support Group. Children could sing or volunteer at a local nursing home. Some groups help provide food or clothes for the poor or unwed mothers at a local crisis pregnancy center. However, any charitable work should be on a limited basis, based on just what families are really able to do without infringing on family life.

Catholic support groups may have field trips, but if so, be sure this is a time when you can keep close control of your children and not allow this to be a time to visit with the other mothers. Your support group is a "witness" to the community about Catholic Home Schooling, and you want to be sure it is a positive witness.

Home schooling families use the public library frequently, usually once a week. Catholic parents should read the books their children are reading, however, because many, especially fiction, promote the secular values we are trying to avoid. Books in science or history may be promoting "politically correct" views. Catholic support groups should try to promote and praise good books to the librarian, and criticize the spending of tax money for anti-Christian materials.

One Catholic support group donates good books to their library. As a matter of policy, libraries have not purchased books considered textbooks, but with the numbers of home schoolers, libraries should be changing their policy. Another Catholic support group met with the librarian and persuaded her to purchase good textbooks and supplemental materials for home schoolers' curriculums. A Catholic support group in a large city found that the librarian was unfriendly toward home schoolers, and the group started their own library. They ask for book donations from older citizens who have excellent books now out of print.

The local parish should be a place where the pastor and members of the parish support home schooling families in various ways. While we see little of this at this time, I believe this is going to change. Home school families tend to congregate at the same parish church. When they become active in the church, as altar boys, and as daily communicants, and as members of parish organizations, the pastor necessarily will take a second look. He eventually may be pleased. Hopefully, support groups will start meeting at the parish church, with priests helping out with talks, or with religion books, or offering space for a speaker.

The Catholic support group should maintain contact with the state home schooling association so that Catholic families can be kept aware of important events or legislative activity. Most state home schooling organizations publish a state manual as well as a monthly newsletter. It is important that these are available for the families at the meetings.

Catholic home schooling support group discussions often focus on good Catholic literature, specifically on that which pertains to Catholic family life and home schooling. Each family might buy one book a month or subscribe to a good Catholic magazine or newspaper which can be shared with others. Perhaps the support group could have a revolving library so that parents may borrow books each month.

As the group grows, be sure that several parents share the burden of leadership. The support group will be stronger if more mothers are involved in arranging the meetings, not simply attending the meetings. Children, by the way, can be very helpful in the business of the support group. They can fold meeting notices, address and seal envelopes, print from the computer, and input names and addresses into the computer. Don't worry about being a large group. Families in small groups can work together more closely and help each other more effectively than in large groups.

Support group meetings should help parents share ideas and good times together. There should be no constitution or officers or dues, though donations might be needed to pay postage for monthly notices.

Networking

The purpose of the local Catholic support group is to help Catholic families on a day-by-day basis as family or home schooling problems and questions arise. This is the main purpose, and sometimes it should be the only purpose.

However, some small groups, particularly those in rural communities, may find a networking system helpful for arranging an annual regional meeting or Catholic home schooling family picnic. Such gatherings can be very encouraging to the parents as well as providing an opportunity for the children to meet a large group of people who are all home schooling. This convinces some relatives, husbands, and children that in fact other people in other parts of the world think home schooling is great, too!

A statewide or regional meeting is not necessary, but with wide publicity, it can attract new families to consider home schooling. A statewide meeting need not be an all-day event. It could be a Friday evening speaker, or a Saturday morning event involving two or three speakers. Keep in mind though, that for people traveling a good distance, an all-day event is more of an attraction.

As for exhibiting curriculum materials, remember that non-Catholic materials can be obtained at the Protestant or State home schooling conventions. It is better to have fewer materials which you know are Catholic than to have an abundance of tables with possibly questionable materials. Inexperienced mothers trust that you are providing accurate and authentically Catholic materials. Do not be careless with that trust.

Consider leadership

Before a teaching parent undertakes a leadership role in a support group, parents should consider the possibility of sharing leadership. We are all extremely busy teaching our own children, raising our families, managing a household, and trying to be good parents and spouses while we are at it. Be honest before God, pray about what your responsibilities can and should be, and move into leadership cautiously. Look around for a mother who has finished home schooling her children and see if she might become an active leader. Younger mothers need to be careful not to jeopardize their own home schooling.

Leading organizations in Catholic home schooling

In mid 1998, there are many local Catholic home school support groups. Some are formed as diocesan support groups. The purpose of these organizations is to provide an opportunity for parents, kids, and families to come together and share their home schooling experience, to help each other in the home schooling endeavor, and to grow in the practice of the Catholic Faith. These groups meet weekly for kids, and usually monthly for parents, with an additional monthly Saturday morning breakfast for moms. They meet to celebrate the liturgical holy days, and try to maintain Catholic cultural events.

A national organization called TORCH, or Traditions of Roman Catholic Homes (not just for home schoolers), has been in existence for a few years, the stated purpose being to help Catholic home schooling support groups to have activities or events to celebrate the feasts of the liturgical year.

This kind of Catholic support group is very good, but sometimes parents have reported that there are so many activities connected with these groups, and so many responsibilities for mothers to carry out the activities, that their home schooling has been compromised. Consequently, I would simply caution parents to keep their priorities clear when becoming involved in a very active support group.

TORCH has recently become involved in political activities—inadvertently, I would assume, because some of its officers were also in NACHE (see below). Since some of the leadership of TORCH is now changing, we will probably be seeing the group return to its original purpose.

Every state now has a Catholic home education association of some kind. Some are now putting on statewide conventions. The one in Michigan puts on two or three a year,

but most put on only one a year, or one every other year.
The Georgia convention in Atlanta in 1998 will be having
a graduate receive her graduation certification at the conference. I foresee that graduations will eventually become a
part of the Catholic state conventions.

Almost all of the Catholic state organizations have newsletters and maintain networks to help people contact others
in the state. Some put out very elaborate and informative
newsletters, especially about state legislation and potential
federal legislation. Others concentrate on discussing discipline or phonics, reading good Catholic books, and suggest-
ing ways to celebrate feast days.

NACHE, the National Association of Catholic Home Educators, was established about five years ago. They publish a
quarterly magazine, and their stated purpose is to help state
organizations to put on Catholic state home schooling conferences, to publish a magazine, and to maintain a network.

Because this organization was headed up immediately by
recent converts, it got off to a difficult start. While young
and new home schooling parents were attracted to it, older
home schooling leaders who had been through the battles
with the diocesan schools and departments of religious education were somewhat concerned about home schooling leaders who had so little experience in the Catholic Church and
in dealing with Church officials.

To get a history of the leadership in the Catholic Home
Schooling movement, one needs to realize that three Catholic
home schools have existed for many years, since the 1970's:
first, Our Lady of Victory, which began in California then
moved to Idaho; second, Seton Home Study School, started
in Virginia; and third, Our Lady of the Rosary, which began
in Virginia then moved to Kentucky.

These three organizations were the leaders in the movement. Seton had begun publishing a leadership newsletter
almost immediately, sending it to any state leaders or people who seemed to be maintaining a network, either locally
or statewide. The topics in the leadership newsletter dealt
with national or diocesan issues. After several years, Seton
organized an annual meeting of these leaders, called The

Round Table. This was not a Seton meeting, but was organized by Seton to encourage leaders to share ideas and consider the issues they were dealing with, mainly relating to diocesan school departments, to diocesan religious education departments, and to bishops and pastors.

Early on, it was evident that NACHE had a different perspective on the diocesan situations than did the leaders at The Round Table. This came to a head when The Round Table sent a letter to the National Catholic Education Association, basically stating, in blunt terms, that home schooling families were not under NCEA jurisdiction. NACHE followed this up with their own letter, undermining The Round Table letter, which The Round Table discovered only when the letter was published in NACHE's magazine.

It was after this that several leaders in The Round Table felt they needed a national organization (not just an annual meeting) to publish a newsletter to explain their position and to deal with issues relating to dioceses. Thus the Catholic Home Schooling Network of America (CHSNA) was formed. It publishes *The Domestic Church* a few times a year.

Catholic support group leaders should be aware of these two national organizations and should subscribe to their newsletters to understand the different perspectives on diocesan and national Church issues.

Suggestions from support groups

A Catholic home schooling group in Michigan reports that they are trying to locate other Catholic home schoolers by inquiring with the nearby La Leche League, Catholics United for the Faith, pro-life groups, and crisis pregnancy centers.

A Catholic home schooling group in New Jersey had a Rosary-making field trip at a monastery, and the children donated their rosaries to different Catholic charities. They planned a birthday party for the Blessed Mother in September, and an All Saints Day party on October 31. For the latter, the children were to dress up as saints.

A parish priest in Florida agreed to have a blessing for

the children and their parents in a Catholic home schooling support group. He also agreed to bless their school materials. The pastor has become more responsive, and the parents had a joint meeting with the Religious Education Director to show them the Catholic home schooling materials. The group meets on First Fridays for Mass and fellowship.

In Oregon, a Catholic home schooling support group meets for discussions on self-discipline, organization, and scheduling; testing children; ideas for Lent and Holy Week; a review of a "hands-on Chemistry book for the home"; and the importance of prayer and practicing Christian virtues. The group meets at a Catholic church where the priest built an additional room for the use of the home schooling families.

A group in Virginia publishes a Catholic Home School Support Newsletter. They have reported on their field trips, especially their visit to a monastery and to a home for retired nuns. They also meet for First Friday Mass, pray the Rosary and have activities for the children. The group had a priest come to recite the Rosary with them and perform some juggling tricks! A field trip was planned for visiting the National Shrine of St. Elizabeth Ann Seton in Emmitsburg. The group also plans an All Saints Day Party at a local parish. They have started three small clubs for the children: a math club, a writing club, and a geography club.

A Catholic home school group in the Philadelphia area scheduled a retreat for home schooled boys at a local seminary. A group in Ohio visit a convent weekly where the nuns help the home schooled children learn Catholic music. The priest gives the children talks each week.

Here in Front Royal, Virginia, one of the mothers arranged for our pastor to have Benediction and a ceremony in honor of the Infant of Prague before the new school year started. The church was half full of home schooling families. Father brought out his most ornate candelabra. After saying the prayers to the Infant, he led the Benediction songs in Latin, an historic event. He ended the ceremony by blessing us all with holy water.

Conclusion

The examples of activities of Catholic home school support groups as noted above represent just a tiny fraction of the reports we receive regularly from Catholic families. Catholic home schooling support groups are growing in importance for the Catholic home schooling families. They are evidently supplying religious and social opportunities as well as moral support. We consider support groups very important for the success of home schooling in Catholic families.

Chapter 17:
Home Schooling Laws, Regulations, & Fantasies

by Kenneth Clark

Kenneth Clark has been the general counsel for Seton Home Study School since 1988.

Catholic home schooling parents should be aware of the home schooling laws within their own state as well as have a picture of the general home schooling situation throughout the country. This will help them not only to speak intelligently to other Catholic parents who ask questions, but also to be informed if the family must consider relocating. In addition, state legislators often propose legislation which they think is working in other states, so it helps to be knowledgeable about the laws in other states.

In essence, there are three different types of home schooling statutes, or states, in this country. These three are first, states where the parents must seek approval before they can home school; second, states where parents must notify the public school authorities that they plan to be home schooling; and third, states where home schools are treated as private schools and neither approval nor notification is necessary. Private school states are the states where parents enjoy the most freedom.

Approval states

The most restrictive states are those where prior approval is required. Typically, in an Approval state, the parent must write to the local superintendent and ask for permission before the parent is allowed to home school.

Fortunately, the trend is toward fewer Approval states. In fact, as of this writing (1998), there are at most only four states that could be considered "Approval." Maine, Massachusetts, Rhode Island and Utah use the word "approve" in their statutes.

Generally, in an Approval state, the parents must submit information showing that the course of instruction at home is equivalent to that being offered in the public schools. This normally means that parents must submit an outline of the curriculum, as well as a list of textbooks to be used. In addition, the parents also must assure the school superintendents that the children will be home schooling for the same number of days as the state requires for compulsory school attendance.

Typically, Approval states require that parents submit a great deal of paperwork to the school, and they are not "allowed" to begin the actual home schooling until approval has been granted them by the school authorities.

Opinion

It is my view that Approval statutes are, by their very nature, unconstitutional. The right to educate one's children in a certain manner has been held to be a "fundamental" right by the United States Supreme Court. However, the courts also have declared that the state has the right to insure that citizens are educated. According to constitutional law, when a person's fundamental constitutional right is in conflict with a compelling state interest, as in the home schooling situation, the state must effectuate its interest in a way that causes the least infringement upon the person's rights. This means that *Approval* legislation for home education must be the least restrictive method possible for effectuating the state's interest in education. However, it is evident that Approval legislation is *not* the least restrictive means because there are many states that require no Approval, in fact require only a notice of intent. Thus these Approval statutes must be unconstitutional, in my legal opinion.

What is required in Approval States?

In the Approval states, for the most part, there are no specific parent-teacher qualifications. Most of the Approval states require that parents submit some form of assessment

at the end of the year, whether it is a nationally standardized test, a narrative progress report, or some other means
of assessment, such as a report card from a home study
school in which the child is enrolled.

Though burdensome and unconstitutional, Approval statutes
are not a serious hindrance to home schooling. Seton always
has been able to work with the Approval states to insure
that our parents are permitted to home school "legally." Nevertheless, parents living in "Approval" states are encouraged
to join the Home School Legal Defense Association (HSLDA)
as insurance. More will be explained about HSLDA in the
next chapter.

Notice-of-Intent States

By far the most common of the three types of home
schooling states are the Notice-of-Intent states. Approximately thirty-five states currently are Notice-of-Intent states,
or have an option that allows for Notice-of-Intent.

In a Notice state, parents need to send a notice or letter to the local school authorities, usually the local superintendent or board of education, informing them that they
intend to home school their children. The notice usually
needs to include the name and address of the parents, as
well as the names, ages, and grade levels of the children.

Please remember that this is a very generalized overview.
With thirty-five states being Notice-of-Intent, the law dif-
fers slightly from state to state.

Religious reasons

In addition to the minimal requirement of name and
address, parents who are giving Notice-of-Intent to the local
school (and this also applies to the people who are seeking approval) would do well to put two other paragraphs in
their Notice-of-Intent letters.

In one paragraph, parents should describe why they are
home schooling, especially if it is for religious reasons. In
our experience, we have found that superintendents are less

likely to antagonize parents who are home schooling because of their sincerely held religious beliefs. The superintendents see these parents as being very strongly committed to the home schooling mission and as being the type who would be unwilling to swerve from their decision simply because pressure is brought to bear upon them. As a result, superintendents tend to be less inclined to attempt discouraging them from home schooling.

The paragraph outlining reasons for home schooling should focus on the positive reasons. The religious reason is the strongest and most positive reason for home schooling. Other reasons, such as strengthening your family relationships or wanting to focus on your child's specific needs in a particular academic area, give evidence of positive and thoughtful consideration. Do not even mention the negatives of the school, as superintendents or principals would consider that a personal attack on them, their professional abilities, or the school.

If home schooling parents plan to have their children enrolled in a home study program, this information should be included in another paragraph with the Notice-of-Intent. Superintendents are less likely to harass home schooling parents who are enrolled in a formal program. They believe that an objective third-party, a correspondence program with teachers overseeing the work, relieves them of some responsibility to oversee it.

If your children are enrolled in a religious program such as Seton Home Study School, your paragraph should include that it is a religious home study program. If you are using Seton's program, you should state that Seton is accredited by the Northwest Association of Schools and Colleges. School officials believe, in general, that they should not be involved with families choosing a religious program, and that accreditation indicates there has been an objective evaluation of the program by professional educators.

Teacher qualifications

As for teacher qualifications, forty-one states have no requirements at all for parent-teachers. In those states which do require certain parent-teacher qualifications, there does not seem to be much of a pattern. Some states require that home instruction must be by a "competent" or "qualified" teacher, but this is automatically considered to be the parent without further discussion.

Teacher qualifications for parents are, of course, unconstitutional because the U. S. Supreme Court has declared that parents have a "fundamental" right to choose the educational means which they consider best for their children. In addition, and most important, the natural law and the law of God give parents the right to teach their own children. No parent-teacher qualifications can be placed in the way of these parental rights.

Assessment requirements

Regarding assessment of the home schooled child's progress, the Notice-of-Intent states are divided, with about half requiring no form of assessment, and the other half requiring standardized test scores or some other assessment to be submitted.

Some states require the attainment of certain percentage scores on nationally standardized tests. These required scores range from the fifteenth to the fortieth percentile. However, if for some reason a student cannot perform at these percentiles, other forms of assessment of progress are usually permitted. Other states require remediation or an evaluation to determine if a learning problem exists. Thus, scoring below a mandated percentile does not mean automatic termination of home schooling.

Even among those states that require standardized tests, regulations differ as to how often the test must be administered. Some states legislate that it be given every year, some require it every other year, and some require that it be administered in certain grades, this latter being in line with the public school regulations.

In many states, the assessment may be a written account of the student's progress or an evaluation made by someone acceptable to the school district and the parent. Some states will accept report cards from a home study school. In short, there are many different options for academic assessment.

Opinion

Requiring standardized tests or some other form of narrative assessment is not terribly burdensome to home schooling families. Such a requirement is not unconstitutional, as long as the scores are used simply as evidence of progress. However, since parents have the right under the natural law and the law of God to teach their own children, the state has no authority to set any kind of test score or certain progress standard as a requirement either to begin or to continue home schooling.

In addition, the requirements placed on home schoolers, to be in line with constitutional law, must be no more burdensome than those placed on children enrolled in the public schools. At present, the states give standardized tests to the government public school children at three different grade levels, while nearly all states require the home schooled students to be tested every year. This is unconstitutional.

No standardized test scores are used to retain government public school children in a grade level, nor are standardized test scores used to send children out of a school. Consequently, in justice, and to be constitutional, home schooled students should not be required to take annual tests, nor should scores play any part in determining whether home schooling may continue. After all, if a student at home must score above the fourteenth percentile to be able to continue home schooling, what is being done with the lowest fourteen percent of the government public school students? The percentile score is not based on how much the student knows on a particular test. The percentile score is determined by how the student achieves in relation to other students.

More comments on testing

There are four main standardized tests in use in the public schools in this country: SRA, CTBS, Stanford, and Iowa. While these companies generally are not happy with parents administering the tests, the instructions are very simple and parents have no trouble administering the tests to their children.

Realistically, at the present time, testing is the least restrictive means available for the state to ascertain student progress. However, there obviously needs to be further refining of the requirements in order to maintain justice for home schooling families. Remember, however, the state may not interfere with the curriculum for home schooling families. If the tests begin to adopt politically correct questions, this would be a problem. At present, while some of the reading comprehension paragraphs are not Christian in their perspective, so far Catholics have been able to tolerate the test material.

Furthermore, it should be emphasized that the test must be given in the student's normal learning environment, that is the home, and the regular parent-teacher should be allowed to administer the tests. Some of the school districts are trying to force home schoolers to take the test at the local school, under the supervision of a stranger. This is unduly stressing the home schooled student as he is tested in an unfamiliar environment. This negates the accuracy of the test and deals an injustice to the home schooler who must be placed in a tense situation. In addition, no certification requirement for parents to administer the tests should be tolerated, as this appears to be an attempt to prevent parents from home schooling, or to control the testing situation.

As long as Notice-of-Intent requirements are minimal, such as giving the names and addresses of the children, and there is minimal state involvement, such as only the receipt of test scores, the Notice statutes are usually not burdensome and are usually constitutional.

Private School states

The best type of home schooling statutes, if we must have any statutes at all, are those by which states consider the home school a private school.

The number of states with this type of law is growing. There are now about twelve Private School states, including Illinois, Indiana, Michigan, Oklahoma, Kansas, and Texas. Since the home school is considered a private school, and since private schools which do not accept federal or state money are basically unregulated, home schools in these states have no Approval requirements, no parent-teacher requirements, no Notice-of-Intent requirements, and no testing or assessment requirements. (Some other states treat home schoolers like private schools, but require notice.)

In the eyes of the Private School states, the home school would be similar to Catholic parochial schools before they accepted public tax money, or similar to some of the private Protestant schools. The state and local authorities are supposed to have a hands-off policy.

Just as you would not notify the state Department of Education that your child is planning to attend Our Lady of Mount Carmel Elementary School, so too you need not notify the Private School states that your child is attending Our Lady of Mount Carmel Home School. The Private School states are by far the best states in the country as far as home schooling goes.

Conclusion

This, then, is a general overview of the various types of home schooling statutes in the United States. Again, please remember that this is very generalized. Every state is unique; no two states are exactly the same in the way that they have written their laws.

The other fact to keep in mind is that this is my own interpretation of the state codes as being either Approval, Notice, or Private School states. Other attorneys may consider some of the Notice states to be what I term Private

School states, and vice versa. If you have a question about your state, contact a home school attorney in your state, or your state home schooling association, or the Home School Legal Defense Association if you are a member.

Please also remember that home schooling state laws are subject to change. In fact, you should assume that any education law is likely to change when you realize the number of lobbyists working in each state.

Since 1982, 35 states have adopted or modified existing home schooling statutes or regulations, and in all cases, the new regulations were an improvement over those in the past. In other words, an Approval state might have become a Notice state, and a Notice state might have become a Private School state. When the law has changed, it has changed in our favor.

Other regulations affecting home education

Catholic parents should be aware that legislation is constantly being introduced in the state legislatures which can directly or indirectly affect home schooling families. Usually when legislation is introduced, legislators are not thinking about how the legislation might affect home schoolers. This is why it is necessary that the state home schooling associations have lobbyists at the statehouse during the legislative session. Catholics can keep aware of such pending legislation by becoming members of the state home schooling association and by receiving the state home schooling newsletter.

The most common ancillary regulation affecting home schoolers is the regulation adopted in most states that young adults under the compulsory attendance age cannot obtain a driver's license unless they are enrolled in a school. Legislators should have exempted home schoolers, but the National Education Association is delighted at the outcome. This means that home schoolers are constantly being identified and cannot remain free from regulations if they want to obtain a driver's license. In addition, it means that home schoolers will have difficulty if they are not enrolled in a home schooling program, or that they must seek a signature from a local school superintendent.

Other curriculum regulations also can affect home schoolers, such as requirements for sex education or AIDS education or homosexual education, now being mandated in some states for the schools receiving federal and state money.

Many parents are concerned that Outcome Based Education plans may affect home schoolers. We need to keep a watchful eye on these developments.

Regulations related to receiving Social Security benefits affect home schoolers when it is insisted the students be enrolled in a "school." Another regulation that can affect home schoolers is the daytime curfew.

Laws can and do change. The best source of current legislative information is your own state home schooling association. Copies of your state laws relevant to homeschooling are usually available.

Fantasies

Many school board members, counselors for home-bound students, school superintendents, and principals have fantasies about home schoolers. Their over-arching fantasy is that home schooling students need to be under their protection. They believe they know what is best for each child in their geographical jurisdiction. These fantasies lead them to make incorrect statements and judgments, and even lead them to harass home schooling families.

It is wise to pray for these people that they learn reality, that they learn the truth about the rights of parents. It is wise for home schooling parents to recognize that these people honestly believe their fantasies. We need to be able to recognize them and deal with them appropriately.

In the next chapter, there will be tips about how to respond to educational authorities; but keep alert about what is going on in your state legislature and stand up for your rights. Do not give up the rights we have fought so hard to gain. Keep fighting for what is right, keep teaching what is right, and trust in God.

More on testing

There has been some controversy, in fact a great deal of controversy, about the various testing requirements on home schooling students throughout the United States. However, the discussions have hardly scratched the surface. Most home schoolers, justifiably, want only to be home schooling their children. They do not have the time, energy, or money to endlessly debate issues which they feel probably have little chance of changing anyway; but in the area of required testing, home schooling parents should be aware of the serious problems and implications involved.

Standardized-test laws make state legislators believe that they are keeping minimal tabs on home schoolers, without adding any onerous burdens to anyone. They believe that if public schools must administer tests, then home schoolers ought to do the same. And they believe they must be responsive to the desires of the largest, most well-financed, and most influential of all political action committees, the National Education Association and its state affiliates.

As is well-known, the state and local education associations are financially supportive of many state legislators' campaigns. The occupation most represented among state legislators, after lawyers, is public school educators.

You might say we have a politically stacked deck!

Currently 26 states require either standardized testing or some alternative evaluation. Sixteen of the 26 provide for an alternative to testing, e.g., portfolio or report card. Nine states require specific percentile achievement on these tests, ranging from a low percentile of 13 in Colorado to a high percentile of 40 in West Virginia and New Hampshire. Most of the other states require that in some way the test scores be used to determine whether the child is "progressing academically."

Some states, such as Alaska, do not attach any penalties to low percentile scores. Most states, however, use low scores to require more state involvement in the home school. In Tennessee, if test scores show lack of progress, the parents must consult with a licensed teacher to "design a remedial course." In other states, low test scores put the family on "probation." In some states, poor scores begin a process which may eventually force the end of home schooling.

Despite the implicit threat that test-score laws create, ironically most parents do not oppose such laws. Generally the percentile required is fairly low, and most parents believe that their children can easily pass. Statistically, hardly any home-educated students fail to reach the required percentiles. Many parents like the positive reinforcement they receive when their children do well on standardized tests.

It seems, then, that standardized-testing laws are something that everyone can agree on. Legislators like them, and parents either like them, or do not really mind.

BUT...

A major problem is that, as a reliable measure of an individual student's ability, standardized tests are practically useless.

Really.

In 1988, George Cizek, who works for the American College Testing Program (ACT), wrote an article in the journal *Educational Measurement: Issues and Practice.* The article, entitled "Applying Standardized Testing to Home-Based Education Programs: Reasonable or Customary?", vol. 7, #3, Fall 1988, disputes whether standardized testing has any valid application to home schoolers.

To understand the issue of whether testing is valid, one must understand something about the tests themselves. Generally speaking, there are two types of tests. "Norm-referenced" or "percentile" tests are tests which measure students against other students. Thus, a student in the 90th percentile scored as well as or better than 90% of the students who took the test. Percentile test scores bear no relation to how many questions were actually answered right or wrong.

"Content-based" tests, on the other hand, test the actual mastery of subject-matter by the student. In other words, the student who correctly answers 90% of the questions receives a grade of 90%. The matter of how other students performed on the test is irrelevant.

Content-based tests are the tests with which we are generally familiar. Standardized achievement tests in the government's public schools are about the only educational application of percentile tests. In fact, students in classrooms would have a rebellion if teachers suddenly instituted percentile tests. A student in a "norm-referenced classroom" could easily fail a spelling test while missing only two out of 20 words. Most people would consider such grading unfair.

Mr. Cizek is quite adamant in stating that norm-referenced tests are inappropriate measures of educational ability. He writes,

> Without measures of absolute abilities or skill levels and aptitude, the data reported from a norm-referenced test are an inadequate—and improper—source of information for use in assessing the quality/acceptability of a child's home-school program.

Coming from an expert in the field of testing, this is a very strong statement.

Here is why

Mr. Cizek makes several important points about standardized testing. Perhaps the most important is that by definition, a certain percentage of test-takers will do "poorly" as a percentile, no matter how well they do on an absolute scale.

To use relative, percentile-type testing as the basis of a home schooling law is particularly unfair. Most of our laws are absolutes. In other words, you must pay the exact tax you owe, you cannot go at all on a red light, and you cannot steal anything. Percentile-test laws are like passing a law putting the 40% least honest people into jail. Every year, 40% of the people would go to jail.

Statistically, 40% of all test takers should be at or below the fortieth percentile on a standardized test. Statistically, almost half of all home schoolers in West Virginia, where currently the fortieth percentile is required, should receive impermissibly low scores every year. The fact that they do not is due only to the efforts of the children and their parents to do better than average. The legislators who passed the law ought to have expected that 40% of all test-takers would fail!

Standardized testing has a particularly adverse effect on students who simply do poorly at test taking. It also penalizes those who attended inferior schools before starting home education. Students at inferior schools may start off at a very low level on standardized tests. Indeed, parents might withdraw their child from a school for this very reason. But when the parent begins a home-education program, the student is expected to reach as high as the fortieth percentile in one year's time, or possibly be returned to the school from which he came!

Indeed, one can see how the testing provision probably falls hardest on poor and minority families. In general, public schools in poor areas are the worst academically, and parents usually have no option for private schooling. In such a case, home schooling is the only alternative to public schooling. However, unless the student can make exceptional progress right away, the state may step in (in some states) and end the home schooling, leaving the parents with no educational alternatives whatsoever. The children most in need of home schooling are the ones who are most likely to be denied the opportunity.

Another major problem with norm-referenced tests is that they are quite unreliable tools for young students in the primary grades. As Mr. Cizek writes, "It is well established that the reliability of almost every psychological measure increases with the age of the subject." The government's public schools do not give standardized tests or report the scores until grade four because of this well-documented fact. Because most children start a home-schooling program in the early grades, home schooled students will begin to be tested as early as kindergarten, and their scores reported, at an age when the tests are least reliable.

An interesting further point is that schools often purchase practice tests for their students. This gives the students an opportunity to familiarize themselves with at least the kind of questions asked before they move on to the real test. Most home schooling parents cannot afford the extra expense of administering multiple tests, so their children are put at a disadvantage. Even if they could afford it, practice tests are not readily available to home schooling families.

The American Psychological Association

Because of the invalidity of these scores as a reliable gauge of absolute achievement, guidelines offered by the American Psychological Association state that

> in elementary or secondary education, a decision or characterization that will have a major impact on a test taker should not automatically be made on the basis of a single test score....A student should not be placed in special classes or schools, for example, solely on the basis of an ability test score.

Mr. Cizek reports that, in fact, in schools "neither teachers nor administrators rely to any great degree on test results in making decisions about individual students."

According to Mr. Cizek, standardized tests were never meant to measure *individual students*. Educators are aware of this, though educator-legislators want to forget it, as do the NEA lobbyists. Parents are not aware of this.

Rather, declared Mr. Cizek, nationally standardized tests are meant as general *measures of a school* or a school system, enabling them to compare themselves to other schools or school systems. Mr. Cizek writes,

> Thus it is not merely a misapplication of test instruments to use the norm-reference test to assess individual progress, but it also marks a break with the traditional role of standardized tests if they are now proposed as a solution to the problem of monitoring the educational

progress of students in individualized home education programs.

Educational setting

Finally, as Mr. Cizek points out, the educational experience of home-educated students is vastly different from that of school-based students. Standardized tests are meant to test within a highly similar group. As Mr. Cizek writes, however,

> In the case of a home-based educational program, the student can be seen as differing from the norm group on only one variable—educational setting. However, that one difference should call into question the applicability of national norms to the home-schooled child.... Student/teacher ratios, teaching methods, psychological security, teaching materials, educational level of the teacher, educational philosophy of the teacher, teacher's level of commitment to the individual student, and curriculum are only a few and most obvious of the many ways...[that] setting significantly affects other aspects of the child's educational experience.

Wow!

Most parents choose home education because they want to create a curriculum and atmosphere that is *significantly* different from public schooling. Yet, all standardized tests developed to date have been developed for children in public schools. In fact, tests have many questions on them which reflect a bias toward group education. Mr. Cizek gives a practical example of this from a recent Michigan Educational Assessment Program (MEAP) test. Three of the questions ask the students to choose who would be the best person to help them if they had the flu, had a toothache, or were buying a toothbrush. None of the questions even lists "parent" as an optional answer!

Our conclusion

There is certainly a place for testing in the evaluation of home schoolers, but percentile tests should not be used for this purpose. Rather, content-based tests should be used. If a student should be able to read and understand *Macbeth* in order to graduate from high school, then that should be the criterion. The student should not be expected to be in the top sixty percent of all students who understand *Macbeth*.

Moreover, home schoolers themselves should be included in the development of content-based tests. The tests should take into account the special strengths, and perhaps weaknesses, of home-schooling programs. If this is done, then legislators and parents can be satisfied that their testing measures something real.

In the meantime, home schooling parents and support groups should make legislators aware of these problems with norm-referenced tests. If legislators are to make regulations regarding home education, they at least ought to be sure that the regulations they make are reasonable. Mandating norm-referenced test-taking by home school students does not meet the reasonability test.

Chapter 18:
Responding to Authorities
by Kenneth Clark

When dealing with government authorities, you must consider two things. First, what are your legal rights? Second, how should a Christian respond to requests or demands from the government?

The first section of this chapter deals with the legislative and judicial system in our country to serve as a background for the second section, which gives Catholic home schooling parents practical hints on dealing with authorities—educational, social, and legal authorities.

The U.S. Constitution

The supreme law of our land is the United States Constitution. All laws, both state and federal, as well as all decisions of state courts, must comply and be in agreement with the federal Constitution. Any state or local law which is held to be unconstitutional by the U.S. Supreme Court is considered not to be a law. Thus, when either the federal Congress or state legislatures pass laws, they must be written so that they pass "constitutional muster." As a result of this, the United States Supreme Court is the most powerful group of people in the United States, since they must agree that any law passed by Congress or by the states is legal.

For home schoolers, this means that even if a President, or a governor, or state legislature is hostile to home schooling, we are still guaranteed certain protections under the federal Constitution. Thankfully, the Supreme Court has ruled, based on the Constitution, that parents have a "fundamental right" to choose the kind of education they want for their children. The only way to change the Constitution is to amend it. This is a very difficult process, as is witnessed by the fact that in the past 200 years, the Constitution has been amended only sixteen times since the passage of the Bill of Rights. Most important, then, is the federal Constitution and the rights it guarantees to all Americans.

Federal statutes

After the U. S. Constitution, federal statutes are the most important laws. Federal statutes are those passed by the United States Congress; these laws apply equally in every state. Most federal legislation deals specifically with issues which involve the whole country. Thus Congress passes statutes dealing with interstate commerce and with federal taxation.

As far as education is concerned, schooling has always been the primary responsibility of the individual states, not of the federal government. There is only one federal statute governing education, which is the Education of All the Handicapped Act. This is the only educational legislation which currently exists at the federal level.

The U.S. Department of Education greatly influences the schools and educational situation throughout the country, though it can make no laws. This department researches and studies various aspects of education and of the schools. In addition, it is involved in the distribution of federal funds to the states.

For instance, the Department of Education has pressured Congress to allot funds to the states for schools to carry out certain programs. If schools were not integrated, for instance, that could affect whether a state would receive federal funding.

While the people working at the U.S. Department of Education are not elected, they, along with the private but powerful National Education Association, greatly influence what is happening in the schools of the nation. Nevertheless, final legislation regarding schools in a state must be passed by state legislators.

State statutes

Most important after federal statutes are the state statutes. State statutes apply only in those states in which they are passed. This is where we find home schooling laws. There are fifty states and thus fifty different state home schooling statutes. No two states have identical state home schooling laws. State statutes, however, must be in conformity with both the federal and the state constitutions.

Each state has a constitution, and those differ as widely from state to state as do the home schooling laws. The protections granted by the state constitutions, however, can sometimes be greater than that granted by the federal Constitution. It often has been said that the federal Constitution provides a "floor" of protection, not a "ceiling." In other words, the federal Constitution grants us a minimum of protection, over and above which the states can grant more. In some states, the right to home school is guaranteed, even if not specifically, by the state constitution.

The state constitution is interpreted by the state supreme court, as the federal Constitution is interpreted by our United States Supreme Court. Thus, we have our federal Constitution and federal statutes, and the state constitutions and state statutes. State constitutions are somewhat easier to amend than the federal Constitution, but they too are difficult to amend.

State administrative regulations

After the state statutes, we have what we call administrative regulations. Administrative regulations are adopted by various state agencies, such as the State Department of Education and the State Department of Transportation. These state administrative agencies usually work out the details for people to fulfill the requirements generally mandated by the state statutes. In other words, if the state passes a statute dealing with home education, the statute might read that home education is legal in this state, and that the State Department of Education will promulgate regulations governing it. These regulations might deal with such things as testing and parent-teacher qualifications.

Two examples of states which have home schooling laws which are procedurally explained and administered by State Department of Education regulations are Hawaii and Nevada. The administrative rules of both states further implement a state statute. Using Hawaii as an example, the statute would be worded something like, "A child is exempt from compulsory attendance when enrolled in an appropriate alternative education program as approved by the superintendent." This, of course, is very general. What does "approved by the superintendent" mean exactly? Approved how? As to teachers, curriculum, test scores, what? According to the Hawaii administrative rules, this means parents must provide a notice, the parent automatically is deemed a qualified instructor, and so on.

Administrative regulations, while not laws or statutes themselves, do have the force of law, because the state legislature has empowered the administrative agency with some of its legislative power. It has delegated some of its authority in a certain area—in the case of the Department of Education, only over the education of the state citizens—to pass these regulations. Although administrative regulations have the force of law, there is no penalty within them, but rather in the law passed by the state which authorizes the passage of the administrative regulations.

However, administrative regulations, as with anything else, must be in compliance with both the federal Constitution and the applicable state constitution. Administrative regulations are much easier to change than laws. It is at this level that state home schooling associations or even individual home schooling parents have the best opportunity to make changes. Regrettably, many state agency regulations are not in compliance with the state or the federal Constitution.

Pronouncements by local school district

The last form of regulation which home schoolers often have to deal with is pronouncements handed down either by a local superintendent or by a local school board. These do not have the force of law and parents are not required to follow these local "regulations." For instance, a superintendent might declare that children in his school district should take a standardized test, even though the state law says nothing about it and there are no administrative regulations on the subject.

Local school district pronouncements have no force of law. However, sometimes superintendents or school boards feel that the force of their authority comes from their position. A person may believe sincerely that by the mere virtue of his being on a school board, or being a superintendent, he has some legal authority. This authority is limited, however, to those areas where it has been granted specifically by the state legislature through a statute or through administrative regulation.

It is very important to realize that superintendents may make pronouncements, but whether or not they actually have the lawful authority to back them up is something else entirely. Parents need to be exceedingly cautious when dealing with such a situation. They must realize that the question of whether the superintendent's "requirement" is good or bad, lawful or unlawful, is immaterial. *If he does not have the authority granted him by the state, his "requirements" are no more than suggestions, and the parents are not obliged to comply with them.*

We urge parents to be very, very careful about complying with "regulations" from a superintendent. Even if it is something which is not particularly onerous, we must seriously consider whether to comply with local pronouncements because it would set a precedent which could affect future legislation. It is likely that the superintendent will inform the state legislature or the State Department of Education that he has been requiring students, for instance, to take standardized testing in his school district for the last couple of years. If the parents have not objected to it or have complied even while objecting, he may suggest to the Department of Education that it should now be an administrative regulation, or even a state law. The further up the chain a law or regulation goes, the more difficult it is to change.

Summary

To summarize: the most important and powerful law in the land is the United States Constitution, our federal Constitution. This is followed by federal statutes, followed by state statutes and the state constitution, with which the state statutes may not be in conflict. This is followed by administrative regulations from the various state agencies, and finally by pronouncements from a local government figure.

Parents should not be afraid to home school, as we have many decisions by the United States Supreme Court, as well as by state supreme courts, upholding the right of parents to educate their children. This parental right has even been called a "fundamental right." The list of Supreme Court cases supporting such parental rights goes back to the 1920's, with *Meyer vs. Nebraska, Pierce vs. Society of Sisters, Prince vs. Massachusetts,* and other cases, all the way up to the present, where we are steadily winning victories in the state courts and in the federal courts, protecting the rights of parents to teach their children at home.

It should be noted that while all the state laws and regulations *should* be conforming to the federal and state constitutions, this does not necessarily mean they do in fact. There are numerous state laws and regulations which do not conform to the Constitution. The problem is that it takes money and time for a person or a group to go to court claiming that a law is unconstitutional. Christians often interpret a law as just or unjust based on the Bible or Church teachings or the Natural Law, but with judges who are not Christian, or who are not approaching the law from a Christian viewpoint, such time and money is often wasted. Needless to say, injustice abounds.

Home School Legal Defense Association

Consider joining the Home School Legal Defense Association. Their number is (540) 338-5600, or you can write to them at P.O. Box 159, Paeonian Springs, VA 22129. The cost of membership is $100 per year ($85 for Seton families). It is the most effective legal protection for home schoolers. If you are a member, and you do run into a legal problem, they will provide you with an attorney and go into court. In fact, they will take the case to the United States Supreme Court if that is necessary.

The $100 annual fee becomes very small when you consider that some HSLDA cases have cost them $50,000 or $100,000. The main reason they are able to charge so little is that they are able to avoid most legal problems by talking to superintendents and persuading them not to follow through on a threat of prosecution or the like. While there are many families in the HSLDA organization, very few ever have legal difficulty. Statistically speaking, only one home schooling family in a hundred will ever be contacted in any sort of negative way, and only one in one hundred of that group will have any kind of serious legal trouble such as a trial or charges filed against them. That means that only about one in every ten thousand families will have a serious legal problem. But this can only continue if parents keep themselves informed, and join HSLDA.

Though it is very unlikely that you will wind up in legal trouble, in some states it is more important to be a member of the HSLDA than in others. Home schooling families in Massachusetts should definitely, at the present time, join HSLDA, since their state is currently trying to harass home schoolers. However, families enrolled with Seton, an accredited program, have experienced fewer problems even there.

Also, I would highly recommend membership for single parents and for families with handicapped children.

Superintendents know the reputation of HSLDA, and if you let them know that you are with HSLDA, local authorities often will back down just for that reason. They know that HSLDA is very aggressive and will fight to the finish.

Enrollment in a program

Consider enrolling in a home study program. The fact is that home schooling families enrolled in a program have far fewer problems with local or state authorities.

When considering a program, you need to consider whether accreditation is important to you. Seton is accredited by the Northwest Association of Schools and Colleges, which is a private accrediting organization, not a state or government organization. Seton became accredited with the hope that our families would have less trouble with superintendents, and this has proved to be true.

Accreditation is important to school superintendents. We are pleased that the very fact that we are an accredited school will make superintendents back down from harassment. Often they will not even look at the curriculum, but are satisfied that an objective professional organization has evaluated and accredited our program.

In general, we have found that superintendents are more cooperative when a family is enrolled in a program. They like it when there is a third party involved in overseeing the home schooling. They also are much more impressed with a professionally prepared curriculum than one which is done by the family themselves. They like the idea that the family can phone a counselor for assistance in their home schooling venture.

Many times a problem with the local superintendent can be easily resolved by the home study school through a letter or telephone call. Often the superintendent merely wants to see an outline of the curriculum. At Seton, we call this a "scope and sequence." Probably nine out of ten "problems" we have ever had with superintendents have been resolved by sending them a scope and sequence of our courses for the student involved.

Statement of philosophy

Compose a written statement of philosophy or religious belief, that is, the reasons you are home schooling, especially if it is for religious reasons. Even though states do not require that you explain why you are home schooling when you notify the superintendent or the school board, we suggest that you do.

In our experience, those who are home schooling for religious reasons are stronger in their commitment than those who are home schooling for any other reason. Superintendents realize this as well, and tend not to harass home schoolers who are religiously committed to their decision to home school.

Your statement of philosophy is basically a declaration that this is required by your faith, and that you are obliged by God to teach your children at home. Although you may not include all your reasons in the letter that you write to the school superintendent, you should enumerate all your reasons for Catholic home schooling in a written statement for yourself and for your family. It is better to have it as a reminder and as a frequent review. Hopefully, you will not need it.

How to handle an official contact

In this section, we will deal with two topics: first, how to handle a contact from a government authority regarding your children's education; and second, some hints on how to avoid legal troubles.

How should a Catholic home schooling parent handle a contact by educational authorities?

There are two very important rules which should govern not only how you handle contacts, but are also good rules for almost any social situation. The first rule in handling any contact, whether by phone, letter, or in person, is to be polite. Be friendly, be a good Christian. "A soft answer turneth away wrath."

In many situations, the contact person is someone just doing a job. He has nothing personal against you and probably no axe to grind against home schooling. He has been informed that you are home schooling, or perhaps has been told that your children are in some sort of school. He is merely doing his job in coming out to investigate a complaint and knows nothing about home schooling. You will be the one to make a first impression on him regarding home schooling and what it is all about. Try to give a good Christian impression.

The second rule is this: while being friendly and polite, do not do anything that makes you feel uncomfortable. Whether it is answering a particular question, letting a person into your house, letting him see your children, or whatever, follow your instincts. If the person wants information you do not want to give him, you are probably correct in wanting to withhold it. If you are uncomfortable with his coming into your house, you are right not to let him in. Be polite, be friendly, but do not do anything which makes you feel uncomfortable. Trust in your instincts. God will not allow you to go wrong when you trust in Him.

Telephone contact

With those two general rules in mind, let us address the different types of contacts. The first is a contact by telephone. Always ask the caller to put a request in writing and send it to you on business stationery. You need to do this for a number of reasons. First, you do not absolutely know to whom you are speaking. If someone calls up saying that he is from the State Department of Education, or from the local superintendent's office, or from the principal's office, you really don't have any way to verify that over the telephone. Unless you know the voice of the person who is calling, it could be anyone calling up to get information. There have been occasions when unauthorized persons have called home schooling families and asked some very personal questions about their home schooling and their lives. Never give personal information over the phone to a stranger. The person on the end of the phone is a stranger if you cannot verify who he is.

Also, do not promise to answer the questions which may be sent to you in writing. After talking with your spouse, or the home school lawyer where you are enrolled, or a local attorney, you may find you are not required to answer the questions. In Virginia, our Seton parents can easily claim the religious exemption, but because the local superintendents send forms in the mail to home schooling families, never mentioning the exemption, many parents just fill out the forms and subject themselves to the unnecessary regulations.

The second reason you want the request to be put in writing is that, many times, it will never be mailed to you. Many of these officials are very busy; it is much easier for them to pick up a telephone and ask a couple of questions than it is to sit down and type or dictate a letter. As a result, there have been many occasions where parents have received telephone calls requesting information, and when parents ask for the request to be put in writing, for one reason or another they never do receive a written request.

Someone at your door

All this is fine, but what if someone comes to the door? Again, be polite, but do not do anything that makes you feel uncomfortable. The most important rule, and the one which cannot be over-emphasized, is that if someone comes to your door, you do not have to let him into your house unless the person has a search warrant. *Let me repeat: if someone comes to your door, anyone at all, you do not have to let him into your home unless the person has a search warrant.*

On a couple of occasions, someone came to our door when I was being home schooled, asking questions about the school we attended. Mother, even though not dressed completely appropriately for the outside weather, stepped out onto the porch, closing the door behind her. The visitors were never asked to sit down on the porch, nor allowed in, and Mother's hand remained on the doorknob. Identification was asked and given before any questions were answered. Not all questions were answered, either.

When you are meeting with a government official, such as a principal or superintendent, or someone from their office, he represents the government. You do not have to allow government representatives into your home without a search warrant. This applies to the police, the FBI, anyone from Social Services or the school district, or any other governmental agent.

The Fourth Amendment

You have a very important Constitutional right, the Fourth Amendment right, which protects you against unlawful searches and seizures. Basically, this means that a person's home is his or her castle. You are not required to let anyone into your castle unless the person has a search warrant.

Obtaining a search warrant is not simple. It requires the person who wishes to search to go to a judge and present that judge with probable cause that some crime is being committed. In other words, the police, social service worker, or superintendent, must go to a judge and claim, "Your Honor, I have reason to believe, based upon testimony from an informant, that Mr. and Mrs. Smith are committing a crime because they are home schooling." But home schooling is not a crime. A judge will not grant a search warrant unless there is truly evidence of a crime. In many cases when unfounded accusations are made about "child abuse," there was no search warrant but the mother allowed herself to be intimidated and allowed officials into her home.

Sometimes mothers or fathers unwittingly call Social Services for help, and find that Social Services are not really wanting to help, but to control. One Catholic father was at work while his wife was sick in bed when he called Social Services to see if someone would pick up his children and take them home. The Social Services people decided to place the children in foster homes. Though the mother does have chronic problems, she is able to walk around the house and take care of herself and could take care of the children. But the parents are not allowed to see their children except on weekends, and they will have to fight the local social service bureaucracy to have their children returned to them. The lesson to be learned: *do not assume that social agencies exist to help you or your children!*

Short of exigent circumstances (that is, short of hearing the children screaming and yelling in pain), short of imminent physical danger to the children, no one is allowed to enter your home without a search warrant.

If you have heard of cases where social workers or police have entered the home of a home schooler with a search warrant, it is likely that an unfriendly neighbor gave an anonymous "tip" about possible child abuse. If you have a sudden problem at your door, call your attorney, or any nearby attorney, immediately. Have that attorney come to your house immediately. Do not answer any questions until an attorney is present. If necessary, have the person at the door talk to your attorney on the phone. Hand him the phone through the door, and make him talk to your attorney outside on your porch or front yard. (Just as you need to know the number of your doctor in case of emergency, you should also know the number of your attorney.)

Obtaining a search warrant is a very difficult and time-consuming process, except in a child abuse charge. *Do not be intimidated into allowing people into your house* simply because they tell you they CAN obtain a search warrant or the police. If they say that, tell them you are very sorry, but you will not allow them in, and if they want to get a search warrant, it is up to them. If they want to call the police, that is also up to them. This gives you TIME to contact an attorney or your state or local home schooling organization.

How to proceed at the door

When someone comes to your door asking questions, the first thing to do is ask for identification. If he is unable or unwilling to provide it, do not speak with him. Step back into your house, close the door, and lock it. If he continues to stay on your property, call the police. Anyone who really is from the superintendent's office or from Social Services should provide you with identification. There is no reason not to, and in fact, in many states, government representatives are required by law to provide identification, which is usually a badge with a photograph.

In addition to seeing identification, ask for a business card. If you have a business card with the person's name, address, and phone number, there is less chance that he will be rude when speaking with you, because he knows that you would be able to report him. Also, you will want to contact an attorney after the conversation. Your attorney must know with whom you spoke, and thus whom to call at the Department of Education or Social Services.

Remember that anyone coming to your door from Social Services is very overworked. Local Social Services agencies

have a staff of forty or fifty people, and it is virtually impossible to find someone if you do not have a name, and
that means a business card. Many parents, after such an
encounter at their door, are too upset and cannot remember
the name. So please obtain the business card, or write down
the name, address, and phone number.

Whether or not to answer questions

After you have the identification and business card, the
person at the door will probably want to ask you some questions about your home schooling.   At this point, you will
have to decide whether to talk with the person or not. Nothing requires you to answer the questions.
   You have a Fifth Amendment right not to answer any
questions, the right against self-incrimination.   Even if you
have not broken the law, the person at your door is asking
questions which might lead him to believe that you have
broken the law.   Therefore, whatever answer you give, no
matter how proper, could be self-incriminating in the eyes of
the official.   Thus, you have a perfect right not to answer on
the grounds of possible self-incrimination.   However, do not
use those words to your visitor.   Simply say, "I would rather
have legal counsel before answering your questions."
   If you feel comfortable talking with the person at your
door, fine.   Remember, however, that if you have no third
party witness, anything you say may be written down, either
accurately or inaccurately. It would be the word of the government agent against yours if any future proceedings should
follow.
   If you decide not to talk with the person, just say that
you are busy, that you do not have time right now, but if he
will put the request for information in writing, you will get
back to him.   This gives you time to contact your spouse,
think about what you want to do, pray about it, contact an
attorney, or contact your local or state home schooling support group.
   If you decide to answer the questions, I strongly urge
you to speak with the person *outside* the house.   Step out-

side, close the door behind you, and talk with the person outside. No matter what the weather is. Whether you are in sunny southern California or blizzard weather in North Dakota, I would say to the person, "I'll step outside and we can talk for a few minutes." Keep your children away from sight if at all possible. You would be surprised how a social worker can use an inconsequential item, like a child without his shoes on, as evidence for child neglect.

Outside the door

Once outside, you should not answer any question that makes you feel uncomfortable. Even if the person asks you something he might be entitled to know, politely ask which law gives him permission to ask for test scores, for your teacher's credentials, or whatever. In fact, ask him to cite the law so that you or an attorney can look it up. Tell him you want to write down the State Code number so you can look it up later. And then do look it up!

You may be familiar with the law yourself, sometimes more so than the person at the door. You must decide whether you will show that you know the law, or simply to let the person speak without adding your comments.

If you know what the home schooling law is in your state, you may or may not want to quote it to them. If your visitor says, "It's the compulsory educational law," you could respond, "But isn't it true, according to the statute section such-and-such of the educational code, that I don't have to be a certified teacher? And isn't it also true that I don't need to administer an achievement test?" However, this kind of a discussion is usually not too productive. Authority figures do not like to be informed by the person they are supposed to be informing!

Some parents feel "called" to have a discussion with the government representative. If so, keep in mind that God will be with you, say a prayer, and rely on God to help you through and to help you give the best possible answers, so as to convince the person not only that what you are doing is right, but that what other home schoolers are doing is right. Next time he receives a call about home schooling, he may have a better understanding of it, know the type of people who are doing it, and treat parents' concerns for their children as real and legitimate.

If you have a copy of the law, you might want to keep it available so that you can produce it and say, "This is what the law says; I have a copy." Normally, having things in writing is better than quoting something.

Hints to avoid trouble

There are many practical hints to avoid legal trouble. Some are more important than others, and I will try to emphasize the hints which I think are very important that you do, as opposed to those I only suggest you consider.

Keep good records

The first hint is one that I emphasize very strongly. I give it first because it is extremely important. It is to keep good records. Many states require that you keep records such as standardized test scores, or grades, or attendance records. Some elementary schools and all high schools require transcripts if you transfer. Records should be kept for two or three years, or until your child graduates from high school. Transcripts for all four years of high school should be kept for a few years. These records should be handy and easily available. Even if your children are enrolled in a home study program, keep a copy of the records for yourself.

If you are planning to send your children to college, you are going to need records, especially a high school transcript, or diploma. Every college in the country requests the prospective student's high school transcript.

Attendance records are very important, and most states consider this the most important school document. The compulsory laws are for attendance, not for education. Attendance records prove to the state or school district which days your children have been in school, and how many days. Even if you think you may never need them, keep attendance records.

Report cards are required by schools if you ever transfer back into a school. Though only a few states require them by law, it is a protection against future problems. Grades should be given quarterly. They do not necessarily have to be numerical grades.

About half the states now require nationally standardized tests, such as the SRA, Iowa, CTBS, or Stanford. They usually are required to be given to home schooled students each year. The standardized test scores prove (though somewhat inaccurately), in an objective way, that education is taking place. If you can show that your child has scored in a high percentile on his standardized tests for the last four years, it would be very difficult for someone to step in and claim that he is not learning anything, or is being educationally deprived.

Keep samples of work

The records we have been talking about are just one page each, but I also recommend that samples of school work be kept. Some states call this a "portfolio," and it includes samples of papers the children have done, sample quizzes they have taken, sample workbooks, or whatever. Ideally, all the children's work for a particular year should be put in a box, stored, and kept for a year or two. It does not need to be kept as long as records. You probably will never need this, and it can be stored away in an attic. However, it will be important if there is ever a problem. It also is nice to have for your children when they get older. They like to look back at what they did when they were young and show their old school papers to their own children.

Keeping records and samples of work is important because it proves without a doubt that education is taking place. If a home schooling family has trouble, it is often because they have been unable to demonstrate that education is taking place. There is no finer evidence that can be presented to a judge than samples of books and papers with your child's handwriting on them. At Seton, we help parents by keeping the records on our computer. Seton automatically provides parents with report cards, a standardized test at the end of each year, as well as achievement awards and diplomas. Test papers are returned with grades and teacher's comments. Seton's counseling to parents shows official schooling supervision.

Be organized

Be organized in your home schooling, and look organized. You should have a class schedule. You may not follow the schedule exactly each day, but you should be able to demonstrate what a typical day looks like. There was one case which parents lost because they could not demonstrate that they had a daily plan for their home schooling. At the beginning of the year, write out a class schedule.

There is much discussion among home schoolers about structure and non-structure. But if parents are ever asked by local or legal authorities, they need to produce some sort of organized plan showing classes at certain times of the day. It is not unusual for parents to be asked to explain a typical home schooling day.

Know the law

Read, study, and learn your state's home schooling law. Keep a copy easily available for quick reference. Knowledge is power. If someone comes to your door claiming that the law says one thing when you know it says something else, it gives you confidence and a comforting peace. It is amazing how often superintendents, or people from their offices, will mislead home schoolers, whether through ignorance of the law on their part or merely for the sake of trying to gain an advantage. Whatever the reason, if you know the law, you are able to respond without fear, in whatever way you believe is best.

You can find a copy of the State Code or state laws at your local library. Look in the index under "Education," and you can find all the laws in your state relating to education, as well as references to legal cases. State home schooling associations publish an information packet with the current state home schooling laws. Every lawyer has a copy of the state laws, also. Copies of each state's home schooling laws are available at Seton.

Always double-check anything anyone tells you about the law that does not sound correct. Remember that the U.S. Supreme Court has ruled that no state may outlaw home schooling, nor may a state make regulations which would, in effect, make home schooling impossible.

The home schooling laws, although difficult in some states, always contain some loopholes which will allow parents to home school. Never in my experience have I encountered a situation where a family who truly wanted to home school was unable to do so because of the state law. Fortunately, as stated earlier, the state laws are changing in the direction of allowing more freedom for homeschooling.

Contact your state association

Contact your state home schooling association. Although the primary home schooling support group you will want to be involved with is your Catholic home schooling association, your state home schooling association will probably be more helpful regarding laws and regulations. You can subscribe to their newsletter even if you do not join the state association.

State home schooling associations are not Catholic, but that is because approximately 90% of the home schoolers in this country are Protestant. Most of the state organizations are evangelical and fundamentalist. Protestant home schooling families agree with us on many moral issues. They are pro-life. You should be somewhat careful, though, and we have even heard of a few state home schooling organizations that are actively anti-Catholic.

The state association can help home schooling families with information and support. Every state organization publishes a monthly or quarterly newsletter. They keep you up to date with proposed legislation in your state. They monitor state legislation and lobby for better home schooling laws. Catholics should be willing to help their state association fight for better legislation for home schooling families.

Home schoolers are trying not only to maintain the victories we have had, but also to increase the freedom or decrease the regulations. It is the state organizations which are in the forefront of this important effort.

Know your own school district

Know where your local school district stands on home schooling. Although the superintendent does not have any authority in law to pass home schooling regulations, he may make some pronouncements. Knowing the "politics" of your local school district is very beneficial, because many times this will give you an indication of how you wish to proceed when and if you notify your superintendent.

Learn your local district's position on home schooling by contacting your state or local support group. Local and state organizations are very knowledgeable about the local politics, because they are very active in them, and have gone through experiences with the superintendent already. They know what is going on, who has been naughty and who has been nice, and they can give you some good insight into how to proceed.

If you feel so inclined, consider becoming involved in local politics, and encourage other home schoolers to do so as well. It is much harder for local politicians to harass home schoolers when home schoolers have political influence. Running for the school board or the town council or even minor town or county positions, or joining your county political organization is not that hard to do.

A letter

In the state of Virginia, parents are given a religious exemption from attendance at school and from the home schooling regulations. While the details of the following letter may not exactly meet your own state regulations, it gives you ideas on how you might write your local superintendent when you are declaring that you cannot follow a certain regulation. The letter was notarized to give a certain formality, legality, and seriousness to this statement of religious convictions.

Also, such a letter is a good idea if you decide to follow a certain regulation for prudential reasons, but philosophically you believe you have the right not to follow the regulation. Your letter might start: "As a matter of courtesy, we are enclosing the following form [or test scores, or whatever]. However, we (name of mother and name of father) are teaching our children at home because of our religious convictions."

Dr. Clark sent the following letter, notarized, to the local superintendent, and to all the school board members, by certified mail. It was sent only after her name was in the newspaper so many times regarding her home schooling lobbying efforts at the state capitol, that she received a phone call from the local school district. Otherwise, she would never have made any contact with the local school district, as she believes her right to home school is from God. Many home school attorneys recommend not to contact any school district authorities until and unless you are first contacted. If your children have been enrolled in the public schools, this would not be possible. Obviously, such a decision as not to notify when the law calls for it must be made with considered thought, prayer, and prudence.

Here is her letter:

Dear Dr. D.,

According to the Code of Virginia, 22.1-256-A: The provisions of this article (22.1-254, Compulsory Attendance) shall not apply to: 4. Children excused under 22.1-256 of this article.

The section 22.1-256 lists the groups of children excused from school attendance. It states that "A. A school board: ...2. Shall excuse from attendance at school any pupil who, together with his parents, by reason of bona fide religious training or belief, is conscientiously opposed to attendance at school."

The section further states that "C. As used in paragraph A 2 of this section, the term 'bona fide religious training or belief' does not include essentially political, sociological, or philosophical views, or a personal moral code."

The Code does not elaborate on the procedure for parents to notify the school board members of their religious convictions. Therefore, we wish to use this notarized letter to inform each Warren County School Board member of the following:

We, Bruce and Mary Kay Clark, are teaching our children at home because of our religious convictions or bona fide religious beliefs. These are not essentially political, sociological, or philosophical views, or a merely personal moral code.

[Note: This last statement uses wording in conformity to the Virginia home schooling law. However, the law is unconstitutional. In fact, it is so blatantly unconstitutional against parents' rights, that a home schooling attorney once said of it: "You could drive a constitutional Mack truck through this one!" According to the U.S. Supreme Court, parents have the right to teach their children at home for *any* reason!]

Though we realize our rights are a natural right of all parents, nevertheless we are also following the principles of our church, as outlined in the Charter of the Rights of the Family. Pope John Paul II states that a) Parents have the right to educate their children in conformity with their moral and religious convictions. b) Parents have the right to choose freely schools or other means necessary to educate their children in keeping with their convictions. c) Parents have the right to ensure that their children are not compelled to attend classes which are not in agreement with their own moral and religious convictions.

In conclusion, we note that our excuse from the 22.1-254 article includes the specifics of the home schooling regulations, such as up-front qualifications, curriculum approval, and annual testing.

Sincerely

Be not afraid

Each one of us must decide exactly where we are going to stand and which laws we believe we can obey, in accord with the teachings of the Church. Just where you believe your position should be is a matter for serious prayer. No one of us home schooling parents should judge the decisions of other home schooling parents. We each need to follow the graces God gives us to make decisions for our own family.

Be not afraid to home school, but be prudent in the way you run your home schooling. Be cautious in not letting your children play outside during school hours if you live in a neighborhood where other parents might call local authorities to complain. Home schooling is legal, and you should not hide your children or yourself from the world, but you should be prudent.

Do not be secretive as you teach your children. You are more likely to get into trouble by acting strangely. If you act as if you are doing something wrong, your children will get the impression that what they are doing is wrong. We do not want them to believe that their parents are being deceptive or doing something illegal, because then the children will become fearful, which is certainly not what home schooling is about.

Nevertheless, the vast majority of home schooling parents who are reported for truancy, child abuse, or child neglect are turned in by neighbors who see the children outside during regular school hours. While the situation can be remedied fairly quickly, it can cause a rather unpleasant situation for a few days. Such reports go on records, and remain there for several years, even if no problems are actually discovered.

A brief point for Catholics

Other chapters in this book show that our right to home school comes from God. This is clearly taught in the Bible and in our Catholic Church documents. While we need to be aware of the state laws, actually they have little relation to the reality that God gives parents the right to teach their own children. So no matter how you deal with local authorities, remain firm in your beliefs and convictions based on the Catholic Church and the Bible. No laws or regulations made by man can stop you from your God-given rights. Nor should they stop you, because they are God-given responsibilities as well.

We Catholics are law-abiding citizens and have a difficult time even considering breaking a law which may not be legal or constitutional or morally correct. We need to think about the blacks who sat in the front of the bus in the early days of their fight for their civil rights. As serious as those rights were, they do not compare with the rights of parents to teach their children true religious and moral values at home. In the future, there may be other laws and regulations which limit our rights to have children as well as how to educate our children. We need to understand now, before such laws are made, how we intend to respond, both spiritually and legally.

Prayers

Finally, start and end every day with prayer; start every class with a prayer. God provides the best legal protection. You need His strength to home school, and to see you through any hurdles you may face. You need Him every day, and the graces He provides to overcome the legal obstacles. God is always with you, and will give you the graces you need to succeed in dealing with educational, social, or legal authorities.

Chapter 19:
Catholic Home Schooling in Our American Democracy

Anyone who favors radical school choice is eventually accused of being un-American.

American public schools, from the very beginning, have been devoted to preparing a certain kind of citizen for this country, rather than giving students a good general education. From the beginning, anyone who questioned the value of these temples of democracy was reviled by educrats. Horace Mann, the father of public schools, wrote long ago what he thought of public school detractors:

> Anything which tends to lessen the value of our free schools is hostile to the designs of our pious ancestors. Any man, who through pride or parsimony permits these schools to decline, can hardly be regarded as a friend to his country. I speak with plainness, for I am pleading the cause of humanity and of God. And I say that any man who designs the destruction of our free schools is a traitor to the cause of liberty and equality, and would, if it were in his power, reduce us to a state of vassalhood.

Although the educrats have stopped talking about being on God's side, they still view the public schools as essential to the continuing democracy of this country. The late Albert Shanker, head of the American Federation of Teachers, once said

> The purpose of education in our schools is to get all kids in our country to learn to live with and respect each other.... [To support private schools is to] destroy something that is extremely important as the glue of the United States of America.

More extreme is the head of the California Teachers Association, Del Weber, who wrote this about private school choice: "There are some proposals which are so evil that they should never even be presented to the voters."

The view of the public school as the temple of democracy traces its roots back to the Puritans who came to this country almost 400 years ago. They saw America as the promised land in which they could build the Biblical "shining city on a hill." America was to be the earthly reflection of the coming life in Heaven.

Indeed, this idea of America being a radically different and singularly special place on earth has not lessened, despite the rejection of God by many Americans. In 1992, a Republican party draft platform reflected this view by calling America the "last, best hope for mankind." Ironically, it was Christians, separating themselves from the Puritan tradition, who objected to this language on the platform committee, saying that Jesus Christ is the last, best hope of mankind.

Unfortunately, Catholics have not been immune from the idea that American democracy is somehow God-ordained. Along with this idea, many Catholics have come to believe the central democratic idea that all authority, as well as concepts of right and wrong, come from the majority vote of the people.

It is interesting to note that the first bishop of the United States, John Carroll, was not appointed by the Pope, but was elected by the clergy of the United States. The Pope reluctantly agreed to this election after being warned by Carroll that an appointment of a bishop by Rome would "shock the political prejudices of this Country." The unwillingness of the leading colonial Catholics in the United States to submit to the authority of Rome shows how deeply they accepted the principle of democratic rule even in matters of church governance.

The Holy Father, Pope Leo XIII, wrote an apostolic letter, *Testem Benevolentiae*, to Cardinal Gibbons in 1899, specifically to warn against the heresy commonly called "Americanism." The basic principle of Americanism, as defined by the Pope, is that the Catholic Church should "adapt herself somewhat" and "relaxing her ancient rigor, show some indulgence to modern popular theories." This is understood not only in regard to rules of life but also in regard to doctrines. The Pope explains that the Church doctrines are not theories, but a divine deposit to be carefully guarded and infallibly declared.

While certain rules of life, said the Pope, can be modified according to the diversity of time and place, it is up to the Church, not to individuals, to judge how to adapt itself. Pope Leo XIII further points out that the Church is of divine right, and other associations exist by the free will of men. Public prosperity, he wrote, "should thrive without setting aside the authority and wisdom of the Church." The natural law and the natural virtues need supernatural and divine help. The holy men of the past, "by humbleness of spirit, by obedience and abstinence, were powerful in word and work, were of the greatest help not only to religion but to the State and society."

The very concept of separation of Church and State, as we have come to know it in America, implies that eternal truths cannot be used as a basis for public laws. In this country, abortion is not considered evil because it is a horrible crime which God has condemned. It is evil only if one can convince 51% of the voters that it is evil. Such a situation implies that no real moral law exists, and any principle can be changed simply by holding another election. The concept of separation of God and State has come to mean Separation of Truth and State. How can it be that such a fundamentally evil principle could be a central tenet of a great and powerful nation?

To understand why moral principles based on God's laws are so anathema to American government, we have to go back to the early history of this country. In the founding days of the Republic, when all the documents guaranteeing religious liberty were written, separation of Church and State really was meant to guarantee that Catholics could not get control of the government. There was to be no established national religion similar to the established national religions in England and European countries; nor were the constitutional laws to be dictated by any power other than by the governed people themselves.

But Protestantism was the underlying faith of this

country's new leaders, and there was precious little separation between Protestantism and government.

Even if the Protestants had really meant what they said about separation of Church and State, this concept would have been radically un-Catholic. The Catholic Church has always taught that the state has an obligation to acknowledge that its authority comes from God, through the Church of Jesus Christ. Pope Boniface VIII's *Unam Sanctam* in 1302 made clear the Church's teaching on the relationship of Church and State:

> We learn from the words of the Gospel that in this Church and in her power are two swords, the spiritual and the temporal....Both of these, that is, the spiritual and the temporal swords, are under the control of the Church. The first is wielded by the Church; the second is wielded on behalf of the Church. The first is wielded by the hand of the priest, the second by the hand of the kings and soldiers but at the wish and by the permissions of the priests. Sword must be subordinated to sword, and it is only fitting that the temporal authority should be subject to the spiritual.

As you recall, King Saul was reprimanded severely by the priests for going to war before consulting them and making sacrifices at the altar. Throughout Christendom, until the Protestant Revolt, kings and nations submitted to the authority of the Pope, recognizing his authority as the Vicar of Christ. Henry VIII, defying the Church in the laws regarding marriage, drew his whole nation into a conflict with the Church.

Of course, it is easy to understand why the early Catholics in colonial America were only too happy to support separation of Church and State. The colonies at the time had established state churches, and they were, of course, Protestant. Many of the colonies, even after the Revolution, actively persecuted Catholics. The Catholics in the colonies realized that if any church were to be recognized as the official church of the country, it would not be the Catholic Church.

Most of the Catholics in the American colonies were Irish, and most of them either knew firsthand of the terrible persecution of Catholics going on in Ireland at the time, or they heard of them from others. Most Americans today, even those of Irish heritage, know little about the extent of the persecution that Catholics suffered in Ireland. This persecution, however, was extensive and brutal. Legally, Irish Catholics were not permitted to buy land, or to inherit property, or to educate their children in the Catholic Faith, or to send children to Catholic schools overseas, or to have Catholic churches, and could not even live in some towns. The great legislator Edmund Burke said that the Penal Laws in Ireland were "as well fitted for the oppression, impoverishment, and degradation of a feeble people...as ever proceeded from the perverted ingenuity of man."

The legal persecution of Catholics in the American colonies was generally not nearly as bad as it was in Ireland or England. Thankfully, some of the laws passed against Catholics went largely unenforced. The anti-Catholicism which existed manifested itself mainly in not permitting Catholics to vote. The anti-Catholicism at the time of the conversion of Elizabeth Ann Seton in Philadelphia was so great, however, that Catholic men had to keep her surrounded to protect her from Protestant neighbors who aimed to verbally and physically abuse her.

Despite the nominal ban on establishment of religion, the public schools in this country started out as thoroughly Protestant institutions. Indeed, when public schools were first instituted, they were simply Protestant schools paid for with public funds.

The mass immigrations of the Irish began in the 1840's, just about the time that compulsory education was instituted. This brought about the problem of Catholic children being forced to attend schools which were instituted to teach against the Catholic religion. For this reason, the bishops of the United States determined to set up a Catholic school system which exists, after a fashion, to this day.

Although the strict separation of morality from the state was never envisioned by the Protestant founding fathers, the language of the Constitution came to be used to enforce this separation starting in the 1950's, when prayer was first banned from public schools. Beginning with that ill-fated decision have come decisions that Christmas cannot be acknowledged with creches on government property, that abortion must be allowed, that contraception is a basic human right, and that prayer may not be allowed at public school graduations. God has been forced from the public square, and the minions of Satan have hastily sought to erect shrines to the dragon in place of the lamb.

We see now that indifferentism, if not hostility, to eternal truth is not only enshrined in legislative halls, but also in the public schools. In New York State a new curriculum mandates that children as young as first grade be introduced to favorable presentations of homosexual "families." This curriculum is said to teach "tolerance" and "respect" for homosexuals, just as we need to respect blacks, say the proponents. What it really teaches is that homosexuality and homosexual "families" are good, that those who oppose them are un-American, and that it is un-American not to tolerate evil in our diverse and pluralistic American society.

The Catholic Church in America is not immune to erroneous ideas about the necessity of democracy to learn truth. How many times have we heard that the Church should change its teaching on birth control because polls show Catholics do not like it? The very idea that public opinion polls should determine Church teaching is ludicrous and insane, but is extremely popular among many theologians and Church "leaders."

In a sense it is true that Catholicism is un-American, if being American is believing that majority rule, or a Supreme Court decision, determines truth. But in a larger sense it is true that being a good Catholic is the most patriotic of acts. To do what is right and good is always to do what is best, both in one's personal life, and in the life of nations. John F. Kennedy once stated that if he felt that the interests of the nation were in conflict with his Catholic faith, he would resign the presidency. But, properly understood, such a situation is impossible, because a wrong act is never best.

When the people of our country are saying that it is all right to kill babies, the patriotic thing to do is to remind them that babies are the future of the nation. When the people of our country are saying that homosexuality is a good thing, it is the patriotic thing to tell them that homosexuality breeds contempt for families and encourages the use of others, even children, for personal lust. When the people of our country tell us that the old and infirm must be disposed of, it is the patriotic thing to tell them that unless we respect the life of each human being, no one will ever be safe in our nation.

Home schooling is in the best interests of America, because it can only be good to raise up a new generation committed to living in harmony with God's will. Home schooling is intensely patriotic because it trains up future leaders of this country who will not be afraid to proclaim that the eternal law of the universe must also be the law of our land. In the end, the glue which holds our country together is not the public schools, but the civic virtue which leads each citizen to care for his fellow man. Our social problems, whether low test scores or abortion or homelessness, can never be solved until the people in this country live by the Christian rule:

> Thou shalt love the Lord Thy God with thy whole heart and with thy whole soul and with thy whole mind and with thy whole strength. This is the first commandment. And the second is like to it: Thou shalt love thy neighbor as thyself. There is no other commandment greater than these.

Alexis de Tocqueville, in his masterful work *Democracy in America*, wrote many years ago, "America is great because she is good. If she ever ceases to be good, she will cease to be great."

Chapter 20:
The Future of Catholic Home Schooling

With the ascent of a "new Democrat" to the White House, many Catholic home schooling parents are concerned about the future of home schooling. They are worried that a strong partnership between the President and the National Education Association could bring new restrictions on the rights of parents. Indeed, the Home School Legal Defense Association reports that they have received thousands of calls from anxious parents since the election.

In addition, there is anxiety about Outcome Based Education (OBE). Many see OBE as another plan by the National Education Association and New Agers to continue to shape children according to their social "politically correct" agenda rather than emphasizing reading, writing, and arithmetic. One of these "outcomes" aims to convince children to accept or to be "tolerant" of "alternative" life styles. Mothers are reporting to us that gay couples are being invited to speak to students in the schools, teaching them the American virtue of "tolerance" towards gays as they should have tolerance toward African Americans and other minority groups.

Those of us in the home schooling apostolate know we need to be concerned about what is happening in the schools, do what we can to influence legislators, and pray that God will protect the rights of home schooling families. As we pray, we need to have trust in Him, because He works in ways we may not be thinking about at all.

In fact, the whole enterprise of education is going in directions we may not be considering. Several factors and movements in this country will bring positive and strong support for us in our Catholic home schooling, though they are not directly connected with home schooling. These factors include television, the new computer technology, work coming home, employment based on learning, educational vouchers, honest school teachers, the culture war, American women re-examining their role in society, home school graduates, and American bishops and priests willing to be counted.

Television

When we Catholics think about television, we think of the anti-Christian values that television promotes. But the television *can* be used for good Christian purposes. Certainly Eternal Word Television Network (EWTN), Mother Angelica's Catholic television network, is evidence that television can be used for the best of purposes, helping to bring us all closer to understanding and living our faith.

There are a few Catholic stations around the country, such as Father Kenneth Baker's stations in Chicago, St. Louis, and Minneapolis, and two independent stations in Laredo and Corpus Christi. There are several Christian television stations in large metropolitan areas. Television can bring the Faith to more people. Television can and will be used to bring Catholic educational programs to home schooling families.

The new computer technology

School's Out, by Lewis J. Perelman, is a new book about *Hyperlearning, The New Technology, and The End of Education*, as the subtitle reads. Its message is that soon anyone will be able to learn anything at any time at any place with the new technology. The material to be learned can be adjusted, or directed, to the individual needs of the learner. Perelman believes that this rapidly advancing technology is going to put the institution of school out of business.

School's Out is tangentially about home schooling. But more than that, it is about learning in the best way, the most efficient way, the fastest way, and the cheapest way. And that is anyplace, anytime—not confined by geography or buildings. The rapidly advancing technology makes it not only possible but necessary in a changing, competitive world to quickly learn what needs to be learned to be successful at whatever we do.

"Hyperlearning" is Perelman's phrase referring to the "universe" of new technology. It refers to the extraordinary speed and scope of the new information technology, and the "connectedness" of knowledge, experience, media, and experts.

The movement of the communications and computer industries is toward connectedness and openness, that is, being more concerned to share information rather than keeping it for great profits. The value of information grows the more it can be connected to other information, making information available by connecting with larger library or informational systems.

An exciting new technological development in wiring will enable computer networks to carry vastly more information. Television and some of the other media have been using copper wires for transmission. These have a limited bandwidth for transmission. Most telephone systems, on the other hand, are using fiber optics, or glass, which has a nearly unlimited bandwidth for transmission. Whereas 50 channels is common now, the future could see 10,000 or more available channels. As this is developed more and more, home televisions and personal computers will be replaced by a multimedia computer terminal using the fiber optics. The author believes we can, and will, have "hyperlearning" in our own homes.

Information is quickly being made available to the public. Soon, all the world's knowledge is going to be on-line, that is, easily available at all times, and globally networked. Even now, the entire texts of large numbers of books are available on CD-ROM. For example, a popular U. S. History CD-ROM disk contains the entire text of over 70 history books! Home schoolers will have more materials available to them via CD-ROM than they could find at any one local or even university library.

On May 17, 1993, Time-Warner, the biggest producer of informational/educational/recreational software programs, announced a joint venture with U.S. West, a huge telephone and fiber optics communications company. In five years, they hope that 20% of American homes will have computers hooked up to their telephones so they can obtain educational and other useful programs available from anywhere in the United States.

As the computer technology develops, everything becomes smaller and smaller. With "galloping miniaturization," we will be able to carry around our computer terminals as easily as wearing our clothes, says Perelman. The cost will go down as more and more people buy, and, as with television, knowledge will be available to everyone, rich and poor.

Within the next 30 years, information storage will be so compact that all the information a person could consume in a lifetime will be stored in an object about the size of a book, an object we can easily carry around with us. This would include magazine articles, newspaper articles, encyclopedia articles, as well as textbooks.

Hypermedia

"Hypermedia" is a term that describes learning with full-motion video, sounds, pictures, words, graphs, and so on. And in addition, it is interactive, allowing the learner to respond, to move in different directions as he learns.

If you visit Radio Shack, you can see the latest hypermedia by Tandy. For only $700 (in 1993), you can buy their multi-media computer, with full-motion video and sound, which connects to the television. At no additional charge, the system includes an up-to-date complete encyclopedia. The user may select to learn this way or that way, go in that direction or this direction. For instance, if you want to learn about Prohibition, you could choose to learn about bootlegging or Al Capone or Eliot Ness or the St. Valentine's Day Massacre, in the order you choose, for as long or as short a time as you wish to receive the message.

The hyperlearning and hypermedia technology is like the old programmed learning in that the software can test the learner regularly and frequently during the learning process, and even move the student back to the content area if the student has not learned the concepts. There is no such thing as failure!

The author declares that multimedia will have an effect on all future communications as profound as the invention of writing. The hyperlearning and hypermedia technology will profoundly affect the future of home schooling as well. And the only direction is up!

Work is coming home

Another factor affecting the future of home schooling is that more and more employees are bringing their work home. One-third of all U.S. homes have a home office or workspace. By 1994, 50 million people will be working out of their homes. One survey in California indicates only 20 to 30 percent of work will NOT eventually be done by workers telecommuting from home. This may be overly optimistic, but certainly the move is in this direction. The more people work at home, the more they will see the feasibility of teaching their children at home.

Historically, members of a family have lived and worked together. Children learned skills from their parents. With the Industrial Revolution and the rise of large cities, fathers left their families for work. In the past twenty years, mothers also have been leaving their families for work. With father and mother gone, children spend practically no time at home. However, with the new technology, parents can work at home on their computers and send their work into the office via a modem. More and more people are working at home, or are using the home as a base for service jobs. Many home schooling parents are looking for "cottage industries" so they can be at home to raise their children and to help them with their education. The more parents work at home, the more families will be considering home schooling.

Employers

Employers are becoming more concerned about what people know or what skills they have than from which school they graduated. Some employers train new employees in the new technology. Home schooling students often apprentice with local businesses while they are in high school. The employers train them on the job, and often the students, guided by their employers, select job-related high school courses, such as bookkeeping, accounting, and word processing.

Employers are finding that home schooled students are

serious workers, are more mature, are able to relate to different age groups, and are better educated. Mrs. Swann of New Mexico, who has home schooled ten children, was featured on national television in the spring of 1993 because two of her daughters, at 17 years old, not only graduated from college, but were hired by a local college as teachers!

With employers less concerned about the place and more concerned about the quality of education, parents will be less fearful about teaching their children at home.

Education in America costs too much

The cost per student in this country varies from $3,000 to $10,000 if the student is in a public school. The average cost of correspondence schools is about $400 a year per student. Individual parents as well as school districts will find it cheaper to finance home schooled students than those in the classroom.

It was reported on ABC television evening news in late 1992 that the state of Kansas doubled the taxes in nine counties in western Kansas, yet decreased the amount of money for their schools. The tax increases were supposed to bring about equal funding in all school districts. The western Kansas counties were so enraged that they wanted to secede from the state of Kansas and set up their own state called West Kansas!

Ninety percent of all schools in this country are owned or operated or financed or regulated by the government. Like other government services, schools cost more and more, but clients receive less and less. More students have more and more degrees, and less and less learning. The nation is at risk. Our freedoms are at risk.

Educational vouchers

In studies showing how groups of students achieve, students with the highest achievement scores are always those whose families help at home with learning, whose parents are actively involved in their education, and whose homes are filled with books and other educational media. It is the home and family of the student which makes the difference. Many parents and employers are going to ask (or demand) why we should not encourage families to teach their children with educational vouchers or tax credits.

Educational vouchers, or tax credits, are going to come about in some fashion. Vouchers could be used like food stamps, and go to the individual learner to buy only educational materials; or, they could go directly to schools which parents select.

Many people are realizing that educational vouchers would decrease many of the problems in the schools. Just getting kids out of the moral relativism of the local public high school could alleviate many school-induced problems such as drug use, the high rate of pregnancy among young girls, violent crimes, and AIDS among young people. It also would solve the problem of poor schools competing with rich schools, with rural western-Kansas type schools fighting for rights and money with urban eastern-Kansas schools.

Educational vouchers, if given out today, would immediately increase in American homes VCR's, cable TV, satellite TV with educational networks, fax machines, computers, video cameras, copiers, desktop publishing, educational software, CD-ROM drives, and so on. Distance and poverty would not be barriers to educational choice. The whole nation would advance educationally with low cost high technology in the home.

In 1989, 20% of high school boys and girls were using computers at home, and this has certainly increased markedly as can be seen by the very inexpensive programs available at discount stores. Visit a Radio Shack. See how many teens and younger kids are browsing around the latest computers. Hear them talking. You may not understand them, but they are picking up quickly on the technology. With educational vouchers, these young people would be increasing purchases substantially.

In Canada, the school districts pay for the education of all students, no matter which school or tutor or correspondence program they choose. After the efforts of home schoolers in Alberta, that province now pays for the tuition, books, and even the shipping of materials for the home schoolers. In the spring of 1993, Alberta starting paying for computers and educational software for the home schoolers. If educational vouchers in our country would cover all educational material, including computers and educational software, there would be no stopping the educational advancement of our brightest young home schooling students.

Honest school teachers

Another factor which will cause the general population to consider home schooling is honest school teachers. More and more teachers are home schooling their own children. More and more teachers are speaking out about the current disaster in the schools, as the New York Teacher of the Year, John Gatto, has done. More and more parents are learning about teachers who are home schooling.

Several of our Seton home schooling parents have been school teachers, or are still school teachers. Some of our home schooling parents are on their local school boards, both public and Catholic. These people serve as witnesses to their concern about the system yet are willing to make extra sacrifices so their own children will not be exposed to the problems. As parents meet teachers and other educators who are home schooling, more parents will investigate and consider teaching their own children at home.

One honest teacher

Family Matters: Why Homeschooling Makes Sense was written by David Guterson, a high school English teacher who teaches his own children at home. Some book reviewers think that Mr. Guterson is quite unusual, not realizing that a large number of public school teachers quietly teach their own children at home.

Family Matters is one of the most important books to be published in recent years. It is being promoted as mainstream, a Conservative Book Club feature, and is published by a mainline publisher, Harcourt, Brace, Jovanovich. Harcourt is one of the largest publishers of public school textbooks.

The author is a high school teacher, a home schooling father, and an excellent writer. His book can be read easily and quickly. It will be a book read by teachers and curious parents. Written from a man's perspective, this is an especially good book for fathers reluctant to home school.

Mr. Guterson discusses standardized test scores and declares that the educational establishment, which loves these tests as measures of academic success, should admit that "by its own definition, home schooling is an astonishing success." He explains how well home schoolers are doing in college. He reviews recent books about our educational system and is surprised that while so many conclude that *families* make the difference in how students achieve, they seem to carefully omit stating the possibility that perhaps families alone could do better than schools in educating children.

"Curiously, however, few of our educational experts...have focused their attention on families or on how to nurture academic success in the homes of all Americans. Instead they offer endless new curricula and novel ways of organizing schools on the assumption that by so doing they will somehow negate the truth of the Coleman Report — that education begins at home."

And succeeds at home!

Socialization

In the chapter, "Homeschoolers Among Others," Guterson discusses the socialization issue. The results of recent studies show how well socialized home schooling children are. He describes the many social activities of his own children and other home schoolers. Then he explains the social complexities of the public school system. Guterson describes the "jocks" and "burnouts," the competitiveness, and the many graduates who tell him how they are "thankful that the long battle for school status is behind them." He is seriously concerned about the peer group pressure, the peer worldview, the "obsessive nature" of children's friendships, and the clique mentality—all part of mass schooling.

> Having passed their formative years chiefly among
> their peers in a world devoid of the very old and very
> young, a highly structured world best characterized as
> competitive and cliquish, they are ill-prepared for mem-
> bership in their own communities even if adequately
> prepared to function in our economy.

Guterson believes that home schoolers, interrelating with
the elderly and the young, with clerks and gardeners, plumb-
ers and electricians, professionals and non-professionals, interrelating with the community members almost daily, are
more prepared for the larger society than those restricted to
the classroom for so many hours a day for many years.

Family Matters, as important as it is, is just a start.
More books and magazine articles by honest teachers are
bound to be published and will help the general public consider making changes in the way their children are being
educated. Honest teachers will surely help educators and
authorities to accept home schooling as an acceptable alternative.

The culture war

Another factor influencing the general population to consider the appropriateness of home schooling is the culture
war. Obviously, those who are promoting the current secular
humanistic culture do not want home schooling and the influence of parents over children. They want to continue the
control that schools have over children, and to continue influencing them to accept the homosexual and contraceptive
mentality. In general, the schools are promoting low standards in art, music, and entertainment, as well as low standards in educational achievements and social relationships.

Families who are against the current secular humanistic
culture will help to foster home schooling as they begin to
understand the culture war. The latest decision by a judge
against the teaching of abstinence in a public school sex
education curriculum because abstinence is a "religious" value

should be the final straw that breaks the camel's back for many Christian families.

In *The De-Valuing of America: The Fight for Our Culture and Our Children* by William J. Bennett, a Jesuit-educated Catholic and former U. S. Secretary of Education, the author forcefully argues that Christian principles should be taught in schools. Quoting himself in a speech before the National Catholic Education Association, Mr. Bennett said:

> All parents, regardless of income, should be able to choose places where they know their children will learn. And they should be able to choose environments where their own values will be extended instead of lost.

While Mr. Bennett does not discuss home schooling, his comments about the Culture War and the failure of schools to promote American Christian culture will help families to consider other alternatives. His book will be influencing parents for a long time to come, helping them realize the battle over culture, the battle between Christian values and the government, NEA-dominated schools. As the lines are more clearly drawn, many will choose home schooling.

In a new magazine called *Dimensions: The Journal of the American Heartland,*" Patrick J. Buchanan, another well-known Catholic, in an article in October, 1992, entitled "The Battle for America's Heart and Soul," wrote:

> The battle over our schools is part of a war to separate parents from their children, one generation from another, and Americans from their heritage....One public policy change that would put power back in the hands of parents is tuition vouchers that could be redeemed at all schools, including religious academies.

While Mr. Buchanan does not mention home schools here, he has personally told me that he supports home schooling.

> But the war for the soul of America will only be won with basic truths, and the basic truths western civilization has discovered are simple and straightforward.

They are spelled out explicitly in the Old and New Testaments.

In the spring of 1993, Patrick Buchanan held his first conference for a new educational organization called *The American Cause.* The theme of the conference was "Winning the Culture War." I was privileged to speak briefly about home schooling, in an effort to show how it can solve many of the problems of our society.

Since the Clinton presidency, many more people have been speaking out about the culture war and about schools which are promoting an un-American and anti-Christian culture. This is causing Christian parents to consider home schooling.

Former feminists

Another factor which will influence the general community to accept home schooling in the future is women who have discovered that the feminist agenda is not quite so wonderful after all. More and more books and articles are being written by women who are rejecting the unfulfilling career lifestyles and who are trying to take back their true vocation as wives and mothers.

Mary Pride's two books, *The Way Home* and *All the Way Home,* have had almost miraculous results in turning women away from the feminist me-first agenda to the truly fulfilling authentic Christian family life.

Organizations are springing up, such as "Mothers at Home" and "Formerly Employed Mothers at Loose Ends," to name only two, which are encouraging mothers to learn the value of family and of sacrificing for their children. In a recent article in a women's magazine called *First,* an article appeared called "The Stay-at-Home Option." It discussed how two paychecks may not be necessary to keep the family afloat. Said one mother, "My schedule is crazy, but I'm more involved with my kids now." As these former career women or feminists, most well educated, turn to home and family, home schooling is going to be seriously considered.

Recent home schooling graduates

Seton is now beginning to enroll the children of graduates of Seton Home Study. These educated young parents
are choosing home education for *their* children. Each year,
more and more home educated students are graduating and
getting married. These young people are open to life, will
be having large families, and will choose home schooling.

In addition, our young home schooling graduates are taking up the banner to fight for the Catholic Church. Parents
are taking their home schooling teens to various meetings and
conferences, so they can see for themselves the feminist influences or the "arguments" for New Age positions. Recently,
a New York mother phoned to tell me that she took her home
schooled sixteen-year-old daughter to a meeting at the parish
where all kinds of crazy and "nutty" anti-Catholic ideas were
being promoted by a pro-feminist group. During the session,
her daughter defended a Catholic position that was being
attacked. "When I was sixteen," the mother said, "I certainly
could not have defended my beliefs the way she did. And
she spoke out in a public meeting with older adults." The
mother was justifiably very proud of her daughter.

The future for Catholic home schooling is bright as our
young people witness to the truth in the parish communities. Young people will be leaders, will be independent
thinkers, will not be afraid to speak in front of elders or
bishops, and, God willing, will help lead their nation out
of bondage.

The Catholic clergy

An encouraging sign for Catholic home schooling parents is the growing number of priests who are beginning to
recognize the value of Catholic home schooling. Many priests
have agreed to be chaplains for Catholic home schooling
groups. Some priests are giving regular talks for home schooling groups, other priests are willing to have home schoolers meet in their parish hall or have an activity at the church.
Catholic home schooled children are having a quiet influ-

ence on the hearts of pastors in the parish churches where they attend Mass or serve as altar boys.

Priests are beginning to ask, "What can I do to help these families who are willing to make the personal sacrifice to teach their own children?"

Antagonism by clergy toward home schoolers has been breaking down with a speed we never predicted. We can only conclude that the prayers of the innocent children have had an effect on the hearts and souls of parish priests.

It is a difficult situation for some of the clergy to respond to the home schooling movement among Catholics. Priests and bishops have a dilemma in supporting the home schoolers publicly. While some of them know the Church's teachings in support of parents taking this responsibility for the education of their children, at the same time they believe they cannot publicly endorse home schooling when the parochial schools are struggling to survive.

We cannot as yet expect public endorsement from our pastors and bishops, and yet we have seen more and more miracles as priests and bishops encourage home schooling parents in a variety of ways.

His Eminence Bernard Cardinal Law, Archbishop of Boston, sent Seton a letter some years ago, encouraging us in our good work for home schoolers. Several other bishops have also encouraged home schooling publicly. Bishop Austin Vaughan, Auxiliary Bishop of New York, spoke encouraging words to a Catholic Home Schooling Conference in Washington, D.C., in June of 1992. Bishop John Sullivan of Kansas City-St. Joseph said Mass for the home schoolers at a Catholic Family and Home Schooling Conference in February, 1993. Bishop James Sullivan of Fargo, North Dakota, wrote a letter asking Seton to promote vocations among our students because he believed so many vocations are coming from home schooling families. The late Bishop John Keating of Arlington, Virginia, was friendly toward Seton Home Study School, which we deeply appreciated.

Priests are speaking publicly at Catholic home schooling conferences. The late Father Vincent Miceli, an outstanding moral theologian and author, was a chaplain for

Seton Home Study School, and spoke at various conferences supporting home schooling.

Father Robert Fox, internationally known for his tours for young people to Fatima and his Fatima Family Apostolate, has been endorsing home schooling for years.

Father Charles Fiore of Madison, Wisconsin, speaks regularly on home schooling at Seton conferences and at Human Life International conferences. Priests from the Legionaries of Christ, whose seminaries are attracting numerous vocations from home schooling families, give encouragement at home schooling conferences. Father Pablo Straub, who has regular programs on EWTN, spoke at a Seton Home Schooling Conference. He has produced a series of video tapes on catechetics, especially for home schooling families. Father George Rutler, after a speech at Christendom College, gave parents an endorsement of home schooling.

Father Paul Marx and Father Matthew Habiger, both with Human Life International, have spoken at Catholic Family and Home Schooling conferences, and regularly sponsor home schooling speakers at their conferences. Mother Angelica of Eternal Word Television Network has interviewed me and others on home schooling.

The most public priest to support Catholic home schooling parents is the renowned Father John Hardon, S.J. He is the author of numerous books including *The Catholic Catechism, Modern Catholic Dictionary, Question and Answer Catholic Catechism, The Treasury of Catholic Wisdom,* and *The Catholic Lifetime Reading Plan.* Father visits the Vatican several times a year, works directly with the Vatican on a variety of American projects, and is the religious support behind the Catholic Home Schooling conference sponsored in Washington, D.C.

A hopeful future

God is working in many diverse ways to help Catholic parents to keep home schooling in this country. It is an important mission we have, and, as we have seen, many factors are helping us.

Father John Hardon believes that the difficult times we are having in our country are simply the persecution before a Golden Age of Christianity. If he is correct, we home schooling parents need to prepare our children to be leaders in that Golden Age to come.

Bibliography

Cover Story

*Dias, Joao S. Cla. *The Mother of Good Counsel of Genazzano*. Sunbury, PA: Western Hemisphere Cultural Society, 1992.

Chapter One

Eakman, B. K. *Educating for the New World Order*. Portland, Oregon: Halcyon House, 1991.

Engel, Randy. *Sex Education: The Final Plague*. Gaithersburg, MD: Human Life International, 1989; TAN, 1993.

Flesch, Rudolf. *Why Johnny Still Can't Read: A New Look at the Scandal of our Schools*. New York: Harper & Row, 1981.

Kilpatrick, William. *Why Johnny Can't Tell Right from Wrong*. New York: Simon & Schuster, 1992.

Morris, Barbara M. *Change Agents in the Schools*. Upland, CA: Barbara M. Morris Report, 1979.

Schlafly, Phyllis, Editor. *Child Abuse in the Classroom*. Alton, IL: Pere Marquette Press, 1984.

Wrenn, Msgr. Michael J. *Catechisms and Controversies: Religious Education in the Postconciliar Years*. San Francisco: Ignatius Press, 1991.

Chapter Two

The Catholic Hearth. Monthly Catholic family magazine for children. Long Prairie, MN: The Neumann Press.

*Starred items are available from Seton Home Study School.

Chapter Three

Encyclicals:
Casti Connubii, or *On Christian Marriage*.
Humanae Vitae, or *Of Human Life*.
Sapientiae Christianae
Militantis Ecclesiae
Divini Illius Magistri, or *On Christian Education of Youth*.

Other Vatican Documents:
Catechesi Tradendae, or *Catechesis in Our Time*
Charter of the Rights of the Family
Declaration on Christian Education, Second Vatican Council
Familiaris Consortio, or *The Role of the Christian Family in the Modern World*.
Canon Law Society. *Code of Canon Law*. Washington, DC: Canon Law Society of America, 1983.

Other Books:

*Daughters of St. Paul. *The Family, Center of Love and Life*. Boston: Daughters of St. Paul, 1981. [Selection of documents of Pope Paul VI, Pope John Paul I, Pope John Paul II].

*Hardon, Rev. John. *The Catholic Family in the Modern World*. St. Paul, MN: Leaflet Missal Company, 1991.

Krason, Stephen M., Editor. *Parental Rights*. Front Royal, VA: Christendom College Press, 1988.

*Peters, Dr. Edward. *Home Schooling and the New Code of Canon Law*. Front Royal, VA: Christendom College Press, 1988.

Chapter Four

The Bible. Douay-Rheims (most accurate translation). Rockford, IL: TAN, 1989. (1899 Edition.)

Matatics, Gerry. Audio tapes on Biblical foundations for what we
    Catholics believe. Front Royal, VA: Biblical Foundations,
    1992.

Navarre Bible Commentaries. Available for each book of the Bible.
    Seton offers the four Gospels of Matthew, Mark, Luke, John.
    Includes the words of the Gospel above the commentary.

Chapters Five and Six

*Video. Home School Legal Defense Association. *Home Schooling:
    A Foundation for Excellence*. Paeonian Springs, VA: HSLDA,
    1992. 30 minutes.

*Video. Seton Home Study School, Editor. *Bringing the Children
    Home*. Front Royal, VA: Seton, 1992. 6 hours.

*Video. Seton Home Study School, Editor. *Keeping the Children
    Home*. Front Royal, VA: Seton, 1993. 6 hours.

Chapter Seven

Ball, Ann. *A Handbook of Catholic Sacramentals*. Huntington, IN:
    Our Sunday Visitor, 1991.

Eternal Word Television Network, Irondale, AL 35210.

Isaacs, David. *Character Building*. Great Britain: Four Courts Press,
    1993. Available from Sceptre Press, Princeton, NJ.

TAN Books and Publishers, Inc., Rockford, IL.

Chapter Nine

*Dobson, Dr. James. *The Strong-Willed Child*. Wheaton, IL: Tyndale
    House, 1978.   [Christian]

Phillips, Phil. *Saturday Morning Mind Control*. Nashville, TN: Oliver Nelson Books, 1991.

*Walsh, Marion. *The Christian Family Coping*. Omaha, NE: Help of Christians Publications, 1986.   [Catholic]

Wood, Steve. *The Training and Discipline of Children*. Audio tapes. Port Charlotte, FL: Family Life Center (P.O. Box 6060, Port Charlotte, FL 33949-6060), 1992. [Catholic]

Chapter Twelve

Barkley, Russell A. *Attention Deficit Hyperactivity Disorder: A Handbook for Diagnosis and Treatment*. New York: The Guilford Press, 1990.

Lidden, Craig B., Newman, Roberta L., and Zalenski, Jane R. *Pay Attention!!! Answers to Common Questions about the Diagnosis and Treatment of Attention Deficit Disorder*. Monroeville, PA: Transact Health Systems, Inc., 1989.

Martin, David L. *Handbook for Creative Teaching*. Crockett, KY: Rod and Staff Publishers, 1986. [Christian]

Stevens, Suzanne. *Classroom Success for the Learning Disabled*. Winston-Salem, NC: Blair Publishers, 1984.

—————. *The Learning Disabled Child: Ways That Parents Can Help*. Winston-Salem, NC: Blair Publishers, 1980.

Chapter Seventeen

*Farris, Michael. *Home Schooling and the Law*. Paeonian Springs, VA: Home School Legal Defense Association, 1990.

*Klicka, Christopher. *The Right Choice: An Academic, Historical, Practical, and Legal Perspective*. Gresham, OR: Noble Publishing Associates, 1992.

Chapter Eighteen

Farris, Michael. *Where Do I Draw the Line*. Paeonian Springs, VA: Home School Legal Defense Association, 1992.

Chapter Nineteen

Carthy, M.P. "Catholicism in English-Speaking Lands." *The Twentieth Century Encyclopedia of Catholicism*. Vol. 92. New York: Hawthorn, 1964.

*Davies, Michael. *The Reign of Christ the King*, Rockford, IL: TAN Book and Publishers, 1992.

McAvoy, Thomas. *The Great Crisis in American Catholic History, 1895 - 1900*. Chicago: Regnery, 1957.

*Pope Pius XII. *On the Function of the State in the Modern World*. Rome: Vatican, 1939.

Woodruff, Douglas. "Church and State." *The Twentieth Century Encyclopedia of Catholicism*. Vol. 89. New York: Hawthorn, 1961.

Chapter Twenty

Bennett, William J. *The De-Valuing of America: The Fight for our Culture and our Children*. New York: Summit Books, 1992.

Guterson, David. *Family Matters*. New York: Harcourt, 1992.

*Perelman, Lewis J. *School's Out: Hyperlearning, the New Technology, and the End of Education*. New York: Morrow, 1992.

Appendix A:
Father John Hardon on
Catholic Home Schooling
Selected Statements from Speeches

Father John Hardon has been most generous in his support of Catholic Home Schooling, giving speeches to encourage parents across America. An outstanding and prolific writer and speaker, Father Hardon is recognized as an eminent Catholic Moral Theologian. A former professor at Loyola University, Father was the founder of the famous Loyola Correspondence School for Catholic college students, which was outstanding in its success. Father holds a Doctorate in Theology from the Gregorian University in Rome.

Father Hardon is the author of numerous books, including *The Catholic Catechism, The Modern Catholic Dictionary, The Question and Answer Catholic Catechism, The Treasury of Catholic Wisdom, The Catholic Lifetime Reading Plan,* and *The Catholic Family in the Modern World.* Father visits the Vatican several times a year, works directly with the Vatican on a variety of American projects, and has been the main support behind the Catholic Home Schooling conference sponsored in Washington, D.C.

Not only has Father Hardon spoken specifically to home schooling audiences on several occasions, and supported Catholic home schooling in talks relating to pro-life and catechetics, but Father is also "breaking new ground," in my opinion, in explaining the meaning of Marriage and Education for the Catholic Family struggling with twentieth century American society.

In June, 1991, in a speech for Catholic home schoolers in the Washington, D.C. area, Father Hardon helped us to understand Catholic home schooling. He defined Catholic home schooling as a process of teaching "that which has been believed by professed and practicing Catholics over the centuries. Catholic home schooling and education over the centuries have been provided especially for the young by professed and practicing Catholics. Moreover, it is Catholic home schooling when what is taught is that which has been proclaimed by the Church's magisterium from the time of the first Vicar of Christ, bishop of Rome, to the present day."

He further stated that home schooling is in the tradition of the Catholic Church. It began in the womb of Mary and continued at Nazareth when Jesus allowed Himself to be taught by Mary and Joseph. "God became Man to teach us. Even as *He* began, so we ought to follow His example. The first, most fundamental, most indispensable education for a child is at home."

While Father spoke about the serious problems in the Church, such as Catholic school closings and the lack of religious vocations, he also said that this "crisis in institutionalized education in materially super-developed countries like the United States is an act of Providence to awaken parents to their responsibility."

Home schooling is the most ancient form of Catholic education in Christianity. For the first 300 years of the Church's history, the churches were in catacombs. For the first three centuries, the Catholic Faith was established and strengthened uniquely and exclusively through home schooling.

For the next 500 years, home schooled Christians spread the Catholic Faith throughout the world. During the following 700 years, home schooling spread the Catholic Faith from "the northern tip of Scotland to the southern tip of South Africa."

"Never in the history of the Church have the majority of Catholics been educated in institutional Catholic schools."

For nineteen centuries, the Catholic Faith has flourished because of home schooling. Catholic home schooling is "necessary and indispensable" today for the Catholic Faith to survive and continue to grow.

When Christ instituted the Sacrament of Matrimony, He provided parents with the graces which they need to remain faithful to one another, as well as the graces to make home schooling possible. Father emphasized that you cannot teach the Catholic Faith unless you have "the grace of God." And only parents are "sacramentally *guaranteed*" the grace to teach their children.

We should not be surprised at the problems with the state authorities because since the dawn of Christianity, the secular powers of the state have been at war with Christ and His followers. St. Augustine said, "There are many people organized, and using civil authority, trying to dominate, control, and if possible, crush the Catholic Church, especially in education."

"There is nothing more important for the survival of the Catholic Church in our country—I speak with a deep conviction—than sound Catholic Home Schooling...mainly because of the widespread secularization of what was once strong Catholic education," according to Father Hardon.

Father ended this talk by pointing out to parents that "You've got to be powerfully, powerfully, powerfully motivated." In addition, parents need to learn the Catholic Faith themselves, and must learn to understand their Faith more thoroughly. And thirdly, both Mother and Father should cooperate in teaching the children and in living the Catholic Faith.

In October, 1991, Father Hardon gave a speech to home schoolers at a Seton-sponsored Catholic Family and Home Schooling conference in St. Paul, Minnesota. Father defined Catholic home schooling as "the planned and organized teaching and training of children at home, for their peaceful and effective life in this world, and for their eternal salvation in the world to come."

Father explained that the teaching refers to the mind, while the training refers to the will. We should be **teaching the mind to motivate the will to do good.** When Christ commanded His Apostles to teach all nations, He was referring to the mind, and when He said to "observe all things that I have commanded you," He was referring to the training of the will to be motivated to do God's will.

"Home Schooling in the United States is the necessary

concomitant of a culture in which the Church is being opposed on every level of her existence; and as a consequence, given the widespread secularization in our country, Home Schooling is not only valuable or useful, **in my judgment, Home Schooling is absolutely necessary for the survival of the Catholic Church in our country.**"

He further stated that the purpose of Home Schooling is "to preserve the Catholic Faith in the family, and to preserve the Catholic Faith in our country."

"There are four principal reasons why Catholic home schooling is necessary." The first reason is that Catholic home schooling has been necessary since the founding of the Church. Although there is a current crisis in the Church, it is not the current emergency which makes home schooling necessary. "Home schooling is an absolute necessity, and has been in every age of the Church's history."

The second reason why Catholic home schooling is necessary is that the Catholic Church has always taught that Catholic home schooling is necessary. (Cf. *Christian Education of Youth.*) "There is no single aspect of religious instruction—none—which, over the centuries, the Church has more frequently, or more insistently, taught the faithful, than of the parents providing for the religious and therefore also human education and upbringing of their offspring. So true is this that it is the second and co-equal primary purpose for which Christ instituted the Sacrament of Matrimony: the procreation and the education of children...by the parents. That is why Christ instituted the Sacrament of Matrimony."

The third reason Catholic home schooling is necessary is that, historically, the Church has survived "only where home schooling over the centuries by the Catholic parents has been taken so seriously that they considered it their most sacred duty."

The fourth reason Catholic home schooling is necessary is seen from experience. Experience teaches us that the Catholic Faith not only survives but "thrives only where parents take seriously as a God-given responsibility" the responsibility of home schooling.

Whereas parents from the beginning of human history had a natural necessity to teach and train their children about God, since the coming of Christ the necessity becomes a supernatural necessity or responsibility. The same ones who brought the children physically into the world have a natural obligation, binding under Natural Law, to provide for the mental, moral and social upbringing of their children. But since God became Man, the necessity, and therefore the corresponding obligation, becomes supernatural.

Parents cannot pass on, cannot teach and train their children in the Faith (let alone morals), unless they have it themselves.

How are parents to provide Catholic home schooling or the supernatural life to their children? First, they themselves must live strong Catholic lives. In fact, to live the good Catholic life in our day requires "heroic virtue." "Only heroic parents will survive the massive, the demonic secularization of materially super-developed countries like America."

Home schooling will not be easy: "Catholic parents must not only endure the cross, resign themselves to living the cross, they are to choose the cross...When you chose home schooling, you chose a cross-ridden form of education...*This* is the age of martyrs. This *is* the age of martyrs. This is the *age of martyrs*. A martyr is one who suffers for his faith. There is bloody martyrdom and unbloody martyrdom. God will use you and provide you with the knowledge and the wisdom, provided you are living the authentic, and, in today's America, heroic Catholic life."

In addition, if you want to teach and train your children, you need to know the Faith. Learn the Faith better. Understand the Faith. Learn as much as you can about the Faith.

Catholic home schooling must be schooling. Mother and Father must cooperate. "There must be a schedule. There must be a program."

Catholic home schooling "must be sacramental. In other words, the Church that Christ founded is the Church of the seven Sacraments, and here it means especially the Sacraments of the Eucharist and Confession...Train your children in living a sacramental life...The single, most fundamental thing you can teach your children, barring none, is to know the necessity and method of prayer."

Father ended this talk by telling parents they themselves must pray. The principal way for parents to gain grace for their children is through prayer.

Father Hardon gave a third Catholic Home Schooling talk in the Washington, D.C. area in June of 1992. He started this talk by stating that he had just returned from Rome and that the Holy Father was "deeply gratified" that home schooling programs are doing their duty. "These [programs] will provide you with a sound training for yourselves as parents, and with the methodology on how to share the Faith with the children you have physically brought into the world."

Father declared that parents are the primary teachers of their children by divine right: "It is by divine right that parents are the primary, principal teachers of the children that they have brought into the world. It is a right that you parents have which is inalienable; it is not conferred by any human authority, but by God Himself, and cannot be taken away by any human power."

Parents are given children by God in order that they may give them back to God. We are commanded by God to teach and train our children so that they reach their heavenly destiny. Consequently, home schooling today is not an option but "an obligation for which you are gravely responsible before God, entrusted with your children to take care of them in this world and bring them into a heavenly eternity. That's the only reason you have children. The only reason you have children in this life is to bring those children with you into a heavenly eternity...

"There are powerful forces in our country, highly organized, carefully planned, very strategic, highly subsidized financially, that are consciously and deliberately working to destroy the Catholic Church in America...

"Home Education...is fast becoming not merely important but imperative to ensure the propagation and preservation of the true Faith in our own still, to some extent,
free United States."

The state has a monopoly over the laws regarding marriage, laws regarding the family, laws regarding education
in the schools.

"The State determines who may teach, what conditions
the teacher must fulfill, which subjects may be taught, how
they are to be taught, under whose supervision, what books
may be used, what may not be used, what must be in the
books approved by civil authorities."

We are living in a totalitarian society. Catholic parents
need to become aware of what is happening and that their
educational rights are being taken away from them. Children
are quickly becoming wards of the State intellectually and
ideologically.

Grace can do what is humanly impossible. For 2,000
years, grace received through the Sacraments has helped parents teach and train their children "most effectively, most
deeply, most lastingly, most practically."

"In today's increasingly de-Christianized America,
secularized American culture, and paganized American society, Parents, I repeat, you've got no option. You must under
God, and with His light and strength, become the principal
teachers of your children. Of course, this presumes that you
parents know your Catholic Faith..."

"Learn your Faith."

"You shall be as effective...as you are yourselves united
with God...Your own union with God, your holiness, your
patience, your humility, your chastity, your selfless love as
parents, husband and wife loving one another selflessly, your
loving your children with the love that only Christ can enable you to practice" will make you effective.

In a speech at a Marian congress, Father Hardon spoke
about the necessary restoration of the Catholic family. He
made this statement at the Marian Congress in South Dakota
some years ago and repeated it in an article in Father Robert

Fox's magazine, *Fatima Family Messenger*. His statement was that "ordinary Catholic families cannot survive" the paganism of our current super-materialistic society. Catholic families must be "extra-ordinary, heroic, and holy." Other families will disappear as families.

Home schooling in our present society is extra-ordinary and heroic. Our aim is to live an authentic Catholic family life through our home schooling.

Father Hardon has said that the ordinary practice of the Faith will not be sufficient. The devil is so active through the media that the ordinary family is "no match for the devil." He declared that "the only Catholic families which will remain alive and thriving by the year 2000 are the families of martyrs." This is a frightening statement, but he has explained elsewhere that this martyrdom can be a dry martyrdom or persecution for the Faith.

The normal condition of the Church, says Father, is persecution. But "the blood of martyrs is the seed of the Church." In a speech in New Orleans, in the Fall of 1992, at a Human Life International conference, Father stated that IF Catholic families respond by living the extraordinary, heroic, and holy life, there will be a new century of flourishing of the Faith which will be unmatched by any period of Catholic Church history.

"Family life can be restored only by the apostolic zeal of wholly holy Catholic families reaching out to other Catholic families who are in such desperate need." Like the Holy Father, Father Hardon speaks about the importance of the apostolate of families to families, mothers to mothers, fathers to fathers, children to children. So while we have a "personal duty to grow in holiness," we also have a "social duty as families reaching out to other families."

Father said he is pleased to see that, although society is literally committing crimes against the family, Catholic families are being given "miraculous graces." It is these miraculous graces which are helping families to home school their children.

Father encourages families to look to the Blessed Mother

for obtaining graces. He has a special devotion to the Miraculous Medal, and encourages us all to wear it. We recall that the Blessed Mother told St. Catherine Laboure that she has many graces to give, but they are not all even asked for.

Father reminds families that we should try to imitate the virtues of the Blessed Mother. Specifically, he recommends the family praying the daily Rosary together, saying the Angelus together, dedicating Saturdays to the Blessed Mother, going to Holy Communion daily, receiving the Sacrament of Penance as often as possible, having pictures of the Blessed Mother in our homes, wearing the scapular, being enrolled in the Confraternity of the Miraculous Medal, reading books about Mary, and having a statue of Mary or a Marian shrine in our home.

In addition, Father Hardon reminds us that we need to "imitate Our Lady in the practice of virtues as an important means of sanctification." The three virtues which he believes are most important for us today are Faith, Chastity, and Charity. Faith, he says, means living and believing our Faith, even if we do not fully understand it. "The family that believes together stays together...Faith is the bedrock of the sanctity of Family Life." He said we need to have faith in the Vicar of Christ, the Pope, and faith in the Real Presence of Jesus Christ in the Eucharist.

As for Chastity, he believes that every member of the family "must practice Christ-like Chastity." Father Hardon declares that the pagans of the Roman Empire were eventually converted because they saw Christians "living the faithful and chaste family life." To practice chastity, Father reminds us to "rely on the power of God, and remember that nothing is impossible with God."

Charity is the virtue, Father said, which makes a family a family. Husbands need to love their wives, wives need to love their husbands, brothers and sisters need to love each other. All members of the family need to be kind to each other and to be patient with each other.

Father encourages mothers not to be seduced by the

appeals of the pagan world but to see Mary as a model of true freedom and model for authentic Catholic family life. "Follow Mary, and entrust your freedom to the will of God."

Appendix B:
Seton Home Study School
by Mary Claire Robinson

Mary Claire Robinson currently lives in California with her husband Keith and their eight children. She has been home schooling for years, and has helped hundreds of home schooling families. Mary has spoken at several Seton Family and Home Schooling conferences.

Over the past four [now nine] years, my son and daughter have attended Seton Home Study. Looking back now as my daughter is a freshman at Thomas Aquinas College, I can see and appreciate how beneficial Seton's program was for her. In this essay I would like to call to your attention these facets of Seton's high school: namely, their strong college prep program, detailed syllabuses, flexible school schedule, meticulous writing tutorial, dedication to ensuring that the material is learned, paramount staff, invaluable religion · courses, and extraordinary phone service.

This last year's challenging academic college courses manifested to my daughter, Mary Elizabeth, Seton's excellent college prep program. Through her twenty-nine units at Seton she was prepared for college with good books and texts. Lesson planning, daily assignments, term and research papers, and the various quarterly and semester exams occupied her time, efforts, and energy. Academically, Seton had provided her with the ideal Catholic high school, structured enough to provide adequate self-discipline and complex enough to ensure that she was always pushed to the maximum of her potential.

Being a mother with lots of younger children, my time with Mary Elizabeth in high school was significantly limited. As a result, she and I both expected her to coordinate, read, plan, and execute her high school work herself. The lesson plans were very thorough, detailed, and quite liberally salted with additional comments or anecdotes. Due to the fact that some subjects use textbooks from secular or Protestant publishers, supplements in the lesson plans clarify vague entries. If a selection or assignment from a textbook was erroneous, heretical, or misguiding, then the lesson plans always included explanations which clarified the truth and expounded the Church's position. The thoroughness of the lesson plans allowed Mary Elizabeth to complete her four years with confidence that she could follow detailed directions successfully.

Although the lesson plans are detailed and specific, the student is free to incorporate flexibility within structured parameters. Mary Elizabeth liked schedules and quickly learned time management techniques that worked for her. Certain subjects, like math and English, she felt she must do every day. Other subjects, such as history and foreign language, she did more successfully by concentrating a large block of time towards the task. Reading a short selection of a novel for a month often resulted in forgetting large parts of the book, making it difficult to answer multiple choice questions, short essays, and other longer themes about it. Thus, Mary Elizabeth often decided to read and complete a month of Literature assignments in one week and proceed to religion or history for the next week. Mary Elizabeth learned to structure her day to include a balance of prayer, school work, play, gardening, cooking, and being mother's helper. The flexibility which Seton Home Study makes possible helped Mary Elizabeth to have the confidence that she could manage her time well the rest of her life.

Home schools and computers are a perfect complement for each other and Seton Home Study utilizes computers well. By Mary Elizabeth's senior year there were three high schoolers and two computers in our house. Naturally, assignments in a home school include lots of writing, and the computer facilitates this. Seton gradually helps its students, through development of grammar, vocabulary, and experience, to become good writers. A thorough job is done in the sophomore year to teach the mechanics of research and term papers. With the computer, word processing and layout software, and a nice printer, school assignments can be corrected easily by the student, his brothers and sisters, and by

Mom and Dad numerous times. Everyone noticed different things, and this was a great education in itself for the whole family. With every year, Mary Elizabeth learned to read her papers from a new perspective and to catch more errors. This ability to communicate one's thoughts and ideas succinctly and clearly on paper has already reaped many important benefits for Mary Elizabeth.

One example of Seton's commitment to learning is the ability to "redo" an assignment for a higher grade. When an assignment has been sent to the school for grading and the tutor feels the student could have done the task better, the teacher will request a "redo." This allows the student to address his mistakes and resubmit the assignment. This feature clearly shows the student that everyone is doing his part to help him truly grasp the subject matter.

Every test, paper, and assignment sent to Seton is given written comments as well as a letter grade and a most thorough grammar, punctuation, and spelling overview. In Seton my children came to expect detailed explanations of a point missed and personalized comments on work well done. When my son realized that his history teacher and he shared some in-depth knowledge of a given area, his answers reflected it. My children felt a kind of dialogue between themselves and their teachers at Seton through the comments which came back on their assignments. This personalized interest in a student and his academic progress reflects the high ideals of the staff at Seton.

Taking the time and effort to find the best staff is the hallmark of Seton. Long before my husband and I were looking for a high school, we had discovered the excellent works of Warren and Anne Carroll, who have to be among the few truly objective historians alive. Even a cursory viewing of the Carrolls' histories reveals how beneficial they are. Their books reflect a perspective upon history which is centered upon the truth. Anne Carroll has written an excellent history of the world, with Jesus Christ as the central focus and theme. She chronicles everything prior to His coming as the preparation for, and everything after His Resurrection as the fulfillment of, His Kingdom. Warren Carroll, after some exceptional smaller period pieces, is writing a six volume *History of Christendom.* These are the kinds of authors which Seton employs to develop their excellent high school curriculum. My children feel they have received an excellent education from both past and contemporary writers.

I cannot extol the merits of Seton's academics and staff without discussing the most important subject which motivates our lives: our Faith. Anne Carroll's expertise naturally extends beyond history, and she wrote the senior religion course. The greatest praise of that course had to be when my daughter called from college and asked me to copy ten chapters for a fellow student who was asking her questions about our Faith. It is one thing to enjoy a course, but it is truly life-changing when you attempt to use it in real life evangelizing. The religion courses at Seton show a true understanding of the state of the Church today.

In the ninth grade, students are introduced to the doctrines of the Catholic Faith and taught how to defend these doctrines rationally. During the sophomore year they learn how to live a moral life and how to gain graces through the Sacraments. In the junior year the focus is on the Bible and Mary and students learn to know Christ so they can love Him. In the senior year Anne Carroll's book features practical applications of moral principles as she helps the student to apply the truths of our Faith to the world today. Everyone who completes Seton's religion course in high school knows his Faith and is capable of being a better servant of Christ and His Church for the rest of his life.

In our home, Dad and Mom thrive on reading and discussing our Faith and how to live it, and naturally our children strive to join in. Seton's high school complemented our children's efforts to participate in and initiate these conversations. Dinner became a part of the school day when Dad asked, "What did you learn in school today?" Seton's curriculum enabled the high schoolers always to have something of merit and interest. They could bring up subjects and summarize points, books, or theological arguments succinctly and completely. Regularly during a conversation they would cite a reference, then go to the bookshelf and bring back an answer or relevant point. They not only had a great grasp of what was said, but remembered where they had heard it and knew how to share this information with everyone.

No explanation of Seton Home Study would be complete without a discussion of their 7:00 a.m. through midnight, six days a week phone service. Whenever questions that stumped my children arose in Latin, Science, or Advanced Math courses, they could always call Seton to receive either an immediate answer and explanation or a referral to another staff member, sometimes even in another state, who could best answer their questions. Time and time again the availability of my children's tutors by telephone was able to save us from frustrating situations.

These, then, are Seton's strengths. They have a strong academic core which develops self-discipline and scheduling talents in the students while providing an intense program of the best high school classes. Through an arduous program Seton's staff manifests a very authentic concern and desire to help the students master their subjects. Syllabuses are made as meticulous and detailed as possible so that the parent or student can have a first reference for answers. Seton's phone service is always available to clear up any more difficult questions, and my children were always impressed with the numerous constructive complaints and criticisms that the tutors made on their papers. Of course, redos were always available when a tutor thought that the student had either not reached his potential or not clearly understood the material when the test was given. Further, an outstanding quality of Seton's program is that it lends itself to discussions about the Faith or other truths at the dinner table. Seton's program has stretched my children academically, socially, and spiritually.

Appendix C:
Catholic Publishers and Mail Order Houses
of Interest to Home Schoolers

Bethlehem Books
15605 County Road 15
Minto, ND 58261
(800) 757-6831
Wonderful children's books—early grades, adolescent, and teen. Good selection of historical fiction and adventure novels. Books stress solid family values and Christian morals.

Catholic Heritage Curricula
P.O. Box 125
Twain Harte, CA 95383-0125
Beautiful selection of children's books, games, stationery, jigsaw puzzles, crosswords, toys, doll clothes (nuns and priests), miniature Mass kit, CD-roms, and more—all 100% Catholic and fun.

Christendom College Press
134 Christendom Drive
Front Royal,VA 22630
(800) 877-5456
Variety of titles, but especially the excellent readable historical titles by Dr. Warren Carroll.

Human Life International
4 Family Life
Front Royal, VA 22630
(540) 635-7884
Largest selection of pro-life, pro-family books, booklets, pamphlets, posters, postcards, flyers, handouts, periodicals, and audio tapes.

Ignatius Press
P.O. Box 1339
Fort Collins, CO 80522
(800) 651-1531

Catholic books and videos. "Faith and Life" catechism series and reprints of the classic "Vision Books" series of the lives of the saints for children.

Intermirifica
2812 Jutland Road
Kensington, MD 20895
(301) 942-9577
Books by Father John Hardon, S.J.

Fatima Family Messenger
P.O. Box 55
Redfield, SD 57469
Books and magazines by Father Robert Fox.

Keep the Faith
810 Belmont Avenue, P. O. Box 8261
North Haledon, NJ 07508
(201) 423-5395
Huge selection of Catholic audio tapes. Topics include religion, history, current events, as well as conferences and books on tape. Much of the work of Dr. William Marra and the late Fr. Vincent Miceli. Large selection of Catholic videos, including many on the lives of the saints.

St. Martin de Porres Lay Dominican Community
New Hope, Kentucky 40052-9989
(800) 789-9494
Publishers of Inside the Vatican, Envoy, *tracts on the New Catechism, and pro-life tracts.*

Mother of Our Savior Co.
P.O. Box 100
Pekin, IN 47165
(800) 451-3993
Large selection of religious books, missals, statues, holy cards, stickers, pictures, videos, music.

Neumann Press
Route 2, Box 30
Long Prairie, MN 56347
(320) 732-6358
Fine selection of reprinted Catholic classics, including many children's titles, readers, history texts; Catholic phonics. Beautiful hardbound books.

Our Lady's Book Service
Servants of Jesus and Mary
P.O. Box 93
Constable, NY 12926
(800) 263-8160
Very good selection of religious books, as well as religious articles (rosaries, scapulars, medals, statues).

Roman Catholic Books
P.O. Box 2286
Fort Collins, CO 80522-2286
Reprints from many fine Catholic authors; lovely hardbound editions.

Seton Educational Media
1350 Progress Drive
Front Royal, VA 22630
(540) 636-9996
Large selection of home schooling materials, textbooks, workbooks, audio and video tapes, software, aids for parents, also Byzantine Catholic materials. Seton is the largest publisher of authentically Catholic curricula today.

St. Paul Book and Media Center
Daughters of St. Paul
50 St. Paul's Avenue
Boston, MA 02130
Source for papal encyclicals.

Sophia Institute Press

P.O. Box 5284
Manchester, NH 03108
(800) 888-9344
Books by St. Thomas Aquinas, Dietrich von Hildebrand, St. Francis de Sales, and many others. Also offers a fine selection of Catholic religious art reproductions.

TAN Books and Publishers, Inc.

P.O. Box 424
Rockford, IL 61105
(800) 437-5876
http://www.tanbooks.com
E-mail: tan@tanbooks.com
The best source of Catholic books for adults, also Catholic history texts (some with answer keys), coloring books and biographies of saints for children, catechisms, Church histories, spiritual reading, reference, etc. Write or call for free catalog.

Western Hemisphere Cultural Society

P.O. Box 417
Sunbury, PA 17801
Small selection of fine quality, visually beautiful Catholic books. Publisher of Our Mother of Good Counsel, *a book explaining in vivid photos the Shrine and the history of the devotion.*

Appendix D:
Periodicals of Interest to Catholic Home Schooling Parents

(Check with publishers for current subscription rates)

Catholic Family News, monthly newspaper, M.P.O. Box 7433, Niagara Falls, NY 14302.

Christifidelis, monthly newsletter "to defend Catholic truth and uphold Catholic rights," St. Joseph Foundation, 11107 Wurzbach, No. 601B, San Antonio, TX 78230-2570. Phone (210) 697-0717.

Christ or Chaos, monthly newsletter "connecting man's spiritual life in Christ with his social life as a citizen." Written by Dr. Thomas Drolesky, noted *Wanderer* columnist. P.O. Box 428807, Cincinnati, OH 45242.

Conservative Chronicle, weekly newspaper presenting articles by many national columnists and cartoonists. Many are by Catholics, such as columnists Joseph Sobran, Phyllis Schlafly, and Pat Buchanan. Articles often deal with education; home schooling is supported. Box 11297, Des Moines, IA 50340-1297.

Education Reporter, monthly newspaper, by well-known Catholic writer and researcher Phyllis Schlafly. Latest happenings in schools. P.O. Box 618, Alton, IL 62002.

HLI Reports and *HLI Special Reports,* monthly from Human Life International, 4 Family Life, Front Royal, VA 22630. Phone (540) 635-7884. Fax (540) 636-7363.

Homiletic and Pastoral Review, 11 issues per year. Father Kenneth Baker's well-respected magazine on Church issues. Ignatius Press, 2515 McAllister Street, San Francisco, CA 94118. Phone (800) 651-1531.

Inside the Vatican, monthly magazine on timely issues in

the Eternal City. Many lovely color photographs of Vatican treasures in each issue. St. Martin de Porres Lay Dominican Community, publishers, New Hope, Kentucky 40052-9989. Phone (800) 789-9494.

National Catholic Register, weekly newspaper presenting different articles than the *Wanderer.* More opinion articles than news articles. Can often be obtained free in parish book racks. P.O. Box 5158, Hamden, CT 06518-5158. Phone (800) 421-3230.

The Remnant, bi-weekly Catholic newspaper supporting the traditional Latin liturgy, etc. 2539 Morrison Avenue, St. Paul, MN 55117.

The Phyllis Schlafly Report, monthly newsletter on topics ranging from education to family, government, and world issues. P.O. Box 618, Alton, IL 62002.

Sursum Corda!, quarterly magazine on positive and hopeful trends in the Church; regularly featured home schooling section. Foundation for Catholic Reform, Subscription Department, 1331 Red Cedar Circle, Fort Collins, CO 80524.

The Wanderer, a weekly newspaper to keep up with what is happening in the Catholic Church. Also, there are many ads for new, used, and out-of-print books helpful for the home schooler. 201 Ohio Street, St. Paul, MN 55107.

Voices, Voices, Voices, published by *Women for Faith and Family,* headed by journalist Helen Hull Hitchcock. P.O. Box 8326, St. Louis, MO 63132. Phone (314) 863-8385.

Catholic home schooling periodicals

The Catholic Hearth, monthly magazine, republished Catholic short stories long out of print. These endearing, instructive stories will be eagerly read by children as well as adults. Rt. 2, Long Prairie, MN 56347. Phone (800) 746-2521.

Catholic Home Schoolers of Pennsylvania, newsletter, Mrs. Ellen Kramer, 101 S. College Street, Myerstown, PA 17067.

The Domestic Church, quarterly newsletter of the Catholic Home School Network of America (CHSNA), information on parental rights, catechesis, curricula, canon law, and other matters of interest to Catholic home school families. P.O. Box 6343, River Forest, IL 60305-6343. Fax (708) 386-3380.

Gabriel's Trumpet, monthly newsletter of Our Lady of the Angels Catholic Home Schoolers, 2132 N. Sycamore Avenue, Rialto, CA 92377.

Homefront, newsletter, 10 issues, written by a veteran Catholic home schooling mother. Offers product reviews and gives practical tips for home schooling. Gilhouse Communications, 525 Shadowridge Drive,Wildwood, MO 63011-1701.

Let The Little Children Come Unto Me, 6 issues, a Catholic newsletter for children, K-4th grade. Maria Ballesteros, P.O. Box 861, Lilburn, GA 30226.

Life After Sunday, 10 issues, a newsletter of Catholic customs for families. Each issue explains a saint and a devotion for the month; includes a children's page. Many ideas for making a home the "domestic church." P.O. Box 1761, Silver Spring, MD 20915. Phone (800) 473-7980.

Mother's Messages, 6 issues. This newsletter's goal is to "inspire, encourage, and provide positive help for Catholic mothers to sanctify themselves and their families through the duties of daily life." Dept. #CFN, P.O. Box 82, O'Neill, NE 68763.

Mother's Watch, newsletter, P.O. Box 2780, Montgomery Village, MD 20886-2780. Phone (410) 756-2370. Fax (410) 756-1171.

Parents' Rights, newsletter, P.O. Box 224, Hilltown, PA 18927-0224.

Regina Pacis, newsletter, 401 Fieldcrest Drive, San Jose, CA 95123-5231.

St. Joseph's Covenant Keepers, monthly newsletter, provides support for the Catholic father. 3872-C Tamiami Trail, Port Charlotte, FL 33952. Phone (941) 764-8565.

Seton Home Study Newsletter, monthly, home schooling advice, book reviews, updates on education, legislation, upcoming conferences, papal statements. 1350 Progress Drive, Front Royal, VA 22630.

Appendix E:
Catholic Home Schooling Organizations

Since this book was first published in 1993, we now have, in addition to the original State home schooling associations (which were mostly staffed by Protestants), a whole array of Catholic home schooling associations. Some are state, some are local. There is at least one per state.

However, we have found that the addresses and contact persons for the Catholic home schooling associations change quite frequently. Therefore, instead of giving a list here which would soon be outdated, we are inviting those interested in this information to consult Seton's website, where we keep these names, addresses, phone numbers and e-mail addresses updated continually.

Seton's website address is: www.setonhome.org

Seton's E-mail address is: info@SetonHome.org

Those who do not have access to the Internet may simply call Seton to receive the name and address of a Catholic home schooling organization in their area. This includes Puerto Rico, Canada and Australia. Call 540-636-9990.

Appendix F:
Other Organizations of Interest
to Home Schoolers

Catholic Home School Network of America (CHSNA)
174 Morningside
Niles, OH 44446
Catherine A. Moran, President
(330) 652-4923 — Voice
(330) 652-5322 — Fax
E-mail: Moran@netdotcom.com
http://home.att.net/~harryl/
Organized in 1996 as the "action arm" of the Round Table of Catholic Home School Leaders. CHSNA links state and regional support groups, as well as individual families through its network of local coordinators. CHSNA keeps the Catholic hierarchy informed about the goals and achievements of Catholic home school students and families.

Catholic League for Religious and Civil Rights
1011 First Avenue
New York, NY 10022
(212) 371-3191 — Voice
(212) 371-3394 — Fax
www.catholicleague.org
This organization is a highly effective fighter of anti-Catholic attacks. Membership will give you a subscription to their very informative monthly newsletter.

Catholics United for the Faith, Inc. (CUF)
827 North Fourth Street
Steubenville, OH 43952
(800) 693-2484 — Order line
Founded to educate Catholics of the great dangers of faulty catechesis and sex education, this organization, now international, has local chapters nationwide. CUF publishes Lay Witness *magazine.*

Eternal Word Television Network (EWTN)
5817 Old Leeds Road
Birmingham, AL 35210
(205) 271-2900
www.ewtn.com
Mother Angelica's 24-hour Catholic television network. Provides live coverage of papal trips, NCCB meetings, etc. Televised daily Mass, Chaplet of Divine Mercy, talk shows with timely Catholic guests, children's fare. Also on shortwave radio.

Home School Legal Defense Association (HSLDA)
P.O. Box 159
Paeonian Springs, VA 22129
(540) 338-5600
For a minimal membership fee, HSLDA will provide complete and legal representation to any member family. The HSLDA legal staff is first-rate, and many of the attorneys are home schooling parents themselves. Seton recommends it to all home schooling families. All attorneys' fees and costs are paid in full by HSLDA. Consider it insurance.

Saint Joseph Covenant Keepers
3872-C Tamiami Trail
Port Charlotte, FL 33952
(941) 764-8565 — Voice
(941) 743-5352 — Fax
E-mail: sjck@sunline.net
http://www.dads.org
An excellent organization providing leadership, guidance and support for Catholic fathers.

St. Joseph Foundation
11107 Wurzbach, No. 601B
San Antonio, TX 78230-2570
(210) 697-0717
A team of Catholic lawyers well versed in Canon law with ties to the Roman Curia. Provides assistance and representation to Catholics either in civil or ecclesiastical courts when rights have been violated. Monthly newsletter, Christifidelis, *sent to donors.*

Keeping It Catholic (the Network) (KIC)
P.O. Box 381224
Clinton Township, MI 48038-0078
(810) 412-1959 — Voice
(810) 412-3973 — Fax
E-mail: Keepitcatholic@usa.net
http://members.tripod.com/~catholic_homeschool/index.html
Offers contacts, educational reviews, recommendations, "buyer beware" alerts, and more to Catholic homeschoolers via its newsletter, Internet, e-mail listserve, Web pages, and Keeping It Catholic Big Book of Homeschooling — Reviews and More. *KIC utilizes the great encyclical* Christian Education of Youth *as its guiding compass for reviewing all educational sources. E-mail for more info on joining the listserve. (free)*

National Coalition of Clergy and Laity (NCCL)
621 Jordan Circle
Whitehall, PA 18052-7119
(610) 435-4190 — Voice
(610) 435-6360 — Fax
E-mail: COALITION@aol.com
An apostolate comprised of priests, religious and laity dedicated to genuine Catholic restoration. Firmly committed to working for a universal ban on classroom sex-ed, advancing the authentic teachings of the Church. "Helping Catholic parents navigate a Catholic course for their children through the minefields of our pagan society." For over a decade the NCCL has assisted Catholics—in concrete and practical ways—to live the Holy Faith authentically, to home school, and to strive for holiness in these troubled times.

Roman Catholic Faithful, Inc. (RCF)
P.O. Box 109
Petersburg, IL 62675
(217) 632-5920 — Voice
(217) 632-7054 — Fax
http://www.rcf.org
Offers assistance in dealing with ecclesiastical abuses.

T.O.R.C.H.
1306 Christopher Court
Bel Air, MD 21014
Organization promoting "Traditions Of Roman Catholic Homes."

Appendix G:
Pope John Paul II's Letter to Families

Since the first edition of *Catholic Home Schooling,* Pope John Paul II published a document called *Letter to Families,* on February 2, 1994. The purpose of this document was to celebrate the Year of the Family, as well as to emphasize that the family is God's plan for the path for people to follow to enter heaven. Jesus Christ entered the world through a family in order to teach us His Gospel. For this reason, the "Church considers serving the family to be one of her essential duties."

Most of the sections of this document are concerned with marriage and the family, such as The Marital Covenant, The Unity of the Two, The Common Good of Marriage and the Family, Responsible Fatherhood and Motherhood. These are all sections which we Catholic home schooling families should read.

The most important section for our Catholic home schooling, however, is the section titled Education. It is in this section that one of the quotes has become rather famous for home schooling parents: You are educators because you are parents.

The following are some selections from this section on Education. (Emphases in original English edition, Pauline Books and Media, Boston, 1995; Vatican translation.)

"What is involved in raising children? In answering this question, two fundamental truths should be kept in mind: first, that man is called to live in truth and love; and second, that everyone finds fulfillment through the sincere gift of self. This is true both for the educator and for the one being educated. Education is thus a unique process for which the mutual communion of persons has immense importance. *The educator* is a person who *"begets" in a spiritual sense.* From this point of view, *raising children can be considered a genuine apostolate.* It is a living means of communication, which not only creates a profound relationship between the educator and the one being educated, but also makes them

441

both sharers in truth and love, that final goal to which everyone is called by God the Father, Son, and Holy Spirit.

"...In the raising of children, conjugal love is expressed as authentic parental love. The "communion of persons" expressed as conjugal love at the beginning of the family, is thus completed and brought to fulfillment in the raising of children.... This is a *process of exchange* in which the parents-educators are in turn to a certain degree educated themselves.

"...If it is true that by giving life *parents* share in God's creative work, it is also true that by raising their children, *they become sharers in His paternal and at the same time maternal way of teaching.*

"Parents are the first and most important educators of their own children, and they also possess *a fundamental competence* in this area: they are *educators because they are parents.* They share their educational mission with other individuals or institutions, such as the Church and the State. But the mission of education must always be carried out in accordance with a proper application of the *principle of subsidiarity.* This implies the legitimacy and indeed the need of giving assistance to the parents, but finds its intrinsic and absolute limit in their prevailing right and their actual capabilities. The principle of subsidiarity is thus at the service of parental love, meeting the good of the family unit. For parents by themselves are not capable of satisfying every requirement of the whole process of raising children, especially in matters concerning their schooling and the entire gamut of socialization. Subsidiarity thus complements paternal and maternal love and confirms its fundamental nature, inasmuch as all other participants in the process of education are only able to carry out their responsibilities *in the name of the parents, with their consent,* and to a certain degree, *with their authorization.*

"...Against this background, we can see the meaning of the fourth commandment, *"Honor your father and your mother"* in a new way. It is closely linked to the whole process of education.

"...In the sphere of education, *the Church* has a specific role to play. In the light of Tradition and the teaching of the Council, it can be said that it is not only a matter of *entrusting the Church* with the person's religious and moral education, but of promoting the entire process of the person's education *"together with"* the *Church.* The family is called to carry out its task of education *in the Church,* thus sharing in her life and mission. The Church wishes to carry out her educational mission above all *through families,* who are made capable of undertaking this task by the Sacrament of Matrimony, through the "grace of state" which follows from it, and the specific "charism" proper to the entire family community.

"Certainly one area in which the family has an irreplaceable role is that of *religious education,* which enables the family to grow as a "domestic church." Religious education and the catechesis of children make the family a true *subject of evangelization and the apostolate* within the Church. We are speaking of a right intrinsically linked to the *principle of religious liberty.* Families, and more specifically parents, are free to choose for their children a particular kind of religious and moral education consonant with their own convictions. Even when they entrust these responsibilities to ecclesiastical institutions or to schools administered by religious personnel, their educational presence ought to continue to be *constant and active.*

"...The Church's constant and trusting prayer during the Year of the Family is *for the education of man,* so that families will persevere in their task of education with courage, trust, and hope, in spite of the difficulties occasionally so serious as to appear insuperable. The Church prays that the forces of the "civilization of love," which have their source in the love of God, will be triumphant. These are forces which the Church ceaselessly expends for the good of the whole human family."

Index

For more information on
Seton Home Study School,
please call or write:

SETON HOME STUDY SCHOOL
1350 Progress Drive
Front Royal, VA 22630
(540) 636-9990

Internet: www.setonhome.org
E-Mail: info@SetonHome.org

---

*Additional copies of this book may be purchased from TAN
Books and Publishers, Inc. at the following discounts:*

1 or more— $18.00 per copy*
10 or more— $15.00 per copy
25 or more— $12.50 per copy
50 or more— $11.00 per copy
100 or more— $10.00 per copy

*Regular discounts to the Book Trade.

U.S. & CAN. POST./HDLG.: If total order = $1-$10, add $2;
$10.01-20, add $3; $20.01-$30, add $4; $30.01-$50, add $5;
$50.01-$75, add $6; $75.01-up, add $7.

(Prices subject to change)

CALL TOLL FREE: 1-800-437-5876

TAN BOOKS AND PUBLISHERS, INC.
P. O. Box 424
Rockford, Illinois 61105

6 BOOKS BY FR. JOHN LAUX!!

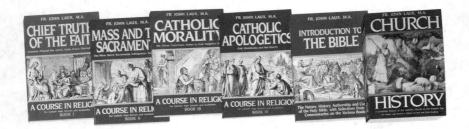

First published in 1928—contain timeless Catholic doctrine. A perfect bridge between the Baltimore Catechism and full-fledged theology! Packed with facts.

1084 CHIEF TRUTHS OF THE FAITH—Book I. 179 pp. PB. Impr. 54 Illus. Index. Includes many Scriptural quotes. A solid Catholic grounding for the rest of one's life. The Blessed Trinity, creation, Scripture & Tradition, Sanctifying & Actual Grace, Heaven, Hell, Purgatory, etc.   **10.00**

1085 MASS AND THE SACRAMENTS—Book II. 199 pp. PB. Impr. 72 Illus. Index. Doctrine & history of the 7 Sacraments, plus Indulgences & Sacramentals. Scriptural background of the Sacraments, institution, requirements for receiving, effects in the soul, matter & form of each, etc.   **10.00**

1086 CATHOLIC MORALITY—Book III. 164 pp. PB. Impr. 40 Illus. Index. Based upon reason and the teachings of Christ. Law, conscience, the virtues, sin, the religious state, duties to God, self, neighbor, etc., temptation, punishment, doubts against faith, lies & mental reservation, love & fear, much more.   **10.00**

1087 CATHOLIC APOLOGETICS—Book IV. 134 pp. PB. Impr. 38 Illus. Index. Dozens of well-reasoned answers to the classic objections to the Catholic Church. Includes existence of God, immortality of the soul, science & faith, authenticity of the Gospels, divinity of Christ, papal infallibility, etc. Excellent!   **10.00**

1083 INTRODUCTION TO THE BIBLE. 326 pp. PB. Impr. 57 Illus. Index. Based on the Douay-Rheims Bible. Covers divine inspiration, the Church as official interpreter, etc. Excellent intro. to individual books of the Bible, with sample passages. A true Catholic understanding of God's holy Word.   **16.50**

0231 CHURCH HISTORY. 621 pp. PB. Impr. 141 Illus. Index. Covers all of Church history: popes, saints, events, etc., with selections from famous writings. Designed for both students and adults. Also a tremendous reference that belongs in every Catholic home. Best l-volume Church history in print!   **24.00**

1088 SET of all 4 Fr. Laux High School Religion books above (Nos. 1084, 1085, 1086, 1087—40.00 value):   **30.00**

1106 SET of all 4 Fr. Laux High School Religion books above plus *Introduction to the Bible* ($56.50 value):   **40.00**

1089 SET of all 4 Fr. Laux High School Religion books above, plus *Church History* and *Introduction to the Bible* ($80.50 value):   **55.00**

Prices subject to change.

WONDERFUL CATHOLIC HISTORY TEXTS!!

1228 CHRIST THE KING—LORD OF HISTORY. Anne W. Carroll. 474 pp. PB. Index. High school—adult. Fast paced, enjoyable history of western civilization since ancient times. Shows the central role of the Catholic Church. Nothing else like it available. Great!   **24.00**

1387 CHRIST AND THE AMERICAS. Anne W. Carroll. 440 pp. PB. Index. High school—adult. Very interesting history of the U.S. and Central and South America through the 1990's, including the Catholic dimension. Fascinating stories, great insights!   **24.00**

1002 THE OLD WORLD AND AMERICA. Most Rev. Philip Furlong. 384 pp. PB. Impr. 200 Illus. Index. 5th-8th grade. From creation through early exploration of the New World. Introduction to the famous persons, places, events and concepts from a Catholic perspective. 37 Chapters, Study Questions, Activities. A great asset for home-schoolers!   **18.00**

1550 THE OLD WORLD AND AMERICA—ANSWER KEY. 80 pp. PB. Clear and complete. A tremendous help for the busy homeschooling parent!   **10.00**

1396 OUR PIONEERS AND PATRIOTS. Most Rev. Philip Furlong. 505 pp. PB. Impr. 235 Illus. & Maps. Index. 5th-8th grade. Famous Catholic U.S. history text written in 1940. Teaches *a lot* in a simple manner—with love for Church and country. 55 Chapters, Study Questions, Activities. Gives a tremendous foundation in U.S. history!   **21.00**

1529 OUR PIONEERS AND PATRIOTS—ANSWER KEY. 90 pp. PB. Clear and complete A tremendous help for the busy homeschooling parent!
10.00

Prices subject to change.

U.S. & CAN. POST./HDLG.: $1-$10, add $2; $10.01-$20, add $3;
$20.01-$30, add $4; $30.01-$50, add $5; $50.01-$75, add $6; $75.01-up, add $7.

**At your Bookdealer or direct from the Publisher.
Call Toll Free 1-800-437-5876**

Dr. Mary Kay Clark and her husband Bruce with their seven sons and their wives and children.